core SERVLETS AND JAVASERVER PAGES

VOLUME 1: CORE TECHNOLOGIES

2ND EDITION

core SERVLETS AND JAVASERVER PAGES

VOLUME 1: CORE TECHNOLOGIES

2ND EDITION

MARTY HALL
LARRY BROWN

PRENTICE HALL
Professional Technical Reference
Upper Saddle River, NJ 07458
www.phptr.com

Sun Microsystems Press
A Prentice Hall Title

Production Editor and Compositor: *Vanessa Moore*
Copy Editor: *Mary Lou Nohr*
Full-Service Production Manager: *Anne R. Garcia*
Executive Editor: *Gregory G. Doench*
Editorial Assistant: *Brandt Kenna*
Cover Design Director: *Jerry Votta*
Cover Designer: *Design Source*
Art Director: *Gail Cocker-Bogusz*
Manufacturing Manager: *Alexis R. Heydt-Long*
Marketing Manager: *Debby vanDijk*

Sun Microsystems Press Publisher: *Myrna Rivera*

10 9 8 7 6 5 4 3 2 1

ISBN: 0-13-009229-0

Sun Microsystems Press
A Prentice Hall Title

Contents

CHAPTER 6

CHAPTER 7

CHAPTER 8

CHAPTER 11
INVOKING JAVA CODE WITH JSP SCRIPTING ELEMENTS 318

CHAPTER 15

CHAPTER 16
SIMPLIFYING ACCESS TO JAVA CODE: THE JSP 2.0 EXPRESSION LANGUAGE 464

CHAPTER 18
CONFIGURING MS ACCESS, MYSQL, AND ORACLE9I 554

CHAPTER 19
CREATING AND PROCESSING HTML FORMS 606

Acknowledgments

Many people helped us with this book. Without their assistance, we would still be on the third chapter. Brian Baldwin (Atlantic Coast Telesys), John Guthrie (Psynapse Technologies), Randal Hanford (Boeing, University of Washington), Martha McNeil (JHU), Rich Slywczak (NASA), and Dan Unger (Eagle Design and Management) provided valuable technical feedback on many different chapters. Their recommendations improved the book considerably.

Others providing useful suggestions or corrections include Evan Atkinson, Abhay Bakshi, Eliezer Bulka, Joe Bunag, Bob Caviness, Brian Deitte, Pete Fritsch, David Geary, Darryn Graham, Peter Gray, Vladimir Gubanov, Kalman Hazins, Lis Immer, Mike Jenkins, George Jensen, Lian Jin, Rob King, Ashley Lan, Christian Malone, Doug Parker, Ann Platoff, Alexander Pyle, Patrick Quinn-O'Brien, Mark Roth, Hong Sung, Frank Tanner, Jeff Thorn, Alex Turetsky, Kris Uebersax, and Elissa Weidaw. I hope I learned from their advice.

Mary Lou "Eagle Eyes" Nohr spotted my errant commas, awkward sentences, typographical errors, and grammatical inconsistencies. She improved the result immensely. Vanessa Moore designed the book layout and produced the final version; she did a great job despite my many last-minute changes. Greg Doench of Prentice Hall believed in the concept from before the first edition and encouraged us to write a second edition. Thanks to all.

Most of all, Marty would like to thank B.J., Lindsay, and Nathan for their patience and encouragement, and Larry would like to thank Lee for her loving and unfailing support. God has blessed us with great families.

About the Authors

Marty Hall is president of coreservlets.com, Inc., a small company that provides training courses and consulting services related to server-side Java technology. He also teaches Java and Web programming in the Johns Hopkins University part-time graduate program in Computer Science, where he directs the Distributed Computing and Web Technology concentration areas. Marty is the author of four books from Prentice Hall and Sun Microsystems Press: the first edition of *Core Servlets and JavaServer Pages*, *More Servlets and JavaServer Pages*, and the first and second editions of *Core Web Programming*. You can reach Marty at hall@coreservlets.com; you can find out about his JSP, servlet, and general Java training courses at http://courses.coreservlets.com/.

Larry Brown is a Senior Network Engineer and Oracle DBA for the U.S. Navy (NSWCCD), where he specializes in developing and deploying network and Web solutions in an enterprise environment. He is also a Computer Science faculty member at the Johns Hopkins University, where he teachers server-side programming, distributed Web programming, and Java user interface development for the part-time graduate program. Larry is the co-author of the second edition of *Core Web Programming*, also from Prentice Hall and Sun Microsystems Press. You can reach Larry at brown@coreservlets.com.

Introduction

Suppose your company wants to sell products online. You have a database that gives the price and inventory status of each item. But, your database doesn't speak HTTP, the protocol that Web browsers use. Nor does it output HTML, the format Web browsers need. What can you do? Once users know what they want to buy, how do you gather that information? You want to customize your site for visitors' preferences and interests—how? You want to keep track of user's purchases as they shop at your site—what techniques are required to implement this behavior? When your Web site becomes popular, you might want to compress pages to reduce bandwidth. How can you do this without causing your site to fail for the 30% of visitors whose browsers don't support compression? In all these cases, you need a program to act as the intermediary between the browser and some server-side resource. This book is about using the Java platform for this type of program.

"Wait a second," you say. "Didn't you *already* write a book about that?" Well, yes. In May of 2000, Sun Microsystems Press and Prentice Hall released Marty's second book, *Core Servlets and JavaServer Pages*. It was successful beyond everyone's wildest expectations, selling approximately 100,000 copies, getting translated into Bulgarian, Chinese simplified script, Chinese traditional script, Czech, French, German, Hebrew, Japanese, Korean, Polish, Russian, and Spanish, and being chosen by Amazon.com as one of the top five computer programming books of 2001. Even better, Marty was swamped with requests for what he *really* likes doing: teaching training courses for developers in industry. Despite having to decline most of the requests, he was still able to teach servlet and JSP short courses in Australia, Canada, Japan, Puerto Rico, the Philippines, and at dozens of U.S. venues. What fun!

Since then, use of servlets and JSP has continued to grow at a phenomenal rate. The Java 2 Platform has become the technology of choice for developing e-commerce applications, dynamic Web sites, and Web-enabled applications and service. Servlets and JSP continue to be the foundation of this platform—they provide the link between Web clients and server-side applications. Virtually all major Web servers for Windows, Unix (including Linux), MacOS, VMS, and mainframe operating systems now support servlet and JSP technology either natively or by means of a plugin. With only a small amount of configuration, you can run servlets and JSP in Microsoft IIS, the Apache Web Server, IBM WebSphere, BEA WebLogic, Oracle9i AS, and dozens of other servers. Performance of both commercial and open-source servlet and JSP engines has improved significantly.

However, the field continues to evolve rapidly. For example:

- The official servlet and JSP reference implementation is no longer developed by Sun. Instead, it is Apache Tomcat, an open-source product developed by a team from many different organizations. So, we provide great detail on Tomcat configuration and usage.
- Except for Tomcat, the servers popular when the book was first released are no longer widely used. So, we cover Macromedia JRun and Caucho Resin instead.
- Version 2.4 of the servlet specification was released in late 2003. Many APIs have been added or have changed. So, we have upgraded the book to be consistent with these APIs.
- Version 2.0 of the JSP specification was released (also late 2003). This version lets you use a shorthand expression language to access bean properties and collection elements. So, we cover both "classic" scripting and use of the JSP 2.0 expression language.
- Two new versions of JDBC have been released, providing many useful new features. So, we explain database access in the context of these new features.
- MySQL has emerged as a popular free database. So, we explain how to download, configure, and use MySQL (we also cover Oracle9i and Microsoft Access, of course).

Whew. Lots of action in the server-side Java community. Yup; and to reflect this fact, the book has been completely and totally rewritten from top to bottom. Many new capabilities are now covered. Experienced developer Larry Brown was brought in to add his expertise, especially in database applications. Many hard-learned lessons are explained in detail. Many techniques are now approached differently.

The new version provides a thorough and up-to-date introduction to servlet and JSP programming. We hope you find it useful.

Who Should Read This Book

This book is aimed at two main groups.

The primary audience is developers who are familiar with the basics of the Java programming language itself but have little or no experience with server-side applications. For you, virtually the entire book should be valuable; with the possible exception of the JSP 2.0 expression language (which is not applicable if you are using a server that is compliant only with JSP 1.2), you are likely to use capabilities from almost *every* chapter in almost *every* real-world application.

The second group is composed of people who are familiar with basic servlet and JSP development and want to learn how to make use of the new capabilities we just described. If you are in this category, you can skim many of the chapters, focusing on the capabilities that are new in servlets 2.4, JSP 2.0, or JDBC 3.0.

Although this book is well suited for both experienced servlet and JSP programmers and newcomers to the technology, it assumes that you are familiar with basic Java programming. You don't have to be an expert Java developer, but if you know nothing about the Java programming language, this is not the place to start. After all, servlet and JSP technology is an *application* of the Java programming language. If you don't know the language, you can't apply it. So, if you know nothing about basic Java development, start with a good introductory book like *Thinking in Java*, *Core Java*, or *Core Web Programming*. Come back here after you are comfortable with at least the basics.

Volume 2

This first volume of the book focuses on core technologies: the servlet and JSP capabilities that you are likely to use in almost every real-life project. The second volume focuses on advanced capabilities: features that you use less frequently but that are extremely valuable in complex applications.

These topics include servlet and JSP filters, declarative and programmatic Web application security, custom tag libraries, the JSP Standard Tag Library (JSTL), Apache Struts, JavaServer Faces (JSF), Java Architecture for XML Binding (JAXB), database connection pooling, advanced JDBC features, and use of Ant for deployment.

For information on the release date of Volume 2, please see the book's Web site at http://www.coreservlets.com/.

Distinctive Features

This book has five important characteristics that set it apart from many other similar-sounding books:

- **Integrated coverage of servlets and JSP.** The two technologies are closely related; you should learn and use them together.
- **Real code.** Complete, working, documented programs are essential to learning; we provide lots of them.
- **Step-by-step instructions.** Complex tasks are broken down into simple steps that are illustrated with real examples.
- **Server configuration and usage details.** We supply lots of concrete examples to get you going quickly.
- **Design strategies.** We give lots of experience-based tips on best approaches and practices.

Integrated Coverage of Servlets and JSP

One of the key philosophies behind *Core Servlets and JavaServer Pages* is that servlets and JSP should be learned (and used!) together, not separately. After all, they aren't two entirely distinct technologies: JSP is just a different way of writing servlets. If you don't know servlet programming, you can't use servlets when they are a better choice than JSP, you can't use the MVC architecture to integrate servlets and JSP, you can't understand complex JSP constructs, and you can't understand how JSP scripting elements work (since they are really just servlet code). If you don't understand JSP development, you can't use JSP when it is a better option than servlet technology, you can't use the MVC architecture, and you are stuck using `print` statements even for pages that consist almost entirely of static HTML.

Servlets and JSP go together! Learn them together!

Real Code

Sure, small code snippets are useful for introducing concepts. The book has lots of them. But, for you to *really* understand how to use various techniques, you also need to see the techniques in the context of complete working programs. Not huge programs: just ones that have no missing pieces and thus really run. We provide plenty of such programs, all of them documented and available for unrestricted use at http://www.coreservlets.com.

Step-by-Step Instructions

When Marty was a Computer Science graduate student (long before Java existed), he had an Algorithms professor who stated in class that he was a believer in step-by-step instructions. Marty was puzzled: wasn't everyone? Not at all. Sure, most instructors explained simple tasks that way, but this professor took even highly theoretical concepts and said "first you do *this*, then you do *that*," and so on. The other instructors didn't explain things this way; neither did his textbooks. But, it helped Marty enormously.

If such an approach works even for theoretical subjects, how much more should it work with applied tasks like those described in this book?

Server Configuration and Usage Details

When Marty first tried to learn server-side programming, he grabbed a couple of books, the official specifications, and some online papers. Almost without fail, they said something like "since this technology is portable, you need to read your server's documentation to know how to execute servlets or JSP pages." Aargh! He couldn't even get started. After hunting around, he downloaded a server. He wrote some code. How did he compile it? Where did he put it after it was compiled? How did he invoke it? How about some help here?

Servlet and JSP *code* is portable. The *APIs* are standardized. But, server structure and organization are not standardized. The directory in which you place your code is different on Tomcat than it is on JRun. You set up Web applications differently with Resin than you do with other servers. These details are important.

Now, we're not saying that this is a book that is specific to any particular server. We're just saying that when a topic requires server-specific knowledge, it is important to say so. Furthermore, specific examples are helpful. So, when we describe a topic that requires server-specific information like the directory in which to place a Web application, we first explain the general pattern that servers tend to follow. Then, we give very specific details for three of the most popular servers that are available without cost for desktop development: Apache Tomcat, Macromedia JRun, and Caucho Resin.

Design Strategies

Sure, it is valuable to know what capabilities the APIs provide. And yes, syntax details are important. But, you also need the big picture. When is a certain approach best? Why? What gotchas do you have to watch out for? Servlet and JSP technology is not perfect; how should you design your system to maximize its strengths and minimize its weaknesses? What strategies simplify the long-term maintenance of your projects? What approaches should you avoid?

We're not new to servlet and JSP technology. We've been doing it for years. And, we've gotten feedback from hundreds of readers and students from Marty's training courses. So, we don't just show you how to use individual features; we explain how these features fit into overall system design and highlight best practices and strategies.

How This Book Is Organized

This book consists of three parts: servlet technology, JSP technology, and supporting technologies.

Part I: Servlet Technology

- Downloading and configuring a free server
- Setting up your development environment
- Deploying servlets and JSP pages: some options
- Organizing projects in Web applications
- Building basic servlets
- Understanding the servlet life cycle
- Dealing with multithreading problems
- Debugging servlets and JSP pages
- Reading form parameters
- Handling missing and malformed data
- Dealing with incomplete form submissions
- Using HTTP request headers
- Compressing pages
- Customizing pages based on browser types or how users got there
- Manipulating HTTP status codes and response headers
- Redirecting requests
- Building Excel spread sheets with servlets
- Generating custom JPEG images from servlets
- Sending incremental updates to the user
- Handling cookies
- Remembering user preferences
- Tracking sessions
- Differentiating between browser and server sessions
- Accumulating user purchases
- Implementing shopping carts

Part II: JSP Technology

- Understanding the need for JSP
- Evaluating strategies for invoking Java code from JSP pages
- Invoking Java code with classic JSP scripting elements
- Using the predefined JSP variables (implicit objects)
- Controlling code structure with the `page` directive
- Generating Excel spread sheets with JSP pages
- Controlling multithreading behavior
- Including pages at request time
- Including pages at compile time
- Using JavaBeans components
- Setting bean properties automatically
- Sharing beans
- Integrating servlets and JSP pages with the MVC architecture
- Using `RequestDispatcher`
- Comparing MVC data-sharing options
- Accessing beans with the JSP 2.0 expression language
- Using uniform syntax to access array elements, `List` items, and `Map` entries
- Using expression language operators

Part III: Supporting Technologies

- Accessing databases with JDBC
- Simplifying JDBC usage
- Using precompiled (parameterized) queries
- Executing stored procedures
- Controlling transactions
- Using JDO and other object-to-relational mappings
- Configuring Oracle, MySQL, and Microsoft Access for use with JDBC
- Creating HTML forms
- Surveying all legal HTML form elements
- Debugging forms with a custom Web server

Conventions

Throughout the book, concrete programming constructs or program output are presented in a monospaced font. For example, when abstractly discussing server-side programs that use HTTP, we might refer to "HTTP servlets" or just "servlets," but when we say `HttpServlet` we are talking about a specific Java class.

User input is indicated in boldface, and command-line prompts are either generic (`Prompt>`) or indicate the operating system to which they apply (`DOS>`). For instance, the following indicates that "`Some Output`" is the result when "`java SomeProgram`" is executed on any platform.

```
Prompt> java SomeProgram
Some Output
```

URLs, filenames, and directory names are presented in a sansserif font. So, for example, we would say "the `StringTokenizer` class" (monospaced because we're talking about the class name) and "Listing such and such shows SomeFile.java" (sansserif because we're talking about the filename). Paths use forward slashes as in URLs unless they are specific to the Windows operating system. So, for instance, we would use a forward slash when saying "look in *install_dir*/bin" (OS neutral) but use backslashes when saying "see C:\Windows\Temp" (Windows specific).

Important standard techniques are indicated by specially marked entries, as in the following example.

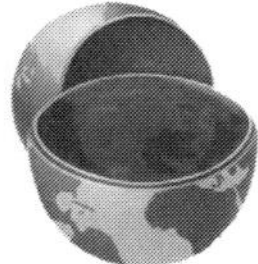

Core Approach

Pay particular attention to items in "Core Approach" sections. They indicate techniques that should always or almost always be used.

Notes and warnings are called out in a similar manner.

About the Web Site

The book has a companion Web site at http://www.coreservlets.com/. This free site includes:

- Documented source code for all examples shown in the book; this code can be downloaded for unrestricted use
- Links to all URLs mentioned in the text of the book
- Up-to-date download sites for servlet and JSP software
- Information on book discounts
- Book additions, updates, and news

About the Training Courses

Hands-on JSP and servlet training courses based on the book are also available. These courses are personally developed and taught by the lead author of the book (Marty). Open-enrollment versions based on the first and second volumes are available at public venues; customizable on-site versions can also be taught at *your* organization. See http://courses.coreservlets.com/ for details.

core

SERVLETS AND JAVASERVER PAGES

VOLUME 1: CORE TECHNOLOGIES

2ND EDITION

An Overview of Servlet and JSP Technology

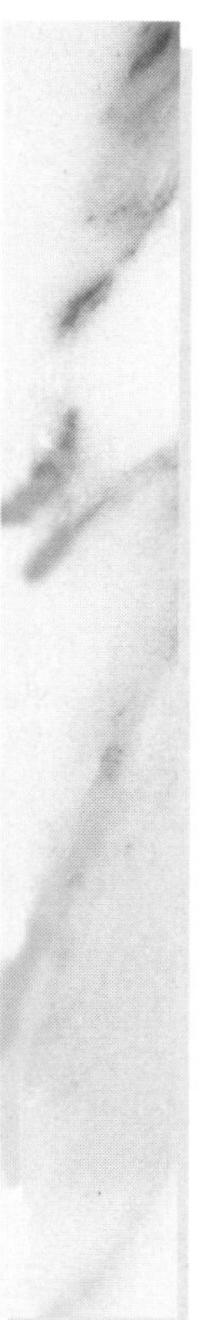

Topics in This Chapter

- Understanding the role of servlets
- Building Web pages dynamically
- Looking at servlet code
- Evaluating servlets vs. other technologies
- Understanding the role of JSP

Chapter 1

Servlet and JSP technology has become the technology of choice for developing online stores, interactive Web applications, and other dynamic Web sites. Why? This chapter gives a high-level overview of the technology and some of the reasons for its popularity. Later chapters provide specific details on programming techniques.

1.1 A Servlet's Job

Servlets are Java programs that run on Web or application servers, acting as a middle layer between requests coming from Web browsers or other HTTP clients and databases or applications on the HTTP server. Their job is to perform the following tasks, as illustrated in Figure 1–1.

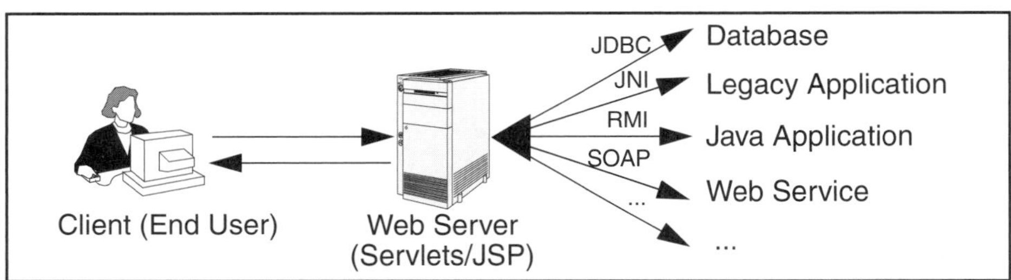

Figure 1–1 The role of Web middleware.

1. **Read the explicit data sent by the client.**
   The end user normally enters this data in an HTML form on a Web page. However, the data could also come from an applet or a custom HTTP client program. Chapter 4 discusses how servlets read this data.
2. **Read the implicit HTTP request data sent by the browser.**
   Figure 1–1 shows a single arrow going from the client to the Web server (the layer where servlets and JSP execute), but there are really *two* varieties of data: the explicit data that the end user enters in a form and the behind-the-scenes HTTP information. Both varieties are critical. The HTTP information includes cookies, information about media types and compression schemes the browser understands, and so forth; it is discussed in Chapter 5.
3. **Generate the results.**
   This process may require talking to a database, executing an RMI or EJB call, invoking a Web service, or computing the response directly. Your real data may be in a relational database. Fine. But your database probably doesn't speak HTTP or return results in HTML, so the Web browser can't talk directly to the database. Even if it could, for security reasons, you probably would not want it to. The same argument applies to most other applications. You need the Web middle layer to extract the incoming data from the HTTP stream, talk to the application, and embed the results inside a document.
4. **Send the explicit data (i.e., the document) to the client.**
   This document can be sent in a variety of formats, including text (HTML or XML), binary (GIF images), or even a compressed format like gzip that is layered on top of some other underlying format. But, HTML is by far the most common format, so an important servlet/JSP task is to wrap the results inside of HTML.
5. **Send the implicit HTTP response data.**
   Figure 1–1 shows a single arrow going from the Web middle layer (the servlet or JSP page) to the client. But, there are really *two* varieties of data sent: the document itself and the behind-the-scenes HTTP information. Again, both varieties are critical to effective development. Sending HTTP response data involves telling the browser or other client what type of document is being returned (e.g., HTML), setting cookies and caching parameters, and other such tasks. These tasks are discussed in Chapters 6 and 7.

1.2 Why Build Web Pages Dynamically?

After Marty wrote the first edition of *Core Servlets and JavaServer Pages*, various of his non-software-savvy friends and relations would ask him what his book was about. Marty would launch into a long, technical discussion of Java, object-oriented programming, and HTTP, only to see their eyes immediately glaze over. Finally, in exasperation, they would ask, "Oh, so your book is about how to make Web pages, right?"

"Well, no," the answer would be, "They are about how to make *programs* that make Web pages."

"Huh? Why wait until the client requests the page and then have a program build the result? Why not just build the Web page ahead of time?"

Yes, many client requests can be satisfied by prebuilt documents, and the server would handle these requests without invoking servlets. In many cases, however, a static result is not sufficient, and a page needs to be generated for each request. There are a number of reasons why Web pages need to be built on-the-fly:

- **The Web page is based on data sent by the client.**
  For instance, the results page from search engines and order-confirmation pages at online stores are specific to particular user requests. You don't know what to display until you read the data that the user submits. Just remember that the user submits two kinds of data: explicit (i.e., HTML form data) and implicit (i.e., HTTP request headers). Either kind of input can be used to build the output page. In particular, it is quite common to build a user-specific page based on a cookie value.
- **The Web page is derived from data that changes frequently.**
  If the page changes for every request, then you certainly need to build the response at request time. If it changes only periodically, however, you could do it two ways: you could periodically build a new Web page on the server (independently of client requests), or you could wait and only build the page when the user requests it. The right approach depends on the situation, but sometimes it is more convenient to do the latter: wait for the user request. For example, a weather report or news headlines site might build the pages dynamically, perhaps returning a previously built page if that page is still up to date.
- **The Web page uses information from corporate databases or other server-side sources.**
  If the information is in a database, you need server-side processing even if the client is using dynamic Web content such as an applet. Imagine using an applet by itself for a search engine site:

"Downloading 50 terabyte applet, please wait!" Obviously, that is silly; you need to talk to the database. Going from the client to the Web tier to the database (a three-tier approach) instead of from an applet directly to a database (a two-tier approach) provides increased flexibility and security with little or no performance penalty. After all, the database call is usually the rate-limiting step, so going through the Web server does not slow things down. In fact, a three-tier approach is often faster because the middle tier can perform caching and connection pooling.

In principle, servlets are not restricted to Web or application servers that handle HTTP requests but can be used for other types of servers as well. For example, servlets could be embedded in FTP or mail servers to extend their functionality. And, a servlet API for SIP (Session Initiation Protocol) servers was recently standardized (see http://jcp.org/en/jsr/detail?id=116). In practice, however, this use of servlets has not caught on, and we'll only be discussing HTTP servlets.

1.3 A Quick Peek at Servlet Code

Now, this is hardly the time to delve into the depths of servlet syntax. Don't worry, you'll get plenty of that throughout the book. But it is worthwhile to take a quick look at a simple servlet, just to get a feel for the basic level of complexity.

Listing 1.1 shows a simple servlet that outputs a small HTML page to the client. Figure 1–2 shows the result.

The code is explained in detail in Chapter 3 (Servlet Basics), but for now, just notice four points:

- **It is regular Java code.** There are new APIs, but no new syntax.
- **It has unfamiliar import statements.** The servlet and JSP APIs are not part of the Java 2 Platform, Standard Edition (J2SE); they are a separate specification (and are also part of the Java 2 Platform, Enterprise Edition—J2EE).
- **It extends a standard class (`HttpServlet`).** Servlets provide a rich infrastructure for dealing with HTTP.
- **It overrides the `doGet` method.** Servlets have different methods to respond to different types of HTTP commands.

Listing 1.1 HelloServlet.java

```
import java.io.*;
import javax.servlet.*;
import javax.servlet.http.*;

public class HelloServlet extends HttpServlet {
  public void doGet(HttpServletRequest request,
                    HttpServletResponse response)
      throws ServletException, IOException {
    response.setContentType("text/html");
    PrintWriter out = response.getWriter();
    String docType =
      "<!DOCTYPE HTML PUBLIC \"-//W3C//DTD HTML 4.0 " +
      "Transitional//EN\">\n";
    out.println(docType +
                "<HTML>\n" +
                "<HEAD><TITLE>Hello</TITLE></HEAD>\n" +
                "<BODY BGCOLOR=\"#FDF5E6\">\n" +
                "<H1>Hello</H1>\n" +
                "</BODY></HTML>");
  }
}
```

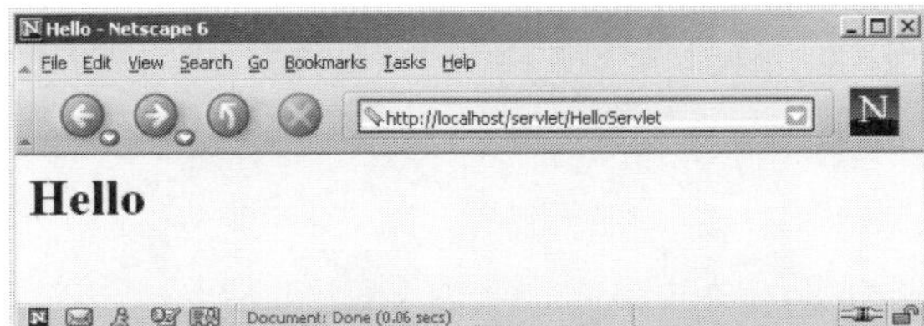

Figure 1–2 Result of `HelloServlet`.

1.4 The Advantages of Servlets Over "Traditional" CGI

Java servlets are more efficient, easier to use, more powerful, more portable, safer, and cheaper than traditional CGI and many alternative CGI-like technologies.

Efficient

With traditional CGI, a new process is started for each HTTP request. If the CGI program itself is relatively short, the overhead of starting the process can dominate the execution time. With servlets, the Java virtual machine stays running and handles each request with a lightweight Java thread, not a heavyweight operating system process. Similarly, in traditional CGI, if there are *N* requests to the same CGI program, the code for the CGI program is loaded into memory *N* times. With servlets, however, there would be *N* threads, but only a single copy of the servlet class would be loaded. This approach reduces server memory requirements and saves time by instantiating fewer objects. Finally, when a CGI program finishes handling a request, the program terminates. This approach makes it difficult to cache computations, keep database connections open, and perform other optimizations that rely on persistent data. Servlets, however, remain in memory even after they complete a response, so it is straightforward to store arbitrarily complex data between client requests.

Convenient

Servlets have an extensive infrastructure for automatically parsing and decoding HTML form data, reading and setting HTTP headers, handling cookies, tracking sessions, and many other such high-level utilities. In CGI, you have to do much of this yourself. Besides, if you already know the Java programming language, why learn Perl too? You're already convinced that Java technology makes for more reliable and reusable code than does Visual Basic, VBScript, or C++. Why go back to those languages for server-side programming?

Powerful

Servlets support several capabilities that are difficult or impossible to accomplish with regular CGI. Servlets can talk directly to the Web server, whereas regular CGI programs cannot, at least not without using a server-specific API. Communicating with the Web server makes it easier to translate relative URLs into concrete path names, for instance. Multiple servlets can also share data, making it easy to implement database connection pooling and similar resource-sharing optimizations. Servlets can also maintain information from request to request, simplifying techniques like session tracking and caching of previous computations.

Portable

Servlets are written in the Java programming language and follow a standard API. Servlets are supported directly or by a plugin on virtually *every* major Web server. Consequently, servlets written for, say, Macromedia JRun can run virtually unchanged on Apache Tomcat, Microsoft Internet Information Server (with a separate plugin), IBM WebSphere, iPlanet Enterprise Server, Oracle9i AS, or StarNine WebStar. They are part of the Java 2 Platform, Enterprise Edition (J2EE; see http://java.sun.com/j2ee/), so industry support for servlets is becoming even more pervasive.

Inexpensive

A number of free or very inexpensive Web servers are good for development use or deployment of low- or medium-volume Web sites. Thus, with servlets and JSP you can start with a free or inexpensive server and migrate to more expensive servers with high-performance capabilities or advanced administration utilities only after your project meets initial success. This is in contrast to many of the other CGI alternatives, which require a significant initial investment for the purchase of a proprietary package.

Price and portability are somewhat connected. For example, Marty tries to keep track of the countries of readers that send him questions by email. India was near the top of the list, probably #2 behind the U.S. Marty also taught one of his JSP and servlet training courses (see http://courses.coreservlets.com/) in Manila, and there was great interest in servlet and JSP technology there.

Now, why are India and the Philippines both so interested? We surmise that the answer is twofold. First, both countries have large pools of well-educated software developers. Second, both countries have (or had, at that time) highly unfavorable currency exchange rates against the U.S. dollar. So, buying a special-purpose Web server from a U.S. company consumed a large part of early project funds.

But, with servlets and JSP, they could start with a free server: Apache Tomcat (either standalone, embedded in the regular Apache Web server, or embedded in Microsoft IIS). Once the project starts to become successful, they could move to a server like Caucho Resin that had higher performance and easier administration but that is not free. But none of their servlets or JSP pages have to be rewritten. If their project becomes even larger, they might want to move to a distributed (clustered) environment. No problem: they could move to Macromedia JRun Professional, which supports distributed applications (Web farms). Again, none of their servlets or JSP pages have to be rewritten. If the project becomes quite large and complex, they might want to use Enterprise JavaBeans (EJB) to encapsulate their business logic. So, they might switch to BEA WebLogic or Oracle9i AS. Again, none of their servlets or JSP pages have to be rewritten. Finally, if their project becomes even bigger, they might move it off of their Linux box and onto an IBM mainframe running IBM WebSphere. But once again, none of their servlets or JSP pages have to be rewritten.

Secure

One of the main sources of vulnerabilities in traditional CGI stems from the fact that the programs are often executed by general-purpose operating system shells. So, the CGI programmer must be careful to filter out characters such as backquotes and semicolons that are treated specially by the shell. Implementing this precaution is harder than one might think, and weaknesses stemming from this problem are constantly being uncovered in widely used CGI libraries.

A second source of problems is the fact that some CGI programs are processed by languages that do not automatically check array or string bounds. For example, in C and C++ it is perfectly legal to allocate a 100-element array and then write into the 999th "element," which is really some random part of program memory. So, programmers who forget to perform this check open up their system to deliberate or accidental buffer overflow attacks.

Servlets suffer from neither of these problems. Even if a servlet executes a system call (e.g., with `Runtime.exec` or JNI) to invoke a program on the local operating system, it does not use a shell to do so. And, of course, array bounds checking and other memory protection features are a central part of the Java programming language.

Mainstream

There are a lot of good technologies out there. But if vendors don't support them and developers don't know how to use them, what good are they? Servlet and JSP technology is supported by servers from Apache, Oracle, IBM, Sybase, BEA, Macromedia, Caucho, Sun/iPlanet, New Atlanta, ATG, Fujitsu, Lutris, Silverstream, the World Wide Web Consortium (W3C), and many others. Several low-cost plugins add support to Microsoft IIS and Zeus as well. They run on Windows, Unix/Linux, MacOS, VMS, and IBM mainframe operating systems. They are the single most popular application of the Java programming language. They are arguably the most popular choice for developing medium to large Web applications. They are used by the airline industry (most United Airlines and Delta Airlines Web sites), e-commerce (ofoto.com), online banking (First USA Bank, Banco Popular de Puerto Rico), Web search engines/portals (excite.com), large financial sites (American Century Investments), and hundreds of other sites that you visit every day.

Of course, popularity alone is no proof of good technology. Numerous counter-examples abound. But our point is that you are not experimenting with a new and unproven technology when you work with server-side Java.

1.5 The Role of JSP

A somewhat oversimplified view of servlets is that they are Java programs with HTML embedded inside of them. A somewhat oversimplified view of JSP documents is that they are HTML pages with Java code embedded inside of them.

For example, compare the sample servlet shown earlier (Listing 1.1) with the JSP page shown below (Listing 1.2). They look totally different; the first looks mostly like a regular Java class, whereas the second looks mostly like a normal HTML page. The interesting thing is that, despite the huge apparent difference, behind the scenes they are the same. In fact, a JSP document is just another way of writing a servlet. JSP pages get translated into servlets, the servlets get compiled, and it is the servlets that run at request time.

Listing 1.2 Store.jsp

```
<!DOCTYPE HTML PUBLIC "-//W3C//DTD HTML 4.0 Transitional//EN">
<HTML>
<HEAD><TITLE>Welcome to Our Store</TITLE></HEAD>
<BODY BGCOLOR="#FDF5E6">
<H1>Welcome to Our Store</H1>
<SMALL>Welcome,
<!-- User name is "New User" for first-time visitors -->
<%= coreservlets.Utils.getUserNameFromCookie(request) %>
To access your account settings, click
<A HREF="Account-Settings.html">here.</A></SMALL>
<P>
Regular HTML for  rest of online store's Web page
</BODY></HTML>
```

So, the question is, If JSP technology and servlet technology are essentially equivalent in power, does it matter which you use? The answer is, Yes, yes, yes! The issue is not power, but convenience, ease of use, and maintainability. For example, anything you can do in the Java programming language you could do in assembly language. Does this mean that it does not matter which you use? Hardly.

JSP is discussed in great detail starting in Chapter 10. But, it is worthwhile mentioning now how servlets and JSP fit together. JSP is focused on simplifying the creation and maintenance of the HTML. Servlets are best at invoking the business logic and performing complicated operations. A quick rule of thumb is that servlets are best for tasks oriented toward *processing*, whereas JSP is best for tasks oriented toward *presentation*. For some requests, servlets are the right choice. For other requests, JSP is a better option. For still others, neither servlets alone nor JSP alone is best, and a combination of the two (see Chapter 15, "Integrating Servlets and JSP: The Model View Controller (MVC) Architecture") is best. But the point is that you need *both* servlets and JSP in your overall project: almost no project will consist entirely of servlets or entirely of JSP. You want both.

OK, enough talk. Move on to the next chapter and get started!

SERVLET TECHNOLOGY

Part 

SERVER SETUP AND CONFIGURATION

Topics in This Chapter

- Installing and configuring Java
- Downloading and setting up a server
- Configuring your development environment
- Testing your setup
- Simplifying servlet and JSP deployment
- Locating files in Tomcat, JRun, and Resin
- Organizing projects into Web applications

Chapter 2

Before you can start learning specific servlet and JSP techniques, you need to have the right software and know how to use it. This introductory chapter explains how to obtain, configure, test, and use free versions of all the software needed to run servlets and JavaServer Pages (JSP). The initial setup involves seven steps, as outlined below.

1. **Download and install the Java Software Development Kit (SDK).** This step involves downloading an implementation of the Java 2 Platform, Standard Edition and setting your `PATH` appropriately. It is covered in Section 2.1.
2. **Download a server.** This step involves obtaining a server that implements the Servlet 2.3 (JSP 1.2) or Servlet 2.4 (JSP 2.0) APIs. It is covered in Section 2.2.
3. **Configure the server.** This step involves telling the server where the SDK is installed, changing the port to 80, and possibly making several server-specific customizations. The general approach is outlined in Section 2.3, with Sections 2.4–2.6 providing specific details for Apache Tomcat, Macromedia JRun, and Caucho Resin.
4. **Set up your development environment.** This step involves setting your `CLASSPATH` to include your top-level development directory and the JAR file containing the servlet and JSP classes. It is covered in Section 2.7.
5. **Test your setup.** This step involves checking the server home page and trying some simple JSP pages and servlets. It is covered in Section 2.8.

6. **Establish a simplified deployment method.** This step involves choosing an approach for copying resources from your development directory to the server's deployment area. It is covered in Section 2.9.
7. **Create custom Web applications.** This step involves creating a separate directory for your application and modifying web.xml to give custom URLs to your servlets. This step can be postponed until you are comfortable with basic servlet and JSP development. It is covered in Section 2.11.

2.1 Download and Install the Java Software Development Kit (SDK)

You probably have already installed the Java Platform, but if not, doing so should be your first step. Current versions of the servlet and JSP APIs require the Java 2 Platform (Standard Edition—J2SE—or Enterprise Edition—J2EE). If you aren't using J2EE features like Enterprise JavaBeans (EJB) or Java Messaging Service (JMS), we recommend that you use the standard edition. Your server will supply the classes needed to add servlet and JSP support to Java 2 Standard Edition.

But what Java version do you need? Well, it depends on what servlet/JSP API you are using, and whether you are using a full J2EE-compliant application server (e.g., WebSphere, WebLogic, or JBoss) or a standalone servlet/JSP container (e.g., Tomcat, JRun, or Resin). If you are starting from scratch, we recommend that you use the latest Java version (1.4); doing so will give you the best performance and guarantee that you are compatible with future releases. But, if you want to know the minimum supported version, here is a quick summary.

- **Servlets 2.3 and JSP 1.2** (standalone servers). Java 1.2 or later.
- **J2EE 1.3** (which includes servlets 2.3 and JSP 1.2). Java 1.3 or later.
- **Servlets 2.4 and JSP 2.0** (standalone servers). Java 1.3 or later.
- **J2EE 1.4** (which includes servlets 2.4 and JSP 2.0). Java 1.4 or later.

We use Java 1.4 in our examples.

For Solaris, Windows, and Linux, obtain Java 1.4 at http://java.sun.com/j2se/1.4/ and 1.3 at http://java.sun.com/j2se/1.3/. Be sure to download the SDK (Software Development Kit), not just the JRE (Java Runtime Environment)—the JRE is intended only for executing already compiled Java class files and lacks a compiler. For other platforms, check first whether a Java 2 implementation comes preinstalled as it does with MacOS X. If not, see Sun's list of third-party Java implementations at http://java.sun.com/cgi-bin/java-ports.cgi.

Your Java implementation should come with complete configuration instructions, but the key point is to set the PATH (not CLASSPATH!) environment variable to refer to the directory that contains java and javac, typically *java_install_dir*/bin. For example, if you are running Windows and installed the SDK in C:\j2sdk1.4.1_01, you might put the following line in your C:\autoexec.bat file. Remember that the autoexec.bat file is executed only when the system is booted.

```
set PATH=C:\j2sdk1.4.1_01\bin;%PATH%
```

If you want to download an already configured autoexec.bat file that contains the PATH setting and the other settings discussed in this chapter, go to http://www.coreservlets.com/, go to the source code archive, and select Chapter 2.

On Windows NT/2000/XP, you could also right-click on My Computer, select Properties, then Advanced, then Environment Variables. Then, you would update the PATH value and press the OK button.

On Unix (Solaris, Linux, etc.), if the SDK is installed in /usr/j2sdk1.4.1_01 and you use the C shell, you would put the following into your .cshrc file.

```
setenv PATH /usr/j2sdk1.4.1_01/bin:$PATH
```

After rebooting (Windows; not necessary if you set the variables interactively) or logging out and back in (Unix), verify that the Java setup is correct by opening a DOS window (Windows) or shell (Unix) and typing `java -version` and `javac -help`. You should see a real result *both* times, not an error message about an unknown command. Alternatively, if you use an Integrated Development Environment (IDE) like Borland JBuilder, Eclipse, IntelliJ IDEA, or Sun ONE Studio, compile and run a simple program to confirm that the IDE knows where you installed Java.

2.2 Download a Server for Your Desktop

Your second step is to download a server (often called a "servlet container" or "servlet engine") that implements the Servlet 2.3 Specification (JSP 1.2) or the Servlet 2.4 Specification (JSP 2.0) for use on your desktop. In fact, we typically keep *three* servers (Apache Tomcat, Macromedia JRun, and Caucho Resin) installed on our desktops and test applications on all the servers, to keep us aware of cross-platform deployment issues and to prevent us from accidentally using nonportable features. We'll give details on each of these servers throughout the book.

Regardless of the server that you use for final deployment, you will want at least one server *on your desktop* for development. Even if the deployment server is in the office next to you connected by a lightning-fast network connection, you still don't want to use it for your development. Even a test server on your intranet that is inaccessible to customers is much less convenient for development purposes than a server right on your desktop. Running a development server on your desktop simplifies development in a number of ways, as compared to deploying to a remote server each and every time you want to test something. Here is why:

- **It is faster to test.** With a server on your desktop, there is no need to use FTP or another upload program. The harder it is for you to test changes, the less frequently you will test. Infrequent testing will let errors persist that will slow you down in the long run.
- **It is easier to debug.** When running on your desktop, many servers display the standard output in a normal window. This is in contrast to deployment servers on which the standard output is almost always either hidden or only available in a log file after execution is completed. So, with a desktop server, plain old `System.out.println` statements become useful tracing and debugging utilities.
- **It is simple to restart.** During development, you will find that you frequently need to restart the server or reload your Web application. For example, the server typically reads the web.xml file (see Section 2.11, "Web Applications: A Preview") only when the server starts or a server-specific command is given to reload a Web application. So, you normally have to restart the server or reload the Web application each time you modify web.xml. Even when servers have an interactive method of reloading web.xml, tasks such as clearing session data, resetting the `ServletContext`, or replacing modified class files used indirectly by servlets or JSP pages (e.g., beans or utility classes) may still necessitate that the server be restarted. Some older servers also need to be restarted because they implement servlet reloading unreliably. (Normally, servers instantiate the class that corresponds to a servlet only once and keep the instance in memory between requests. With *servlet reloading*, a server automatically replaces servlets that are in memory but whose class files have changed on the disk.) Besides, some deployment servers recommend completely disabling servlet reloading to increase performance. So, it is much more productive to develop in an environment in which you can restart the server or reload the Web application with a click of the mouse—without asking for permission from other developers who might be using the server.
- **It is more reliable to benchmark.** Although it is difficult to collect accurate timing results for short-running programs even in the best of circumstances, running benchmarks on multiuser systems that have heavy and varying system loads is notoriously unreliable.

- **It is under your control.** As a developer, you may not be the administrator of the system on which the test or deployment server runs. You might have to ask some system administrator every time you want the server restarted. Or, the remote system may be down for a system upgrade at the most critical juncture of your development cycle. Not fun.
- **It is easy to install.** Downloading and configuring a server takes no more than an hour. By using a server on your desktop instead of a remote one, you'll probably save yourself that much time the very first day you start developing.

If you can run the same server on your desktop that you use for deployment, all the better. So, if you are deploying on BEA WebLogic, IBM WebSphere, Oracle9i AS, etc., and your license permits you to also run the server on your desktop, by all means do so. But one of the beauties of servlets and JSP is that you don't *have* to; you can develop with one server and deploy with another.

Following are some of the most popular free options for desktop development servers. In all cases, the free version runs as a standalone Web server. In most cases, you have to pay for the deployment version that can be integrated with a regular Web server like Microsoft IIS, iPlanet/Sun ONE Server, Zeus, or the Apache Web Server. However, the performance difference between using one of the servers as a servlet and JSP engine within a regular Web server and using it as a complete standalone Web server is not significant enough to matter during development. See http://java.sun.com/products/servlet/industry.html for a more complete list of servers and server plugins that support servlets and JSP.

- **Apache Tomcat.** Tomcat 5 is the official reference implementation of the servlet 2.4 and JSP 2.0 specifications. Tomcat 4 is the official reference implementation for servlets 2.3 (JSP 1.2). Both versions can be used as standalone servers during development or can be plugged into a standard Web server for use during deployment. Like all Apache products, Tomcat is entirely free and has complete source code available. Of all the servers, it also tends to be the one that is most compliant with the latest servlet and JSP specifications. However, the commercial servers tend to be better documented, easier to configure, and faster. To download Tomcat, start at http://jakarta.apache.org/tomcat/, go to the binaries download section, and choose the latest release build of Tomcat.
- **Macromedia JRun.** JRun is a servlet and JSP engine that can be used in standalone mode for development or plugged into most common commercial Web servers for deployment. It is free for development purposes, but you must purchase a license before deploying with it. It is a popular choice among developers looking for easier administration than Tomcat. For details, see http://www.macromedia.com/software/jrun/.

- **Caucho's Resin.** Resin is a fast servlet and JSP engine with extensive XML support. Along with Tomcat and JRun, it is one of the three most popular servers used by commercial Web hosting companies that provide servlet and JSP support. It is free for development and noncommercial deployment purposes. For details, see http://caucho.com/products/resin/.
- **New Atlanta's ServletExec.** ServletExec is another popular servlet and JSP engine that can be used in standalone mode for development or, for deployment, plugged into the Microsoft IIS, Apache, and Sun ONE servers. You can download and use it for free, but some of the high-performance capabilities and administration utilities are disabled until you purchase a license. The ServletExec Debugger is the configuration you would use as a standalone desktop development server. For details, see http://www.newatlanta.com/products/servletexec/.
- **Jetty.** Jetty is an open-source server that supports servlets and JSP technology and is free for both development and deployment. It is often used as a complete standalone server (rather than integrated inside a non-Java Web server), even for deployment. For details, see http://jetty.mortbay.org/jetty/.

2.3 Configure the Server

Once you have downloaded and installed both the Java Platform itself and a server that supports servlets and JSP, you need to configure your server to run on your system. This configuration involves the following generic steps; the following three sections give specific details for Tomcat, JRun, and Resin.

Please note that these directions are geared toward using the server as a standalone Web server for use in desktop development. For deployment, you often set up your server to act as plugin within a traditional Web server like Apache or IIS. This configuration is beyond the scope of this book; use the wizard that comes with the server or read the configuration instructions in the vendor's documentation.

1. **Identifying the SDK installation directory.** To compile JSP pages, the server needs to know the location of the Java classes that are used by the Java compiler (e.g., `javac` or `jikes`). With most servers, either the server installation wizard detects the location of the SDK directory or you need to set the `JAVA_HOME` environment variable to refer to that directory. `JAVA_HOME` should list the base SDK installation directory, not the `bin` subdirectory.

2. **Specifying the port.** Most servers come preconfigured to use a non-standard port, just in case an existing server is already using port 80. If no server is already using port 80, for convenience, set your newly installed server to use that port.
3. **Making server-specific customizations.** These settings vary from server to server. Be sure to read your server's installation directions.

2.4 Configuring Apache Tomcat

Of all of the popular servlet and JSP engines, Tomcat is the hardest to configure. Tomcat is also the most fluid of the popular servers: compared to most other servers, Tomcat has more frequent releases and each version has more significant changes to the setup and configuration instructions. So, to handle new versions of Tomcat, we maintain an up-to-date Web page at http://www.coreservlets.com/ for installing and configuring Tomcat. Our online Tomcat configuration page includes sample versions of the three major files you need to edit: autoexec.bat, server.xml, and web.xml. If you use a version of Tomcat later than 4.1.24, you may want to refer to that Web site for details. Instructions consistent with release 4.1.24 follow.

Your first step is to download the Tomcat zip file from http://jakarta.apache.org/tomcat/. Click on Binaries and choose the latest release version. Assuming you are using JDK 1.4, select the "LE" version (e.g., tomcat-4.1.24-LE-jdk14.zip). Next, unzip the file into a location of your choosing. The only restriction is that the location cannot be protected from write access: Tomcat creates temporary files when it runs, so Tomcat must be installed in a location to which the user who starts Tomcat has write access. Unzipping Tomcat will result in a top-level directory similar to C:\jakarta-tomcat-4.1.24-LE-jdk14 (hereafter referred to as *install_dir*). Once you have downloaded and unzipped the Tomcat files, configuring the server involves the following steps. We give a quick summary below, then provide details in the following subsections.

1. **Setting the `JAVA_HOME` variable.** Set this variable to list the base SDK installation directory.
2. **Specifying the server port.** Edit *install_dir*/conf/server.xml and change the value of the `port` attribute of the `Connector` element from 8080 to 80.
3. **Enabling servlet reloading.** Add a `DefaultContext` element to *install_dir*/conf/server.xml to tell Tomcat to reload servlets that have been loaded into the server's memory but whose class files have changed on disk since they were loaded.

4. **Enabling the ROOT context.** To enable the default Web application, uncomment the following line in *install_dir*/conf/server.xml. `<Context path="" docBase="ROOT" debug="0"/>`
5. **Turning on the invoker servlet.** To permit you to run servlets without making changes to your web.xml file, some versions of Tomcat require you to uncomment the `/servlet/*` `servlet-mapping` element in *install_dir*/conf/web.xml.
6. **Increasing DOS memory limits.** On older Windows versions, tell the operating system to reserve more space for environment variables.
7. **Setting `CATALINA_HOME`.** Optionally, set the `CATALINA_HOME` environment variable to refer to the base Tomcat installation directory.

The following subsections give details on each of these steps. Please note that this section describes the use of Tomcat as a standalone server for servlet and JSP *development*. It requires a totally different configuration to deploy Tomcat as a servlet and JSP container integrated within a regular Web server (e.g., with `mod_webapp` in the Apache Web Server). For information on the use of Tomcat for deployment, see http://jakarta.apache.org/tomcat/tomcat-4.1-doc/.

Setting the JAVA_HOME Variable

The most critical Tomcat setting is the `JAVA_HOME` environment variable—an improper setting stops Tomcat from finding the classes used by `javac` and thus prevents Tomcat from handling JSP pages. This variable should list the base SDK installation directory, not the bin subdirectory. For example, if you are running Windows and you installed the SDK in C:\j2sdk1.4.1_01, you might put the following line in your C:\autoexec.bat file. Remember that the autoexec.bat file is executed only when the system is booted.

```
set JAVA_HOME=C:\j2sdk1.4.1_01
```

On Windows NT/2000/XP, you could also right-click on My Computer, select Properties, then Advanced, then Environment Variables. Then, you would enter the `JAVA_HOME` value and click OK.

On Unix (Solaris, Linux, MacOS X, AIX, etc.), if the SDK is installed in /usr/local/java1.4 and you use the C shell, you would put the following into your .cshrc file.

```
setenv JAVA_HOME /usr/local/java1.4
```

Rather than setting the `JAVA_HOME` environment variable globally in the operating system, some developers prefer to edit the Tomcat startup script and set the variable there. If you prefer this strategy, edit *install_dir*/bin/catalina.bat (Windows) and insert the following line at the top of the file, after the first set of comments.

```
set JAVA_HOME=C:\j2sdk1.4.1_01
```

Be sure to make a backup copy of catalina.bat before making the changes. Unix users would make similar changes to catalina.sh.

Specifying the Server Port

Most of the free servers listed in Section 2.2 use a nonstandard default port to avoid conflicts with other Web servers that may already be using the standard port (80). Tomcat is no exception: it uses port 8080 by default. However, if you are using Tomcat in standalone mode (i.e., as a complete Web server, not just as a servlet and JSP engine integrated within another Web server) and have no other server running permanently on port 80, you will find it more convenient to use port 80. That way, you don't have to use the port number in every URL you type in your browser. Note, however, that on Unix, you must have system administrator privileges to start services on port 80 or other port numbers below 1024. You probably have such privileges on your desktop machine; you do not necessarily have them on deployment servers. Furthermore, many Windows XP Professional implementations have Microsoft IIS already registered on port 80; you'll have to disable IIS if you want to run Tomcat on port 80. You can permanently disable IIS from the Administrative Tools/Internet Information Services section of the Control Panel.

Modifying the port number involves editing *install_dir*/conf/server.xml, changing the `port` attribute of the `Connector` element from 8080 to 80, and restarting the server. Replace *install_dir* with the base Tomcat installation location. For example, if you downloaded the Java 1.4 version of Tomcat 4.1.24 and unzipped it into the C directory, you would edit C:\jakarta-tomcat-4.1.24-LE-jdk14\conf\server.xml.

With Tomcat, the original element will look something like the following:

```
<Connector className="org.apache.coyote.tomcat4.CoyoteConnector"
           port="8080" minProcessors="5" maxProcessors="75"
           ... />
```

It should change to something like the following:

```
<Connector className="org.apache.coyote.tomcat4.CoyoteConnector"
           port="80" minProcessors="5" maxProcessors="75"
           ... />
```

Note that this element varies a bit from one Tomcat version to another. The easiest way to find the correct entry is to search for 8080 in server.xml; there should be only one noncomment occurrence. Be sure to make a backup of server.xml before you edit it, just in case you make a mistake that prevents the server from running. Also, remember that XML is case sensitive, so, for instance, you cannot replace `port` with `Port` or `Connector` with `connector`.

Enabling Servlet Reloading

The next step is to tell Tomcat to check the modification dates of the class files of requested servlets and reload ones that have changed since they were loaded into the server's memory. This slightly degrades performance in deployment situations, so is turned off by default. However, if you fail to turn it on for your development server, you'll have to restart the server or reload your Web application every time you recompile a servlet that has already been loaded into the server's memory.

To turn on servlet reloading, edit *install_dir*/conf/server.xml by adding a `DefaultContext` subelement to the main `Service` element and supply `true` for the `reloadable` attribute. The easiest way to do this is to find the following comment:

```
<!-- Define properties for each web application. ...
... -->
```

and insert the following line just below it:

```
<DefaultContext reloadable="true"/>
```

Again, be sure to make a backup copy of server.xml before making this change.

Enabling the ROOT Context

The ROOT context is the default Web application in Tomcat; it is convenient to use when you are first learning about servlets and JSP (although you'll use your own Web applications once you're more experienced—see Section 2.11). The default Web application is already enabled in Tomcat 4.0 and some versions of Tomcat 4.1. But, in Tomcat 4.1.24, it is disabled by default. To enable it, uncomment the following line in *install_dir*/conf/server.xml:

```
<Context path="" docBase="ROOT" debug="0"/>
```

Turning on the Invoker Servlet

The invoker servlet lets you run servlets without first making changes to the WEB-INF/web.xml file in your Web application. Instead, you just drop your servlet into WEB-INF/classes and use the URL http://*host*/servlet/*ServletName* (for the default Web application) or http://*host*/*webAppPrefix*/servlet/*ServletName* (for custom Web applications). The invoker servlet is extremely convenient when you are first learning and even when you are in the initial development phase of real projects. But, as discussed at length later in the book, you do not want it on at deployment time. Up until Apache Tomcat 4.1.12, the invoker was enabled by default. However, a security flaw was recently uncovered whereby the invoker servlet could be used to see the source code of servlets that were generated from JSP pages. Although this may not matter in most cases, it might reveal proprietary code to outsiders, so, as of Tomcat 4.1.12, the invoker was disabled by default. We suspect that the Jakarta project will fix the problem soon and reenable the invoker servlet in upcoming Tomcat releases. In the meantime, however, you almost certainly want to enable it when learning. Just be sure that you do so only on a desktop development machine that is not accessible to the outside world.

To enable the invoker servlet, uncomment the following `servlet-mapping` element in *install_dir*/conf/web.xml. Note that the filename is web.xml, not server.xml, and do not confuse this Tomcat-specific web.xml file with the standard one that goes in the WEB-INF directory of each Web application.

```
<servlet-mapping>
  <servlet-name>invoker</servlet-name>
  <url-pattern>/servlet/*</url-pattern>
</servlet-mapping>
```

Increasing DOS Memory Limits

If you use an old version of Windows (i.e., Windows 98/Me or earlier), you may have to change the DOS memory settings for the startup and shutdown scripts. If you get an "Out of Environment Space" error message when you start the server, you will need to right-click on *install_dir*/bin/startup.bat, select Properties, select Memory, and change the Initial Environment entry from Auto to at least 2816. Repeat the process for *install_dir*/bin/shutdown.bat.

Setting CATALINA_HOME

In some cases, it is also helpful to set the `CATALINA_HOME` environment variable to refer to the base Tomcat installation directory. This variable identifies the location of various Tomcat files to the server. However, if you are careful to avoid copying the server startup and shutdown scripts and instead use only shortcuts (called "symbolic links" on Unix) instead, you are *not* required to set this variable. See Section 2.9 (Establish a Simplified Deployment Method) for more information on using these shortcuts.

Testing the Basic Server Setup

To verify that you have configured Tomcat successfully, double-click on *install_dir*/bin/startup.bat (Windows) or execute *install_dir*/bin/startup.sh (Unix/Linux). Open a browser and enter http://localhost/ (http://localhost:8080/

if you chose not to change the port to 80). You should see something similar to Figure 2–1. Shut down the server by double-clicking on *install_dir*/bin/shutdown.bat (Windows) or executing *install_dir*/bin/shutdown.sh (Unix). If you cannot get Tomcat to run, try going to *install_dir*/bin and typing `catalina run`; this will prevent Tomcat from starting a separate window and will let you see error messages such as those that stem from the port being in use or `JAVA_HOME` being defined incorrectly.

After you customize your development environment (see Section 2.7), be sure to perform the more exhaustive tests listed in Section 2.8.

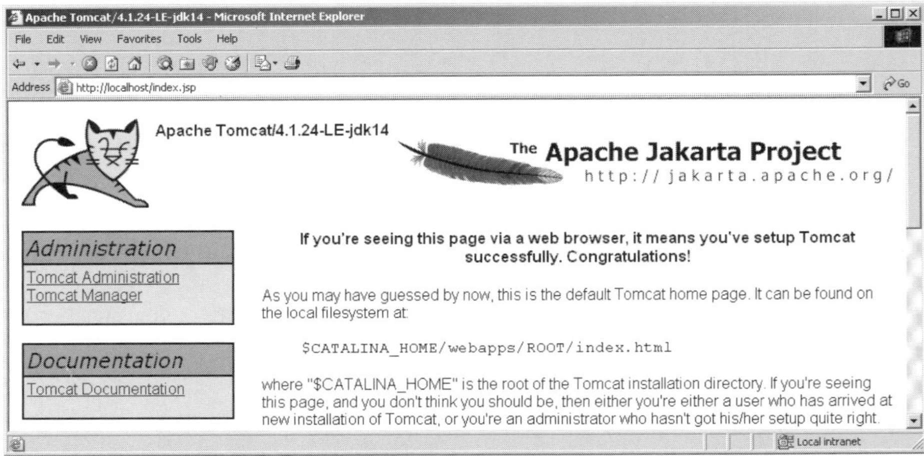

Figure 2–1 Tomcat home page.

2.5 Configuring Macromedia JRun

To use JRun on your desktop, your first step is to download the free development version of JRun from http://www.macromedia.com/software/jrun/ and run the installation wizard. Most of the configuration settings are specified during installation. There are seven main settings you are likely to want to specify. The following list gives a quick summary; details are given in the subsections that follow the list.

1. **The serial number.** Leave it blank for the free development server.
2. **User restrictions.** You can limit the use of JRun to your account or make it available to anyone on your system.
3. **The SDK installation location.** Specify the base directory, not the bin subdirectory.

4. **The server installation directory.** In most cases, you just accept the default.
5. **The administrator username and password.** You will need these values for making additional customizations later.
6. **The autostart capability.** During development, you do *not* want JRun to start automatically. In particular, on Windows, you should *not* identify JRun as a Windows service.
7. **The server port.** You will probably want to change it from 8100 to 80.

The JRun Serial Number

Using JRun in development mode (i.e., where only requests from the local machine are accepted) does not require a serial number. So, unless you are using a full deployment version of the server, leave the serial number blank when prompted for it. You can upgrade to a deployment version later without reinstalling the server. See Figure 2–2.

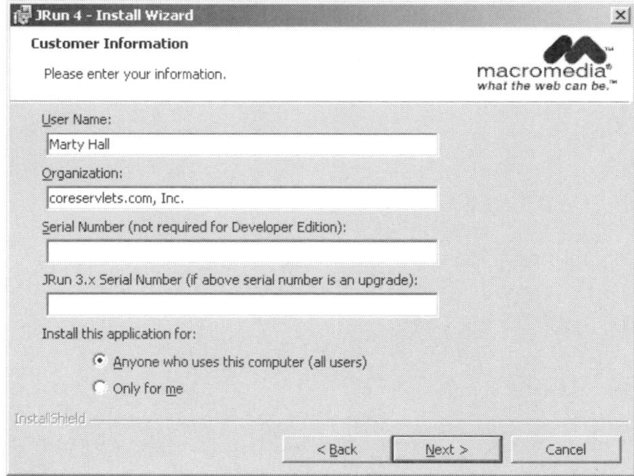

Figure 2–2 Omit the serial number if you are using the free development version of JRun.

JRun User Restrictions

When you install JRun, you will be asked whether you want the server to be available to all users on your system or only to your account. See Figure 2–2. Select whichever is appropriate.

The Java Installation Location

The installation wizard will search for a Java installation and present its base directory as the default choice. If that choice refers to your most recent Java version, accept the default. However, if the installation wizard finds an older version of Java, choose Browse and select an alternative location. In such a case, make sure you supply the location of the base directory, not the bin subdirectory. Also, be sure that you designate the location of the full SDK (called "JDK" in Java 1.3 and earlier), not of the JRE (Java Runtime Environment)—the JRE directory lacks the classes needed to compile JSP pages. See Figure 2–3.

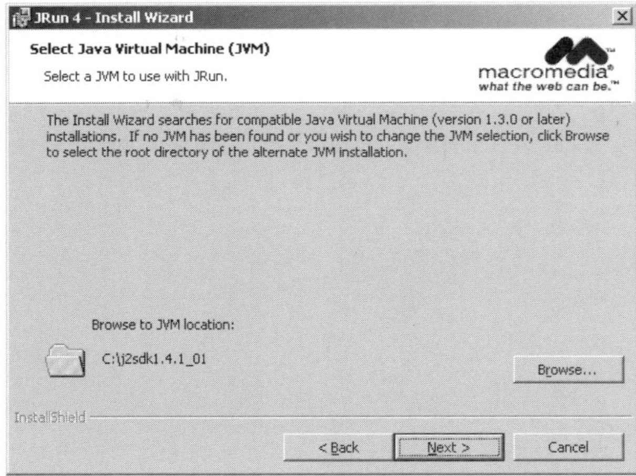

Figure 2–3 Be sure the JVM location refers to the base installation directory of your latest Java version.

The Server Installation Location

You can choose whatever directory you want for this option. Most users simply accept the default, which, on Windows, is C:\JRun4.

The Administrator Username and Password

The installation wizard will prompt you for a name and password. The values you supply are arbitrary, but be sure to remember what you specified; you will need them to customize the server later. See Figure 2–4.

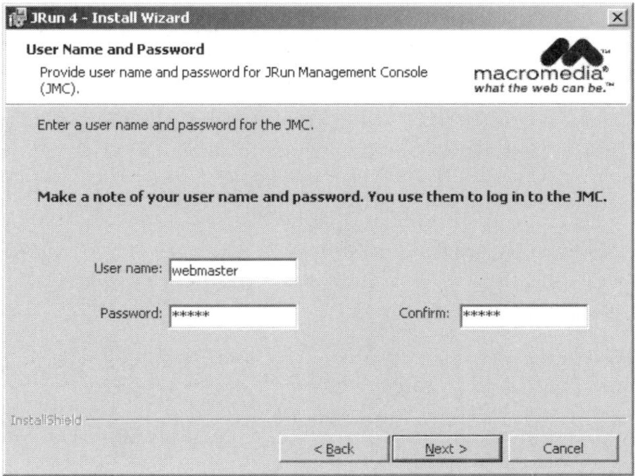

Figure 2–4 Be sure to remember the administrator username and password.

The Autostart Capability

When using JRun as a development server, you will find it much more convenient to start and stop JRun manually than to have the operating system start JRun automatically. So, when prompted whether you want JRun to be a Windows service, leave the choice unchecked. See Figure 2–5.

JRun 4 - Install Wizard
Install JRun Services
Specify how JRun starts.
macromedia®
what the web can be.™
You can manually start JRun, or you can specify that JRun starts automatically when you start your computer. To start JRun automatically, select Install JRun as a Windows service.
We recommend that you install JRun as a Windows service for deployment but not for development.
Install JRun as a Windows service.
InstallShield
< Back
Next >
Cancel

Figure 2–5 Do *not* install JRun as a Windows service.

The Server Port

After completing the installation, go to the Start menu, select Programs, select Macromedia JRun 4, and choose JRun Launcher. Select the admin server and press Start. Do the same for the default server. See Figure 2–6.

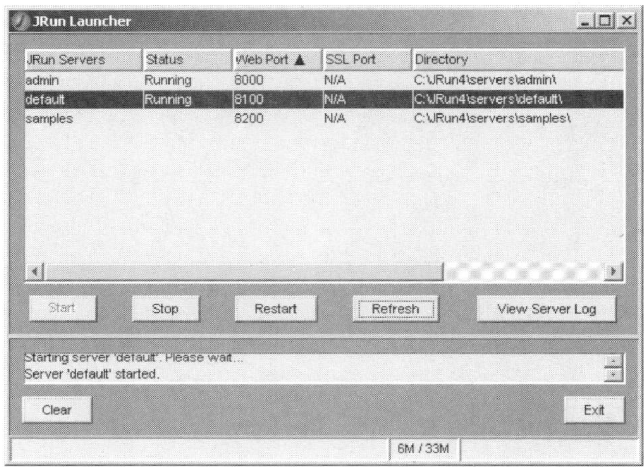

Figure 2–6 You use the JRun Launcher to start and stop the administration and default servers.

Next, either open a browser and enter the URL http://localhost:8000/ or go to the Start menu, select Programs, select Macromedia JRun 4, and choose JRun Management Console. Either option will result in a Web page that prompts you for a username and password. Enter the values you specified during installation, then select Services under the default server in the left-hand pane. This will yield a result similar to Figure 2–7. Next, choose WebService, change the port from 8100 to 80, press Apply, and stop and restart the server.

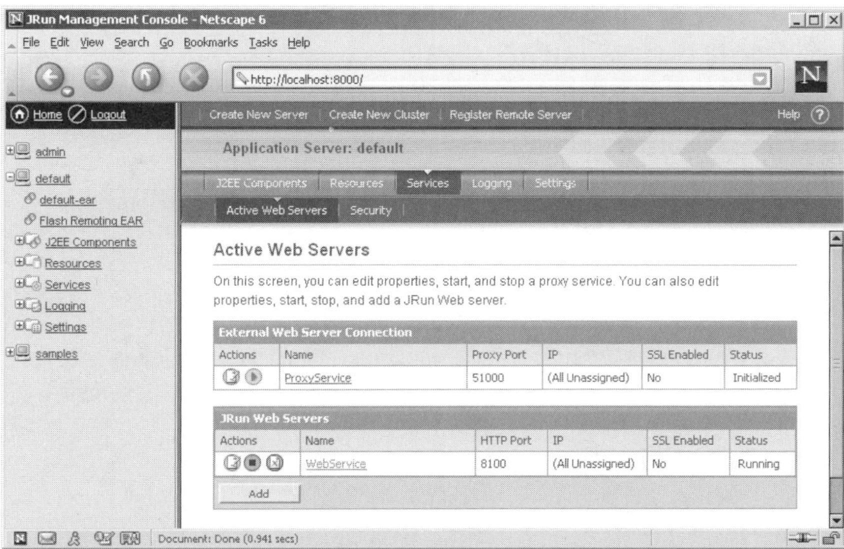

Figure 2–7 After selecting Services under the default server, choose WebService to edit the port of the default JRun server.

Testing the Basic Server Setup

To verify that you have configured JRun successfully, open the JRun Launcher by going to the Start menu, selecting Programs, choosing Macromedia JRun 4, and designating JRun Launcher. If you just changed the server port, the server is probably already running. (Note that you do not need to start the admin server unless you want to modify additional server options.) Open a browser and enter http://localhost/ (http://localhost:8100/ if you chose not to change the port to 80). You should see something similar to Figure 2–8. Shut down the server by pressing Stop in the JRun Launcher.

After you customize your development environment (see Section 2.7), be sure to perform the more exhaustive tests listed in Section 2.8.

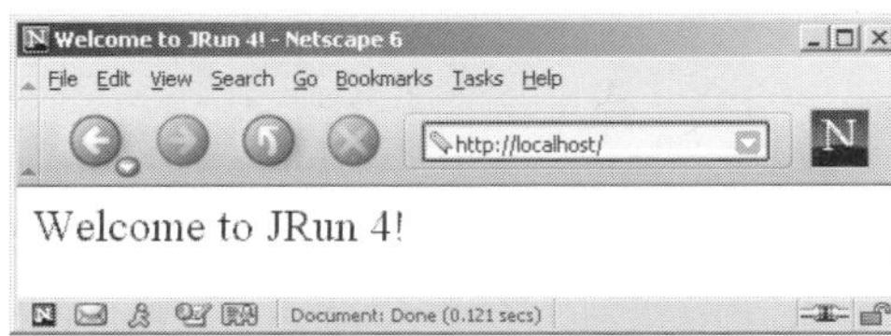

Figure 2–8 The JRun home page.

2.6 Configuring Caucho Resin

To run Resin on your desktop, you should first download the Resin zip file from http://caucho.com/products/resin/ and unzip it into a location of your choosing (hereafter referred to as *install_dir*). Once you have done so, configuring the server involves two simple steps.

1. **Setting the `JAVA_HOME` variable.** Set this variable to list the base SDK installation directory.
2. **Specifying the port.** Edit *install_dir*/conf/resin.conf and change the value of the `port` attribute of the `http` element from 8080 to 80.

Details are given in the following subsections.

Setting the JAVA_HOME Variable

The most important setting is the `JAVA_HOME` environment variable. This variable should refer to the base SDK installation directory. Details are given in Section 2.4 (Configuring Apache Tomcat), but for a quick example, if you are using Java 1.4.1 on Windows, you might put the following line in C:\autoexec.bat.

```
set JAVA_HOME=C:\j2sdk1.4.1_01
```

Specifying the Resin Port

To avoid conflicts with preexisting servers, Resin uses port 8080 by default. However, if you won't be simultaneously running another server, you will probably find it convenient to change Resin to use port 80, the standard HTTP port. To do this, edit *install_dir*/conf/resin.conf and change `<http **port='8080'**/>` to `<http **port='80'**/>`.

Testing the Basic Server Setup

To verify that you have configured Resin successfully, double-click on *install_dir*/bin/httpd.exe. Open a browser and enter http://localhost/ (http://localhost:8080/ if you chose not to change the port to 80). You should see something similar to Figure 2–9. Shut down the server by selecting Stop in the small dialog box that pops up when you start the server.

After you customize your development environment (see Section 2.7), be sure to perform the more exhaustive tests listed in Section 2.8.

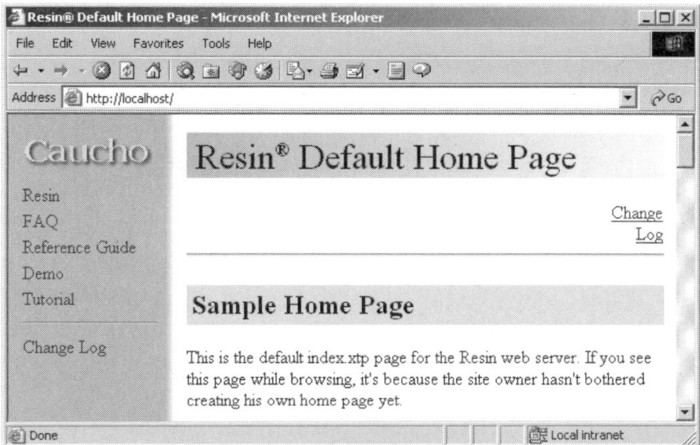

Figure 2–9 Resin home page.

2.7 Set Up Your Development Environment

You configured and tested the server, so you're all set, right? Well, no, not quite. That's just the local *deployment* environment. You still have to set up your personal *development* environment. Otherwise, you won't be able to compile servlets and auxiliary Java classes that you write. Configuring your development environment involves the following steps.

1. **Creating a development directory.** Choose a location in which to develop your servlets, JSP documents, and supporting classes.
2. **Setting your `CLASSPATH`.** Tell the compiler about the servlet and JSP JAR file and the location of your development directory. *Setting this variable incorrectly is the single most common cause of problems for beginners.*
3. **Making shortcuts to start and stop the server.** Make sure it is convenient to start and stop the server.
4. **Bookmarking or installing the servlet and JSP API documentation.** You'll refer to this documentation frequently, so keep it handy.

The following subsections give details on each of these steps.

Creating a Development Directory

The first thing you should do is create a directory in which to place the servlets and JSP documents that you develop. This directory can be in your home directory (e.g., ~/ServletDevel on Unix) or in a convenient general location (e.g., C:\ServletDevel on Windows). It should *not*, however, be in the server's installation directory.

Eventually, you will organize this development directory into different Web applications (each with a common structure—see Section 2.11, "Web Applications: A Preview"). For initial testing of your environment, however, you can just put servlets either directly in the development directory (for packageless servlets) or in a subdirectory that matches the servlet package name. After compiling, you can simply copy the class files to the server's default Web application.

Many developers put all their code in the server's deployment directory (see Section 2.10). We strongly discourage this practice and instead recommend one of the approaches described in Section 2.9 (Establish a Simplified Deployment Method). Although developing in the deployment directory seems simpler at the beginning since it requires no copying of files, it significantly complicates matters in the long run. Mixing development and deployment locations makes it hard to separate an operational version from a version you are testing, makes it difficult to test on multiple servers, and makes organization much more complicated. Besides, your desktop is almost certainly not the final deployment server, so you'll eventually have to develop a good system for deploying anyhow.

Core Warning

Don't use the server's deployment directory as your development location. Instead, keep a separate development directory.

Setting Your CLASSPATH

Since servlets and JSP are not part of the Java 2 Platform, Standard Edition, you must identify the servlet classes to the compiler. The *server* already knows about the servlet classes, but the *compiler* (i.e., `javac`) you use for development probably doesn't. So, if you don't set your `CLASSPATH`, attempts to compile servlets, tag libraries, or other classes that use the servlet API will fail with error messages about unknown classes. The exact location of the servlet JAR file varies from server to server. In most cases, you can hunt around in the *install_dir*/lib directory. Or, read your server's documentation to discover the location. Once you find the JAR file, add the location to your development `CLASSPATH`. Here are the locations for some common development servers:

- **Tomcat.**
  install_dir/common/lib/servlet.jar
- **JRun.**
  install_dir/lib/jrun.jar
- **Resin.**
  install_dir/lib/jsdk23.jar

In addition to the servlet JAR file, you also need to put your development directory in the `CLASSPATH`. Although this is not necessary for simple packageless servlets, once you gain experience you will almost certainly use packages. Compiling a file that is in a package and that uses another class in the same package requires the `CLASSPATH` to include the directory that is at the top of the package hierarchy. In this case, that's the development directory we discussed in the first subsection. Forgetting this setting is perhaps *the* most common mistake made by beginning servlet programmers.

Core Approach

Remember to add your development directory to your `CLASSPATH`. Otherwise, you will get "Unresolved symbol" error messages when you attempt to compile servlets that are in packages and that make use of other classes in the same package.

Finally, you should include "." (the current directory) in the `CLASSPATH`. Otherwise, you will only be able to compile packageless classes that are in the top-level development directory.

Here are a few representative methods of setting the `CLASSPATH`. They assume that your development directory is C:\ServletDevel (Windows) or /usr/ServletDevel (Unix) and that you are using Tomcat 4. Replace ***install_dir*** with the actual base installation location of the server. Be sure to use the appropriate case for the filenames; they are case sensitive (even on a Windows platform!). If a Windows path contains spaces (e.g., C:\Documents and Settings*Your Name*\My Documents\...), enclose it in double quotes. Note that these examples represent only one approach for setting the `CLASSPATH`. For example, you could create a script that invokes `javac` with a designated value for the `-classpath` option. In addition, many Java integrated development environments have a global or project-specific setting that accomplishes the same result. But those settings are totally IDE specific and aren't discussed here.

- **Windows 95/98/Me.** Put the following in C:\autoexec.bat. (Note that this all goes on one line with no spaces—it is broken here for readability.)
```
set CLASSPATH=.;
               C:\ServletDevel;
               install_dir\common\lib\servlet.jar
```
- **Windows NT/2000/XP.** Use the autoexec.bat file as above, or right-click on My Computer, select Properties, then System, then Advanced, then Environment Variables. Then, enter the `CLASSPATH` value from the previous bullet and click OK.
- **Unix (C shell).** Put the following in your .cshrc. (Again, in the real file it goes on a single line without spaces.)
```
setenv CLASSPATH .:
                 /usr/ServletDevel:
                 install_dir/common/lib/servlet.jar
```

Making Shortcuts to Start and Stop the Server

During our development, we find ourselves frequently restarting the server. As a result, we find it convenient to place shortcuts to the server startup and shutdown icons inside the main development directory or on the desktop. You will likely find it convenient to do the same.

For example, for Tomcat on Windows, go to *install_dir*/bin, right-click on startup.bat, and select Copy. Then go to your development directory, right-click in the window, and select Paste Shortcut (not just Paste). Repeat the process for *install_dir*/bin/shutdown.bat. Some users like to put the shortcuts on the desktop or their Start menu. If you put the shortcuts there, you can even right-click on the shortcut, select Properties, then enter a keyboard shortcut by typing a key in the "Keyboard shortcut" text field. That way, you can start and stop the server just by pressing Control-Alt-*SomeKey* on your keyboard.

On Unix, you would use `ln -s` to make a symbolic link to startup.sh, tomcat.sh (needed even though you don't directly invoke this file), and shutdown.sh.

For JRun on Windows, go to the Start menu, select Programs, select Macromedia JRun 4, right-click on the JRun Launcher icon, and select Copy. Then go to your development directory, right-click in the window, and select Paste Shortcut (not just Paste). Repeat the process for the JRun Management Console if you so desire. There is no separate shutdown icon; the JRun Launcher lets you both start and stop the server.

For Resin on Windows, right-click on *install_dir*/bin/httpd.exe, and select Copy. Then go to your development directory, right-click in the window, and select Paste Shortcut (not just Paste). There is no separate shutdown icon; invoking httpd.exe results in a popup window with a Quit button that lets you stop the server.

Bookmarking or Installing the Servlet and JSP API Documentation

Just as no serious programmer should develop general-purpose Java applications without access to the Java 1.4 or 1.3 API documentation (in Javadoc format), no serious programmer should develop servlets or JSP pages without access to the API for classes in the `javax.servlet` packages. Here is a summary of where to find the API. (Remember that the source code archive at http://www.coreservlets.com/ has up-to-date links to all URLs cited in the book, in addition to the source code for all examples.)

- **http://java.sun.com/products/jsp/download.html**
  This site lets you download the Javadoc files for the servlet 2.4 (JSP 2.0) or servlet 2.3 (JSP 1.2) APIs. You will probably find this API so useful that it will be worth having a local copy instead of browsing it online. However, some servers bundle this documentation, so check before downloading. (See the next bullet.)
- **On your local server**
  Some servers come bundled with the servlet and JSP Javadocs. For example, with Tomcat, you can access the API by going to the default home page (http://localhost/) and clicking on Tomcat Documentation and then Servlet/JSP Javadocs. Or, bookmark *install_dir*/webapps/tomcat-docs/catalina/docs/api/index.html; doing so lets you access the documentation even when Tomcat is not running. Neither JRun nor Resin bundles the API, however.
- **http://java.sun.com/products/servlet/2.3/javadoc/**
  This site lets you browse the servlet 2.3 API online.
- **http://java.sun.com/j2ee/sdk_1.3/techdocs/api/**
  This address lets you browse the complete API for version 1.3 of the Java 2 Platform, Enterprise Edition (J2EE), which includes the servlet 2.3 and JSP 1.2 packages.
- **http://java.sun.com/j2ee/1.4/docs/api/**
  This address lets you browse the complete API for version 1.4 of the Java 2 Platform, Enterprise Edition (J2EE), which includes the servlet 2.4 and JSP 2.0 packages.

2.8 Test Your Setup

Before trying your own servlets or JSP pages, you should make sure that the SDK, the server, and your development environment are all configured properly. Verification involves the three steps summarized below; more details are given in the subsections following the list.

1. **Verifying your SDK installation.** Be sure that both `java` and `javac` work properly.
2. **Checking your basic server configuration.** Access the server home page, a simple user-defined HTML page, and a simple user-defined JSP page.
3. **Compiling and deploying some simple servlets.** Try a basic packageless servlet, a servlet that uses packages, and a servlet that uses both packages and a utility (helper) class.

Verifying Your SDK Installation

Open a DOS window (Windows) or shell (Unix) and type `java -version` and `javac -help`. You should see a real result *both* times, not an error message about an unknown command. Alternatively, if you use an Integrated Development Environment (IDE), compile and run a simple program to confirm that the IDE knows where you installed Java. If either of these tests fails, review Section 2.1 (Download and Install the Java Software Development Kit (SDK)) and double-check the installation instructions that came with the SDK.

Checking Your Basic Server Configuration

First, start the server and access the standard home page (http://localhost/, or http://localhost:*port*/ if you did not change the port to 80). If this fails, review the instructions of Sections 2.3–2.6 and double-check your server's installation instructions.

After you have verified that the server is running, you should make sure that you can install and access simple HTML and JSP pages. This test, if successful, shows two important things. First, successfully accessing an HTML page shows that you understand which directories should hold HTML and JSP files. Second, successfully accessing a new JSP page shows that the Java compiler (not just the Java virtual machine) is configured properly.

Eventually, you will almost certainly want to create and use your own Web applications (see Section 2.11, "Web Applications: A Preview"), but for initial testing we recommend that you use the default Web application. Although Web applications follow a common directory structure, the exact location of the default Web application is server specific. Check your server's documentation for definitive instructions, but we summarize the locations for Tomcat, JRun, and Resin in the following list. Where we list *SomeDirectory* you can use any directory name you like. (But you are never allowed to use WEB-INF or META-INF as directory names. For the default Web application, you also must avoid a directory name that matches the URL prefix of any existing Web application such as samples or examples.) If you are running on your local machine, you can use localhost where we list *host* in the URLs.

- **Tomcat HTML/JSP directory.**
  install_dir/webapps/ROOT
  (or *install_dir*/webapps/ROOT/*SomeDirectory*)
- **JRun HTML/JSP directory.**
  install_dir/servers/default/default-ear/default-war
  (or *install_dir*/servers/default/default-ear/default-war/*SomeDirectory*)
- **Resin HTML/JSP directory.**
  install_dir/doc
  (or *install_dir*/doc/*SomeDirectory*)
- **Corresponding URLs.**
  http://*host*/Hello.html
  (or http://*host*/*SomeDirectory*/Hello.html)
  http://*host*/Hello.jsp
  (or http://*host*/*SomeDirectory*/Hello.jsp)

For your first tests, we suggest you simply drop Hello.html (Listing 2.1, Figure 2–10) and Hello.jsp (Listing 2.2, Figure 2–11) into the appropriate locations. For now, don't worry about what the JSP document does; we'll cover that later. The code for these files, as well as *all* the code from the book, is available online at http://www.coreservlets.com/. That Web site also contains links to all URLs cited in the book, updates, additions, information on training courses, and other servlet and JSP resources. It also contains a frequently updated page on Tomcat configuration (since Tomcat changes more often than the other servers).

If neither the HTML file nor the JSP file works (e.g., you get File Not Found—404—errors), you probably are either using the wrong directory for the files or misspelling the URL (e.g., using a lowercase h in Hello.jsp). If the HTML file works but the JSP file fails, you probably have incorrectly specified the base SDK directory (e.g., with the `JAVA_HOME` variable) and should review Section 2.7 (Set Up Your Development Environment).

Listing 2.1 Hello.html

```
<!DOCTYPE HTML PUBLIC "-//W3C//DTD HTML 4.0 Transitional//EN">
<HTML>
<HEAD><TITLE>HTML Test</TITLE></HEAD>
<BODY BGCOLOR="#FDF5E6">
<H1>HTML Test</H1>
Hello.
</BODY></HTML>
```

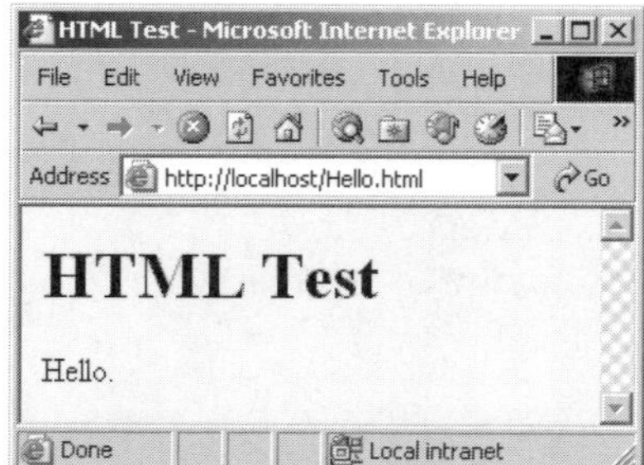

Figure 2–10 Result of Hello.html.

Listing 2.2 Hello.jsp

```
<!DOCTYPE HTML PUBLIC "-//W3C//DTD HTML 4.0 Transitional//EN">
<HTML>
<HEAD><TITLE>JSP Test</TITLE></HEAD>
<BODY BGCOLOR="#FDF5E6">
<H1>JSP Test</H1>
Time: <%= new java.util.Date() %>
</BODY>
</HTML>
```

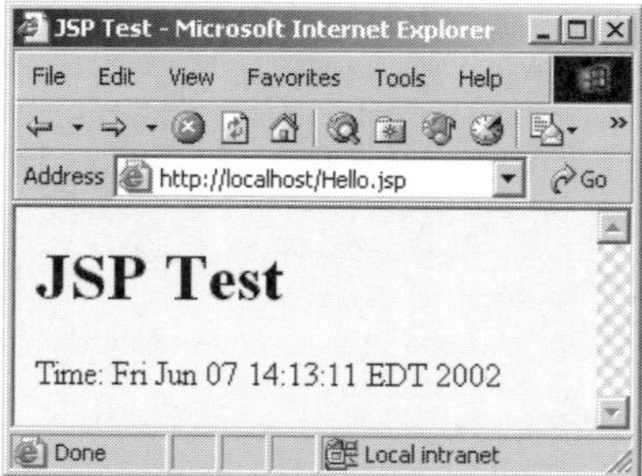

Figure 2–11 Result of Hello.jsp.

Compiling and Deploying Some Simple Servlets

OK, so your development environment is all set. At least you *think* it is. It would be nice to confirm that hypothesis. Following are three test servlets that help verify it.

Test 1: A Servlet That Does Not Use Packages

The first servlet to try is a basic one: no packages, no utility (helper) classes, just simple HTML output. Rather than writing your own test servlet, you can just download HelloServlet.java (Listing 2.3) from the book's source code archive at http://www.coreservlets.com/. Again, don't worry about how this servlet works—that is covered in detail in the next chapter—the point here is just to test your setup. If you get compilation errors, go back and check your CLASSPATH settings (Section 2.7)—you most likely erred in listing the location of the JAR file that contains the servlet classes (e.g., servlet.jar).

Once you compile HelloServlet.java, put HelloServlet.class in the appropriate location (usually the WEB-INF/classes directory of your server's default Web application). Check your server's documentation for this location, or see the following list for a summary of the locations used by Tomcat, JRun, and Resin. Then, access the servlet with the URL http://*host*/servlet/HelloServlet (or http://*host*:*port*/servlet/HelloServlet if you chose not to change the port number as described in Section 2.3). Use localhost for ***host*** if you are running the server on your desktop system. You should get something similar to Figure 2–12. If this URL fails but the test of the server itself succeeded, you probably put the class file in the wrong directory.

Notice that you use servlet (not servlets!) in the URL even though there is no real directory named servlet. URLs of the form .../servlet/*ServletName* are just an instruction to a special servlet (called the *invoker servlet*) to run the servlet with the specified name. The servlet code itself is in any of the locations the server normally uses (usually, .../WEB-INF/classes for individual class files or .../WEB-INF/lib for JAR files that contain servlets). Using default URLs like this is convenient during your initial development, but once you are ready to deploy, you will almost certainly disable this capability and register a separate URL for each servlet. See Section 2.11 (Web Applications: A Preview) for details. In fact, servers are not strictly required to support these default URLs, and some of the high-end application servers, most notably BEA WebLogic, do not.

- **Tomcat directory for Java .class files.**
  install_dir/webapps/ROOT/WEB-INF/classes
  (Note: in many Tomcat versions, you'll have to manually create the classes directory.)
- **JRun directory for Java .class files.**
  install_dir/servers/default/default-ear/default-war/WEB-INF/classes
- **Resin directory for Java .class files.**
  install_dir/doc/WEB-INF/classes
- **Corresponding URL.**
  http://*host*/servlet/HelloServlet

Listing 2.3 HelloServlet.java

```
import java.io.*;
import javax.servlet.*;
import javax.servlet.http.*;

/** Simple servlet used to test server. */

public class HelloServlet extends HttpServlet {
  public void doGet(HttpServletRequest request,
                    HttpServletResponse response)
      throws ServletException, IOException {
    response.setContentType("text/html");
    PrintWriter out = response.getWriter();
    String docType =
      "<!DOCTYPE HTML PUBLIC \"-//W3C//DTD HTML 4.0 " +
      "Transitional//EN\">\n";
    out.println(docType +
                "<HTML>\n" +
                "<HEAD><TITLE>Hello</TITLE></HEAD>\n" +
                "<BODY BGCOLOR=\"#FDF5E6\">\n" +
                "<H1>Hello</H1>\n" +
                "</BODY></HTML>");
  }
}
```

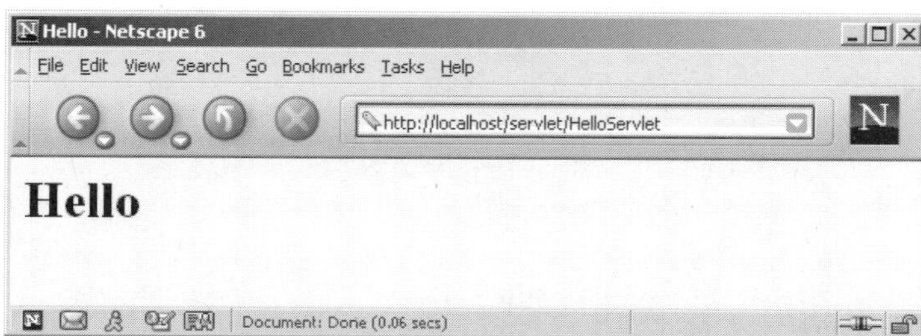

Figure 2–12 Result of http://localhost/servlet/HelloServlet.

Test 2: A Servlet That Uses Packages

The second servlet to try is one that uses packages but no utility classes. Packages are the standard mechanism for preventing class name conflicts in the Java programming language. There are three standard rules to remember:

1. **Insert package declarations in the code.** If a class is in a package, it must have "`package` *`packageName`*`;`" as the first noncomment line in the source code.
2. **Use a directory that matches the package name.** If a class is in a package, it must be in a directory that matches its package name. This is true for class files in both development and deployment locations.
3. **From Java code, use dots after packages.** When you refer to classes that are in packages either from within Java code or in a URL, you use a dot, not a slash, between the package name and the class name.

Again, rather than writing your own test, you can grab HelloServlet2.java (Listing 2.4) from the book's source code archive at http://www.coreservlets.com/. Since this servlet is in the `coreservlets` package, it should go in the coreservlets directory, *both* during development *and* when deployed to the server. If you get compilation errors, go back and check your `CLASSPATH` settings (Section 2.7)—you most likely forgot to include "." (the current directory). Once you compile HelloServlet2.java, put HelloServlet2.class in the coreservlets subdirectory of whatever directory the server uses for servlets that are not in custom Web applications (usually the WEB-INF/classes directory of the default Web application). Check your server's documentation for this location, or see the following list for a summary of the locations for Tomcat, JRun, and Resin. For now, you can simply copy the class file from the development directory to the deployment directory, but Section 2.9 (Establish a Simplified Deployment Method) provides some options for simplifying the process.

Once you have placed the servlet in the proper directory, access it with the URL http://localhost/servlet/coreservlets.HelloServlet2. Note that there is a dot, not a slash, between the package name and the servlet name in the URL. You should get something similar to Figure 2–13. If this test fails, you probably either typed the URL wrong (e.g., failed to maintain the proper case) or put HelloServlet2.class in the wrong location (e.g., directly in the server's WEB-INF/classes directory instead of in the coreservlets subdirectory).

- **Tomcat directory for packaged Java classes.**
  install_dir/webapps/ROOT/WEB-INF/classes/coreservlets
- **JRun directory for packaged Java classes.**
  install_dir/servers/default/default-ear/default-war/WEB-INF/classes/coreservlets
- **Resin directory for packaged Java classes.**
  install_dir/doc/WEB-INF/classes/coreservlets
- **Corresponding URL.**
  http://*host*/servlet/coreservlets.HelloServlet2

Listing 2.4 coreservlets/HelloServlet2.java

```
package coreservlets;

import java.io.*;
import javax.servlet.*;
import javax.servlet.http.*;

/** Simple servlet for testing the use of packages. */

public class HelloServlet2 extends HttpServlet {
  public void doGet(HttpServletRequest request,
                    HttpServletResponse response)
      throws ServletException, IOException {
    response.setContentType("text/html");
    PrintWriter out = response.getWriter();
    String docType =
      "<!DOCTYPE HTML PUBLIC \"-//W3C//DTD HTML 4.0 " +
      "Transitional//EN\">\n";
    out.println(docType +
                "<HTML>\n" +
                "<HEAD><TITLE>Hello (2)</TITLE></HEAD>\n" +
                "<BODY BGCOLOR=\"#FDF5E6\">\n" +
                "<H1>Hello (2)</H1>\n" +
                "</BODY></HTML>");
  }
}
```

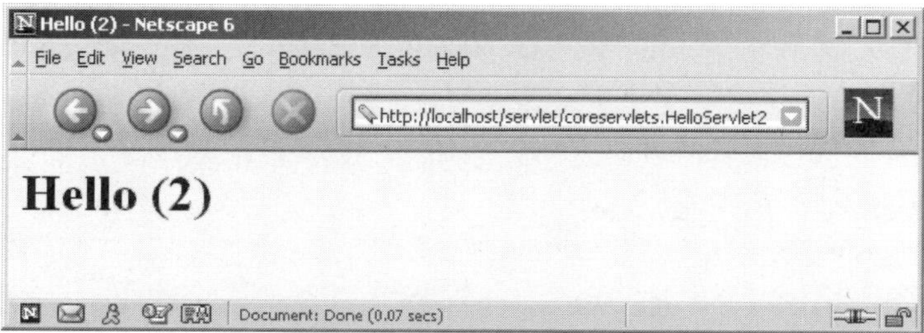

Figure 2–13 Result of http://localhost/servlet/coreservlets.HelloServlet2. Note that it is a dot, not a slash, between the package name and the class name.

Test 3: A Servlet That Uses Packages and Utilities

The final servlet you should test to verify the configuration of your server and development environment is one that uses both packages and utility classes. Listing 2.5 presents **HelloServlet3.java**, a servlet that uses the `ServletUtilities` class (Listing 2.6) to simplify the generation of the `DOCTYPE` (specifies the HTML version—useful when using HTML validators) and `HEAD` (specifies the title) portions of the HTML page. Those two parts of the page are useful (technically required, in fact) but are tedious to generate with servlet `println` statements. Again, the source code can be found at **http://www.coreservlets.com/**.

Since both the servlet and the utility class are in the `coreservlets` package, they should go in the **coreservlets** directory. If you get compilation errors, go back and check your `CLASSPATH` settings (Section 2.7)—you most likely forgot to include the top-level development directory. We've said it before, but we'll say it again: your `CLASSPATH` must include the top-level directory of your package hierarchy before you can compile a packaged class that makes use of another class that is in the same package or in any other user-defined (nonsystem) package. This requirement is not particular to servlets; it is the way packages work on the Java platform in general. Nevertheless, many servlet developers are unaware of this fact, and it is one of the (perhaps *the*) most common problems that beginning developers encounter. Furthermore, as we will see later, you *must* put all utility classes you write into packages if you want to use them from JSP pages, so virtually all the auxiliary classes (and most of the servlets) you write will be in packages. You might as well get used to the process of using packages now.

Core Warning

Your `CLASSPATH` must include your top-level development directory. Otherwise, you will get "unresolved symbol" errors when you attempt to compile servlets that are in packages and that also use user-defined classes that are in packages.

Once you compile **HelloServlet3.java** (which will automatically cause **ServletUtilities.java** to be compiled), put **HelloServlet3.class** and **ServletUtilities.class** in the **coreservlets** subdirectory of whatever directory the server uses for servlets that are not in custom Web applications (usually the **WEB-INF/classes** directory of the default Web application). Check your server's documentation for this location, or see the following list for a summary of the locations used by Tomcat, JRun, and Resin. Then, access the servlet with the URL http://localhost/servlet/coreservlets.HelloServlet3. You should get something similar to Figure 2–14.

- **Tomcat directory for packaged Java classes.**
  install_dir/webapps/ROOT/WEB-INF/classes/coreservlets
- **JRun directory for packaged Java classes.**
  install_dir/servers/default/default-ear/default-war/WEB-INF/classes/coreservlets
- **Resin directory for packaged Java classes.**
  install_dir/doc/WEB-INF/classes/coreservlets
- **Corresponding URL.**
  http://*host*/servlet/coreservlets.HelloServlet3

Listing 2.5 coreservlets/HelloServlet3.java

```
package coreservlets;

import java.io.*;
import javax.servlet.*;
import javax.servlet.http.*;

/** Simple servlet for testing the use of packages
 *  and utilities from the same package.
 */

public class HelloServlet3 extends HttpServlet {
  public void doGet(HttpServletRequest request,
                    HttpServletResponse response)
      throws ServletException, IOException {
    response.setContentType("text/html");
    PrintWriter out = response.getWriter();
    String title = "Hello (3)";
    out.println(ServletUtilities.headWithTitle(title) +
                "<BODY BGCOLOR=\"#FDF5E6\">\n" +
                "<H1>" + title + "</H1>\n" +
                "</BODY></HTML>");
  }
}
```

Listing 2.6 coreservlets/ServletUtilities.java (Excerpt)

```
package coreservlets;

import javax.servlet.*;
import javax.servlet.http.*;

/** Some simple time savers. Note that most are static methods. */

public class ServletUtilities {
  public static final String DOCTYPE =
    "<!DOCTYPE HTML PUBLIC \"-//W3C//DTD HTML 4.0 " +
    "Transitional//EN\">";

  public static String headWithTitle(String title) {
    return(DOCTYPE + "\n" +
           "<HTML>\n" +
           "<HEAD><TITLE>" + title + "</TITLE></HEAD>\n");
  }

  ...
}
```

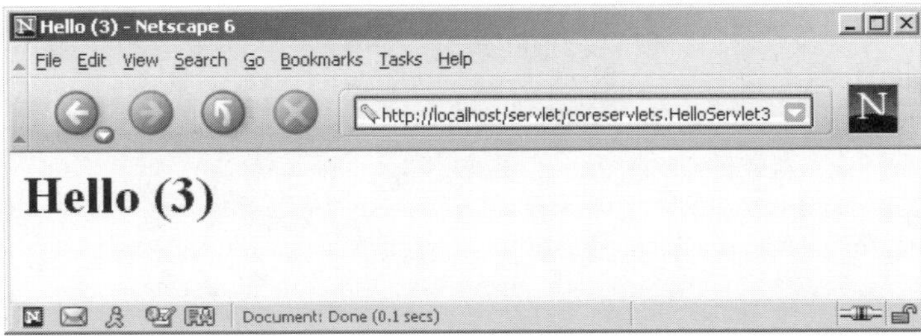

Figure 2–14 Result of http://localhost/servlet/coreservlets.HelloServlet3.

2.9 Establish a Simplified Deployment Method

OK, so you have a development directory. You can compile servlets with or without packages. You know which directory the servlet classes belong in. You know the URL that should be used to access them (at least the default URL; in Section 2.11, "Web Applications: A Preview," you'll see how to customize that address). But how do you move the class files from the development directory to the deployment directory? Copying each one by hand every time is tedious and error prone. Once you start using Web applications (see Section 2.11), copying individual files becomes even more cumbersome.

There are several ways to simplify the process. Here are a few of the most popular ones. If you are just beginning with servlets and JSP, you probably want to start with the first option and use it until you become comfortable with the development process. Note that we do *not* list the option of putting your code directly in the server's deployment directory. Although this is one of the most common choices among beginners, it scales so poorly to advanced tasks that we recommend you steer clear of it from the start.

1. **Copying to a shortcut or symbolic link.**
2. **Using the `-d` option of `javac`.**
3. **Letting your IDE take care of deployment.**
4. **Using `ant` or a similar tool.**

Details on these four options are given in the following subsections.

Copying to a Shortcut or Symbolic Link

On Windows, go to the server's default Web application, right-click on the classes directory, and select Copy. Then go to your development directory, right-click, and select Paste Shortcut (not just Paste). Now, whenever you compile a packageless servlet, just drag the class files onto the shortcut. When you develop in packages, use the *right* mouse button to drag the entire directory (e.g., the coreservlets directory) onto the shortcut, release the mouse button, and select Copy. See Figure 2–15 for an example setup that simplifies testing of this chapter's examples on Tomcat, JRun, and Resin. On Unix, you can use symbolic links (created with `ln -s`) in a manner similar to that for Windows shortcuts.

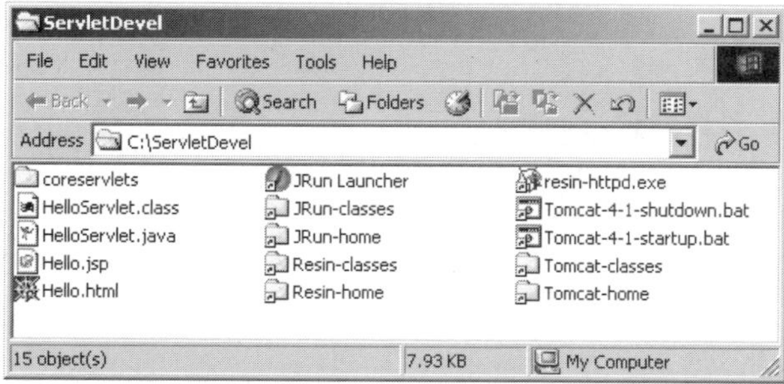

Figure 2–15 Using shortcuts to simplify deployment.

An advantage of this approach is that it is simple. So, it is good for beginners who want to concentrate on learning servlets and JSP, not deployment tools. Another advantage is that a variation applies once you start using your own Web applications (see Section 2.11). Just make a shortcut to the main Web application directory (typically one level up from the top of the default Web application), and copy the entire Web application each time by using the right mouse button to drag the directory that contains your Web application onto this shortcut and selecting Copy.

One disadvantage of this approach is that it requires repeated copying if you use multiple servers. For example, we keep three different servers (Tomcat, JRun, and Resin) on our development system and regularly test the code on all three servers. A second disadvantage is that this approach copies both the Java source code files and the class files to the server, whereas only the class files are needed. This may not matter much on your desktop server, but when you get to the "real" deployment server, you won't want to include the source code files.

Using the -d Option of javac

By default, the Java compiler (`javac`) places class files in the same directory as the source code files that they came from. However, `javac` has an option (`-d`) that lets you designate a different location for the class files. You need only specify the top-level directory for class files—`javac` will automatically put packaged classes in subdirectories that match the package names. So, for example, with Tomcat you could compile the `HelloServlet2` servlet (Listing 2.4, Section 2.8) as follows (line break added only for clarity; omit it in real life).

```
javac -d install_dir/webapps/ROOT/WEB-INF/classes
         HelloServlet2.java
```

You could even make a Windows batch file or Unix shell script or alias that makes a command like `servletc` expand to `javac -d` *`install_dir`*`/.../classes`. See http://java.sun.com/j2se/1.4/docs/tooldocs/win32/javac.html for more details on `-d` and other `javac` options.

An advantage of this approach is that it requires no manual copying of class files. Furthermore, the exact same command can be used for classes in different packages since `javac` automatically puts the class files in a subdirectory matching the package.

The main disadvantage is that this approach applies only to Java class files; it won't work for deploying HTML and JSP pages, much less entire Web applications.

Letting Your IDE Take Care of Deployment

Most servlet- and JSP-savvy development environments (e.g., IBM WebSphere Studio Application Developer, Sun ONE Studio, Borland JBuilder, Eclipse) have options that let you specify where to deploy class files for your project. Then, when you tell the IDE to build the project, the class files are automatically deployed to the proper location (package-specific subdirectories and all).

An advantage of this approach, at least in some IDEs, is that it can deploy HTML and JSP pages and even entire Web applications, not just Java class files. A disadvantage is that it is an IDE-specific technique and thus is not portable across systems.

Using ant or a Similar Tool

Developed by the Apache foundation, `ant` is a tool similar to the Unix `make` utility. However, `ant` is written in the Java programming language (and thus is portable) and is touted to be both simpler to use and more powerful than `make`. Many servlet and JSP developers use `ant` for compiling and deploying. The use of `ant` is especially popular among Tomcat users and with those developing Web applications (see Section 2.11). Use of `ant` is discussed in Volume 2 of this book.

For general information on using `ant`, see http://jakarta.apache.org/ant/manual/. See http://jakarta.apache.org/tomcat/tomcat-4.1-doc/appdev/processes.html for specific guidance on using `ant` with Tomcat.

The main advantage of this approach is flexibility: `ant` is powerful enough to handle everything from compiling the Java source code to copying files to producing Web archive (WAR) files (see Section 2.11, "Web Applications: A Preview"). The disadvantage of `ant` is the overhead of learning to use it; there is a steeper learning curve with `ant` than with the other techniques in this section.

2.10 Deployment Directories for Default Web Application: Summary

The following subsections summarize the way to deploy and access HTML files, JSP pages, servlets, and utility classes in Apache Tomcat, Macromedia JRun, and Caucho Resin. The summary assumes that you are deploying files in the default Web application, have changed the port number to 80 (see Section 2.3), and are accessing servlets through the default URL (i.e., http://host/servlet/ServletName). Section 2.11 explains how to deploy user-defined Web applications and how to customize the URLs. But you'll probably want to start with the defaults just to confirm that everything is working properly. The Appendix (Server Organization and Structure) gives a unified summary of the directories used by Tomcat, JRun, and Resin for both the default Web application and custom Web applications.

If you are using a server on your desktop, you can use localhost for the *host* portion of each of the URLs in this section.

Tomcat

HTML and JSP Pages

- **Main Location.**
  install_dir/webapps/ROOT
- **Corresponding URLs.**
  http://*host*/*SomeFile*.html
  http://*host*/*SomeFile*.jsp
- **More Specific Location (Arbitrary Subdirectory).**
  install_dir/webapps/ROOT/*SomeDirectory*
- **Corresponding URLs.**
  http://*host*/*SomeDirectory*/*SomeFile*.html
  http://*host*/*SomeDirectory*/*SomeFile*.jsp

Individual Servlet and Utility Class Files

- **Main Location (Classes without Packages).**
  install_dir/webapps/ROOT/WEB-INF/classes
- **Corresponding URL (Servlets).**
  http://*host*/servlet/*ServletName*
- **More Specific Location (Classes in Packages).**
  install_dir/webapps/ROOT/WEB-INF/classes/*packageName*
- **Corresponding URL (Servlets in Packages).**
  http://*host*/servlet/*packageName.ServletName*

Servlet and Utility Class Files Bundled in JAR Files

- **Location.**
  install_dir/webapps/ROOT/WEB-INF/lib
- **Corresponding URLs (Servlets).**
  http://*host*/servlet/*ServletName*
  http://*host*/servlet/*packageName.ServletName*

JRun

HTML and JSP Pages

- **Main Location.**
  install_dir/servers/default/default-ear/default-war
- **Corresponding URLs.**
  http://*host*/*SomeFile*.html
  http://*host*/*SomeFile*.jsp

- **More Specific Location (Arbitrary Subdirectory).**
  install_dir/servers/default/default-ear/default-war/*SomeDirectory*
- **Corresponding URLs.**
  http://*host*/*SomeDirectory*/*SomeFile*.html
  http://*host*/*SomeDirectory*/*SomeFile*.jsp

Individual Servlet and Utility Class Files

- **Main Location (Classes without Packages).**
  install_dir/servers/default/default-ear/default-war/WEB-INF/classes
- **Corresponding URL (Servlets).**
  http://*host*/servlet/*ServletName*
- **More Specific Location (Classes in Packages).**
  install_dir/servers/default/default-ear/default-war/WEB-INF/classes/*packageName*
- **Corresponding URL (Servlets in Packages).**
  http://*host*/servlet/*packageName.ServletName*

Servlet and Utility Class Files Bundled in JAR Files

- **Location.**
  install_dir/servers/default/default-ear/default-war/WEB-INF/lib
- **Corresponding URLs (Servlets).**
  http://*host*/servlet/*ServletName*
  http://*host*/servlet/*packageName.ServletName*

Resin

HTML and JSP Pages

- **Main Location.**
  install_dir/doc
- **Corresponding URLs.**
  http://*host*/*SomeFile*.html
  http://*host*/*SomeFile*.jsp
- **More Specific Location (Arbitrary Subdirectory).**
  install_dir/doc/*SomeDirectory*
- **Corresponding URLs.**
  http://*host*/*SomeDirectory*/*SomeFile*.html
  http://*host*/*SomeDirectory*/*SomeFile*.jsp

Individual Servlet and Utility Class Files

- **Main Location (Classes without Packages).**
  install_dir/doc/WEB-INF/classes
- **Corresponding URL (Servlets).**
  http://*host*/servlet/*ServletName*
- **More Specific Location (Classes in Packages).**
  install_dir/doc/WEB-INF/classes/*packageName*
- **Corresponding URL (Servlets in Packages).**
  http://*host*/servlet/*packageName.ServletName*

Servlet and Utility Class Files Bundled in JAR Files

- **Location.**
  install_dir/doc/WEB-INF/lib
- **Corresponding URLs (Servlets).**
  http://*host*/servlet/*ServletName*
  http://*host*/servlet/*packageName.ServletName*

2.11 Web Applications: A Preview

Up to this point, we've been using the server's default Web application for our servlets. Most servers come preinstalled with a default Web application, and most servers let you invoke servlets in that application with URLs of the form http://*host*/servlet/*ServletName* or http://*host*/servlet/*packageName.ServletName*. Use of the default Web application and URL is very convenient when you are learning how to use servlets; you probably want to stick with these defaults when you first practice the techniques described throughout the book. So, if you are new to servlet and JSP development, skip this section for now.

However, once you have learned the basics of both servlets and JSP and are ready to start on real applications, you'll want to use your own Web application instead of the default one. Web applications are discussed in great detail in Volume 2 of this book, but a quick preview of the basics is presented in this section.

Core Approach

*When first learning, use the default Web application and default servlet URLs. For serious applications, use custom Web applications and URLs that are assigned in the deployment descriptor (**web.xml**).*

Most servers (including the three used as examples in this book) have server-specific administration consoles that let you create and register Web applications from within a Web browser. These consoles are discussed in Volume 2; for now, we restrict ourselves to the basic manual approach that is nearly identical on all servers. The following list summarizes the steps; the subsections that follow the steps give details.

1. **Make a directory whose structure mirrors the structure of the default Web application.** HTML (and, eventually, JSP) documents go in the top-level directory, the web.xml file goes in the WEB-INF subdirectory, and servlets and other classes go either in WEB-INF/classes or in a subdirectory of WEB-INF/classes that matches the package name.
2. **Update your `CLASSPATH`.** Add webAppDir/WEB-INF/classes to it.
3. **Register the Web application with the server.** Tell the server where the Web application directory (or JAR file created from it) is located and what prefix in the URL (see the next item) should be used to invoke the application. For example, with Tomcat, just drop the Web application directory in *install_dir*/webapps and then restart the server. The name of the directory becomes the Web application prefix.
4. **Use the designated URL prefix to invoke servlets or HTML/JSP pages from the Web application.** Invoke unpackaged servlets with a default URL of http://*host*/***webAppPrefix***/servlet/*ServletName*, packaged servlets with http://*host*/***webAppPrefix***/servlet/*packageName.ServletName*, and HTML pages from the top-level Web application directory with http://*host*/***webAppPrefix***/*filename*.html.
5. **Assign custom URLs for all your servlets.** Use the `servlet` and `servlet-mapping` elements of web.xml to give a URL of the form http://*host*/*webAppPrefix*/*someName* to each servlet.

Making a Web Application Directory

To make a Web application, create a directory in your development folder. That new directory should have the same general layout as the default Web application:

- HTML and, eventually, JSP documents go in the top-level directory (or any subdirectory other than WEB-INF).
- The web.xml file (sometimes called "the deployment descriptor") goes in the WEB-INF subdirectory.
- Servlets and other classes go either in WEB-INF/classes or, more commonly, in a subdirectory of WEB-INF/classes that matches the package name.

The easiest way to make such a directory is to copy an existing Web application. For instance, with Tomcat, you could copy the ROOT directory to your development folder and rename it to testApp, resulting in something like C:\Servlets+JSP\testApp. As with the default Web application, we strongly advise against developing directly in the server's Web application directory. Keep a separate directory, and deploy it whenever you are ready to test. The easiest deployment option is to simply copy the directory to the server's standard location, but Section 2.9 (Establish a Simplified Deployment Method) gives several other alternatives.

Updating Your CLASSPATH

Recall from Section 2.7 (Set Up Your Development Environment) that your CLASSPATH needs to contain the top-level directory of .class files. This is true whether or not you are using custom Web applications, so add webAppDir/classes to the CLASSPATH.

Registering the Web Application with the Server

In this step, you tell the server where the Web application directory (or JAR file created from it) is located and what prefix in the URL (see the next subsection) should be used to invoke the application. There are various server-specific mechanisms for doing this registration, many of which involve the use of an interactive administration console. But, on most servers, you can also register a Web application simply by dropping the Web application directory in a standard location and then restarting the server. In such a case, the name of the Web application directory is used as the URL prefix. Here are the standard locations for Web application directories with the three servers used throughout the book.

- **Tomcat Web application autodeploy directory.**
  install_dir/webapps
- **JRun Web application autodeploy directory.**
  install_dir/servers/default
- **Resin Web application autodeploy directory.**
  install_dir/webapps

For example, we created a directory called testApp with the following structure:

- testApp/Hello.html
  The sample HTML file of Section 2.8 (Listing 2.1).
- testApp/Hello.jsp
  The sample JSP file of Section 2.8 (Listing 2.2).
- testApp/WEB-INF/classes/HelloServlet.class
  The sample packageless servlet of Section 2.8 (Listing 2.3).
- testApp/WEB-INF/classes/coreservlets/HelloServlet2.class
  The first sample packaged servlet of Section 2.8 (Listing 2.4).

- testApp/WEB-INF/classes/coreservlets/HelloServlet3.class
  The second sample packaged servlet of Section 2.8 (Listing 2.5).
- testApp/WEB-INF/classes/coreservlets/ServletUtilities.class
  The utility class (Listing 2.6) used by `HelloServlet3`.

WAR Files

Web ARchive (WAR) files provide a convenient way of bundling Web applications in a single file. Having a single large file instead of many small files makes it easier to transfer the Web application from server to server.

A WAR file is really just a JAR file with a .war extension, and you use the normal `jar` command to create it. For example, to bundle the entire testApp Web app into a WAR file named testApp2.war, you would just change directory to the testApp directory and execute the following command.

```
jar cvf testApp2.war *
```

There are a few options you can use in advanced applications (we discuss these in Volume 2 of the book), but for simple WAR files, that's it!

Again, the exact details of deployment are server dependent, but most servers let you simply drop a WAR file in the autodeploy directory, and the base name of the WAR file becomes the Web application prefix. For example, you would drop testApp2.war into the same directory you dropped testApp, restart the server, then invoke the test resources shown in Figures 2–16 through 2–20 by merely changing testApp to testApp2 in the URLs.

Using the URL Prefix

When you use Web applications, a special prefix is part of all URLs. For example:

- Unpackaged servlets are invoked with a default URL of
  http://*host*/***webAppPrefix***/servlet/*ServletName*
- Packaged servlets are invoked with
  http://*host*/***webAppPrefix***/servlet/*packageName.ServletName*
- Registered servlets (see the next subsection) are invoked with
  http://*host*/***webAppPrefix***/*customName*
- HTML pages from the top-level Web application directory are invoked with http://*host*/***webAppPrefix***/*filename*.html.
- HTML pages from subdirectories are invoked with
  http://*host*/***webAppPrefix***/*subdirectoryName*/*filename*.html.
- JSP pages are placed in the same locations as HTML pages and invoked in the same way (except that the file extension is .jsp instead of .html).

Most servers let you choose arbitrary prefixes, but, by default, the name of the directory (or the base name of the WAR file) becomes the Web application prefix. For example, we copied the **testApp** directory to the appropriate Web application directory (***install_dir*/webapps** for Tomcat and Resin, ***install_dir*/servers/default** for JRun) and restarted the server. Then, we invoked the resources by using URLs identical to those of Section 2.8 except for the addition of **testApp** after the hostname. See Figures 2–16 through 2–20.

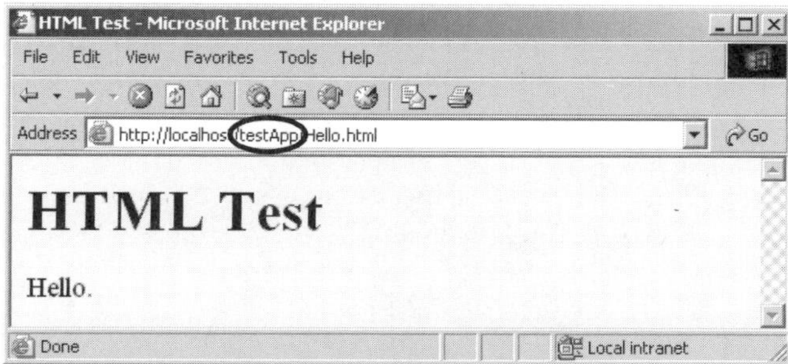

Figure 2–16 Hello.html invoked within a Web application.

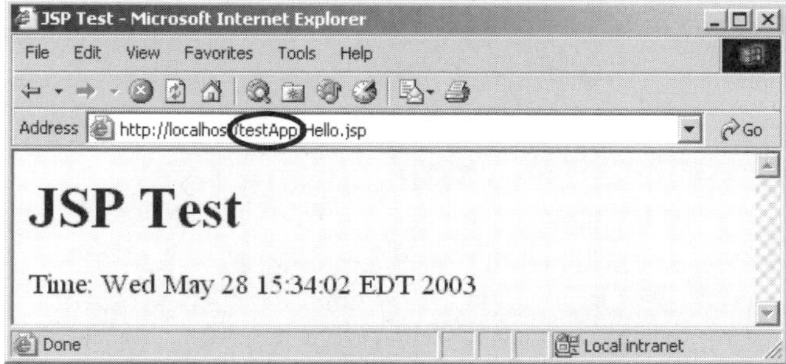

Figure 2–17 Hello.jsp invoked within a Web application.

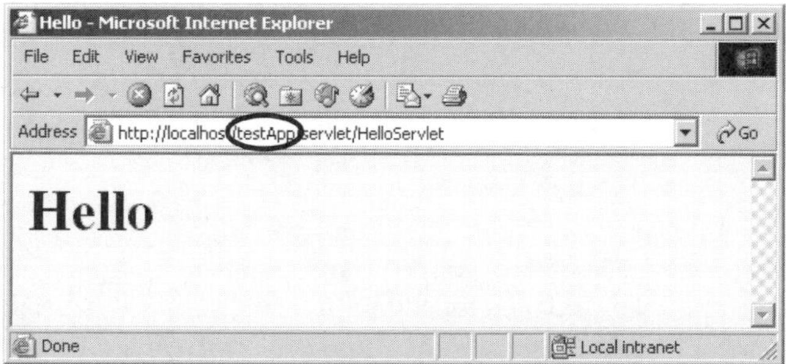

Figure 2–18 HelloServlet.class invoked with the default URL within a Web application.

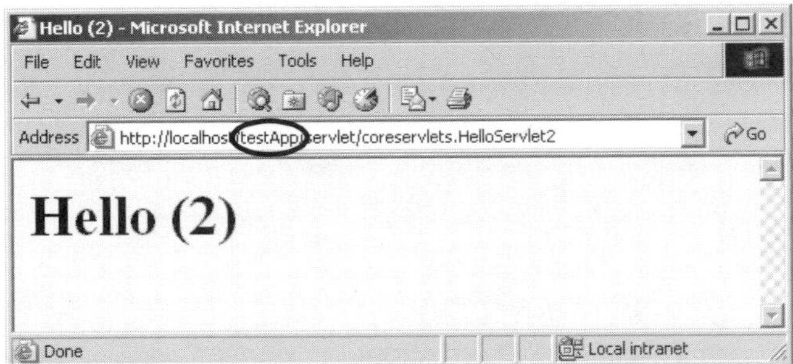

Figure 2–19 HelloServlet2.class invoked with the default URL within a Web application.

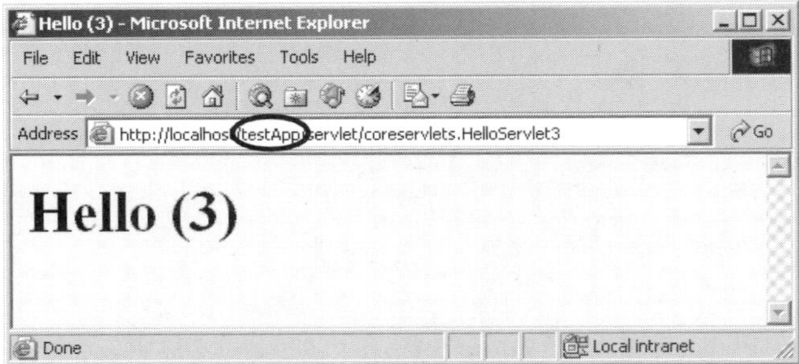

Figure 2–20 HelloServlet3.class invoked with the default URL within a Web application.

Assigning Custom URLs to Your Servlets

During initial development, it is very convenient to drop a servlet in WEB-INF/classes and immediately invoke it with http://*host*/*webAppPrefix*/servlet/*ServletName*. For deploying serious applications, however, you always want to define custom URLs.

You assign the URLs by using the `servlet` and `servlet-mapping` elements of web.xml (the deployment descriptor). The web.xml file is discussed in great detail in Volume 2 of the book, but for the purpose of registering custom URLs, you simply need to know five things:

- **The file location.** It *always* goes in WEB-INF.
- **The base form.** It starts with an XML header and a `DOCTYPE` declaration, and it contains a `web-app` element.
- **The way to give names to servlets.** You use `servlet` with `servlet-name` and `servlet-class` subelements.
- **The way to give URLs to named servlets.** You use `servlet-mapping` with `servlet-name` and `url-pattern` subelements.
- **When the web.xml file is read.** It is read *only* when the server starts.

Locating the Deployment Descriptor

The web.xml file always goes in the WEB-INF directory of your Web application. That is the *only* portable location; other locations (e.g., *install_dir*/conf for Tomcat) are nonstandard server extensions that you should steer clear of.

Defining the Base Format

A web.xml file that is compatible with both servlets 2.3 (JSP 1.2) and servlets 2.4 (JSP 2.0) has the following basic form:

```
<?xml version="1.0" encoding="ISO-8859-1"?>
<!DOCTYPE web-app
  PUBLIC "-//Sun Microsystems, Inc.//DTD Web Application 2.3//EN"
  "http://java.sun.com/dtd/web-app_2_3.dtd">
<web-app>

</web-app>
```

Deployment descriptors that are specific to servlets 2.4 (JSP 2.0) are discussed in Volume 2 of the book.

Naming Servlets

To name a servlet, you use the `servlet` element within `web-app`, with `servlet-name` (any name) and `servlet-class` (the fully qualified class name) subelements. For example, to give the name `Servlet2` to `HelloServlet2`, you would use the following.

```
<servlet>
  <servlet-name>Servlet2</servlet-name>
  <servlet-class>coreservlets.HelloServlet2</servlet-class>
</servlet>
```

Giving URLs

To give a URL to a named servlet, you use the `servlet-mapping` element, with `servlet-name` (the previously assigned name) and `url-pattern` (the URL suffix, starting with a slash) subelements. For example, to give the URL http://*host*/*webAppPrefix*/servlet2 to the servlet named `Servlet2`, you would use the following.

```
<servlet-mapping>
  <servlet-name>Servlet2</servlet-name>
  <url-pattern>/servlet2</url-pattern>
</servlet-mapping>
```

Note that *all* the `servlet` elements must come before *any* of the `servlet-mapping` elements: you cannot intermingle them.

Reading the Deployment Descriptor

Many servers have "hot deploy" capabilities or methods to interactively restart Web applications. For example, JRun automatically restarts Web applications whose **web.xml** files have changed. By default, however, the **web.xml** file is read *only* when the server starts. So, unless you make use of a server-specific feature, you have to restart the server every time you modify the **web.xml** file.

Example

Listing 2.7 gives the full **web.xml** file for the **testApp** Web application. The file was placed in the **WEB-INF** directory of **testApp**, the **testApp** directory was copied to the server's Web application directory (e.g., ***install_dir*/webapps** for Tomcat and Resin, ***install_dir*/servers/default** for JRun), and the server was restarted. Figures 2–21 through 2–23 show the three sample servlets invoked with the registered URLs.

Listing 2.7 WEB-INF/web.xml

```
<?xml version="1.0" encoding="ISO-8859-1"?>
<!DOCTYPE web-app
   PUBLIC "-//Sun Microsystems, Inc.//DTD Web Application 2.3//EN"
   "http://java.sun.com/dtd/web-app_2_3.dtd">
<web-app>
  <servlet>
    <servlet-name>Servlet1</servlet-name>
    <servlet-class>HelloServlet</servlet-class>
  </servlet>
  <servlet>
    <servlet-name>Servlet2</servlet-name>
    <servlet-class>coreservlets.HelloServlet2</servlet-class>
  </servlet>
  <servlet>
    <servlet-name>Servlet3</servlet-name>
    <servlet-class>coreservlets.HelloServlet3</servlet-class>
  </servlet>
  <servlet-mapping>
    <servlet-name>Servlet1</servlet-name>
    <url-pattern>/servlet1</url-pattern>
  </servlet-mapping>
  <servlet-mapping>
    <servlet-name>Servlet2</servlet-name>
    <url-pattern>/servlet2</url-pattern>
  </servlet-mapping>
```

Listing 2.7 WEB-INF/web.xml *(continued)*

```
  <servlet-mapping>
    <servlet-name>Servlet3</servlet-name>
    <url-pattern>/servlet3</url-pattern>
  </servlet-mapping>
</web-app>
```

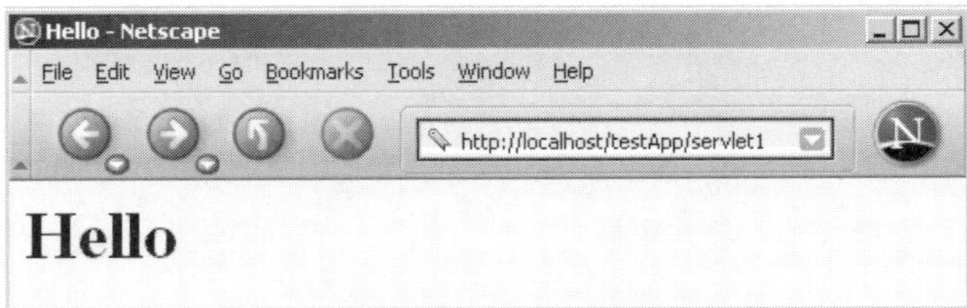

Figure 2–21 `HelloServlet` invoked with a custom URL.

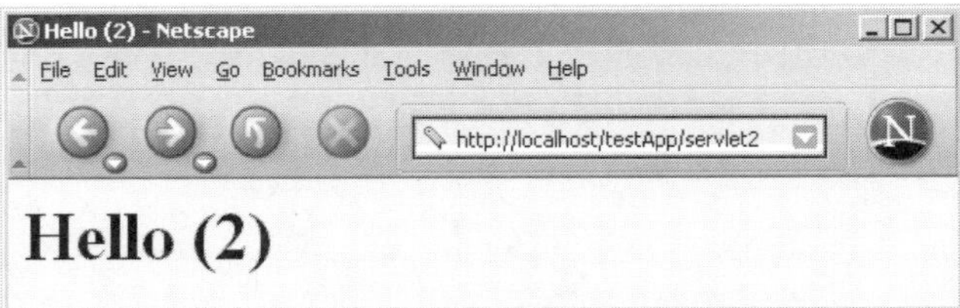

Figure 2–22 `HelloServlet2` invoked with a custom URL.

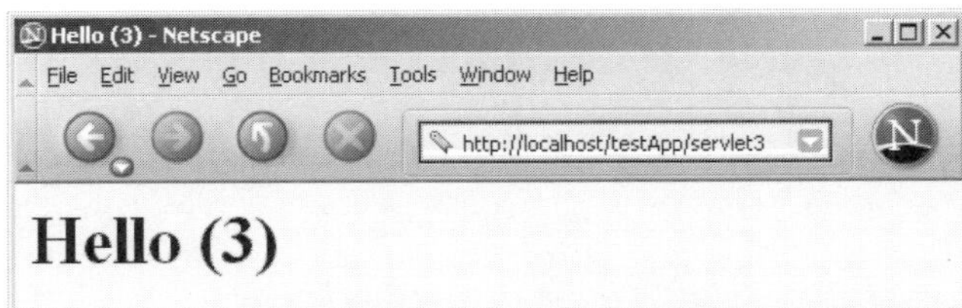

Figure 2–23 `HelloServlet3` invoked with a custom URL.

SERVLET BASICS

Topics in This Chapter

- The basic structure of servlets
- A simple servlet that generates plain text
- A servlet that generates HTML
- Servlets and packages
- Some utilities that help build HTML
- The servlet life cycle
- How to deal with multithreading problems
- Tools for interactively talking to servlets
- Servlet debugging strategies

Chapter 3

As discussed in Chapter 1, servlets are programs that run on a Web or application server and act as a middle layer between a request coming from a Web browser or other HTTP client and databases or applications on the HTTP server. Their job is to perform the following tasks, as illustrated in Figure 3–1.

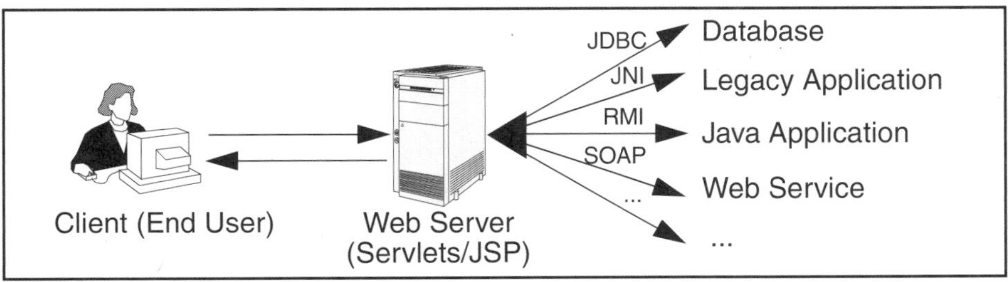

Figure 3–1 The role of Web middleware.

1. **Read the explicit data sent by the client.**
   The end user normally enters this data in an HTML form on a Web page. However, the data could also come from an applet or a custom HTTP client program.
2. **Read the implicit HTTP request data sent by the browser.**
   Figure 3–1 shows a single arrow going from the client to the Web server (the layer in which servlets and JSP pages execute), but there are really *two* varieties of data: the explicit data the end user enters in

a form and the behind-the-scenes HTTP information. Both types of data are critical to effective development. The HTTP information includes cookies, media types and compression schemes the browser understands, and so forth; it is discussed in Chapter 5.

3. **Generate the results.**
   This process may require talking to a database, executing an RMI or CORBA call, invoking a Web service, or computing the response directly. Your real data may be in a relational database. Fine. But your database probably doesn't speak HTTP or return results in HTML, so the Web browser can't talk directly to the database. The same argument applies to most other applications. You need the Web middle layer to extract the incoming data from the HTTP stream, talk to the application, and embed the results inside a document.
4. **Send the explicit data (i.e., the document) to the client.**
   This document can be sent in a variety of formats, including text (HTML or XML), binary (GIF images), Excel, or even a compressed format like gzip that is layered on top of some other underlying format.
5. **Send the implicit HTTP response data.**
   Figure 3–1 shows a single arrow going from the Web middle layer (the servlet or JSP page) to the client, but there are really *two* varieties of data sent: the document itself and the behind-the-scenes HTTP information. Both types of data are critical to effective development. Sending HTTP response data involves telling the browser or other client what type of document is being returned (e.g., HTML), setting cookies and caching parameters, and other such tasks. These tasks are discussed in Chapters 6–8.

In principle, servlets are not restricted to Web or application servers that handle HTTP requests but can be used for other types of servers as well. For example, servlets could be embedded in FTP or mail servers to extend their functionality. In practice, however, this use of servlets has not caught on, and we discuss only HTTP servlets.

3.1 Basic Servlet Structure

Listing 3.1 outlines a basic servlet that handles `GET` requests. `GET` requests, for those unfamiliar with HTTP, are the usual type of browser requests for Web pages. A browser generates this request when the user enters a URL on the address line, follows a link from a Web page, or submits an HTML form that either does not specify a METHOD or specifies METHOD="GET". Servlets can also easily handle POST requests, which are generated when someone submits an HTML form that specifies METHOD="POST". For details on the use of HTML forms and the distinctions between GET and POST, see Chapter 19 (Creating and Processing HTML Forms).

Listing 3.1 ServletTemplate.java

```
import java.io.*;
import javax.servlet.*;
import javax.servlet.http.*;

public class ServletTemplate extends HttpServlet {
  public void doGet(HttpServletRequest request,
                    HttpServletResponse response)
      throws ServletException, IOException {

    // Use "request" to read incoming HTTP headers
    // (e.g., cookies) and query data from HTML forms.

    // Use "response" to specify the HTTP response status
    // code and headers (e.g., the content type, cookies).

    PrintWriter out = response.getWriter();
    // Use "out" to send content to browser.
  }
}
```

Servlets typically extend HttpServlet and override doGet or doPost, depending on whether the data is being sent by GET or by POST. If you want a servlet to take the same action for both GET and POST requests, simply have doGet call doPost, or vice versa.

Both doGet and doPost take two arguments: an HttpServletRequest and an HttpServletResponse. The HttpServletRequest lets you get at all of the *incoming* data; the class has methods by which you can find out about information such as form (query) data, HTTP request headers, and the client's hostname. The HttpServletResponse lets you specify *outgoing* information such as HTTP status codes (200, 404, etc.) and response headers (Content-Type, Set-Cookie, etc.). Most importantly, HttpServletResponse lets you obtain a PrintWriter that you use to send document content back to the client. For simple servlets, most of the effort is spent in println statements that generate the desired page. Form data, HTTP request headers, HTTP responses, and cookies are all discussed in the following chapters.

Since doGet and doPost throw two exceptions (ServletException and IOException), you are required to include them in the method declaration. Finally, you must import classes in java.io (for PrintWriter, etc.), javax.servlet (for HttpServlet, etc.), and javax.servlet.http (for HttpServletRequest and HttpServletResponse).

However, there is no need to memorize the method signature and import statements. Instead, simply download the preceding template from the source code archive at http://www.coreservlets.com/ and use it as a starting point for your servlets.

3.2 A Servlet That Generates Plain Text

Listing 3.2 shows a simple servlet that outputs plain text, with the output shown in Figure 3–2. Before we move on, it is worth spending some time reviewing the process of installing, compiling, and running this simple servlet. See Chapter 2 (Server Setup and Configuration) for a much more detailed description of the process.

First, be sure that you've already verified the basics:

- That your server is set up properly as described in Section 2.3 (Configure the Server).
- That your development CLASSPATH refers to the necessary three entries (the servlet JAR file, your top-level development directory, and ".") as described in Section 2.7 (Set Up Your Development Environment).
- That all of the test cases of Section 2.8 (Test Your Setup) execute successfully.

Second, type "javac HelloWorld.java" or tell your development environment to compile the servlet (e.g., by clicking Build in your IDE or selecting Compile from the emacs JDE menu). This step will compile your servlet to create HelloWorld.class.

Third, move HelloWorld.class to the directory that your server uses to store servlets that are in the default Web application. The exact location varies from server to server, but is typically of the form *install_dir*/.../WEB-INF/classes (see Section 2.10 for details). For Tomcat you use *install_dir*/webapps/ROOT/WEB-INF/classes, for JRun you use *install_dir*/servers/default/default-ear/default-war/WEB-INF/classes, and for Resin you use *install_dir*/doc/WEB-INF/classes. Alternatively, you can use one of the techniques of Section 2.9 (Establish a Simplified Deployment Method) to automatically place the class files in the appropriate location.

Finally, invoke your servlet. This last step involves using either the default URL of http://*host*/servlet/*ServletName* or a custom URL defined in the web.xml file as described in Section 2.11 (Web Applications: A Preview). During initial development, you will almost certainly find it convenient to use the default URL so that you don't have to edit the web.xml file each time you test a new servlet. When you deploy real applications, however, you almost always disable the default URL and assign explicit URLs in the web.xml file (see Section 2.11, "Web Applications: A Preview"). In fact, servers are not absolutely required to support the default URL, and a few, most notably BEA WebLogic, do not.

Figure 3–2 shows the servlet being accessed by means of the default URL, with the server running on the local machine.

Listing 3.2 HelloWorld.java

```
import java.io.*;
import javax.servlet.*;
import javax.servlet.http.*;

public class HelloWorld extends HttpServlet {
  public void doGet(HttpServletRequest request,
                    HttpServletResponse response)
      throws ServletException, IOException {
    PrintWriter out = response.getWriter();
    out.println("Hello World");
  }
}
```

Figure 3–2 Result of http://localhost/servlet/HelloWorld.

3.3 A Servlet That Generates HTML

Most servlets generate HTML, not plain text as in the previous example. To generate HTML, you add three steps to the process just shown:

1. Tell the browser that you're sending it HTML.
2. Modify the `println` statements to build a legal Web page.
3. Check your HTML with a formal syntax validator.

You accomplish the first step by setting the HTTP `Content-Type` response header to `text/html`. In general, headers are set by the `setHeader` method of `HttpServletResponse`, but setting the content type is such a common task that there is also a special `setContentType` method just for this purpose. The way to designate HTML is with a type of `text/html`, so the code would look like this:

```
response.setContentType("text/html");
```

Although HTML is the most common kind of document that servlets create, it is not unusual for servlets to create other document types. For example, it is quite common to use servlets to generate Excel spreadsheets (content type `application/vnd.ms-excel`—see Section 7.3), JPEG images (content type `image/jpeg`—see Section 7.5), and XML documents (content type `text/xml`). Also, you rarely use servlets to generate HTML pages that have relatively fixed formats (i.e., whose layout changes little for each request); JSP is usually more convenient in such a case. JSP is discussed in Part II of this book (starting in Chapter 10).

Don't be concerned if you are not yet familiar with HTTP response headers; they are discussed in Chapter 7. However, you should note now that you need to set response headers *before* actually returning any of the content with the `PrintWriter`. That's because an HTTP response consists of the status line, one or more headers, a blank line, and the actual document, *in that order*. The headers can appear in any order, and servlets buffer the headers and send them all at once, so it is legal to set the status code (part of the first line returned) even after setting headers. But servlets do not necessarily buffer the document itself, since users might want to see partial results for long pages. Servlet engines are permitted to partially buffer the output, but the size of the buffer is left unspecified. You can use the `getBufferSize` method of `HttpServletResponse` to determine the size, or you can use `setBufferSize` to specify it. You can set headers until the buffer fills up and is actually sent to the client. If you aren't sure whether the buffer has been sent, you can use the `isCommitted` method to check. Even so, the best approach is to simply put the `setContentType` line before any of the lines that use the `PrintWriter`.

Core Warning

*You must set the content type **before** transmitting the actual document.*

The second step in writing a servlet that builds an HTML document is to have your `println` statements output HTML, not plain text. Listing 3.3 shows HelloServlet.java, the sample servlet used in Section 2.8 to verify that the server is functioning properly. As Figure 3–3 illustrates, the browser formats the result as HTML, not as plain text.

Listing 3.3 HelloServlet.java

```
import java.io.*;
import javax.servlet.*;
import javax.servlet.http.*;

/** Simple servlet used to test server. */

public class HelloServlet extends HttpServlet {
  public void doGet(HttpServletRequest request,
                    HttpServletResponse response)
      throws ServletException, IOException {
    response.setContentType("text/html");
    PrintWriter out = response.getWriter();
    String docType =
      "<!DOCTYPE HTML PUBLIC \"-//W3C//DTD HTML 4.0 " +
      "Transitional//EN\">\n";
    out.println(docType +
                "<HTML>\n" +
                "<HEAD><TITLE>Hello</TITLE></HEAD>\n" +
                "<BODY BGCOLOR=\"#FDF5E6\">\n" +
                "<H1>Hello</H1>\n" +
                "</BODY></HTML>");
  }
}
```

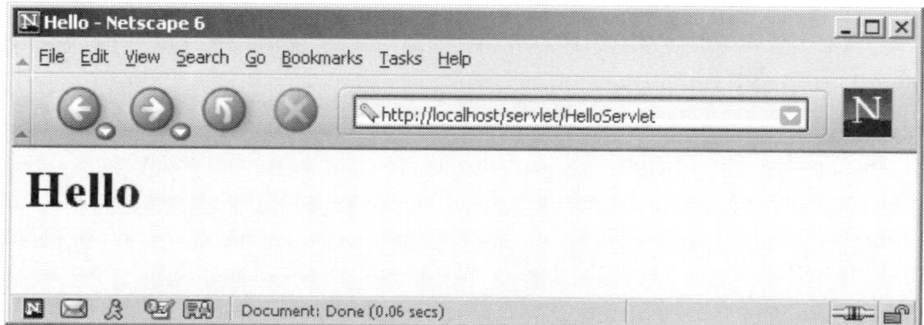

Figure 3–3 Result of http://localhost/servlet/HelloServlet.

The final step is to check that your HTML has no syntax errors that could cause unpredictable results on different browsers. See Section 3.5 (Simple HTML-Building Utilities) for a discussion of HTML validators.

3.4 Servlet Packaging

In a production environment, multiple programmers can be developing servlets for the same server. So, placing all the servlets in the same directory results in a massive, hard-to-manage collection of classes and risks name conflicts when two developers inadvertently choose the same name for a servlet or a utility class. Now, Web applications (see Section 2.11) help with this problem by dividing things up into separate directories, each with its own set of servlets, utility classes, JSP pages, and HTML files. However, since even a single Web application can be large, you still need the standard Java solution for avoiding name conflicts: packages. Besides, as you will see later, custom classes used by JSP pages should *always* be in packages. You might as well get in the habit early.

When you put your servlets in packages, you need to perform the following two additional steps.

1. **Place the files in a subdirectory that matches the intended package name.** For example, we'll use the `coreservlets` package for most of the rest of the servlets in this book. So, the class files need to go in a subdirectory called coreservlets. Remember that case matters for both package names and directory names, regardless of what operating system you are using.
2. **Insert a package statement in the class file.** For instance, for a class to be in a package called `somePackage`, the class should be in the somePackage directory and the *first* non-comment line of the file should read

```
package somePackage;
```

For example, Listing 3.4 presents a variation of the `HelloServlet` class that is in the `coreservlets` package and thus the **coreservlets** directory. As discussed in Section 2.8 (Test Your Setup), the class file should be placed in ***install_dir*/webapps/ROOT/WEB-INF/classes/coreservlets** for Tomcat, ***install_dir*/servers/default/default-ear/default-war/WEB-INF/classes/coreservlets** for JRun, and ***install_dir*/doc/WEB-INF/classes/coreservlets** for Resin. Other servers have similar installation locations.

Figure 3–4 shows the servlet accessed by means of the default URL.

Listing 3.4 coreservlets/HelloServlet2.java

```
package coreservlets;

import java.io.*;
import javax.servlet.*;
import javax.servlet.http.*;

/** Simple servlet for testing the use of packages. */

public class HelloServlet2 extends HttpServlet {
  public void doGet(HttpServletRequest request,
                    HttpServletResponse response)
      throws ServletException, IOException {
    response.setContentType("text/html");
    PrintWriter out = response.getWriter();
    String docType =
      "<!DOCTYPE HTML PUBLIC \"-//W3C//DTD HTML 4.0 " +
      "Transitional//EN\">\n";
    out.println(docType +
                "<HTML>\n" +
                "<HEAD><TITLE>Hello (2)</TITLE></HEAD>\n" +
                "<BODY BGCOLOR=\"#FDF5E6\">\n" +
                "<H1>Hello (2)</H1>\n" +
                "</BODY></HTML>");
  }
}
```

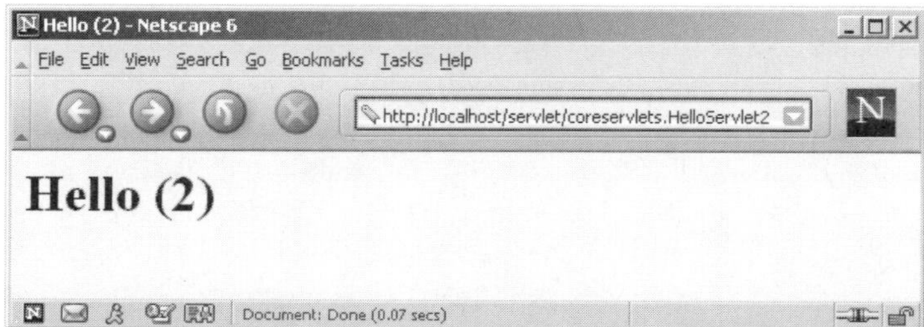

Figure 3–4 Result of http://localhost/servlet/coreservlets.HelloServlet2.

3.5 Simple HTML-Building Utilities

As you probably already know, an HTML document is structured as follows:

```
<!DOCTYPE ...>
<HTML>
<HEAD><TITLE>...</TITLE>...</HEAD>
<BODY ...>...</BODY>
</HTML>
```

When using servlets to build the HTML, you might be tempted to omit part of this structure, especially the `DOCTYPE` line, noting that virtually all major browsers ignore it even though the HTML specifications require it. We strongly discourage this practice. The advantage of the `DOCTYPE` line is that it tells HTML validators which version of HTML you are using so they know which specification to check your document against. These validators are valuable debugging services, helping you catch HTML syntax errors that your browser guesses well on but that other browsers will have trouble displaying.

The two most popular online validators are the ones from the World Wide Web Consortium (http://validator.w3.org/) and from the Web Design Group (http://www.html-help.com/tools/validator/). They let you submit a URL, then they retrieve the page, check the syntax against the formal HTML specification, and report any errors to you. Since, to a client, a servlet that generates HTML looks exactly like a regular Web page, it can be validated in the normal manner unless it requires `POST` data to return its result. Since `GET` data is attached to the URL, you can even send the validators a URL that includes `GET` data. If the servlet is available only inside your corporate firewall, simply run it, save the HTML to disk, and choose the validator's File Upload option.

Core Approach

Use an HTML validator to check the syntax of pages that your servlets generate.

Admittedly, it is sometimes a bit cumbersome to generate HTML with `println` statements, especially long tedious lines like the `DOCTYPE` declaration. Some people address this problem by writing lengthy HTML-generation utilities, then use the utilities throughout their servlets. We're skeptical of the usefulness of such an extensive library. First and foremost, the inconvenience of generating HTML programmatically is one of the main problems addressed by JavaServer Pages (see Chapter 10, "Overview of JSP Technology"). Second, HTML generation routines can be cumbersome and tend not to support the full range of HTML attributes (`CLASS` and `ID` for style sheets, JavaScript event handlers, table cell background colors, and so forth).

Despite the questionable value of a full-blown HTML generation library, if you find you're repeating the same constructs many times, you might as well create a simple utility class that simplifies those constructs. After all, you're working with the Java programming language; don't forget the standard object-oriented programming principle of reusing, not repeating, code. Repeating identical or nearly identical code means that you have to change the code lots of different places when you inevitably change your approach.

For standard servlets, two parts of the Web page (`DOCTYPE` and `HEAD`) are unlikely to change and thus could benefit from being incorporated into a simple utility file. These are shown in Listing 3.5, with Listing 3.6 showing a variation of the `HelloServlet` class that makes use of this utility. We'll add a few more utilities throughout the book.

Listing 3.5 coreservlets/ServletUtilities.java

```
package coreservlets;

import javax.servlet.*;
import javax.servlet.http.*;

/** Some simple time savers. Note that most are static methods. */

public class ServletUtilities {
  public static final String DOCTYPE =
    "<!DOCTYPE HTML PUBLIC \"-//W3C//DTD HTML 4.0 " +
    "Transitional//EN\">";
```

Listing 3.5 coreservlets/ServletUtilities.java *(continued)*

```
  public static String headWithTitle(String title) {
    return(DOCTYPE + "\n" +
           "<HTML>\n" +
           "<HEAD><TITLE>" + title + "</TITLE></HEAD>\n");
  }

  ...
}
```

Listing 3.6 coreservlets/HelloServlet3.java

```
package coreservlets;

import java.io.*;
import javax.servlet.*;
import javax.servlet.http.*;

/** Simple servlet for testing the use of packages
 *  and utilities from the same package.
 */

public class HelloServlet3 extends HttpServlet {
  public void doGet(HttpServletRequest request,
                    HttpServletResponse response)
      throws ServletException, IOException {
    response.setContentType("text/html");
    PrintWriter out = response.getWriter();
    String title = "Hello (3)";
    out.println(ServletUtilities.headWithTitle(title) +
                "<BODY BGCOLOR=\"#FDF5E6\">\n" +
                "<H1>" + title + "</H1>\n" +
                "</BODY></HTML>");
  }
}
```

After you compile HelloServlet3.java (which results in ServletUtilities.java being compiled automatically), you need to move the two class files to the coreservlets subdirectory of the server's default deployment location (.../WEB-INF/classes; review Section 2.8 for details). If you get an "Unresolved symbol" error when compiling HelloServlet3.java, go back and review the CLASSPATH settings described in Section 2.7 (Set Up Your Development Environment), especially the part about including the top-level development directory in the CLASSPATH. Figure 3–5 shows the result when the servlet is invoked with the default URL.

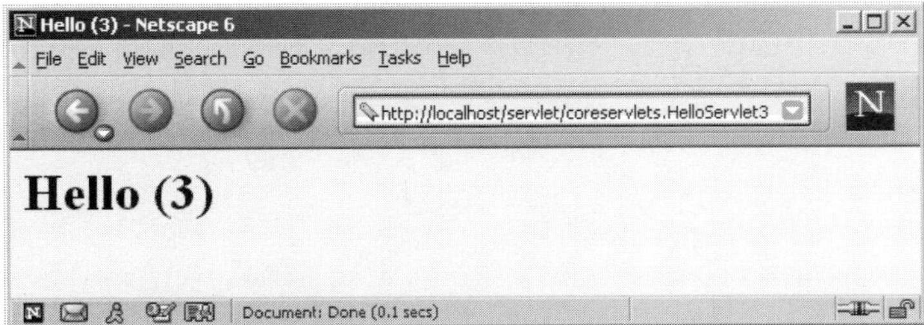

Figure 3–5 Result of http://localhost/servlet/coreservlets.HelloServlet3.

3.6 The Servlet Life Cycle

In Section 1.4 (The Advantages of Servlets Over "Traditional" CGI) we referred to the fact that only a single instance of each servlet gets created, with each user request resulting in a new thread that is handed off to `doGet` or `doPost` as appropriate. We'll now be more specific about how servlets are created and destroyed, and how and when the various methods are invoked. We summarize here, then elaborate in the following subsections.

When the servlet is first created, its `init` method is invoked, so `init` is where you put one-time setup code. After this, each user request results in a thread that calls the `service` method of the previously created instance. Multiple concurrent requests normally result in multiple threads calling `service` simultaneously, although your servlet can implement a special interface (`SingleThreadModel`) that stipulates that only a single thread is permitted to run at any one time. The `service` method then calls `doGet`, `doPost`, or another `doXxx` method, depending on the type of HTTP request it received. Finally, if the server decides to unload a servlet, it first calls the servlet's `destroy` method.

The service Method

Each time the server receives a request for a servlet, the server spawns a new thread and calls `service`. The `service` method checks the HTTP request type (`GET`, `POST`, `PUT`, `DELETE`, etc.) and calls `doGet`, `doPost`, `doPut`, `doDelete`, etc., as appropriate. A `GET` request results from a normal request for a URL or from an HTML form that has no `METHOD` specified. A `POST` request results from an HTML form that specifically lists `POST` as the `METHOD`. Other HTTP requests are generated only by custom clients. If you aren't familiar with HTML forms, see Chapter 19 (Creating and Processing HTML Forms).

Now, if you have a servlet that needs to handle both POST and GET requests identically, you may be tempted to override service directly rather than implementing both doGet and doPost. This is not a good idea. Instead, just have doPost call doGet (or vice versa), as below.

```
public void doGet(HttpServletRequest request,
                  HttpServletResponse response)
    throws ServletException, IOException {
  // Servlet code
}

public void doPost(HttpServletRequest request,
                   HttpServletResponse response)
    throws ServletException, IOException {
  doGet(request, response);
}
```

Although this approach takes a couple of extra lines of code, it has several advantages over directly overriding service. First, you can later add support for other HTTP request methods by adding doPut, doTrace, etc., perhaps in a subclass. Overriding service directly precludes this possibility. Second, you can add support for modification dates by adding a getLastModified method, as illustrated in Listing 3.7. Since getLastModified is invoked by the default service method, overriding service eliminates this option. Finally, service gives you automatic support for HEAD, OPTION, and TRACE requests.

Core Approach

If your servlet needs to handle both GET and POST identically, have your doPost method call doGet, or vice versa. Don't override service.

The doGet, doPost, and doXxx Methods

These methods contain the real meat of your servlet. Ninety-nine percent of the time, you only care about GET or POST requests, so you override doGet and/or doPost. However, if you want to, you can also override doDelete for DELETE requests, doPut for PUT, doOptions for OPTIONS, and doTrace for TRACE. Recall, however, that you have automatic support for OPTIONS and TRACE.

Normally, you do not need to implement doHead in order to handle HEAD requests (HEAD requests stipulate that the server should return the normal HTTP headers, but no associated document). You don't normally need to implement doHead because the system automatically calls doGet and uses the resultant status line and header settings to answer HEAD requests. However, it is occasionally useful to implement `doHead` so that you can generate responses to `HEAD` requests (i.e., requests from custom clients that want just the HTTP headers, not the actual document) more quickly—without building the actual document output.

The init Method

Most of the time, your servlets deal only with per-request data, and `doGet` or `doPost` are the only life-cycle methods you need. Occasionally, however, you want to perform complex setup tasks when the servlet is first loaded, but not repeat those tasks for each request. The `init` method is designed for this case; it is called when the servlet is first created, and *not* called again for each user request. So, it is used for one-time initializations, just as with the `init` method of applets. The servlet is normally created when a user first invokes a URL corresponding to the servlet, but you can also specify that the servlet be loaded when the server is first started (see the chapter on the web.xml file in Volume 2 of this book).

The `init` method definition looks like this:

```
public void init() throws ServletException {
  // Initialization code...
}
```

The `init` method performs two varieties of initializations: general initializations and initializations controlled by initialization parameters.

General Initializations

With the first type of initialization, `init` simply creates or loads some data that will be used throughout the life of the servlet, or it performs some one-time computation. If you are familiar with applets, this task is analogous to an applet calling `getImage` to load image files over the network: the operation only needs to be performed once, so it is triggered by `init`. Servlet examples include setting up a database connection pool for requests that the servlet will handle or loading a data file into a `HashMap`.

Listing 3.7 shows a servlet that uses `init` to do two things.

First, it builds an array of 10 integers. Since these numbers are based upon complex calculations, we don't want to repeat the computation for each request. So, `doGet` looks up the values that `init` computed, instead of generating them each time. The results of this technique are shown in Figure 3–6.

Second, since the output of the servlet does not change except when the server is rebooted, `init` also stores a page modification date that is used by the `getLastModified` method. This method should return a modification time expressed in milliseconds since 1970, as is standard with Java dates. The time is automatically converted to a date in GMT appropriate for the `Last-Modified` header. More importantly, if the server receives a conditional `GET` request (one specifying that the client only wants pages marked `If-Modified-Since` a particular date), the system compares the specified date to that returned by `getLastModified`, returning the page only if it has been changed after the specified date. Browsers frequently make these conditional requests for pages stored in their caches, so supporting conditional requests helps your users (they get faster results) and reduces server load (you send fewer complete documents). Since the `Last-Modified` and `If-Modified-Since` headers use only whole seconds, the `getLastModified` method should round times down to the nearest second.

Listing 3.7 coreservlets/LotteryNumbers.java

```
package coreservlets;

import java.io.*;
import javax.servlet.*;
import javax.servlet.http.*;

/** Example using servlet initialization and the
 *  getLastModified method.
 */

public class LotteryNumbers extends HttpServlet {
  private long modTime;
  private int[] numbers = new int[10];

  /** The init method is called only when the servlet is first
   *  loaded, before the first request is processed.
   */

  public void init() throws ServletException {
    // Round to nearest second (i.e., 1000 milliseconds)
    modTime = System.currentTimeMillis()/1000*1000;
    for(int i=0; i<numbers.length; i++) {
      numbers[i] = randomNum();
    }
  }

  /** Return the list of numbers that init computed. */

  public void doGet(HttpServletRequest request,
                    HttpServletResponse response)
      throws ServletException, IOException {
    response.setContentType("text/html");
    PrintWriter out = response.getWriter();
    String title = "Your Lottery Numbers";
    String docType =
      "<!DOCTYPE HTML PUBLIC \"-//W3C//DTD HTML 4.0 " +
      "Transitional//EN\">\n";
```

Listing 3.7 coreservlets/LotteryNumbers.java *(continued)*

```
    out.println(docType +
                "<HTML>\n" +
                "<HEAD><TITLE>" + title + "</TITLE></HEAD>\n" +
                "<BODY BGCOLOR=\"#FDF5E6\">\n" +
                "<H1 ALIGN=CENTER>" + title + "</H1>\n" +
                "<B>Based upon extensive research of " +
                "astro-illogical trends, psychic farces, " +
                "and detailed statistical claptrap, " +
                "we have chosen the " + numbers.length +
                " best lottery numbers for you.</B>" +
                "<OL>");
    for(int i=0; i<numbers.length; i++) {
      out.println("  <LI>" + numbers[i]);
    }
    out.println("</OL>" +
                "</BODY></HTML>");
  }

  /** The standard service method compares this date against
   *  any date specified in the If-Modified-Since request header.
   *  If the getLastModified date is later or if there is no
   *  If-Modified-Since header, the doGet method is called
   *  normally. But if the getLastModified date is the same or
   *  earlier, the service method sends back a 304 (Not Modified)
   *  response and does <B>not</B> call doGet. The browser should
   *  use its cached version of the page in such a case.
   */

  public long getLastModified(HttpServletRequest request) {
    return(modTime);
  }

  // A random int from 0 to 99.

  private int randomNum() {
    return((int)(Math.random() * 100));
  }
}
```

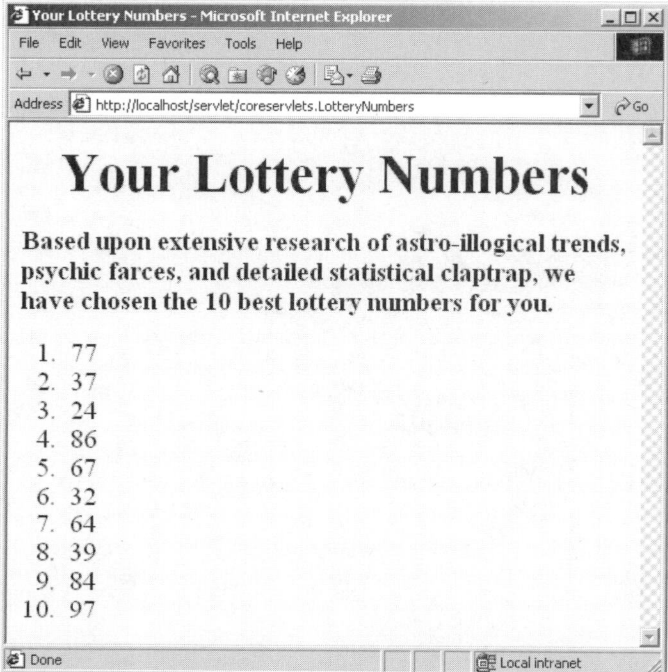

Figure 3–6 Result of the `LotteryNumbers` servlet.

Figures 3–7 and 3–8 show the result of requests for the same servlet with two slightly different `If-Modified-Since` dates. To set the request headers and see the response headers, we used `WebClient`, a Java application that lets you interactively set up HTTP requests, submit them, and see the "raw" results. The code for `WebClient` is available at the source code archive on the book's home page (http://www.coreservlets.com/).

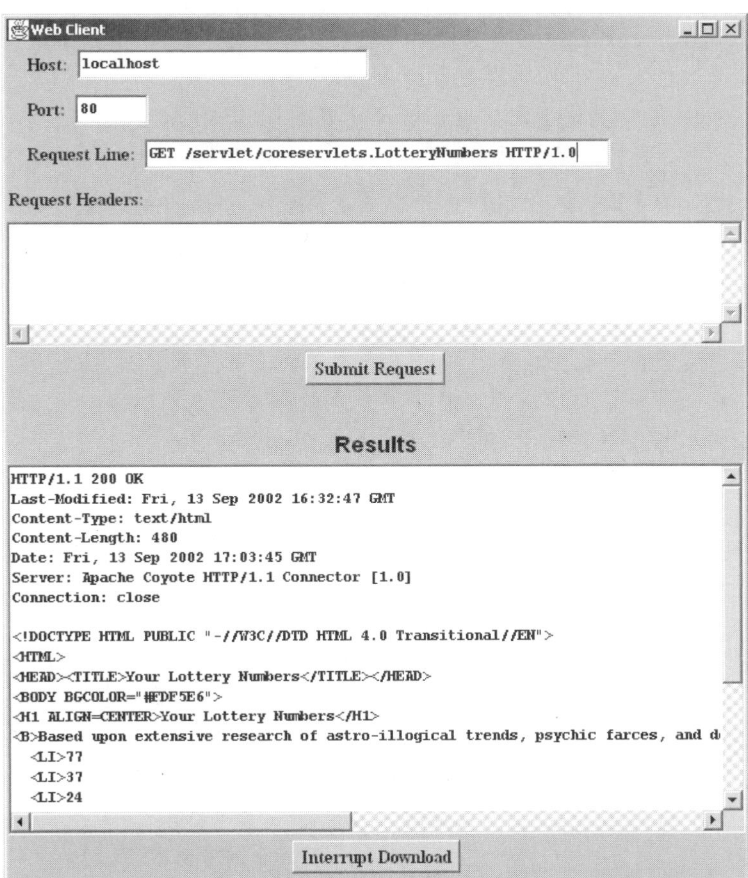

Figure 3–7 Accessing the `LotteryNumbers` servlet results in normal response (with the document sent to the client) in two situations: when there is an unconditional `GET` request or when there is a conditional request that specifies a date before servlet initialization. Code for the `WebClient` program (used here to interactively connect to the server) is available at the book's source code archive at http://www.coreservlets.com/.

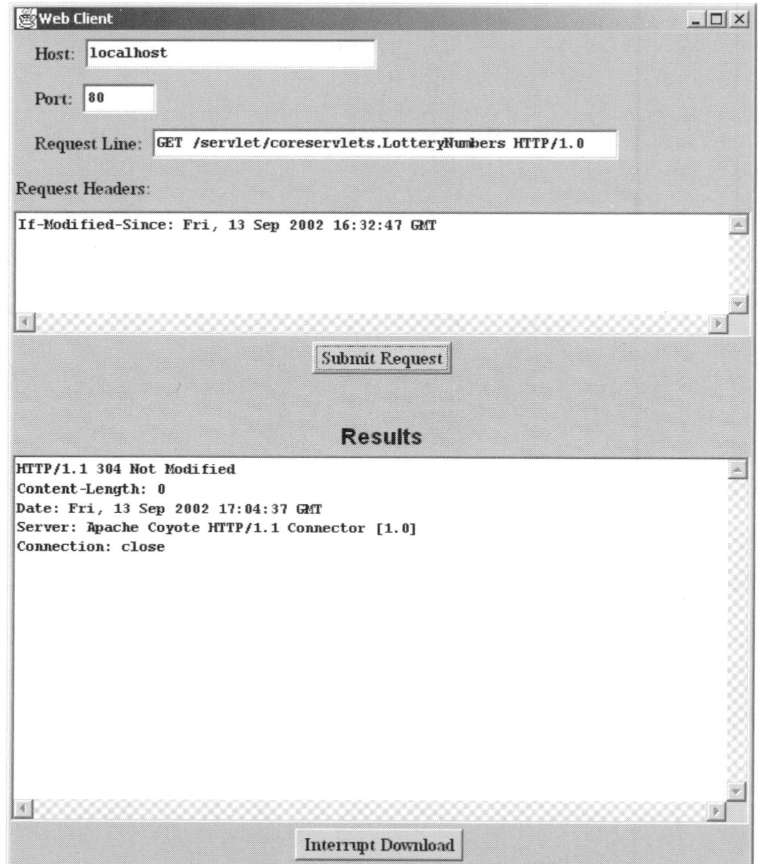

Figure 3–8 Accessing the `LotteryNumbers` servlet results in a 304 (Not Modified) response with no actual document in one situation: when a conditional `GET` request is received that specifies a date at or after servlet initialization.

Initializations Controlled by Initialization Parameters

In the previous example, the `init` method computed some data that was used by the `doGet` and `getLastModified` methods. Although this type of general initialization is quite common, it is also common to control the initialization by the use of initialization parameters. To understand the motivation for init parameters, you need to understand the categories of people who might want to customize the way a servlet or JSP page behaves. There are three such groups:

1. Developers.
2. End users.
3. Deployers.

Developers change the behavior of a servlet by changing the code. End users change the behavior of a servlet by providing data to an HTML form (assuming that the developer has written the servlet to look for this data). But what about deployers? There needs to be a way to let administrators move servlets from machine to machine and change certain parameters (e.g., the address of a database, the size of a connection pool, or the location of a data file) without modifying the servlet source code. Providing this capability is the purpose of init parameters.

Because the use of servlet initialization parameters relies heavily on the deployment descriptor (web.xml), we postpone details and examples on init parameters until the deployment descriptor chapter in Volume 2 of this book. But, here is a brief preview:

1. Use the web.xml `servlet` element to give a name to your servlet.
2. Use the web.xml `servlet-mapping` element to assign a custom URL to your servlet. You never use default URLs of the form http://.../**servlet**/*ServletName* when using init parameters. In fact, these default URLs, although extremely convenient during initial development, are almost never used in deployment scenarios.
3. Add `init-param` subelements to the web.xml `servlet` element to assign names and values of initialization parameters.
4. From within your servlet's `init` method, call `getServletConfig` to obtain a reference to the `ServletConfig` object.
5. Call the `getInitParameter` method of `ServletConfig` with the name of the init parameter. The return value is the value of the init parameter or `null` if no such init parameter is found in the web.xml file.

The destroy Method

The server may decide to remove a previously loaded servlet instance, perhaps because it is explicitly asked to do so by the server administrator or perhaps because the servlet is idle for a long time. Before it does, however, it calls the servlet's `destroy` method. This method gives your servlet a chance to close database connections, halt background threads, write cookie lists or hit counts to disk, and perform other such cleanup activities. Be aware, however, that it is possible for the Web server to crash (remember those California power outages?). So, don't count on `destroy` as the *only* mechanism for saving state to disk. If your servlet performs activities like counting hits or accumulating lists of cookie values that indicate special access, you should also proactively write the data to disk periodically.

3.7 The SingleThreadModel Interface

Normally, the system makes a single instance of your servlet and then creates a new thread for each user request. This means that if a new request comes in while a previous request is still executing, multiple threads can concurrently be accessing the same servlet object. Consequently, your `doGet` and `doPost` methods must be careful to synchronize access to fields and other shared data (if any) since multiple threads may access the data simultaneously. Note that local variables are not shared by multiple threads, and thus need no special protection.

In principle, you can prevent multithreaded access by having your servlet implement the `SingleThreadModel` interface, as below.

```
public class YourServlet extends HttpServlet
    implements SingleThreadModel {
  ...
}
```

If you implement this interface, the system guarantees that there is never more than one request thread accessing a single instance of your servlet. In most cases, it does so by queuing all the requests and passing them one at a time to a single servlet instance. However, the server is permitted to create a pool of multiple instances, each of which handles one request at a time. Either way, this means that you don't have to worry about simultaneous access to regular fields (instance variables) of the servlet. You *do*, however, still have to synchronize access to class variables (`static` fields) or shared data stored outside the servlet.

Although `SingleThreadModel` prevents concurrent access in principle, in practice there are two reasons why it is usually a poor choice.

First, synchronous access to your servlets can significantly hurt performance (latency) if your servlet is accessed frequently. When a servlet waits for I/O, the server cannot handle pending requests for the same servlet. So, think twice before using the `SingleThreadModel` approach. Instead, consider synchronizing only the part of the code that manipulates the shared data.

The second problem with `SingleThreadModel` stems from the fact that the specification permits servers to use pools of instances instead of queueing up the requests to a single instance. As long as each instance handles only one request at a time, the pool-of-instances approach satisfies the requirements of the specification. But, it is a bad idea.

Suppose, on one hand, that you are using regular non-static instance variables (fields) to refer to shared data. Sure, `SingleThreadModel` prevents concurrent access, but it does so by throwing out the baby with the bath water: each servlet instance has a separate copy of the instance variables, so the data is no longer shared properly.

On the other hand, suppose that you are using static instance variables to refer to the shared data. In that case, the pool-of-instances approach to `SingleThreadModel` provides no advantage whatsoever; multiple requests (using different instances) can still concurrently access the static data.

Now, `SingleThreadModel` is still occasionally useful. For example, it can be used when the instance variables are reinitialized for each request (e.g., when they are used merely to simplify communication among methods). But, the problems with `SingleThreadModel` are so severe that it is deprecated in the servlet 2.4 (JSP 2.0) specification. You are much better off using explicit `synchronized` blocks.

Core Warning

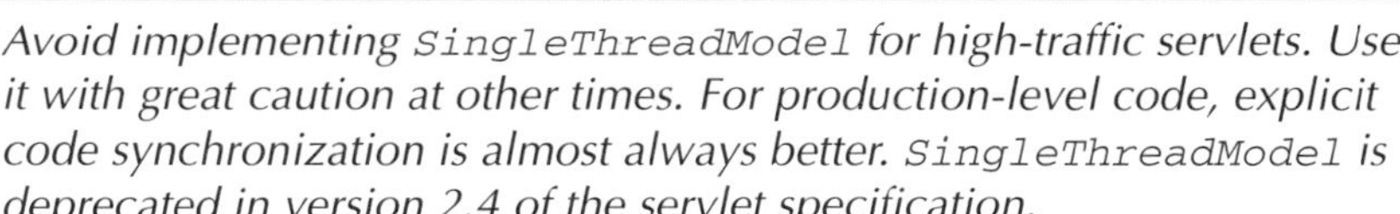

Avoid implementing `SingleThreadModel` for high-traffic servlets. Use it with great caution at other times. For production-level code, explicit code synchronization is almost always better. `SingleThreadModel` is deprecated in version 2.4 of the servlet specification.

For example, consider the servlet of Listing 3.8 that attempts to assign unique user IDs to each client (unique until the server restarts, that is). It uses an instance variable (field) called `nextID` to keep track of which ID should be assigned next, and uses the following code to output the ID.

```
String id = "User-ID-" + nextID;
out.println("<H2>" + id + "</H2>");
nextID = nextID + 1;
```

Now, suppose you were very careful in testing this servlet. You put it in a subdirectory called **coreservlets**, compiled it, and copied the **coreservlets** directory to the **WEB-INF/classes** directory of the default Web application (see Section 2.10, "Deployment Directories for Default Web Application: Summary"). You started the server. You repeatedly accessed the servlet with **http://localhost/servlet/coreservlets.UserIDs**. Every time you accessed it, you got a different value (Figure 3–9). So the code is correct, right? Wrong! The problem occurs only when there are multiple simultaneous accesses to the servlet. Even then, it occurs only once in a while. But, in a few cases, the first client could read the `nextID` field and have its thread preempted before it incremented the field. Then, a second client could read the field and get the same value as the first client. Big trouble! For example, there have been real-world e-commerce applications where customer purchases were occasionally charged to the wrong client's credit card, precisely because of such a race condition in the generation of user IDs.

Now, if you are familiar with multithreaded programming, the problem was very obvious to you. The question is, what is the proper solution? Here are three possibilities.

1. **Shorten the race.** Remove the third line of the code snippet and change the first line to the following.

   ```
   String id = "User-ID-" + nextID++;
   ```

   Boo! This approach decreases the likelihood of an incorrect answer, but does not eliminate the possibility. In many scenarios, lowering the probability of a wrong answer is a bad thing, not a good thing: it merely means that the problem is less likely to be detected in testing, and more likely to occur after being fielded.
2. **Use `SingleThreadModel`.** Change the servlet class definition to the following.

   ```
   public class UserIDs extends HttpServlet
                             implements SingleThreadModel {
   ```

   Will this work? If the server implements `SingleThreadModel` by queueing up all the requests, then, yes, this will work. But at a performance cost if there is a lot of concurrent access. Even worse, if the server implements `SingleThreadModel` by making a pool of servlet instances, this approach will totally fail because each instance will have its own `nextID` field. Either server implementation approach is legal, so this "solution" is no solution at all.
3. **Synchronize the code explicitly.** Use the standard synchronization construct of the Java programming language. Start a `synchronized` block just before the first access to the shared data, and end the block just after the last update to the data, as follows.

   ```
   synchronized(this) {
     String id = "User-ID-" + nextID;
     out.println("<H2>" + id + "</H2>");
     nextID = nextID + 1;
   }
   ```

   This technique tells the system that, once a thread has entered the above block of code (or any other `synchronized` section labelled with the same object reference), no other thread is allowed in until the first thread exits. This is the solution you have always used in the Java programming language. It is the right one here, too. Forget error-prone and low-performance `SingleThreadModel` shortcuts; fix race conditions the right way.

Listing 3.8 coreservlets/UserIDs.java

```
package coreservlets;

import java.io.*;
import javax.servlet.*;
import javax.servlet.http.*;

/** Servlet that attempts to give each user a unique
 *  user ID. However, because it fails to synchronize
 *  access to the nextID field, it suffers from race
 *  conditions: two users could get the same ID.
 */

public class UserIDs extends HttpServlet {
  private int nextID = 0;

  public void doGet(HttpServletRequest request,
                    HttpServletResponse response)
      throws ServletException, IOException {
    response.setContentType("text/html");
    PrintWriter out = response.getWriter();
    String title = "Your ID";
    String docType =
      "<!DOCTYPE HTML PUBLIC \"-//W3C//DTD HTML 4.0 " +
      "Transitional//EN\">\n";
    out.println(docType +
                "<HTML>\n" +
                "<HEAD><TITLE>" + title + "</TITLE></HEAD>\n" +
                "<CENTER>\n" +
                "<BODY BGCOLOR=\"#FDF5E6\">\n" +
                "<H1>" + title + "</H1>\n");
    String id = "User-ID-" + nextID;
    out.println("<H2>" + id + "</H2>");
    nextID = nextID + 1;
    out.println("</BODY></HTML>");
  }
}
```

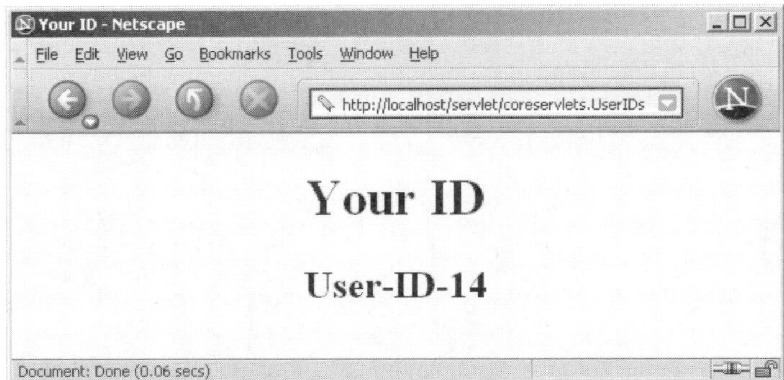

Figure 3–9 Result of the `UserIDs` servlet.

3.8 Servlet Debugging

Naturally, when *you* write servlets, you never make mistakes. However, some of your colleagues might make an occasional error, and you can pass this advice on to them. Seriously, though, debugging servlets can be tricky because you don't execute them directly. Instead, you trigger their execution by means of an HTTP request, and they are executed by the Web server. This remote execution makes it difficult to insert break points or to read debugging messages and stack traces. So, approaches to servlet debugging differ somewhat from those used in general development. Here are 10 general strategies that can make your life easier.

1. **Use print statements.**
With most server vendors, if you run the server on your desktop, a window pops up that displays standard output (i.e., the result of `System.out.println` statements). "What?" you say, "Surely you aren't advocating something as old-fashioned as print statements?" Well, true, there are more sophisticated debugging techniques. And if you are familiar with them, by all means use them. But you'd be surprised how useful it is to just gather basic information about how your program is operating. The `init` method doesn't seem to work? Insert a print statement, restart the server, and see if the print statement is displayed in the standard output window. Perhaps you declared `init` incorrectly, so your version isn't being called? Get a `NullPointerException`? Insert a couple of print statements to find out which line of code generated the error and which object on that line was `null`. When in doubt, gather more information.

2. **Use an integrated debugger in your IDE.**
   Many integrated development environments (IDEs) have sophisticated debugging tools that can be integrated with your servlet and JSP container. The Enterprise editions of IDEs like Borland JBuilder, Oracle JDeveloper, IBM WebSphere Studio, Eclipse, BEA WebLogic Studio, Sun ONE Studio, etc., typically let you insert breakpoints, trace method calls, and so on. Some will even let you connect to a server running on a remote system.
3. **Use the log file.**
   The `HttpServlet` class has a method called `log` that lets you write information into a logging file on the server. Reading debugging messages from the log file is a bit less convenient than watching them directly from a window as with the two previous approaches, but using the log file is an option even when running on a remote server; in such a situation, print statements are rarely useful and only the advanced IDEs support remote debugging. The `log` method has two variations: one that takes a `String`, and the other that takes a `String` and a `Throwable` (an ancestor class of `Exception`). The exact location of the log file is server-specific, but is generally clearly documented or can be found in subdirectories of the server installation directory.
4. **Use Apache Log4J.**
   Log4J is a package from the Apache Jakarta Project—the same project that manages Tomcat (one of the sample servers used in the book) and Struts (an MVC framework discussed in Volume 2 of this book). With Log4J, you semi-permanently insert debugging statements in your code and use an XML-based configuration file to control which are invoked at request time. Log4J is fast, flexible, convenient, and becoming more popular by the day. For details, see http://jakarta.apache.org/log4j/.
5. **Write separate classes.**
   One of the basic principles of good software design is to put commonly used code into a separate function or class so you don't need to keep rewriting it. That principle is even more important when you are writing servlets, since these separate classes can often be tested independently of the server. You can even write a test routine, with a `main`, that can be used to generate hundreds or thousands of test cases for your routines—not something you are likely to do if you have to submit each test case by hand in a browser.
6. **Plan ahead for missing or malformed data.**
   Are you reading form data from the client (Chapter 4)? Remember to check whether it is `null` or an empty string. Are you processing HTTP request headers (Chapter 5)? Remember that the headers are optional and thus might be `null` in any particular request. Every time

you
process data that comes directly or indirectly from a client, be sure to consider the possibility that it was entered incorrectly or omitted altogether.

7. **Look at the HTML source.**
   If the result you see in the browser looks odd, choose View Source from the browser's menu. Sometimes a small HTML error like `<TABLE>` instead of `</TABLE>` can prevent much of the page from being viewed. Even better, use a formal HTML validator on the servlet's output. See Section 3.5 (Simple HTML-Building Utilities) for a discussion of this approach.
8. **Look at the request data separately.**
   Servlets read data from the HTTP request, construct a response, and send it back to the client. If something in the process goes wrong, you want to discover if the cause is that the client is sending the wrong data or that the servlet is processing it incorrectly. The `EchoServer` class, discussed in Chapter 19 (Creating and Processing HTML Forms), lets you submit HTML forms and get a result that shows you *exactly* how the data arrived at the server. This class is merely a simple HTTP server that, for all requests, constructs an HTML page showing what was sent. Full source code is online at http://www.coreservlets.com/.
9. **Look at the response data separately.**
   Once you look at the request data separately, you'll want to do the same for the response data. The `WebClient` class, discussed in the `init` example of Section 3.6 (The Servlet Life Cycle), lets you connect to the server interactively, send custom HTTP request data, and see everything that comes back—HTTP response headers and all. Again, you can download the source code from http://www.coreservlets.com/.
10. **Stop and restart the server.**
    Servers are supposed to keep servlets in memory between requests, not reload them each time they are executed. However, most servers support a development mode in which servlets are supposed to be automatically reloaded whenever their associated class file changes. At times, however, some servers can get confused, especially when your only change is to a lower-level class, not to the top-level servlet class. So, if it appears that changes you make to your servlets are not reflected in the servlet's behavior, try restarting the server. Similarly, the `init` method is run only when a servlet is first loaded, the web.xml file (see Section 2.11) is read only when a Web application is first loaded (although many servers have a custom extension for reloading it), and certain Web application listeners (see Volume 2) are triggered only when the server first starts. Restarting the server will simplify debugging in all of those situations.

HANDLING THE CLIENT REQUEST: FORM DATA

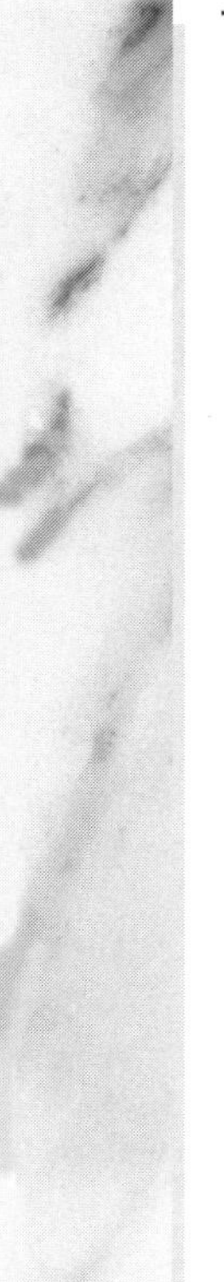

Topics in This Chapter

- Reading individual request parameters
- Reading the entire set of request parameters
- Handling missing and malformed data
- Filtering special characters out of the request parameters
- Automatically filling in a data object with request parameter values
- Dealing with incomplete form submissions

Chapter 4

One of the main motivations for building Web pages dynamically is so that the result can be based upon user input. This chapter shows you how to access that input (Sections 4.1–4.4). It also shows you how to use default values when some of the expected parameters are missing (Section 4.5), how to filter < and > out of the request data to avoid messing up the HTML results (Section 4.6), how to create "form beans" that can be automatically populated from the request data (Section 4.7), and how, when required request parameters are missing, to redisplay the form with the missing values highlighted (Section 4.8).

4.1 The Role of Form Data

If you've ever used a search engine, visited an online bookstore, tracked stocks on the Web, or asked a Web-based site for quotes on plane tickets, you've probably seen funny-looking URLs like http://*host*/*path*?user=Marty+Hall&origin=bwi&dest=sfo. The part after the question mark (i.e., user=Marty+Hall&origin=bwi&dest=sfo) is known as *form data* (or *query data*) and is the most common way to get information from a Web page to a server-side program. Form data can be attached to the end of the URL after a question mark (as above) for `GET` requests; form data can also be sent to the server on a separate line for `POST` requests. If you're not familiar with

HTML forms, Chapter 19 (Creating and Processing HTML Forms) gives details on how to build forms that collect and transmit data of this sort. However, here are the basics.

1. **Use the `FORM` element to create an HTML form.** Use the `ACTION` attribute to designate the address of the servlet or JSP page that will process the results; you can use an absolute or relative URL. For example:

   ```
   <FORM ACTION="...">...</FORM>
   ```

   If `ACTION` is omitted, the data is submitted to the URL of the current page.
2. **Use input elements to collect user data.** Place the elements between the start and end tags of the `FORM` element and give each input element a `NAME`. Textfields are the most common input element; they are created with the following.

   ```
   <INPUT TYPE="TEXT" NAME="...">
   ```
3. **Place a submit button near the bottom of the form.** For example:

   ```
   <INPUT TYPE="SUBMIT">
   ```

   When the button is pressed, the URL designated by the form's `ACTION` is invoked. With `GET` requests, a question mark and name/value pairs are attached to the end of the URL, where the names come from the `NAME` attributes in the HTML input elements and the values come from the end user. With `POST` requests, the same data is sent, but on a separate request line instead of attached to the URL.

Extracting the needed information from this form data is traditionally one of the most tedious parts of server-side programming.

First of all, before servlets you generally had to read the data one way for `GET` requests (in traditional CGI, this is usually through the `QUERY_STRING` environment variable) and a different way for `POST` requests (by reading the standard input in traditional CGI).

Second, you have to chop the pairs at the ampersands, then separate the parameter names (left of the equal signs) from the parameter values (right of the equal signs).

Third, you have to *URL-decode* the values: reverse the encoding that the browser uses on certain characters. Alphanumeric characters are sent unchanged by the browser, but spaces are converted to plus signs and other characters are converted to *%XX*, where *XX* is the ASCII (or ISO Latin-1) value of the character, in hex. For example, if someone enters a value of "`~hall, ~gates, and ~mcnealy`" into a textfield with the name `users` in an HTML form, the data is sent as "`users=%7Ehall%2C+%7Egates%2C+and+%7Emcnealy`", and the server-side program has to reconstitute the original string.

Finally, the fourth reason that it is tedious to parse form data with traditional server-side technologies is that values can be omitted (e.g., "`param1=val1&`**`param2=`**`¶m3=val3`") or a parameter can appear more than once (e.g., "**`param1=val1`**`¶m2=val2&`**`param1=val3`**"), so your parsing code needs special cases for these situations.

Fortunately, servlets help us with much of this tedious parsing. That's the topic of the next section.

4.2 Reading Form Data from Servlets

One of the nice features of servlets is that all of this form parsing is handled automatically. You call `request.getParameter` to get the value of a form parameter. You can also call `request.getParameterValues` if the parameter appears more than once, or you can call `request.getParameterNames` if you want a complete list of all parameters in the current request. In the rare cases in which you need to read the raw request data and parse it yourself, call `getReader` or `getInputStream`.

Reading Single Values: getParameter

To read a request (form) parameter, you simply call the `getParameter` method of `HttpServletRequest`, supplying the case-sensitive parameter name as an argument. You supply the parameter name exactly as it appeared in the HTML source code, and you get the result exactly as the end user entered it; any necessary URL-decoding is done automatically. Unlike the case with many alternatives to servlet technology, you use `getParameter` exactly the same way when the data is sent by `GET` (i.e., from within the `doGet` method) as you do when it is sent by `POST` (i.e., from within `doPost`); the servlet knows which request method the client used and automatically uses the appropriate method to read the data. An empty `String` is returned if the parameter exists but has no value (i.e., the user left the corresponding textfield empty when submitting the form), and `null` is returned if there was no such parameter.

Parameter names are case sensitive so, for example, `request.getParameter("Param1")` and `request.getParameter("param1")` are *not* interchangeable.

Core Warning

The values supplied to `getParameter` and `getParameterValues` are case sensitive.

Reading Multiple Values: getParameterValues

If the same parameter name might appear in the form data more than once, you should call `getParameterValues` (which returns an array of strings) instead of `getParameter` (which returns a single string corresponding to the first occurrence of the parameter). The return value of `getParameterValues` is `null` for nonexistent parameter names and is a one-element array when the parameter has only a single value.

Now, if you are the author of the HTML form, it is usually best to ensure that each textfield, checkbox, or other user interface element has a unique name. That way, you can just stick with the simpler `getParameter` method and avoid `getParameterValues` altogether. However, you sometimes write servlets or JSP pages that handle other people's HTML forms, so you have to be able to deal with all possible cases. Besides, multiselectable list boxes (i.e., HTML `SELECT` elements with the `MULTIPLE` attribute set; see Chapter 19 for details) repeat the parameter name for each selected element in the list. So, you cannot always avoid multiple values.

Looking Up Parameter Names: getParameterNames and getParameterMap

Most servlets look for a specific set of parameter names; in most cases, if the servlet does not know the name of the parameter, it does not know what to do with it either. So, your primary tool should be `getParameter`. However, it is sometimes useful to get a full list of parameter names. The primary utility of the full list is debugging, but you occasionally use the list for applications where the parameter names are very dynamic. For example, the names themselves might tell the system what to do with the parameters (e.g., `row-1-col-3-value`), the system might build a database update assuming that the parameter names are database column names, or the servlet might look for a few specific names and then pass the rest of the names to another application.

Use `getParameterNames` to get this list in the form of an `Enumeration`, each entry of which can be cast to a `String` and used in a `getParameter` or `getParameterValues` call. If there are no parameters in the current request, `getParameterNames` returns an empty `Enumeration` (not `null`). Note that `Enumeration` is an interface that merely guarantees that the actual class will have `hasMoreElements` and `nextElement` methods: there is no guarantee that any particular underlying data structure will be used. And, since some common data structures (hash tables, in particular) scramble the order of the elements, you should not count on `getParameterNames` returning the parameters in the order in which they appeared in the HTML form.

Core Warning

Don't count on `getParameterNames` returning the names in any particular order.

An alternative to `getParameterNames` is `getParameterMap`. This method returns a `Map`: the parameter names (strings) are the table keys and the parameter values (string arrays as returned by `getParameterNames`) are the table values.

Reading Raw Form Data and Parsing Uploaded Files: getReader or getInputStream

Rather than reading individual form parameters, you can access the query data directly by calling `getReader` or `getInputStream` on the `HttpServletRequest` and then using that stream to parse the raw input. Note, however, that if you read the data in this manner, it is not guaranteed to be available with `getParameter`.

Reading the raw data is a bad idea for regular parameters since the input is neither parsed (separated into entries specific to each parameter) nor URL-decoded (translated so that plus signs become spaces and %*XX* is replaced by the original ASCII or ISO Latin-1 character corresponding to the hex value *XX*). However, reading the raw input is of use in two situations.

The first case in which you might read and parse the data yourself is when the data comes from a custom client rather than by an HTML form. The most common custom client is an applet; applet-servlet communication of this nature is discussed in Volume 2 of this book.

The second situation in which you might read the data yourself is when the data is from an uploaded file. HTML supports a `FORM` element (`<INPUT TYPE="FILE" ...>`) that lets the client upload a file to the server. Unfortunately, the servlet API defines no mechanism to read such files. So, you need a third-party library to do so. One of the most popular ones is from the Apache Jakarta Project. See http://jakarta.apache.org/commons/fileupload/ for details.

Reading Input in Multiple Character Sets: setCharacterEncoding

By default, `request.getParameter` interprets input using the server's current character set. To change this default, use the `setCharacterEncoding` method of `ServletRequest`. But, what if input could be in more than one character set? In such a case, you cannot simply call `setCharacterEncoding` with a normal character set name. The reason for this restriction is that `setCharacterEncoding` must be called *before* you access any request parameters, and in many cases you use a request parameter (e.g., a checkbox) to determine the character set.

So, you are left with two choices: read the parameter in one character set and convert it to another, or use an autodetect feature provided with some character sets.

For the first option, you would read the parameter of interest, use `getBytes` to extract the raw bytes, then pass those bytes to the `String` constructor along with the name of the desired character set. Here is an example that converts a parameter to Japanese:

```
String firstNameWrongEncoding = request.getParameter("firstName");
String firstName =
  new String(firstNameWrongEncoding.getBytes(), "Shift_JIS");
```

For the second option, you would use a character set that supports detection and conversion from the default set. A full list of character sets supported in Java is available at http://java.sun.com/j2se/1.4.1/docs/guide/intl/encoding.doc.html. For example, to allow input in either English or Japanese, you might use the following.

```
request.setCharacterEncoding("JISAutoDetect");
String firstName = request.getParameter("firstName");
```

4.3 Example: Reading Three Parameters

Listing 4.1 presents a simple servlet called `ThreeParams` that reads form parameters named `param1`, `param2`, and `param3` and places their values in a bulleted list. Although you are required to specify *response* settings (see Chapters 6 and 7) before beginning to generate the content, you are not required to read the *request* parameters at any particular place in your code. So, we read the parameters only when we are ready to use them. Also recall that since the `ThreeParams` class is in the `coreservlets` package, it is deployed to the coreservlets subdirectory of the WEB-INF/classes directory of your Web application (the default Web application in this case).

As we will see later, this servlet is a perfect example of a case that would be dramatically simpler with JSP. See Section 11.6 (Comparing Servlets to JSP Pages) for an equivalent JSP version.

Listing 4.1 ThreeParams.java

```
package coreservlets;

import java.io.*;
import javax.servlet.*;
import javax.servlet.http.*;

/** Simple servlet that reads three parameters from the
 *  form data.
 */

public class ThreeParams extends HttpServlet {
  public void doGet(HttpServletRequest request,
                    HttpServletResponse response)
      throws ServletException, IOException {
    response.setContentType("text/html");
    PrintWriter out = response.getWriter();
    String title = "Reading Three Request Parameters";
    String docType =
      "<!DOCTYPE HTML PUBLIC \"-//W3C//DTD HTML 4.0 " +
      "Transitional//EN\">\n";
    out.println(docType +
                "<HTML>\n" +
                "<HEAD><TITLE>" + title + "</TITLE></HEAD>\n" +
                "<BODY BGCOLOR=\"#FDF5E6\">\n" +
                "<H1 ALIGN=\"CENTER\">" + title + "</H1>\n" +
                "<UL>\n" +
                "  <LI><B>param1</B>: "
                + request.getParameter("param1") + "\n" +
                "  <LI><B>param2</B>: "
                + request.getParameter("param2") + "\n" +
                "  <LI><B>param3</B>: "
                + request.getParameter("param3") + "\n" +
                "</UL>\n" +
                "</BODY></HTML>");
  }
}
```

Listing 4.2 shows an HTML form that collects user input and sends it to this servlet. By using an `ACTION` URL beginning with a slash (/servlet/coreservlets.ThreeParams), you can install the form anywhere in the default Web application; you can move the HTML form to another directory or move both the HTML form and the servlet to another machine, all without editing the HTML form or the servlet. The general principle that form URLs beginning with slashes increases portability holds true even when you use custom Web applications, but you have to include the Web application prefix in the URL. See Section 2.11 (Web Applications: A Preview) for details on Web applications. There are other ways to write the URLs that also simplify portability, but the most important point is to use relative URLs (no host name), not absolute ones (i.e., http://*host*/...). If you use absolute URLs, you have to edit the forms whenever you move the Web application from one machine to another. Since you almost certainly develop on one machine and deploy on another, use of absolute URLs should be strictly avoided.

Core Approach

Use form ACTION URLs that are relative, not absolute.

Listing 4.2 ThreeParamsForm.html

```
<!DOCTYPE HTML PUBLIC "-//W3C//DTD HTML 4.0 Transitional//EN">
<HTML><HEAD><TITLE>Collecting Three Parameters</TITLE></HEAD>
<BODY BGCOLOR="#FDF5E6">
<H1 ALIGN="CENTER">Collecting Three Parameters</H1>

<FORM ACTION="/servlet/coreservlets.ThreeParams">
  First Parameter:  <INPUT TYPE="TEXT" NAME="param1"><BR>
  Second Parameter: <INPUT TYPE="TEXT" NAME="param2"><BR>
  Third Parameter:  <INPUT TYPE="TEXT" NAME="param3"><BR>
  <CENTER><INPUT TYPE="SUBMIT"></CENTER>
</FORM>

</BODY></HTML>
```

Recall that the location of the default Web application varies from server to server. HTML forms go in the top-level directory or in subdirectories other than WEB-INF. If we place the HTML page in the form-data subdirectory and access it from the local machine, then the full installation location on the three sample servers used in the book is as follows:

- **Tomcat Location**
  install_dir/webapps/ROOT/form-data/ThreeParamsForm.html
- **JRun Location**
  install_dir/servers/default/default-ear/default-war/form-data/ThreeParamsForm.html

- **Resin Location**
  install_dir/doc/form-data/ThreeParamsForm.html
- **Corresponding URL**
  http://localhost/form-data/ThreeParamsForm.html

Figure 4–1 shows the HTML form when the user has entered the home directory names of three famous Internet personalities. OK, OK, only two of them are famous,[1] but the point here is that the tilde (~) is a nonalphanumeric character and will be URL-encoded by the browser when the form is submitted. Figure 4–2 shows the result of the servlet; note the URL-encoded values on the address line but the original form field values in the output: `getParameter` always returns the values as the end user typed them in, regardless of how they were sent over the network.

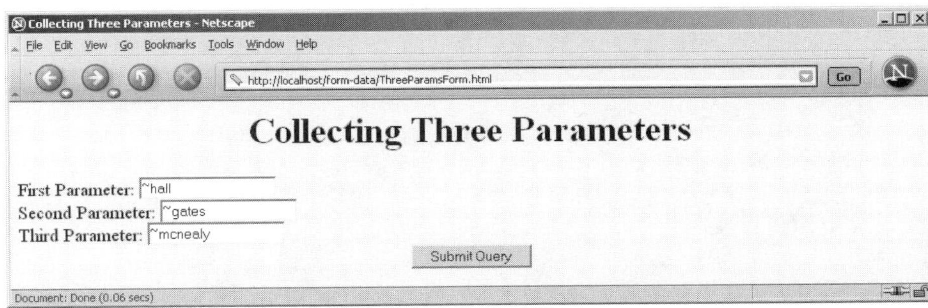

Figure 4–1 Front end to parameter-processing servlet.

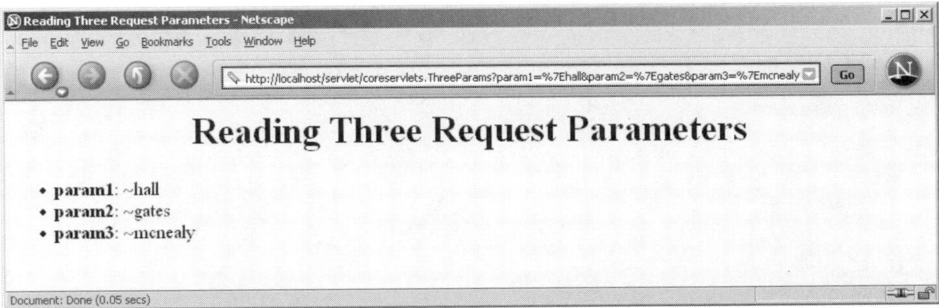

Figure 4–2 Result of parameter-processing servlet: request parameters are URL-decoded automatically.

1. Gates isn't *that* famous, after all.

4.4 Example: Reading All Parameters

The previous example extracts parameter values from the form data according to prespecified parameter names. It also assumes that each parameter has exactly one value. Here's an example that looks up *all* the parameter names that are sent and puts their values in a table. It highlights parameters that have missing values as well as ones that have multiple values. Although this approach is rarely used in production servlets (if you don't know the names of the form parameters, you probably don't know what to do with them), it is quite useful for debugging.

First, the servlet looks up all the parameter names with the `getParameterNames` method of `HttpServletRequest`. This method returns an `Enumeration` that contains the parameter names in an unspecified order. Next, the servlet loops down the `Enumeration` in the standard manner, using `hasMoreElements` to determine when to stop and using `nextElement` to get each parameter name. Since `nextElement` returns an `Object`, the servlet casts the result to a `String` and passes that to `getParameterValues`, yielding an array of strings. If that array is one entry long and contains only an empty string, then the parameter had no values and the servlet generates an italicized "No Value" entry. If the array is more than one entry long, then the parameter had multiple values and the values are displayed in a bulleted list. Otherwise, the single value is placed directly into the table.

The source code for the servlet is shown in Listing 4.3; Listing 4.4 shows the HTML code for a front end you can use to try out the servlet. Figures 4–3 and 4–4 show the result of the HTML front end and the servlet, respectively.

Listing 4.3 ShowParameters.java

```
package coreservlets;

import java.io.*;
import javax.servlet.*;
import javax.servlet.http.*;
import java.util.*;

/** Shows all the parameters sent to the servlet via either
 *  GET or POST. Specially marks parameters that have
 *  no values or multiple values.
 */
```

Listing 4.3 ShowParameters.java *(continued)*

```
public class ShowParameters extends HttpServlet {
  public void doGet(HttpServletRequest request,
                    HttpServletResponse response)
      throws ServletException, IOException {
    response.setContentType("text/html");
    PrintWriter out = response.getWriter();
    String docType =
    "<!DOCTYPE HTML PUBLIC \"-//W3C//DTD HTML 4.0 " +
    "Transitional//EN\">\n";
    String title = "Reading All Request Parameters";
    out.println(docType +
                "<HTML>\n" +
                "<HEAD><TITLE>" + title + "</TITLE></HEAD>\n" +
                "<BODY BGCOLOR=\"#FDF5E6\">\n" +
                "<H1 ALIGN=CENTER>" + title + "</H1>\n" +
                "<TABLE BORDER=1 ALIGN=CENTER>\n" +
                "<TR BGCOLOR=\"#FFAD00\">\n" +
                "<TH>Parameter Name<TH>Parameter Value(s)");
    Enumeration paramNames = request.getParameterNames();
    while(paramNames.hasMoreElements()) {
      String paramName = (String)paramNames.nextElement();
      out.print("<TR><TD>" + paramName + "\n<TD>");
      String[] paramValues =
        request.getParameterValues(paramName);
      if (paramValues.length == 1) {
        String paramValue = paramValues[0];
        if (paramValue.length() == 0)
          out.println("<I>No Value</I>");
        else
          out.println(paramValue);
      } else {
        out.println("<UL>");
        for(int i=0; i<paramValues.length; i++) {
          out.println("<LI>" + paramValues[i]);
        }
        out.println("</UL>");
      }
    }
    out.println("</TABLE>\n</BODY></HTML>");
  }

  public void doPost(HttpServletRequest request,
                     HttpServletResponse response)
      throws ServletException, IOException {
    doGet(request, response);
  }
}
```

Notice that the servlet uses a `doPost` method that simply calls `doGet`. That's because we want it to be able to handle *both* `GET` and `POST` requests. This approach is a good standard practice if you want HTML interfaces to have some flexibility in how they send data to the servlet. See the discussion of the `service` method in Section 3.6 (The Servlet Life Cycle) for a discussion of why having `doPost` call `doGet` (or vice versa) is preferable to overriding `service` directly. The HTML form from Listing 4.4 uses `POST`, as should *all* forms that have password fields (for details, see Chapter 19, "Creating and Processing HTML Forms"). However, the `ShowParameters` servlet is not specific to that particular front end, so the source code archive site at http://www.coreservlets.com/ includes a similar HTML form that uses `GET` for you to experiment with.

Listing 4.4 ShowParametersPostForm.html

```
<!DOCTYPE HTML PUBLIC "-//W3C//DTD HTML 4.0 Transitional//EN">
<HTML><HEAD><TITLE>A Sample FORM using POST</TITLE></HEAD>
<BODY BGCOLOR="#FDF5E6">
<H1 ALIGN="CENTER">A Sample FORM using POST</H1>
<FORM ACTION="/servlet/coreservlets.ShowParameters"
      METHOD="POST">
  Item Number: <INPUT TYPE="TEXT" NAME="itemNum"><BR>
  Description: <INPUT TYPE="TEXT" NAME="description"><BR>
  Price Each: <INPUT TYPE="TEXT" NAME="price" VALUE="$"><BR>
  <HR>
  First Name: <INPUT TYPE="TEXT" NAME="firstName"><BR>
  Last Name: <INPUT TYPE="TEXT" NAME="lastName"><BR>
  Middle Initial: <INPUT TYPE="TEXT" NAME="initial"><BR>
  Shipping Address:
  <TEXTAREA NAME="address" ROWS=3 COLS=40></TEXTAREA><BR>
  Credit Card:<BR>
    <INPUT TYPE="RADIO" NAME="cardType"
                     VALUE="Visa">Visa<BR>
    <INPUT TYPE="RADIO" NAME="cardType"
                     VALUE="MasterCard">MasterCard<BR>
    <INPUT TYPE="RADIO" NAME="cardType"
                     VALUE="Amex">American Express<BR>
    <INPUT TYPE="RADIO" NAME="cardType"
                     VALUE="Discover">Discover<BR>
    <INPUT TYPE="RADIO" NAME="cardType"
                     VALUE="Java SmartCard">Java SmartCard<BR>
```

Listing 4.4 ShowParametersPostForm.html *(continued)*

```
  Credit Card Number:
  <INPUT TYPE="PASSWORD" NAME="cardNum"><BR>
  Repeat Credit Card Number:
  <INPUT TYPE="PASSWORD" NAME="cardNum"><BR><BR>
  <CENTER><INPUT TYPE="SUBMIT" VALUE="Submit Order"></CENTER>
</FORM>
</BODY></HTML>
```

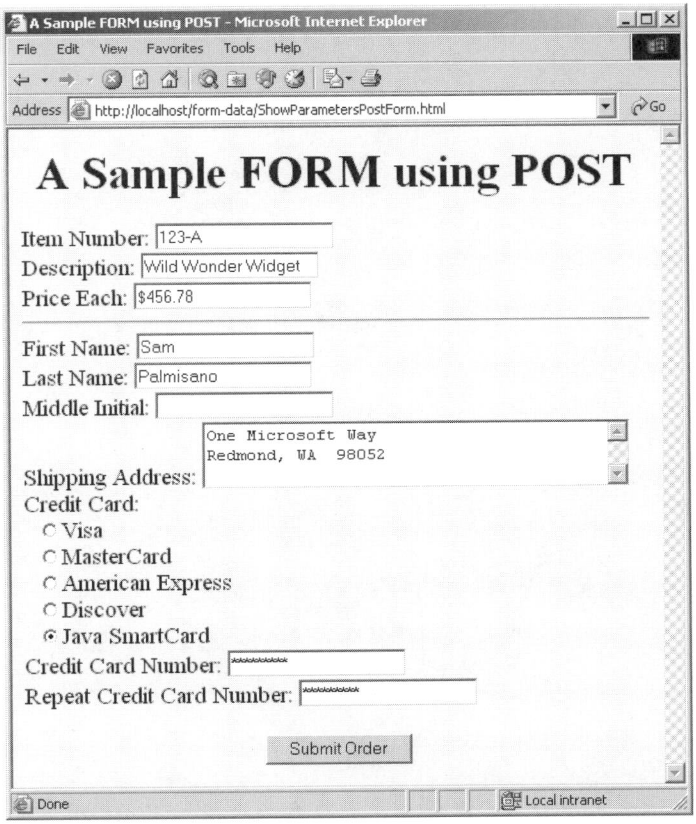

Figure 4–3 HTML form that collects data for the ShowParameters servlet.

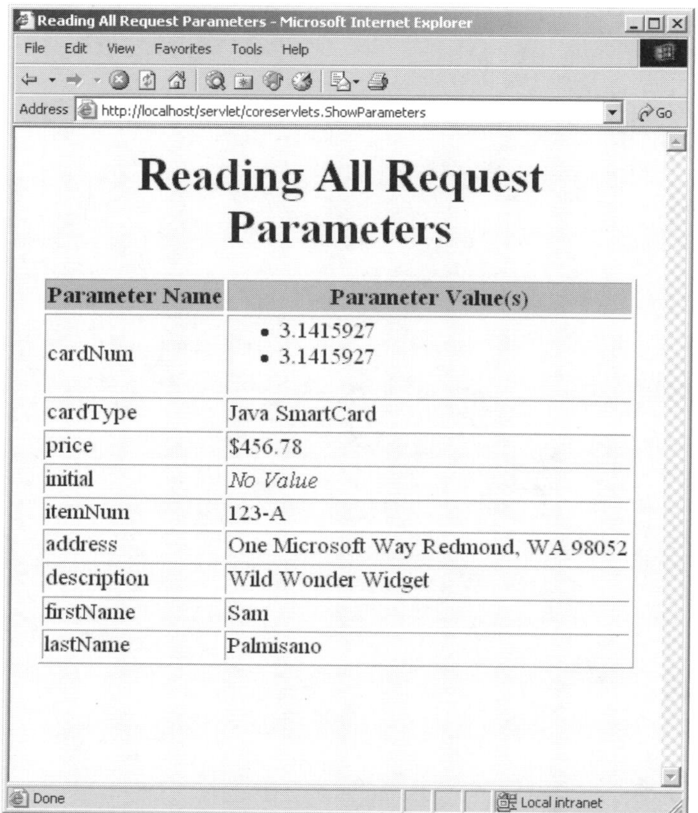

Figure 4–4 Result of the `ShowParameters` servlet.

4.5 Using Default Values When Parameters Are Missing or Malformed

Online job services have become increasingly popular of late. A reputable site provides a useful service to job seekers by giving their skills wide exposure and provides a useful service to employers by giving them access to a large pool of prospective employees. This section presents a servlet that handles part of such a site: the creation of online résumés from user-submitted data. Now, the question is: what should the servlet do when the user fails to supply the necessary information? This question has two answers: use default values or redisplay the form (prompting the user for missing values). This section illustrates the use of default values; Section 4.8 illustrates redisplay of the form.

DILBERT reprinted by permission of United Feature Syndicate, Inc.

When examining request parameters, you need to check for three conditions:

1. **The value is `null`.** A call to `request.getParameter` returns `null` if the form contains no textfield or other element of the expected name so that the parameter name does not appear in the request at all. This can happen when the end user uses an incorrect HTML form or when a bookmarked URL containing `GET` data is used but the parameter names have changed since the URL was bookmarked. To avoid a `NullPointerException`, you have to check for `null` *before* you try to call any methods on the string that results from `getParameter`.
2. **The value is an empty string.** A call to `request.getParameter` returns an empty string (i.e., `""`) if the associated textfield is empty when the form is submitted. To check for an empty string, compare the string to `""` by using `equals` or compare the length of the string to 0. *Do not use the == operator*; in the Java programming language, == always tests whether the two arguments are the same object (at the same memory location), not whether the two objects look similar. Just to be safe, it is also a good idea to call `trim` to remove any white space that the user may have entered, since in most scenarios you want to treat pure white space as missing data. So, for example, a test for missing values might look like the following.

```
String param = request.getParameter("someName");
if ((param == null) || (param.trim().equals(""))) {
  doSomethingForMissingValues(...);
} else {
  doSomethingWithParameter(param);
}
```

3. **The value is a nonempty string of the wrong format.** What defines the wrong format is application specific: you might expect certain textfields to contain only numeric values, others to have exactly seven characters, and others to only contain single letters.

Note that the use of JavaScript for client-side validation does not remove the need for also doing this type of checking on the server. After all, you are responsible for the server-side application, and often another developer or group is responsible for the forms. You do not want *your* application to crash if *they* fail to detect every type of illegal input. Besides, clients can use their own HTML forms, can manually edit URLs that contain `GET` data, and can disable JavaScript.

Core Approach

Design your servlets to gracefully handle parameters that are missing (`null` or empty string) or improperly formatted. Test your servlets with missing and malformed data as well as with data in the expected format.

Listing 4.5 and Figure 4–5 show the HTML form that acts as the front end to the résumé-processing servlet. If you are not familiar with HTML forms, see Chapter 19. The form uses `POST` to submit the data and it gathers values for various parameter names. The important thing to understand here is what the servlet does with missing and malformed data. This process is summarized in the following list. Listing 4.6 shows the complete servlet code.

- **`name`**, **`title`**, **`email`**, **`languages`**, **`skills`**
  These parameters specify various parts of the résumé. Missing values should be replaced by default values specific to the parameter. The servlet uses a method called `replaceIfMissing` to accomplish this task.
- **`fgColor`**, **`bgColor`**
  These parameters give the colors of the foreground and background of the page. Missing values should result in black for the foreground and white for the background. The servlet again uses `replaceIfMissing` to accomplish this task.
- **`headingFont`**, **`bodyFont`**
  These parameters designate the font to use for headings and the main text, respectively. A missing value or a value of "default" should result in a sans-serif font such as Arial or Helvetica. The servlet uses a method called `replaceIfMissingOrDefault` to accomplish this task.
- **`headingSize`**, **`bodySize`**
  These parameters specify the point size for main headings and body text, respectively. Subheadings will be displayed in a slightly smaller size than the main headings. Missing values or nonnumeric values should result in a default size (32 for headings, 18 for body). The servlet uses a call to `Integer.parseInt` and a `try/catch` block for `NumberFormatException` to handle this case.

Listing 4.5 SubmitResume.html

```
<!DOCTYPE HTML PUBLIC "-//W3C//DTD HTML 4.0 Transitional//EN">
<HTML><HEAD><TITLE>Free Resume Posting</TITLE>
  <LINK REL=STYLESHEET
        HREF="jobs-site-styles.css"
        TYPE="text/css">
</HEAD>
<BODY>
<H1>hot-computer-jobs.com</H1>
<P CLASS="LARGER">
To use our <I>free</I> resume-posting service, simply fill
out the brief summary of your skills below. Use "Preview"
to check the results, then press "Submit" once it is
ready. Your mini-resume will appear online within 24 hours.</P>
<HR>
<FORM ACTION="/servlet/coreservlets.SubmitResume"
      METHOD="POST">
<DL>
<DT><B>First, give some general information about the look of
your resume:</B>
<DD>Heading font:
    <INPUT TYPE="TEXT" NAME="headingFont" VALUE="default">
<DD>Heading text size:
    <INPUT TYPE="TEXT" NAME="headingSize" VALUE=32>
<DD>Body font:
    <INPUT TYPE="TEXT" NAME="bodyFont" VALUE="default">
<DD>Body text size:
    <INPUT TYPE="TEXT" NAME="bodySize" VALUE=18>
<DD>Foreground color:
    <INPUT TYPE="TEXT" NAME="fgColor" VALUE="BLACK">
<DD>Background color:
    <INPUT TYPE="TEXT" NAME="bgColor" VALUE="WHITE">

<DT><B>Next, give some general information about yourself:</B>
<DD>Name: <INPUT TYPE="TEXT" NAME="name">
<DD>Current or most recent title:
    <INPUT TYPE="TEXT" NAME="title">
<DD>Email address: <INPUT TYPE="TEXT" NAME="email">
<DD>Programming Languages:
    <INPUT TYPE="TEXT" NAME="languages">

<DT><B>Finally, enter a brief summary of your skills and
    experience:</B> (use &lt;P&gt; to separate paragraphs.
    Other HTML markup is also permitted.)
<DD><TEXTAREA NAME="skills"
              ROWS=10 COLS=60 WRAP="SOFT"></TEXTAREA>
```

Listing 4.5 SubmitResume.html *(continued)*

```
</DL>
  <CENTER>
    <INPUT TYPE="SUBMIT" NAME="previewButton" Value="Preview">
    <INPUT TYPE="SUBMIT" NAME="submitButton" Value="Submit">
  </CENTER>
</FORM>
<HR>
<P CLASS="TINY">See our privacy policy
<A HREF="we-will-spam-you.html">here</A>.</P>
</BODY></HTML>
```

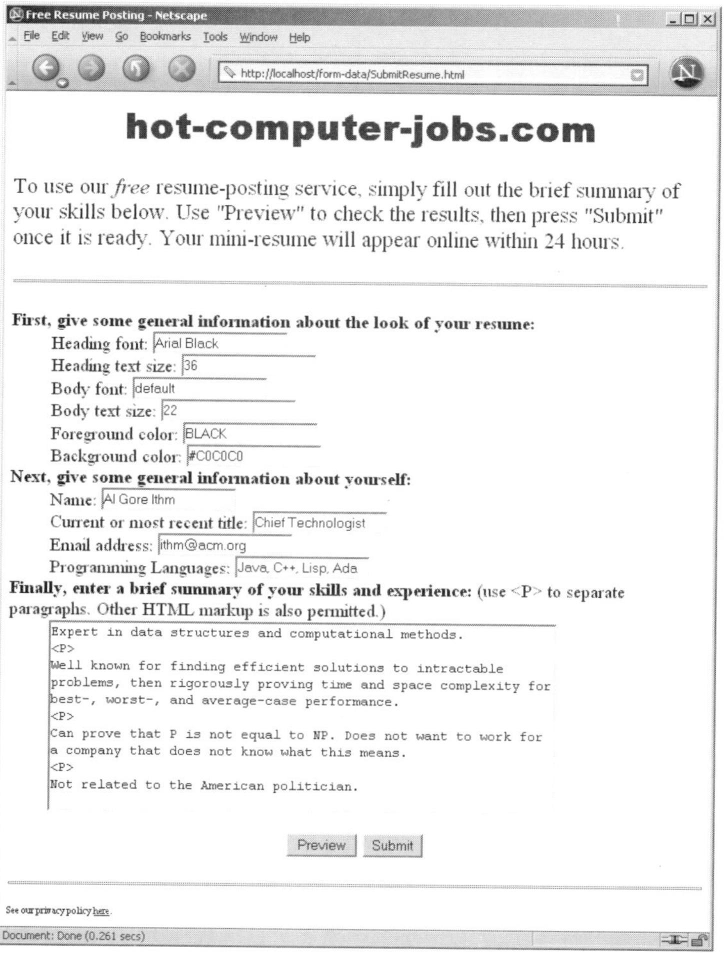

Figure 4–5 Front end to résumé-previewing servlet.

Listing 4.6 SubmitResume.java

```
package coreservlets;

import java.io.*;
import javax.servlet.*;
import javax.servlet.http.*;
import java.util.*;

/** Servlet that handles previewing and storing resumes
 *  submitted by job applicants.
 */

public class SubmitResume extends HttpServlet {
  public void doPost(HttpServletRequest request,
                     HttpServletResponse response)
      throws ServletException, IOException {
    response.setContentType("text/html");
    PrintWriter out = response.getWriter();
    if (request.getParameter("previewButton") != null) {
      showPreview(request, out);
    } else {
      storeResume(request);
      showConfirmation(request, out);
    }
  }

  /** Shows a preview of the submitted resume. Takes
   *  the font information and builds an HTML
   *  style sheet out of it, then takes the real
   *  resume information and presents it formatted with
   *  that style sheet.
   */

  private void showPreview(HttpServletRequest request,
                           PrintWriter out) {
    String headingFont = request.getParameter("headingFont");
    headingFont = replaceIfMissingOrDefault(headingFont, "");
    int headingSize =
      getSize(request.getParameter("headingSize"), 32);
    String bodyFont = request.getParameter("bodyFont");
    bodyFont = replaceIfMissingOrDefault(bodyFont, "");
    int bodySize =
      getSize(request.getParameter("bodySize"), 18);
    String fgColor = request.getParameter("fgColor");
    fgColor = replaceIfMissing(fgColor, "BLACK");
    String bgColor = request.getParameter("bgColor");
```

Listing 4.6 SubmitResume.java *(continued)*

```
    bgColor = replaceIfMissing(bgColor, "WHITE");
    String name = request.getParameter("name");
    name = replaceIfMissing(name, "Lou Zer");
    String title = request.getParameter("title");
    title = replaceIfMissing(title, "Loser");
    String email = request.getParameter("email");
    email =
      replaceIfMissing(email, "contact@hot-computer-jobs.com");
    String languages = request.getParameter("languages");
    languages = replaceIfMissing(languages, "<I>None</I>");
    String languageList = makeList(languages);
    String skills = request.getParameter("skills");
    skills = replaceIfMissing(skills, "Not many, obviously.");
    out.println
      (ServletUtilities.DOCTYPE + "\n" +
       "<HTML><HEAD><TITLE>Resume for " + name + "</TITLE>\n" +
       makeStyleSheet(headingFont, headingSize,
                      bodyFont, bodySize,
                      fgColor, bgColor) + "\n" +
       "</HEAD>\n" +
       "<BODY>\n" +
       "<CENTER>\n"+
       "<SPAN CLASS=\"HEADING1\">" + name + "</SPAN><BR>\n" +
       "<SPAN CLASS=\"HEADING2\">" + title + "<BR>\n" +
       "<A HREF=\"mailto:" + email + "\">" + email +
           "</A></SPAN>\n" +
       "</CENTER><BR><BR>\n" +
       "<SPAN CLASS=\"HEADING3\">Programming Languages" +
       "</SPAN>\n" +
       makeList(languages) + "<BR><BR>\n" +
       "<SPAN CLASS=\"HEADING3\">Skills and Experience" +
       "</SPAN><BR><BR>\n" +
       skills + "\n" +
       "</BODY></HTML>");
  }

  /** Builds a cascading style sheet with information
   *  on three levels of headings and overall
   *  foreground and background cover. Also tells
   *  Internet Explorer to change color of mailto link
   *  when mouse moves over it.
   */
```

Listing 4.6 SubmitResume.java *(continued)*

```
private String makeStyleSheet(String headingFont,
                              int heading1Size,
                              String bodyFont,
                              int bodySize,
                              String fgColor,
                              String bgColor) {
  int heading2Size = heading1Size*7/10;
  int heading3Size = heading1Size*6/10;
  String styleSheet =
    "<STYLE TYPE=\"text/css\">\n" +
    "<!--\n" +
    ".HEADING1 { font-size: " + heading1Size + "px;\n" +
    "            font-weight: bold;\n" +
    "            font-family: " + headingFont +
                   "Arial, Helvetica, sans-serif;\n" +
    "}\n" +
    ".HEADING2 { font-size: " + heading2Size + "px;\n" +
    "            font-weight: bold;\n" +
    "            font-family: " + headingFont +
                   "Arial, Helvetica, sans-serif;\n" +
    "}\n" +
    ".HEADING3 { font-size: " + heading3Size + "px;\n" +
    "            font-weight: bold;\n" +
    "            font-family: " + headingFont +
                   "Arial, Helvetica, sans-serif;\n" +
    "}\n" +
    "BODY { color: " + fgColor + ";\n" +
    "       background-color: " + bgColor + ";\n" +
    "       font-size: " + bodySize + "px;\n" +
    "       font-family: " + bodyFont +
                  "Times New Roman, Times, serif;\n" +
    "}\n" +
    "A:hover { color: red; }\n" +
    "-->\n" +
    "</STYLE>";
  return(styleSheet);
}

/** Replaces null strings (no such parameter name) or
 *  empty strings (e.g., if textfield was blank) with
 *  the replacement. Returns the original string otherwise.
 */
```

Listing 4.6 SubmitResume.java *(continued)*

```
  private String replaceIfMissing(String orig,
                                  String replacement) {
    if ((orig == null) || (orig.trim().equals(""))) {
      return(replacement);
    } else {
      return(orig);
    }
  }

  // Replaces null strings, empty strings, or the string
  // "default" with the replacement.
  // Returns the original string otherwise.

  private String replaceIfMissingOrDefault(String orig,
                                           String replacement) {
    if ((orig == null) ||
        (orig.trim().equals("")) ||
        (orig.equals("default"))) {
      return(replacement);
    } else {
      return(orig + ", ");
    }
  }

  // Takes a string representing an integer and returns it
  // as an int. Returns a default if the string is null
  // or in an illegal format.

  private int getSize(String sizeString, int defaultSize) {
    try {
      return(Integer.parseInt(sizeString));
    } catch(NumberFormatException nfe) {
      return(defaultSize);
    }
  }

  // Given "Java,C++,Lisp", "Java C++ Lisp" or
  // "Java, C++, Lisp", returns
  // "<UL>
  //    <LI>Java
  //    <LI>C++
  //    <LI>Lisp
  //  </UL>"
```

Listing 4.6 SubmitResume.java *(continued)*

```
  private String makeList(String listItems) {
    StringTokenizer tokenizer =
      new StringTokenizer(listItems, ", ");
    String list = "<UL>\n";
    while(tokenizer.hasMoreTokens()) {
      list = list + "  <LI>" + tokenizer.nextToken() + "\n";
    }
    list = list + "</UL>";
    return(list);
  }

  /** Shows a confirmation page when the user clicks the
   *  "Submit" button.
   */

  private void showConfirmation(HttpServletRequest request,
                                PrintWriter out) {
    String title = "Submission Confirmed.";
    out.println(ServletUtilities.headWithTitle(title) +
                "<BODY>\n" +
                "<H1>" + title + "</H1>\n" +
                "Your resume should appear online within\n" +
                "24 hours. If it doesn't, try submitting\n" +
                "again with a different email address.\n" +
                "</BODY></HTML>");
  }

  /** Why it is bad to give your email address to
   *  untrusted sites.
   */

  private void storeResume(HttpServletRequest request) {
    String email = request.getParameter("email");
    putInSpamList(email);
  }

  private void putInSpamList(String emailAddress) {
    // Code removed to protect the guilty.
  }
}
```

Once the servlet has meaningful values for each of the font and color parameters, it builds a cascading style sheet out of them. Style sheets are a standard way of specifying the font faces, font sizes, colors, indentation, and other formatting information in an HTML 4.0 Web page. Style sheets are usually placed in a separate file so that several

Web pages at a site can share the same style sheet, but in this case it is more convenient to embed the style information directly in the page by use of the `STYLE` element. For more information on style sheets, see http://www.w3.org/TR/REC-CSS1.

After creating the style sheet, the servlet places the job applicant's name, job title, and email address centered under each other at the top of the page. The heading font is used for these lines, and the email address is placed inside a `mailto:` hypertext link so that prospective employers can contact the applicant directly by clicking on the address. The programming languages specified in the `languages` parameter are parsed by `StringTokenizer` (assuming spaces or commas are used to separate the language names) and placed in a bulleted list beneath a "Programming Languages" heading. Finally, the text from the `skills` parameter is placed at the bottom of the page beneath a "Skills and Experience" heading.

Figures 4–6 and 4–7 show results when the required data is supplied and omitted, respectively. Figure 4–8 shows the result of clicking Submit instead of Preview.

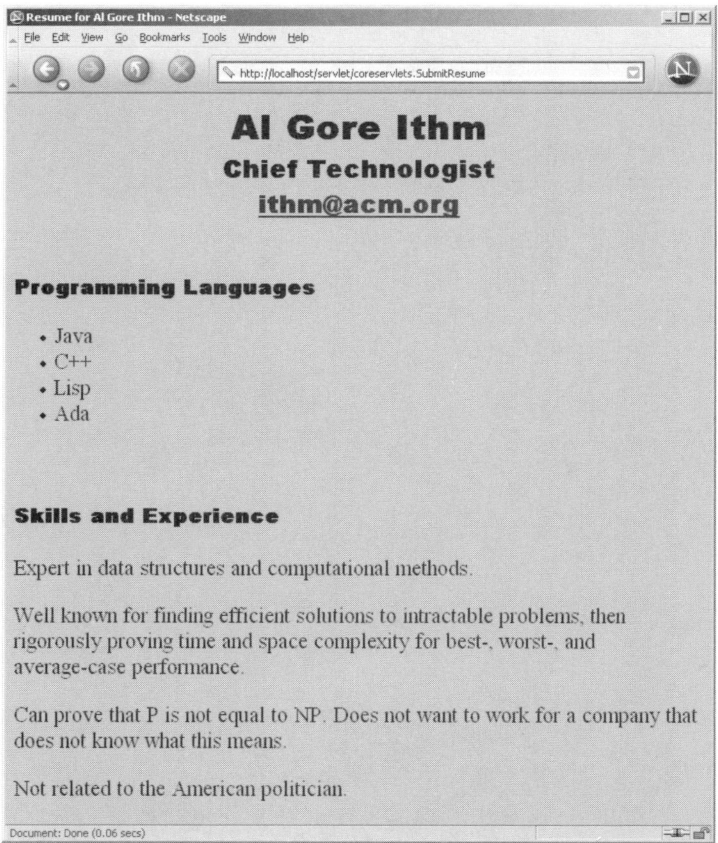

Figure 4–6 Preview of a résumé submission that contained the required form data.

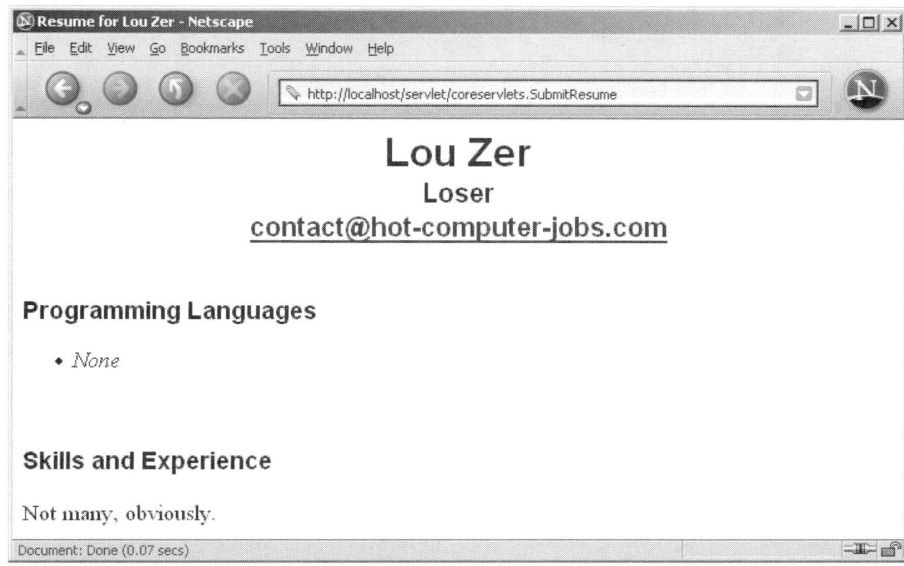

Figure 4–7 Preview of a submission that was missing much of the required data: default values replace the omitted values.

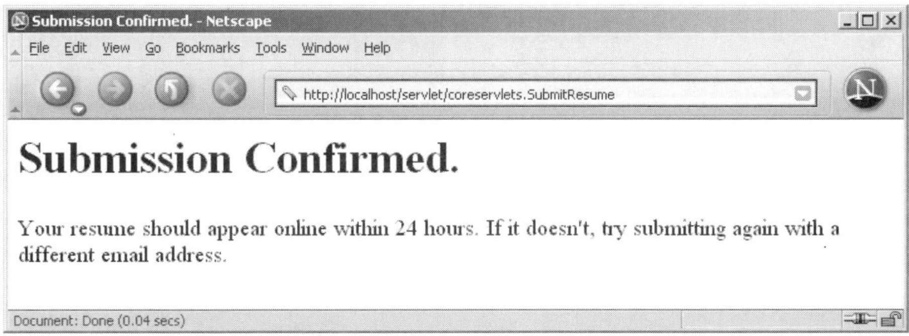

Figure 4–8 Result of submitting the résumé to the database.

4.6 Filtering Strings for HTML-Specific Characters

Normally, when a servlet wants to generate HTML that will contain characters like < or >, it simply uses < or >, the standard HTML character entities. Similarly, if a servlet wants a double quote or an ampersand to appear inside an HTML attribute value, it uses " or &. Failing to make these substitutions results in malformed HTML code, since < or > will often be interpreted as part of an HTML markup tag, a double quote in an attribute value may be interpreted as the end of the value, and ampersands are just plain illegal in attribute values. In most cases, it is easy to note the special characters and use the standard HTML replacements. However, there are two cases in which it is not so easy to make this substitution manually.

The first case in which manual conversion is difficult occurs when the string is derived from a program excerpt or another source in which it is already in some standard format. Going through manually and changing all the special characters can be tedious in such a case, but forgetting to convert even one special character can result in your Web page having missing or improperly formatted sections.

The second case in which manual conversion fails is when the string is derived from HTML form data. Here, the conversion absolutely must be performed at runtime, since of course the query data is not known at compile time. If the user accidentally or deliberately enters HTML tags, the generated Web page will contain spurious HTML tags and can have completely unpredictable results (the HTML specification tells browsers what to do with legal HTML; it says nothing about what they should do with HTML containing illegal syntax).

Core Approach

If you read request parameters and display their values in the resultant page, you should filter out the special HTML characters. Failing to do so can result in output that has missing or oddly formatted sections.

Failing to do this filtering for externally accessible Web pages also lets your page become a vehicle for the *cross-site scripting attack*. Here, a malicious programmer embeds GET parameters in a URL that refers to one of your servlets (or any other server-side program). These GET parameters expand to HTML tags (usually <SCRIPT> elements) that exploit known browser bugs. So, an attacker could embed the code in a URL that refers to your site and distribute only the URL, not the malicious Web page itself. That way, the attacker can remain undiscovered more easily and can also exploit trusted relationships to make users think the scripts are coming from a trusted source (your organization). For more details on this issue, see http://www.cert.org/advisories/CA-2000-02.html and http://www.microsoft.com/technet/security/topics/ExSumCS.asp.

Code for Filtering

Replacing <, >, `"`, and `&` in strings is a simple matter, and a number of different approaches can accomplish the task. However, it is important to remember that Java strings are immutable (i.e., can't be modified), so repeated string concatenation involves copying and then discarding many string segments. For example, consider the following two lines:

```
String s1 = "Hello";
String s2 = s1 + " World";
```

Since `s1` cannot be modified, the second line makes a copy of `s1` and appends `"World"` to the copy, then the copy is discarded. To avoid the expense of generating and copying these temporary objects, whenever you perform repeated concatenation within a loop, you should use a mutable data structure; and `StringBuffer` is the natural choice.

Core Approach

If you do string concatenation from within a loop, use `StringBuffer`, not `String`.

Listing 4.7 shows a static `filter` method that uses a `StringBuffer` to efficiently copy characters from an input string to a filtered version, replacing the four special characters along the way.

Listing 4.7 ServletUtilities.java (Excerpt)

```
package coreservlets;
import javax.servlet.*;
import javax.servlet.http.*;

public class ServletUtilities {
  ...

  /** Replaces characters that have special HTML meanings
   *  with their corresponding HTML character entities.
   */
```

Listing 4.7 ServletUtilities.java (Excerpt) *(continued)*

```
  // Note that Javadoc is not used for the more detailed
  // documentation due to the difficulty of making the
  // special chars readable in both plain text and HTML.
  //
  //  Given a string, this method replaces all occurrences of
  //  '<' with '&lt;', all occurrences of '>' with
  //  '&gt;', and (to handle cases that occur inside attribute
  //  values), all occurrences of double quotes with
  //  '&quot;' and all occurrences of '&' with '&amp;'.
  //  Without such filtering, an arbitrary string
  //  could not safely be inserted in a Web page.

  public static String filter(String input) {
    if (!hasSpecialChars(input)) {
      return(input);
    }
    StringBuffer filtered = new StringBuffer(input.length());
    char c;
    for(int i=0; i<input.length(); i++) {
      c = input.charAt(i);
      switch(c) {
        case '<': filtered.append("&lt;"); break;
        case '>': filtered.append("&gt;"); break;
        case '"': filtered.append("&quot;"); break;
        case '&': filtered.append("&amp;"); break;
        default: filtered.append(c);
      }
    }
    return(filtered.toString());
  }

  private static boolean hasSpecialChars(String input) {
    boolean flag = false;
    if ((input != null) && (input.length() > 0)) {
      char c;
      for(int i=0; i<input.length(); i++) {
        c = input.charAt(i);
        switch(c) {
          case '<': flag = true; break;
          case '>': flag = true; break;
          case '"': flag = true; break;
          case '&': flag = true; break;
        }
      }
    }
    return(flag);
  }
}
```

Example: A Servlet That Displays Code Snippets

As an example, consider the HTML form of Listing 4.8 that gathers a snippet of the Java programming language and sends it to the servlet of Listing 4.9 for display.

Now, when the user enters normal input, the result is fine, as illustrated by Figure 4–9. However, as shown in Figure 4–10, the result can be unpredictable when the input contains special characters like < and >. Different browsers can give different results since the HTML specification doesn't say what to do in this case, but most browsers think that the "`<b>`" in "`if (a<b) {`" starts an HTML tag. But, since the characters after the `b` are unrecognized, browsers ignore them until the next >, which is at the end of the `</PRE>` tag. Thus, not only does most of the code snippet disappear, but the browser does not interpret the `</PRE>` tag, so the text after the code snippet is improperly formatted, with a fixed-width font and line wrapping disabled.

Listing 4.10 shows a servlet that works exactly like the previous one except that it filters the special characters from the request parameter value before displaying it. Listing 4.11 shows an HTML form that sends data to it (except for the `ACTION` URL, this form is identical to that shown in Listing 4.8). Figure 4–11 shows the result of the input that failed for the previous servlet: no problem here.

Listing 4.8 CodeForm1.html

```
<!DOCTYPE HTML PUBLIC "-//W3C//DTD HTML 4.0 Transitional//EN">
<HTML><HEAD><TITLE>Submit Code Sample</TITLE></HEAD>
<BODY BGCOLOR="#FDF5E6">
<CENTER>
<H1 ALIGN="CENTER">Submit Code Sample</H1>
<FORM ACTION="/servlet/coreservlets.BadCodeServlet">
  Code:<BR>
  <TEXTAREA ROWS="6" COLS="40" NAME="code"></TEXTAREA><P>
  <INPUT TYPE="SUBMIT" VALUE="Submit Code">
</FORM>
</CENTER></BODY></HTML>
```

Listing 4.9 BadCodeServlet.java

```
package coreservlets;

import java.io.*;
import javax.servlet.*;
import javax.servlet.http.*;

/** Servlet that reads a code snippet from the request
 *  and displays it inside a PRE tag. Fails to filter
 *  the special HTML characters.
 */

public class BadCodeServlet extends HttpServlet {
  public void doGet(HttpServletRequest request,
                    HttpServletResponse response)
      throws ServletException, IOException {
    response.setContentType("text/html");
    PrintWriter out = response.getWriter();
    String title = "Code Sample";
    String docType =
      "<!DOCTYPE HTML PUBLIC \"-//W3C//DTD HTML 4.0 " +
      "Transitional//EN\">\n";
    out.println(docType +
                "<HTML>\n" +
                "<HEAD><TITLE>" + title + "</TITLE></HEAD>\n" +
                "<BODY BGCOLOR=\"#FDF5E6\">\n" +
                "<H1 ALIGN=\"CENTER\">" + title + "</H1>\n" +
                "<PRE>\n" +
                getCode(request) +
                "</PRE>\n" +
                "Now, wasn't that an interesting sample\n" +
                "of code?\n" +
                "</BODY></HTML>");
  }

  protected String getCode(HttpServletRequest request) {
    return(request.getParameter("code"));
  }
}
```

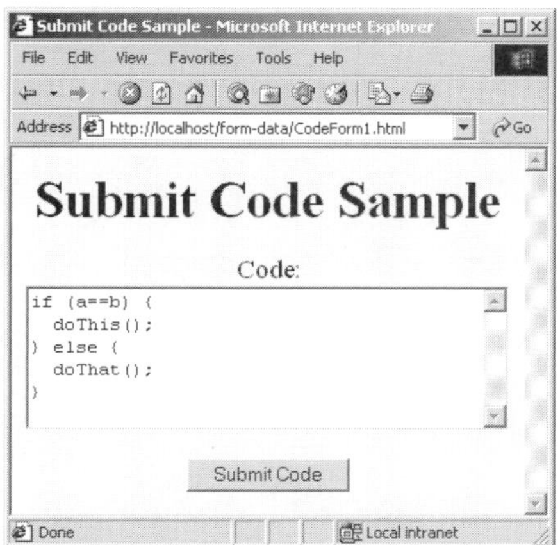

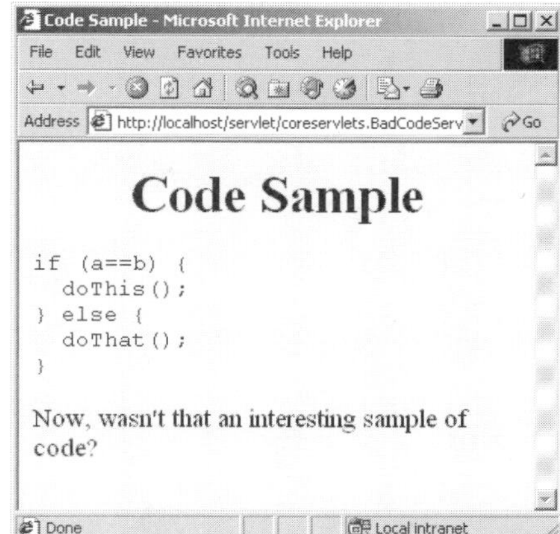

Figure 4–9 `BadCodeServlet`: result is fine when request parameters contain no special characters.

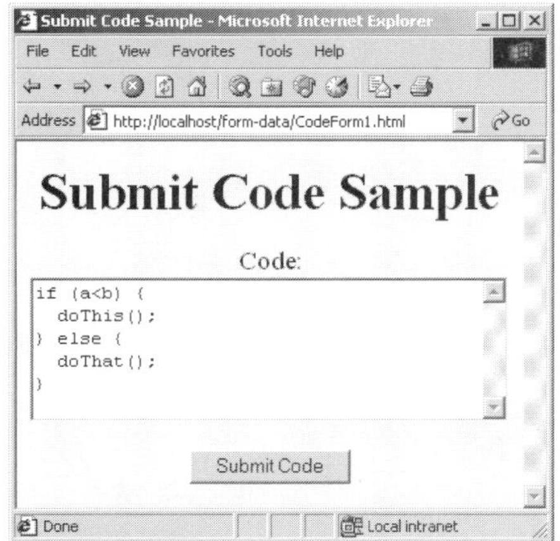

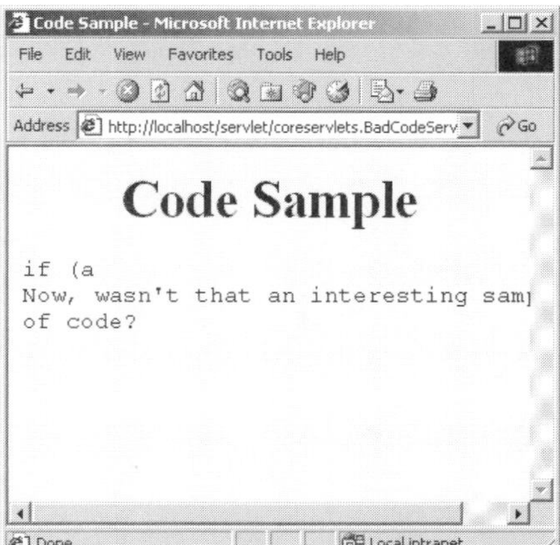

Figure 4–10 `BadCodeServlet`: result has missing and incorrectly formatted sections when request parameters contain special characters.

Listing 4.10 GoodCodeServlet.java

```
package coreservlets;

import javax.servlet.http.*;

/** Servlet that reads a code snippet from the request and displays
 *  it inside a PRE tag. Filters the special HTML characters.
 */

public class GoodCodeServlet extends BadCodeServlet {
  protected String getCode(HttpServletRequest request) {
    return(ServletUtilities.filter(super.getCode(request)));
  }
}
```

Listing 4.11 CodeForm2.html

```
<!DOCTYPE HTML PUBLIC "-//W3C//DTD HTML 4.0 Transitional//EN">
<HTML><HEAD><TITLE>Submit Code Sample</TITLE></HEAD>
<BODY BGCOLOR="#FDF5E6">
<CENTER>
<H1 ALIGN="CENTER">Submit Code Sample</H1>
<FORM ACTION="/servlet/coreservlets.GoodCodeServlet">
  Code:<BR>
  <TEXTAREA ROWS="6" COLS="40" NAME="code"></TEXTAREA><P>
  <INPUT TYPE="SUBMIT" VALUE="Submit Code">
</FORM>
</CENTER></BODY></HTML>
```

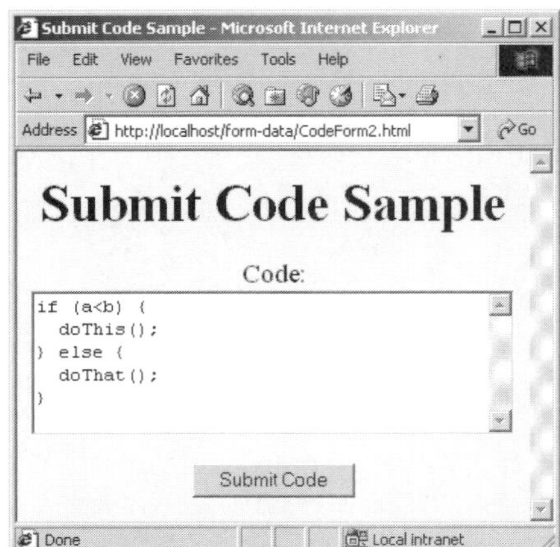

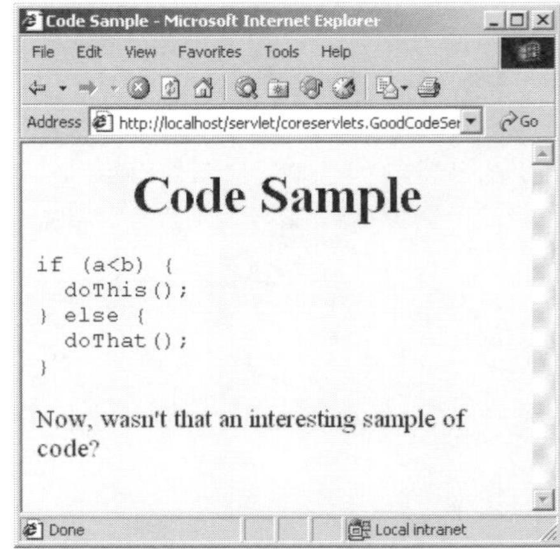

Figure 4–11 `GoodCodeServlet`: result is fine even when request parameters contain special characters.

4.7 Automatically Populating Java Objects from Request Parameters: Form Beans

The `getParameter` method makes it easy to read incoming request parameters: you use the same method from `doGet` as from `doPost`, and the value returned is automatically URL-decoded (i.e., in the format that the end user typed it in, not necessarily in the format in which it was sent over the network). Since the return value of `getParameter` is `String`, however, you have to parse the value yourself (checking for missing or malformed data, of course) if you want other types of values. For example, if you expect `int` or `double` values, you have to pass the result of `getParameter` to `Integer.parseInt` or `Double.parseDouble` and enclose the code inside a `try/catch` block that looks for `NumberFormatException`. If you have many request parameters, this procedure can be quite tedious.

For example, suppose that you have a data object with three `String` fields, two `int` fields, two `double` fields, and a `boolean`. Filling in the object based on a form submission would require eight separate calls to `getParameter`, two calls each to `Integer.parseInt` and `Double.parseDouble`, and some special-purpose code to set the `boolean` flag. It would be nice to do this work automatically.

Now, in JSP, you can use the JavaBeans component architecture to greatly simplify the process of reading request parameters, parsing the values, and storing the results in Java objects. This process is discussed in detail in Chapter 14 (Using JavaBeans Components in JSP Documents). If you are unfamiliar with the idea of beans, refer to that chapter for details. The gist, though, is that an ordinary Java object is considered to be a *bean* if the class uses private fields and has methods that follow the get/set naming convention. The names of the methods (minus the word "get" or "set" and with the first character in lower case) are called *properties*. For example, an arbitrary Java class with a `getName` and `setName` method is said to define a bean that has a property called `name`.

As discussed in Chapter 14, there is special JSP syntax (`property="*"` in a `jsp:setProperty` call) that you can use to populate a bean in one fell swoop. Specifically, this setting indicates that the system should examine all incoming request parameters and pass them to bean properties that match the request parameter name. In particular, if the request parameter is named `param1`, the parameter is passed to the `setParam1` method of the object. Furthermore, simple type conversions are performed automatically. For instance, if there is a request parameter called `numOrdered` and the object has a method called `setNumOrdered` that expects an `int` (i.e., the bean has a `numOrdered` property of type `int`), the `numOrdered` request parameter is automatically converted to an `int` and the resulting value is automatically passed to the `setNumOrdered` method.

Now, if you can do this in JSP, you would think you could do it in servlets as well. After all, as discussed in Chapter 10, JSP pages are really servlets in disguise: each JSP page gets translated into a servlet, and it is the servlet that runs at request time. Furthermore, as we see in Chapter 15 (Integrating Servlets and JSP: The Model View Controller (MVC) Architecture), in complicated scenarios it is often best to combine servlets and JSP pages in such a way that the servlets do the programming work and the JSP pages do the presentation work. So, it is really more important for servlets to be able to read request parameters easily than it is for JSP pages to do so. Surprisingly, however, the servlet specification provides no such capability: the code behind the `property="*"` JSP process is not exposed through a standard API.

Fortunately, the widely used Jakarta Commons package (see **http://jakarta.apache.org/commons/**) from The Apache Software Foundation contains classes that make it easy to build a utility to automatically associate request parameters with bean properties (i.e., with `set`*`Xxx`* methods). The next subsection provides information on obtaining the Commons packages, but the important point here is that a static `populateBean` method takes a bean (i.e., a Java object with at least some methods that follow the get/set naming convention) and a `Map` as input and passes all `Map` values to the bean property that matches the associated `Map` key name. This utility also does type conversion automatically, using default values (e.g., 0 for numeric values) instead of throwing exceptions when the corresponding request parameter is malformed. If the bean has no property matching the name, the `Map` entry is ignored; again, no exception is thrown.

Listing 4.12 presents a utility that uses the Jakarta Commons utility to automatically populate a bean according to incoming request parameters. To use it, simply pass the bean and the request object to `BeanUtilities.populateBean`. That's it! You want to put two request parameters into a data object? No problem: one method call is all that's needed. Fifteen request parameters plus type conversion? Same one method call.

Listing 4.12 BeanUtilities.java

```
package coreservlets.beans;

import java.util.*;
import javax.servlet.http.*;
import org.apache.commons.beanutils.BeanUtils;

/** Some utilities to populate beans, usually based on
 *  incoming request parameters. Requires three packages
 *  from the Apache Commons library: beanutils, collections,
 *  and logging. To obtain these packages, see
 *  http://jakarta.apache.org/commons/. Also, the book's
 *  source code archive (see http://www.coreservlets.com/)
```

Listing 4.12 BeanUtilities.java *(continued)*

```
 *  contains links to all URLs mentioned in the book, including
 *  to the specific sections of the Jakarta Commons package.
 *  <P>
 *  Note that this class is in the coreservlets.beans package,
 *  so must be installed in .../coreservlets/beans/.
 */

public class BeanUtilities {
  /** Examines all of the request parameters to see if
   *  any match a bean property (i.e., a setXxx method)
   *  in the object. If so, the request parameter value
   *  is passed to that method. If the method expects
   *  an int, Integer, double, Double, or any of the other
   *  primitive or wrapper types, parsing and conversion
   *  is done automatically. If the request parameter value
   *  is malformed (cannot be converted into the expected
   *  type), numeric properties are assigned zero and boolean
   *  properties are assigned false: no exception is thrown.
   */

  public static void populateBean(Object formBean,
                                  HttpServletRequest request) {
    populateBean(formBean, request.getParameterMap());
  }

  /** Populates a bean based on a Map: Map keys are the
   *  bean property names; Map values are the bean property
   *  values. Type conversion is performed automatically as
   *  described above.
   */

  public static void populateBean(Object bean,
                                  Map propertyMap) {
    try {
      BeanUtils.populate(bean, propertyMap);
    } catch(Exception e) {
      // Empty catch. The two possible exceptions are
      // java.lang.IllegalAccessException and
      // java.lang.reflect.InvocationTargetException.
      // In both cases, just skip the bean operation.
    }
  }
}
```

Putting BeanUtilities to Work

Listing 4.13 shows a servlet that gathers insurance information about an employee, presumably to use it to determine available insurance plans and associated costs. To perform this task, the servlet needs to fill in an insurance information data object (InsuranceInfo.java, Listing 4.14) with information on the employee's name and ID (both of type `String`), number of children (`int`), and whether or not the employee is married (`boolean`). Since this object is represented as a bean, `BeanUtilities.populateBean` can be used to fill in the required information with a single method call. Listing 4.15 shows the HTML form that gathers the data; Figures 4–12 and 4–13 show typical results.

Listing 4.13 SubmitInsuranceInfo.java

```
package coreservlets;

import java.io.*;
import javax.servlet.*;
import javax.servlet.http.*;
import coreservlets.beans.*;

/** Example of simplified form processing. Illustrates the
 *  use of BeanUtilities.populateBean to automatically fill
 *  in a bean (Java object with methods that follow the
 *  get/set naming convention) from request parameters.
 */

public class SubmitInsuranceInfo extends HttpServlet {
  public void doGet(HttpServletRequest request,
                    HttpServletResponse response)
      throws ServletException, IOException {
    InsuranceInfo info = new InsuranceInfo();
    BeanUtilities.populateBean(info, request);
    response.setContentType("text/html");
    PrintWriter out = response.getWriter();
    String docType =
      "<!DOCTYPE HTML PUBLIC \"-//W3C//DTD HTML 4.0 " +
      "Transitional//EN\">\n";
    String title = "Insurance Info for " + info.getName();
    out.println(docType +
                "<HTML>\n" +
                "<HEAD><TITLE>" + title + "</TITLE></HEAD>\n" +
                "<BODY BGCOLOR=\"#FDF5E6\">\n" +
                "<CENTER>\n" +
                "<H1>" + title + "</H1>\n" +
```

Listing 4.13 SubmitInsuranceInfo.java *(continued)*

```
                "<UL>\n" +
                "   <LI>Employee ID: " +
                   info.getEmployeeID() + "\n" +
                "   <LI>Number of children: " +
                   info.getNumChildren() + "\n" +
                "   <LI>Married?: " +
                   info.isMarried() + "\n" +
                "</UL></CENTER></BODY></HTML>");
  }
}
```

Listing 4.14 InsuranceInfo.java

```
package coreservlets.beans;

import coreservlets.*;

/** Simple bean that represents information needed to
 *  calculate an employee's insurance costs. Has String,
 *  int, and boolean properties. Used to demonstrate
 *  automatically filling in bean properties from request
 *  parameters.
 */

public class InsuranceInfo {
  private String name = "No name specified";
  private String employeeID = "No ID specified";
  private int numChildren = 0;
  private boolean isMarried = false;

  public String getName() {
    return(name);
  }

  /** Just in case user enters special HTML characters,
   *  filter them out before storing the name.
   */

  public void setName(String name) {
    this.name = ServletUtilities.filter(name);
  }

  public String getEmployeeID() {
    return(employeeID);
  }
```

Listing 4.14 InsuranceInfo.java *(continued)*

```
  /** Just in case user enters special HTML characters,
   *  filter them out before storing the name.
   */

  public void setEmployeeID(String employeeID) {
    this.employeeID = ServletUtilities.filter(employeeID);
  }

  public int getNumChildren() {
    return(numChildren);
  }

  public void setNumChildren(int numChildren) {
    this.numChildren = numChildren;
  }

  /** Bean convention: name getter method "isXxx" instead
   *  of "getXxx" for boolean methods.
   */

  public boolean isMarried() {
    return(isMarried);
  }

  public void setMarried(boolean isMarried) {
    this.isMarried = isMarried;
  }
}
```

Listing 4.15 InsuranceForm.html

```
<!DOCTYPE HTML PUBLIC "-//W3C//DTD HTML 4.0 Transitional//EN">
<HTML><HEAD><TITLE>Employee Insurance Signup</TITLE></HEAD>
<BODY BGCOLOR="#FDF5E6">
<CENTER>
<H1>Employee Insurance Signup</H1>

<FORM ACTION="/servlet/coreservlets.SubmitInsuranceInfo">
  Name:  <INPUT TYPE="TEXT" NAME="name"><BR>
  Employee ID: <INPUT TYPE="TEXT" NAME="employeeID"><BR>
  Number of Children:  <INPUT TYPE="TEXT" NAME="numChildren"><BR>
  <INPUT TYPE="CHECKBOX" NAME="married" VALUE="true">Married?<BR>
  <CENTER><INPUT TYPE="SUBMIT"></CENTER>
</FORM>

</CENTER></BODY></HTML>
```

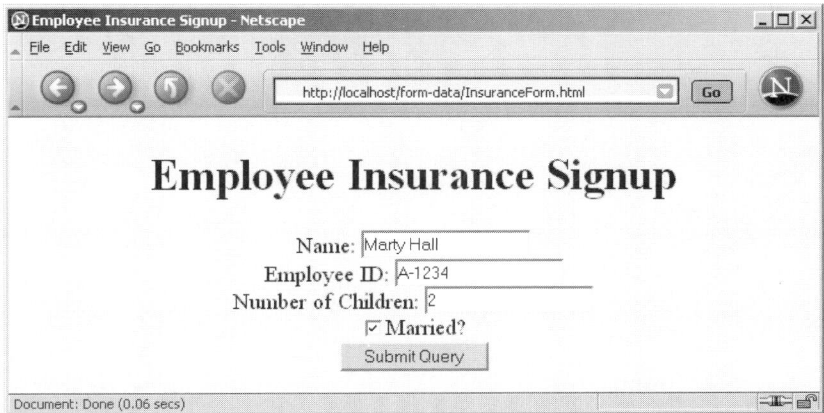

Figure 4–12 Front end to insurance-processing servlet.

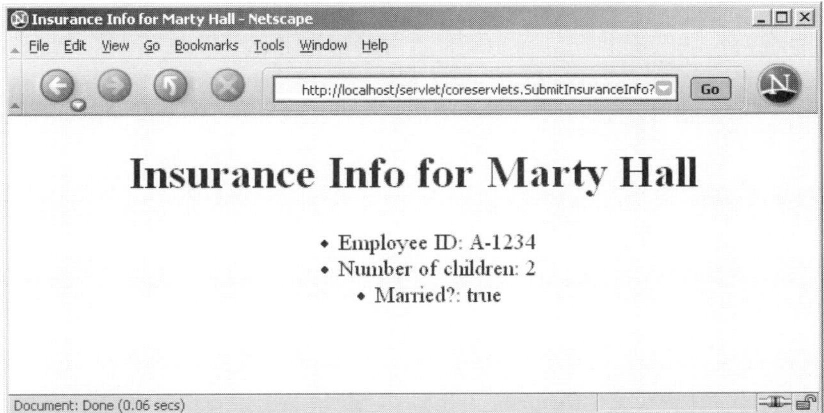

Figure 4–13 Insurance-processing servlet: the gathering of request data is greatly simplified by use of `BeanUtilities.populateBean`.

Obtaining and Installing the Jakarta Commons Packages

Most of the work of our `BeanUtilities` class is done by the Jakarta Commons `BeanUtils` component. This component performs the reflection (determination of what writable bean properties—`set`*`Xxx`* methods—the object has) and the type conversion (parsing a String as an `int`, `double`, `boolean`, or other primitive or wrapper type). So, `BeanUtilities` will not work unless you install the Jakarta

Commons `BeanUtils`. However, since `BeanUtils` depends on two other Jakarta Commons components—`Collections` and `Logging`—you have to download and install all three.

To download these components, start at http://jakarta.apache.org/commons/, look for the "Components Repository" heading in the left column, and, for each of the three components, download the JAR file for the latest version. (Our code is based on version 1.5 of the `BeanUtils`, but it is likely that any recent version will work identically.) Perhaps the easiest way to download the components is to go to http://www.coreservlets.com/, go to Chapter 4 of the source code archive, and look for the direct links to the three JAR files.

The most portable way to install the components is to follow the standard approach:

- For development, list the three JAR files in your `CLASSPATH`.
- For deployment, put the three JAR files in the WEB-INF/lib directory of your Web application.

When dealing with JAR files like these—used in multiple Web applications—many developers use server-specific features that support sharing of JAR files across Web applications. For example, Tomcat permits common JAR files to be placed in *tomcat_install_dir*/common/lib. Another shortcut that many people use on their development machines is to drop the three JAR files into *sdk_install_dir*/jre/lib/ext. Doing so makes the JAR files automatically accessible both to the development environment and to the locally installed server. These are both useful tricks as long as you remember that *your-web-app*/WEB-INF/lib is the only standardized location on the deployment server.

4.8 Redisplaying the Input Form When Parameters Are Missing or Malformed

It sometimes makes sense to use default values when the user fails to fill in certain form fields. Other times, however, there are no reasonable default values to use, and the form should be redisplayed to the user. Two desirable capabilities make the use of a normal HTML form impossible in this scenario:

- Users should not have to reenter values that they already supplied.
- Missing form fields should be marked prominently.

Redisplay Options

So, what can be done to implement these capabilities? Well, a full description of the possible approaches is a bit complicated and requires knowledge of several techniques (e.g., Struts, JSTL) that are not covered in Volume 1 of this book. So, you should refer to Volume 2 for details, but here is a quick preview.

- **Have the same servlet present the form, process the data, and present the results.** The servlet first looks for incoming request data: if it finds none, it presents a blank form. If the servlet finds partial request data, it extracts the partial data, puts it back into the form, and marks the other fields as missing. If the servlet finds the full complement of required data, it processes the request and displays the results. The form omits the `ACTION` attribute so that form submissions automatically go to the same URL as the form itself. This is the only approach for which we have already covered all of the necessary techniques, so this is the approach illustrated in this section.
- **Have one servlet present the form; have a second servlet process the data and present the results.** This option is better than the first since it divides up the labor and keeps each servlet smaller and more manageable. However, using this approach requires two techniques we have not yet covered: how to transfer control from one servlet to another and how to access user-specific data in one servlet that was created in another. Transferring from one servlet to another can be done with `response.sendRedirect` (see Chapter 6, "Generating the Server Response: HTTP Status Codes") or the `forward` method of `RequestDispatcher` (see Chapter 15, "Integrating Servlets and JSP: The Model View Controller (MVC) Architecture"). The easiest way to pass the data from the processing servlet back to the form-display servlet is to store it in the `HttpSession` object (see Chapter 9, "Session Tracking").
- **Have a JSP page "manually" present the form; have a servlet or JSP page process the data and present the results.** This is an excellent option, and it is widely used. However, it requires knowledge of JSP in addition to knowledge of the two techniques mentioned in the previous bullet (how to transfer the user from the data-processing servlet to the form page and how to use session tracking to store user-specific data). In particular, you need to know how to use JSP expressions (see Chapter 11, "Invoking Java Code with JSP Scripting Elements") or `jsp:getProperty` (see Chapter 14, "Using JavaBeans Components in JSP Documents") to extract the partial data from the data object and put it into the HTML form.

- **Have a JSP page present the form, automatically filling in the fields with values obtained from a data object. Have a servlet or JSP page process the data and present the results.** This is perhaps the best option of all. But, in addition to the techniques described in the previous bullet, it requires custom JSP tags that mimic HTML form elements but use designated values automatically. You can write these tags yourself or you can use ready-made versions such as those that come with JSTL or Apache Struts (see Volume 2 for coverage of custom tags, JSTL, and Struts).

A Servlet That Processes Auction Bids

To illustrate the first of the form-redisplay options, consider a servlet that processes bids at an auction site. Figures 4–14 through 4–16 show the desired outcome: the servlet initially displays a blank form, redisplays the form with missing data marked when partial data is submitted, and processes the request when complete data is submitted.

To accomplish this behavior, the servlet (Listing 4.16) performs the following steps.

1. Fills in a `BidInfo` object (Listing 4.17) from the request data, using `BeanUtilities.populateBean` (see Section 4.7, "Automatically Populating Java Objects from Request Parameters: Form Beans") to automatically match up request parameter names with bean properties and to perform simple type conversion.
2. Checks whether that `BidInfo` object is completely empty (no fields changed from the default). If so, it calls `showEntryForm` to display the initial input form.
3. Checks whether the `BidInfo` object is partially empty (some, but not all, fields changed from the default). If so, it calls `showEntryForm` to display the input form with a warning message and with the missing fields highlighted. Fields in which the user already entered data keep their previous values.
4. Checks whether the `BidInfo` object is completely filled in. If so, it calls `showBid` to process the data and present the result.

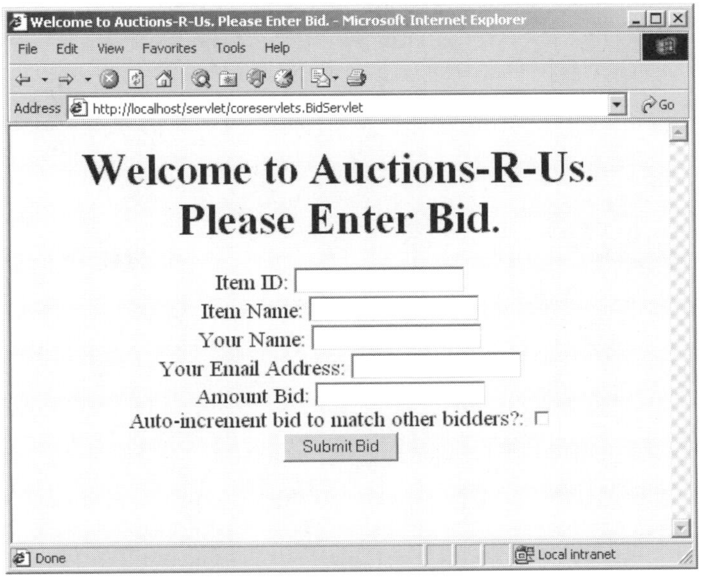

Figure 4–14 Original form of servlet: it presents a form to collect data about a bid at an auction.

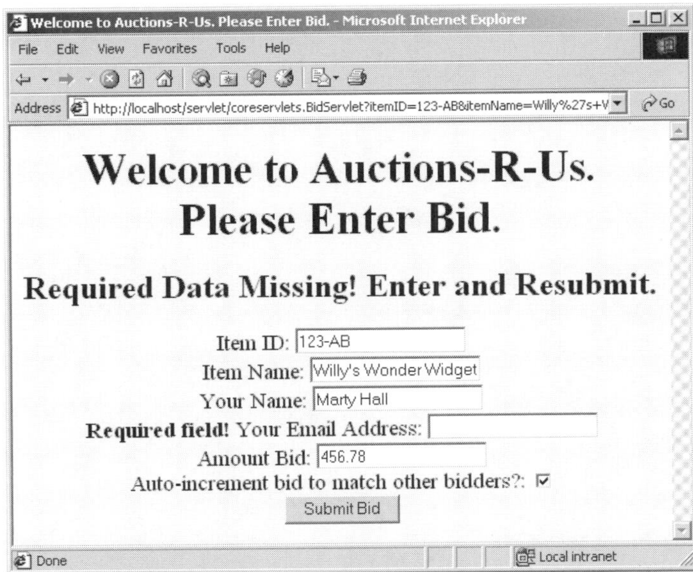

Figure 4–15 Bid servlet with incomplete data. If the user submits a form that is not fully filled in, the bid servlet redisplays the form. The user's previous partial data is maintained, and missing fields are highlighted.

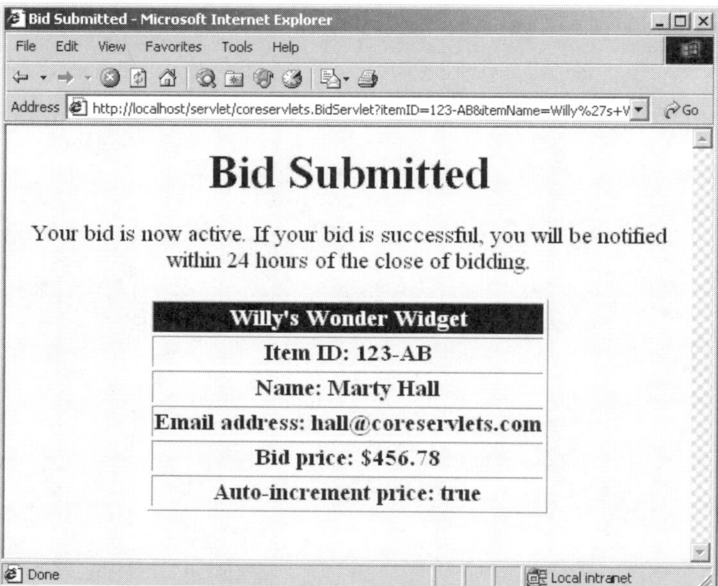

Figure 4–16 Bid servlet with complete data: it presents the results.

Listing 4.16 BidServlet.java

```
package coreservlets;

import java.io.*;
import javax.servlet.*;
import javax.servlet.http.*;
import coreservlets.beans.*;

/** Example of simplified form processing. Shows two features:
 *  <OL>
 *    <LI>Automatically filling in a bean based on the
 *        incoming request parameters.
 *    <LI>Using the same servlet both to generate the input
 *        form and to process the results. That way, when
 *        fields are omitted, the servlet can redisplay the
 *        form without making the user reenter previously
 *        entered values.
 *  </UL>
 */
```

Listing 4.16 BidServlet.java *(continued)*

```
public class BidServlet extends HttpServlet {

  /** Try to populate a bean that represents information
   *  in the form data sent by the user. If this data is
   *  complete, show the results. If the form data is
   *  missing or incomplete, display the HTML form
   *  that gathers the data.
   */

  public void doGet(HttpServletRequest request,
                    HttpServletResponse response)
      throws ServletException, IOException {
    BidInfo bid = new BidInfo();
    BeanUtilities.populateBean(bid, request);
    if (bid.isComplete()) {
      // All required form data was supplied: show result.
      showBid(request, response, bid);
    } else {
      // Form data was missing or incomplete: redisplay form.
      showEntryForm(request, response, bid);
    }
  }

  /** All required data is present: show the results page. */

  private void showBid(HttpServletRequest request,
                       HttpServletResponse response,
                       BidInfo bid)
      throws ServletException, IOException {
    submitBid(bid);
    response.setContentType("text/html");
    PrintWriter out = response.getWriter();
    String title = "Bid Submitted";
    out.println
      (DOCTYPE +
       "<HTML>\n" +
       "<HEAD><TITLE>" + title + "</TITLE></HEAD>\n" +
       "<BODY BGCOLOR=\"#FDF5E6\"><CENTER>\n" +
       "<H1>" + title + "</H1>\n" +
       "Your bid is now active. If your bid is successful,\n" +
       "you will be notified within 24 hours of the close\n" +
       "of bidding.\n" +
       "<P>\n" +
       "<TABLE BORDER=1>\n" +
       "  <TR><TH BGCOLOR=\"BLACK\"><FONT COLOR=\"WHITE\">" +
       bid.getItemName() + "</FONT>\n" +
       "  <TR><TH>Item ID: " +
```

Listing 4.16 BidServlet.java *(continued)*

```
        bid.getItemID() + "\n" +
        "  <TR><TH>Name: " +
        bid.getBidderName() + "\n" +
        "  <TR><TH>Email address: " +
        bid.getEmailAddress() + "\n" +
        "  <TR><TH>Bid price: $" +
        bid.getBidPrice() + "\n" +
        "  <TR><TH>Auto-increment price: " +
        bid.isAutoIncrement() + "\n" +
        "</TABLE></CENTER></BODY></HTML>");
  }

  /** If the required data is totally missing, show a blank
   *  form. If the required data is partially missing,
   *  warn the user, fill in form fields that already have
   *  values, and prompt user for missing fields.
   */

  private void showEntryForm(HttpServletRequest request,
                             HttpServletResponse response,
                             BidInfo bid)
      throws ServletException, IOException {
    boolean isPartlyComplete = bid.isPartlyComplete();
    response.setContentType("text/html");
    PrintWriter out = response.getWriter();
    String title =
      "Welcome to Auctions-R-Us. Please Enter Bid.";
    out.println
      (DOCTYPE +
       "<HTML>\n" +
       "<HEAD><TITLE>" + title + "</TITLE></HEAD>\n" +
       "<BODY BGCOLOR=\"#FDF5E6\"><CENTER>\n" +
       "<H1>" + title + "</H1>\n" +
       warning(isPartlyComplete) +
       "<FORM>\n" +
       inputElement("Item ID", "itemID",
                    bid.getItemID(), isPartlyComplete) +
       inputElement("Item Name", "itemName",
                    bid.getItemName(), isPartlyComplete) +
       inputElement("Your Name", "bidderName",
                    bid.getBidderName(), isPartlyComplete) +
       inputElement("Your Email Address", "emailAddress",
                    bid.getEmailAddress(), isPartlyComplete) +
       inputElement("Amount Bid", "bidPrice",
                    bid.getBidPrice(), isPartlyComplete) +
```

Listing 4.16 BidServlet.java *(continued)*

```
      checkbox("Auto-increment bid to match other bidders?",
               "autoIncrement", bid.isAutoIncrement()) +
      "<INPUT TYPE=\"SUBMIT\" VALUE=\"Submit Bid\">\n" +
      "</CENTER></BODY></HTML>");
  }

  private void submitBid(BidInfo bid) {
    // Some application-specific code to record the bid.
    // The point is that you pass in a real object with
    // properties populated, not a bunch of strings.
  }

  private String warning(boolean isFormPartlyComplete) {
    if(isFormPartlyComplete) {
      return("<H2>Required Data Missing! " +
             "Enter and Resubmit.</H2>\n");
    } else {
      return("");
    }
  }

  /** Create a textfield for input, prefaced by a prompt.
   *  If this particular textfield is missing a value but
   *  other fields have values (i.e., a partially filled form
   *  was submitted), then add a warning telling the user that
   *  this textfield is required.
   */

  private String inputElement(String prompt,
                              String name,
                              String value,
                              boolean shouldPrompt) {
    String message = "";
    if (shouldPrompt && ((value == null) || value.equals(""))) {
      message = "<B>Required field!</B> ";
    }
    return(message + prompt + ": " +
           "<INPUT TYPE=\"TEXT\" NAME=\"" + name + "\"" +
           " VALUE=\"" + value + "\"><BR>\n");
  }

  private String inputElement(String prompt,
                              String name,
                              double value,
                              boolean shouldPrompt) {
```

Listing 4.16 BidServlet.java *(continued)*

```
    String num;
    if (value == 0.0) {
      num = "";
    } else {
      num = String.valueOf(value);
    }
    return(inputElement(prompt, name, num, shouldPrompt));
  }

  private String checkbox(String prompt,
                          String name,
                          boolean isChecked) {
    String result =
      prompt + ": " +
      "<INPUT TYPE=\"CHECKBOX\" NAME=\"" + name + "\"";
    if (isChecked) {
      result = result + " CHECKED";
    }
    result = result + "><BR>\n";
    return(result);
  }

  private final String DOCTYPE =
    "<!DOCTYPE HTML PUBLIC \"-//W3C//DTD HTML 4.0 " +
    "Transitional//EN\">\n";
}
```

Listing 4.17 BidInfo.java

```
package coreservlets.beans;

import coreservlets.*;

/** Bean that represents information about a bid at
 *  an auction site. Used to demonstrate redisplay of forms
 *  that have incomplete data.
 */

public class BidInfo {
  private String itemID = "";
  private String itemName = "";
  private String bidderName = "";
  private String emailAddress = "";
  private double bidPrice = 0;
  private boolean autoIncrement = false;
```

Listing 4.17 BidInfo.java *(continued)*

```
public String getItemName() {
  return(itemName);
}

public void setItemName(String itemName) {
  this.itemName = ServletUtilities.filter(itemName);
}

public String getItemID() {
  return(itemID);
}

public void setItemID(String itemID) {
  this.itemID = ServletUtilities.filter(itemID);
}

public String getBidderName() {
  return(bidderName);
}

public void setBidderName(String bidderName) {
  this.bidderName =  ServletUtilities.filter(bidderName);
}

public String getEmailAddress() {
  return(emailAddress);
}

public void setEmailAddress(String emailAddress) {
  this.emailAddress = ServletUtilities.filter(emailAddress);
}

public double getBidPrice() {
  return(bidPrice);
}

public void setBidPrice(double bidPrice) {
  this.bidPrice = bidPrice;
}

public boolean isAutoIncrement() {
  return(autoIncrement);
}
```

Listing 4.17 BidInfo.java *(continued)*

```
  public void setAutoIncrement(boolean autoIncrement) {
    this.autoIncrement = autoIncrement;
  }

  /** Has all the required data been entered? Everything except
      autoIncrement must be specified explicitly (autoIncrement
      defaults to false).
  */

  public boolean isComplete() {
    return(hasValue(getItemID()) &&
           hasValue(getItemName()) &&
           hasValue(getBidderName()) &&
           hasValue(getEmailAddress()) &&
           (getBidPrice() > 0));
  }

  /** Has any of the data been entered? */

  public boolean isPartlyComplete() {
    boolean flag =
           (hasValue(getItemID()) ||
           hasValue(getItemName()) ||
           hasValue(getBidderName()) ||
           hasValue(getEmailAddress()) ||
           (getBidPrice() > 0) ||
           isAutoIncrement());
    return(flag);
  }

  private boolean hasValue(String val) {
    return((val != null) && (!val.equals("")));
  }
}
```

Handling the Client Request: HTTP Request Headers

Topics in This Chapter

- Reading HTTP request headers
- Building a table of all the request headers
- Understanding the various request headers
- Reducing download times by compressing pages
- Differentiating among types of browsers
- Customizing pages according to how users got there
- Accessing the standard CGI variables

Chapter 5

One of the keys to creating effective servlets is understanding how to manipulate the HyperText Transfer Protocol (HTTP). Thoroughly understanding this protocol is not an esoteric, theoretical concept, but rather a practical issue that can have an immediate impact on the performance and usability of your servlets. This section discusses the HTTP information that is sent from the browser to the server in the form of request headers. It explains the most important HTTP 1.1 request headers, summarizing how and why they would be used in a servlet. As we see later, request headers are read and applied the same way in JSP pages as they are in servlets.

Note that HTTP request headers are distinct from the form (query) data discussed in the previous chapter. Form data results directly from user input and is sent as part of the URL for `GET` requests and on a separate line for `POST` requests. Request headers, on the other hand, are indirectly set by the browser and are sent immediately following the initial `GET` or `POST` request line. For instance, the following example shows an HTTP request that might result from a user submitting a book-search request to a servlet at http://www.somebookstore.com/servlet/Search. The request includes the headers `Accept`, `Accept-Encoding`, `Connection`, `Cookie`, `Host`, `Referer`, and `User-Agent`, all of which might be important to the operation of the servlet, but none of which can be derived from the form data or deduced automatically: the servlet needs to explicitly read the request headers to make use of this information.

```
GET /servlet/Search?keywords=servlets+jsp HTTP/1.1
Accept: image/gif, image/jpg, */*
Accept-Encoding: gzip
Connection: Keep-Alive
Cookie: userID=id456578
```

```
Host: www.somebookstore.com
Referer: http://www.somebookstore.com/findbooks.html
User-Agent: Mozilla/4.0 (compatible; MSIE 6.0; Windows NT 5.0)
```

5.1 Reading Request Headers

Reading headers is straightforward; just call the `getHeader` method of `HttpServletRequest` with the name of the header. This call returns a `String` if the specified header was supplied in the current request, `null` otherwise. In HTTP 1.0, all request headers are optional; in HTTP 1.1, only `Host` is required. So, always check for `null` before using a request header.

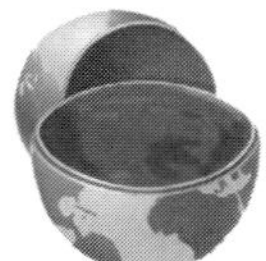

Core Approach

Always check that the result of `request.getHeader` is non-`null` before using it.

Header names are not case sensitive. So, for example, `request.getHeader("Connection")` is interchangeable with `request.getHeader("connection")`.

Although `getHeader` is the general-purpose way to read incoming headers, a few headers are so commonly used that they have special access methods in `HttpServletRequest`. Following is a summary.

- **`getCookies`**
  The `getCookies` method returns the contents of the `Cookie` header, parsed and stored in an array of `Cookie` objects. This method is discussed in more detail in Chapter 8 (Handling Cookies).
- **`getAuthType` and `getRemoteUser`**
  The `getAuthType` and `getRemoteUser` methods break the `Authorization` header into its component pieces.
- **`getContentLength`**
  The `getContentLength` method returns the value of the `Content-Length` header (as an `int`).
- **`getContentType`**
  The `getContentType` method returns the value of the `Content-Type` header (as a `String`).

- **getDateHeader and getIntHeader**
  The getDateHeader and getIntHeader methods read the specified headers and then convert them to Date and int values, respectively.

- **getHeaderNames**
  Rather than looking up one particular header, you can use the getHeaderNames method to get an Enumeration of all header names received on this particular request. This capability is illustrated in Section 5.2 (Making a Table of All Request Headers).

- **getHeaders**
  In most cases, each header name appears only once in the request. Occasionally, however, a header can appear multiple times, with each occurrence listing a separate value. Accept-Language is one such example. You can use getHeaders to obtain an Enumeration of the values of all occurrences of the header.

Finally, in addition to looking up the request headers, you can get information on the main request line itself (i.e., the first line in the example request just shown), also by means of methods in HttpServletRequest. Here is a summary of the four main methods.

- **getMethod**
  The getMethod method returns the main request method (normally, GET or POST, but methods like HEAD, PUT, and DELETE are possible).

- **getRequestURI**
  The getRequestURI method returns the part of the URL that comes after the host and port but before the form data. For example, for a URL of http://randomhost.com/servlet/search.BookSearch?subject=jsp, getRequestURI would return "/servlet/search.BookSearch".

- **getQueryString**
  The getQueryString method returns the form data. For example, with http://randomhost.com/servlet/search.BookSearch?subject=jsp, getQueryString would return "subject=jsp".

- **getProtocol**
  The getProtocol method returns the third part of the request line, which is generally HTTP/1.0 or HTTP/1.1. Servlets should usually check getProtocol before specifying *response* headers (Chapter 7) that are specific to HTTP 1.1.

5.2 Making a Table of All Request Headers

Listing 5.1 shows a servlet that simply creates a table of all the headers it receives, along with their associated values. It accomplishes this task by calling `request.getHeaderNames` to obtain an `Enumeration` of headers in the current request. It then loops down the `Enumeration`, puts the header name in the left table cell, and puts the result of `getHeader` in the right table cell. Recall that `Enumeration` is a standard interface in Java; it is in the `java.util` package and contains just two methods: `hasMoreElements` and `nextElement`.

The servlet also prints three components of the main request line (method, URI, and protocol). Figures 5–1 and 5–2 show typical results with Netscape and Internet Explorer.

Listing 5.1 ShowRequestHeaders.java

```
package coreservlets;

import java.io.*;
import javax.servlet.*;
import javax.servlet.http.*;
import java.util.*;

/** Shows all the request headers sent on the current request. */

public class ShowRequestHeaders extends HttpServlet {
  public void doGet(HttpServletRequest request,
                    HttpServletResponse response)
      throws ServletException, IOException {
    response.setContentType("text/html");
    PrintWriter out = response.getWriter();
    String title = "Servlet Example: Showing Request Headers";
    String docType =
      "<!DOCTYPE HTML PUBLIC \"-//W3C//DTD HTML 4.0 " +
      "Transitional//EN\">\n";
    out.println(docType +
                "<HTML>\n" +
                "<HEAD><TITLE>" + title + "</TITLE></HEAD>\n" +
                "<BODY BGCOLOR=\"#FDF5E6\">\n" +
                "<H1 ALIGN=\"CENTER\">" + title + "</H1>\n" +
                "<B>Request Method: </B>" +
                request.getMethod() + "<BR>\n" +
                "<B>Request URI: </B>" +
                request.getRequestURI() + "<BR>\n" +
                "<B>Request Protocol: </B>" +
```

Listing 5.1 ShowRequestHeaders.java *(continued)*

```
                request.getProtocol() + "<BR><BR>\n" +
                "<TABLE BORDER=1 ALIGN=\"CENTER\">\n" +
                "<TR BGCOLOR=\"#FFAD00\">\n" +
                "<TH>Header Name<TH>Header Value");
    Enumeration headerNames = request.getHeaderNames();
    while(headerNames.hasMoreElements()) {
      String headerName = (String)headerNames.nextElement();
      out.println("<TR><TD>" + headerName);
      out.println("    <TD>" + request.getHeader(headerName));
    }
    out.println("</TABLE>\n</BODY></HTML>");
  }

  /** Since this servlet is for debugging, have it
   *  handle GET and POST identically.
   */

  public void doPost(HttpServletRequest request,
                     HttpServletResponse response)
      throws ServletException, IOException {
    doGet(request, response);
  }
}
```

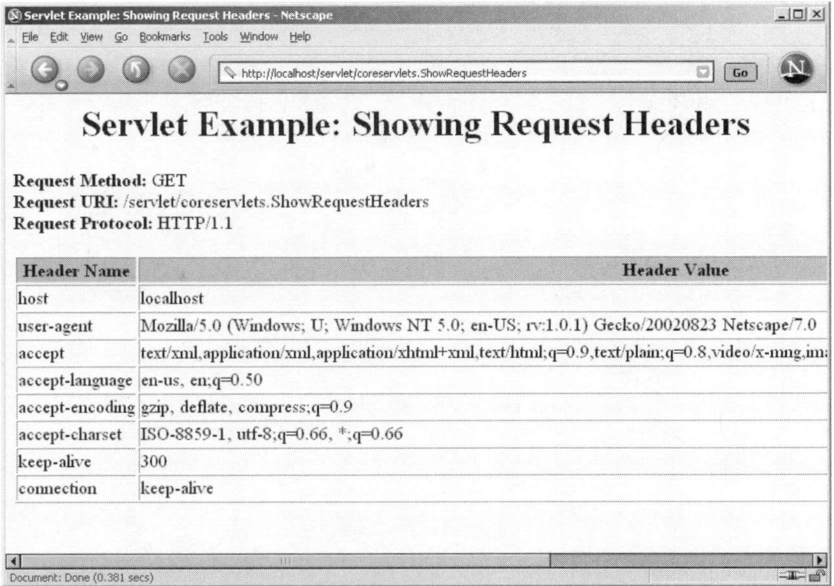

Figure 5–1 Request headers sent by Netscape 7 on Windows 2000.

Figure 5–2 Request headers sent by Internet Explorer 6 on Windows 2000.

5.3 Understanding HTTP 1.1 Request Headers

Access to the request headers permits servlets to perform a number of optimizations and to provide a number of features not otherwise possible. This section summarizes the headers most often used by servlets; for additional details on these and other headers, see the HTTP 1.1 specification, given in RFC 2616. The official RFCs are archived in a number of places; your best bet is to start at http://www.rfc-editor.org/ to get a current list of the archive sites. Note that HTTP 1.1 supports a superset of the headers permitted in HTTP 1.0.

Accept

This header specifies the MIME types that the browser or other clients can handle. A servlet that can return a resource in more than one format can examine the `Accept` header to decide which format to use. For example, images in PNG format have some compression advantages over those in GIF, but not all browsers support PNG. If you have images in both formats, your servlet can call `request.getHeader("Accept")`, check for `image/png`, and if it finds a match, use *blah*.png filenames in all the `IMG` elements it generates. Otherwise, it would just use *blah*.gif.

See Table 7.1 in Section 7.2 (Understanding HTTP 1.1 Response Headers) for the names and meanings of the common MIME types.

Note that Internet Explorer 5 and 6 have a bug whereby the `Accept` header is sent improperly when you reload a page. It is sent properly in the original request, however.

Accept-Charset

This header indicates the character sets (e.g., ISO-8859-1) the browser can use.

Accept-Encoding

This header designates the types of encodings that the client knows how to handle. If the server receives this header, it is free to encode the page by using one of the formats specified (usually to reduce transmission time), sending the `Content-Encoding` response header to indicate that it has done so. This encoding type is completely distinct from the MIME type of the actual document (as specified in the `Content-Type` response header), since this encoding is reversed *before* the browser decides what to do with the content. On the other hand, using an encoding the browser doesn't understand results in incomprehensible pages. Consequently, it is critical that you explicitly check the `Accept-Encoding` header before using any type of content encoding. Values of `gzip` or `compress` are the two most common possibilities.

Compressing pages before returning them is a valuable service because the cost of decoding is likely to be small compared with the savings in transmission time. See Section 5.4 in which gzip compression is used to reduce download times by a factor of more than 10.

Accept-Language

This header specifies the client's preferred languages in case the servlet can produce results in more than one language. The value of the header should be one of the standard language codes such as `en`, `en-us`, `da`, etc. See RFC 1766 for details (start at http://www.rfc-editor.org/ to get a current list of the RFC archive sites).

Authorization

This header is used by clients to identify themselves when accessing password-protected Web pages. For details, see the chapters on Web application security in Volume 2 of this book.

Connection

This header indicates whether the client can handle persistent HTTP connections. Persistent connections permit the client or other browser to retrieve multiple files (e.g., an HTML file and several associated images) with a single socket connection, thus saving the overhead of negotiating several independent connections. With an HTTP 1.1 request, persistent connections are the default, and the client must specify a value of `close` for this header to use old-style connections. In HTTP 1.0, a value of `Keep-Alive` means that persistent connections should be used.

Each HTTP request results in a new invocation of a servlet (i.e., a thread calling the servlet's `service` and `doXxx` methods), regardless of whether the request is a separate connection. That is, the server invokes the servlet only after the server has already read the HTTP request. This means that servlets need to cooperate with the server to handle persistent connections. Consequently, the servlet's job is just to make it *possible* for the server to use persistent connections; the servlet does so by setting the `Content-Length` response header. For details, see Chapter 7 (Generating the Server Response: HTTP Response Headers).

Content-Length

This header is applicable only to `POST` requests and gives the size of the `POST` data in bytes. Rather than calling `request.getIntHeader("Content-Length")`, you can simply use `request.getContentLength()`. However, since servlets take care of reading the form data for you (see Chapter 4), you rarely use this header explicitly.

Cookie

This header returns cookies to servers that previously sent them to the browser. Never read this header directly because doing so would require cumbersome low-level parsing; use `request.getCookies` instead. For details, see Chapter 8 (Handling Cookies). Technically, `Cookie` is not part of HTTP 1.1. It was originally a Netscape extension but is now widely supported, including in both Netscape and Internet Explorer.

Host

In HTTP 1.1, browsers and other clients are *required* to specify this header, which indicates the host and port as given in the original URL. Because of the widespread use of virtual hosting (one computer handling Web sites for multiple domain names), it is quite possible that the server could not otherwise determine this information. This header is not new in HTTP 1.1, but in HTTP 1.0 it was optional, not required.

If-Modified-Since

This header indicates that the client wants the page only if it has been changed after the specified date. The server sends a 304 (`Not Modified`) header if no newer result is available. This option is useful because it lets browsers cache documents and reload them over the network only when they've changed. However, servlets don't need to deal directly with this header. Instead, they should just implement the `getLastModified` method to have the system handle modification dates automatically. For an example, see the lottery numbers servlet in Section 3.6 (The Servlet Life Cycle).

If-Unmodified-Since

This header is the reverse of `If-Modified-Since`; it specifies that the operation should succeed only if the document is older than the specified date. Typically, `If-Modified-Since` is used for `GET` requests ("give me the document only if it is newer than my cached version"), whereas `If-Unmodified-Since` is used for `PUT` requests ("update this document only if nobody else has changed it since I generated it"). This header is new in HTTP 1.1.

Referer

This header indicates the URL of the referring Web page. For example, if you are at Web page 1 and click on a link to Web page 2, the URL of Web page 1 is included in the `Referer` header when the browser requests Web page 2. Most major browsers set this header, so it is a useful way of tracking where requests come from. This capability is helpful for tracking advertisers who refer people to your site, for slightly changing content depending on the referring site, for identifying when users first enter your application, or simply for keeping track of where your traffic comes from. In the last case, most people rely on Web server log files, since the `Referer` is typically recorded there. Although the `Referer` header is useful, don't rely too heavily on it since it can easily be spoofed by a custom client. Also, note that, owing to a spelling mistake by one of the original HTTP authors, this header is `Referer`, not the expected `Referrer`.

Finally, note that some browsers (Opera), ad filters (Web Washer), and personal firewalls (Norton) screen out this header. Besides, even in normal situations, the header is only set when the user follows a link. So, be sure to follow the approach you should be using with all headers anyhow: check for `null` before using the header.

See Section 5.6 (Changing the Page According to How the User Got There) for details and an example.

User-Agent

This header identifies the browser or other client making the request and can be used to return different content to different types of browsers. Be wary of this use when dealing only with Web browsers; relying on a hard-coded list of browser versions and associated features can make for unreliable and hard-to-modify servlet code. Whenever possible, use something specific in the HTTP headers instead. For example, instead of trying to remember which browsers support gzip on which platforms, simply check the `Accept-Encoding` header.

However, the `User-Agent` header is quite useful for distinguishing among different *categories* of client. For example, Japanese developers might see whether the `User-Agent` is an Imode cell phone (in which case they would redirect to a chtml page), a Skynet cell phone (in which case they would redirect to a wml page), or a Web browser (in which case they would generate regular HTML).

Most Internet Explorer versions list a "Mozilla" (Netscape) version first in their `User-Agent` line, with the real browser version listed parenthetically. The Opera browser does the same thing. This deliberate misidentification is done for compatibility with JavaScript; JavaScript developers often use the `User-Agent` header to determine which JavaScript features are supported. So, if you want to differentiate Netscape from Internet Explorer, you have to check for the string "MSIE" or something more specific, not just the string "Mozilla." Also note that this header can be easily spoofed, a fact that calls into question the reliability of sites that use this header to "show" market penetration of various browser versions.

See Section 5.5 (Differentiating Among Different Browser Types) for details and an example.

5.4 Sending Compressed Web Pages

Gzip is a text compression scheme that can dramatically reduce the size of HTML (or plain text) pages. Most recent browsers know how to handle gzipped content, so the server can compress the document and send the smaller document over the network, after which the browser will automatically reverse the compression (no user action required) and treat the result in the normal manner. Sending such compressed content can be a real time saver since the time required to compress the document on the server and then uncompress it on the client is typically dwarfed by the time saved in download time, especially when dialup connections are used.

DILBERT reprinted by permission of United Feature Syndicate, Inc.

However, although most recent browsers support this capability, not all do. If you send gzipped content to browsers that don't support this capability, the browsers will not be able to display the page at all. Fortunately, browsers that support this feature indicate that they do so by setting the `Accept-Encoding` request header. Browsers that support content encoding include most versions of Netscape for Unix, most versions of Internet Explorer for Windows, and Netscape 4.7 and later for Windows. Earlier Netscape versions on Windows and Internet Explorer on non-Windows platforms generally do not support content encoding.

Listing 5.2 shows a servlet that checks the `Accept-Encoding` header, sending a compressed Web page to clients that support gzip encoding (as determined by the `isGzipSupported` method of Listing 5.3) and sending a regular Web page to those that don't. The result (see Figure 5–3) yielded a compression of over *300*-fold and a speedup of more than a factor of *10* when a dialup connection was used. In repeated tests with Netscape and Internet Explorer on a 28.8K modem connection, the compressed page averaged less than 5 seconds to completely download, whereas the uncompressed page consistently took more than 50 seconds. Results were less dramatic with faster connections, but the improvement was still significant. Gzip compression is such a useful technique that we later present a filter that lets you apply gzip compression to designated servlets or JSP pages without changing the actual code of the individual resources. For details, see the chapter on servlet and JSP filters in Volume 2 of this book.

Core Tip

Gzip compression can dramatically reduce the download time of long text pages.

Implementing compression is straightforward since support for the gzip format is built in to the Java programming language by classes in `java.util.zip`. The servlet first checks the `Accept-Encoding` header to see if it contains an entry for gzip. If so, it uses a `PrintWriter` wrapped around a `GZIPOutputStream` and specifies `gzip` as the value of the `Content-Encoding` response header. If gzip is not supported, the servlet uses the normal `PrintWriter` and omits the `Content-Encoding` header. To make it easy to compare regular and compressed performance with the same browser, we also added a feature whereby we can suppress compression by including `?disableGzip` at the end of the URL.

Listing 5.2 LongServlet.java

```
package coreservlets;

import java.io.*;
import javax.servlet.*;
import javax.servlet.http.*;

/** Servlet with <B>long</B> output. Used to test
 *  the effect of the gzip compression.
 */

public class LongServlet extends HttpServlet {
  public void doGet(HttpServletRequest request,
                    HttpServletResponse response)
      throws ServletException, IOException {
    response.setContentType("text/html");

    // Change the definition of "out" depending on whether
    // or not gzip is supported.
    PrintWriter out;
    if (GzipUtilities.isGzipSupported(request) &&
        !GzipUtilities.isGzipDisabled(request)) {
      out = GzipUtilities.getGzipWriter(response);
      response.setHeader("Content-Encoding", "gzip");
    } else {
      out = response.getWriter();
    }

    // Once "out" has been assigned appropriately, the
    // rest of the page has no dependencies on the type
    // of writer being used.
```

Listing 5.2 LongServlet.java *(continued)*

```
    String docType =
      "<!DOCTYPE HTML PUBLIC \"-//W3C//DTD HTML 4.0 " +
      "Transitional//EN\">\n";
    String title = "Long Page";
    out.println
      (docType +
       "<HTML>\n" +
       "<HEAD><TITLE>" + title + "</TITLE></HEAD>\n" +
       "<BODY BGCOLOR=\"#FDF5E6\">\n" +
       "<H1 ALIGN=\"CENTER\">" + title + "</H1>\n");
    String line = "Blah, blah, blah, blah, blah. " +
                  "Yadda, yadda, yadda, yadda.";
    for(int i=0; i<10000; i++) {
      out.println(line);
    }
    out.println("</BODY></HTML>");
    out.close(); // Needed for gzip; optional otherwise.
  }
}
```

Listing 5.3 GzipUtilities.java

```
package coreservlets;

import java.io.*;
import javax.servlet.*;
import javax.servlet.http.*;
import java.util.zip.*;

/** Three small static utilities to assist with gzip encoding.
 *  <UL>
 *    <LI>isGzipSupported: does the browser support gzip?
 *    <LI>isGzipDisabled: has the user passed in a flag
 *        saying that gzip encoding should be disabled for
 *        this request? (Useful so that you can measure
 *        results with and without gzip on the same browser).
 *    <LI>getGzipWriter: return a gzipping PrintWriter.
 *  </UL>
 */

public class GzipUtilities {

  /** Does the client support gzip? */
```

Listing 5.3 GzipUtilities.java *(continued)*

```
  public static boolean isGzipSupported
      (HttpServletRequest request) {
    String encodings = request.getHeader("Accept-Encoding");
    return((encodings != null) &&
           (encodings.indexOf("gzip") != -1));
  }

  /** Has user disabled gzip (e.g., for benchmarking)? */

  public static boolean isGzipDisabled
      (HttpServletRequest request) {
    String flag = request.getParameter("disableGzip");
    return((flag != null) && (!flag.equalsIgnoreCase("false")));
  }

  /** Return gzipping PrintWriter for response. */

  public static PrintWriter getGzipWriter
      (HttpServletResponse response) throws IOException {
    return(new PrintWriter
            (new GZIPOutputStream
              (response.getOutputStream())));
  }
}
```

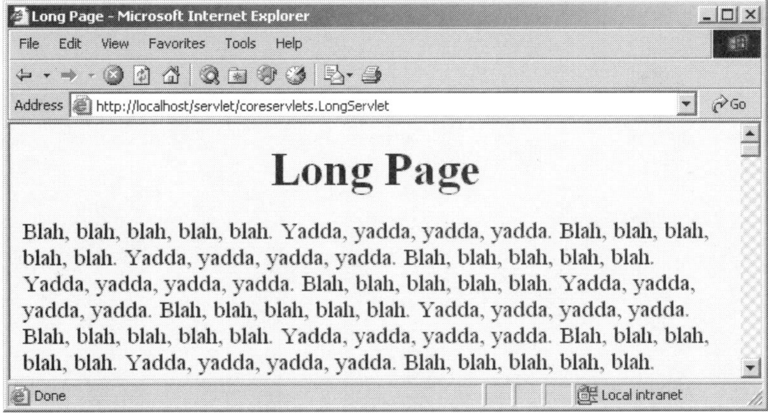

Figure 5–3 Since the Windows version of Internet Explorer 6 supports gzip, this page was sent gzipped over the network and automatically reconstituted by the browser, resulting in a large saving in download time.

5.5 Differentiating Among Different Browser Types

The `User-Agent` header identifies the specific browser that is making the request. Although use of this header appears straightforward at first glance, a few subtleties are involved:

- **Use `User-Agent` only when necessary.** Otherwise, you will have difficult-to-maintain code that consists of tables of browser versions and associated capabilities. For example, instead of remembering that the Windows version of Internet Explorer 5 supports gzip compression but the MacOS version doesn't, check the `Accept-Encoding` header. Instead of remembering which browsers support Java and which don't, use the `APPLET` tag with fallback code between `<APPLET>` and `</APPLET>`.
- **Check for `null`.** Sure, all major browser versions send the `User-Agent` header. But, the header is not *required* by the HTTP 1.1 specification, some browsers let you disable it (e.g., Opera), and custom clients (e.g., Web spiders or link verifiers) might not use the header at all. In fact, you should *always* check that the result of `request.getHeader` is non-`null` before trying to use it, regardless of which header you are dealing with.
- **To differentiate between Netscape and Internet Explorer, check for "MSIE," not "Mozilla."** Both Netscape and Internet Explorer say "Mozilla" at the beginning of the header, even though Mozilla is the Godzilla-like Netscape mascot. This characteristic is for compatibility with JavaScript.
- **Note that the header can be faked.** Some browsers let the user change the value of this header. Even if the browser didn't allow this, the user could always use a custom client. If a client fakes this header, the servlet cannot tell the difference.

Listing 5.4 shows a servlet that sends browser-specific insults to users. For the sake of simplicity, it assumes that Internet Explorer and Netscape are the only two browsers being used. Specifically, it assumes that any browser whose `User-Agent` contains "MSIE" is Internet Explorer and any whose `User-Agent` does not is Netscape. Figures 5–4 and 5–5 show the results.

Listing 5.4 BrowserInsult.java

```
package coreservlets;

import java.io.*;
import javax.servlet.*;
import javax.servlet.http.*;

/** Servlet that gives browser-specific insult.
 *  Illustrates how to use the User-Agent
 *  header to tell browsers apart.
 */

public class BrowserInsult extends HttpServlet {
  public void doGet(HttpServletRequest request,
                    HttpServletResponse response)
      throws ServletException, IOException {
    response.setContentType("text/html");
    PrintWriter out = response.getWriter();
    String title, message;
    // Assume for simplicity that Netscape and IE are
    // the only two browsers.
    String userAgent = request.getHeader("User-Agent");
    if ((userAgent != null) &&
        (userAgent.indexOf("MSIE") != -1)) {
      title = "Microsoft Minion";
      message = "Welcome, O spineless slave to the " +
                "mighty empire.";
    } else {
      title = "Hopeless Netscape Rebel";
      message = "Enjoy it while you can. " +
                "You <I>will</I> be assimilated!";
    }
    String docType =
      "<!DOCTYPE HTML PUBLIC \"-//W3C//DTD HTML 4.0 " +
      "Transitional//EN\">\n";
    out.println(docType +
                "<HTML>\n" +
                "<HEAD><TITLE>" + title + "</TITLE></HEAD>\n" +
                "<BODY BGCOLOR=\"#FDF5E6\">\n" +
                "<H1 ALIGN=CENTER>" + title + "</H1>\n" +
                message + "\n" +
                "</BODY></HTML>");
  }
}
```

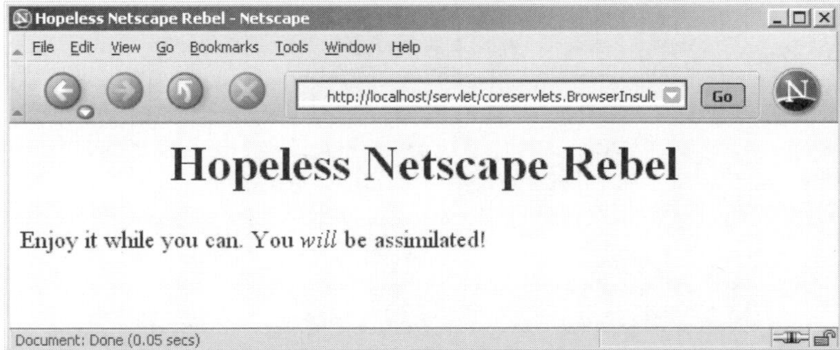

Figure 5–4 The `BrowserInsult` servlet as viewed by a Netscape user.

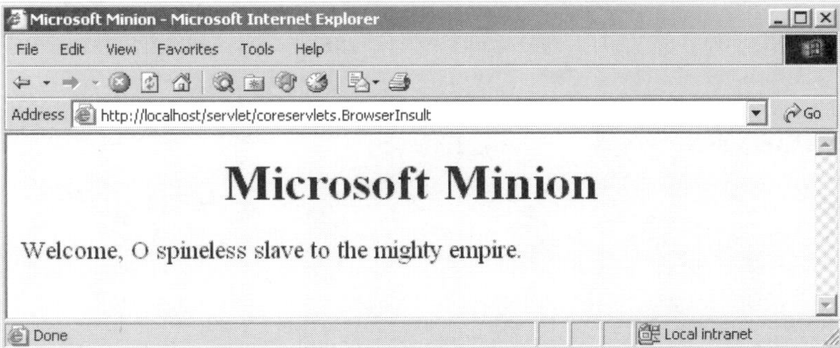

Figure 5–5 The `BrowserInsult` servlet as viewed by an Internet Explorer user.

5.6 Changing the Page According to How the User Got There

The `Referer` header designates the location of the page users were on when they clicked a link to get to the current page. If users simply type the address of a page, the browser sends no `Referer` at all and `request.getHeader("Referer")` returns `null`.

This header enables you to customize the page depending on how the user reached it. For example, you could use this header to do the following:

- Create a jobs/careers site that takes on the look and feel of the associated site that links to it.
- Change the content of a page depending on whether the link came from inside or outside the firewall. (Do not use this trick for secure applications, however; the `Referer` header, like all headers, is easily forged.)

- Supply links that take users back to the page they came from.
- Track the effectiveness of banner ads or record click-through rates from various different sites that display your ads.

Listing 5.5 shows a servlet that uses the `Referer` header to customize the image it displays. If the address of the referring page contains the string "JRun," the servlet displays the logo of Macromedia JRun. If the address contains the string "Resin," the servlet displays the logo of Caucho Resin. Otherwise, the servlet displays the logo of Apache Tomcat. The servlet also displays the address of the referring page.

Listing 5.6 shows the HTML pages used to link to the servlet. We created three *identical* pages named JRun-Referer.html, Resin-Referer.html, and Tomcat-Referer.html; the servlet uses the name of the referring page, not form data, to distinguish among the three. Recall that HTML pages are placed in the top-level directory of your Web application (or an arbitrary subdirectory thereof), whereas servlet code is placed in a subdirectory of WEB-INF/classes that matches the package name. So, for example, with Tomcat and the default Web application, the HTML pages are placed in *install_dir*/webapps/ROOT/request-headers/ and accessed with URLs of the form http://*hostname*/request-headers/*Xxx*-Referer.html.

Figures 5–6 through 5–9 show some representative results.

Listing 5.5 CustomizeImage.java

```
package coreservlets;

import java.io.*;
import javax.servlet.*;
import javax.servlet.http.*;

/** Servlet that displays referer-specific image. */

public class CustomizeImage extends HttpServlet {
  public void doGet(HttpServletRequest request,
                    HttpServletResponse response)
      throws ServletException, IOException {
    response.setContentType("text/html");
    PrintWriter out = response.getWriter();
    String referer = request.getHeader("Referer");
    if (referer == null) {
      referer = "<I>none</I>";
    }
    String title = "Referring page: " + referer;
    String imageName;
    if (contains(referer, "JRun")) {
      imageName = "jrun-powered.gif";
```

Listing 5.5 CustomizeImage.java *(continued)*

```
    } else if (contains(referer, "Resin")) {
      imageName = "resin-powered.gif";
    } else {
      imageName = "tomcat-powered.gif";
    }
    String imagePath = "../request-headers/images/" + imageName;
    String docType =
      "<!DOCTYPE HTML PUBLIC \"-//W3C//DTD HTML 4.0 " +
      "Transitional//EN\">\n";
    out.println(docType +
                "<HTML>\n" +
                "<HEAD><TITLE>" + title + "</TITLE></HEAD>\n" +
                "<BODY BGCOLOR=\"#FDF5E6\">\n" +
                "<CENTER><H2>" + title + "</H2>\n" +
                "<IMG SRC=\"" + imagePath + "\">\n" +
                "</CENTER></BODY></HTML>");
  }

  private boolean contains(String mainString,
                           String subString) {
    return(mainString.indexOf(subString) != -1);
  }
}
```

Listing 5.6 JRun-Referer.html (identical to Tomcat-Referer.html and Resin-Referer.html)

```
<!DOCTYPE HTML PUBLIC "-//W3C//DTD HTML 4.0 Transitional//EN">
<HTML><HEAD><TITLE>Referer Test</TITLE></HEAD>
<BODY BGCOLOR="#FDF5E6">
<H1 ALIGN="CENTER">Referer Test</H1>
Click <A HREF="/servlet/coreservlets.CustomizeImage">here</A>
to visit the servlet.
</BODY></HTML>
```

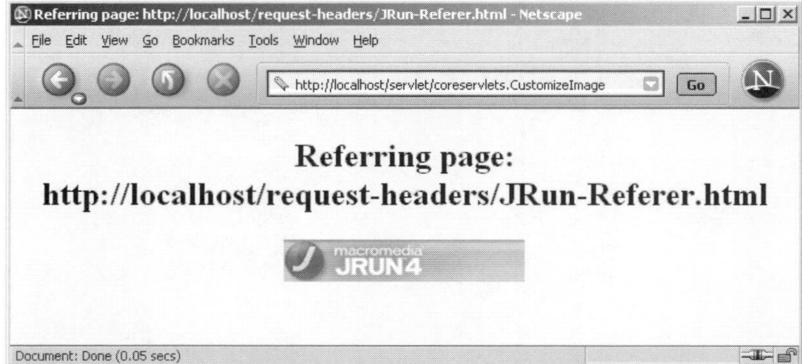

Figure 5–6 The `CustomizeImage` servlet when the address of the referring page contains the string "JRun."

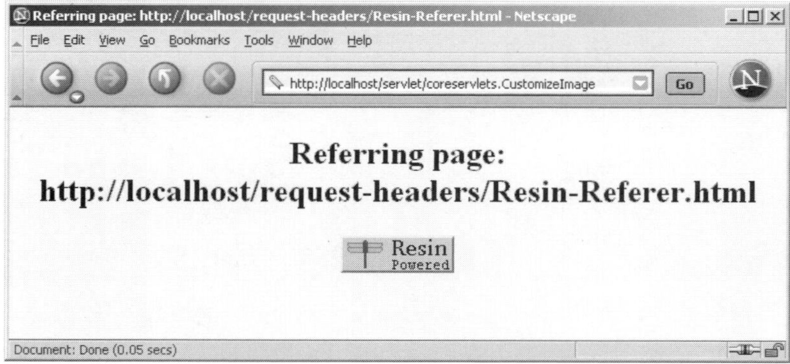

Figure 5–7 The `CustomizeImage` servlet when the address of the referring page contains the string "Resin."

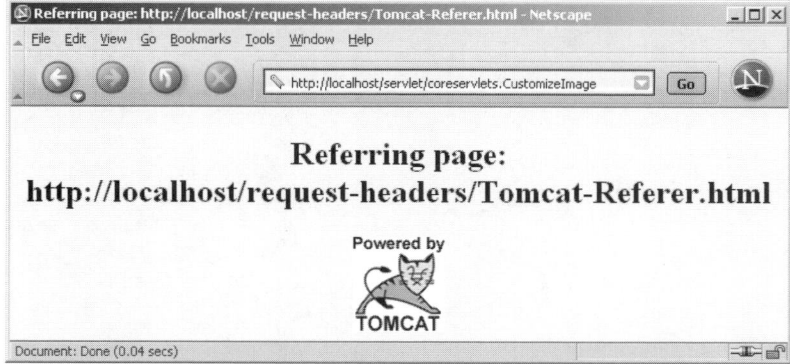

Figure 5–8 The `CustomizeImage` servlet when the address of the referring page contains neither "JRun" nor "Resin."

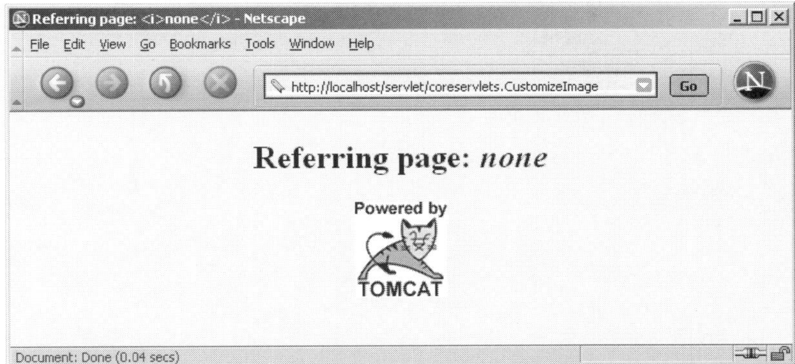

Figure 5–9 The `CustomizeImage` servlet when the `Referer` header is missing. When using the `Referer` header, always handle the case in which the result of `getHeader` is `null`.

5.7 Accessing the Standard CGI Variables

If you come to servlets with a background in traditional Common Gateway Interface (CGI) programming, you are probably used to the idea of "CGI variables." These are a somewhat eclectic collection of information about the current request. Some are based on the HTTP request line and headers (e.g., form data), others are derived from the socket itself (e.g., the name and IP address of the requesting host), and still others are taken from server installation parameters (e.g., the mapping of URLs to actual paths).

Although it probably makes more sense to think of different sources of data (request data, server information, etc.) as distinct, experienced CGI programmers may find it useful to see the servlet equivalent of each of the CGI variables. If you don't have a background in traditional CGI, first, count your blessings; servlets are easier to use, more flexible, and more efficient than standard CGI. Second, just skim this section, noting the parts not directly related to the incoming HTTP request. In particular, observe that you can use `getServletContext().getRealPath` to map a URI (the part of the URL that comes after the host and port) to an actual path and that you can use `request.getRemoteHost` and `request.getRemoteAddress` to get the name and IP address of the client.

Servlet Equivalent of CGI Variables

For each standard CGI variable, this subsection summarizes its purpose and the means of accessing it from a servlet. Assume `request` is the `HttpServletRequest` supplied to the `doGet` and `doPost` methods.

AUTH_TYPE

If an `Authorization` header was supplied, this variable gives the scheme specified (`basic` or `digest`). Access it with `request.getAuthType()`.

CONTENT_LENGTH

For `POST` requests only, this variable stores the number of bytes of data sent, as given by the `Content-Length` request header. Technically, since the `CONTENT_LENGTH` CGI variable is a string, the servlet equivalent is `String.valueOf(request.getContentLength())` or `request.getHeader("Content-Length")`. You'll probably want to just call `request.getContentLength()`, which returns an `int`.

CONTENT_TYPE

`CONTENT_TYPE` designates the MIME type of attached data, if specified. See Table 7.1 in Section 7.2 (Understanding HTTP 1.1 Response Headers) for the names and meanings of the common MIME types. Access `CONTENT_TYPE` with `request.getContentType()`.

DOCUMENT_ROOT

The `DOCUMENT_ROOT` variable specifies the real directory corresponding to the URL `http://host/`. Access it with `getServletContext().getRealPath("/")`. Also, you can use `getServletContext().getRealPath` to map an arbitrary URI (i.e., URL suffix that comes after the hostname and port) to an actual path on the local machine.

HTTP_XXX_YYY

Variables of the form `HTTP_HEADER_NAME` are how CGI programs access arbitrary HTTP request headers. The `Cookie` header becomes `HTTP_COOKIE`, `User-Agent` becomes `HTTP_USER_AGENT`, `Referer` becomes `HTTP_REFERER`, and so forth. Servlets should just use `request.getHeader` or one of the shortcut methods described in Section 5.1 (Reading Request Headers).

PATH_INFO
This variable supplies any path information attached to the URL after the address of the servlet but before the query data. For example, with http://host/servlet/coreservlets.SomeServlet/foo/bar?baz=quux, the path information is `/foo/bar`. Since servlets, unlike standard CGI programs, can talk directly to the server, they don't need to treat path information specially. Path information could be sent as part of the regular form data and then translated by `getServletContext().getRealPath`. Access the value of `PATH_INFO` by using `request.getPathInfo()`.

PATH_TRANSLATED
`PATH_TRANSLATED` gives the path information mapped to a real path on the server. Again, with servlets there is no need to have a special case for path information, since a servlet can call `getServletContext().getRealPath` to translate partial URLs into real paths. This translation is not possible with standard CGI because the CGI program runs entirely separately from the server. Access this variable by means of `request.getPathTranslated()`.

QUERY_STRING
For `GET` requests, this variable gives the attached data as a single string with values still URL-encoded. You rarely want the raw data in servlets; instead, use `request.getParameter` to access individual parameters, as described in Section 5.1 (Reading Request Headers). However, if you do want the raw data, you can get it with `request.getQueryString()`.

REMOTE_ADDR
This variable designates the IP address of the client that made the request, as a `String` (e.g., `"198.137.241.30"`). Access it by calling `request.getRemoteAddr()`.

REMOTE_HOST
`REMOTE_HOST` indicates the fully qualified domain name (e.g., `whitehouse.gov`) of the client that made the request. The IP address is returned if the domain name cannot be determined. You can access this variable with `request.getRemoteHost()`.

REMOTE_USER
If an `Authorization` header was supplied and decoded by the server itself, the `REMOTE_USER` variable gives the user part, which is useful for session tracking in protected sites. Access it with `request.getRemoteUser()`. For decoding `Authorization` information directly in servlets, see the chapters on Web application security in Volume 2 of this book.

REQUEST_METHOD

This variable stipulates the HTTP request type, which is usually `GET` or `POST` but is occasionally `HEAD`, `PUT`, `DELETE`, `OPTIONS`, or `TRACE`. Servlets rarely need to look up `REQUEST_METHOD` explicitly, since each of the request types is typically handled by a different servlet method (`doGet`, `doPost`, etc.). An exception is `HEAD`, which is handled automatically by the `service` method returning whatever headers and status codes the `doGet` method would use. Access this variable by means of `request.getMethod()`.

SCRIPT_NAME

This variable specifies the path to the servlet, relative to the server's root directory. It can be accessed through `request.getServletPath()`.

SERVER_NAME

`SERVER_NAME` gives the host name of the server machine. It can be accessed by means of `request.getServerName()`.

SERVER_PORT

This variable stores the port the server is listening on. Technically, the servlet equivalent is `String.valueOf(request.getServerPort())`, which returns a `String`. You'll usually just want `request.getServerPort()`, which returns an `int`.

SERVER_PROTOCOL

The `SERVER_PROTOCOL` variable indicates the protocol name and version used in the request line (e.g., `HTTP/1.0` or `HTTP/1.1`). Access it by calling `request.getProtocol()`.

SERVER_SOFTWARE

This variable gives identifying information about the Web server. Access it by means of `getServletContext().getServerInfo()`.

A Servlet That Shows the CGI Variables

Listing 5.7 presents a servlet that creates a table showing the values of all the CGI variables other than `HTTP_XXX_YYY`, which are just the HTTP request headers described in Section 5.3. Figure 5–10 shows the result for a typical request.

Listing 5.7 ShowCGIVariables.java

```
package coreservlets;

import java.io.*;
import javax.servlet.*;
import javax.servlet.http.*;
import java.util.*;

/** Creates a table showing the current value of each
 *  of the standard CGI variables.
 */

public class ShowCGIVariables extends HttpServlet {
  public void doGet(HttpServletRequest request,
                    HttpServletResponse response)
      throws ServletException, IOException {
    response.setContentType("text/html");
    PrintWriter out = response.getWriter();
    String[][] variables =
      { { "AUTH_TYPE", request.getAuthType() },
        { "CONTENT_LENGTH",
          String.valueOf(request.getContentLength()) },
        { "CONTENT_TYPE", request.getContentType() },
        { "DOCUMENT_ROOT",
          getServletContext().getRealPath("/") },
        { "PATH_INFO", request.getPathInfo() },
        { "PATH_TRANSLATED", request.getPathTranslated() },
        { "QUERY_STRING", request.getQueryString() },
        { "REMOTE_ADDR", request.getRemoteAddr() },
        { "REMOTE_HOST", request.getRemoteHost() },
        { "REMOTE_USER", request.getRemoteUser() },
        { "REQUEST_METHOD", request.getMethod() },
        { "SCRIPT_NAME", request.getServletPath() },
        { "SERVER_NAME", request.getServerName() },
        { "SERVER_PORT",
          String.valueOf(request.getServerPort()) },
        { "SERVER_PROTOCOL", request.getProtocol() },
        { "SERVER_SOFTWARE",
          getServletContext().getServerInfo() }
      };
    String title = "Servlet Example: Showing CGI Variables";
    String docType =
      "<!DOCTYPE HTML PUBLIC \"-//W3C//DTD HTML 4.0 " +
      "Transitional//EN\">\n";
```

Listing 5.7 ShowCGIVariables.java *(continued)*

```
    out.println(docType +
                "<HTML>\n" +
                "<HEAD><TITLE>" + title + "</TITLE></HEAD>\n" +
                "<BODY BGCOLOR=\"#FDF5E6\">\n" +
                "<CENTER>\n" +
                "<H1>" + title + "</H1>\n" +
                "<TABLE BORDER=1>\n" +
                "  <TR BGCOLOR=\"#FFAD00\">\n" +
                "    <TH>CGI Variable Name<TH>Value");
    for(int i=0; i<variables.length; i++) {
      String varName = variables[i][0];
      String varValue = variables[i][1];
      if (varValue == null)
        varValue = "<I>Not specified</I>";
      out.println("  <TR><TD>" + varName + "<TD>" + varValue);
    }
    out.println("</TABLE></CENTER></BODY></HTML>");
  }

  /** POST and GET requests handled identically. */

  public void doPost(HttpServletRequest request,
                     HttpServletResponse response)
      throws ServletException, IOException {
    doGet(request, response);
  }
}
```

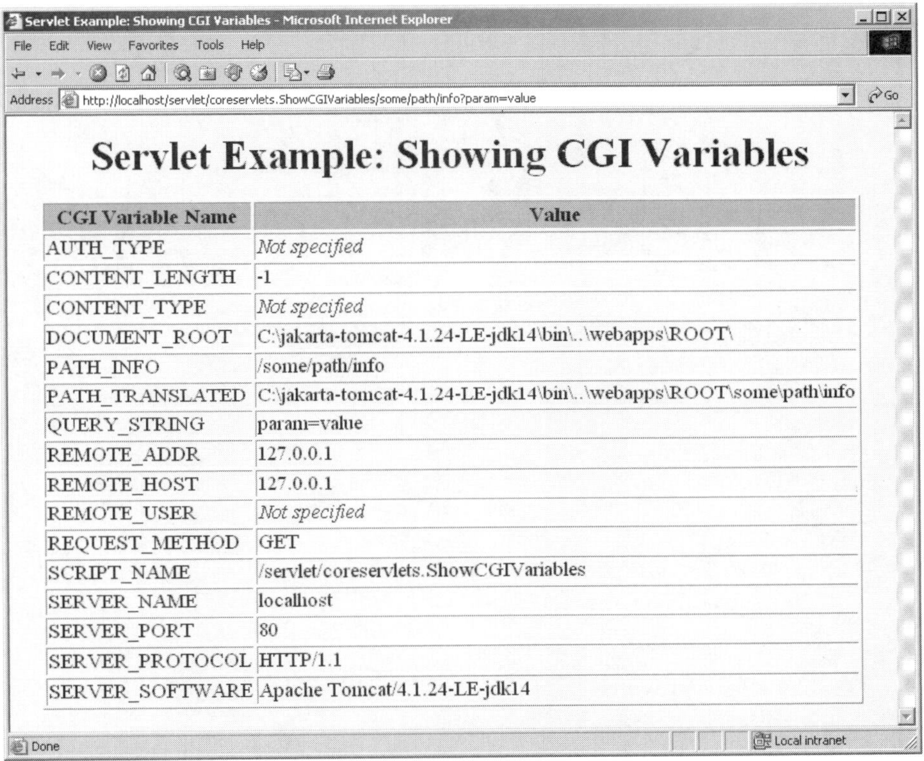

Figure 5–10 The standard CGI variables for a typical request.

Generating the Server Response: HTTP Status Codes

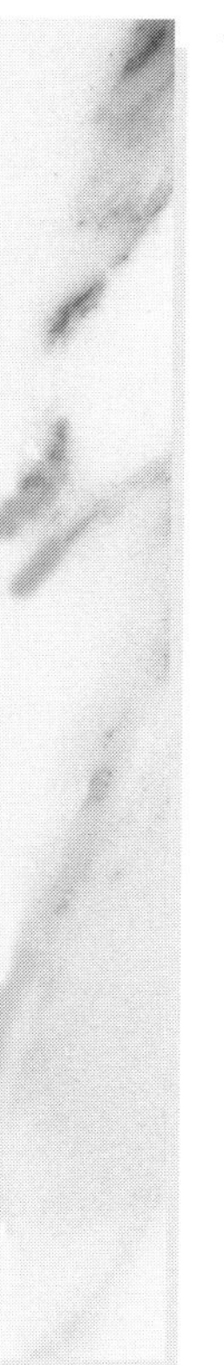

Topics in This Chapter

- Format of the HTTP response
- How to set status codes
- What the status codes are good for
- Shortcut methods for redirection and error pages
- A servlet that redirects users to browser-specific pages
- A front end to various search engines

Chapter 6

As we saw in the previous chapter, a request from a browser or other client consists of an HTTP command (usually `GET` or `POST`), zero or more request headers (one or more in HTTP 1.1, since `Host` is required), a blank line, and, only in the case of `POST` requests, some query data. A typical request looks like the following.

```
GET /servlet/SomeName HTTP/1.1
Host: ...
Header2: ...
...
HeaderN:
  (Blank Line)
```

When a Web server responds to a request, the response typically consists of a status line, some response headers, a blank line, and the document. A typical response looks like this:

```
HTTP/1.1 200 OK
Content-Type: text/html
Header2: ...
...
HeaderN: ...
  (Blank Line)
<!DOCTYPE ...>
<HTML>
<HEAD>...</HEAD>
<BODY>
...
</BODY></HTML>
```

The status line consists of the HTTP version (`HTTP/1.1` in the preceding example), a status code (an integer; `200` in the example), and a very short message corresponding to the status code (`OK` in the example). In most cases, the headers are optional except for `Content-Type`, which specifies the MIME type of the document that follows. Although most responses contain a document, some don't. For example, responses to `HEAD` requests should never include a document, and various status codes essentially indicate failure or redirection (and thus either don't include a document or include only a short error-message document).

Servlets can perform a variety of important tasks by manipulating the status line and the response headers. For example, they can forward the user to other sites; indicate that the attached document is an image, Adobe Acrobat file, or HTML file; tell the user that a password is required to access the document; and so forth. This chapter summarizes the most important status codes and describes what can be accomplished with them; the following chapter discusses the response headers.

6.1 Specifying Status Codes

As just described, the HTTP response status line consists of an HTTP version, a status code, and an associated message. Since the message is directly associated with the status code and the HTTP version is determined by the server, all a servlet needs to do is to set the status code. A code of 200 is set automatically, so servlets don't usually need to specify a status code at all. When they *do* want to, they use `response.setStatus`, `response.sendRedirect`, or `response.sendError`.

Setting Arbitrary Status Codes: setStatus

When you want to set an arbitrary status code, do so with the `setStatus` method of `HttpServletResponse`. If your response includes a special status code and a document, be sure to call `setStatus` *before* actually returning any of the content with the `PrintWriter`. The reason is that an HTTP response consists of the status line, one or more headers, a blank line, and the actual document, *in that order*. Servlets do not necessarily buffer the document, so you have to either set the status code before using the `PrintWriter` or carefully check that the buffer hasn't been flushed and content actually sent to the browser.

Core Approach

*Set status codes **before** sending any document content to the client.*

The `setStatus` method takes an `int` (the status code) as an argument, but instead of using explicit numbers, for readability and to avoid typos, use the constants defined in `HttpServletResponse`. The name of each constant is derived from the standard HTTP 1.1 message for each constant, all upper case with a prefix of `SC` (for *Status Code*) and spaces changed to underscores. Thus, since the message for 404 is Not Found, the equivalent constant in `HttpServletResponse` is `SC_NOT_FOUND`. There is one minor exception, however: the constant for code 302 is derived from the message defined by HTTP 1.0 (Moved Temporarily), not the HTTP 1.1 message (Found).

Setting 302 and 404 Status Codes: sendRedirect and sendError

Although the general method of setting status codes is simply to call `response.setStatus(int)`, there are two common cases for which a shortcut method in `HttpServletResponse` is provided. Just be aware that both of these methods throw `IOException`, whereas `setStatus` does not. Since the `doGet` and `doPost` methods already throw `IOException`, this difference only matters if you pass the response object to another method.

- **`public void sendRedirect(String url)`**
  The 302 status code directs the browser to connect to a new location. The `sendRedirect` method generates a 302 response along with a `Location` header giving the URL of the new document. Either an absolute or a relative URL is permitted; the system automatically translates relative URLs into absolute ones before putting them in the `Location` header.
- **`public void sendError(int code, String message)`**
  The 404 status code is used when no document is found on the server. The `sendError` method sends a status code (usually 404) along with a short message that is automatically formatted inside an HTML document and sent to the client.

Setting a status code does not necessarily mean that you omit the document. For example, although most servers automatically generate a small File Not Found message for 404 responses, a servlet might want to customize this response. Again, remember that if you do send output, you have to call `setStatus` or `sendError` *first*.

6.2 HTTP 1.1 Status Codes

In this section we describe the most important status codes available for use in servlets talking to HTTP 1.1 clients, along with the standard message associated with each code. A good understanding of these codes can dramatically increase the capabilities of your servlets, so you should at least skim the descriptions to see what options are at your disposal. You can come back for details when you are ready to use the capabilities.

The complete HTTP 1.1 specification is given in RFC 2616. In general, you can access RFCs online by going to http://www.rfc-editor.org/ and following the links to the latest RFC archive sites, but since this one came from the World Wide Web Consortium, you can just go to http://www.w3.org/Protocols/. Codes that are new in HTTP 1.1 are noted since some browsers support only HTTP 1.0. You should only send the new codes to clients that support HTTP 1.1, as verified by checking `request.getRequestProtocol`.

The rest of this section describes the specific status codes available in HTTP 1.1. These codes fall into five general categories:

- **100–199**
  Codes in the 100s are informational, indicating that the client should respond with some other action.
- **200–299**
  Values in the 200s signify that the request was successful.
- **300–399**
  Values in the 300s are used for files that have moved and usually include a `Location` header indicating the new address.
- **400–499**
  Values in the 400s indicate an error by the client.
- **500–599**
  Codes in the 500s signify an error by the server.

The constants in `HttpServletResponse` that represent the various codes are derived from the standard messages associated with the codes. In servlets, you usually refer to status codes only by means of these constants. For example, you would use `response.setStatus(response.SC_NO_CONTENT)` rather than `response.setStatus(204)`, since the latter is unclear to readers and is prone to typographical errors. However, you should note that servers are allowed to vary the messages slightly, and clients pay attention only to the numeric value. So, for example, you might see a server return a status line of `HTTP/1.1 200 Document Follows` instead of `HTTP/1.1 200 OK`.

100 (Continue)
If the server receives an `Expect` request header with a value of `100-continue`, it means that the client is asking if it can send an attached document in a follow-up request. In such a case, the server should either respond with status 100 (`SC_CONTINUE`) to tell the client to go ahead or use 417 (`SC_EXPECTATION_FAILED`) to tell the browser it won't accept the document. This status code is new in HTTP 1.1.

200 (OK)
A value of 200 (`SC_OK`) means that everything is fine; the document follows for `GET` and `POST` requests. This status is the default for servlets; if you don't use `setStatus`, you'll get 200.

202 (Accepted)
A value of 202 (`SC_ACCEPTED`) tells the client that the request is being acted upon but processing is not yet complete.

204 (No Content)
A status code of 204 (`SC_NO_CONTENT`) stipulates that the browser should continue to display the previous document because no new document is available. This behavior is useful if the user periodically reloads a page by pressing the Reload button and you can determine that the previous page is already up-to-date.

205 (Reset Content)
A value of 205 (`SC_RESET_CONTENT`) means that there is no new document but the browser should reset the document view. Thus, this status code is used to instruct browsers to clear form fields. It is new in HTTP 1.1.

301 (Moved Permanently)
The 301 (`SC_MOVED_PERMANENTLY`) status indicates that the requested document is elsewhere; the new URL for the document is given in the `Location` response header. Browsers should automatically follow the link to the new URL.

302 (Found)
This value is similar to 301, except that in principle the URL given by the `Location` header should be interpreted as a temporary replacement, not a permanent one. In practice, most browsers treat 301 and 302 identically. Note: in HTTP 1.0, the message was `Moved Temporarily` instead of `Found`, and the constant in `HttpServletResponse` is `SC_MOVED_TEMPORARILY`, not the expected `SC_FOUND`.

Core Note

The constant representing 302 is `SC_MOVED_TEMPORARILY`, not `SC_FOUND`.

Status code 302 is useful because browsers automatically follow the reference to the new URL given in the `Location` response header. Note that the browser reconnects to the new URL immediately; no intermediate output is displayed. This behavior distinguishes *redirects* from *refreshes* where an intermediate page is temporarily displayed (see the next chapter for details on the `Refresh` header). With redirects, another site, not the servlet itself, generates the results. So why use a servlet at all? Redirects are useful for the following tasks:

- **Computing destinations.** If you know the final destination for the user in advance, your hypertext link or HTML form could send the user directly there. But, if you need to look at the data before deciding where to obtain the necessary results, a redirection is useful. For example, you might want to send users to a standard site that gives information on stocks, but you need to look at the stock symbol before deciding whether to send them to the New York Stock Exchange, NASDAQ, or a non-U.S. site.
- **Tracking user behavior.** If you send users a page that contains a hypertext link to another site, you have no way to know if they actually click on the link. But perhaps this information is important in analyzing the usefulness of the different links you send them. So, instead of sending users the direct link, you can send them a link to your own site, where you can then record some information and then redirect them to the real site. For example, several search engines use this trick to determine which of the results they display are most popular.
- **Performing side effects.** What if you want to send users to a certain site but set a cookie on the user's browser first? No problem: return both a `Set-Cookie` response header (by means of `response.addCookie`—see Chapter 8) *and* a 302 status code (by means of `response.sendRedirect`).

The 302 status code is so useful, in fact, that there is a special method for it, `sendRedirect`. Using `response.sendRedirect(url)` has a couple of advantages over using `response.setStatus(response.SC_MOVED_TEMPORARILY)` and `response.setHeader("Location", url)`. First, it is shorter and easier. Second, with `sendRedirect`, the servlet automatically builds a page containing the link to show to older browsers that don't automatically follow redirects. Finally, `sendRedirect` can handle relative URLs, automatically translating them into absolute ones.

Technically, browsers are supposed to automatically follow the redirection only if the original request was `GET`. For details, see the discussion of the 307 status code.

303 (See Other)

The 303 (`SC_SEE_OTHER`) status is similar to 301 and 302, except that if the original request was `POST`, the new document (given in the `Location` header) should be retrieved with `GET`. See status code 307. This code is new in HTTP 1.1.

304 (Not Modified)

When a client has a cached document, it can perform a conditional request by supplying an `If-Modified-Since` header to signify that it wants the document only if it has been changed since the specified date. A value of 304 (`SC_NOT_MODIFIED`) means that the cached version is up-to-date and the client should use it. Otherwise, the server should return the requested document with the normal (200) status code. Servlets normally should not set this status code directly. Instead, they should implement the `getLastModified` method and let the default `service` method handle conditional requests based upon this modification date. For an example, see the `LotteryNumbers` servlet in Section 3.6 (The Servlet Life Cycle).

307 (Temporary Redirect)

The rules for how a browser should handle a 307 status are identical to those for 302. The 307 value was added to HTTP 1.1 since many browsers erroneously follow the redirection on a 302 response even if the original message is a `POST`. Browsers are supposed to follow the redirection of a `POST` request only when they receive a 303 response status. This new status is intended to be unambiguously clear: follow redirected `GET` *and* `POST` requests in the case of 303 responses; follow redirected `GET` *but not* `POST` requests in the case of 307 responses. This status code is new in HTTP 1.1.

400 (Bad Request)

A 400 (`SC_BAD_REQUEST`) status indicates bad syntax in the client request.

401 (Unauthorized)

A value of 401 (`SC_UNAUTHORIZED`) signifies that the client tried to access a password-protected page but that the request did not have proper identifying information in the `Authorization` header. The response must include a `WWW-Authenticate` header. For details, see the chapter on programmatic Web application security in Volume 2 of this book.

403 (Forbidden)

A status code of 403 (`SC_FORBIDDEN`) means that the server refuses to supply the resource, regardless of authorization. This status is often the result of bad file or directory permissions on the server.

404 (Not Found)

The infamous 404 (`SC_NOT_FOUND`) status tells the client that no resource could be found at that address. This value is the standard "no such page" response. It is such a common and useful response that there is a special method for it in the `HttpServletResponse` class: `sendError("message")`. The advantage of `sendError` over `setStatus` is that with `sendError`, the server automatically generates an error page showing the error message. 404 errors need not merely say "Sorry, the page cannot be found." Instead, they can give information on why the page couldn't be found or supply search boxes or alternative places to look. The sites at www.microsoft.com and www.ibm.com have particularly good examples of useful error pages (to see them, just make up a nonexistent URL at either site). In fact, there is an entire site dedicated to the good, the bad, the ugly, and the bizarre in 404 error messages: http://www.plinko.net/404/. We find http://www.plinko.net/404/links.asp?type=cat&key=13 (amusing 404 error messages) particularly funny.

Unfortunately, however, the default behavior of Internet Explorer in version 5 and later is to ignore the error page you send back and to display its own static (and relatively useless) error message, even though doing so explicitly contradicts the HTTP specification. To turn off this setting, go to the Tools menu, select Internet Options, choose the Advanced tab, and make sure the "Show friendly HTTP error messages" box is *not* checked. Regrettably, few users are aware of this setting, so this "feature" prevents most users of Internet Explorer from seeing any informative messages you return. Other major browsers and version 4 of Internet Explorer properly display server-generated error pages.

Core Warning

By default, Internet Explorer versions 5 and later improperly ignore server-generated error pages.

Fortunately, it is relatively uncommon for individual servlets to build their own 404 error pages. A more common approach is to set up error pages for an entire Web application; see Section 2.11 (Web Applications: A Preview) for details.

405 (Method Not Allowed)

A 405 (`SC_METHOD_NOT_ALLOWED`) value signifies that the request method (`GET`, `POST`, `HEAD`, `PUT`, `DELETE`, etc.) was not allowed for this particular resource. This status code is new in HTTP 1.1.

415 (Unsupported Media Type)

A value of 415 (`SC_UNSUPPORTED_MEDIA_TYPE`) means that the request had an attached document of a type the server doesn't know how to handle. This status code is new in HTTP 1.1.

417 (Expectation Failed)

If the server receives an `Expect` request header with a value of `100-continue`, it means that the client is asking if it can send an attached document in a follow-up request. In such a case, the server should either respond with this status (417) to tell the browser it won't accept the document or use 100 (`SC_CONTINUE`) to tell the client to go ahead. This status code is new in HTTP 1.1.

500 (Internal Server Error)

500 (`SC_INTERNAL_SERVER_ERROR`) is the generic "server is confused" status code. It often results from CGI programs or (heaven forbid!) servlets that crash or return improperly formatted headers.

501 (Not Implemented)

The 501 (`SC_NOT_IMPLEMENTED`) status notifies the client that the server doesn't support the functionality to fulfill the request. It is used, for example, when the client issues a command like `PUT` that the server doesn't support.

503 (Service Unavailable)

A status code of 503 (`SC_SERVICE_UNAVAILABLE`) signifies that the server cannot respond because of maintenance or overloading. For example, a servlet might return this header if some thread or database connection pool is currently full. The server can supply a `Retry-After` header to tell the client when to try again.

505 (HTTP Version Not Supported)

The 505 (SC_HTTP_VERSION_NOT_SUPPORTED) code means that the server doesn't support the version of HTTP named in the request line. This status code is new in HTTP 1.1.

6.3 A Servlet That Redirects Users to Browser-Specific Pages

Recall from Chapter 5 that the User-Agent request header designates the specific browser (or cell phone or other client) making the request. Recall further that most major browsers contain the string Mozilla in their User-Agent header, but only Microsoft Internet Explorer contains the string MSIE.

Listing 6.1 shows a servlet that makes use of this fact to send Internet Explorer users to the Netscape home page, and all other users to the Microsoft home page. The servlet accomplishes this task by using the sendRedirect method to send a 302 status code and a Location response header to the browser. Figures 6–1 and 6–2 show results for Internet Explorer and Netscape, respectively.

Listing 6.1 WrongDestination.java

```
package coreservlets;

import java.io.*;
import javax.servlet.*;
import javax.servlet.http.*;

/** Servlet that sends IE users to the Netscape home page and
 *  Netscape (and all other) users to the Microsoft home page.
 */

public class WrongDestination extends HttpServlet {
  public void doGet(HttpServletRequest request,
                    HttpServletResponse response)
      throws ServletException, IOException {
    String userAgent = request.getHeader("User-Agent");
    if ((userAgent != null) &&
        (userAgent.indexOf("MSIE") != -1)) {
      response.sendRedirect("http://home.netscape.com");
    } else {
      response.sendRedirect("http://www.microsoft.com");
    }
  }
}
```

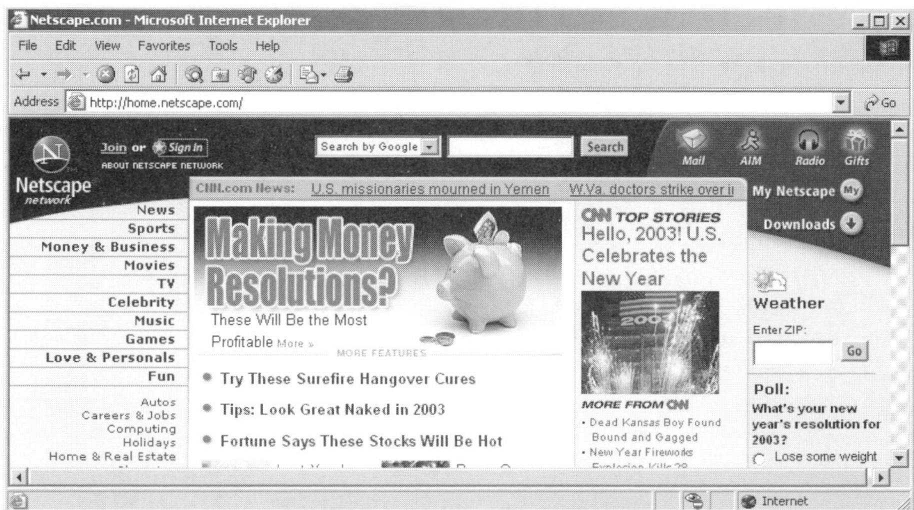

Figure 6–1 Result of http://*host*/servlet/coreservlets.WrongDestination in Internet Explorer.

Figure 6–2 Result of http://*host*/servlet/coreservlets.WrongDestination in Netscape.

6.4 A Front End to Various Search Engines

Suppose that you want to make a "one-stop searching" site that lets users search any of the most popular search engines without having to remember many different URLs. You want to let users enter a query, select the search engine, and then send them to that search engine's results page for that query. If users omit the search keywords or fail to select a search engine, you have no site to redirect them to, so you want to display an error page informing them of this fact.

Listing 6.2 (SearchEngines.java) presents a servlet that accomplishes these tasks by making use of the 302 (`Found`) and 404 (`Not Found`) status codes—the two most common status codes other than 200. The 302 code is set by the shorthand `sendRedirect` method of `HttpServletResponse`, and 404 is specified by `sendError`.

In this application, a servlet builds an HTML form (see Figure 6–3 and the source code in Listing 6.5) that displays a page to let the user specify a search string and select the search engine to use. When the form is submitted, the servlet extracts those two parameters, constructs a URL with the parameters embedded in a way appropriate to the search engine selected (see the `SearchSpec` and `SearchUtilities` classes of Listings 6.3 and 6.4), and redirects the user to that URL (see Figure 6–4). If the user fails to choose a search engine or specify search terms, an error page informs the client of this fact (see Figure 6–5, but recall warnings about Internet Explorer under the 404 status code in the previous section).

Listing 6.2 SearchEngines.java

```
package coreservlets;

import java.io.*;
import javax.servlet.*;
import javax.servlet.http.*;
import java.net.*;

/** Servlet that takes a search string and a search
 *  engine name, sending the query to
 *  that search engine. Illustrates manipulating
 *  the response status code. It sends a 302 response
 *  (via sendRedirect) if it gets a known search engine,
 *  and sends a 404 response (via sendError) otherwise.
 */
```

Listing 6.2 SearchEngines.java *(continued)*

```
public class SearchEngines extends HttpServlet {
  public void doGet(HttpServletRequest request,
                    HttpServletResponse response)
      throws ServletException, IOException {
    String searchString = request.getParameter("searchString");
    if ((searchString == null) ||
        (searchString.length() == 0)) {
      reportProblem(response, "Missing search string");
      return;
    }
    // The URLEncoder changes spaces to "+" signs and other
    // non-alphanumeric characters to "%XY", where XY is the
    // hex value of the ASCII (or ISO Latin-1) character.
    // Browsers always URL-encode form values, and the
    // getParameter method decodes automatically. But since
    // we're just passing this on to another server, we need to
    // re-encode it to avoid characters that are illegal in
    // URLs. Also note that JDK 1.4 introduced a two-argument
    // version of URLEncoder.encode and deprecated the one-arg
    // version. However, since version 2.3 of the servlet spec
    // mandates only the Java 2 Platform (JDK 1.2 or later),
    // we stick with the one-arg version for portability.
    searchString = URLEncoder.encode(searchString);

    String searchEngineName =
      request.getParameter("searchEngine");
    if ((searchEngineName == null) ||
        (searchEngineName.length() == 0)) {
      reportProblem(response, "Missing search engine name");
      return;
    }
    String searchURL =
      SearchUtilities.makeURL(searchEngineName, searchString);
    if (searchURL != null) {
      response.sendRedirect(searchURL);
    } else {
      reportProblem(response, "Unrecognized search engine");
    }
  }

  private void reportProblem(HttpServletResponse response,
                             String message)
      throws IOException {
    response.sendError(response.SC_NOT_FOUND, message);
  }
}
```

Listing 6.3 SearchSpec.java

```
package coreservlets;

/** Small class that encapsulates how to construct a
 *  search string for a particular search engine.
 */

public class SearchSpec {
  private String name, baseURL;

  public SearchSpec(String name,
                    String baseURL) {
    this.name = name;
    this.baseURL = baseURL;
  }

  /** Builds a URL for the results page by simply concatenating
   *  the base URL (http://...?someVar=") with the URL-encoded
   *  search string (jsp+training).
   */

  public String makeURL(String searchString) {
    return(baseURL + searchString);
  }

  public String getName() {
    return(name);
  }
}
```

Listing 6.4 SearchUtilities.java

```
package coreservlets;

/** Utility with static method to build a URL for any
 *  of the most popular search engines.
 */

public class SearchUtilities {
  private static SearchSpec[] commonSpecs =
    { new SearchSpec("Google",
                     "http://www.google.com/search?q="),
      new SearchSpec("AllTheWeb",
                     "http://www.alltheweb.com/search?q="),
```

Listing 6.4 SearchUtilities.java *(continued)*

```
      new SearchSpec("Yahoo",
                     "http://search.yahoo.com/bin/search?p="),
      new SearchSpec("AltaVista",
                     "http://www.altavista.com/web/results?q="),
      new SearchSpec("Lycos",
                     "search.lycos.com/default.asp?query="),
      new SearchSpec("HotBot",
                     "http://hotbot.com/default.asp?query="),
      new SearchSpec("MSN",
                     "http://search.msn.com/results.asp?q="),
    };

  public static SearchSpec[] getCommonSpecs() {
    return(commonSpecs);
  }

  /** Given a search engine name and a search string, builds
   *  a URL for the results page of that search engine
   *  for that query. Returns null if the search engine name
   *  is not one of the ones it knows about.
   */

  public static String makeURL(String searchEngineName,
                               String searchString) {
    SearchSpec[] searchSpecs = getCommonSpecs();
    String searchURL = null;
    for(int i=0; i<searchSpecs.length; i++) {
      SearchSpec spec = searchSpecs[i];
      if (spec.getName().equalsIgnoreCase(searchEngineName)) {
        searchURL = spec.makeURL(searchString);
        break;
      }
    }
    return(searchURL);
  }
}
```

Figure 6–3 Front end to the `SearchEngines` servlet. See Listing 6.5 for the source code.

Figure 6–4 Results of the `SearchEngines` servlet when the form of Figure 6–3 is submitted. Although the form is submitted to the `SearchEngines` servlet, that servlet generates no output and the end user sees only the result of the redirection.

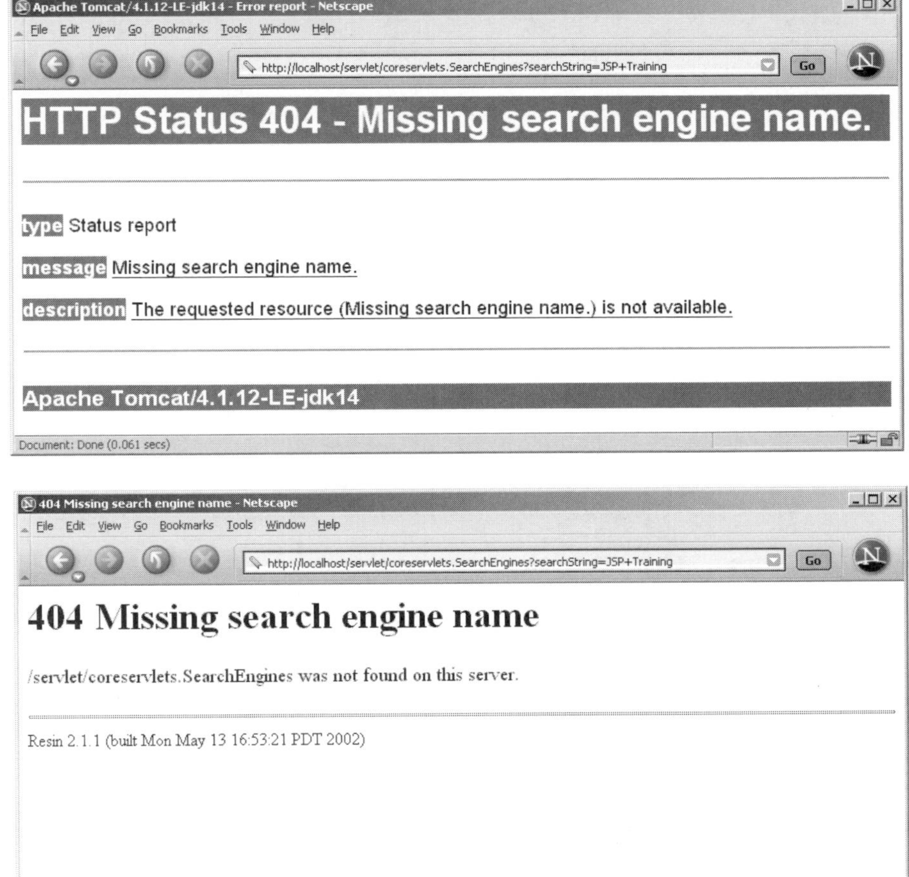

Figure 6–5 Results of the `SearchEngines` servlet upon submission of a form that has no search engine specified. These results are for Tomcat 4.1 and Resin 4.0; results will vary slightly among servers and will incorrectly omit the "Missing search string" message in JRun 4. In Internet Explorer, you must modify the browser settings as described in the previous section (see the 404 entry) to see the error message.

Listing 6.5 SearchEngineForm.java

```
package coreservlets;

import java.io.*;
import javax.servlet.*;
import javax.servlet.http.*;

/** Servlet that builds the HTML form that gathers input
 *  for the search engine servlet. This servlet first
 *  displays a textfield for the search query, then looks up
 *  the search engine names known to SearchUtilities and
 *  displays a list of radio buttons, one for each search
 *  engine.
 */

public class SearchEngineForm extends HttpServlet {
  public void doGet(HttpServletRequest request,
                    HttpServletResponse response)
      throws ServletException, IOException {
    response.setContentType("text/html");
    PrintWriter out = response.getWriter();
    String title = "One-Stop Web Search!";
    String actionURL = "/servlet/coreservlets.SearchEngines";
    String docType =
      "<!DOCTYPE HTML PUBLIC \"-//W3C//DTD HTML 4.0 " +
      "Transitional//EN\">\n";
    out.println
      (docType +
       "<HTML>\n" +
       "<HEAD><TITLE>" + title + "</TITLE></HEAD>\n" +
       "<BODY BGCOLOR=\"#FDF5E6\">\n" +
       "<CENTER>\n" +
       "<H1>" + title + "</H1>\n" +
       "<FORM ACTION=\"" + actionURL + "\">\n" +
       "  Search keywords: \n" +
       "  <INPUT TYPE=\"TEXT\" NAME=\"searchString\"><P>\n");
    SearchSpec[] specs = SearchUtilities.getCommonSpecs();
    for(int i=0; i<specs.length; i++) {
      String searchEngineName = specs[i].getName();
      out.println("<INPUT TYPE=\"RADIO\" " +
                  "NAME=\"searchEngine\" " +
                  "VALUE=\"" + searchEngineName + "\">\n");
      out.println(searchEngineName + "<BR>\n");
    }
    out.println
      ("<BR>  <INPUT TYPE=\"SUBMIT\">\n" +
       "</FORM>\n" +
       "</CENTER></BODY></HTML>");
  }
}
```

GENERATING THE SERVER RESPONSE: HTTP RESPONSE HEADERS

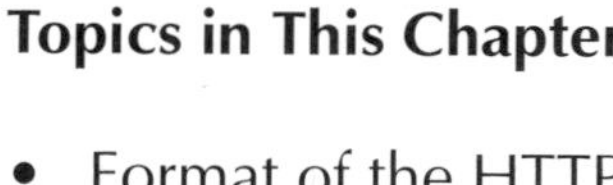

Topics in This Chapter

- Format of the HTTP response
- Setting response headers
- Understanding what response headers are good for
- Building Excel spread sheets
- Generating JPEG images dynamically
- Sending incremental updates to the browser

Chapter 7

As discussed in the previous chapter, a response from a Web server normally consists of a status line, one or more response headers (one of which must be `Content-Type`), a blank line, and the document. To get the most out of your servlets, you need to know how to use the status line and response headers effectively, not just how to generate the document.

Setting the HTTP response headers often goes hand in hand with setting the status codes in the status line, as discussed in the previous chapter. For example, all the "document moved" status codes (300 through 307) have an accompanying `Location` header, and a 401 (`Unauthorized`) code always includes an accompanying `WWW-Authenticate` header. However, specifying headers can also play a useful role even when no unusual status code is set. Response headers can be used to specify cookies, to supply the page modification date (for client-side caching), to instruct the browser to reload the page after a designated interval, to give the file size so that persistent HTTP connections can be used, to designate the type of document being generated, and to perform many other tasks. This chapter shows how to generate response headers, explains what the various headers are used for, and gives several examples.

7.1 Setting Response Headers from Servlets

The most general way to specify headers is to use the `setHeader` method of `HttpServletResponse`. This method takes two strings: the header name and the header value. As with setting status codes, you must specify headers *before* returning the actual document.

- **`setHeader(String headerName, String headerValue)`**
  This method sets the response header with the designated name to the given value.

In addition to the general-purpose `setHeader` method, `HttpServletResponse` also has two specialized methods to set headers that contain dates and integers:

- **`setDateHeader(String header, long milliseconds)`**
  This method saves you the trouble of translating a Java date in milliseconds since 1970 (as returned by `System.currentTimeMillis`, `Date.getTime`, or `Calendar.getTimeInMillis`) into a GMT time string.
- **`setIntHeader(String header, int headerValue)`**
  This method spares you the minor inconvenience of converting an `int` to a `String` before inserting it into a header.

HTTP allows multiple occurrences of the same header name, and you sometimes want to add a new header rather than replace any existing header with the same name. For example, it is quite common to have multiple `Accept` and `Set-Cookie` headers that specify different supported MIME types and different cookies, respectively. The methods `setHeader`, `setDateHeader`, and `setIntHeader` *replace* any existing headers of the same name, whereas `addHeader`, `addDateHeader`, and `addIntHeader` *add* a header regardless of whether a header of that name already exists. If it matters to you whether a specific header has already been set, use `containsHeader` to check.

Finally, `HttpServletResponse` also supplies a number of convenience methods for specifying common headers. These methods are summarized as follows.

- **`setContentType(String mimeType)`**
  This method sets the `Content-Type` header and is used by the majority of servlets.

- **`setContentLength(int length)`**
  This method sets the `Content-Length` header, which is useful if the browser supports persistent (keep-alive) HTTP connections.
- **`addCookie(Cookie c)`**
  This method inserts a cookie into the `Set-Cookie` header. There is no corresponding `setCookie` method, since it is normal to have multiple `Set-Cookie` lines. See Chapter 8 (Handling Cookies) for a discussion of cookies.
- **`sendRedirect(String address)`**
  As discussed in the previous chapter, the `sendRedirect` method sets the `Location` header as well as setting the status code to 302. See Sections 6.3 (A Servlet That Redirects Users to Browser-Specific Pages) and 6.4 (A Front End to Various Search Engines) for examples.

7.2 Understanding HTTP 1.1 Response Headers

Following is a summary of the most useful HTTP 1.1 response headers. A good understanding of these headers can increase the effectiveness of your servlets, so you should at least skim the descriptions to see what options are at your disposal. You can come back for details when you are ready to use the capabilities.

These headers are a superset of those permitted in HTTP 1.0. The official HTTP 1.1 specification is given in RFC 2616. The RFCs are online in various places; your best bet is to start at http://www.rfc-editor.org/ to get a current list of the archive sites. Header names are not case sensitive but are traditionally written with the first letter of each word capitalized.

Be cautious in writing servlets whose behavior depends on response headers that are available only in HTTP 1.1, especially if your servlet needs to run on the WWW "at large" rather than on an intranet—some older browsers support only HTTP 1.0. It is best to explicitly check the HTTP version with `request.getRequestProtocol` before using HTTP-1.1-specific headers.

Allow

The `Allow` header specifies the request methods (`GET`, `POST`, etc.) that the server supports. It is required for 405 (`Method Not Allowed`) responses. The default `service` method of servlets automatically generates this header for `OPTIONS` requests.

Cache-Control

This useful header tells the browser or other client the circumstances in which the response document can safely be cached. It has the following possible values.

- **`public`.** Document is cacheable, even if normal rules (e.g., for password-protected pages) indicate that it shouldn't be.
- **`private`.** Document is for a single user and can only be stored in private (nonshared) caches.
- **`no-cache`.** Document should never be cached (i.e., used to satisfy a later request). The server can also specify "`no-cache="header1,header2,...,headerN"`" to stipulate the headers that should be omitted if a cached response is later used. Browsers normally do not cache documents that were retrieved by requests that include form data. However, if a servlet generates different content for different requests even when the requests contain no form data, it is critical to tell the browser not to cache the response. Since older browsers use the `Pragma` header for this purpose, the typical servlet approach is to set *both* headers, as in the following example.

  ```
  response.setHeader("Cache-Control", "no-cache");
  response.setHeader("Pragma", "no-cache");
  ```

- **`no-store`.** Document should never be cached and should not even be stored in a temporary location on disk. This header is intended to prevent inadvertent copies of sensitive information.
- **`must-revalidate`.** Client must revalidate document with original server (not just intermediate proxies) each time it is used.
- **`proxy-revalidate`.** This is the same as `must-revalidate`, except that it applies only to shared caches.
- **`max-age=xxx`.** Document should be considered stale after *xxx* seconds. This is a convenient alternative to the `Expires` header but only works with HTTP 1.1 clients. If both `max-age` and `Expires` are present in the response, the `max-age` value takes precedence.
- **`s-max-age=xxx`.** Shared caches should consider the document stale after *xxx* seconds.

The `Cache-Control` header is new in HTTP 1.1.

Connection

A value of `close` for this response header instructs the browser not to use persistent HTTP connections. Technically, persistent connections are the default when the client supports HTTP 1.1 and does *not* specify a

`Connection: close` request header (or when an HTTP 1.0 client specifies `Connection: keep-alive`). However, since persistent connections require a `Content-Length` response header, there is no reason for a servlet to explicitly use the `Connection` header. Just omit the `Content-Length` header if you aren't using persistent connections.

Content-Disposition

The `Content-Disposition` header lets you request that the browser ask the user to save the response to disk in a file of the given name. It is used as follows:

```
Content-Disposition: attachment; filename=some-file-name
```

This header is particularly useful when you send the client non-HTML responses (e.g., Excel spreadsheets as in Section 7.3 or JPEG images as in Section 7.5). `Content-Disposition` was not part of the original HTTP specification; it was defined later in RFC 2183. Recall that you can download RFCs by going to http://rfc-editor.org/ and following the instructions.

Content-Encoding

This header indicates the way in which the page was encoded during transmission. The browser should reverse the encoding before deciding what to do with the document. Compressing the document with gzip can result in huge savings in transmission time; for an example, see Section 5.4 (Sending Compressed Web Pages).

Content-Language

The `Content-Language` header signifies the language in which the document is written. The value of the header should be one of the standard language codes such as `en`, `en-us`, `da`, etc. See RFC 1766 for details on language codes (you can access RFCs online at one of the archive sites listed at http://www.rfc-editor.org/).

Content-Length

This header indicates the number of bytes in the response. This information is needed only if the browser is using a persistent (keep-alive) HTTP connection. See the `Connection` header for determining when the browser supports persistent connections. If you want your servlet to take advantage of persistent connections when the browser supports them, your servlet should write the document into a `ByteArrayOutputStream`, look up its size when done, put that into the `Content-Length` field with `response.setContentLength`, then send the content by `byteArrayStream.writeTo(response.getOutputStream())`.

Content-Type

The `Content-Type` header gives the MIME (Multipurpose Internet Mail Extension) type of the response document. Setting this header is so common that there is a special method in `HttpServletResponse` for it: `setContentType`. MIME types are of the form *`maintype/subtype`* for officially registered types and of the form *`maintype/x-subtype`* for unregistered types. Most servlets specify `text/html`; they can, however, specify other types instead. This is important partly because servlets directly generate other MIME types (as in the Excel and JPEG examples of this chapter), but also partly because servlets are used as the glue to connect other applications to the Web. OK, so you have Adobe Acrobat to generate PDF, GhostScript to generate PostScript, and a database application to search indexed MP3 files. But you still need a servlet to answer the HTTP request, invoke the helper application, and set the `Content-Type` header, even though the servlet probably simply passes the output of the helper application directly to the client.

In addition to a basic MIME type, the `Content-Type` header can also designate a specific character encoding. If this is not specified, the default is `ISO-8859_1` (Latin). For example, the following instructs the browser to interpret the document as HTML in the `Shift_JIS` (standard Japanese) character set.

```
response.setContentType("text/html; charset=Shift_JIS");
```

Table 7.1 lists some of the most common MIME types used by servlets. RFC 1521 and RFC 1522 list more of the common MIME types (again, see http://www.rfc-editor.org/ for a list of RFC archive sites). However, new MIME types are registered all the time, so a dynamic list is a better place to look. The officially registered types are listed at http://www.isi.edu/in-notes/iana/assignments/media-types/media-types. For common unregistered types, http://www.ltsw.se/knbase/internet/mime.htp is a good source.

Table 7.1 Common MIME Types

Type	Meaning
application/msword	Microsoft Word document
application/octet-stream	Unrecognized or binary data
application/pdf	Acrobat (.pdf) file
application/postscript	PostScript file

Table 7.1 Common MIME Types *(continued)*

Type	Meaning
application/vnd.lotus-notes	Lotus Notes file
application/vnd.ms-excel	Excel spreadsheet
application/vnd.ms-powerpoint	PowerPoint presentation
application/x-gzip	Gzip archive
application/x-java-archive	JAR file
application/x-java-serialized-object	Serialized Java object
application/x-java-vm	Java bytecode (`.class`) file
application/zip	Zip archive
audio/basic	Sound file in .au or .snd format
audio/midi	MIDI sound file
audio/x-aiff	AIFF sound file
audio/x-wav	Microsoft Windows sound file
image/gif	GIF image
image/jpeg	JPEG image
image/png	PNG image
image/tiff	TIFF image
image/x-xbitmap	X Windows bitmap image
text/css	HTML cascading style sheet
text/html	HTML document
text/plain	Plain text
text/xml	XML
video/mpeg	MPEG video clip
video/quicktime	QuickTime video clip

Expires

This header stipulates the time at which the content should be considered out-of-date and thus no longer be cached. A servlet might use this header for a document that changes relatively frequently, to prevent the browser from displaying a stale cached value. Furthermore, since some older browsers support `Pragma` unreliably (and `Cache-Control` not at all), an `Expires` header with a date in the past is often used to prevent browser caching. However, some browsers ignore dates before January 1, 1980, so do not use 0 as the value of the `Expires` header.

For example, the following would instruct the browser not to cache the document for more than 10 minutes.

```
long currentTime = System.currentTimeMillis();
long tenMinutes = 10*60*1000; // In milliseconds
response.setDateHeader("Expires",
                       currentTime + tenMinutes);
```

Also see the `max-age` value of the `Cache-Control` header.

Last-Modified

This very useful header indicates when the document was last changed. The client can then cache the document and supply a date by an `If-Modified-Since` request header in later requests. This request is treated as a conditional `GET`, with the document being returned only if the `Last-Modified` date is later than the one specified for `If-Modified-Since`. Otherwise, a 304 (`Not Modified`) status line is returned, and the client uses the cached document. If you set this header explicitly, use the `setDateHeader` method to save yourself the bother of formatting GMT date strings. However, in most cases you simply implement the `getLastModified` method (see the lottery number servlet of Section 3.6, "The Servlet Life Cycle") and let the standard `service` method handle `If-Modified-Since` requests.

Location

This header, which should be included with all responses that have a status code in the 300s, notifies the browser of the document address. The browser automatically reconnects to this location and retrieves the new document. This header is usually set indirectly, along with a 302 status code, by the `sendRedirect` method of `HttpServletResponse`. See Sections 6.3 (A Servlet That Redirects Users to Browser-Specific Pages) and 6.4 (A Front End to Various Search Engines) for examples.

Pragma

Supplying this header with a value of `no-cache` instructs HTTP 1.0 clients not to cache the document. However, support for this header was inconsistent with HTTP 1.0 browsers, so `Expires` with a date in the past is often used instead. In HTTP 1.1, `Cache-Control: no-cache` is a more reliable replacement.

Refresh

This header indicates how soon (in seconds) the browser should ask for an updated page. For example, to tell the browser to ask for a new copy in 30 seconds, you would specify a value of 30 with

```
response.setIntHeader("Refresh", 30);
```

Note that `Refresh` does not stipulate continual updates; it just specifies when the *next* update should be. So, you have to continue to supply `Refresh` in all subsequent responses. This header is extremely useful because it lets servlets return partial results quickly while still letting the client see the complete results at a later time. For an example, see Section 7.4 (Persistent Servlet State and Auto-Reloading Pages).

Instead of having the browser just reload the current page, you can specify the page to load. You do this by supplying a semicolon and a URL after the refresh time. For example, to tell the browser to go to **http://*host*/*path*** after 5 seconds, you would do the following.

```
response.setHeader("Refresh", "5; URL=http://host/path/");
```

This setting is useful for "splash screens" on which an introductory image or message is displayed briefly before the real page is loaded.

Note that this header is commonly set indirectly by putting

```
<META HTTP-EQUIV="Refresh"
      CONTENT="5; URL=http://host/path/">
```

in the `HEAD` section of the HTML page, rather than as an explicit header from the server. That usage came about because automatic reloading or forwarding is something often desired by authors of static HTML pages. For servlets, however, setting the header directly is easier and clearer.

This header is not officially part of HTTP 1.1 but is an extension supported by both Netscape and Internet Explorer.

Retry-After

This header can be used in conjunction with a 503 (`Service Unavailable`) response to tell the client how soon it can repeat its request.

Set-Cookie

The `Set-Cookie` header specifies a cookie associated with the page. Each cookie requires a separate `Set-Cookie` header. Servlets should not use `response.setHeader("Set-Cookie", ...)` but instead should use the special-purpose `addCookie` method of `HttpServletResponse`. For details, see Chapter 8 (Handling Cookies). Technically, `Set-Cookie` is not part of HTTP 1.1. It was originally a Netscape extension but is now widely supported, including in both Netscape and Internet Explorer.

WWW-Authenticate

This header is always included with a 401 (`Unauthorized`) status code. It tells the browser what authorization type (`BASIC` or `DIGEST`) and realm the client should supply in its `Authorization` header. For examples of the use of `WWW-Authenticate` and a discussion of the various security mechanisms available to servlets and JSP pages, see the chapters on Web application security in Volume 2 of this book.

7.3 Building Excel Spreadsheets

Although servlets usually generate HTML output, they are not required to do so. HTTP is fundamental to servlets; HTML is not. Now, it is sometimes useful to generate Microsoft Excel content so that users can save the results in a report and so that you can make use of the built-in formula support in Excel. Excel accepts input in at least three distinct formats: tab-separated data, HTML tables, and a native binary format.

In this section, we illustrate the use of tab-separated data to generate spreadsheets. In Chapter 12 (Controlling the Structure of Generated Servlets: The JSP page Directive), we show how to build Excel spreadsheets by using HTML-table format. No matter the format, the key is to use the `Content-Type` response header to tell the client that you are sending a spreadsheet. You use the shorthand `setContentType` method to set the `Content-Type` header, and the MIME type for Excel spreadsheets is `application/vnd.ms-excel`. So, to generate Excel spreadsheets, just do:

```
response.setContentType("application/vnd.ms-excel");
PrintWriter out = response.getWriter();
```

Then, simply print some entries with tabs (`\t` in Java strings) in between. That's it: no `DOCTYPE`, no `HEAD`, no `BODY`: those are all HTML-specific things.

Listing 7.1 presents a simple servlet that builds an Excel spreadsheet that compares apples and oranges. Note that =SUM(*col*:*col*) sums a range of columns in Excel. Figure 7–1 shows the results.

Listing 7.1 AppleAndOranges.java

```
package coreservlets;

import java.io.*;
import javax.servlet.*;
import javax.servlet.http.*;

/** Servlet that creates Excel spreadsheet comparing
 *  apples and oranges.
 */

public class ApplesAndOranges extends HttpServlet {
  public void doGet(HttpServletRequest request,
                    HttpServletResponse response)
      throws ServletException, IOException {
      response.setContentType("application/vnd.ms-excel");
      PrintWriter out = response.getWriter();
      out.println("\tQ1\tQ2\tQ3\tQ4\tTotal");
      out.println("Apples\t78\t87\t92\t29\t=SUM(B2:E2)");
      out.println("Oranges\t77\t86\t93\t30\t=SUM(B3:E3)");
  }
}
```

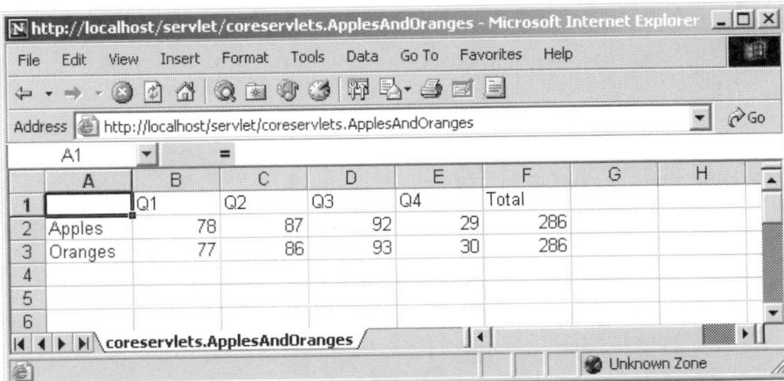

Figure 7–1 Result of the ApplesAndOranges servlet in Internet Explorer on a system that has Microsoft Office installed.

7.4 Persistent Servlet State and Auto-Reloading Pages

Suppose your servlet or JSP page performs a calculation that takes a long time to complete: say, 20 seconds or more. In such a case, it is not reasonable to complete the computation and then send the results to the client—by that time the client may have given up and left the page or, worse, have hit the Reload button and restarted the process. To deal with requests that take a long time to process (or whose results periodically change), you need the following capabilities:

- **A way to store data between requests.** For data that is not specific to any one client, store it in a field (instance variable) of the servlet. For data that is specific to a user, store it in the `HttpSession` object (see Chapter 9, "Session Tracking"). For data that needs to be available to other servlets or JSP pages, store it in the `ServletContext` (see the section on sharing data in Chapter 14, "Using JavaBeans Components in JSP Documents").
- **A way to keep computations running after the response is sent to the user.** This task is simple: just start a `Thread`. The thread started by the system to answer requests automatically finishes when the response is finished, but other threads can keep running. The only subtlety: set the thread priority to a low value so that you do not slow down the server.
- **A way to get the updated results to the browser when they are ready.** Unfortunately, because browsers do not maintain an open connection to the server, there is no easy way for the server to proactively send the new results to the browser. Instead, the browser needs to be told to ask for updates. That is the purpose of the `Refresh` response header.

Finding Prime Numbers for Use with Public Key Cryptography

Here is an example that lets you ask for a list of some large, randomly chosen prime numbers. As you are probably aware, access to large prime numbers is the key to most public-key cryptography systems, the kind of encryption systems used on the Web (e.g., for SSL and X509 certificates). Finding prime numbers may take some time for very large numbers (e.g., 100 digits), so the servlet immediately returns initial results but then keeps calculating, using a low-priority thread so that it won't degrade Web server performance. If the calculations are not complete, the servlet instructs the browser to ask for a new page in a few seconds by sending it a `Refresh` header.

In addition to illustrating the value of HTTP response headers (`Refresh` in this case), this example shows two other valuable servlet capabilities. First, it shows that the same servlet can handle multiple simultaneous connections, each with its own thread. So, while one thread is finishing a calculation for one client, another client can connect and still see partial results.

Second, this example shows how easy it is for servlets to maintain state between requests, something that is cumbersome to implement in most competing technologies (even .NET, which is perhaps the best of the alternatives). Only a single instance of the servlet is created, and each request simply results in a new thread calling the servlet's `service` method (which calls `doGet` or `doPost`). So, shared data simply has to be placed in a regular instance variable (field) of the servlet. Thus, the servlet can access the appropriate ongoing calculation when the browser reloads the page and can keep a list of the *N* most recently requested results, returning them immediately if a new request specifies the same parameters as a recent one. Of course, the normal rules that require authors to synchronize multithreaded access to shared data still apply to servlets. Servlets can also store persistent data in the `ServletContext` object that is available through the `getServletContext` method. `ServletContext` has `setAttribute` and `getAttribute` methods that let you store arbitrary data associated with specified keys. The difference between storing data in instance variables and storing it in the `ServletContext` is that the `ServletContext` is shared by all servlets and JSP pages in the Web application.

Listing 7.2 shows the main servlet class. First, it receives a request that specifies two parameters: `numPrimes` and `numDigits`. These values are normally collected from the user and sent to the servlet by means of a simple HTML form. Listing 7.3 shows the source code and Figure 7–2 shows the result. Next, these parameters are converted to integers by means of a simple utility that uses `Integer.parseInt` (see Listing 7.6). These values are then matched by the `findPrimeList` method to an `ArrayList` of recent or ongoing calculations to see if a previous computation corresponds to the same two values. If so, that previous value (of type `PrimeList`) is used; otherwise, a new `PrimeList` is created and stored in the ongoing-calculations `Vector`, potentially displacing the oldest previous list. Next, that `PrimeList` is checked to determine whether it has finished finding all of its primes. If not, the client is sent a `Refresh` header to tell it to come back in five seconds for updated results. Either way, a bulleted list of the current values is returned to the client. See Figures 7–3 through 7–5 for representative results.

Listing 7.2 PrimeNumberServlet.java

```
package coreservlets;

import java.io.*;
import javax.servlet.*;
import javax.servlet.http.*;
import java.util.*;

/** Servlet that processes a request to generate n
 *  prime numbers, each with at least m digits.
 *  It performs the calculations in a low-priority background
 *  thread, returning only the results it has found so far.
 *  If these results are not complete, it sends a Refresh
 *  header instructing the browser to ask for new results a
 *  little while later. It also maintains a list of a
 *  small number of previously calculated prime lists
 *  to return immediately to anyone who supplies the
 *  same n and m as a recently completed computation.
 */

public class PrimeNumberServlet extends HttpServlet {
  private ArrayList primeListCollection = new ArrayList();
  private int maxPrimeLists = 30;

  public void doGet(HttpServletRequest request,
                    HttpServletResponse response)
      throws ServletException, IOException {
    int numPrimes =
      ServletUtilities.getIntParameter(request,
                                       "numPrimes", 50);
    int numDigits =
      ServletUtilities.getIntParameter(request,
                                       "numDigits", 120);
    PrimeList primeList =
      findPrimeList(primeListCollection, numPrimes, numDigits);
    if (primeList == null) {
      primeList = new PrimeList(numPrimes, numDigits, true);
      // Multiple servlet request threads share the instance
      // variables (fields) of PrimeNumbers. So
      // synchronize all access to servlet fields.
      synchronized(primeListCollection) {
        if (primeListCollection.size() >= maxPrimeLists)
          primeListCollection.remove(0);
        primeListCollection.add(primeList);
      }
    }
    ArrayList currentPrimes = primeList.getPrimes();
    int numCurrentPrimes = currentPrimes.size();
    int numPrimesRemaining = (numPrimes - numCurrentPrimes);
```

Listing 7.2 PrimeNumberServlet.java *(continued)*

```
    boolean isLastResult = (numPrimesRemaining == 0);
    if (!isLastResult) {
      response.setIntHeader("Refresh", 5);
    }
    response.setContentType("text/html");
    PrintWriter out = response.getWriter();
    String title = "Some " + numDigits + "-Digit Prime Numbers";
    out.println(ServletUtilities.headWithTitle(title) +
                "<BODY BGCOLOR=\"#FDF5E6\">\n" +
                "<H2 ALIGN=CENTER>" + title + "</H2>\n" +
                "<H3>Primes found with " + numDigits +
                " or more digits: " + numCurrentPrimes +
                ".</H3>");
    if (isLastResult)
      out.println("<B>Done searching.</B>");
    else
      out.println("<B>Still looking for " + numPrimesRemaining +
                  " more<BLINK>...</BLINK></B>");
    out.println("<OL>");
    for(int i=0; i<numCurrentPrimes; i++) {
      out.println("  <LI>" + currentPrimes.get(i));
    }
    out.println("</OL>");
    out.println("</BODY></HTML>");
  }

  // See if there is an existing ongoing or completed
  // calculation with the same number of primes and number
  // of digits per prime. If so, return those results instead
  // of starting a new background thread. Keep this list
  // small so that the Web server doesn't use too much memory.
  // Synchronize access to the list since there may be
  // multiple simultaneous requests.

  private PrimeList findPrimeList(ArrayList primeListCollection,
                                  int numPrimes,
                                  int numDigits) {
      for(int i=0; i<primeListCollection.size(); i++) {
        PrimeList primes =
          (PrimeList)primeListCollection.get(i);
    synchronized(primeListCollection) {
        if ((numPrimes == primes.numPrimes()) &&
            (numDigits == primes.numDigits()))
          return(primes);
      }
      return(null);
    }
  }
}
```

Listing 7.3 PrimeNumbers.html

```
<!DOCTYPE HTML PUBLIC "-//W3C//DTD HTML 4.0 Transitional//EN">
<HTML>
<HEAD>
  <TITLE>Finding Large Prime Numbers</TITLE>
</HEAD>
<BODY BGCOLOR="#FDF5E6">
<CENTER>
<H2>Finding Large Prime Numbers</H2>
<BR><BR>
<FORM ACTION="/servlet/coreservlets.PrimeNumberServlet">
  <B>Number of primes to calculate:</B>
  <INPUT TYPE="TEXT" NAME="numPrimes" VALUE=25 SIZE=4><BR>
  <B>Number of digits:</B>
  <INPUT TYPE="TEXT" NAME="numDigits" VALUE=150 SIZE=3><BR>
  <INPUT TYPE="SUBMIT" VALUE="Start Calculating">
</FORM>
</CENTER>
</BODY></HTML>
```

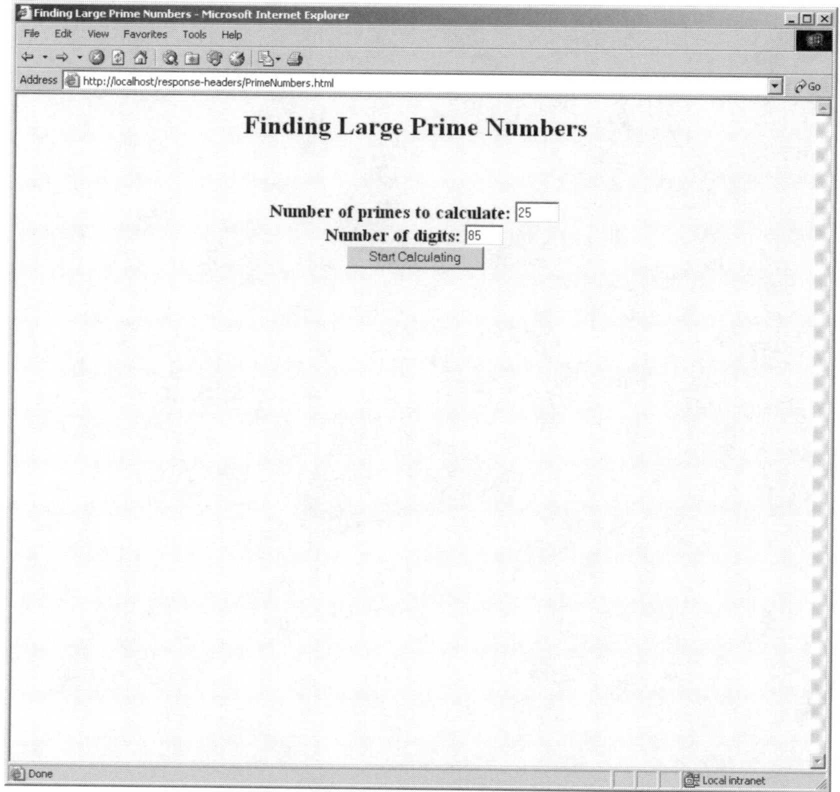

Figure 7–2 Front end to the prime-number-generation servlet.

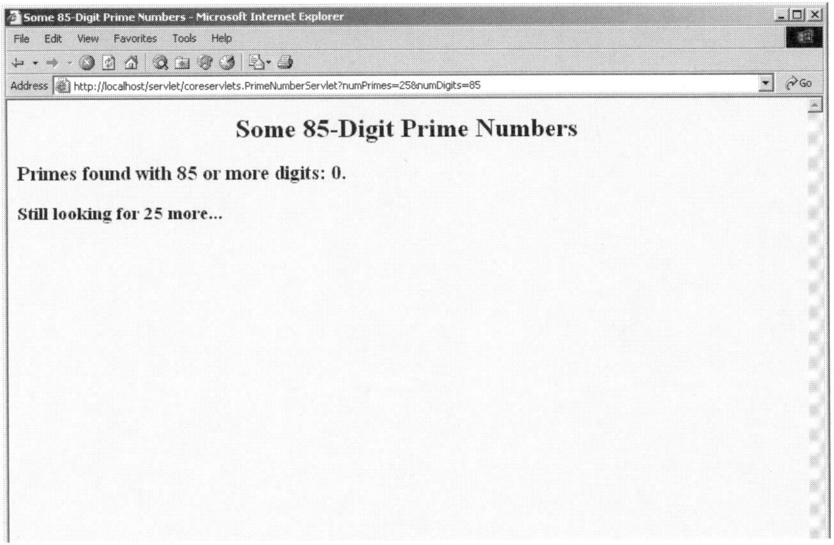

Figure 7–3 Initial results of the prime-number-generation servlet. A quick result is sent to the browser, along with instructions (in the `Refresh` header) to reconnect for an update in five seconds.

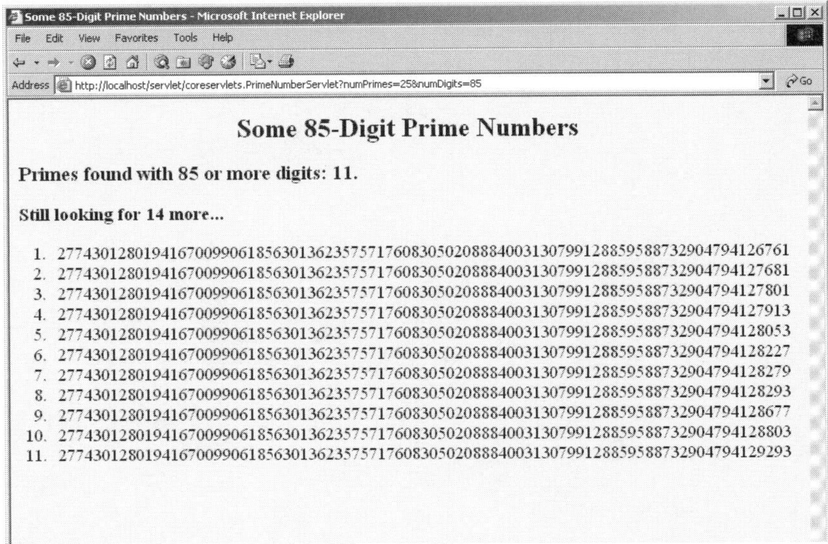

Figure 7–4 Intermediate results of the prime-number-generation servlet. The servlet stores the previous computations and matches the current request with the stored values by comparing the request parameters (the size and number of primes to compute). Other clients that request the same parameters see the same already computed results.

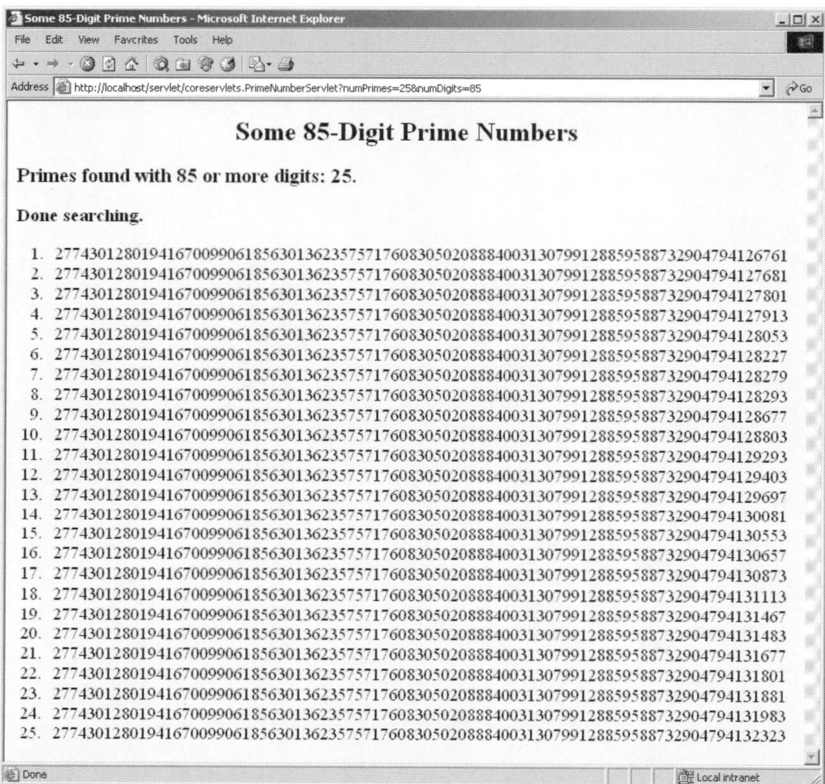

Figure 7–5 Final results of the prime-number-generation servlet. Since the servlet has computed as many primes as the user requested, no `Refresh` header is sent to the browser and the page is no longer reloaded automatically.

Listings 7.4 (**PrimeList.java**) and 7.5 (**Primes.java**) present auxiliary code used by the servlet. **PrimeList.java** handles the background thread for the creation of a list of primes for a specific set of values. The point of this example is twofold: that servlets can maintain data between requests by storing it in instance variables (or the `ServletContext`) and that the servlet can use the `Refresh` header to instruct the browser to return for updates. However, if you care about the gory details of prime-number generation, **Primes.java** contains the low-level algorithms for choosing a random number of a specified length and then finding a prime at or above that value. It uses built-in methods in the `BigInteger` class; the algorithm for determining if the number is prime is a probabilistic one and thus has a chance of being mistaken. However, the probability of being wrong can be specified, and we use an error value of 100. Assuming that the algorithm used in most Java implementations is the

Miller-Rabin test, the likelihood of falsely reporting a composite (i.e., non-prime) number as prime is provably less than 2^{100}. This is almost certainly smaller than the likelihood of a hardware error or random radiation causing an incorrect response in a deterministic algorithm, and thus the algorithm can be considered deterministic.

Listing 7.4 PrimeList.java

```
package coreservlets;

import java.util.*;
import java.math.BigInteger;

/** Creates an ArrayList of large prime numbers, usually in
 *  a low-priority background thread. Provides a few small
 *  thread-safe access methods.
 */

public class PrimeList implements Runnable {
  private ArrayList primesFound;
  private int numPrimes, numDigits;

  /** Finds numPrimes prime numbers, each of which is
   *  numDigits long or longer. You can set it to return
   *  only when done, or have it return immediately,
   *  and you can later poll it to see how far it
   *  has gotten.
   */

  public PrimeList(int numPrimes, int numDigits,
                   boolean runInBackground) {
    primesFound = new ArrayList(numPrimes);
    this.numPrimes = numPrimes;
    this.numDigits = numDigits;
    if (runInBackground) {
      Thread t = new Thread(this);
      // Use low priority so you don't slow down server.
      t.setPriority(Thread.MIN_PRIORITY);
      t.start();
    } else {
      run();
    }
  }
```

Listing 7.4 PrimeList.java *(continued)*

```
  public void run() {
    BigInteger start = Primes.random(numDigits);
    for(int i=0; i<numPrimes; i++) {
      start = Primes.nextPrime(start);
      synchronized(this) {
        primesFound.add(start);
      }
    }
  }

  public synchronized boolean isDone() {
    return(primesFound.size() == numPrimes);
  }

  public synchronized ArrayList getPrimes() {
    if (isDone())
      return(primesFound);
    else
      return((ArrayList)primesFound.clone());
  }

  public int numDigits() {
    return(numDigits);
  }

  public int numPrimes() {
    return(numPrimes);
  }

  public synchronized int numCalculatedPrimes() {
    return(primesFound.size());
  }
}
```

Listing 7.5 Primes.java

```
package coreservlets;

import java.math.BigInteger;

/** A few utilities to generate a large random BigInteger,
 *  and find the next prime number above a given BigInteger.
 */

public class Primes {
  // Note that BigInteger.ZERO and BigInteger.ONE are
  // unavailable in JDK 1.1.
  private static final BigInteger ZERO = BigInteger.ZERO;
  private static final BigInteger ONE = BigInteger.ONE;
  private static final BigInteger TWO = new BigInteger("2");

  // Likelihood of false prime is less than 1/2^ERR_VAL.
  // Presumably BigInteger uses the Miller-Rabin test or
  // equivalent, and thus is NOT fooled by Carmichael numbers.
  // See section 33.8 of Cormen et al.'s Introduction to
  // Algorithms for details.
  private static final int ERR_VAL = 100;

  public static BigInteger nextPrime(BigInteger start) {
    if (isEven(start))
      start = start.add(ONE);
    else
      start = start.add(TWO);
    if (start.isProbablePrime(ERR_VAL))
      return(start);
    else
      return(nextPrime(start));
  }

  private static boolean isEven(BigInteger n) {
    return(n.mod(TWO).equals(ZERO));
  }

  private static StringBuffer[] digits =
    { new StringBuffer("0"), new StringBuffer("1"),
      new StringBuffer("2"), new StringBuffer("3"),
      new StringBuffer("4"), new StringBuffer("5"),
      new StringBuffer("6"), new StringBuffer("7"),
      new StringBuffer("8"), new StringBuffer("9") };
```

Listing 7.5 Primes.java *(continued)*

```
  private static StringBuffer randomDigit(boolean isZeroOK) {
    int index;
    if (isZeroOK) {
      index = (int)Math.floor(Math.random() * 10);
    } else {
      index = 1 + (int)Math.floor(Math.random() * 9);
    }
    return(digits[index]);
  }

  /** Create a random big integer where every digit is
   *  selected randomly (except that the first digit
   *  cannot be a zero).
   */

  public static BigInteger random(int numDigits) {
    StringBuffer s = new StringBuffer("");
    for(int i=0; i<numDigits; i++) {
      if (i == 0) {
        // First digit must be non-zero.
        s.append(randomDigit(false));
      } else {
        s.append(randomDigit(true));
      }
    }
    return(new BigInteger(s.toString()));
  }

  /** Simple command-line program to test. Enter number
   *  of digits, and the program picks a random number of that
   *  length and then prints the first 50 prime numbers
   *  above that.
   */

  public static void main(String[] args) {
    int numDigits;
    try {
      numDigits = Integer.parseInt(args[0]);
    } catch (Exception e) { // No args or illegal arg.
      numDigits = 150;
    }
    BigInteger start = random(numDigits);
    for(int i=0; i<50; i++) {
      start = nextPrime(start);
      System.out.println("Prime " + i + " = " + start);
    }
  }
}
```

Listing 7.6 ServletUtilities.java (Excerpt)

```
package coreservlets;

import javax.servlet.*;
import javax.servlet.http.*;

/** Some simple time savers. Note that most are static methods. */

public class ServletUtilities {
  // ...

  /** Read a parameter with the specified name, convert it
   *  to an int, and return it. Return the designated default
   *  value if the parameter doesn't exist or if it is an
   *  illegal integer format.
   */

  public static int getIntParameter(HttpServletRequest request,
                                    String paramName,
                                    int defaultValue) {
    String paramString = request.getParameter(paramName);
    int paramValue;
    try {
      paramValue = Integer.parseInt(paramString);
    } catch(NumberFormatException nfe) { // null or bad format
      paramValue = defaultValue;
    }
    return(paramValue);
  }
}
```

7.5 Using Servlets to Generate JPEG Images

Although servlets often generate HTML output, they certainly don't *always* do so. For example, Section 7.3 (Building Excel Spreadsheets) shows a servlet that builds Excel spreadsheets and returns them to the client. Here, we show you how to generate JPEG images.

First, let us summarize the two main steps servlets have to perform to build multimedia content.

1. **Inform the browser of the content type they are sending.** To accomplish this task, servlets set the `Content-Type` response header by using the `setContentType` method of `HttpServletResponse`.
2. **Send the output in the appropriate format.** This format varies among document types, of course, but in most cases you send binary data, not strings as you do with HTML documents. Consequently, servlets will usually get the raw output stream by using the `getOutputStream` method, rather than getting a `PrintWriter` by using `getWriter`.

Putting these two steps together, servlets that generate non-HTML content usually have a section of their `doGet` or `doPost` method that looks like this:

```
response.setContentType("type/subtype");
OutputStream out = response.getOutputStream();
```

Those are the two general steps required to build non-HTML content. Next, let's look at the specific steps required to generate JPEG images.

1. **Create a `BufferedImage`.**
   You create a `java.awt.image.BufferedImage` object by calling the `BufferedImage` constructor with a width, a height, and an image representation type as defined by one of the constants in the `BufferedImage` class. The representation type is not important, since we do not manipulate the bits of the `BufferedImage` directly and since most types yield identical results when converted to JPEG. We use `TYPE_INT_RGB`. Putting this all together, here is the normal process:

```
int width = ...;
int height = ...;
BufferedImage image =
  new BufferedImage(width, height,
                    BufferedImage.TYPE_INT_RGB);
```

2. **Draw into the `BufferedImage`.**
   You accomplish this task by calling the image's `getGraphics` method, casting the resultant `Graphics` object to `Graphics2D`, then making use of Java 2D's rich set of drawing operations, coordinate transformations, font settings, and fill patterns to perform the drawing. Here is a simple example.

```
Graphics2D g2d = (Graphics2D)image.getGraphics();
g2d.setXxx(...);
g2d.fill(someShape);
g2d.draw(someShape);
```

3. **Set the `Content-Type` response header.**
   As already discussed, you use the `setContentType` method of `HttpServletResponse` for this task. The MIME type for JPEG images is `image/jpeg`. Thus, the code is as follows.

   ```
   response.setContentType("image/jpeg");
   ```

4. **Get an output stream.**
   As discussed previously, if you are sending binary data, you should call the `getOutputStream` method of `HttpServletResponse` rather than the `getWriter` method. For instance:

   ```
   OutputStream out = response.getOutputStream();
   ```

5. **Send the `BufferedImage` in JPEG format to the output stream.**
   Before JDK 1.4, accomplishing this task yourself required quite a bit of work. So, most people used a third-party utility for this purpose. In JDK 1.4 and later, however, the `ImageIO` class greatly simplifies this task. If you are using an application server that supports J2EE 1.4 (which includes servlets 2.4 and JSP 2.0), you are guaranteed to have JDK 1.4 or later. However, standalone servers are not absolutely required to use JDK 1.4, so be aware that this code depends on the Java version. When you use the `ImageIO` class, you just pass a `BufferedImage`, an image format type (`"jpg"`, `"png"`, etc.—call `ImageIO.getWriterFormatNames` for a complete list), and either an `OutputStream` or a `File` to the `write` method of `ImageIO`. Except for catching the required `IOException`, that's it! For example:

   ```
   try {
     ImageIO.write(image, "jpg", out);
   } catch(IOException ioe) {
     System.err.println("Error writing JPEG file: " + ioe);
   }
   ```

Listing 7.7 shows a servlet that reads `message`, `fontName`, and `fontSize` parameters and passes them to the `MessageImage` utility (Listing 7.8) to create a JPEG image showing the message in the designated face and size, with a gray, oblique-shadowed version of the message shown behind the main string. If the user presses the Show Font List button, then instead of building an image, the servlet displays a list of font names available on the server.

Listing 7.7 ShadowedText.java

```
package coreservlets;

import java.io.*;
import javax.servlet.*;
import javax.servlet.http.*;
import java.awt.*;

/** Servlet that generates JPEG images representing
 *  a designated message with an oblique-shadowed
 *  version behind it.
 */

public class ShadowedText extends HttpServlet {
  public void doGet(HttpServletRequest request,
                    HttpServletResponse response)
      throws ServletException, IOException {
    String wantsList = request.getParameter("showList");
    if (wantsList != null) {
      showFontList(response);
    } else {
      String message = request.getParameter("message");
      if ((message == null) || (message.length() == 0)) {
        message = "Missing 'message' parameter";
      }
      String fontName = request.getParameter("fontName");
      if ((fontName == null) || (fontName.length() == 0)) {
        fontName = "Serif";
      }
      String fontSizeString = request.getParameter("fontSize");
      int fontSize;
      try {
        fontSize = Integer.parseInt(fontSizeString);
      } catch(NumberFormatException nfe) {
        fontSize = 90;
      }
      response.setContentType("image/jpeg");
      MessageImage.writeJPEG
        (MessageImage.makeMessageImage(message,
                                       fontName,
                                       fontSize),
         response.getOutputStream());
    }
  }
```

Listing 7.7 ShadowedText.java *(continued)*

```
  private void showFontList(HttpServletResponse response)
      throws IOException {
    PrintWriter out = response.getWriter();
    String docType =
      "<!DOCTYPE HTML PUBLIC \"-//W3C//DTD HTML 4.0 " +
      "Transitional//EN\">\n";
    String title = "Fonts Available on Server";
    out.println(docType +
                "<HTML>\n" +
                "<HEAD><TITLE>" + title + "</TITLE></HEAD>\n" +
                "<BODY BGCOLOR=\"#FDF5E6\">\n" +
                "<H1 ALIGN=CENTER>" + title + "</H1>\n" +
                "<UL>");
    String[] fontNames = MessageImage.getFontNames();
    for(int i=0; i<fontNames.length; i++) {
      out.println("  <LI>" + fontNames[i]);
    }
    out.println("</UL>\n" +
                "</BODY></HTML>");
  }
}
```

Listing 7.8 MessageImage.java

```
package coreservlets;

import java.awt.*;
import java.awt.geom.*;
import java.awt.image.*;
import java.io.*;
import javax.imageio.*;

/** Utilities for building images showing shadowed messages.
 *  <P>
 *  Requires JDK 1.4 since it uses the ImageIO class.
 *  JDK 1.4 is standard with J2EE-compliant app servers
 *  with servlets 2.4 and JSP 2.0. However, standalone
 *  servlet/JSP engines require only JDK 1.3 or later, and
 *  version 2.3 of the servlet spec requires only JDK
 *  1.2 or later. So, although most servers run on JDK 1.4,
 *  this code is not necessarily portable across all servers.
 */
```

Listing 7.8 MessageImage.java *(continued)*

```
public class MessageImage {

  /** Creates an Image of a string with an oblique
   *  shadow behind it. Used by the ShadowedText servlet.
   */

  public static BufferedImage makeMessageImage(String message,
                                               String fontName,
                                               int fontSize) {

    Font font = new Font(fontName, Font.PLAIN, fontSize);
    FontMetrics metrics = getFontMetrics(font);
    int messageWidth = metrics.stringWidth(message);
    int baselineX = messageWidth/10;
    int width = messageWidth+2*(baselineX + fontSize);
    int height = fontSize*7/2;
    int baselineY = height*8/10;
    BufferedImage messageImage =
      new BufferedImage(width, height,
                        BufferedImage.TYPE_INT_RGB);
    Graphics2D g2d = (Graphics2D)messageImage.getGraphics();
    g2d.setBackground(Color.white);
    g2d.clearRect(0, 0, width, height);
    g2d.setFont(font);
    g2d.translate(baselineX, baselineY);
    g2d.setPaint(Color.lightGray);
    AffineTransform origTransform = g2d.getTransform();
    g2d.shear(-0.95, 0);
    g2d.scale(1, 3);
    g2d.drawString(message, 0, 0);
    g2d.setTransform(origTransform);
    g2d.setPaint(Color.black);
    g2d.drawString(message, 0, 0);
    return(messageImage);
  }

  public static void writeJPEG(BufferedImage image,
                               OutputStream out) {
    try {
      ImageIO.write(image, "jpg", out);
    } catch(IOException ioe) {
      System.err.println("Error outputting JPEG: " + ioe);
    }
  }
```

Listing 7.8 MessageImage.java *(continued)*

```
  public static void writeJPEG(BufferedImage image,
                               File file) {
    try {
      ImageIO.write(image, "jpg", file);
    } catch(IOException ioe) {
      System.err.println("Error writing JPEG file: " + ioe);
    }
  }

  public static String[] getFontNames() {
    GraphicsEnvironment env =
      GraphicsEnvironment.getLocalGraphicsEnvironment();
    return(env.getAvailableFontFamilyNames());
  }

  /** We need a Graphics object to get a FontMetrics object
   *  (an object that says how big strings are in given fonts).
   *  But, you need an image from which to derive the Graphics
   *  object. Since the size of the "real" image will depend on
   *  how big the string is, we create a very small temporary
   *  image first, get the FontMetrics, figure out how
   *  big the real image should be, then use a real image
   *  of that size.
   */

  private static FontMetrics getFontMetrics(Font font) {
    BufferedImage tempImage =
      new BufferedImage(1, 1, BufferedImage.TYPE_INT_RGB);
    Graphics2D g2d = (Graphics2D)tempImage.getGraphics();
    return(g2d.getFontMetrics(font));
  }
}
```

Listing 7.9 (Figure 7–6) shows an HTML form used as a front end to the servlet. Figures 7–7 through 7–10 show some possible results. Just to simplify experimentation, Listing 7.10 presents an interactive application that lets you specify the message and font name on the command line, outputting the image to a file.

Listing 7.9 ShadowedText.html

```
<!DOCTYPE HTML PUBLIC "-//W3C//DTD HTML 4.0 Transitional//EN">
<HTML>
<HEAD><TITLE>JPEG Generation Service</TITLE></HEAD>
<BODY BGCOLOR="#FDF5E6">
<H1 ALIGN="CENTER">JPEG Generation Service</H1>
Welcome to the <I>free</I> trial edition of our JPEG
generation service. Enter a message, a font name,
and a font size below, then submit the form. You will
be returned a JPEG image showing the message in the
designated font, with an oblique "shadow" of the message
behind it. Once you get an image you are satisfied with,
right-click
on it (or click while holding down the SHIFT key) to save
it to your local disk.
<P>
The server is currently on Windows, so the font name must
be either a standard Java font name (e.g., Serif, SansSerif,
or Monospaced) or a Windows font name (e.g., Arial Black).
Unrecognized font names will revert to Serif. Press the
"Show Font List" button for a complete list.

<FORM ACTION="/servlet/coreservlets.ShadowedText">
  <CENTER>
    Message:
    <INPUT TYPE="TEXT" NAME="message"><BR>
    Font name:
    <INPUT TYPE="TEXT" NAME="fontName" VALUE="Serif"><BR>
    Font size:
    <INPUT TYPE="TEXT" NAME="fontSize" VALUE="90"><P>
    <INPUT TYPE="SUBMIT" VALUE="Build Image"><P>
    <INPUT TYPE="SUBMIT" NAME="showList" VALUE="Show Font List">
  </CENTER>
</FORM>

</BODY></HTML>
```

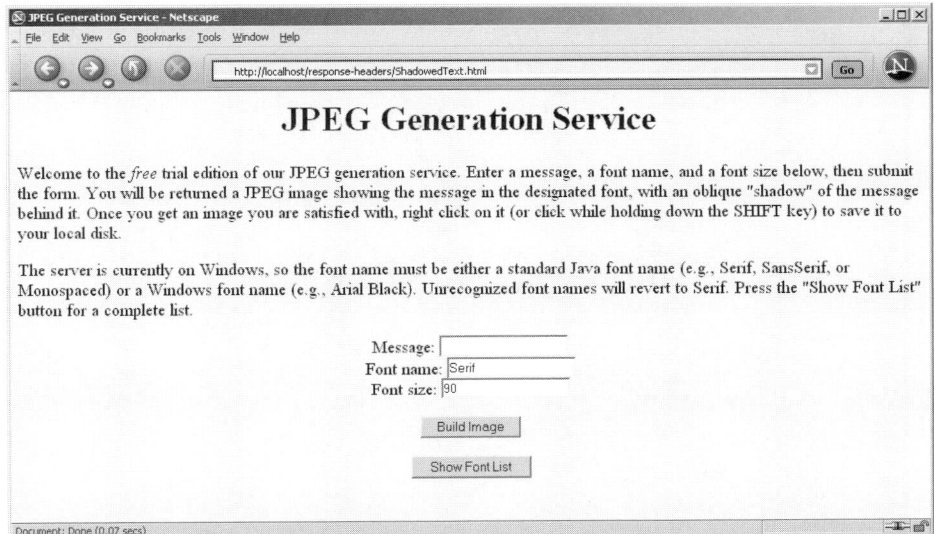

Figure 7–6 Front end to the image-generation servlet.

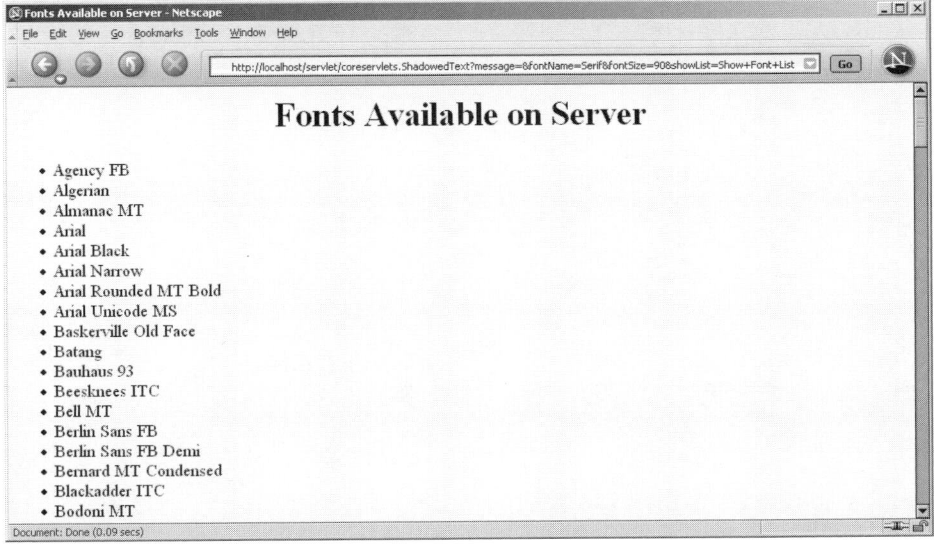

Figure 7–7 Result of servlet when the client selects Show Font List.

Figure 7–8 One possible result of the image-generation servlet. The client can save the image to disk as ***somename*.jpg** and use it in Web pages or other applications.

Figure 7–9 A second possible result of the image-generation servlet.

Figure 7–10 A third possible result of the image-generation servlet.

Listing 7.10 ImageTest.java

```
package coreservlets;

import java.io.*;

public class ImageTest {
  public static void main(String[] args) {
    String message = "Testing";
    String font = "Arial";
    if (args.length > 0) {
      message = args[0];
    }
    if (args.length > 1) {
      font = args[1];
    }
    MessageImage.writeJPEG
      (MessageImage.makeMessageImage(message, font, 40),
       new File("ImageTest.jpg"));
  }
}
```

Handling Cookies

Topics in This Chapter

- Understanding the benefits and drawbacks of cookies
- Sending outgoing cookies
- Receiving incoming cookies
- Tracking repeat visitors
- Specifying cookie attributes
- Differentiating between session cookies and persistent cookies
- Simplifying cookie usage with utility classes
- Modifying cookie values
- Remembering user preferences

Chapter 8

Cookies are small bits of textual information that a Web server sends to a browser and that the browser later returns unchanged when visiting the same Web site or domain. By letting the server read information it sent the client previously, the site can provide visitors with a number of conveniences such as presenting the site the way the visitor previously customized it or letting identifiable visitors in without their having to reenter a password.

This chapter discusses how to explicitly set and read cookies from within servlets, and the next chapter shows how to use the servlet session tracking API (which can use cookies behind the scenes) to keep track of users as they move around to different pages within your site.

8.1 Benefits of Cookies

There are four typical ways in which cookies can add value to your site. We summarize these benefits below, then give details in the rest of the section.

- **Identifying a user during an e-commerce session.** This type of short-term tracking is so important that another API is layered on top of cookies for this purpose. See the next chapter for details.

- **Remembering usernames and passwords.** Cookies let a user log in to a site automatically, providing a significant convenience for users of unshared computers.
- **Customizing sites.** Sites can use cookies to remember user preferences.
- **Focusing advertising.** Cookies let the site remember which topics interest certain users and show advertisements relevant to those interests.

Identifying a User During an E-commerce Session

Many online stores use a "shopping cart" metaphor in which users select items, add them to their shopping carts, then continue shopping. Since the HTTP connection is usually closed after each page is sent, when a user selects a new item to add to the cart, how does the store know that it is the same user who put the previous item in the cart? Persistent (keep-alive) HTTP connections do *not* solve this problem, since persistent connections generally apply only to requests made very close together in time, as when a browser asks for the images associated with a Web page. Besides, many older servers and browsers lack support for persistent connections. Cookies, however, *can* solve this problem. In fact, this capability is so useful that servlets have an API specifically for session tracking, and servlet and JSP authors don't need to manipulate cookies directly to take advantage of it. Session tracking is discussed in Chapter 9.

Remembering Usernames and Passwords

Many large sites require you to register to use their services, but it is inconvenient to remember and enter the username and password each time you visit. Cookies are a good alternative for low-security sites. When a user registers, a cookie containing a unique user ID is sent to him. When the client reconnects at a later date, the user ID is returned automatically, the server looks it up, determines it belongs to a registered user that chose autologin, and permits access without an explicit username and password. The site might also store the user's address, credit card number, and so forth in a database and use the user ID from the cookie as the key to retrieve the data. This approach prevents the user from having to reenter the data each time.

For example, when Marty travels to companies to give onsite JSP and servlet training courses, he typically checks both travelocity.com and expedia.com for flight information. These both require usernames and passwords to search flight schedules, but have different rules about which characters are legal in usernames and how many characters are required for passwords. So, Marty has a difficult time remembering how to log in. Fortunately, both sites use the cookie scheme described in the preceding paragraph, simplifying Marty's access from his personal desktop or laptop machine.

Customizing Sites

Many "portal" sites let you customize the look of the main page. They might let you pick which weather report you want to see (yes, it is still raining in Seattle), what stock symbols should be displayed (yes, your stock is still way down), what sports results you care about (yes, the Orioles are still losing), how search results should be displayed (yes, you want to see more than one result per page), and so forth. Since it would be inconvenient for you to have to set up your page each time you visit their site, they use cookies to remember what you wanted. For simple settings, the site could accomplish this customization by storing the page settings directly in the cookies. For more complex customization, however, the site just sends the client a unique identifier and keeps a server-side database that associates identifiers with page settings.

Focusing Advertising

Most advertiser-funded Web sites charge their advertisers much more for displaying "directed" (or "focused") ads than for displaying "random" ads. Advertisers are generally willing to pay much more to have their ads shown to people that are known to have some interest in the general product category. Sites reportedly charge advertisers as much as 30 times more for directed ads than for random ads. For example, if you go to a search engine and do a search on "Java Servlets," the search site can charge an advertiser much more for showing you an ad for a servlet development environment than for an ad for an online travel agent specializing in Indonesia. On the other hand, if the search had been for "Java Hotels," the situation would be reversed.

Without cookies, sites have to show a random ad when you first arrive and haven't yet performed a search, as well as when you search on something that doesn't match any ad categories. With cookies, they can identify your interests by remembering your previous searches. Since this approach enables them to show directed ads on visits to their home page as well as for their results page, it nearly doubles their advertising revenue.

8.2 Some Problems with Cookies

Providing convenience to the user and added value to the site owner is the purpose behind cookies. And despite much misinformation, cookies are not a serious security threat. Cookies are *never* interpreted or executed in any way and thus cannot be used to insert viruses or attack your system. Furthermore, since browsers generally only accept 20 cookies per site and 300 cookies total, and since browsers can limit each cookie to 4 kilobytes, cookies cannot be used to fill up someone's disk or launch other denial-of-service attacks.

However, even though cookies don't present a serious *security* threat, they can present a significant threat to *privacy*.

First, some people don't like the fact that search engines can remember what they previously searched for. For example, they might search for job openings or sensitive health data and don't want some banner ad tipping off their coworkers or boss next time they do a search. Besides, a search engine need not use a banner ad: a poorly designed one could display a textarea listing your most recent queries ("Jobs anywhere except at this stupid company!"; "Will my SARS infection kill my coworkers?"; etc.). A coworker could see this information if they visited the search engine for your computer or if they looked over your shoulder when you visited it.

Even worse, two sites can share data on a user by each loading small images off the same third-party site, where that third party uses cookies and shares the data with both original sites. For example, suppose that both some-search-site.com and some-random-site.com wanted to display directed ads from some-ad-site.com based on what the user searched for at some-search-site.com. If the user searched for "Java Servlets," the search engine at some-search-site.com could return a page with the following image link:

```
<IMG SRC="http://some-ad-site.com/banner?data=Java+Servlets" ...>
```

Since the browser will make an HTTP connection to some-ad-site.com, some-ad-site.com can return a persistent cookie to the browser. Next, some-random-site.com could return an image link like this:

```
<IMG SRC="http://some-ad-site.com/banner" ...>
```

Since the browser will reconnect to some-ad-site.com—a site from which it got cookies earlier—it will return the cookie it previously received. Assuming that some-ad-site.com sent a unique cookie value and, in its database, associated that cookie value with the "Java Servlets" search, some-ad-site can return a directed banner ad even though it is the user's first visit to some-random-site. The doubleclick.net service was the most famous early example of this technique. (Recent versions of Netscape and Internet Explorer, however, have a nice feature that lets you refuse cookies from sites other than that to which you connected, but without disabling cookies altogether. See Figure 8–1.)

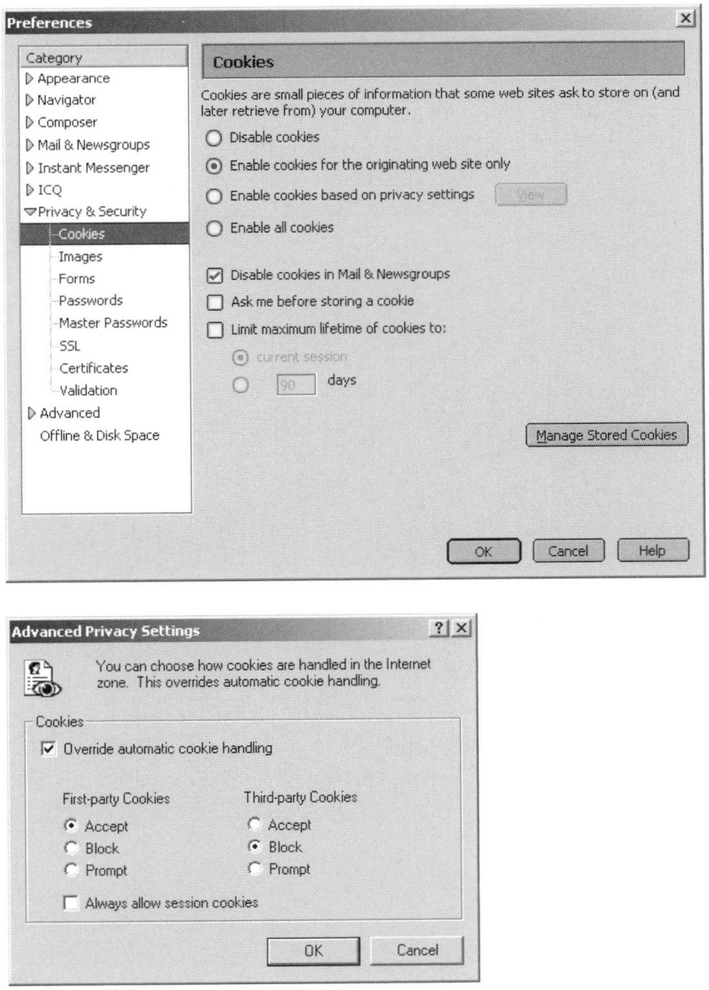

Figure 8–1 Cookie customization settings for Netscape (top) and Internet Explorer (bottom).

This trick of associating cookies with images can even be exploited through email if you use an HTML-enabled email reader that "supports" cookies and is associated with a browser. Thus, people could send you email that loads images, attach cookies to those images, and then identify you (email address and all) if you subsequently visit their Web site. Boo.

A second privacy problem occurs when sites rely on cookies for overly sensitive data. For example, some of the big online bookstores use cookies to remember your registration information and let you order without reentering much of your personal information. This is not a particular problem since they don't actually display your complete credit card number and only let you send books to an address that was specified when you *did* enter the credit card in full or use the username and password. As a result, someone using your computer (or stealing your cookie file) could do no more harm than sending a big book order to your address, where the order could be refused. However, other companies might not be so careful, and an attacker who gained access to someone's computer or cookie file could get online access to valuable personal information. Even worse, incompetent sites might embed credit card or other sensitive information directly in the cookies themselves, rather than using innocuous identifiers that are linked to real users only on the server. This embedding is dangerous, since most users don't view leaving their computer unattended in their office as being tantamount to leaving their credit card sitting on their desk.

The point of this discussion is twofold:

1. Due to real and perceived privacy problems, some users turn off cookies. So, even when you use cookies to give added value to a site, whenever possible your site shouldn't *depend* on them. Dependence on cookies is difficult to avoid in some situations, but if you can provide reasonable functionality for users without cookies enabled, so much the better.
2. As the author of servlets or JSP pages that use cookies, you should be careful not to use cookies for particularly sensitive information, since this would open users up to risks if somebody accessed the user's computer or cookie files.

8.3 Deleting Cookies

You will probably find it easier to experiment with the examples in this chapter if you periodically delete your cookies (or at least the cookies that are associated with localhost or whatever host your server is running on).

To delete your cookies in Internet Explorer, start at the Tools menu and select Internet Options. To delete all cookies, press Delete Cookies. To selectively delete cookies, press Settings, then View Files (cookie files have names that begin with `Cookie:`, but it is easier to find them if you choose Delete Files before View Files). See Figure 8–2.

To delete your cookies in Netscape, start at the Edit menu, then choose Preferences, Privacy and Security, and Cookies. Press the Manage Stored Cookies button to view or delete any or all of your cookies. Again, see Figure 8–2.

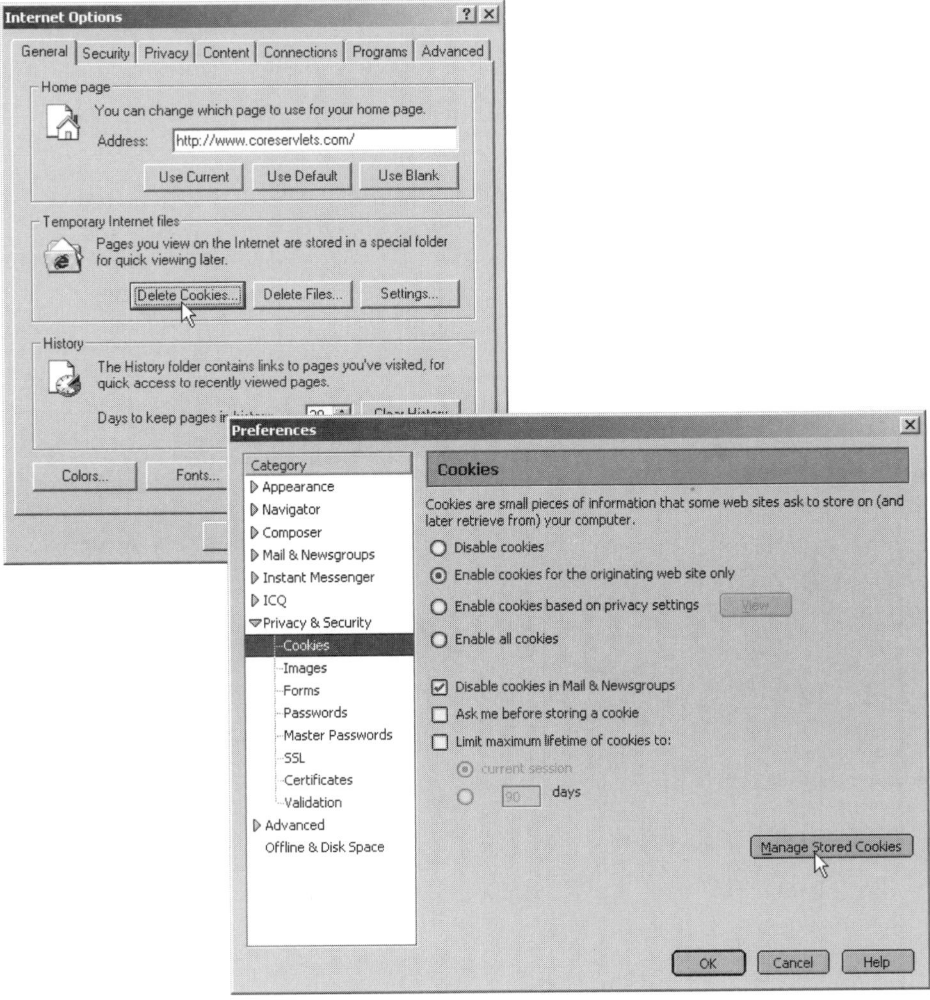

Figure 8–2 Deleting cookies in Internet Explorer and Netscape.

8.4 Sending and Receiving Cookies

To send cookies to the client, a servlet should use the `Cookie` constructor to create one or more cookies with designated names and values, set any optional attributes with `cookie.set`*Xxx* (readable later by `cookie.get`*Xxx*), and insert the cookies into the HTTP response headers with `response.addCookie`.

To read incoming cookies, a servlet should call `request.getCookies`, which returns an array of `Cookie` objects corresponding to the cookies the browser has associated with your site (`null` if there are no cookies in the request). In most cases, the servlet should then loop down this array calling `getName` on each cookie until it finds the one whose name matches the name it was searching for, then call `getValue` on that `Cookie` to see the value associated with the name. Each of these topics is discussed in more detail in the following subsections.

Sending Cookies to the Client

Sending cookies to the client involves three steps (summarized below with details in the following subsections).

1. **Creating a `Cookie` object.** You call the `Cookie` constructor with a cookie name and a cookie value, both of which are strings.
2. **Setting the maximum age.** If you want the browser to store the cookie on disk instead of just keeping it in memory, you use `setMaxAge` to specify how long (in seconds) the cookie should be valid.
3. **Placing the `Cookie` into the HTTP response headers.** You use `response.addCookie` to accomplish this. If you forget this step, no cookie is sent to the browser!

Creating a Cookie Object

You create a cookie by calling the `Cookie` constructor, which takes two strings: the cookie name and the cookie value. Neither the name nor the value should contain white space or any of the following characters:

```
[ ] ( ) = , " / ? @ : ;
```

For example, to create a cookie named `userID` with a value `a1234`, you would use the following.

```
Cookie c = new Cookie("userID", "a1234");
```

Setting the Maximum Age

If you create a cookie and send it to the browser, by default it is a session-level cookie: a cookie that is stored in the browser's memory and deleted when the user quits the browser. If you want the browser to store the cookie on disk, use `setMaxAge` with a time in seconds, as below.

```
c.setMaxAge(60*60*24*7); // One week
```

Since you could use the session-tracking API (Chapter 9) to simplify most tasks for which you use session-level cookies, you almost always use the `setMaxAge` method when using the `Cookie` API.

Setting the maximum age to 0 instructs the browser to delete the cookie.

Core Approach

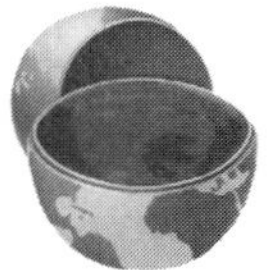

When you create a `Cookie` object, you should normally call `setMaxAge` before sending the cookie to the client.

Note that `setMaxAge` is not the only `Cookie` characteristic that you can modify. The other, less frequently used characteristics are discussed in Section 8.6 (Using Cookie Attributes).

Placing the Cookie in the Response Headers

By creating a `Cookie` object and calling `setMaxAge`, all you have done is manipulate a data structure in the server's memory. You haven't actually sent anything to the browser. If you don't send the cookie to the client, it has no effect. This may seem obvious, but a common mistake by beginning developers is to create and manipulate `Cookie` objects but fail to send them to the client.

Core Warning

Creating and manipulating a `Cookie` object has no effect on the client. You must explicitly send the cookie to the client with `response.addCookie`.

To send the cookie, insert it into a `Set-Cookie` HTTP response header by means of the `addCookie` method of `HttpServletResponse`. The method is called `addCookie`, not `setCookie`, because any previously specified `Set-Cookie` headers are left alone and a new header is set. Also, remember that the response headers must be set before any document content is sent to the client.

Here is an example:

```
Cookie userCookie = new Cookie("user", "uid1234");
userCookie.setMaxAge(60*60*24*365); // Store cookie for 1 year
response.addCookie(userCookie);
```

Reading Cookies from the Client

To send a cookie *to* the client, you create a `Cookie`, set its maximum age (usually), then use `addCookie` to send a `Set-Cookie` HTTP response header. To read the cookies that come back *from* the client, you should perform the following two tasks, which are summarized below and then described in more detail in the following subsections.

1. **Call `request.getCookies`.** This yields an array of `Cookie` objects.
2. **Loop down the array, calling `getName` on each one until you find the cookie of interest.** You then typically call `getValue` and use the value in some application-specific way.

Call request.getCookies

To obtain the cookies that were sent by the browser, you call `getCookies` on the `HttpServletRequest`. This call returns an array of `Cookie` objects corresponding to the values that came in on the `Cookie` HTTP request headers. If the request contains no cookies, `getCookies` should return `null`. Note, however, that an old version of Apache Tomcat (version 3.x) had a bug whereby it returned a zero-length array instead of `null`.

Loop Down the Cookie Array

Once you have the array of cookies, you typically loop down it, calling `getName` on each `Cookie` until you find one matching the name you have in mind. Remember that cookies are specific to your host (or domain), not your servlet (or JSP page). So, although your servlet might send a single cookie, you could get many irrelevant cookies back. Once you find the cookie of interest, you typically call `getValue` on it and finish with some processing specific to the resultant value. For example:

```
String cookieName = "userID";
Cookie[] cookies = request.getCookies();
if (cookies != null) {
  for(int i=0; i<cookies.length; i++) {
    Cookie cookie = cookies[i];
    if (cookieName.equals(cookie.getName())) {
```

```
        doSomethingWith(cookie.getValue());
      }
    }
  }
```

This is such a common process that, in Section 8.8, we present two utilities that simplify retrieving a cookie or cookie value that matches a designated cookie name.

8.5 Using Cookies to Detect First-Time Visitors

Suppose that, at your site, you want to display a prominent banner to first-time visitors, telling them to register. But, you don't want to clutter up the display showing a useless banner to return visitors.

A cookie is the perfect way to differentiate first-timers from repeat visitors. Check for the existence of a uniquely named cookie; if it is there, the client is a repeat visitor. If the cookie is not there, the visitor is a newcomer, and you should set an outgoing "this user has been here before" cookie.

Although this is a straightforward idea, there is one important point to note: you cannot determine if the user is a newcomer by the mere existence of entries in the cookie array. Many beginning servlet programmers erroneously use the following approach.

```
Cookie[] cookies = request.getCookies();
if (cookies == null) {
  doStuffForNewbie();          // Correct.
} else {
  doStuffForReturnVisitor(); // Incorrect.
}
```

Wrong! Sure, if the cookie array is `null`, the client is a newcomer (at least as far as you can tell—he could also have deleted or disabled cookies). But, if the array is non-`null`, it merely shows that the client has been to your *site* (or domain—see `setDomain` in the next section), not that they have been to your *servlet*. Other servlets, JSP pages, and non-Java Web applications can set cookies, and any of those cookies could get returned to your browser, depending on the path settings (see `setPath` in the next section).

Listing 8.1 illustrates the correct approach: checking for a specific cookie. Figures 8–3 and 8–4 show the results of initial and subsequent visits.

Listing 8.1 RepeatVisitor.java

```
package coreservlets;

import java.io.*;
import javax.servlet.*;
import javax.servlet.http.*;

/** Servlet that says "Welcome aboard" to first-time
 *  visitors and "Welcome back" to repeat visitors.
 *  Also see RepeatVisitor2 for variation that uses
 *  cookie utilities from later in this chapter.
 */

public class RepeatVisitor extends HttpServlet {
  public void doGet(HttpServletRequest request,
                    HttpServletResponse response)
      throws ServletException, IOException {
    boolean newbie = true;
    Cookie[] cookies = request.getCookies();
    if (cookies != null) {
      for(int i=0; i<cookies.length; i++) {
        Cookie c = cookies[i];
        if ((c.getName().equals("repeatVisitor")) &&
            // Could omit test and treat cookie name as a flag
            (c.getValue().equals("yes"))) {
          newbie = false;
          break;
        }
      }
    }
    String title;
    if (newbie) {
      Cookie returnVisitorCookie =
        new Cookie("repeatVisitor", "yes");
      returnVisitorCookie.setMaxAge(60*60*24*365); // 1 year
      response.addCookie(returnVisitorCookie);
      title = "Welcome Aboard";
    } else {
      title = "Welcome Back";
    }
    response.setContentType("text/html");
    PrintWriter out = response.getWriter();
    String docType =
      "<!DOCTYPE HTML PUBLIC \"-//W3C//DTD HTML 4.0 " +
      "Transitional//EN\">\n";
```

Listing 8.1 RepeatVisitor.java *(continued)*

```
    out.println(docType +
                "<HTML>\n" +
                "<HEAD><TITLE>" + title + "</TITLE></HEAD>\n" +
                "<BODY BGCOLOR=\"#FDF5E6\">\n" +
                "<H1 ALIGN=\"CENTER\">" + title + "</H1>\n" +
                "</BODY></HTML>");
  }
}
```

Figure 8–3 First visit by a client to the `RepeatVisitor` servlet.

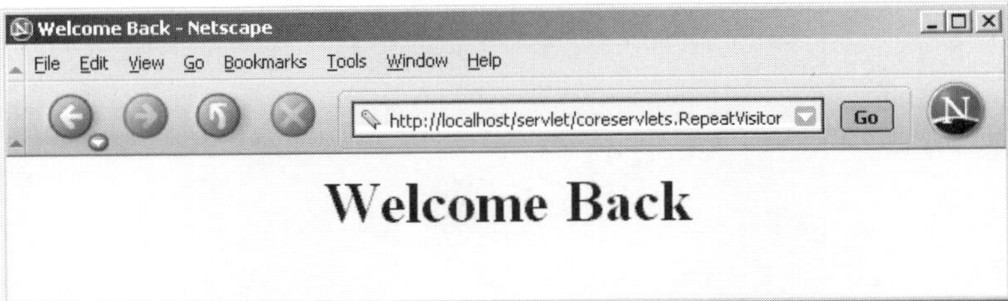

Figure 8–4 Subsequent visits by a client to the `RepeatVisitor` servlet.

8.6 Using Cookie Attributes

Before adding the cookie to the outgoing headers, you can set various characteristics of the cookie by using the following `set`*Xxx* methods, where *Xxx* is the name of the attribute you want to specify.

Although each `set`*Xxx* method has a corresponding `get`*Xxx* method to retrieve the attribute value, note that the attributes are part of the header sent from the server to the browser; they are *not* part of the header returned by the browser to the server. Thus, except for name and value, the cookie attributes apply only to *outgoing* cookies from the server to the client; they aren't set on cookies that come *from* the browser to the server. So, don't expect these attributes to be available in the cookies you get by means of `request.getCookies`. This means that you can't implement continually changing cookie values merely by setting a maximum age on a cookie once, sending it out, finding the appropriate cookie in the incoming array on the next request, reading the value, modifying it, and storing it back in the `Cookie`. You have to call `setMaxAge` again each time (and, of course, pass the `Cookie` to `response.addCookie`).

Here are the methods that set the cookie attributes.

public void setComment(String comment)
public String getComment()
These methods specify or look up a comment associated with the cookie. With version 0 cookies (see the upcoming entry on `setVersion` and `getVersion`), the comment is used purely for informational purposes on the server; it is not sent to the client.

public void setDomain(String domainPattern)
public String getDomain()
These methods set or retrieve the domain to which the cookie applies. Normally, the browser returns cookies only to the exact same hostname that sent the cookies. For instance, cookies sent from a servlet at bali.vacations.com would not normally get returned by the browser to pages at queensland.vacations.com. If the site wanted this to happen, the servlets could specify `cookie.setDomain(".vacations.com")`. To prevent servers from setting cookies that apply to hosts outside their domain, the specified domain must meet the following requirements: it must start with a dot (e.g., .coreservlets.com); it must contain two dots for noncountry domains like .com, .edu, and .gov; and it must contain three dots for country domains like .co.uk and .edu.es.

public void setMaxAge(int lifetime)
public int getMaxAge()
These methods tell how much time (in seconds) should elapse before the cookie expires. A negative value, which is the default, indicates that the cookie will last only for the current browsing session (i.e., until the user quits the browser) and will not be stored on disk. See the `LongLivedCookie` class (Listing 8.4), which defines a subclass of `Cookie` with a maximum age automatically set one year in the future. Specifying a value of 0 instructs the browser to delete the cookie.

public String getName()

The `getName` method retrieves the name of the cookie. The name and the value are the two pieces you virtually *always* care about. However, since the name is supplied to the `Cookie` constructor, there is *no* `setName` method; you cannot change the name once the cookie is created. On the other hand, `getName` is used on almost every cookie received by the server. Since the `getCookies` method of `HttpServletRequest` returns an array of `Cookie` objects, a common practice is to loop down the array, calling `getName` until you have a particular name, then to check the value with `getValue`. For an encapsulation of this process, see the `getCookieValue` method shown in Listing 8.3.

public void setPath(String path)
public String getPath()

These methods set or get the path to which the cookie applies. If you don't specify a path, the browser returns the cookie only to URLs in or below the directory containing the page that sent the cookie. For example, if the server sent the cookie from http://ecommerce.site.com/toys/specials.html, the browser would send the cookie back when connecting to http:// ecommerce.site.com/toys/bikes/beginners.html, but not to http://ecommerce.site.com/cds/classical.html. The `setPath` method can specify something more general. For example, `cookie.setPath("/")` specifies that *all* pages on the server should receive the cookie. The path specified must include the current page; that is, you may specify a more general path than the default, but not a more specific one. So, for example, a servlet at http://host/store/cust-service/request could specify a path of /store/ (since /store/ includes /store/cust-service/) but not a path of /store/cust-service/returns/ (since this directory does not include /store/cust-service/).

Core Approach

To specify that a cookie apply to all *URLs on your site, use* `cookie.setPath("/")`.

public void setSecure(boolean secureFlag)
public boolean getSecure()

This pair of methods sets or gets the boolean value indicating whether the cookie should only be sent over encrypted (i.e., SSL) connections. The default is `false`; the cookie should apply to all connections.

public void setValue(String cookieValue)
public String getValue()

The `setValue` method specifies the value associated with the cookie; `getValue` looks it up. Again, the name and the value are the two parts of a cookie that you *almost always* care about, although in a few cases, a name is used as a boolean flag and its value is ignored (i.e., the existence of a cookie with the designated name is all that matters). However, since the cookie value is supplied to the `Cookie` constructor, `setValue` is typically reserved for cases when you change the values of incoming cookies and then send them back out. For an example, see Section 8.10 (Modifying Cookie Values: Tracking User Access Counts).

public void setVersion(int version)
public int getVersion()

These methods set and get the cookie protocol version with which the cookie complies. Version 0, the default, follows the original Netscape specification (http://wp.netscape.com/newsref/std/cookie_spec.html). Version 1, not yet widely supported, adheres to RFC 2109 (retrieve RFCs from the archive sites listed at http://www.rfc-editor.org/).

8.7 Differentiating Session Cookies from Persistent Cookies

This section illustrates the use of the cookie attributes by contrasting the behavior of cookies with and without a maximum age. Listing 8.2 shows the `CookieTest` servlet, a servlet that performs two tasks:

1. First, the servlet sets six outgoing cookies. Three have no explicit age (i.e., have a negative value by default), meaning that they should apply only in the current browsing session—until the user restarts the browser. The other three use `setMaxAge` to stipulate that the browser should write them to disk and that they should persist for the next hour, regardless of whether the user restarts the browser or reboots the computer to initiate a new browsing session.
2. Second, the servlet uses `request.getCookies` to find all the incoming cookies and display their names and values in an HTML table.

Figure 8–5 shows the result of the initial visit, Figure 8–6 shows a visit immediately after that, and Figure 8–7 shows the result of a visit after the user restarts the browser.

Listing 8.2 CookieTest.java

```
package coreservlets;

import java.io.*;
import javax.servlet.*;
import javax.servlet.http.*;

/** Creates a table of the cookies associated with
 *  the current page. Also sets six cookies: three
 *  that apply only to the current session
 *  (regardless of how long that session lasts)
 *  and three that persist for an hour (regardless
 *  of whether the browser is restarted).
 */

public class CookieTest extends HttpServlet {
  public void doGet(HttpServletRequest request,
                    HttpServletResponse response)
      throws ServletException, IOException {
    for(int i=0; i<3; i++) {
      // Default maxAge is -1, indicating cookie
      // applies only to current browsing session.
      Cookie cookie = new Cookie("Session-Cookie-" + i,
                                 "Cookie-Value-S" + i);
      response.addCookie(cookie);
      cookie = new Cookie("Persistent-Cookie-" + i,
                          "Cookie-Value-P" + i);
      // Cookie is valid for an hour, regardless of whether
      // user quits browser, reboots computer, or whatever.
      cookie.setMaxAge(3600);
      response.addCookie(cookie);
    }
    response.setContentType("text/html");
    PrintWriter out = response.getWriter();
    String docType =
      "<!DOCTYPE HTML PUBLIC \"-//W3C//DTD HTML 4.0 " +
      "Transitional//EN\">\n";
    String title = "Active Cookies";
```

Listing 8.2 CookieTest.java *(continued)*

```
    out.println(docType +
                "<HTML>\n" +
                "<HEAD><TITLE>" + title + "</TITLE></HEAD>\n" +
                "<BODY BGCOLOR=\"#FDF5E6\">\n" +
                "<H1 ALIGN=\"CENTER\">" + title + "</H1>\n" +
                "<TABLE BORDER=1 ALIGN=\"CENTER\">\n" +
                "<TR BGCOLOR=\"#FFAD00\">\n" +
                "  <TH>Cookie Name\n" +
                "  <TH>Cookie Value");
    Cookie[] cookies = request.getCookies();
    if (cookies == null) {
      out.println("<TR><TH COLSPAN=2>No cookies");
    } else {
      Cookie cookie;
      for(int i=0; i<cookies.length; i++) {
        cookie = cookies[i];
        out.println("<TR>\n" +
                    "  <TD>" + cookie.getName() + "\n" +
                    "  <TD>" + cookie.getValue());
      }
    }
    out.println("</TABLE></BODY></HTML>");
  }
}
```

Figure 8–5 Result of initial visit to the `CookieTest` servlet. This is the same result as when visiting the servlet, quitting the browser, waiting an hour, and revisiting the servlet.

Figure 8–6 Result of revisiting the `CookieTest` servlet within an hour of the original visit, in the same browser session (browser stayed open between the original visit and the visit shown here).

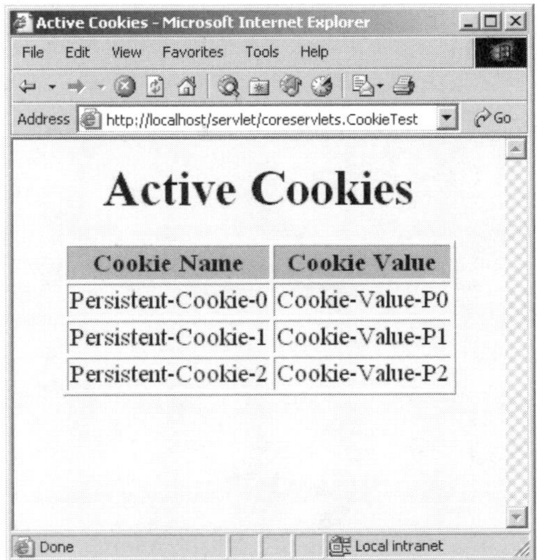

Figure 8–7 Result of revisiting the `CookieTest` servlet within an hour of the original visit, in a different browser session (browser was restarted between the original visit and the visit shown here).

8.8 Basic Cookie Utilities

This section presents some simple but useful utilities for dealing with cookies.

Finding Cookies with Specified Names

Listing 8.3 shows two static methods in the `CookieUtilities` class that simplify the retrieval of a cookie or cookie value, given a cookie name. The `getCookieValue` method loops through the array of available `Cookie` objects, returning the value of any `Cookie` whose name matches the input. If there is no match, the designated default value is returned. So, for example, our typical approach for dealing with cookies is as follows:

```
String color =
  CookieUtilities.getCookieValue(request, "color", "black");
String font =
  CookieUtilities.getCookieValue(request, "font", "Arial");
```

The `getCookie` method also loops through the array comparing names but returns the actual `Cookie` object instead of just the value. That method is for cases when you want to do something with the `Cookie` other than just read its value. The `getCookieValue` method is more commonly used, but, for example, you might use `getCookie` in lieu of `getCookieValue` if you wanted to put a new value into the cookie and send it back out again. Just don't forget that if you use this approach, you have to respecify any cookie attributes such as date, path, and domain: these attributes are not set for incoming cookies.

Listing 8.3 CookieUtilities.java

```
package coreservlets;

import javax.servlet.*;
import javax.servlet.http.*;

/** Two static methods for use in cookie handling. */

public class CookieUtilities {
```

Listing 8.3 CookieUtilities.java *(continued)*

```
  /** Given the request object, a name, and a default value,
   *  this method tries to find the value of the cookie with
   *  the given name. If no cookie matches the name,
   *  the default value is returned.
   */

  public static String getCookieValue
                          (HttpServletRequest request,
                           String cookieName,
                           String defaultValue) {
    Cookie[] cookies = request.getCookies();
    if (cookies != null) {
      for(int i=0; i<cookies.length; i++) {
        Cookie cookie = cookies[i];
        if (cookieName.equals(cookie.getName())) {
          return(cookie.getValue());
        }
      }
    }
    return(defaultValue);
  }

  /** Given the request object and a name, this method tries
   *  to find and return the cookie that has the given name.
   *  If no cookie matches the name, null is returned.
   */

  public static Cookie getCookie(HttpServletRequest request,
                                 String cookieName) {
    Cookie[] cookies = request.getCookies();
    if (cookies != null) {
      for(int i=0; i<cookies.length; i++) {
        Cookie cookie = cookies[i];
        if (cookieName.equals(cookie.getName())) {
          return(cookie);
        }
      }
    }
    return(null);
  }
}
```

Creating Long-Lived Cookies

Listing 8.4 shows a small class that you can use instead of `Cookie` if you want your cookie to automatically persist for a year when the client quits the browser. This class (`LongLivedCookie`) merely extends `Cookie` and calls `setMaxAge` automatically.

Listing 8.4 LongLivedCookie.java

```
package coreservlets;

import javax.servlet.http.*;

/** Cookie that persists 1 year. Default Cookie doesn't
 *  persist past current browsing session.
 */

public class LongLivedCookie extends Cookie {
  public static final int SECONDS_PER_YEAR = 60*60*24*365;

  public LongLivedCookie(String name, String value) {
    super(name, value);
    setMaxAge(SECONDS_PER_YEAR);
  }
}
```

8.9 Putting the Cookie Utilities into Practice

Listing 8.5 redoes the `RepeatVisitor` servlet of Listing 8.1. The new version (`RepeatVisitor2`) has the same functionality as the old version: it says "Welcome Aboard" to first-time visitors and "Welcome Back" to repeat visitors. However, it uses the cookie utilities of Section 8.8 to simplify the code in two ways:

1. Instead of calling `request.getCookies` and looping down that array examining each name, it merely calls `CookieUtilities.getCookieValue`.
2. Instead of creating a `Cookie` object, calculating the number of seconds in a year, and then calling `setMaxAge`, it merely creates a `LongLivedCookie` object.

Figures 8–8 and 8–9 show the results.

Listing 8.5 RepeatVisitor2.java

```
package coreservlets;

import java.io.*;
import javax.servlet.*;
import javax.servlet.http.*;

/** A variation of the RepeatVisitor servlet that uses
 *  CookieUtilities.getCookieValue and LongLivedCookie
 *  to simplify the code.
 */

public class RepeatVisitor2 extends HttpServlet {
  public void doGet(HttpServletRequest request,
                    HttpServletResponse response)
      throws ServletException, IOException {
    boolean newbie = true;
    String value =
      CookieUtilities.getCookieValue(request, "repeatVisitor2",
                                     "no");
    if (value.equals("yes")) {
      newbie = false;
    }
    String title;
    if (newbie) {
      LongLivedCookie returnVisitorCookie =
        new LongLivedCookie("repeatVisitor2", "yes");
      response.addCookie(returnVisitorCookie);
      title = "Welcome Aboard";
    } else {
      title = "Welcome Back";
    }
    response.setContentType("text/html");
    PrintWriter out = response.getWriter();
    String docType =
      "<!DOCTYPE HTML PUBLIC \"-//W3C//DTD HTML 4.0 " +
      "Transitional//EN\">\n";
    out.println(docType +
                "<HTML>\n" +
                "<HEAD><TITLE>" + title + "</TITLE></HEAD>\n" +
                "<BODY BGCOLOR=\"#FDF5E6\">\n" +
                "<H1 ALIGN=\"CENTER\">" + title + "</H1>\n" +
                "</BODY></HTML>");
  }
}
```

Figure 8–8 First visit by a client to the `RepeatVisitor2` servlet.

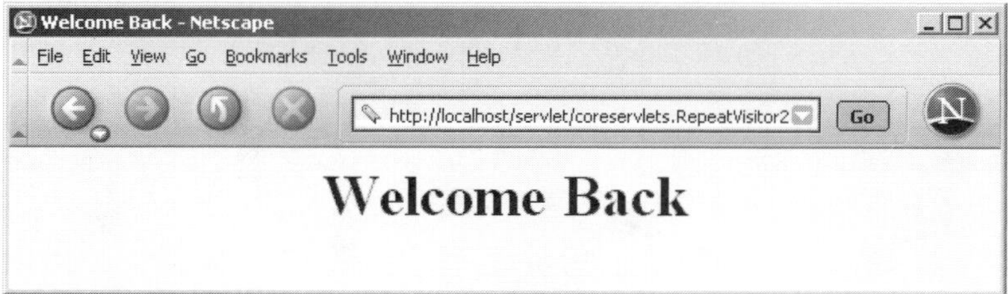

Figure 8–9 Subsequent visit by a client to the `RepeatVisitor2` servlet.

8.10 Modifying Cookie Values: Tracking User Access Counts

In the previous examples, we sent a cookie to the user only on the first visit. Once the cookie had a value, we never changed it. This approach of a single cookie value is surprisingly common since cookies frequently contain nothing but unique user identifiers: all the real user data is stored in a database—the user identifier is merely the database key.

But what if you want to periodically change the value of a cookie? How do you do so?

- To *replace* a previous cookie value, send the same cookie name with a different cookie value. If you actually use the incoming `Cookie` objects, don't forget to do `response.addCookie`; merely calling `setValue` is not sufficient. You also need to reapply any relevant cookie attributes by calling `setMaxAge`, `setPath`, etc.—cookie attributes are not specified for incoming cookies. Reapplying these attributes means that reusing the incoming `Cookie` objects saves you little, so many developers don't bother.

- To instruct the browser to *delete* a cookie, use `setMaxAge` to assign a maximum age of 0.

Listing 8.6 presents a servlet that keeps track of how many times each client has visited the page. It does this by making a cookie whose name is `accessCount` and whose value is the actual count. To accomplish this task, the servlet needs to repeatedly replace the cookie value by resending a cookie with the identical name.

Figure 8–10 shows some typical results.

Listing 8.6 ClientAccessCounts.java

```
package coreservlets;

import java.io.*;
import javax.servlet.*;
import javax.servlet.http.*;

/** Servlet that prints per-client access counts. */

public class ClientAccessCounts extends HttpServlet {
  public void doGet(HttpServletRequest request,
                    HttpServletResponse response)
      throws ServletException, IOException {
    String countString =
      CookieUtilities.getCookieValue(request,
                                     "accessCount",
                                     "1");
    int count = 1;
    try {
      count = Integer.parseInt(countString);
    } catch(NumberFormatException nfe) { }
    LongLivedCookie c =
      new LongLivedCookie("accessCount",
                          String.valueOf(count+1));
    response.addCookie(c);
    response.setContentType("text/html");
    PrintWriter out = response.getWriter();
    String title = "Access Count Servlet";
    String docType =
      "<!DOCTYPE HTML PUBLIC \"-//W3C//DTD HTML 4.0 " +
      "Transitional//EN\">\n";
```

Listing 8.6 ClientAccessCounts.java *(continued)*

```
    out.println(docType +
                "<HTML>\n" +
                "<HEAD><TITLE>" + title + "</TITLE></HEAD>\n" +
                "<BODY BGCOLOR=\"#FDF5E6\">\n" +
                "<CENTER>\n" +
                "<H1>" + title + "</H1>\n" +
                "<H2>This is visit number " +
                count + " by this browser.</H2>\n" +
                "</CENTER></BODY></HTML>");
  }
}
```

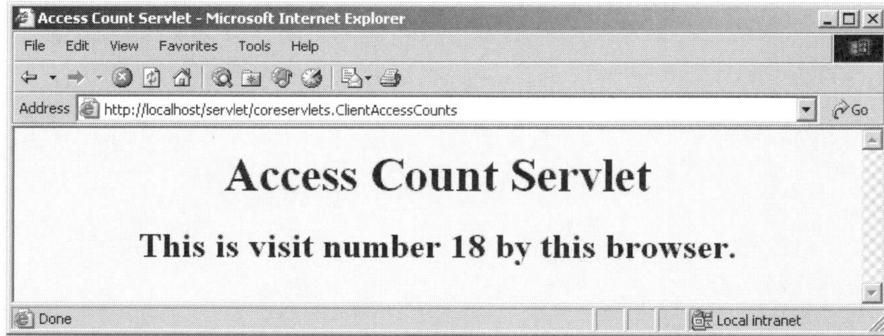

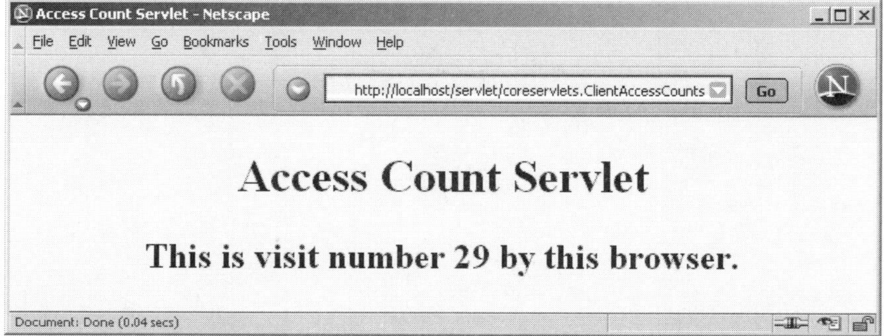

Figure 8–10 Users each see their own access count. Also, Internet Explorer and Netscape maintain cookies separately, so the same user sees independent access counts with the two browsers.

8.11 Using Cookies to Remember User Preferences

One of the most common applications of cookies is to use them to "remember" user preferences. For simple user settings, as here, the preferences can be stored directly in the cookies. For more complex applications, the cookie typically contains a unique user identifier and the preferences are stored in a database.

Listing 8.7 presents a servlet that creates an input form with the following characteristics.

- **The form is redisplayed if it is incomplete when submitted.** The form sends data to a second servlet (Listing 8.8) that checks whether any of the designated request parameters is missing, then stores the parameter values in cookies. If no parameter is missing, the second servlet displays the parameter values. If a parameter is missing, the second servlet redirects the user to the original servlet so that the form can be redisplayed. The original servlet maintains the user's previously entered values by extracting them from the cookies.
- **The form remembers previous entries.** The fields are prepopulated with whatever values the user entered on the most recent request.

Figures 8–11 through 8–13 show some typical results.

Listing 8.7 RegistrationForm.java

```
package coreservlets;

import java.io.*;
import javax.servlet.*;
import javax.servlet.http.*;

/** Servlet that displays an HTML form to collect user's
 *  first name, last name, and email address. Uses cookies
 *  to determine the initial values of each of those
 *  form fields.
 */
```

Listing 8.7 RegistrationForm.java *(continued)*

```
public class RegistrationForm extends HttpServlet {
  public void doGet(HttpServletRequest request,
                    HttpServletResponse response)
      throws ServletException, IOException {
    response.setContentType("text/html");
    PrintWriter out = response.getWriter();
    String actionURL =
      "/servlet/coreservlets.RegistrationServlet";
    String firstName =
      CookieUtilities.getCookieValue(request, "firstName", "");
    String lastName =
      CookieUtilities.getCookieValue(request, "lastName", "");
    String emailAddress =
      CookieUtilities.getCookieValue(request, "emailAddress",
                                     "");
    String docType =
      "<!DOCTYPE HTML PUBLIC \"-//W3C//DTD HTML 4.0 " +
      "Transitional//EN\">\n";
    String title = "Please Register";
    out.println
      (docType +
       "<HTML>\n" +
       "<HEAD><TITLE>" + title + "</TITLE></HEAD>\n" +
       "<BODY BGCOLOR=\"#FDF5E6\">\n" +
       "<CENTER>\n" +
       "<H1>" + title + "</H1>\n" +
       "<FORM ACTION=\"" + actionURL + "\">\n" +
       "First Name:\n" +
       "  <INPUT TYPE=\"TEXT\" NAME=\"firstName\" " +
                "VALUE=\"" + firstName + "\"><BR>\n" +
       "Last Name:\n" +
       "  <INPUT TYPE=\"TEXT\" NAME=\"lastName\" " +
                       "VALUE=\"" + lastName + "\"><BR>\n" +
       "Email Address: \n" +
       "  <INPUT TYPE=\"TEXT\" NAME=\"emailAddress\" " +
                "VALUE=\"" + emailAddress + "\"><P>\n" +
       "<INPUT TYPE=\"SUBMIT\" VALUE=\"Register\">\n" +
       "</FORM></CENTER></BODY></HTML>");
  }
}
```

Listing 8.8 RegistrationServlet.java

```
package coreservlets;

import java.io.*;
import javax.servlet.*;
import javax.servlet.http.*;

/** Servlet that processes a registration form containing
 *  a user's first name, last name, and email address.
 *  If all the values are present, the servlet displays the
 *  values. If any of the values are missing, the input
 *  form is redisplayed. Either way, the values are put
 *  into cookies so that the input form can use the
 *  previous values.
 */

public class RegistrationServlet extends HttpServlet {
  public void doGet(HttpServletRequest request,
                    HttpServletResponse response)
      throws ServletException, IOException {
    response.setContentType("text/html");
    boolean isMissingValue = false;
    String firstName = request.getParameter("firstName");
    if (isMissing(firstName)) {
      firstName = "Missing first name";
      isMissingValue = true;
    }
    String lastName = request.getParameter("lastName");
    if (isMissing(lastName)) {
      lastName = "Missing last name";
      isMissingValue = true;
    }
    String emailAddress = request.getParameter("emailAddress");
    if (isMissing(emailAddress)) {
      emailAddress = "Missing email address";
      isMissingValue = true;
    }
    Cookie c1 = new LongLivedCookie("firstName", firstName);
    response.addCookie(c1);
    Cookie c2 = new LongLivedCookie("lastName", lastName);
    response.addCookie(c2);
    Cookie c3 = new LongLivedCookie("emailAddress",
                                    emailAddress);
    response.addCookie(c3);
    String formAddress =
      "/servlet/coreservlets.RegistrationForm";
    if (isMissingValue) {
      response.sendRedirect(formAddress);
```

Listing 8.8 RegistrationServlet.java *(continued)*

```
    } else {
      PrintWriter out = response.getWriter();
      String docType =
        "<!DOCTYPE HTML PUBLIC \"-//W3C//DTD HTML 4.0 " +
        "Transitional//EN\">\n";
      String title = "Thanks for Registering";
      out.println
        (docType +
         "<HTML>\n" +
         "<HEAD><TITLE>" + title + "</TITLE></HEAD>\n" +
         "<BODY BGCOLOR=\"#FDF5E6\">\n" +
         "<CENTER>\n" +
         "<H1 ALIGN>" + title + "</H1>\n" +
         "<UL>\n" +
         "  <LI><B>First Name</B>: " +
               firstName + "\n" +
         "  <LI><B>Last Name</B>: " +
               lastName + "\n" +
         "  <LI><B>Email address</B>: " +
               emailAddress + "\n" +
         "</UL>\n" +
         "</CENTER></BODY></HTML>");
    }
  }

  /** Determines if value is null or empty. */

  private boolean isMissing(String param) {
    return((param == null) ||
           (param.trim().equals("")));
  }
}
```

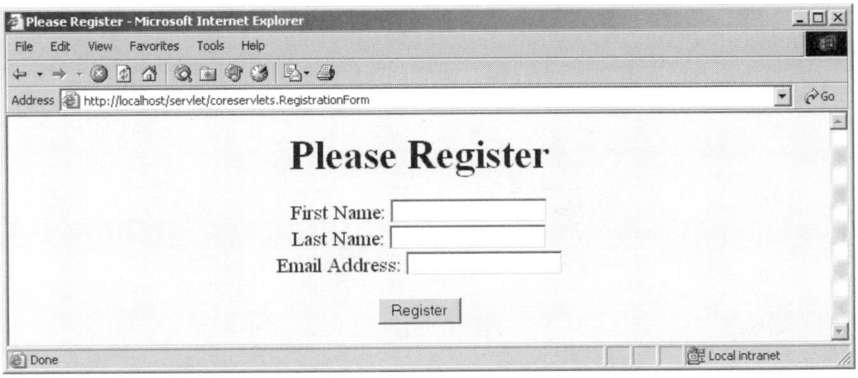

Figure 8–11 Initial result of `RegistrationForm` servlet.

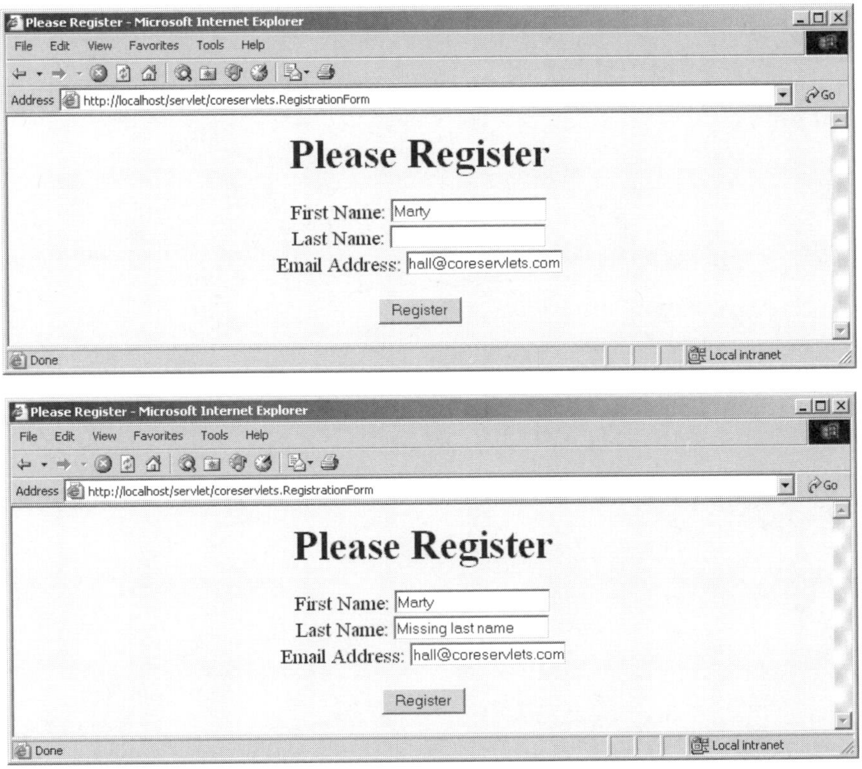

Figure 8–12 When the input form is incompletely filled in (top), the `RegistrationServlet` redirects the user to the `RegistrationForm` (bottom). The `RegistrationForm` uses cookies to determine the values of the form fields that were already filled in.

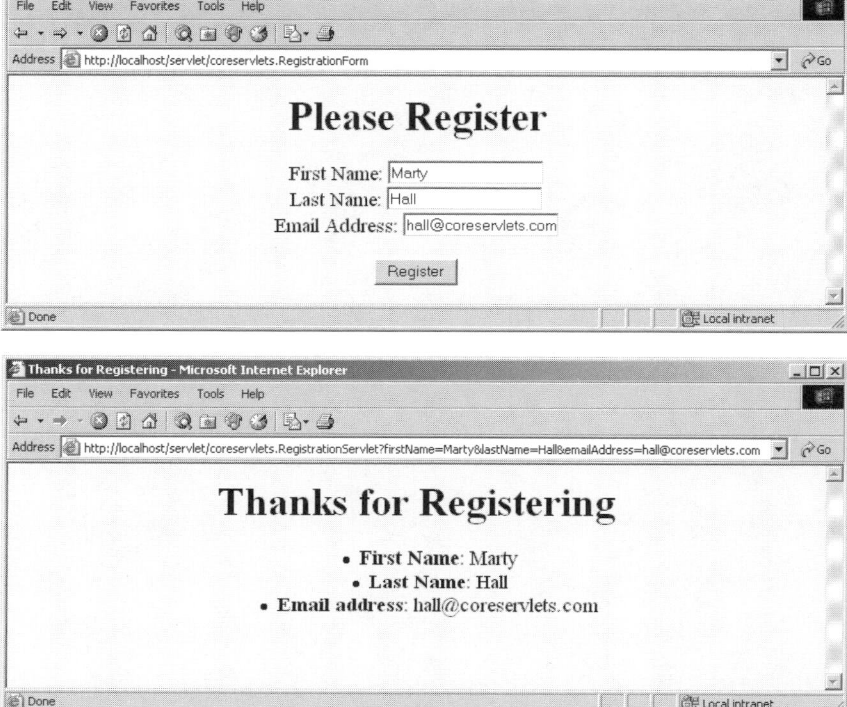

Figure 8–13 When the input form is completely filled in (top), the `RegistrationServlet` (bottom) simply displays the request parameter values. The input form shown here (top) is also representative of how the form will look when the user revisits the input form at some later date: form is prepopulated with the most recently used values.

Session Tracking

Topics in This Chapter

- Implementing session tracking from scratch
- Using basic session tracking
- Understanding the session-tracking API
- Differentiating between server and browser sessions
- Encoding URLs
- Storing immutable objects vs. storing mutable objects
- Tracking user access counts
- Accumulating user purchases
- Implementing a shopping cart
- Building an online store

Chapter 9

This chapter introduces the servlet session-tracking API, which keeps track of user-specific data as visitors move around your site.

9.1 The Need for Session Tracking

HTTP is a "stateless" protocol: each time a client retrieves a Web page, the client opens a separate connection to the Web server and the server does not automatically maintain contextual information about the client. Even with servers that support persistent (keep-alive) HTTP connections and keep sockets open for multiple client requests that occur in rapid succession, there is no built-in support for maintaining contextual information. This lack of context causes a number of difficulties. For example, when clients at an online store add an item to their shopping carts, how does the server know what's already in the carts? Similarly, when clients decide to proceed to checkout, how can the server determine which previously created shopping carts are theirs? These questions seem very simple, yet, because of the inadequacies of HTTP, answering them is surprisingly complicated.

There are three typical solutions to this problem: cookies, URL rewriting, and hidden form fields. The following subsections quickly summarize what would be required if you had to implement session tracking yourself (without using the built-in session-tracking API) for each of the three ways.

Cookies

You can use cookies to store an ID for a shopping session; with each subsequent connection, you can look up the current session ID and then use that ID to extract information about that session from a lookup table on the server machine. So, there would really be two tables: one that associates session IDs with user tables, and the user tables themselves that store user-specific data. For example, on the initial request a servlet could do something like the following:

```
String sessionID = makeUniqueString();
HashMap sessionInfo = new HashMap();
HashMap globalTable = findTableStoringSessions();
globalTable.put(sessionID, sessionInfo);
Cookie sessionCookie = new Cookie("JSESSIONID", sessionID);
sessionCookie.setPath("/");
response.addCookie(sessionCookie);
```

Then, in later requests the server could use the `globalTable` hash table to associate a session ID from the `JSESSIONID` cookie with the `sessionInfo` hash table of user-specific data.

Using cookies in this manner is an excellent solution and is the most widely used approach for session handling. Still, it is nice that servlets have a higher-level API that handles all this plus the following tedious tasks:

- Extracting the cookie that stores the session identifier from the other cookies (there may be many cookies, after all).
- Determining when idle sessions have expired, and reclaiming them.
- Associating the hash tables with each request.
- Generating the unique session identifiers.

URL Rewriting

With this approach, the client appends some extra data on the end of each URL. That data identifies the session, and the server associates that identifier with user-specific data it has stored. For example, with http://host/path/file.html;jsessionid=a1234, the session identifier is attached as jsessionid=a1234, so `a1234` is the ID that uniquely identifies the table of data associated with that user.

URL rewriting is a moderately good solution for session tracking and even has the advantage that it works when browsers don't support cookies or when the user has disabled them. However, if you implement session tracking yourself, URL rewriting has the same drawback as do cookies, namely, that the server-side program has a lot of straightforward but tedious processing to do. Even with a high-level API that handles most of the details for you, you have to be very careful that every URL that references your site and is returned to the user (even by indirect means like `Location` fields in server redirects) has the extra information appended. This restriction means that you cannot have any static HTML pages on your site (at least not any that have links back to dynamic pages at the site). So, every page has to be dynamically generated with servlets or JSP. Even when all the pages are dynamically generated, if the user leaves the session and comes back via a bookmark or link, the session information can be lost because the stored link contains the wrong identifying information.

Hidden Form Fields

As discussed in Chapter 19 (Creating and Processing HTML Forms), HTML forms can have an entry that looks like the following:

```
<INPUT TYPE="HIDDEN" NAME="session" VALUE="a1234">
```

This entry means that, when the form is submitted, the specified name and value are automatically included in the `GET` or `POST` data. This hidden field can be used to store information about the session but has the major disadvantage that it only works if every page is dynamically generated by a form submission. Clicking on a regular (`<A HREF...>`) hypertext link does not result in a form submission, so hidden form fields cannot support general session tracking, only tracking within a specific series of operations such as checking out at a store.

Session Tracking in Servlets

Servlets provide an outstanding session-tracking solution: the `HttpSession` API. This high-level interface is built on top of cookies or URL rewriting. All servers are required to support session tracking with cookies, and most have a setting by which you can globally switch to URL rewriting.

Either way, the servlet author doesn't need to bother with many of the implementation details, doesn't have to explicitly manipulate cookies or information appended to the URL, and is automatically given a convenient place to store arbitrary objects that are associated with each session.

9.2 Session Tracking Basics

Using sessions in servlets is straightforward and involves four basic steps. Here is a summary; details follow.

1. **Accessing the session object associated with the current request.** Call `request.getSession` to get an `HttpSession` object, which is a simple hash table for storing user-specific data.
2. **Looking up information associated with a session.** Call `getAttribute` on the `HttpSession` object, cast the return value to the appropriate type, and check whether the result is `null`.
3. **Storing information in a session.** Use `setAttribute` with a key and a value.
4. **Discarding session data.** Call `removeAttribute` to discard a specific value. Call `invalidate` to discard an entire session. Call `logout` to log the client out of the Web server and invalidate all sessions associated with that user.

Accessing the Session Object Associated with the Current Request

Session objects are of type `HttpSession`, but they are basically just hash tables that can store arbitrary user objects (each associated with a key). You look up the `HttpSession` object by calling the `getSession` method of `HttpServletRequest`, as below.

```
HttpSession session = request.getSession();
```

Behind the scenes, the system extracts a user ID from a cookie or attached URL data, then uses that ID as a key into a table of previously created `HttpSession` objects. But this is all done transparently to the programmer: you just call `getSession`. If no session ID is found in an incoming cookie or attached URL information, the system creates a new, empty session. And, if cookies are being used (the default situation), the system also creates an outgoing cookie named `JSESSIONID` with a unique value representing the session ID. So, although you call `getSession` on the *request*, the call can affect the *response*. Consequently, you are permitted to call `request.getSession` only when it would be legal to set HTTP response headers: before any document content has been sent (i.e., flushed or committed) to the client.

Core Approach

*Call `request.getSession` **before** you send any document content to the client.*

Now, if you plan to add data to the session regardless of whether data was there already, `getSession()` (or, equivalently, `getSession(true)`) is the appropriate method call because it creates a new session if no session already exists. However, suppose that you merely want to print out information on what is already in the session, as you might at a "View Cart" page at an e-commerce site. In such a case, it is wasteful to create a new session when no session exists already. So, you can use `getSession(false)`, which returns `null` if no session already exists for the current client. Here is an example.

```
HttpSession session = request.getSession(false);
if (session == null) {
  printMessageSayingCartIsEmpty();
} else {
  extractCartAndPrintContents(session);
}
```

Looking Up Information Associated with a Session

`HttpSession` objects live on the server; they don't go back and forth over the network; they're just automatically associated with the client by a behind-the-scenes mechanism like cookies or URL rewriting. These session objects have a built-in data structure (a hash table) in which you can store any number of keys and associated values. You use `session.getAttribute("key")` to look up a previously stored value. The return type is `Object`, so you must do a typecast to whatever more specific type of data was associated with that attribute name in the session. The return value is `null` if there is no such attribute, so you need to check for `null` before calling methods on objects associated with sessions.

Here's a representative example.

```
HttpSession session = request.getSession();
SomeClass value =
  (SomeClass)session.getAttribute("someIdentifier");
if (value == null) { // No such object already in session
  value = new SomeClass(...);
  session.setAttribute("someIdentifier", value);
}
doSomethingWith(value);
```

In most cases, you have a specific attribute name in mind and want to find the value (if any) already associated with that name. However, you can also discover all the attribute names in a given session by calling `getAttributeNames`, which returns an `Enumeration`.

Associating Information with a Session

As discussed in the previous subsection, you *read* information associated with a session by using `getAttribute`. To *specify* information, use `setAttribute`. To let your values perform side effects when they are stored in a session, simply have the object you are associating with the session implement the `HttpSessionBindingListener` interface. That way, every time `setAttribute` is called on one of those objects, its `valueBound` method is called immediately afterward.

Be aware that `setAttribute` replaces any previous values; to remove a value without supplying a replacement, use `removeAttribute`. This method triggers the `valueUnbound` method of any values that implement `HttpSessionBindingListener`.

Following is an example of adding information to a session. You can add information in two ways: by adding a new session attribute (as with the bold line in the example) or by augmenting an object that is already in the session (as in the last line of the example). This distinction is fleshed out in the examples of Sections 9.7 and 9.8, which contrast the use of immutable and mutable objects as session attributes.

```
HttpSession session = request.getSession();
SomeClass value =
  (SomeClass)session.getAttribute("someIdentifier");
if (value == null) { // No such object already in session
  value = new SomeClass(...);
  session.setAttribute("someIdentifier", value);
}
doSomethingWith(value);
```

In general, session attributes merely have to be of type `Object` (i.e., they can be anything other than `null` or a primitive like `int`, `double`, or `boolean`). However, some application servers support distributed Web applications in which an application is shared across a cluster of physical servers. Session tracking needs to still work in such a case, so the system needs to be able to move session objects from machine to machine. Thus, if you run in such an environment and you mark your Web application as being distributable, you must meet the additional requirement that session attributes implement the `Serializable` interface.

Discarding Session Data

When you are done with a user's session data, you have three options.

- **Remove only the data your servlet created.** You can call `removeAttribute("key")` to discard the value associated with the specified key. This is the most common approach.

- **Delete the whole session (in the current Web application).** You can call `invalidate` to discard an entire session. Just remember that doing so causes all of that user's session data to be lost, not just the session data that your servlet or JSP page created. So, *all* the servlets and JSP pages in a Web application have to agree on the cases for which `invalidate` may be called.
- **Log the user out and delete all sessions belonging to him or her.** Finally, in servers that support servlets 2.4 and JSP 2.0, you can call `logout` to log the client out of the Web server and invalidate all sessions (at most one per Web application) associated with that user. Again, since this action affects servlets other than your own, be sure to coordinate use of the `logout` command with the other developers at your site.

9.3 The Session-Tracking API

Although the session attributes (i.e., the user data) are the pieces of session information you care most about, other information is sometimes useful as well. Here is a summary of the methods available in the `HttpSession` class.

public Object getAttribute(String name)
This method extracts a previously stored value from a session object. It returns `null` if no value is associated with the given name.

public Enumeration getAttributeNames()
This method returns the names of all attributes in the session.

public void setAttribute(String name, Object value)
This method associates a value with a name. If the object supplied to `setAttribute` implements the `HttpSessionBindingListener` interface, the object's `valueBound` method is called after it is stored in the session. Similarly, if the previous value implements `HttpSessionBindingListener`, its `valueUnbound` method is called.

public void removeAttribute(String name)
This method removes any values associated with the designated name. If the value being removed implements `HttpSessionBindingListener`, its `valueUnbound` method is called.

public void invalidate()

This method invalidates the session and unbinds all objects associated with it. Use this method with caution; remember that sessions are associated with users (i.e., clients), not with individual servlets or JSP pages. So, if you invalidate a session, you might be destroying data that another servlet or JSP page is using.

public void logout()

This method logs the client out of the Web server and invalidates *all* sessions associated with that client. The scope of the logout is the same as the scope of the authentication. For example, if the server implements single sign-on, calling `logout` logs the client out of all Web applications on the server and invalidates all sessions (at most one per Web application) associated with the client. For details, see the chapters on Web application security in Volume 2 of this book.

public String getId()

This method returns the unique identifier generated for each session. It is useful for debugging or logging or, in rare cases, for programmatically moving values out of memory and into a database (however, some J2EE servers can do this automatically).

public boolean isNew()

This method returns `true` if the client (browser) has never seen the session, usually because the session was just created rather than being referenced by an incoming client request. It returns `false` for preexisting sessions. The main reason for mentioning this method is to steer you away from it: `isNew` is much less useful than it appears at first glance. Many beginning developers try to use `isNew` to determine whether users have been to their servlet before (within the session timeout period), writing code like the following:

```
HttpSession session = request.getSession();
if (session.isNew()) {
  doStuffForNewbies();
} else {
  doStuffForReturnVisitors();  // Wrong!
}
```

Wrong! Yes, if `isNew` returns `true`, then as far as you can tell this is the user's first visit (at least within the session timeout). But if `isNew` returns `false`, it merely shows that they have visited the Web application before, not that they have visited your servlet or JSP page before.

public long getCreationTime()
This method returns the time in milliseconds since midnight, January 1, 1970 (GMT) at which the session was first built. To get a value useful for printing, pass the value to the `Date` constructor or the `setTimeInMillis` method of `GregorianCalendar`.

public long getLastAccessedTime()
This method returns the time in milliseconds since midnight, January 1, 1970 (GMT) at which the session was last accessed by the client.

public int getMaxInactiveInterval()
public void setMaxInactiveInterval(int seconds)
These methods get or set the length of time, in seconds, that a session should go without access before being automatically invalidated. A negative value specifies that the session should never time out. Note that the timeout is maintained on the server and is *not* the same as the cookie expiration date. For one thing, sessions are normally based on in-memory cookies, not persistent cookies, so there *is* no expiration date. Even if you intercepted the `JSESSIONID` cookie and sent it out with an expiration date, browser sessions and server sessions are two distinct things. For details on the distinction, see the next section.

9.4 Browser Sessions vs. Server Sessions

By default, session-tracking is based on cookies that are stored in the browser's memory, not written to disk. Thus, unless the servlet explicitly reads the incoming `JSESSIONID` cookie, sets the maximum age and path, and sends it back out, quitting the browser results in the session being broken: the client will not be able to access the session again. The problem, however, is that the server does not know that the browser was closed and thus the server has to maintain the session in memory until the inactive interval has been exceeded.

Consider a physical shopping trip to a Wal-Mart store. You browse around and put some items in a physical shopping cart, then leave that shopping cart at the end of an aisle while you look for another item. A clerk walks up and sees the shopping cart. Can he reshelve the items in it? No—you are probably still shopping and will come back for the cart soon. What if you realize that you have lost your wallet, so you get in your car and drive home? Can the clerk reshelve the items in your shopping cart now? Again, no—the clerk presumably does not *know* that you have left the store. So, what can the clerk do? He can keep an eye on the cart, and if nobody has touched it for some period of time, he can then conclude that it is abandoned and take the items out of it. The only exception is if you brought the cart to him and said "I'm sorry, I left my wallet at home, so I have to leave."

The analogous situation in the servlet world is one in which the server is trying to decide if it can throw away your `HttpSession` object. Just because you are not currently using the session does not mean the server can throw it away. Maybe you will be back (submit a new request) soon? If you quit your browser, thus causing the browser-session-level cookies to be lost, the session is effectively broken. But, as with the case of getting in your car and leaving Wal-Mart, the server does not *know* that you quit your browser. So, the server still has to wait for a period of time to see if the session has been abandoned. Sessions automatically become inactive when the amount of time between client accesses exceeds the interval specified by `getMaxInactiveInterval`. When this happens, objects stored in the `HttpSession` object are removed (unbound). Then, if those objects implement the `HttpSessionBindingListener` interface, they are automatically notified. The one exception to the "the server waits until sessions time out" rule is if `invalidate` or `logout` is called. This is akin to your explicitly telling the Wal-Mart clerk that you are leaving, so the server can immediately remove all the items from the session and destroy the session object.

9.5 Encoding URLs Sent to the Client

By default, servlet containers (engines) use cookies as the underlying mechanism for session tracking. But suppose you reconfigure your server to use URL rewriting instead? How will your code have to change?

The goods news: your core session-tracking code does not need to change at all.

The bad news: lots of *other* code has to change. In particular, if any of your pages contain links back to your own site, you have to explicitly add the session data to the URL. Now, the servlet API provides methods to add this information to whatever URL you specify. The problem is that you have to *call* these methods; it is not technically feasible for the system to examine the output of all of your servlets and JSP pages, figure out which parts contain hyperlinks back to your site, and modify those URLs. You have to tell it which URLs to modify. This requirement means that you cannot have static HTML pages if you use URL rewriting for session tracking, or at least you cannot have static HTML pages that refer to your own site. This is a significant burden in many applications, but worth the price in a few.

Core Warning

If you use URL rewriting for session tracking, most or all of your pages will have to be dynamically generated. You cannot have any static HTML pages that contain hyperlinks to dynamic pages at your site.

There are two possible situations in which you might use URLs that refer to your own site.

The first one is where the URLs are embedded in the Web page that the servlet generates. These URLs should be passed through the `encodeURL` method of `HttpServletResponse`. The method determines if URL rewriting is currently in use and appends the session information only if necessary. The URL is returned unchanged otherwise.

Here's an example:

```
String originalURL = someRelativeOrAbsoluteURL;
String encodedURL = response.encodeURL(originalURL);
out.println("<A HREF=\"" + encodedURL + "\">...</A>");
```

The second situation in which you might use a URL that refers to your own site is in a `sendRedirect` call (i.e., placed into the `Location` response header). In this second situation, different rules determine whether session information needs to be attached, so you cannot use `encodeURL`. Fortunately, `HttpServletResponse` supplies an `encodeRedirectURL` method to handle that case. Here's an example:

```
String originalURL = someURL;
String encodedURL = response.encodeRedirectURL(originalURL);
response.sendRedirect(encodedURL);
```

If you think there is a reasonable likelihood that your Web application will eventually use URL rewriting instead of cookies, it is good practice to plan ahead and encode URLs that reference your own site.

9.6 A Servlet That Shows Per-Client Access Counts

Listing 9.1 presents a simple servlet that shows basic information about the client's session. When the client connects, the servlet uses `request.getSession` either to retrieve the existing session or, if there is no session, to create a new one. The servlet then looks for an attribute called `accessCount` of type `Integer`. If it cannot find such an attribute, it uses 0 as the number of previous accesses. This value is then incremented and associated with the session by `setAttribute`. Finally, the servlet prints a small HTML table showing information about the session.

Note that `Integer` is an *immutable* (nonmodifiable) data structure: once built, it cannot be changed. That means you have to allocate a new `Integer` object on each request, then use `setAttribute` to replace the old object. The following snippet shows the general approach for session tracking when an immutable object will be stored.

```
HttpSession session = request.getSession();
SomeImmutableClass value =
  (SomeImmutableClass)session.getAttribute("someIdentifier");
if (value == null) { // No such object already in session
  value = new SomeImmutableClass(...);
} else {
  value = new SomeImmutableClass(calculatedFrom(value));
}
session.setAttribute("someIdentifier", value);
doSomethingWith(value);
```

This approach contrasts with the approach used in the next section (Section 9.7) with a mutable (modifiable) data structure. In that approach, the object is allocated and `setAttribute` is called only when there is no such object already in the session. That is, the *contents* of the object change each time, but the session maintains the same object *reference*.

Figures 9–1 and 9–2 show the servlet on the initial visit and after the page was reloaded several times.

Listing 9.1 ShowSession.java

```
package coreservlets;

import java.io.*;
import javax.servlet.*;
import javax.servlet.http.*;
import java.util.*;

/** Servlet that uses session tracking to keep per-client
 *  access counts. Also shows other info about the session.
 */

public class ShowSession extends HttpServlet {
  public void doGet(HttpServletRequest request,
                    HttpServletResponse response)
      throws ServletException, IOException {
    response.setContentType("text/html");
    HttpSession session = request.getSession();
```

Listing 9.1 ShowSession.java *(continued)*

```
    String heading;
    Integer accessCount =
      (Integer)session.getAttribute("accessCount");
    if (accessCount == null) {
      accessCount = new Integer(0);
      heading = "Welcome, Newcomer";
    } else {
      heading = "Welcome Back";
      accessCount = new Integer(accessCount.intValue() + 1);
    }
    // Integer is an immutable data structure. So, you
    // cannot modify the old one in-place. Instead, you
    // have to allocate a new one and redo setAttribute.
    session.setAttribute("accessCount", accessCount);
    PrintWriter out = response.getWriter();
    String title = "Session Tracking Example";
    String docType =
      "<!DOCTYPE HTML PUBLIC \"-//W3C//DTD HTML 4.0 " +
      "Transitional//EN\">\n";
    out.println(docType +
                "<HTML>\n" +
                "<HEAD><TITLE>" + title + "</TITLE></HEAD>\n" +
                "<BODY BGCOLOR=\"#FDF5E6\">\n" +
                "<CENTER>\n" +
                "<H1>" + heading + "</H1>\n" +
                "<H2>Information on Your Session:</H2>\n" +
                "<TABLE BORDER=1>\n" +
                "<TR BGCOLOR=\"#FFAD00\">\n" +
                "  <TH>Info Type<TH>Value\n" +
                "<TR>\n" +
                "  <TD>ID\n" +
                "  <TD>" + session.getId() + "\n" +
                "<TR>\n" +
                "  <TD>Creation Time\n" +
                "  <TD>" +
                new Date(session.getCreationTime()) + "\n" +
                "<TR>\n" +
                "  <TD>Time of Last Access\n" +
                "  <TD>" +
                new Date(session.getLastAccessedTime()) + "\n" +
                "<TR>\n" +
                "  <TD>Number of Previous Accesses\n" +
                "  <TD>" + accessCount + "\n" +
                "</TABLE>\n" +
                "</CENTER></BODY></HTML>");
  }
}
```

Figure 9–1 First visit by client to `ShowSession` servlet.

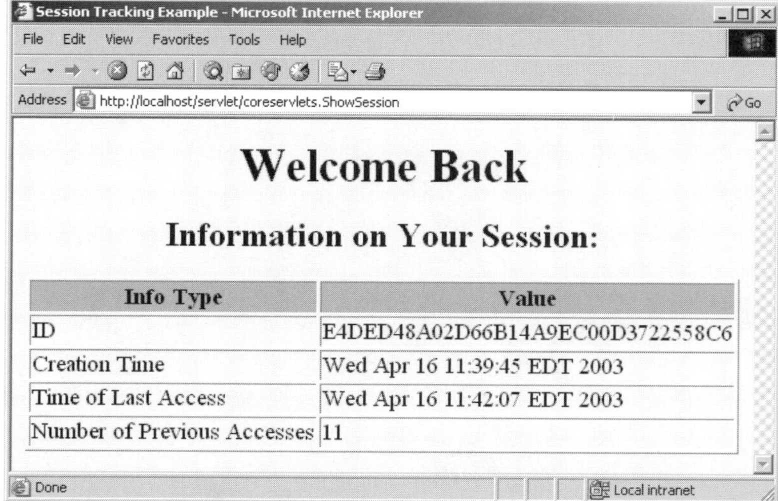

Figure 9–2 Twelfth visit to `ShowSession` servlet. Access count for this client is independent of number of visits by other clients.

9.7 Accumulating a List of User Data

The example of the previous section (Section 9.6) stores user-specific data in the user's HttpSession object. The object stored (an Integer) is an immutable data structure: one that cannot be modified. Consequently, a new Integer is allocated for each request, and that new object is stored in the session with setAttribute, overwriting the previous value.

Another common approach is to use a *mutable* data structure such as an array, List, Map, or application-specific data structure that has writable fields (instance variables). With this approach, you do not need to call setAttribute except when the object is first allocated. Here is the basic template:

```
HttpSession session = request.getSession();
SomeMutableClass value =
  (SomeMutableClass)session.getAttribute("someIdentifier");
if (value == null) { // No such object already in session
  value = new SomeMutableClass(...);
  session.setAttribute("someIdentifier", value);
}
value.updateInternalState(...);
doSomethingWith(value);
```

Mutable data structures are most commonly used to maintain a set of data associated with the user. In this section we present a simplified example in which we maintain a basic list of items that each user has purchased. In the next section (Section 9.8), we present a full-fledged shopping cart example. Most of the code in that example is for automatically building the Web pages that display the items and for the shopping cart itself. Although these application-specific pieces can be somewhat complicated, the basic session tracking is quite simple. Even so, it is useful to see the fundamental approach without the distractions of the application-specific pieces. That's the purpose of the example here.

Listing 9.2 shows an application that uses a simple ArrayList (the Java 2 platform's replacement for Vector) to keep track of the items each user has purchased. In addition to finding or creating the session and inserting the newly purchased item (the value of the newItem request parameter) into it, this example outputs a bulleted list of whatever items are in the "cart" (i.e., the ArrayList). Notice that the code that outputs this list is synchronized on the ArrayList. This precaution is worth taking, but you should be aware that the circumstances that make synchronization necessary are exceedingly rare. Since each user has a separate session, the only way a race condition could occur is if the same user submits two purchases in rapid succession. Although unlikely, this *is* possible, so synchronization is worthwhile.

Listing 9.2 ShowItems.java

```
package coreservlets;

import java.io.*;
import javax.servlet.*;
import javax.servlet.http.*;
import java.util.*;

/** Servlet that displays a list of items being ordered.
 *  Accumulates them in an ArrayList with no attempt at
 *  detecting repeated items. Used to demonstrate basic
 *  session tracking.
 */

public class ShowItems extends HttpServlet {
  public void doGet(HttpServletRequest request,
                    HttpServletResponse response)
      throws ServletException, IOException {
    HttpSession session = request.getSession();
    ArrayList previousItems =
      (ArrayList)session.getAttribute("previousItems");
    if (previousItems == null) {
      previousItems = new ArrayList();
      session.setAttribute("previousItems", previousItems);
    }
    String newItem = request.getParameter("newItem");
    response.setContentType("text/html");
    PrintWriter out = response.getWriter();
    String title = "Items Purchased";
    String docType =
      "<!DOCTYPE HTML PUBLIC \"-//W3C//DTD HTML 4.0 " +
      "Transitional//EN\">\n";
    out.println(docType +
                "<HTML>\n" +
                "<HEAD><TITLE>" + title + "</TITLE></HEAD>\n" +
                "<BODY BGCOLOR=\"#FDF5E6\">\n" +
                "<H1>" + title + "</H1>");
    synchronized(previousItems) {
      if (newItem != null) {
        previousItems.add(newItem);
      }
      if (previousItems.size() == 0) {
        out.println("<I>No items</I>");
```

Listing 9.2 ShowItems.java *(continued)*

```
      } else {
        out.println("<UL>");
        for(int i=0; i<previousItems.size(); i++) {
          out.println("<LI>" + (String)previousItems.get(i));
        }
        out.println("</UL>");
      }
    }
    out.println("</BODY></HTML>");
  }
}
```

Listing 9.3 shows an HTML form that collects values of the `newItem` parameter and submits them to the servlet. Figure 9–3 shows the result of the form; Figures 9–4 and 9–5 show the results of the servlet before the order form is visited and after it is visited several times, respectively.

Listing 9.3 OrderForm.html

```
<!DOCTYPE HTML PUBLIC "-//W3C//DTD HTML 4.0 Transitional//EN">
<HTML>
<HEAD>
  <TITLE>Order Form</TITLE>
</HEAD>
<BODY BGCOLOR="#FDF5E6">
<CENTER>
<H1>Order Form</H1>
<FORM ACTION="servlet/coreservlets.ShowItems">
  New Item to Order:
  <INPUT TYPE="TEXT" NAME="newItem" VALUE="Yacht"><P>
  <INPUT TYPE="SUBMIT" VALUE="Order and Show All Purchases">
</FORM>
</CENTER></BODY></HTML>
```

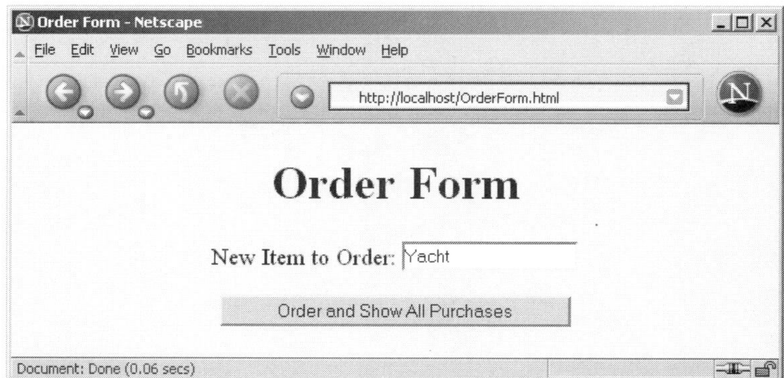

Figure 9–3 Front end to the item display servlet.

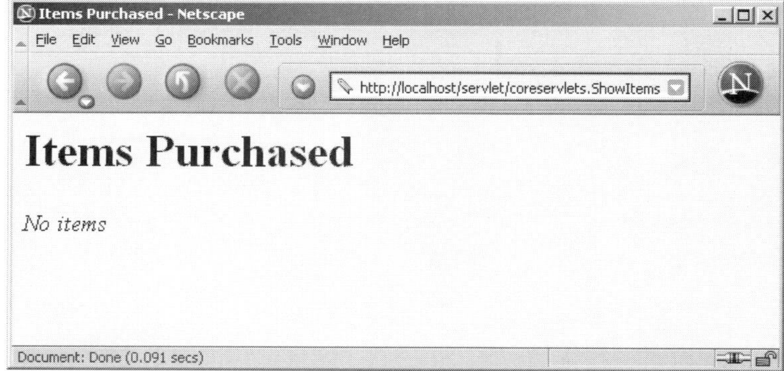

Figure 9–4 The item display servlet before any purchases are made.

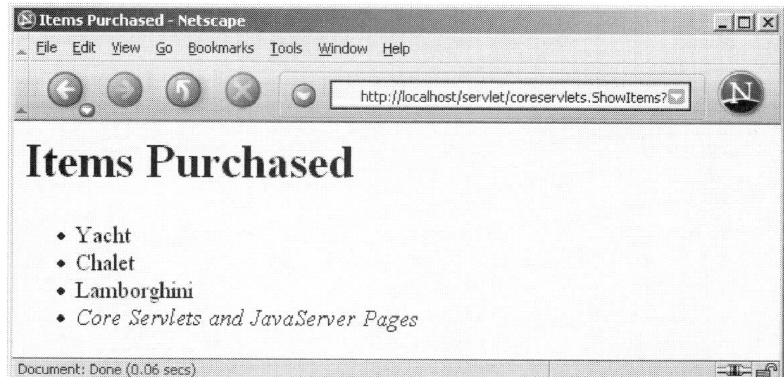

Figure 9–5 The item display servlet after a few valuable items are purchased.

9.8 An Online Store with a Shopping Cart and Session Tracking

This section gives an extended example of how you might build an online store that uses session tracking. The first subsection shows how to build pages that display items for sale. The code for each display page simply lists the page title and the identifiers of the items listed on the page. The actual page is then built automatically by methods in the parent class, based on item descriptions stored in the catalog. The second subsection shows the page that handles the orders. It uses session tracking to associate a shopping cart with each user and permits the user to modify orders for any previously selected item. The third subsection presents the implementation of the shopping cart, the data structures representing individual items and orders, and the catalog.

Creating the Front End

Listing 9.4 presents an abstract base class used as a starting point for servlets that want to display items for sale. It takes the identifiers for the items for sale, looks them up in the catalog, and uses the descriptions and prices found there to present an order page to the user. Listing 9.5 (with the result shown in Figure 9–6) and Listing 9.6 (with the result shown in Figure 9–7) show how easy it is to build actual pages with this parent class.

Listing 9.4 CatalogPage.java

```
package coreservlets;

import java.io.*;
import javax.servlet.*;
import javax.servlet.http.*;

/** Base class for pages showing catalog entries.
 *  Servlets that extend this class must specify
 *  the catalog entries that they are selling and the page
 *  title <I>before</I> the servlet is ever accessed. This
 *  is done by putting calls to setItems and setTitle
 *  in init.
 */
```

Listing 9.4 CatalogPage.java *(continued)*

```
public abstract class CatalogPage extends HttpServlet {
  private CatalogItem[] items;
  private String[] itemIDs;
  private String title;

  /** Given an array of item IDs, look them up in the
   *  Catalog and put their corresponding CatalogItem entry
   *  into the items array. The CatalogItem contains a short
   *  description, a long description, and a price,
   *  using the item ID as the unique key.
   *  <P>
   *  Servlets that extend CatalogPage <B>must</B> call
   *  this method (usually from init) before the servlet
   *  is accessed.
   */

  protected void setItems(String[] itemIDs) {
    this.itemIDs = itemIDs;
    items = new CatalogItem[itemIDs.length];
    for(int i=0; i<items.length; i++) {
      items[i] = Catalog.getItem(itemIDs[i]);
    }
  }

  /** Sets the page title, which is displayed in
   *  an H1 heading in resultant page.
   *  <P>
   *  Servlets that extend CatalogPage <B>must</B> call
   *  this method (usually from init) before the servlet
   *  is accessed.
   */

  protected void setTitle(String title) {
    this.title = title;
  }

  /** First display title, then, for each catalog item,
   *  put its short description in a level-two (H2) heading
   *  with the price in parentheses and long description
   *  below. Below each entry, put an order button
   *  that submits info to the OrderPage servlet for
   *  the associated catalog entry.
   *  <P>
   *  To see the HTML that results from this method, do
   *  "View Source" on KidsBooksPage or TechBooksPage, two
   *  concrete classes that extend this abstract class.
   */
```

Listing 9.4 CatalogPage.java *(continued)*

```
  public void doGet(HttpServletRequest request,
                    HttpServletResponse response)
      throws ServletException, IOException {
    if (items == null) {
      response.sendError(response.SC_NOT_FOUND,
                         "Missing Items.");
      return;
    }
    response.setContentType("text/html");
    PrintWriter out = response.getWriter();
    String docType =
      "<!DOCTYPE HTML PUBLIC \"-//W3C//DTD HTML 4.0 " +
      "Transitional//EN\">\n";
    out.println(docType +
                "<HTML>\n" +
                "<HEAD><TITLE>" + title + "</TITLE></HEAD>\n" +
                "<BODY BGCOLOR=\"#FDF5E6\">\n" +
                "<H1 ALIGN=\"CENTER\">" + title + "</H1>");
    CatalogItem item;
    for(int i=0; i<items.length; i++) {
      out.println("<HR>");
      item = items[i];
      // Show error message if subclass lists item ID
      // that's not in the catalog.
      if (item == null) {
        out.println("<FONT COLOR=\"RED\">" +
                    "Unknown item ID " + itemIDs[i] +
                    "</FONT>");
      } else {
        out.println();
        String formURL =
          "/servlet/coreservlets.OrderPage";
        // Pass URLs that reference own site through encodeURL.
        formURL = response.encodeURL(formURL);
        out.println
          ("<FORM ACTION=\"" + formURL + "\">\n" +
           "<INPUT TYPE=\"HIDDEN\" NAME=\"itemID\" " +
           "       VALUE=\"" + item.getItemID() + "\">\n" +
           "<H2>" + item.getShortDescription() +
           " ($" + item.getCost() + ")</H2>\n" +
           item.getLongDescription() + "\n" +
           "<P>\n<CENTER>\n" +
           "<INPUT TYPE=\"SUBMIT\" " +
           "VALUE=\"Add to Shopping Cart\">\n" +
           "</CENTER>\n<P>\n</FORM>");
      }
    }
    out.println("<HR>\n</BODY></HTML>");
  }
}
```

Listing 9.5 KidsBooksPage.java

```
package coreservlets;

/** A specialization of the CatalogPage servlet that
 *  displays a page selling three famous kids-book series.
 *  Orders are sent to the OrderPage servlet.
 */

public class KidsBooksPage extends CatalogPage {
  public void init() {
    String[] ids = { "lewis001", "alexander001", "rowling001" };
    setItems(ids);
    setTitle("All-Time Best Children's Fantasy Books");
  }
}
```

Listing 9.6 TechBooksPage.java

```
package coreservlets;

/** A specialization of the CatalogPage servlet that
 *  displays a page selling two famous computer books.
 *  Orders are sent to the OrderPage servlet.
 */

public class TechBooksPage extends CatalogPage {
  public void init() {
    String[] ids = { "hall001", "hall002" };
    setItems(ids);
    setTitle("All-Time Best Computer Books");
  }
}
```

Figure 9–6 Result of the `KidsBooksPage` servlet.

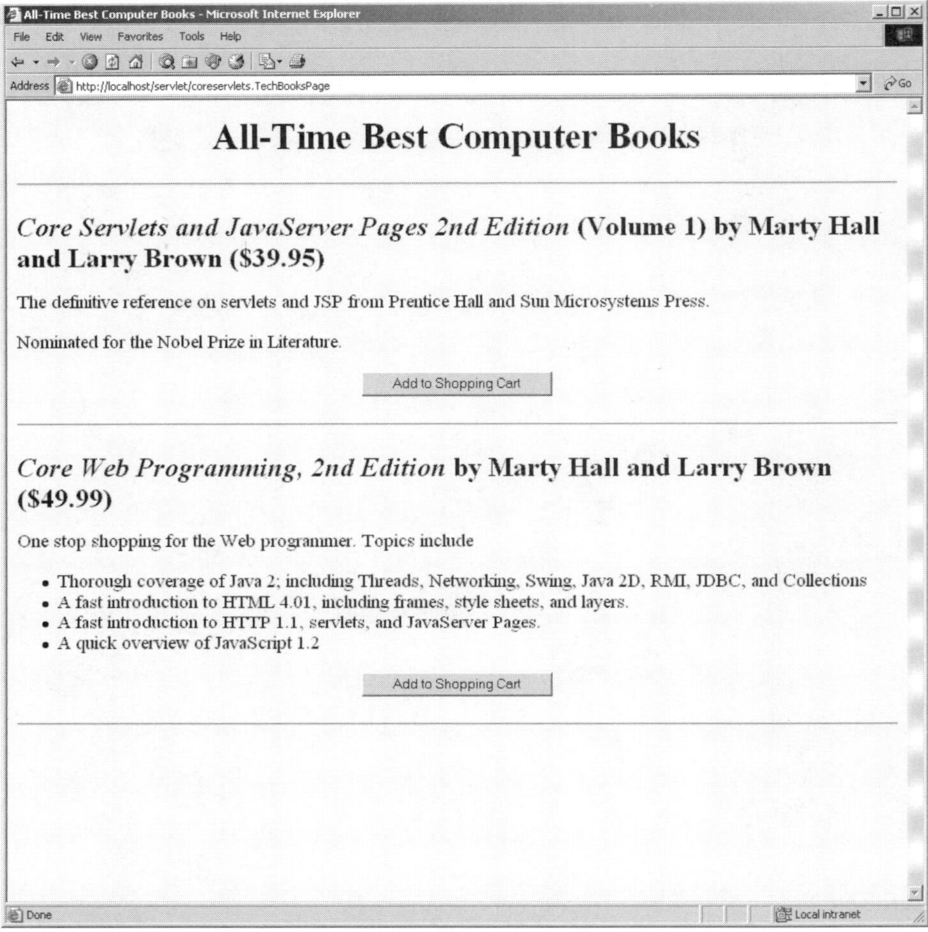

Figure 9–7 Result of the `TechBooksPage` servlet.

Handling the Orders

Listing 9.7 shows the servlet that handles the orders coming from the various catalog pages shown in the previous subsection. It uses session tracking to associate a shopping cart with each user. Since each user has a separate session, it is unlikely that multiple threads will be accessing the same shopping cart simultaneously. However, if you were paranoid, you could conceive of a few circumstances in which concurrent access could occur, such as when a single user has multiple browser windows open and sends updates from more than one in quick succession. So, just to be safe, the code synchronizes access based upon the session object. This synchronization prevents other threads that use the same session from accessing the data concurrently, while still allowing simultaneous requests from different users to proceed. Figures 9–8 and 9–9 show some typical results.

Listing 9.7 OrderPage.java

```
package coreservlets;

import java.io.*;
import javax.servlet.*;
import javax.servlet.http.*;
import java.util.*;
import java.text.*;

/** Shows all items currently in ShoppingCart. Clients
 *  have their own session that keeps track of which
 *  ShoppingCart is theirs. If this is their first visit
 *  to the order page, a new shopping cart is created.
 *  Usually, people come to this page by way of a page
 *  showing catalog entries, so this page adds an additional
 *  item to the shopping cart. But users can also
 *  bookmark this page, access it from their history list,
 *  or be sent back to it by clicking on the "Update Order"
 *  button after changing the number of items ordered.
 */

public class OrderPage extends HttpServlet {
  public void doGet(HttpServletRequest request,
                    HttpServletResponse response)
      throws ServletException, IOException {
    HttpSession session = request.getSession();
    ShoppingCart cart;
    synchronized(session) {
      cart = (ShoppingCart)session.getAttribute("shoppingCart");
      // New visitors get a fresh shopping cart.
      // Previous visitors keep using their existing cart.
      if (cart == null) {
        cart = new ShoppingCart();
        session.setAttribute("shoppingCart", cart);
      }
```

Listing 9.7 OrderPage.java *(continued)*

```
      if (itemID != null) {
        String numItemsString =
          request.getParameter("numItems");
        if (numItemsString == null) {
          // If request specified an ID but no number,
          // then customers came here via an "Add Item to Cart"
          // button on a catalog page.
          cart.addItem(itemID);
        } else {
          // If request specified an ID and number, then
          // customers came here via an "Update Order" button
          // after changing the number of items in order.
          // Note that specifying a number of 0 results
          // in item being deleted from cart.
          int numItems;
          try {
            numItems = Integer.parseInt(numItemsString);
          } catch(NumberFormatException nfe) {
            numItems = 1;
          }
          cart.setNumOrdered(itemID, numItems);
        }
      }
    }
    // Whether or not the customer changed the order, show
    // order status.
    response.setContentType("text/html");
    PrintWriter out = response.getWriter();
    String title = "Status of Your Order";
    String docType =
      "<!DOCTYPE HTML PUBLIC \"-//W3C//DTD HTML 4.0 " +
      "Transitional//EN\">\n";
    out.println(docType +
                "<HTML>\n" +
                "<HEAD><TITLE>" + title + "</TITLE></HEAD>\n" +
                "<BODY BGCOLOR=\"#FDF5E6\">\n" +
                "<H1 ALIGN=\"CENTER\">" + title + "</H1>");
    synchronized(session) {
      List itemsOrdered = cart.getItemsOrdered();
      if (itemsOrdered.size() == 0) {
        out.println("<H2><I>No items in your cart...</I></H2>");
      } else {
        // If there is at least one item in cart, show table
        // of items ordered.
        out.println
```

Listing 9.7 OrderPage.java *(continued)*

```
String itemID = request.getParameter("itemID");
    ("<TABLE BORDER=1 ALIGN=\"CENTER\">\n" +
     "<TR BGCOLOR=\"#FFAD00\">\n" +
     "  <TH>Item ID<TH>Description\n" +
     "  <TH>Unit Cost<TH>Number<TH>Total Cost");
  ItemOrder order;
  // Rounds to two decimal places, inserts dollar
  // sign (or other currency symbol), etc., as
  // appropriate in current Locale.
  NumberFormat formatter =
    NumberFormat.getCurrencyInstance();
  // For each entry in shopping cart, make
  // table row showing ID, description, per-item
  // cost, number ordered, and total cost.
  // Put number ordered in textfield that user
  // can change, with "Update Order" button next
  // to it, which resubmits to this same page
  // but specifying a different number of items.
  for(int i=0; i<itemsOrdered.size(); i++) {
    order = (ItemOrder)itemsOrdered.get(i);
    out.println
      ("<TR>\n" +
       "  <TD>" + order.getItemID() + "\n" +
       "  <TD>" + order.getShortDescription() + "\n" +
       "  <TD>" +
       formatter.format(order.getUnitCost()) + "\n" +
       "  <TD>" +
       "<FORM>\n" +  // Submit to current URL
       "<INPUT TYPE=\"HIDDEN\" NAME=\"itemID\"\n" +
       "       VALUE=\"" + order.getItemID() + "\">\n" +
       "<INPUT TYPE=\"TEXT\" NAME=\"numItems\"\n" +
       "       SIZE=3 VALUE=\"" +
       order.getNumItems() + "\">\n" +
       "<SMALL>\n" +
       "<INPUT TYPE=\"SUBMIT\"\n "+
       "       VALUE=\"Update Order\">\n" +
       "</SMALL>\n" +
       "</FORM>\n" +
       "  <TD>" +
       formatter.format(order.getTotalCost()));
  }
  String checkoutURL =
    response.encodeURL("../Checkout.html");
  // "Proceed to Checkout" button below table
```

Listing 9.7 OrderPage.java *(continued)*

```
        out.println
          ("</TABLE>\n" +
           "<FORM ACTION=\"" + checkoutURL + "\">\n" +
           "<BIG><CENTER>\n" +
           "<INPUT TYPE=\"SUBMIT\"\n" +
           "       VALUE=\"Proceed to Checkout\">\n" +
           "</CENTER></BIG></FORM>");
      }
      out.println("</BODY></HTML>");
    }
  }
}
```

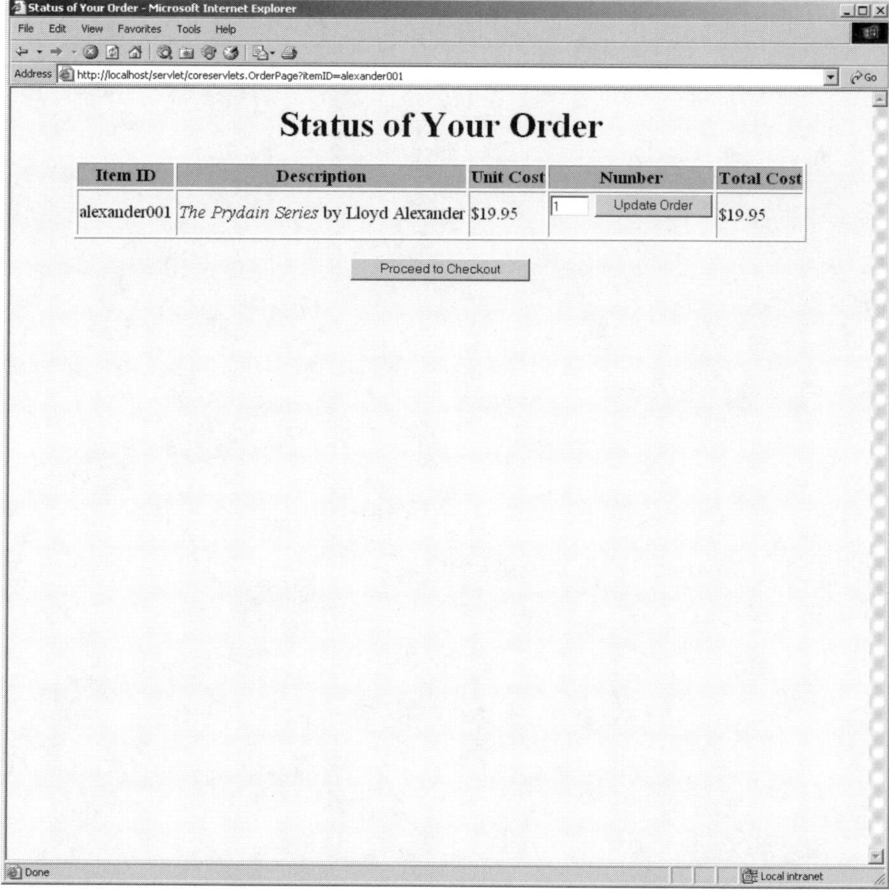

Figure 9–8 Result of `OrderPage` servlet after user clicks on "Add to Shopping Cart" in `KidsBooksPage`.

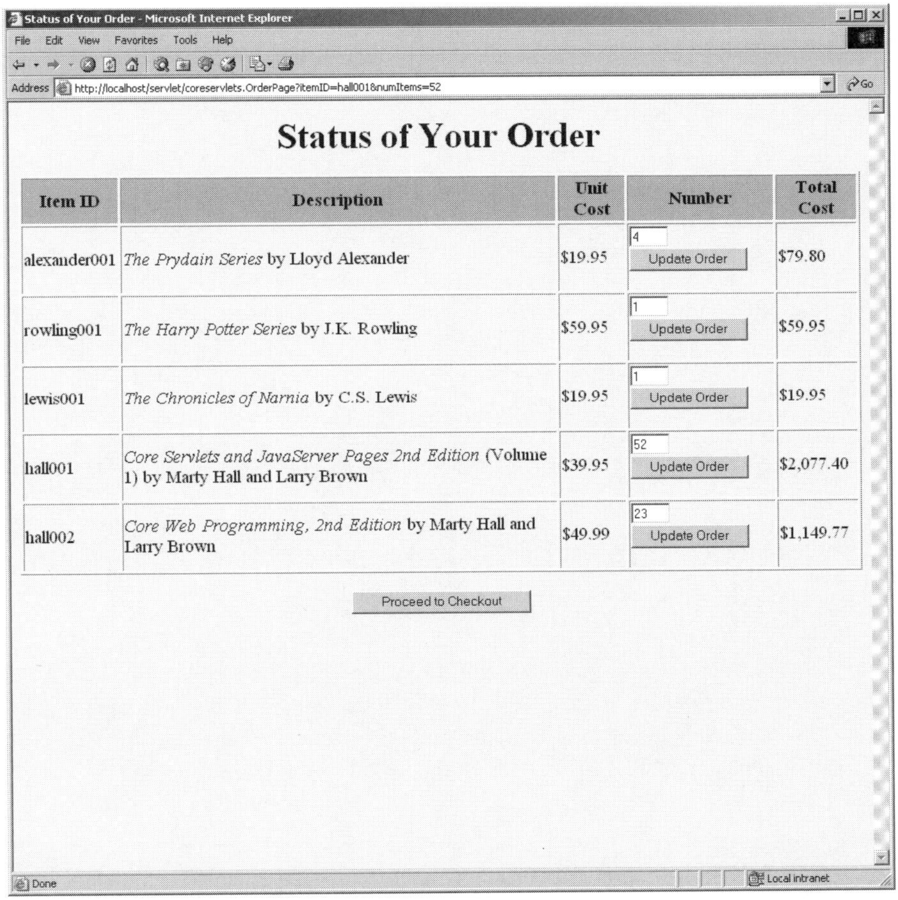

Status of Your Order - Microsoft Internet Explorer

File Edit View Favorites Tools Help

Address http://localhost/servlet/coreservlets.OrderPage?itemID=hall001&numItems=52

Status of Your Order

Item ID	Description	Unit Cost	Number	Total Cost
alexander001	*The Prydain Series* by Lloyd Alexander	$19.95	4 Update Order	$79.80
rowling001	*The Harry Potter Series* by J.K. Rowling	$59.95	1 Update Order	$59.95
lewis001	*The Chronicles of Narnia* by C.S. Lewis	$19.95	1 Update Order	$19.95
hall001	*Core Servlets and JavaServer Pages 2nd Edition* (Volume 1) by Marty Hall and Larry Brown	$39.95	52 Update Order	$2,077.40
hall002	*Core Web Programming, 2nd Edition* by Marty Hall and Larry Brown	$49.99	23 Update Order	$1,149.77

Proceed to Checkout

Done Local intranet

Figure 9–9 Result of `OrderPage` servlet after several additions and changes to the order.

Listing 9.8 Checkout.html

```
<!DOCTYPE HTML PUBLIC "-//W3C//DTD HTML 4.0 Transitional//EN">
<HTML>
<HEAD>
  <TITLE>Checking Out</TITLE>
</HEAD>
<BODY BGCOLOR="#FDF5E6">
<H1 ALIGN="CENTER">Checking Out</H1>
```

Listing 9.8 Checkout.html *(continued)*

```
We are sorry, but our electronic credit-card-processing
system is currently out of order. Please send a check
to:
<PRE>
  Marty Hall
  coreservlets.com, Inc.
  300 Red Brook Blvd., Suite 400
  Owings Mills, MD 21117
</PRE>
Since we have not yet calculated shipping charges, please
sign the check but do not fill in the amount. We will
generously do that for you.
</BODY></HTML>
```

Behind the Scenes: Implementing the Shopping Cart and Catalog Items

Listing 9.9 gives the shopping cart implementation. It simply maintains a `List` of orders, with methods to add and update these orders. Listing 9.10 shows the code for an individual catalog item, Listing 9.11 presents the class representing the order status of a particular item, and Listing 9.12 gives the catalog implementation.

Listing 9.9 ShoppingCart.java

```
package coreservlets;

import java.util.*;

/** A shopping cart data structure used to track orders.
 *  The OrderPage servlet associates one of these carts
 *  with each user session.
 */

public class ShoppingCart {
  private ArrayList itemsOrdered;

  /** Builds an empty shopping cart. */
```

Listing 9.9 ShoppingCart.java *(continued)*

```
public ShoppingCart() {
  itemsOrdered = new ArrayList();
}

/** Returns List of ItemOrder entries giving
 *  Item and number ordered. Declared as List instead
 *  of ArrayList so that underlying implementation
 *  can be changed later.
 */

public List getItemsOrdered() {
  return(itemsOrdered);
}

/** Looks through cart to see if it already contains
 *  an order entry corresponding to item ID. If it does,
 *  increments the number ordered. If not, looks up
 *  Item in catalog and adds an order entry for it.
 */

public synchronized void addItem(String itemID) {
  ItemOrder order;
  for(int i=0; i<itemsOrdered.size(); i++) {
    order = (ItemOrder)itemsOrdered.get(i);
    if (order.getItemID().equals(itemID)) {
      order.incrementNumItems();
      return;
    }
  }
  ItemOrder newOrder = new ItemOrder(Catalog.getItem(itemID));
  itemsOrdered.add(newOrder);
}

/** Looks through cart to find order entry corresponding
 *  to item ID listed. If the designated number
 *  is positive, sets it. If designated number is 0
 *  (or, negative due to a user input error), deletes
 *  item from cart.
 */

public synchronized void setNumOrdered(String itemID,
                                       int numOrdered) {
```

Listing 9.9 ShoppingCart.java *(continued)*

```
      ItemOrder order;
      for(int i=0; i<itemsOrdered.size(); i++) {
        order = (ItemOrder)itemsOrdered.get(i);
        if (order.getItemID().equals(itemID)) {
          if (numOrdered <= 0) {
            itemsOrdered.remove(i);
          } else {
            order.setNumItems(numOrdered);
          }
          return;
        }
      }
      ItemOrder newOrder =
        new ItemOrder(Catalog.getItem(itemID));
      itemsOrdered.add(newOrder);
    }
  }
```

Listing 9.10 CatalogItem.java

```
package coreservlets;

/** Describes a catalog item for an online store. The itemID
 *  uniquely identifies the item, the short description
 *  gives brief info like the book title and author,
 *  the long description describes the item in a couple
 *  of sentences, and the cost gives the current per-item price.
 *  Both the short and long descriptions can contain HTML
 *  markup.
 */

public class CatalogItem {
  private String itemID;
  private String shortDescription;
  private String longDescription;
  private double cost;

  public CatalogItem(String itemID, String shortDescription,
                     String longDescription, double cost) {
    setItemID(itemID);
    setShortDescription(shortDescription);
    setLongDescription(longDescription);
    setCost(cost);
  }
```

Listing 9.10 CatalogItem.java *(continued)*

```
  public String getItemID() {
    return(itemID);
  }

  protected void setItemID(String itemID) {
    this.itemID = itemID;
  }

  public String getShortDescription() {
    return(shortDescription);
  }

  protected void setShortDescription(String shortDescription) {
    this.shortDescription = shortDescription;
  }

  public String getLongDescription() {
    return(longDescription);
  }

  protected void setLongDescription(String longDescription) {
    this.longDescription = longDescription;
  }

  public double getCost() {
    return(cost);
  }

  protected void setCost(double cost) {
    this.cost = cost;
  }
}
```

Listing 9.11 ItemOrder.java

```
package coreservlets;

/** Associates a catalog Item with a specific order by
 *  keeping track of the number ordered and the total price.
 *  Also provides some convenience methods to get at the
 *  CatalogItem data without extracting the CatalogItem
 *  separately.
 */
```

Listing 9.11 ItemOrder.java *(continued)*

```
public class ItemOrder {
  private CatalogItem item;
  private int numItems;

  public ItemOrder(CatalogItem item) {
    setItem(item);
    setNumItems(1);
  }

  public CatalogItem getItem() {
    return(item);
  }

  protected void setItem(CatalogItem item) {
    this.item = item;
  }

  public String getItemID() {
    return(getItem().getItemID());
  }

  public String getShortDescription() {
    return(getItem().getShortDescription());
  }

  public String getLongDescription() {
    return(getItem().getLongDescription());
  }

  public double getUnitCost() {
    return(getItem().getCost());
  }

  public int getNumItems() {
    return(numItems);
  }

  public void setNumItems(int n) {
    this.numItems = n;
  }

  public void incrementNumItems() {
    setNumItems(getNumItems() + 1);
  }
```

Listing 9.11 ItemOrder.java *(continued)*

```
  public void cancelOrder() {
    setNumItems(0);
  }

  public double getTotalCost() {
    return(getNumItems() * getUnitCost());
  }
}
```

Listing 9.12 Catalog.java

```
package coreservlets;

/** A catalog that lists the items available in inventory. */

public class Catalog {
  // This would come from a database in real life.
  // We use a static table for ease of testing and deployment.
  // See JDBC chapters for info on using databases in
  // servlets and JSP pages.
  private static CatalogItem[] items =
    { new CatalogItem
        ("hall001",
         "<I>Core Servlets and JavaServer Pages " +
           "2nd Edition</I> (Volume 1)" +
           " by Marty Hall and Larry Brown",
         "The definitive reference on servlets " +
           "and JSP from Prentice Hall and \n" +
           "Sun Microsystems Press.<P>Nominated for " +
           "the Nobel Prize in Literature.",
         39.95),
      new CatalogItem
        ("hall002",
         "<I>Core Web Programming, 2nd Edition</I> " +
           "by Marty Hall and Larry Brown",
         "One stop shopping for the Web programmer. " +
           "Topics include \n" +
           "<UL><LI>Thorough coverage of Java 2; " +
           "including Threads, Networking, Swing, \n" +
           "Java 2D, RMI, JDBC, and Collections\n" +
           "<LI>A fast introduction to HTML 4.01, " +
           "including frames, style sheets, and layers.\n" +
```

Listing 9.12 Catalog.java *(continued)*

```
        "<LI>A fast introduction to HTTP 1.1, " +
        "servlets, and JavaServer Pages.\n" +
        "<LI>A quick overview of JavaScript 1.2\n" +
        "</UL>",
      49.99),
  new CatalogItem
    ("lewis001",
     "<I>The Chronicles of Narnia</I> by C.S. Lewis",
       "The classic children's adventure pitting " +
       "Aslan the Great Lion and his followers\n" +
       "against the White Witch and the forces " +
       "of evil. Dragons, magicians, quests, \n" +
       "and talking animals wound around a deep " +
       "spiritual allegory. Series includes\n" +
       "<I>The Magician's Nephew</I>,\n" +
       "<I>The Lion, the Witch and the Wardrobe</I>,\n" +
       "<I>The Horse and His Boy</I>,\n" +
       "<I>Prince Caspian</I>,\n" +
       "<I>The Voyage of the Dawn Treader</I>,\n" +
       "<I>The Silver Chair</I>, and \n" +
       "<I>The Last Battle</I>.",
     19.95),
  new CatalogItem
    ("alexander001",
     "<I>The Prydain Series</I> by Lloyd Alexander",
       "Humble pig-keeper Taran joins mighty " +
       "Lord Gwydion in his battle against\n" +
       "Arawn the Lord of Annuvin. Joined by " +
       "his loyal friends the beautiful princess\n" +
       "Eilonwy, wannabe bard Fflewddur Fflam," +
       "and furry half-man Gurgi, Taran discovers " +
       "courage, nobility, and other values along\n" +
       "the way. Series includes\n" +
       "<I>The Book of Three</I>,\n" +
       "<I>The Black Cauldron</I>,\n" +
       "<I>The Castle of Llyr</I>,\n" +
       "<I>Taran Wanderer</I>, and\n" +
       "<I>The High King</I>.",
     19.95),
  new CatalogItem
    ("rowling001",
     "<I>The Harry Potter Series</I> by J.K. Rowling",
     "The first five of the popular stories " +
       "about wizard-in-training Harry Potter\n" +
       "topped both the adult and children's " +
```

Listing 9.12 Catalog.java *(continued)*

```
          "best-seller lists. Series includes\n" +
          "<I>Harry Potter and the Sorcerer's Stone</I>,\n" +
          "<I>Harry Potter and the Chamber of Secrets</I>,\n" +
          "<I>Harry Potter and the " +
          "Prisoner of Azkaban</I>,\n" +
          "<I>Harry Potter and the Goblet of Fire</I>, and\n" +
          "<I>Harry Potter and the "+
          "Order of the Phoenix</I>.\n",
        59.95)
      };

  public static CatalogItem getItem(String itemID) {
    CatalogItem item;
    if (itemID == null) {
      return(null);
    }
    for(int i=0; i<items.length; i++) {
      item = items[i];
      if (itemID.equals(item.getItemID())) {
        return(item);
      }
    }
    return(null);
  }
}
```

JSP Technology

Part II

OVERVIEW OF JSP TECHNOLOGY

Topics in This Chapter

- Understanding the need for JSP
- Evaluating the benefits of JSP
- Comparing JSP to other technologies
- Avoiding JSP misconceptions
- Installing JSP pages
- Surveying JSP syntax

Chapter 10

JavaServer Pages (JSP) technology enables you to mix regular, static HTML with dynamically generated content. You simply write the regular HTML in the normal manner, using familiar Web-page-building tools. You then enclose the code for the dynamic parts in special tags, most of which start with `<%` and end with `%>`.

For example, Listing 10.1 (Figure 10–1) presents a very small JSP page that uses a request parameter to display the title of a book. Notice that the listing is mostly standard HTML; the dynamic code consists entirely of the half line shown in bold in the listing.

Listing 10.1 OrderConfirmation.jsp

```
<!DOCTYPE HTML PUBLIC "-//W3C//DTD HTML 4.0 Transitional//EN">
<HTML>
<HEAD>
<TITLE>Order Confirmation</TITLE>
<LINK REL=STYLESHEET
      HREF="JSP-Styles.css"
      TYPE="text/css">
</HEAD>
<BODY>
<H2>Order Confirmation</H2>
Thanks for ordering <I><%= request.getParameter("title") %></I>!
</BODY></HTML>
```

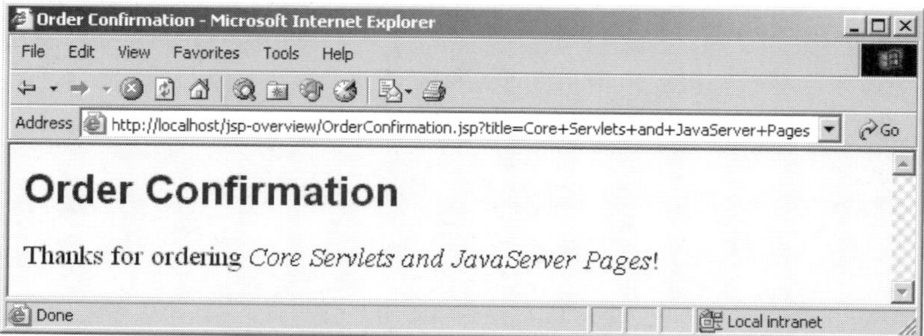

Figure 10–1 Result of OrderConfirmation.jsp.

You can think of servlets as Java code with HTML inside; you can think of JSP as HTML with Java code inside. Now, neither servlets nor JSP pages are restricted to using HTML, but they usually do, and this over-simplified description is a common way to view the technologies.

Now, despite the large apparent differences between JSP pages and servlets, behind the scenes they are the same thing. JSP pages are translated into servlets, the servlets are compiled, and at request time it is the compiled servlets that execute. So, writing JSP pages is really just another way of writing servlets.

Even though servlets and JSP pages are equivalent behind the scenes, they are not equally useful in all situations. Separating the static HTML from the dynamic content provides a number of benefits over servlets alone, and the approach used in JavaServer Pages offers several advantages over competing technologies. This chapter explains the reasons for using JSP, discusses its benefits, dispels some misconceptions, shows you how to install and execute JSP pages, and summarizes the JSP syntax discussed in the rest of the book.

10.1 The Need for JSP

"Hey!" you say, "You just spent several chapters extolling the virtues of servlets. I like servlets. Servlets are convenient to write and efficient to execute. They make it simple to read request parameters and to set up custom code to handle missing and malformed data. They can easily make use of HTTP request headers and can flexibly manipulate HTTP response data. They can customize their behavior based on cookies, track user-specific data with the session-tracking API, and talk to relational databases with JDBC. What more do I need?"

Well, this is a good point. Servlets are indeed useful, and JSP by no means makes them obsolete. However, look at the list of topics for which servlets excel. They are all tasks related to *programming* or data *processing*. But servlets are not so good at *presentation*. Servlets have the following deficiencies when it comes to generating the output:

- **It is hard to write and maintain the HTML.** Using `print` statements to generate HTML? Hardly convenient: you have to use parentheses and semicolons, have to insert backslashes in front of embedded double quotes, and have to use string concatenation to put the content together. Besides, it simply does not look like HTML, so it is harder to visualize. Compare this servlet style with Listing 10.1 where you hardly even notice that the page is not an ordinary HTML document.
- **You cannot use standard HTML tools.** All those great Web-site development tools you have are of little use when you are writing Java code.
- **The HTML is inaccessible to non-Java developers.** If the HTML is embedded within Java code, a Web development expert who does not know the Java programming language will have trouble reviewing and changing the HTML.

10.2 Benefits of JSP

JSP pages are translated into servlets. So, fundamentally, any task JSP pages can perform could also be accomplished by servlets. However, this underlying equivalence does not mean that servlets and JSP pages are equally appropriate in all scenarios. The issue is not the power of the technology, it is the convenience, productivity, and maintainability of one or the other. After all, anything you can do on a particular computer platform in the Java programming language you could also do in assembly language. But it still matters which you choose.

JSP provides the following benefits over servlets alone:

- **It is easier to write and maintain the HTML.** Your static code is ordinary HTML: no extra backslashes, no double quotes, and no lurking Java syntax.
- **You can use standard Web-site development tools.** For example, we use Macromedia Dreamweaver for most of the JSP pages in the book. Even HTML tools that know nothing about JSP can be used because they simply ignore the JSP tags.
- **You can divide up your development team.** The Java programmers can work on the dynamic code. The Web developers can concentrate on the presentation layer. On large projects, this division is very important. Depending on the size of your team and the complexity of your project, you can enforce a weaker or stronger separation between the static HTML and the dynamic content.

Now, this discussion is not to say that you should stop using servlets and use only JSP instead. By no means. Almost all projects will use both. For some requests in your project, you will use servlets. For others, you will use JSP. For still others, you will combine them with the MVC architecture (Chapter 15). You want the appropriate tool for the job, and servlets, by themselves, do not complete your toolkit.

10.3 Advantages of JSP Over Competing Technologies

A number of years ago, the lead author of this book (Marty) was invited to attend a small 20-person industry roundtable discussion on software technology. Sitting in the seat next to Marty was James Gosling, inventor of the Java programming language. Sitting several seats away was a high-level manager from a very large software company in Redmond, Washington. During the discussion, the moderator brought up the subject of Jini, which at that time was a new Java technology. The moderator asked the manager what he thought of it, and the manager responded that it was too early to tell, but that it seemed to be an excellent idea. He went on to say that they would keep an eye on it, and if it seemed to be catching on, they would follow his company's usual "embrace and extend" strategy. At this point, Gosling lightheartedly interjected "You mean *dis*grace and *dis*tend."

Now, the grievance that Gosling was airing was that he felt that this company would take technology from other companies and suborn it for their own purposes. But guess what? The shoe is on the other foot here. The Java community did not invent the idea of designing pages as a mixture of static HTML and dynamic code marked with special tags. For example, ColdFusion did it years earlier. Even ASP (a product from the very software company of the aforementioned manager) popularized this approach before JSP came along and decided to jump on the bandwagon. In fact, JSP not only adopted the general idea, it even used many of the same special tags as ASP did.

So, the question becomes: why use JSP instead of one of these other technologies? Our first response is that we are not arguing that everyone should. Several of those other technologies are quite good and are reasonable options in some situations. In other situations, however, JSP is clearly better. Here are a few of the reasons.

Versus .NET and Active Server Pages (ASP)

.NET is well-designed technology from Microsoft. ASP.NET is the part that directly competes with servlets and JSP. The advantages of JSP are twofold.

First, JSP is portable to multiple operating systems and Web servers; you aren't locked into deploying on Windows and IIS. Although the core .NET platform runs on a few non-Windows platforms, the ASP part does not. You cannot expect to deploy serious ASP.NET applications on multiple servers and operating systems. For some applications, this difference does not matter. For others, it matters greatly.

Second, for some applications the choice of the underlying language matters greatly. For example, although .NET's C# language is very well designed and is similar to Java, fewer programmers are familiar with either the core C# syntax or the many auxiliary libraries. In addition, many developers still use the original version of ASP. With this version, JSP has a clear advantage for the dynamic code. With JSP, the dynamic part is written in Java, not VBScript or another ASP-specific language, so JSP is more powerful and better suited to complex applications that require reusable components.

You could make the same argument when comparing JSP to the previous version of ColdFusion; with JSP you can use Java for the "real code" and are not tied to a particular server product. However, the current release of ColdFusion is within the context of a J2EE server, allowing developers to easily mix ColdFusion and servlet/JSP code.

Versus PHP

PHP (a recursive acronym for "PHP: Hypertext Preprocessor") is a free, open-source, HTML-embedded scripting language that is somewhat similar to both ASP and JSP. One advantage of JSP is that the dynamic part is written in Java, which already has an extensive API for networking, database access, distributed objects, and the like, whereas PHP requires learning an entirely new, less widely used language. A second advantage is that JSP is much more widely supported by tool and server vendors than is PHP.

Versus Pure Servlets

JSP doesn't provide any capabilities that couldn't, in principle, be accomplished with servlets. In fact, JSP documents are automatically translated into servlets behind the scenes. But it is more convenient to write (and to modify!) regular HTML than to use a zillion `println` statements to generate the HTML. Plus, by separating the presentation from the content, you can put different people on different tasks: your Web page design experts can build the HTML by using familiar tools and either leave places for your servlet programmers to insert the dynamic content or invoke the dynamic content indirectly by means of XML tags.

Does this mean that you can just learn JSP and forget about servlets? Absolutely not! JSP developers need to know servlets for four reasons:

1. JSP pages get translated into servlets. You can't understand how JSP works without understanding servlets.
2. JSP consists of static HTML, special-purpose JSP tags, and Java code. What kind of Java code? Servlet code! You can't write that code if you don't understand servlet programming.
3. Some tasks are better accomplished by servlets than by JSP. JSP is good at generating pages that consist of large sections of fairly well structured HTML or other character data. Servlets are better for generating binary data, building pages with highly variable structure, and performing tasks (such as redirection) that involve little or no output.
4. Some tasks are better accomplished by a *combination* of servlets and JSP than by *either* servlets or JSP alone. See Chapter 15 for details.

Versus JavaScript

JavaScript, which is completely distinct from the Java programming language, is normally used to dynamically generate HTML on the *client*, building parts of the Web page as the browser loads the document. This is a useful capability and does not normally overlap with the capabilities of JSP (which runs only on the *server*). JSP pages still include `SCRIPT` tags for JavaScript, just as normal HTML pages do. In fact, JSP can even be used to dynamically generate the JavaScript that will be sent to the client. So, JavaScript is not a competing technology; it is a complementary one.

It is also possible to use JavaScript on the server, most notably on Sun ONE (formerly iPlanet), IIS, and BroadVision servers. However, Java is more powerful, flexible, reliable, and portable.

Versus WebMacro or Velocity

JSP is by no means perfect. Many people have pointed out features that could be improved. This is a good thing, and one of the advantages of JSP is that the specification is controlled by a community that draws from many different companies. So, the technology can incorporate improvements in successive releases.

However, some groups have developed alternative Java-based technologies to try to address these deficiencies. This, in our judgment, is a mistake. Using a third-party tool like Apache Struts (see Volume 2 of this book) that *augments* JSP and servlet technology is a good idea when that tool adds sufficient benefit to compensate for the additional complexity. But using a nonstandard tool that tries to *replace* JSP is a bad idea. When choosing a technology, you need to weigh many factors: standardization, portability, integration, industry support, and technical features. The arguments for JSP alternatives have focused almost exclusively on the technical features part. But portability, standardization, and integration are also very important. For example, as discussed in Section 2.11, the servlet and JSP specifications define a standard directory structure for Web applications and provide standard files (.war files) for deploying Web applications. All JSP-compatible servers must support these standards. Filters (Volume 2) can be set up to apply to any number of servlets or JSP pages, but not to nonstandard resources. The same goes for Web application security settings (see Volume 2).

Besides, the tremendous industry support for JSP and servlet technology results in improvements that mitigate many of the criticisms of JSP. For example, the JSP Standard Tag Library (Volume 2) and the JSP 2.0 expression language (Chapter 16) address two of the most well-founded criticisms: the lack of good iteration constructs and the difficulty of accessing dynamic results without using either explicit Java code or verbose `jsp:useBean` elements.

10.4 Misconceptions About JSP

In this section, we address some of the most common misunderstandings about JSP.

Forgetting JSP Is Server-Side Technology

The book's Web site lists the lead author's email address: hall@coreservlets.com. Furthermore, Marty teaches JSP and servlet training courses for various companies and at public venues. Consequently, he gets a lot of email with servlet and JSP questions. Here are some typical questions he has received (most of them repeatedly).

- Our server is running JDK 1.4. So, how do I put a Swing component in a JSP page?
- How do I put an image into a JSP page? I do not know the proper Java I/O commands to read image files.
- Since Tomcat does not support JavaScript, how do I make images that are highlighted when the user moves the mouse over them?
- Our clients use older browsers that do not understand JSP. What should we do?
- When our clients use "View Source" in a browser, how can I prevent them from seeing the JSP tags?

All of these questions are based upon the assumption that browsers know something about the server-side process. But they do not. Thus:

- For putting applets with Swing components into Web pages, what matters is the browser's Java version—the server's version is irrelevant. If the browser supports the Java 2 platform, you use the normal `APPLET` (or Java plug-in) tag and would do so even if you were using non-Java technology on the server.
- You do not need Java I/O to read image files; you just put the image in the directory for Web resources (i.e., two levels up from WEB-INF/classes) and output a normal `IMG` tag.
- You create images that change under the mouse by using client-side JavaScript, referenced with the `SCRIPT` tag; this does not change just because the server is using JSP.
- Browsers do not "support" JSP at all—they merely see the output of the JSP page. So, make sure your JSP outputs HTML compatible with the browser, just as you would do with static HTML pages.
- And, of course you need not do anything to prevent clients from seeing JSP tags; those tags are processed on the server and are not part of the output that is sent to the client.

Confusing Translation Time with Request Time

A JSP page is converted into a servlet. The servlet is compiled, loaded into the server's memory, initialized, and executed. But which step happens when? To answer that question, remember two points:

- The JSP page is translated into a servlet and compiled only the first time it is accessed after having been modified.
- Loading into memory, initialization, and execution follow the normal rules for servlets.

Table 10.1 gives some common scenarios and tells whether or not each step occurs in that scenario. The most frequently misunderstood entries are highlighted. When referring to the table, note that servlets resulting from JSP pages use the `_jspService` method (called for both `GET` and `POST` requests), not `doGet` or `doPost`. Also, for initialization, they use the `jspInit` method, not the `init` method.

Table 10.1 JSP Operations in Various Scenarios

	JSP page translated into servlet	Servlet compiled	Servlet loaded into server's memory	`jspInit` called	`_jspService` called
			Page first written		
Request 1	Yes	Yes	Yes	Yes	Yes
Request 2	**No**	**No**	**No**	**No**	Yes
			Server restarted		
Request 3	**No**	**No**	Yes	Yes	Yes
Request 4	No	No	No	No	Yes
			Page modified		
Request 5	Yes	Yes	Yes	Yes	Yes
Request 6	No	No	No	No	Yes

Thinking JSP Alone Is Sufficient

There is a small community of developers that are so enamored with JSP that they use it for practically everything. Most of these developers *never* use servlets; many never even use auxiliary helper classes—they just build large complex JSP pages for each and every task.

This is a mistake. JSP is an excellent tool. But the fundamental problem it addresses is *presentation*: the difficulty of creating and maintaining HTML to represent the result of a request. JSP is a good choice for pages with relatively fixed formats and lots of static text. JSP, by itself, is less good for applications that have a variable structure, is poor for applications that have mostly dynamic data, and is totally unsuitable for applications that output binary data or manipulate HTTP without generating explicit output (as with the search engine servlet of Section 6.4). Still other applications are best solved with neither servlets alone nor JSP alone, but with a combination of the two (see Chapter 15).

JSP is a powerful and widely applicable tool. Nevertheless, other tools are sometimes better. Choose the right tool for the job.

Thinking Servlets Alone Are Sufficient

At the other end of the spectrum from the JSP-only camp is the servlets-only camp. Adherents of this camp state, quite rightly, that JSP pages are really just dressed up servlets, so JSP pages cannot accomplish anything that could not also be done with servlets. From this, they conclude that you should stick with servlets, where you have access to the full underlying power, have complete control, and can see exactly what is happening. Hmm, have you heard this argument before? It sounds a lot like the position of the "don't be a wimp; write all your code in assembly language" crowd.

Yes, you could use servlets for any task for which JSP is used. But it is not always equally convenient to do so. For tasks that involve a lot of static HTML content, use of JSP technology (or a combination of JSP and servlets) simplifies the creation and maintenance of the HTML, permits you to use industry standard Web site creation tools, and lets you "divide and conquer" by splitting your effort between the Java developers and the Web developers.

Servlets are powerful and widely applicable tools. Nevertheless, other tools are sometimes better. Choose the right tool for the job.

10.5 Installation of JSP Pages

Servlets require you to set your `CLASSPATH`, use packages to avoid name conflicts, install the class files in servlet-specific locations, and use special-purpose URLs. Not so with JSP pages. JSP pages can be placed in the same directories as normal HTML pages, images, and style sheets; they can also be accessed through URLs of the same form as those for HTML pages, images, and style sheets. Here are a few examples of default installation locations (i.e., locations that apply when you aren't using custom Web applications) and associated URLs. Where we list *SomeDirectory*, you can use any directory name you like, except that you are never allowed to use WEB-INF or META-INF as directory names. When using the default Web application, you also have to avoid a directory name that matches the URL prefix of any other Web application. For information on defining your own Web applications, see Section 2.11.

JSP Directories for Tomcat (Default Web Application)

- **Main Location.**
  install_dir/webapps/ROOT

- **Corresponding URL.**
  http://*host*/*SomeFile*.jsp
- **More Specific Location (Arbitrary Subdirectory).**
  install_dir/webapps/ROOT/*SomeDirectory*
- **Corresponding URL.**
  http://*host*/*SomeDirectory*/*SomeFile*.jsp

JSP Directories for JRun (Default Web Application)

- **Main Location.**
  install_dir/servers/default/default-ear/default-war
- **Corresponding URL.**
  http://*host*/*SomeFile*.jsp
- **More Specific Location (Arbitrary Subdirectory).**
  install_dir/servers/default/default-ear/default-war/*SomeDirectory*
- **Corresponding URL.**
  http://*host*/*SomeDirectory*/*SomeFile*.jsp

JSP Directories for Resin (Default Web Application)

- **Main Location.**
  install_dir/doc
- **Corresponding URL.**
  http://*host*/*SomeFile*.jsp
- **More Specific Location (Arbitrary Subdirectory).**
  install_dir/doc/*SomeDirectory*
- **Corresponding URL.**
  http://*host*/*SomeDirectory*/*SomeFile*.jsp

Note that, although JSP pages *themselves* need no special installation directories, any Java classes called *from* JSP pages still need to go in the standard locations used by servlet classes (e.g., .../WEB-INF/classes/*directoryMatchingPackageName*; see Section 2.10). Note that the Java classes used by JSP pages should *always* be in packages; this point is discussed further in later chapters.

10.6 Basic Syntax

Here is a quick summary of the various JSP constructs you will see in this book.

HTML Text

- **Description:**
  HTML content to be passed unchanged to the client
- **Example:**
  `<H1>Blah</H1>`
- **Discussed in:**
  Section 11.1

HTML Comments

- **Description:**
  HTML comment that is sent to the client but not displayed by the browser
- **Example:**
  `<!-- Blah -->`
- **Discussed in:**
  Section 11.1

Template Text

- **Description:**
  Text sent unchanged to the client. HTML text and HTML comments are just special cases of this.
- **Example:**
  Anything other than the syntax of the following subsections
- **Discussed in:**
  Section 11.1

JSP Comment

- **Description:**
  Developer comment that is not sent to the client
- **Example:**
  `<%-- Blah --%>`

- **Discussed in:**
  Section 11.1

JSP Expression

- **Description:**
  Expression that is evaluated and sent to the client each time the page is requested
- **Example:**
  `<%= Java Value %>`
- **Discussed in:**
  Section 11.4

JSP Scriptlet

- **Description:**
  Statement or statements that are executed each time the page is requested
- **Example:**
  `<% Java Statement %>`
- **Discussed in:**
  Section 11.7

JSP Declaration

- **Description:**
  Field or method that becomes part of class definition when page is translated into a servlet
- **Examples:**
  `<%! Field Definition %>`
  `<%! Method Definition %>`
- **Discussed in:**
  Section 11.10

JSP Directive

- **Description:**
  High-level information about the structure of the servlet code (`page`), code that is included at page-translation time (`include`), or custom tag libraries used (`taglib`)

- **Example:**
`<%@ directive att="val" %>`
- **Discussed in:**
`page`: Chapter 12
`include`: Chapter 13
`taglib` and `tag`: Volume 2

JSP Action

- **Description:**
Action that takes place when the page is requested
- **Example:**
`<jsp:blah>...</jsp:blah>`
- **Discussed in:**
`jsp:include` and related: Chapter 13
`jsp:useBean` and related: Chapter 14
`jsp:invoke` and related: Volume 2

JSP Expression Language Element

- **Description:**
Shorthand JSP expression
- **Example:**
`${ EL Expression }`
- **Discussed in:**
Chapter 16

Custom Tag (Custom Action)

- **Description:**
Invocation of custom tag
- **Example:**
```
<prefix:name>
Body
</prefix:name>
```
- **Discussed in:**
Volume 2

Escaped Template Text

- **Description:**
  Text that would otherwise be interpreted specially. Slash is removed and remaining text is sent to the client
- **Examples:**
  `<\%`
  `%\>`
- **Discussed in:**
  Section 11.1

Invoking Java Code with JSP Scripting Elements

Topics in This Chapter

- Static vs. dynamic text
- Dynamic code and good JSP design
- The importance of packages for JSP helper/utility classes
- JSP expressions
- JSP scriptlets
- JSP declarations
- Servlet code resulting from JSP scripting elements
- Scriptlets and conditional text
- Predefined variables
- Servlets vs. JSP pages for similar tasks

Chapter 11

This chapter discusses the "classic" approach to invoking Java code from within JSP pages. This approach works in both JSP 1 (i.e., JSP 1.2 and earlier) and JSP 2. Chapter 16 discusses the JSP expression language, which provides a concise mechanism to indirectly invoke Java code, but only in JSP 2.0 and later.

11.1 Creating Template Text

In most cases, a large percentage of your JSP document consists of static text (usually HTML), known as *template text*. In almost all respects, this HTML looks just like normal HTML, follows all the same syntax rules, and is simply "passed through" to the client by the servlet created to handle the page. Not only does the HTML look normal, it can be created by whatever tools you already are using for building Web pages. For example, we used Macromedia Dreamweaver for many of the JSP pages in this book.

There are two minor exceptions to the "template text is passed straight through" rule. First, if you want to have `<%` or `%>` in the output, you need to put `<\%` or `%\>` in the template text. Second, if you want a comment to appear in the JSP page but not in the resultant document, use

```
<%-- JSP Comment --%>
```

HTML comments of the form

```
<!-- HTML Comment -->
```

are passed through to the client normally.

11.2 Invoking Java Code from JSP

There are a number of different ways to generate dynamic content from JSP, as illustrated in Figure 11–1. Each of these approaches has a legitimate place; the size and complexity of the project is the most important factor in deciding which approach is appropriate. However, be aware that people err on the side of placing too much code directly in the page much more often than they err on the opposite end of the spectrum. Although putting small amounts of Java code directly in JSP pages works fine for simple applications, using long and complicated blocks of Java code in JSP pages yields a result that is hard to maintain, hard to debug, hard to reuse, and hard to divide among different members of the development team. See Section 11.3 (Limiting the Amount of Java Code in JSP Pages) for details. Nevertheless, many pages are quite simple, and the first two approaches of Figure 11–1 (placing explicit Java code directly in the page) work quite well. This chapter discusses those approaches.

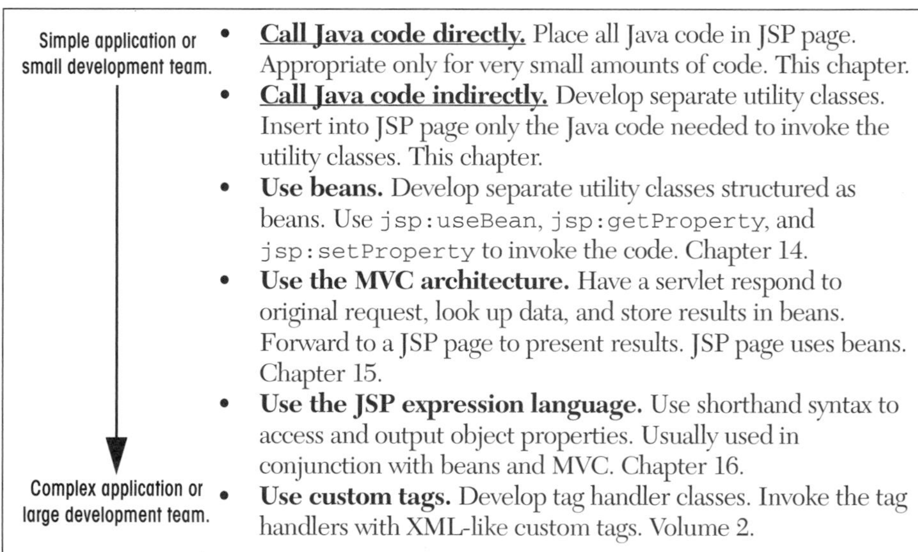

Figure 11–1 Strategies for invoking dynamic code from JSP.

Types of JSP Scripting Elements

JSP scripting elements let you insert Java code into the servlet that will be generated from the JSP page. There are three forms:

1. **Expressions** of the form `<%= Java Expression %>`, which are evaluated and inserted into the servlet's output.
2. **Scriptlets** of the form `<% Java Code %>`, which are inserted into the servlet's `_jspService` method (called by `service`).
3. **Declarations** of the form `<%! Field/Method Declaration %>`, which are inserted into the body of the servlet class, outside any existing methods.

Each of these scripting elements is described in more detail in the following sections.

11.3 Limiting the Amount of Java Code in JSP Pages

You have 25 lines of Java code that you need to invoke. You have two options: (1) put all 25 lines directly in the JSP page, or (2) put the 25 lines of code in a separate Java class, put the Java class in WEB-INF/classes/*directoryMatchingPackageName*, and use one or two lines of JSP-based Java code to invoke it. Which is better? The second. The second. The second! And all the more so if you have 50, 100, 500, or 1000 lines of code. Here's why:

- **Development.** You generally write regular classes in a Java-oriented environment (e.g., an IDE like JBuilder or Eclipse or a code editor like UltraEdit or emacs). You generally write JSP in an HTML-oriented environment like Dreamweaver. The Java-oriented environment is typically better at balancing parentheses, providing tooltips, checking the syntax, colorizing the code, and so forth.
- **Compilation.** To compile a regular Java class, you press the Build button in your IDE or invoke `javac`. To compile a JSP page, you have to drop it in the right directory, start the server, open a browser, and enter the appropriate URL.
- **Debugging.** We know this never happens to you, but when *we* write Java classes or JSP pages, we occasionally make syntax errors. If there is a syntax error in a regular class definition, the compiler tells you right away and it also tells you what line of code contains the error. If

there is a syntax error in a JSP page, the server typically tells you what line *of the servlet* (i.e., the servlet into which the JSP page was translated) contains the error. For tracing output at runtime, with regular classes you can use simple `System.out.println` statements if your IDE provides nothing better. In JSP, you can sometimes use print statements, but where those print statements are displayed varies from server to server.

- **Division of labor.** Many large development teams are composed of some people who are experts in the Java language and others who are experts in HTML but know little or no Java. The more Java code that is directly in the page, the harder it is for the Web developers (the HTML experts) to manipulate it.
- **Testing.** Suppose you want to make a JSP page that outputs random integers between designated 1 and some bound (inclusive). You use `Math.random`, multiply by the range, cast the result to an `int`, and add 1. Hmm, that sounds right. But are you sure? If you do this directly in the JSP page, you have to invoke the page over and over to see if you get all the numbers in the designated range but no numbers outside the range. After hitting the Reload button a few dozen times, you will get tired of testing. But, if you do this in a static method in a regular Java class, you can write a test routine that invokes the method inside a loop (see Listing 11.13), and then you can run hundreds or thousands of test cases with no trouble. For more complicated methods, you can save the output, and, whenever you modify the method, compare the new output to the previously stored results.
- **Reuse.** You put some code in a JSP page. Later, you discover that you need to do the same thing in a different JSP page. What do you do? Cut and paste? Boo! Repeating code in this manner is a cardinal sin because if (when!) you change your approach, you have to change many different pieces of code. Solving the code reuse problem is what object-oriented programming is all about. Don't forget all your good OOP principles just because you are using JSP to simplify the generation of HTML.

"But wait!" you say, "I have an IDE that makes it easier to develop, debug, and and compile JSP pages." OK, good point. There is no hard and fast rule for exactly how much Java code is too much to go directly in the page. But no IDE solves the testing and reuse problems, and your general design strategy should be centered around putting the complex code in regular Java classes and keeping the JSP pages relatively simple.

Core Approach

Limit the amount of Java code that is in JSP pages. At the very least, use helper classes that are invoked from the JSP pages. Once you gain more experience, consider beans, MVC, and custom tags as well.

Almost all experienced developers have seen gross excesses: JSP pages that consist of many lines of Java code followed by tiny snippets of HTML. That is obviously bad: it is harder to develop, compile, debug, divvy up among team members, test, and reuse. A servlet would have been far better. However, some of these developers have overreacted by flatly stating that it is *always* wrong to have *any* Java code directly in the JSP page. Certainly, on some projects it is worth the effort to keep a strict separation between the content and the presentation and to enforce a style where there is no Java syntax in any of the JSP pages. But this is not always necessary (or even beneficial).

A few people go even further by saying that *all* pages in *all* applications should use the Model-View-Controller (MVC) architecture, preferably with the Apache Struts framework. This, in our opinion, is also an overreaction. Yes, MVC (Chapter 15) is a great idea, and we use it all the time on real projects. And, yes, Struts (Volume 2) is a nice framework; we are using it on a large project as the book is going to press. The approaches are great when the situation gets moderately (MVC in general) or highly (Struts) complicated.

But simple situations call for simple solutions. In our opinion, all the approaches of Figure 11–1 have a legitimate place; it depends mostly on the complexity of the application and the size of the development team. Still, be warned: beginners are much more likely to err by making hard-to-manage JSP pages chock-full of Java code than they are to err by using unnecessarily large and elaborate frameworks.

The Importance of Using Packages

Whenever you write Java classes, the class files are deployed in WEB-INF/classes/*directoryMatchingPackageName* (or inside a JAR file that is placed in WEB-INF/lib). This is true regardless of whether the class is a servlet, a regular helper class, a bean, a custom tag handler, or anything else. All code goes in the same place.

With regular servlets, however, it is sometimes reasonable to use the default package, since you can use separate Web applications (see Section 2.11) to avoid name conflicts with servlets from other projects. However, with code called from JSP, you should always use packages. And, since when you write a utility for use from a servlet, you do not know if you will later use it from a JSP page as well, this strategy means that you should *always* use packages for *all* classes used by either servlets or JSP pages.

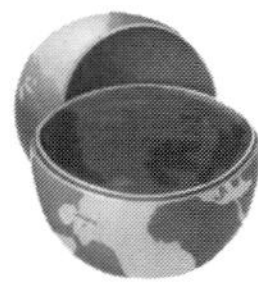

Core Approach

Put all your classes in packages.

Why? To answer that question, consider the following code. The code may or may not contain a `package` declaration but does not contain `import` statements.

```
...
public class SomeClass {
  public String someMethod(...) {
    SomeHelperClass test = new SomeHelperClass(...);
    String someString = SomeUtilityClass.someStaticMethod(...);
    ...
  }
}
```

Now, the question is, what package will the system think that `SomeHelperClass` and `SomeUtilityClass` are in? The answer is, whatever package `SomeClass` is in. What package is that? Whatever is given in the `package` declaration. OK, fine. Elementary Java syntax. No problem. OK, then, consider the following JSP code:

```
...
<%
  SomeHelperClass test = new SomeHelperClass(...);
  String someString = SomeUtilityClass.someStaticMethod(...);
%>
```

Now, same question: what package will the system think that `SomeHelperClass` and `SomeUtilityClass` are in? Same answer: whatever package the current class (the servlet that the JSP page is translated into) is in. What package is that? Hmm, good question. Nobody knows! The package is not standardized by the JSP spec. So, packageless helper classes, when used in this manner, will only work if the system builds a packageless servlet. But they don't always do that, so JSP code like this example can fail. To make matters worse, servers sometimes *do* build packageless servlets out of JSP pages. For example, most Tomcat versions build packageless servlets for JSP pages that are in the top-level directory of the Web application. The problem is that there is absolutely no standard to guide when they do this and when they don't. It would be far better if the JSP code just shown always failed. Instead, it sometimes works and sometimes fails, depending on the server or even depending on what directory the JSP page is in. Boo!

Be safe, be portable, plan ahead. Always use packages!

11.4 Using JSP Expressions

A JSP expression is used to insert values directly into the output. It has the following form:

```
<%= Java Expression %>
```

The expression is evaluated, converted to a string, and inserted in the page. This evaluation is performed at runtime (when the page is requested) and thus has full access to information about the request. For example, the following shows the date/time that the page was requested.

```
Current time: <%= new java.util.Date() %>
```

Predefined Variables

To simplify these expressions, you can use a number of predefined variables (or "implicit objects"). There is nothing magic about these variables; the system simply tells you what names it will use for the local variables in `_jspService` (the method that replaces `doGet` in servlets that result from JSP pages). These implicit objects are discussed in more detail in Section 11.12, but for the purpose of expressions, the most important ones are these:

- **`request`**, the `HttpServletRequest`.
- **`response`**, the `HttpServletResponse`.
- **`session`**, the `HttpSession` associated with the request (unless disabled with the `session` attribute of the `page` directive—see Section 12.4).
- **`out`**, the `Writer` (a buffered version of type `JspWriter`) used to send output to the client.
- **`application`**, the `ServletContext`. This is a data structure shared by all servlets and JSP pages in the Web application and is good for storing shared data. We discuss it further in the chapters on beans (Chapter 14) and MVC (Chapter 15).

Here is an example:

```
Your hostname: <%= request.getRemoteHost() %>
```

JSP/Servlet Correspondence

Now, we just stated that a JSP expression is evaluated and inserted into the page output. Although this is true, it is sometimes helpful to understand what is going on behind the scenes.

It is actually quite simple: JSP expressions basically become `print` (or `write`) statements in the servlet that results from the JSP page. Whereas regular HTML becomes `print` statements with double quotes around the text, JSP expressions become `print` statements with no double quotes. Instead of being placed in the `doGet` method, these `print` statements are placed in a new method called `_jspService` that is called by `service` for both `GET` and `POST` requests. For instance, Listing 11.1 shows a small JSP sample that includes some static HTML and a JSP expression. Listing 11.2 shows a `_jspService` method that might result. Of course, different vendors will produce code in slightly different ways, and optimizations such as reading the HTML from a static byte array are quite common.

Also, we oversimplified the definition of the `out` variable; `out` in a JSP page is a `JspWriter`, so you have to modify the slightly simpler `PrintWriter` that directly results from a call to `getWriter`. So, don't expect the code your server generates to look *exactly* like this.

Listing 11.1 Sample JSP Expression: Random Number

```
<H1>A Random Number</H1>
<%= Math.random() %>
```

Listing 11.2 Representative Resulting Servlet Code: Random Number

```
public void _jspService(HttpServletRequest request,
                        HttpServletResponse response)
    throws ServletException, IOException {
  response.setContentType("text/html");
  HttpSession session = request.getSession();
  JspWriter out = response.getWriter();
  out.println("<H1>A Random Number</H1>");
  out.println(Math.random());
  ...
}
```

If you want to see the exact code that your server generates, you'll have to dig around a bit to find it. In fact, some servers delete the source code files once they are successfully compiled. But here is a summary of the locations used by three common, free development servers.

Tomcat Autogenerated Servlet Source Code

install_dir/work/Standalone/localhost/_
(The final directory is an underscore. More generally, in *install_dir*/work/Standalone/localhost/*webAppName*.
The location varies slightly among various Tomcat versions.)

JRun Autogenerated Servlet Source Code

install_dir/servers/default/default-ear/default-war/WEB-INF/jsp
(More generally, in the WEB-INF/jsp directory of the Web application to which the JSP page belongs. However, note that JRun does not save the .java files unless you change the `keepGenerated` element from `false` to `true` in *install_dir*/servers/default/SERVER-INF/default-web.xml.)

Resin Autogenerated Servlet Source Code

install_dir/doc/WEB-INF/work
(More generally, in the WEB-INF/work directory of the Web application to which the JSP page belongs.)

XML Syntax for Expressions

XML authors can use the following alternative syntax for JSP expressions:

```
<jsp:expression>Java Expression</jsp:expression>
```

In JSP 1.2 and later, servers are required to support this syntax as long as authors don't mix the XML version and the standard JSP version (`<%= ... %>`) in the same page. This means that, to use the XML version, you must use XML syntax in the *entire* page. In JSP 1.2 (but not 2.0), this requirement means that you have to enclose the entire page in a `jsp:root` element. As a result, most developers stick with the classic syntax except when they are either generating XML documents (e.g., xhtml or SOAP) or when the JSP page is itself the output of some XML process (e.g., XSLT).

Note that XML elements, unlike HTML ones, are case sensitive. So, be sure to use `jsp:expression` in lower case.

11.5 Example: JSP Expressions

Listing 11.3 gives an example JSP page called Expressions.jsp. We placed the file in a directory called jsp-scripting, copied the entire directory from our development directory to the top level of the default Web application (in general, to the top-level directory of the Web application—one level up from WEB-INF), and used a URL of http://*host*/jsp-scripting/Expressions.jsp. Figures 11–2 and 11–3 show some typical results.

Notice that we include META tags and a style sheet link in the HEAD section of the JSP page. It is good practice to include these elements, but there are two reasons why they are often omitted from pages generated by normal servlets.

First, with servlets, it is tedious to generate the required println statements. With JSP, however, the format is simpler and you can make use of the code reuse options in your usual HTML building tools. This convenience is an important factor in the use of JSP. JSP pages are not more *powerful* than servlets (they *are* servlets behind the scenes), but they are sometimes more *convenient* than servlets.

Second, servlets cannot use the simplest form of relative URLs (ones that refer to files in the same directory as the current page), since the servlet directories are not mapped to URLs in the same manner as are URLs for normal Web pages. Moreover, servers are expressly prohibited from making content in WEB-INF/classes (or anywhere in WEB-INF) directly accessible to clients. So, it is impossible to put style sheets in the same directory as servlet class files, even if you use the web.xml servlet and servlet-mapping elements (see Section 2.11, "Web Applications: A Preview") to customize servlet URLs. JSP pages, on the other hand, are installed in the normal Web page hierarchy on the server, and relative URLs are resolved properly as long as the JSP page is accessed directly by the client rather than indirectly by means of a RequestDispatcher (see Chapter 15, "Integrating Servlets and JSP: The Model View Controller (MVC) Architecture").

Thus, in most cases style sheets and JSP pages can be kept together in the same directory. The source code for the style sheet, like all code shown or referenced in the book, can be found at http://www.coreservlets.com.

Listing 11.3 Expressions.jsp

```
<!DOCTYPE HTML PUBLIC "-//W3C//DTD HTML 4.0 Transitional//EN">
<HTML>
<HEAD>
<TITLE>JSP Expressions</TITLE>
<META NAME="keywords"
      CONTENT="JSP,expressions,JavaServer Pages,servlets">
<META NAME="description"
      CONTENT="A quick example of JSP expressions.">
```

Listing 11.3 Expressions.jsp *(continued)*

```
<LINK REL=STYLESHEET
      HREF="JSP-Styles.css"
      TYPE="text/css">
</HEAD>
<BODY>
<H2>JSP Expressions</H2>
<UL>
  <LI>Current time: <%= new java.util.Date() %>
  <LI>Server: <%= application.getServerInfo() %>
  <LI>Session ID: <%= session.getId() %>
  <LI>The <CODE>testParam</CODE> form parameter:
      <%= request.getParameter("testParam") %>
</UL>
</BODY></HTML>
```

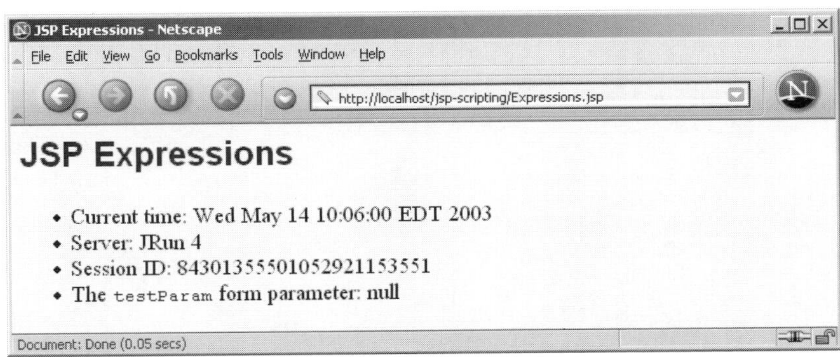

Figure 11–2 Result of Expressions.jsp using Macromedia JRun and omitting the `testParam` request parameter.

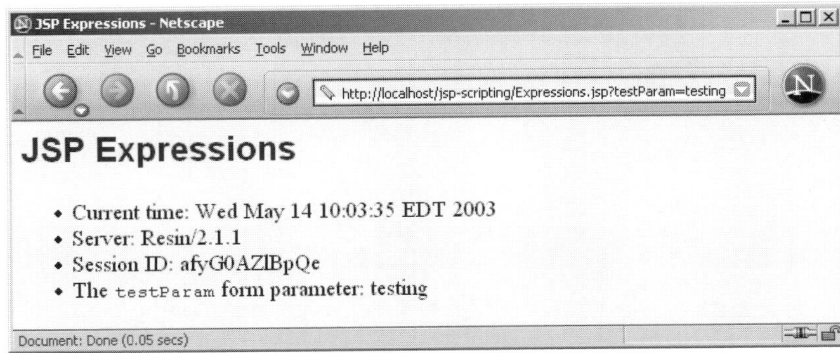

Figure 11–3 Result of Expressions.jsp using Caucho Resin and specifying `testing` as the value of the `testParam` request parameter.

11.6 Comparing Servlets to JSP Pages

In Section 4.3, we presented an example of a servlet that outputs the values of three designated form parameters. The code for that servlet is repeated here in Listing 11.4. Listing 11.5 (Figure 11–4) shows a version rewritten in JSP, using JSP expressions to access the form parameters. The JSP version is clearly superior: shorter, simpler, and easier to maintain.

Now, this is not to say that all servlets will convert to JSP so cleanly. JSP works best when the *structure* of the HTML page is fixed but the *values* at various places need to be computed dynamically. If the structure of the page is dynamic, JSP is less beneficial. Sometimes servlets are better in such a case. And, of course, if the page consists of binary data or has little static content, servlets are clearly superior. Furthermore, sometimes the answer is neither servlets nor JSP alone, but rather a combination of the two. For details, see Chapter 15 (Integrating Servlets and JSP: The Model View Controller (MVC) Architecture).

Listing 11.4 ThreeParams.java

```
package coreservlets;

import java.io.*;
import javax.servlet.*;
import javax.servlet.http.*;

public class ThreeParams extends HttpServlet {
  public void doGet(HttpServletRequest request,
                    HttpServletResponse response)
      throws ServletException, IOException {
    response.setContentType("text/html");
    PrintWriter out = response.getWriter();
    String title = "Reading Three Request Parameters";
    String docType =
      "<!DOCTYPE HTML PUBLIC \"-//W3C//DTD HTML 4.0 " +
      "Transitional//EN\">\n";
    out.println(docType +
                "<HTML>\n" +
                "<HEAD><TITLE>" + title + "</TITLE></HEAD>\n" +
                "<BODY BGCOLOR=\"#FDF5E6\">\n" +
                "<H1 ALIGN=\"CENTER\">" + title + "</H1>\n" +
                "<UL>\n" +
                "  <LI><B>param1</B>: "
                + request.getParameter("param1") + "\n" +
                "  <LI><B>param2</B>: "
```

Listing 11.4 ThreeParams.java *(continued)*

```
                + request.getParameter("param2") + "\n" +
                "  <LI><B>param3</B>: "
                + request.getParameter("param3") + "\n" +
                "</UL>\n" +
                "</BODY></HTML>");
  }
}
```

Listing 11.5 ThreeParams.jsp

```
<!DOCTYPE HTML PUBLIC "-//W3C//DTD HTML 4.0 Transitional//EN">
<HTML>
<HEAD>
<TITLE>Reading Three Request Parameters</TITLE>
<LINK REL=STYLESHEET
      HREF="JSP-Styles.css"
      TYPE="text/css">
</HEAD>
<BODY>
<H1>Reading Three Request Parameters</H1>
<UL>
  <LI><B>param1</B>: <%= request.getParameter("param1") %>
  <LI><B>param2</B>: <%= request.getParameter("param2") %>
  <LI><B>param3</B>: <%= request.getParameter("param3") %>
</UL>
</BODY></HTML>
```

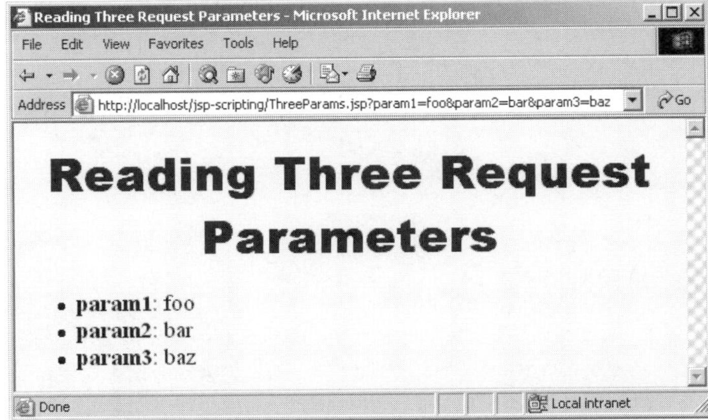

Figure 11–4 Result of ThreeParams.jsp.

11.7 Writing Scriptlets

If you want to do something more complex than output the value of a simple expression, JSP scriptlets let you insert arbitrary code into the servlet's _jspService method (which is called by service). Scriptlets have the following form:

```
<% Java Code %>
```

Scriptlets have access to the same automatically defined variables as do expressions (request, response, session, out, etc.). So, for example, if you want to explicitly send output to the resultant page, you could use the out variable, as in the following example.

```
<%
String queryData = request.getQueryString();
out.println("Attached GET data: " + queryData);
%>
```

In this particular instance, you could have accomplished the same effect more easily by using a combination of a scriptlet and a JSP expression, as below.

```
<% String queryData = request.getQueryString(); %>
Attached GET data: <%= queryData %>
```

Or, you could have used a single JSP expression, as here.

```
Attached GET data: <%= request.getQueryString() %>
```

In general, however, scriptlets can perform a number of tasks that cannot be accomplished with expressions alone. These tasks include setting response headers and status codes, invoking side effects such as writing to the server log or updating a database, or executing code that contains loops, conditionals, or other complex constructs. For instance, the following snippet specifies that the current page is sent to the client as Microsoft Word, not as HTML (which is the default). Since Microsoft Word can import HTML documents, this technique is actually quite useful in real applications.

```
<% response.setContentType("application/msword"); %>
```

It is important to note that you need not set response headers or status codes at the *very* top of a JSP page, even though this capability appears to violate the rule that this type of response data needs to be specified before any document content is sent to the client. It is legal to set headers and status codes after a small amount of document content because servlets that result from JSP pages use a special variety of Writer (of type JspWriter) that partially buffers the document. This buffering behavior can be changed, however; see Chapter 12 (Controlling the Structure of Generated Servlets: The JSP page Directive) for a discussion of the `buffer` and `autoflush` attributes of the `page` directive.

JSP/Servlet Correspondence

It is easy to understand how JSP scriptlets correspond to servlet code: the scriptlet code is just directly inserted into the `_jspService` method: no strings, no `print` statements, no changes whatsoever. For instance, Listing 11.6 shows a small JSP sample that includes some static HTML, a JSP expression, and a JSP scriptlet. Listing 11.7 shows a `_jspService` method that might result. Note that the call to `bar` (the JSP expression) is not followed by a semicolon, but the call to `baz` (the JSP scriptlet) is. Remember that JSP expressions contain Java *values* (which do not end in semicolons), whereas most JSP scriptlets contain Java *statements* (which are terminated by semicolons). To make it even easier to remember when to use a semicolon, simply remember that expressions get placed inside `print` or `write` statements, and `out.print(blah;);` is clearly illegal.

Again, different vendors will produce this code in slightly different ways, and we oversimplified the `out` variable (which is a `JspWriter`, not the slightly simpler `PrintWriter` that results from a call to `getWriter`). So, don't expect the code your server generates to look *exactly* like this.

Listing 11.6 Sample JSP Expression/Scriptlet

```
<H2>foo</H2>
<%= bar() %>
<% baz(); %>
```

Listing 11.7 Representative Resulting Servlet Code: Expression/Scriptlet

```
public void _jspService(HttpServletRequest request,
                        HttpServletResponse response)
    throws ServletException, IOException {
  response.setContentType("text/html");
  HttpSession session = request.getSession();
  JspWriter out = response.getWriter();
  out.println("<H2>foo</H2>");
  out.println(bar());
  baz();
  ...
}
```

XML Syntax for Scriptlets

The XML equivalent of `<% Java Code %>` is

```
<jsp:scriptlet>Java Code</jsp:scriptlet>
```

In JSP 1.2 and later, servers are required to support this syntax as long as authors don't mix the XML version (`<jsp:scriptlet> ... </jsp:scriptlet>`) and the ASP-like version (`<% ... %>`) in the same page; if you use the XML version you must use XML syntax consistently for the entire page. Remember that XML elements are case sensitive; be sure to use `jsp:scriptlet` in lower case.

11.8 Scriptlet Example

As an example of code that is too complex for a JSP expression alone, Listing 11.8 presents a JSP page that uses the `bgColor` request parameter to set the background color of the page. Simply using

```
<BODY BGCOLOR="<%= request.getParameter("bgColor") %>">
```

would violate the cardinal rule of reading form data: always check for missing or malformed data. So, we use a scriptlet instead. JSP-Styles.css is omitted so that the style sheet does not override the background color. Figures 11–5, 11–6, and 11–7 show the default result, the result for a background of `C0C0C0`, and the result for `papayawhip` (one of the oddball X11 color names still supported by most browsers for historical reasons), respectively.

Listing 11.8 BGColor.jsp

```
<!DOCTYPE HTML PUBLIC "-//W3C//DTD HTML 4.0 Transitional//EN">
<HTML>
<HEAD>
  <TITLE>Color Testing</TITLE>
</HEAD>
<%
String bgColor = request.getParameter("bgColor");
if ((bgColor == null) || (bgColor.trim().equals(""))) {
  bgColor = "WHITE";
}
%>
<BODY BGCOLOR="<%= bgColor %>">
<H2 ALIGN="CENTER">Testing a Background of "<%= bgColor %>"</H2>
</BODY></HTML>
```

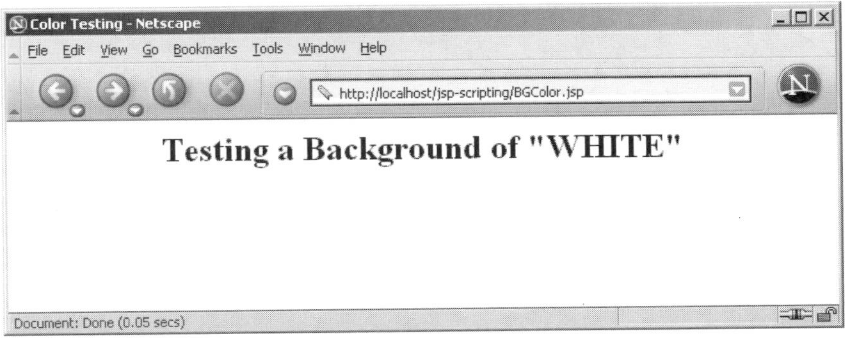

Figure 11–5 Default result of BGColor.jsp.

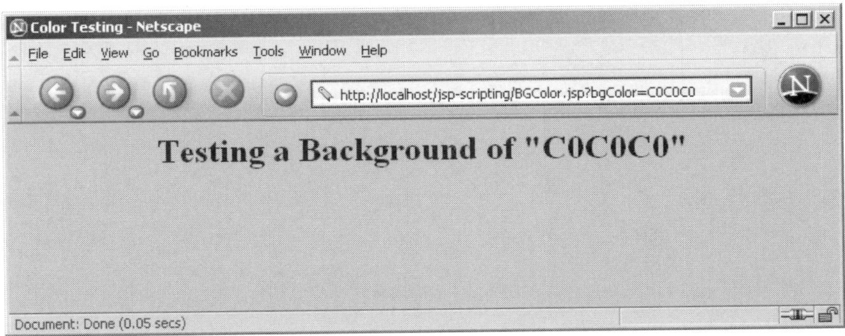

Figure 11–6 Result of BGColor.jsp when accessed with a `bgColor` parameter having the RGB value `C0C0C0`.

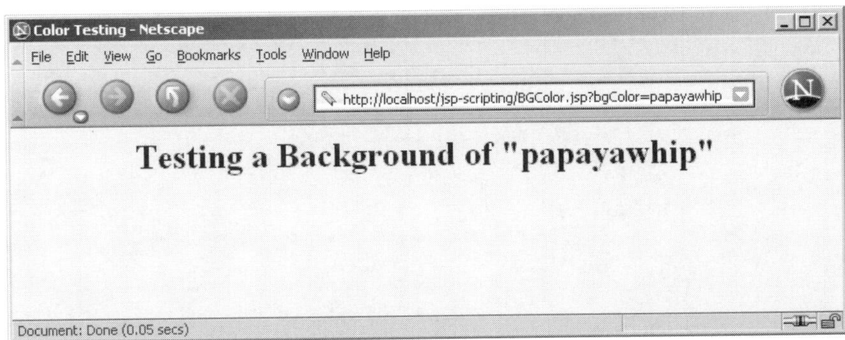

Figure 11–7 Result of BGColor.jsp when accessed with a `bgColor` parameter having the X11 color name `papayawhip`.

11.9 Using Scriptlets to Make Parts of the JSP Page Conditional

Another use of scriptlets is to conditionally output HTML or other content that is *not* within any JSP tag. Key to this approach are the facts that (a) code inside a scriptlet gets inserted into the resultant servlet's `_jspService` method (called by `service`) *exactly* as written and (b) that any static HTML (template text) before or after a scriptlet gets converted to `print` statements. This behavior means that scriptlets need not contain complete Java statements and that code blocks left open can affect the static HTML or JSP outside the scriptlets. For example, consider the JSP fragment of Listing 11.9 that contains mixed template text and scriptlets.

Listing 11.9 DayWish.jsp

```
<!DOCTYPE HTML PUBLIC "-//W3C//DTD HTML 4.0 Transitional//EN">
<HTML>
<HEAD>
<TITLE>Wish for the Day</TITLE>
<LINK REL=STYLESHEET
      HREF="JSP-Styles.css"
      TYPE="text/css">
</HEAD>
<BODY>
<% if (Math.random() < 0.5) { %>
<H1>Have a <I>nice</I> day!</H1>
<% } else { %>
<H1>Have a <I>lousy</I> day!</H1>
<% } %>
</BODY></HTML>
```

You probably find the bold part a bit confusing. We certainly did the first few times we saw constructs of this nature. Neither the "have a nice day" nor the "have a lousy day" lines are contained within a JSP tag, so it seems odd that only one of the two becomes part of the output for any given request. See Figures 11–8 and 11–9.

Don't panic! Simply follow the rules for how JSP code gets converted to servlet code. Once you think about how this example will be converted to servlet code by the JSP engine, you get the following easily understandable result.

```
if (Math.random() < 0.5) {
  out.println("<H1>Have a <I>nice</I> day!</H1>");
} else {
  out.println("<H1>Have a <I>lousy</I> day!</H1>");
}
```

The key is that the first two scriptlets do not contain complete statements, but rather partial statements that have dangling braces. This serves to capture the subsequent HTML within the `if` or `else` clauses.

Figure 11–8 One possible result of DayWish.jsp.

Figure 11–9 Another possible result of DayWish.jsp.

Overuse of this approach can lead to JSP code that is hard to understand and maintain. Avoid using it to conditionalize large sections of HTML, and try to keep your JSP pages as focused on presentation (HTML output) tasks as possible. Nevertheless, there are some situations in which the alternative approaches are also unappealing. The primary example is generation of lists or tables containing an indeterminate number of entries. This happens quite frequently when you are presenting data that is the result of a database query. See Chapter 17 (Accessing Databases with JDBC) for details on database access from Java code. Besides, even if *you* do not use this approach, you are bound to see examples of it in your projects, and you need to understand how and why it works as it does.

11.10 Using Declarations

A JSP declaration lets you define methods or fields that get inserted into the main body of the servlet class (*outside* the `_jspService` method that is called by `service` to process the request). A declaration has the following form:

```
<%! Field or Method Definition %>
```

Since declarations do not generate output, they are normally used in conjunction with JSP expressions or scriptlets. In principle, JSP declarations can contain field (instance variable) definitions, method definitions, inner class definitions, or even static initializer blocks: anything that is legal to put inside a class definition but outside any existing methods. In practice, however, declarations almost always contain field or method definitions.

One caution is warranted, however: do not use JSP declarations to override the standard servlet life-cycle methods (`service`, `doGet`, `init`, etc.). The servlet into which the JSP page gets translated already makes use of these methods. There is no need for declarations to gain access to `service`, `doGet`, or `doPost`, since calls to `service` are automatically dispatched to `_jspService`, which is where code resulting from expressions and scriptlets is put. However, for initialization and cleanup, you can use `jspInit` and `jspDestroy`—the standard `init` and `destroy` methods are guaranteed to call these two methods in servlets that come from JSP.

Core Approach

For initialization and cleanup in JSP pages, use JSP declarations to override `jspInit` or `jspDestroy`, not `init` or `destroy`.

Aside from overriding standard methods like `jspInit` and `jspDestroy`, the utility of JSP declarations for defining methods is somewhat questionable. Moving the methods to separate classes (possibly as static methods) makes them easier to write (since you are using a Java environment, not an HTML-like one), easier to test (no need to run a server), easier to debug (compilation warnings give the right line numbers; no tricks are needed to see the standard output), and easier to reuse (many different JSP pages can use the same utility class). However, using JSP declarations to define instance variables (fields), as we will see shortly, gives you something not easily reproducible with separate utility classes: a place to store data that is persistent between requests.

Core Approach

Define most methods with separate Java classes, not JSP declarations.

JSP/Servlet Correspondence

JSP declarations result in code that is placed inside the servlet class definition but outside the `_jspService` method. Since fields and methods can be declared in any order, it does not matter whether the code from declarations goes at the top or bottom of the servlet. For instance, Listing 11.10 shows a small JSP snippet that includes some static HTML, a JSP declaration, and a JSP expression. Listing 11.11 shows a servlet that might result. Note that the specific name of the resultant servlet is not defined by the JSP specification, and in fact, different servers have different conventions. Besides, as already stated, different vendors will produce this code in slightly different ways, and we oversimplified the `out` variable (which is a `JspWriter`, not the slightly simpler `PrintWriter` that results from a call to `getWriter`). Finally, the servlet will never implement `HttpJspPage` directly, but rather will extend some vendor-specific class that already implements `HttpJspPage`. So, don't expect the code your server generates to look *exactly* like this.

Listing 11.10 Sample JSP Declaration

```
<H1>Some Heading</H1>
<%!
  private String randomHeading() {
    return("<H2>" + Math.random() + "</H2>");
  }
%>
<%= randomHeading() %>
```

Listing 11.11 Representative Resulting Servlet Code: Declaration

```
public class xxxx implements HttpJspPage {
 private String randomHeading() {
   return("<H2>" + Math.random() + "</H2>");
 }
 public void _jspService(HttpServletRequest request,
                         HttpServletResponse response)
    throws ServletException, IOException {
```

Listing 11.11 Representative Resulting Servlet Code: Declaration *(continued)*

```
    response.setContentType("text/html");
    HttpSession session = request.getSession();
    JspWriter out = response.getWriter();
    out.println("<H1>Some Heading</H1>");
    out.println(randomHeading());
    ...
  }

  ...
}
```

XML Syntax for Declarations

The XML equivalent of `<%! Field or Method Definition %>` is

```
<jsp:declaration>Field or Method Definition</jsp:declaration>
```

In JSP 1.2 and later, servers are required to support this syntax as long as authors don't mix the XML version (`<jsp:declaration> ... </jsp:declaration>`) and the standard ASP-like version (`<%! ... %>`) in the same page. The entire page must follow XML syntax if you are going to use the XML form, so most developers stick with the classic syntax except when they are using XML anyhow. Remember that XML elements are case sensitive; be sure to use `jsp:declaration` in lower case.

11.11 Declaration Example

In this example, the following JSP snippet prints the number of times the current page has been requested since the server was booted (or the servlet class was changed and reloaded). A hit counter in two lines of code!

```
<%! private int accessCount = 0; %>
Accesses to page since server reboot:
<%= ++accessCount %>
```

Recall that multiple client requests to the same servlet result only in multiple threads calling the `service` method of a single servlet instance. They do *not* result in the creation of multiple servlet instances except possibly when the servlet implements the now-deprecated `SingleThreadModel` interface (see Section 3.7). Thus, instance variables (fields) of a normal servlet are shared by multiple requests, and `accessCount` does not have to be declared `static`. Now, advanced readers might wonder if the snippet just shown is thread safe; does the code guarantee that each visitor gets a unique count? The answer is no; in unusual situations multiple users could, in principle, see the same value. For access counts, as long as the count is correct in the long run, it does not matter if two different users occasionally see the same count. But, for values such as session identifiers, it is critical to have unique values. For an example that is similar to the previous snippet but that uses `synchronized` blocks to guarantee thread safety, see the discussion of the `isThreadSafe` attribute of the `page` directive in Chapter 12.

Listing 11.12 shows the full JSP page; Figure 11–10 shows a representative result. Now, before you rush out and use this approach to track access to all your pages, a couple of cautions are in order.

First of all, you couldn't use this for a real hit counter, since the count starts over whenever you restart the server. So, a real hit counter would need to use `jspInit` and `jspDestroy` to read the previous count at startup and store the old count when the server is shut down.

Second, even if you use `jspDestroy`, it would be possible for the server to crash unexpectedly (e.g., when a rolling blackout strikes Silicon Valley). So, you would have to periodically write the hit count to disk.

Finally, some advanced servers support distributed applications whereby a cluster of servers appears to the client as a single server. If your servlets or JSP pages might need to support distribution in this way, plan ahead and avoid the use of fields for persistent data. Use a database instead. (Note that session objects are automatically shared across distributed applications as long as the values are `Serializable`. But session values are specific to each user, whereas we need client-independent data in this case.)

Listing 11.12 AccessCounts.jsp

```
<!DOCTYPE HTML PUBLIC "-//W3C//DTD HTML 4.0 Transitional//EN">
<HTML>
<HEAD>
<TITLE>JSP Declarations</TITLE>
<LINK REL=STYLESHEET
      HREF="JSP-Styles.css"
      TYPE="text/css">
</HEAD>
<BODY>
<H1>JSP Declarations</H1>
<%! private int accessCount = 0; %>
<H2>Accesses to page since server reboot:
<%= ++accessCount %></H2>
</BODY></HTML>
```

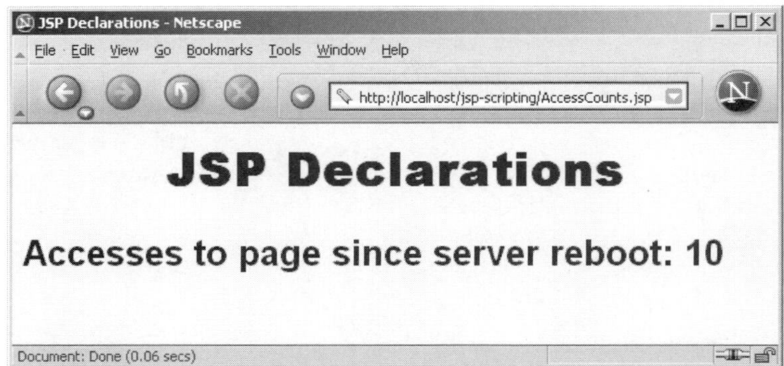

Figure 11–10 Visiting AccessCounts.jsp after it has been requested nine previous times by the same or different clients.

11.12 Using Predefined Variables

When you wrote a doGet method for a servlet, you probably wrote something like this:

```
public void doGet(HttpServletRequest request,
                  HttpServletResponse response)
    throws ServletException, IOException {
  response.setContentType("text/html");
  HttpSession session = request.getSession();
  PrintWriter out = response.getWriter();
  out.println(...);
  ...
}
```

The servlet API told you the types of the arguments to doGet, the methods to call to get the session and writer objects, and their types. JSP changes the method name from doGet to _jspService and uses a JspWriter instead of a PrintWriter. But the idea is the same. The question is, who told you what variable names to use? The answer is, nobody! You chose whatever names you wanted.

For JSP expressions and scriptlets to be useful, you need to know what variable names the autogenerated servlet uses. So, the specification tells you. You are supplied with eight automatically defined local variables in _jspService, sometimes called "implicit objects." Nothing is special about these; they are merely the names of the local variables. *Local* variables. Not constants. Not JSP reserved words. Nothing magic. So, if you are writing code that is not part of the _jspService method, these variables are not available. In particular, since JSP declarations result in code that appears outside the `_jspService` method, these variables are not accessible in declarations. Similarly, they are not available in utility classes that are invoked by JSP pages. If you need a separate method to have access to one of these variables, do what you always do in Java code: pass the variable along.

The available variables are `request`, `response`, `out`, `session`, `application`, `config`, `pageContext`, and `page`. Details for each are given below. An additional variable called `exception` is available, but only in error pages. This variable is discussed in Chapter 12 (Controlling the Structure of Generated Servlets: The JSP page Directive) in the sections on the `errorPage` and `isErrorPage` attributes.

- **`request`**
  This variable is the `HttpServletRequest` associated with the request; it gives you access to the request parameters, the request type (e.g., `GET` or `POST`), and the incoming HTTP headers (e.g., cookies).
- **`response`**
  This variable is the `HttpServletResponse` associated with the response to the client. Since the output stream (see `out`) is normally buffered, it is usually legal to set HTTP status codes and response headers in the body of JSP pages, even though the setting of headers or status codes is not permitted in servlets once any output has been sent to the client. If you turn buffering off, however (see the `buffer` attribute in Chapter 12), you must set status codes and headers before supplying any output.
- **`out`**
  This variable is the `Writer` used to send output to the client. However, to make it easy to set response headers at various places in the JSP page, `out` is not the standard `PrintWriter` but rather a buffered version of `Writer` called `JspWriter`. You can adjust the buffer size through use of the `buffer` attribute of the `page` directive (see Chapter 12). The `out` variable is used almost exclusively in scriptlets since JSP expressions are automatically placed in the output stream and thus rarely need to refer to `out` explicitly.
- **`session`**
  This variable is the `HttpSession` object associated with the request. Recall that sessions are created automatically in JSP, so this variable is bound even if there is no incoming session reference. The one exception is the use of the `session` attribute of the `page` directive (Chapter 12) to disable automatic session tracking. In that case, attempts to reference the `session` variable cause errors at the time the JSP page is translated into a servlet. See Chapter 9 for general information on session tracking and the `HttpSession` class.

- **application**
  This variable is the `ServletContext` as obtained by `getServletContext`. Servlets and JSP pages can store persistent data in the `ServletContext` object rather than in instance variables. `ServletContext` has `setAttribute` and `getAttribute` methods that let you store arbitrary data associated with specified keys. The difference between storing data in instance variables and storing it in the `ServletContext` is that the `ServletContext` is shared by all servlets and JSP pages in the Web application, whereas instance variables are available only to the same servlet that stored the data.
- **config**
  This variable is the `ServletConfig` object for this page. In principle, you can use it to read initialization parameters, but, in practice, initialization parameters are read from `jspInit`, not from `_jspService`.
- **pageContext**
  JSP introduced a class called `PageContext` to give a single point of access to many of the page attributes. The `PageContext` class has methods `getRequest`, `getResponse`, `getOut`, `getSession`, and so forth. The `pageContext` variable stores the value of the `PageContext` object associated with the current page. If a method or constructor needs access to multiple page-related objects, passing `pageContext` is easier than passing many separate references to `request`, `response`, `out`, and so forth.
- **page**
  This variable is simply a synonym for `this` and is not very useful. It was created as a placeholder for the time when the scripting language could be something other than Java.

11.13 Comparing JSP Expressions, Scriptlets, and Declarations

This section contains several similar examples, each of which generates random integers between 1 and 10. They illustrate the difference in how the three JSP scripting elements are typically used. All the pages use the `randomInt` method defined in Listing 11.13.

Listing 11.13 RanUtilities.java

```
package coreservlets; // Always use packages!!

/** Simple utility to generate random integers. */

public class RanUtilities {

  /** A random int from 1 to range (inclusive). */

  public static int randomInt(int range) {
    return(1 + ((int)(Math.random() * range)));
  }

  /** Test routine. Invoke from the command line with
   *  the desired range. Will print 100 values.
   *  Verify that you see values from 1 to range (inclusive)
   *  and no values outside that interval.
   */

  public static void main(String[] args) {
    int range = 10;
    try {
      range = Integer.parseInt(args[0]);
    } catch(Exception e) { // Array index or number format
      // Do nothing: range already has default value.
    }
    for(int i=0; i<100; i++) {
      System.out.println(randomInt(range));
    }
  }
}
```

Example 1: JSP Expressions

In the first example, the goal is to output a bulleted list of five random integers from 1 to 10. Since the structure of this page is fixed and we use a separate helper class for the `randomInt` method, JSP expressions are all that is needed. Listing 11.14 shows the code; Figure 11–11 shows a typical result.

Listing 11.14 RandomNums.jsp

```
<!DOCTYPE HTML PUBLIC "-//W3C//DTD HTML 4.0 Transitional//EN">
<HTML>
<HEAD>
<TITLE>Random Numbers</TITLE>
<LINK REL=STYLESHEET
      HREF="JSP-Styles.css"
      TYPE="text/css">
</HEAD>
<BODY>
<H1>Random Numbers</H1>
<UL>
  <LI><%= coreservlets.RanUtilities.randomInt(10) %>
  <LI><%= coreservlets.RanUtilities.randomInt(10) %>
  <LI><%= coreservlets.RanUtilities.randomInt(10) %>
  <LI><%= coreservlets.RanUtilities.randomInt(10) %>
  <LI><%= coreservlets.RanUtilities.randomInt(10) %>
</UL>
</BODY></HTML>
```

Figure 11–11 Result of RandomNums.jsp. Different values are displayed whenever the page is reloaded.

Example 2: JSP Scriptlets

In the second example, the goal is to generate a list of between 1 and 10 entries (selected at random), each of which is a number between 1 and 10. Because the number of entries in the list is dynamic, a JSP scriptlet is needed. But, should there be a single scriptlet containing a loop that outputs the numbers, or should we use the dangling-brace approach described in Section 11.9 (Using Scriptlets to Make Parts of the JSP Page Conditional)? The choice is not clear here: the first approach yields a more concise result, but the second approach exposes the `<LI>` element to the Web developer, who might want to modify the type of bullet or insert additional formatting elements. So, we present both approaches. Listing 11.15 shows the first approach (a single loop that uses the predefined `out` variable); Listing 11.16 shows the second approach (capturing the "static" HTML into the loop). Figures 11–12 and 11–13 show some typical results.

Listing 11.15 RandomList1.jsp

```
<!DOCTYPE HTML PUBLIC "-//W3C//DTD HTML 4.0 Transitional//EN">
<HTML>
<HEAD>
<TITLE>Random List (Version 1)</TITLE>
<LINK REL=STYLESHEET
      HREF="JSP-Styles.css"
      TYPE="text/css">
</HEAD>
<BODY>
<H1>Random List (Version 1)</H1>
<UL>
<%
int numEntries = coreservlets.RanUtilities.randomInt(10);
for(int i=0; i<numEntries; i++) {
  out.println("<LI>" + coreservlets.RanUtilities.randomInt(10));
}
%>
</UL>
</BODY></HTML>
```

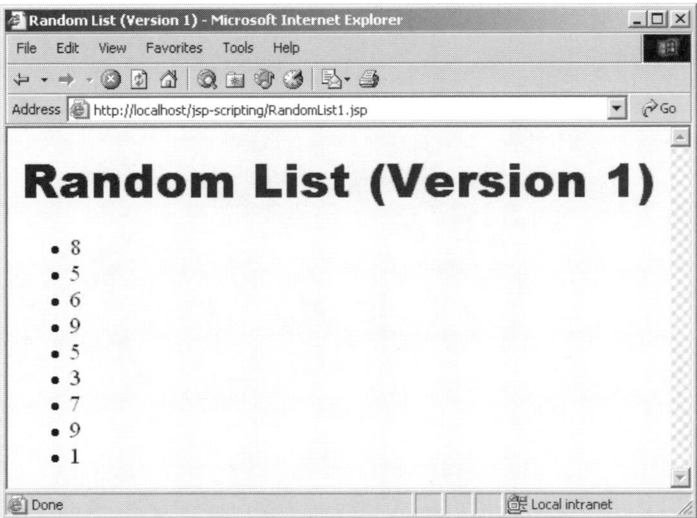

Figure 11–12 Result of RandomList1.jsp. Different values (and a different number of list items) are displayed whenever the page is reloaded.

Listing 11.16 RandomList2.jsp

```
<!DOCTYPE HTML PUBLIC "-//W3C//DTD HTML 4.0 Transitional//EN">
<HTML>
<HEAD>
<TITLE>Random List (Version 2)</TITLE>
<LINK REL=STYLESHEET
      HREF="JSP-Styles.css"
      TYPE="text/css">
</HEAD>
<BODY>
<H1>Random List (Version 2)</H1>
<UL>
<%
int numEntries = coreservlets.RanUtilities.randomInt(10);
for(int i=0; i<numEntries; i++) {
%>
<LI><%= coreservlets.RanUtilities.randomInt(10) %>
<% } %>
</UL>
</BODY></HTML>
```

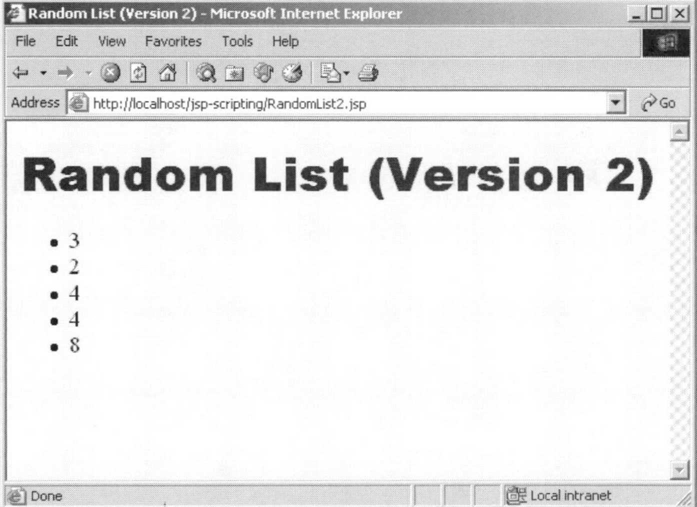

Figure 11–13 Result of RandomList2.jsp. Different values (and a different number of list items) are displayed whenever the page is reloaded.

Example 3: JSP Declarations

In this third example, the requirement is to generate a random number on the first request, then show the *same* number to all users until the server is restarted. Instance variables (fields) are the natural way to accomplish this persistence. The reason is that instance variables are initialized only when the object is built and servlets are built once and remain in memory between requests: a new instance is not allocated for each request. JSP expressions and scriptlets deal only with code inside the `_jspService` method, so they are not appropriate here. A JSP declaration is needed instead. Listing 11.17 shows the code; Figure 11–14 shows a typical result.

Listing 11.17 SemiRandomNumber.jsp

```
<!DOCTYPE HTML PUBLIC "-//W3C//DTD HTML 4.0 Transitional//EN">
<HTML>
<HEAD>
<TITLE>Semi-Random Number</TITLE>
<LINK REL=STYLESHEET
      HREF="JSP-Styles.css"
      TYPE="text/css">
</HEAD>
```

Listing 11.17 SemiRandomNumber.jsp *(continued)*

```
<BODY>
<%!
private int randomNum = coreservlets.RanUtilities.randomInt(10);
%>
<H1>Semi-Random Number:<BR><%= randomNum %></H1>
</BODY>
</HTML>
```

Figure 11–14 Result of SemiRandomNumber.jsp. Until the server is restarted, all clients see the same result.

Controlling the Structure of Generated Servlets: The JSP page Directive

Topics in This Chapter

- Understanding the purpose of the page directive
- Designating which classes are imported
- Specifying the MIME type of the page
- Generating Excel spreadsheets
- Participating in sessions
- Setting the size and behavior of the output buffer
- Designating pages to handle JSP errors
- Controlling threading behavior
- Using XML-compatible syntax for directives

Chapter 12

A JSP *directive* affects the overall structure of the servlet that results from the JSP page. The following templates show the two possible forms for directives. Single quotes can be substituted for the double quotes around the attribute values, but the quotation marks cannot be omitted altogether. To obtain quotation marks within an attribute value, precede them with a backslash, using `\'` for `'` and `\"` for `"`.

```
<%@ directive attribute="value" %>

<%@ directive attribute1="value1"
              attribute2="value2"
              ...
              attributeN="valueN" %>
```

In JSP, there are three main types of directives: `page`, `include`, and `taglib`. The `page` directive lets you control the structure of the servlet by importing classes, customizing the servlet superclass, setting the content type, and the like. A `page` directive can be placed anywhere within the document; its use is the topic of this chapter. The second directive, `include`, lets you insert a file into the JSP page at the time the JSP file is translated into a servlet. An `include` directive should be placed in the document at the point at which you want the file to be inserted; it is discussed in Chapter 13. The third directive, `taglib`, defines custom markup tags; it is discussed at great length in Volume 2 of this book, where there are several chapters on custom tag libraries.

The `page` directive lets you define one or more of the following case-sensitive attributes (listed in approximate order of frequency of use): `import`, `contentType`, `pageEncoding`, `session`, `isELIgnored` (JSP 2.0 only), `buffer`, `autoFlush`, info, errorPage, isErrorPage, isThreadSafe, language, and extends. These attributes are explained in the following sections.

12.1 The import Attribute

The import attribute of the page directive lets you specify the packages that should be imported by the servlet into which the JSP page gets translated. As discussed in Section 11.3 (Limiting the Amount of Java Code in JSP Pages) and illustrated in Figure 12–1, using separate utility (helper) classes makes your dynamic code easier to write, maintain, debug, test, and reuse.

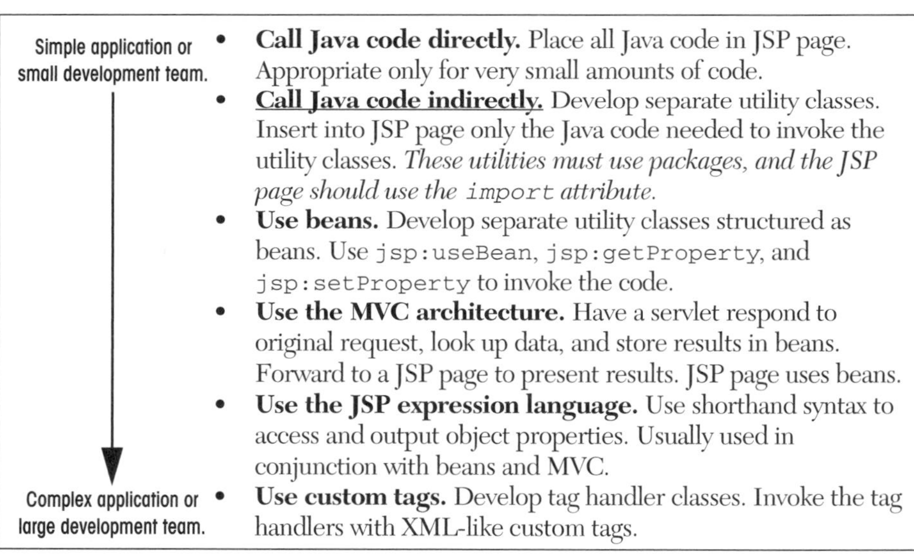

Figure 12–1 Strategies for invoking dynamic code from JSP.

When you use utility classes, remember that they should *always* be in packages. For one thing, packages are a good strategy on any large project because they help protect against name conflicts. With JSP, however, packages are absolutely required. The reason is that, in the absence of packages, classes you reference are assumed to be in the same package as the current class. For example, suppose that a JSP page contains the following scriptlet.

```
<% Test t = new Test(); %>
```

Now, if Test is in an imported package, there is no ambiguity. But, if Test is not in a package or the package to which Test belongs is not explicitly imported, then the system will assume that `Test` is in the same package as the autogenerated servlet. The problem is that the autogenerated servlet's package is not known! It is quite common for servers to create servlets whose package is determined by the directory in which the JSP page is placed. Other servers use different approaches. So, you simply cannot rely on packageless classes working properly. The same argument applies to beans (Chapter 14), since beans are just classes that follow some simple naming and structure conventions.

Core Approach

Always put your utility classes and beans in packages.

By default, the servlet imports `java.lang.*`, `javax.servlet.*`, `javax.servlet.jsp.*`, `javax.servlet.http.*`, and possibly some number of server-specific entries. Never write JSP code that relies on any server-specific classes being imported automatically; doing so makes your code nonportable.

Use of the `import` attribute takes one of the following two forms.

```
<%@ page import="package.class" %>
<%@ page import="package.class1,...,package.classN" %>
```

For example, the following directive signifies that all classes in the `java.util` package should be available to use without explicit package identifiers.

```
<%@ page import="java.util.*" %>
```

The `import` attribute is the only `page` attribute that is allowed to appear multiple times within the same document. Although `page` directives can appear anywhere within the document, it is traditional to place `import` statements either near the top of the document or just before the first place that the referenced package is used.

Note that, although the JSP pages go in the normal HTML directories of the server, the classes you write that are used by JSP pages must be placed in the special Java-code directories (e.g., .../WEB-INF/classes/*directoryMatchingPackageName*). See Sections 2.10 (Deployment Directories for Default Web Application: Summary) and 2.11 (Web Applications: A Preview) for information on these directories.

For example, Listing 12.1 presents a page that illustrates each of the three scripting elements from the previous chapter. The page uses three classes not in the standard JSP import list: `java.util.Date`, `coreservlets.CookieUtilities` (see Listing 8.3), and `coreservlets.LongLivedCookie` (see Listing 8.4). So, to simplify references to these classes, the JSP page uses

```
<%@ page import="java.util.*,coreservlets.*" %>
```

Figures 12–2 and 12–3 show some typical results.

Listing 12.1 ImportAttribute.jsp

```
<!DOCTYPE HTML PUBLIC "-//W3C//DTD HTML 4.0 Transitional//EN">
<HTML>
<HEAD>
<TITLE>The import Attribute</TITLE>
<LINK REL=STYLESHEET
      HREF="JSP-Styles.css"
      TYPE="text/css">
</HEAD>
<BODY>
<H2>The import Attribute</H2>
<%-- JSP page Directive --%>
<%@ page import="java.util.*,coreservlets.*" %>
<%-- JSP Declaration --%>
<%!
private String randomID() {
  int num = (int)(Math.random()*10000000.0);
  return("id" + num);
}
private final String NO_VALUE = "<I>No Value</I>";
%>
<%-- JSP Scriptlet --%>
<%
String oldID =
  CookieUtilities.getCookieValue(request, "userID", NO_VALUE);
if (oldID.equals(NO_VALUE)) {
  String newID = randomID();
  Cookie cookie = new LongLivedCookie("userID", newID);
  response.addCookie(cookie);
}
%>
<%-- JSP Expressions --%>
This page was accessed on <%= new Date() %> with a userID
cookie of <%= oldID %>.
</BODY></HTML>
```

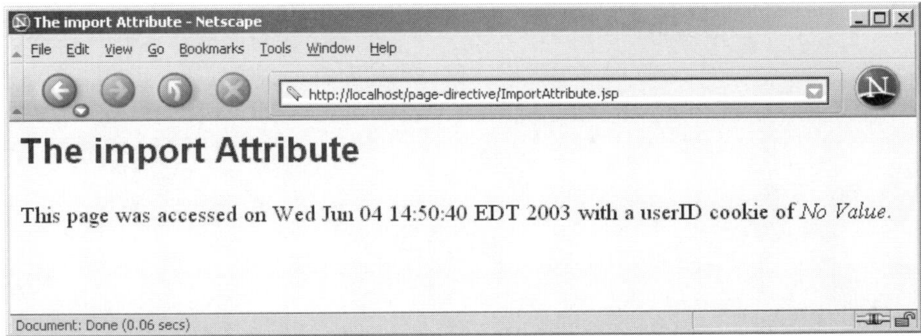

Figure 12–2 ImportAttribute.jsp when first accessed.

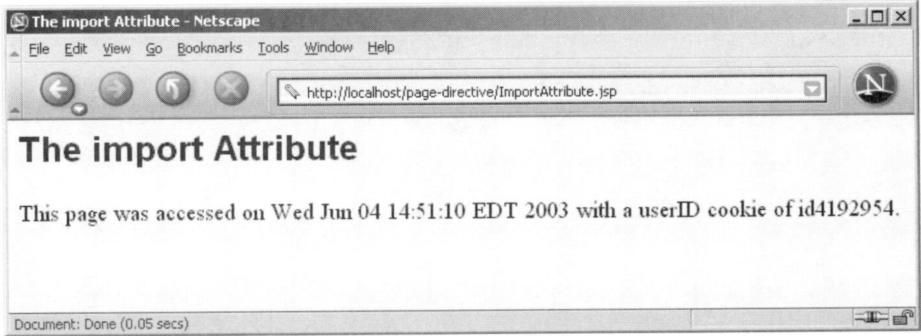

Figure 12–3 ImportAttribute.jsp when accessed in a subsequent request.

12.2 The contentType and pageEncoding Attributes

The `contentType` attribute sets the `Content-Type` response header, indicating the MIME type of the document being sent to the client. For more information on MIME types, see Table 7.1 (Common MIME Types) in Section 7.2 (Understanding HTTP 1.1 Response Headers).

Use of the `contentType` attribute takes one of the following two forms.

```
<%@ page contentType="MIME-Type" %>
<%@ page contentType="MIME-Type; charset=Character-Set" %>
```

For example, the directive

```
<%@ page contentType="application/vnd.ms-excel" %>
```

has the same basic effect as the scriptlet

```
<% response.setContentType("application/vnd.ms-excel"); %>
```

The first difference between the two forms is that `response.setContentType` uses explicit Java code (an approach some developers try to avoid), whereas the `page` directive uses only JSP syntax. The second difference is that directives are parsed specially; they don't directly become `_jspService` code at the location at which they appear. This means that `response.setContentType` can be invoked conditionally whereas the `page` directive cannot be. Setting the content type conditionally is useful when the same content can be displayed in different forms—for an example, see the next section (Conditionally Generating Excel Spreadsheets).

Unlike regular servlets, for which the default MIME type is `text/plain`, the default for JSP pages is `text/html` (with a default character set of `ISO-8859-1`). Thus, JSP pages that output HTML in a Latin character set need not use `contentType` at all. If you want to change both the content type and the character set, you can do the following.

```
<%@ page contentType="someMimeType; charset=someCharacterSet" %>
```

However, if you only want to change the character set, it is simpler to use the `pageEncoding` attribute. For example, Japanese JSP pages might use the following.

```
<%@ page pageEncoding="Shift_JIS" %>
```

Generating Excel Spreadsheets

Listing 12.2 shows a JSP page that uses the `contentType` attribute and tab-separated data to generate Excel output. Note that the `page` directive and comment are at the bottom so that the carriage returns at the ends of the lines don't show up in the Excel document. (Note: JSP does not ignore white space—JSP usually generates HTML in which most white space is ignored by the browser, but JSP itself maintains the white space and sends it to the client.) Figure 12–4 shows the result in Internet Explorer on a system that has Microsoft Office installed.

Listing 12.2 Excel.jsp

```
First	Last	Email Address
Marty	Hall	hall@coreservlets.com
Larry	Brown	brown@coreservlets.com
Steve	Balmer	balmer@ibm.com
Scott	McNealy	mcnealy@microsoft.com
<%@ page contentType="application/vnd.ms-excel" %>
<%-- There are tabs, not spaces, between columns. --%>
```

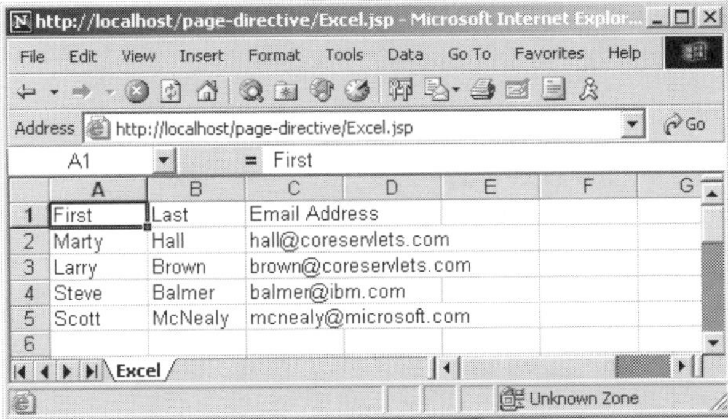

Figure 12–4 Excel document (Excel.jsp) in Internet Explorer.

12.3 Conditionally Generating Excel Spreadsheets

In most cases in which you generate non-HTML content with JSP, you know the content type in advance. In those cases, the `contentType` attribute of the `page` directive is appropriate: it requires no explicit Java syntax and can appear anywhere in the page.

Occasionally, however, you may want to build the same content, but change the listed content type depending on the situation. For example, many word processing and desktop publishing systems can import HTML pages. So, you could arrange to have the page come up either in the publishing system or in the browser, depending on the content type you send. Similarly, Microsoft Excel can import tables that are represented in HTML with the `TABLE` tag. This capability suggests a simple method of returning either HTML or Excel content, depending on which the user prefers: just use an HTML table and set the content type to `application/vnd.ms-excel` only if the user requests the results in Excel.

Unfortunately, this approach brings to light a small deficiency in the page directive: attribute values cannot be computed at runtime, nor can page directives be conditionally inserted as can template text. So, the following attempt results in Excel content regardless of the result of the checkUserRequest method.

```
<% boolean usingExcel = checkUserRequest(request); %>
<% if (usingExcel) { %>
<%@ page contentType="application/vnd.ms-excel" %>
<% } %>
```

Fortunately, there is a simple solution to the problem of conditionally setting the content type: just use scriptlets and the normal servlet approach of response.setContentType, as in the following snippet:

```
<%
String format = request.getParameter("format");
if ((format != null) && (format.equals("excel"))) {
  response.setContentType("application/vnd.ms-excel");
}
%>
```

For example, we once worked on a project that displayed financial (budget) information to authorized users. The data could be displayed in a table in a regular Web page if the user merely wanted to review it, or it could be placed into an Excel spreadsheet if the user wanted to put it into a report. When we first joined the project, there were two entirely separate pieces of code for each task. We changed it to build the same HTML table either way and to merely change the content type. Voila!

Listing 12.3 shows a page that uses this approach; Figures 12–5 and 12–6 show the results. In a real application, of course, the data would almost certainly come from a database. We use static values here for simplicity, but see Chapter 17 (Accessing Databases with JDBC) for information on talking to relational databases from servlets and JSP pages.

Listing 12.3 AppleAndOranges.jsp

```
<!DOCTYPE HTML PUBLIC "-//W3C//DTD HTML 4.0 Transitional//EN">
<HTML>
<HEAD>
<TITLE>Comparing Apples and Oranges</TITLE>
<LINK REL=STYLESHEET
      HREF="JSP-Styles.css"
      TYPE="text/css">
</HEAD>
```

Listing 12.3 AppLesAndOranges.jsp *(continued)*

```
<BODY>
<CENTER>
<H2>Comparing Apples and Oranges</H2>
<%
String format = request.getParameter("format");
if ((format != null) && (format.equals("excel"))) {
  response.setContentType("application/vnd.ms-excel");
}
%>
<TABLE BORDER=1>
  <TR><TH></TH>          <TH>Apples<TH>Oranges
  <TR><TH>First Quarter <TD>2307  <TD>4706
  <TR><TH>Second Quarter<TD>2982  <TD>5104
  <TR><TH>Third Quarter <TD>3011  <TD>5220
  <TR><TH>Fourth Quarter<TD>3055  <TD>5287
</TABLE>
</CENTER></BODY></HTML>
```

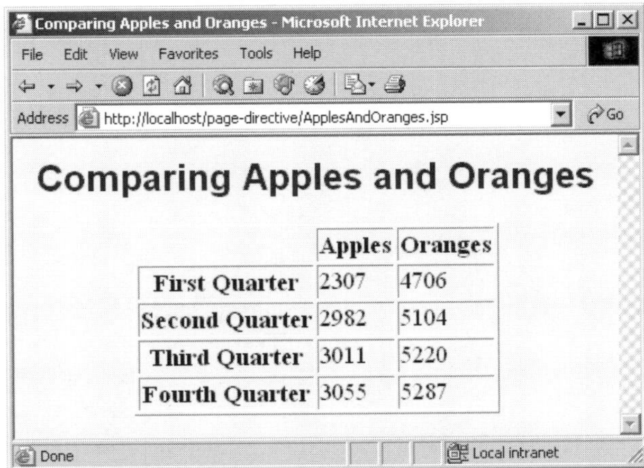

Figure 12–5 The default result of ApplesAndOranges.jsp is HTML content.

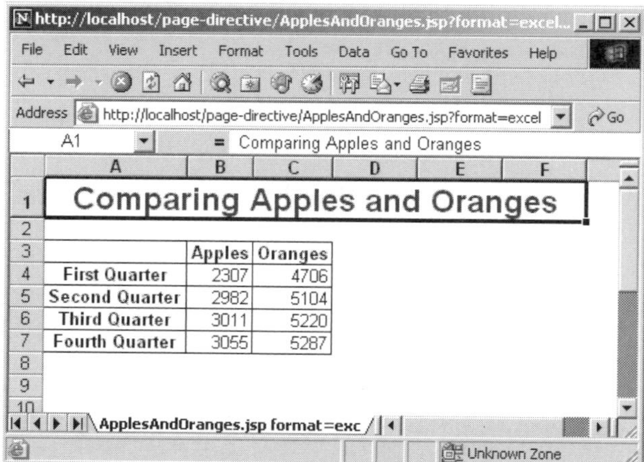

Figure 12–6 Specifying `format=excel` for ApplesAndOranges.jsp results in Excel content.

12.4 The session Attribute

The `session` attribute controls whether the page participates in HTTP sessions. Use of this attribute takes one of the following two forms.

```
<%@ page session="true" %> <%-- Default --%>
<%@ page session="false" %>
```

A value of `true` (the default) signifies that the predefined variable `session` (of type `HttpSession`) should be bound to the existing session if one exists; otherwise, a new session should be created and bound to `session`. A value of `false` means that no sessions will be automatically created and that attempts to access the variable `session` will result in errors at the time the JSP page is translated into a servlet.

Using `session="false"` may save significant amounts of server memory on high-traffic sites. However, note that using `session="false"` does not *disable* session tracking—it merely prevents the JSP page from creating *new* sessions for users who don't have them already. So, since sessions are *user specific*, not *page specific*, it doesn't do any good to turn off session tracking for one page unless you also turn it off for related pages that are likely to be visited in the same client session.

12.5 The isELIgnored Attribute

The `isELIgnored` attribute controls whether the JSP 2.0 Expression Language (EL) is ignored (`true`) or evaluated normally (`false`). This attribute is new in JSP 2.0; it is illegal to use it in a server that supports only JSP 1.2 or earlier. The default value of the attribute depends on the version of **web.xml** you use for your Web application. If your **web.xml** specifies servlets 2.3 (corresponding to JSP 1.2) or earlier, the default is `true` (but it is still legal to change the default—you are permitted to use this attribute in a JSP-2.0-compliant server regardless of the **web.xml** version). If your **web.xml** specifies servlets 2.4 (corresponding to JSP 2.0) or later, the default is `false`. Use of this attribute takes one of the following two forms.

```
<%@ page isELIgnored="false" %>
<%@ page isELIgnored="true" %>
```

JSP 2.0 introduced a concise expression language for accessing request parameters, cookies, HTTP headers, bean properties and `Collection` elements from within a JSP page. For details, see Chapter 16 (Simplifying Access to Java Code: The JSP 2.0 Expression Language). Expressions in the JSP EL take the form `${`*`expression`*`}`. Normally, these expressions are convenient. However, what would happen if you had a JSP 1.2 page that, just by happenstance, contained a string of the form `${...}`? In JSP 2.0, this could cause problems. Using `isELIgnored="true"` prevents these problems.

12.6 The buffer and autoFlush Attributes

The `buffer` attribute specifies the size of the buffer used by the `out` variable, which is of type `JspWriter`. Use of this attribute takes one of two forms:

```
<%@ page buffer="sizekb" %>
<%@ page buffer="none" %>
```

Servers can use a larger buffer than you specify, but not a smaller one. For example, `<%@ page buffer="32kb" %>` means the document content should be buffered and not sent to the client until at least 32 kilobytes are accumulated, the page is completed, or the output is explicitly flushed (e.g., with `response.flushBuffer`). The default buffer size is server specific, but must be at least 8 kilobytes. Be cautious about turning off buffering; doing so requires JSP elements that set headers or status codes to appear at the top of the file, before any HTML content. On the other hand, disabling buffering or using a small buffer is occasionally useful when it takes a very long time to generate each line of the output; in this scenario, users would see each line as soon as it is ready, rather than waiting even longer to see groups of lines.

The `autoFlush` attribute controls whether the output buffer should be automatically flushed when it is full (the default) or whether an exception should be raised when the buffer overflows (`autoFlush="false"`). Use of this attribute takes one of the following two forms.

```
<%@ page autoFlush="true" %> <%-- Default --%>
<%@ page autoFlush="false" %>
```

A value of `false` is illegal when `buffer="none"` is also used. Use of `autoFlush="false"` is exceedingly rare when the client is a normal Web browser. However, if the client is a custom application, you might want to guarantee that the application either receives a complete message or no message at all. A value of `false` could also be used to catch database queries that generate too much data, but it is generally better to place that logic in the data access code, not the presentation code.

12.7 The info Attribute

The `info` attribute defines a string that can be retrieved from the servlet by means of the `getServletInfo` method. Use of `info` takes the following form.

```
<%@ page info="Some Message" %>
```

12.8 The errorPage and isErrorPage Attributes

The `errorPage` attribute specifies a JSP page that should process any exceptions (i.e., something of type `Throwable`) thrown but not caught in the current page. It is used as follows:

```
<%@ page errorPage="Relative URL" %>
```

The exception thrown will automatically be available to the designated error page by means of the `exception` variable.

The `isErrorPage` attribute indicates whether or not the current page can act as the error page for another JSP page. Use of `isErrorPage` takes one of the following two forms:

```
<%@ page isErrorPage="true" %>
<%@ page isErrorPage="false" %> <%-- Default --%>
```

For example, Listing 12.4 shows a JSP page that computes speed based on distance and time parameters. The page neglects to check whether the input parameters are missing or malformed, so an error could easily occur at runtime. However, the page designates SpeedErrors.jsp (Listing 12.5) as the page to handle errors that occur in ComputeSpeed.jsp, so the user does not receive the typical terse JSP error messages. Note that SpeedErrors.jsp is placed in the WEB-INF directory. Because servers prohibit direct client access to WEB-INF, this arrangement prevents clients from accidentally accessing SpeedErrors.jsp directly. When an error occurs, SpeedErrors.jsp is accessed by the *server*, not by the *client*: error pages of this sort do not result in `response.sendRedirect` calls, and the client sees only the URL of the originally requested page, not the URL of the error page.

Figures 12–7 and 12–8 show results when good and bad input parameters are received, respectively.

Note that the `errorPage` attribute designates *page-specific* error pages. To designate error pages that apply to an entire Web application or to various categories of errors within an application, use the `error-page` element in web.xml. For details, see Volume 2 of this book.

Listing 12.4 ComputeSpeed.jsp

```
<!DOCTYPE HTML PUBLIC "-//W3C//DTD HTML 4.0 Transitional//EN">
<HTML>
<HEAD>
<TITLE>Computing Speed</TITLE>
<LINK REL=STYLESHEET
      HREF="JSP-Styles.css"
      TYPE="text/css">
</HEAD>
<BODY>
<%@ page errorPage="/WEB-INF/SpeedErrors.jsp" %>
<TABLE BORDER=5 ALIGN="CENTER">
  <TR><TH CLASS="TITLE">
      Computing Speed</TABLE>
<%!
// Note lack of try/catch for NumberFormatException if
// value is null or malformed.
```

Listing 12.4 ComputeSpeed.jsp *(continued)*

```
private double toDouble(String value) {
  return(Double.parseDouble(value));
}
%>
<%
double furlongs = toDouble(request.getParameter("furlongs"));
double fortnights = toDouble(request.getParameter("fortnights"));
double speed = furlongs/fortnights;
%>
<UL>
  <LI>Distance: <%= furlongs %> furlongs.
  <LI>Time: <%= fortnights %> fortnights.
  <LI>Speed: <%= speed %> furlongs per fortnight.
</UL>
</BODY></HTML>
```

Listing 12.5 SpeedErrors.jsp

```
<!DOCTYPE HTML PUBLIC "-//W3C//DTD HTML 4.0 Transitional//EN">
<HTML>
<HEAD>
<TITLE>Error Computing Speed</TITLE>
<LINK REL=STYLESHEET
      HREF="JSP-Styles.css"
      TYPE="text/css">
</HEAD>
<BODY>
<%@ page isErrorPage="true" %>
<TABLE BORDER=5 ALIGN="CENTER">
  <TR><TH CLASS="TITLE">
      Error Computing Speed</TABLE>
<P>
ComputeSpeed.jsp reported the following error:
<I><%= exception %></I>. This problem occurred in the
following place:
<PRE>
<%@ page import="java.io.*" %>
<% exception.printStackTrace(new PrintWriter(out)); %>
</PRE>
</BODY></HTML>
```

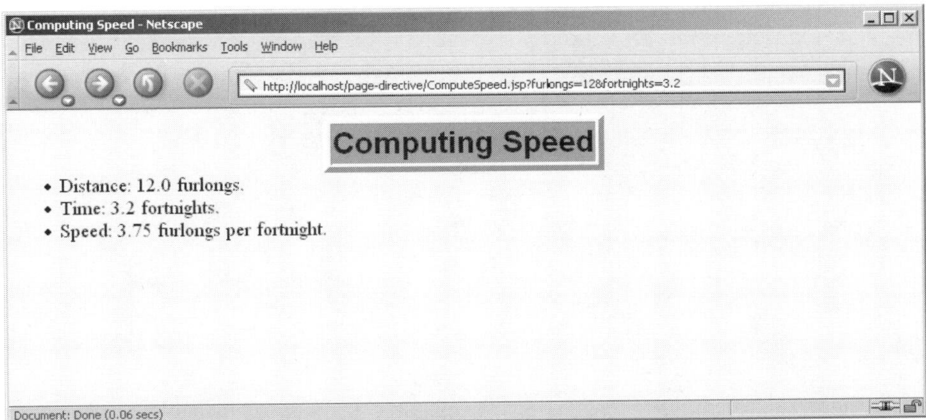

Figure 12–7 ComputeSpeed.jsp when it receives legal values.

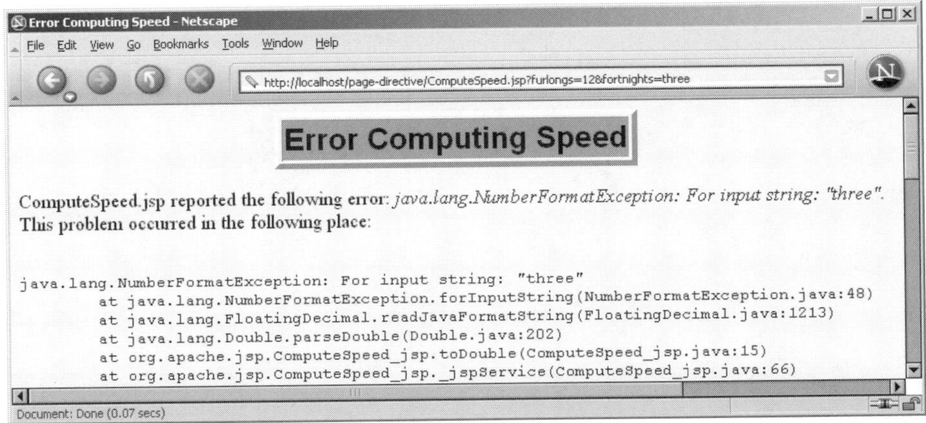

Figure 12–8 ComputeSpeed.jsp when it receives illegal values. Note that the address line shows the URL of ComputeSpeed.jsp, not SpeedErrors.jsp.

12.9 The isThreadSafe Attribute

The `isThreadSafe` attribute controls whether the servlet that results from the JSP page will allow concurrent access (the default) or will guarantee that no servlet instance processes more than one request at a time (`isThreadSafe="false"`). Use of the `isThreadSafe` attribute takes one of the following two forms.

```
<%@ page isThreadSafe="true" %> <%-- Default --%>
<%@ page isThreadSafe="false" %>
```

Unfortunately, the standard mechanism for preventing concurrent access is to implement the `SingleThreadModel` interface (Section 3.7). Although `SingleThreadModel` and `isThreadSafe="false"` were recommended in the early days, recent experience has shown that `SingleThreadModel` was so poorly designed that it is basically useless. So, you should avoid `isThreadSafe` and use explicit synchronization instead.

Core Warning

Do not use `isThreadSafe`. Use explicit synchronization instead.

To understand why `isThreadSafe="false"` is a bad idea, consider the following non-thread-safe snippet to compute user IDs. It is not thread safe since a thread could be preempted after reading `idNum` but before updating it, yielding two users with the same user ID.

```
<%! private int idNum = 0; %>
<%
String userID = "userID" + idNum;
out.println("Your ID is " + userID + ".");
idNum = idNum + 1;
%>
```

The code should have used a `synchronized` block. This construct is written

```
synchronized(someObject) { ... }
```

and means that once a thread enters the block of code, no other thread can enter the same block (or any other block marked with the same object reference) until the first thread exits. So, the previous snippet should have been written in the following manner.

```
<%! private int idNum = 0; %>
<%
synchronized(this) {
  String userID = "userID" + idNum;
  out.println("Your ID is " + userID + ".");
  idNum = idNum + 1;
}
%>
```

There are two reasons why this explicitly synchronized version is superior to the original version with the addition of `<%@ page isThreadSafe="false" %>`.

First, the explicitly synchronized version will probably have much better performance if the page is accessed frequently. The reason is that most JSP pages are not CPU limited but are I/O limited. So, while the system waits for I/O (e.g., a response from a database, the result of an EJB call, output sent over the network to the user), it should be doing something else. Since most servers implement `SingleThreadModel` by queueing up requests and handling them one at a time, high-traffic JSP pages can be *much* slower with this approach.

Even worse, the version that uses `SingleThreadModel` might not even get the right answer! Rather than queueing up requests, servers are permitted to implement `SingleThreadModel` by making a pool of servlet instances, as long as no instance is invoked concurrently. This, of course, totally defeats the purpose of using fields for persistence, since each instance would have a different field (instance variable), and multiple users could still get the same user ID. Defining the `idNum` field as `static` does not solve the problem either; the `this` reference would be different for each servlet instance, so the protection would be ineffective.

These problems are basically intractable. Give up. Forget `SingleThreadModel` and `isThreadSafe="false"`. Synchronize your code explicitly instead.

12.10 The extends Attribute

The `extends` attribute designates the superclass of the servlet that will be generated for the JSP page. It takes the following form.

```
<%@ page extends="package.class" %>
```

This attribute is normally reserved for developers or vendors that implement fundamental changes to the way in which pages operate (e.g., to add in personalization features). Ordinary mortals should steer clear of this attribute except when referring to classes provided by the server vendor for this purpose.

12.11 The language Attribute

At some point, the `language` attribute is intended to specify the scripting language being used, as below.

```
<%@ page language="cobol" %>
```

For now, don't bother with this attribute since `java` is both the default and the only legal choice.

12.12 XML Syntax for Directives

If you are writing XML-compatible JSP pages, you can use an alternative XML-compatible syntax for directives as long as you don't mix the XML syntax and the classic syntax in the same page. These constructs take the following form:

```
<jsp:directive.directiveType attribute="value" />
```

For example, the XML equivalent of

```
<%@ page import="java.util.*" %>
```

is

```
<jsp:directive.page import="java.util.*" />
```

Including Files and Applets in JSP Pages

Topics in This Chapter

- Using `jsp:include` to include pages at request time
- Using `<%@ include ... %>` (the `include` directive) to include files at page translation time
- Understanding why `jsp:include` is usually better than the `include` directive
- Using `jsp:plugin` to include applets for the Java Plug-in

Chapter 13

JSP has three main capabilities for including external pieces into a JSP document:

- **The `jsp:include` action.** The `jsp:include` action lets you include the output of a page at request time. Its main advantage is that it saves you from changing the main page when the included pages change. Its main disadvantage is that since it includes the *output* of the secondary page, not the secondary page's actual *code* as with the `include` directive, the included pages cannot use any JSP constructs that affect the main page as a whole. The advantages generally far outweigh the disadvantages, and you will almost certainly use it much more than the other inclusion mechanisms. Use of `jsp:include` is discussed in Section 13.1.
- **The `include` directive.** This construct lets you insert JSP code into the main page before that main page is translated into a servlet. Its main advantage is that it is powerful: the included code can contain JSP constructs such as field definitions and content-type settings that affect the main page as a whole. Its main disadvantage is that it is hard to maintain: you have to update the main page whenever any of the included pages change. Use of the `include` directive is discussed in Section 13.2.
- **The `jsp:plugin` action.** Although this book is primarily about server-side Java, client-side Java in the form of Web-embedded applets continues to play a role, especially within corporate intranets. The `jsp:plugin` element is used to insert applets that use the Java Plug-in into JSP pages. Its main advantage is that it saves you from

writing long, tedious, and error-prone `OBJECT` and `EMBED` tags in your HTML. Its main disadvantage is that it applies to applets, and applets are relatively infrequently used. Use of `jsp:plugin` is discussed in Section 13.4.

13.1 Including Pages at Request Time: The jsp:include Action

Suppose you have a series of pages, all of which have the same navigation bar, contact information, or footer. What can you do? Well, one common "solution" is to cut and paste the same HTML snippets into all the pages. This is a bad idea because when you change the common piece, you have to change every page that uses it. Another common solution is to use some sort of server-side include mechanism whereby the common piece gets inserted as the page is requested. This general approach is a good one, but the typical mechanisms are server specific. Enter `jsp:include`, a portable mechanism that lets you insert any of the following into the JSP output:

- The content of an HTML page.
- The content of a plain text document.
- The output of JSP page.
- The output of a servlet.

The `jsp:include` action includes the output of a secondary page at the time the main page is requested. Although the *output* of the included pages cannot contain JSP, the pages can be the result of resources that use servlets or JSP to *create* the output. That is, the URL that refers to the included resource is interpreted in the normal manner by the server and thus can be a servlet or JSP page. The server runs the included page in the usual way and places the output into the main page. This is precisely the behavior of the `include` method of the `RequestDispatcher` class (see Chapter 15, "Integrating Servlets and JSP: The Model View Controller (MVC) Architecture"), which is what servlets use if they want to do this type of file inclusion.

The page Attribute: Specifying the Included Page

You designate the included page with the `page` attribute, as shown below. This attribute is required; it should be a relative URL referencing the resource whose output should be included.

```
<jsp:include page="relative-path-to-resource" />
```

Relative URLs that do not start with a slash are interpreted relative to the location of the main page. Relative URLs that start with a slash are interpreted relative to the base Web application directory, *not* relative to the server root. For example, consider a JSP page in the `headlines` Web application that is accessed by the URL http://*host*/headlines/sports/table-tennis.jsp. The table-tennis.jsp file is in the sports subdirectory of whatever directory is used by the `headlines` Web application. Now, consider the following two include statements.

```
<jsp:include page="bios/cheng-yinghua.jsp" />
<jsp:include page="/templates/footer.jsp" />
```

In the first case, the system would look for cheng-yinghua.jsp in the bios subdirectory of sports (i.e., in the sports/bios sub-subdirectory of the main directory of the `headlines` application). In the second case, the system would look for footer.jsp in the templates subdirectory of the `headlines` application, *not* in the templates subdirectory of the server root. The `jsp:include` action *never* causes the system to look at files outside of the current Web application. If you have trouble remembering how the system interprets URLs that begin with slashes, remember this rule: they are interpreted relative to the current Web application whenever the server handles them; they are interpreted relative to the server root only when the client (browser) handles them. For example, the URL in

```
<jsp:include page="/path/file" />
```

is interpreted within the context of the current Web application because the server resolves the URL; the browser never sees it. But, the URL in

```
<IMG SRC="/path/file" ...>
```

is interpreted relative to the server's base directory because the browser resolves the URL; the browser knows nothing about Web applications. For information on Web applications, see Section 2.11.

Core Note

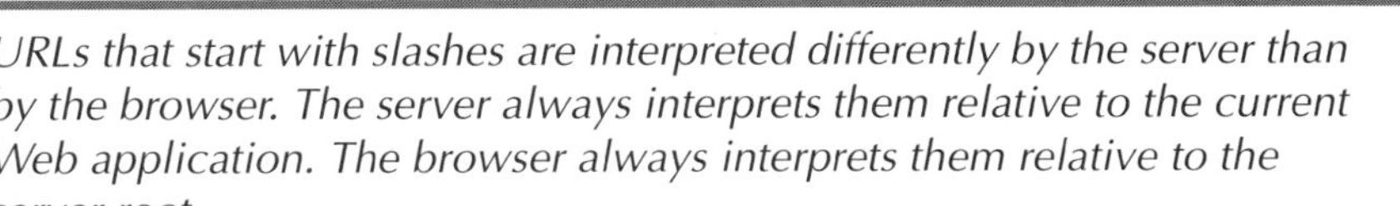

URLs that start with slashes are interpreted differently by the server than by the browser. The server always interprets them relative to the current Web application. The browser always interprets them relative to the server root.

Finally, note that you are permitted to place your pages in the WEB-INF directory. Although the client is prohibited from directly accessing files in this directory, it is the server, not the client, that accesses files referenced by the `page` attribute of jsp:include. In fact, placing the included pages in WEB-INF is a recommended practice; doing so will prevent them from being accidentally accessed by the client (which would be bad, since they are usually incomplete HTML documents).

Core Approach

To prevent the included files from being accessed separately, place them in WEB-INF or a subdirectory thereof.

XML Syntax and jsp:include

The jsp:include action is one of the first JSP constructs we have seen that has only XML syntax, with no equivalent "classic" syntax. If you are unfamiliar with XML, note three things:

- **XML element names can contain colons.** So, do not be thrown off by the fact that the element name is jsp:include. In fact, the XML-compatible version of all standard JSP elements starts with the jsp prefix (or namespace).
- **XML tags are case sensitive.** In standard HTML, it does not matter if you say BODY, body, or Body. In XML, it matters. So, be sure to use jsp:include in all lower case.
- **XML tags must be explicitly closed.** In HTML, there are container elements such as H1 that have both start and end tags (<H1> ... </H1>) as well as standalone elements such as IMG or HR that have no end tags (<HR>). In addition, the HTML specification defines the end tags of some container elements (e.g., TR, P) to be optional. In XML, all elements are container elements, and end tags are never optional. However, as a convenience, you can replace bodyless snippets such as <blah></blah> with <blah/>. So when using jsp:include, be sure to include that trailing slash.

The flush Attribute

In addition to the required page attribute, jsp:include has a second attribute: flush, as shown below. This attribute is optional; it specifies whether the output stream of the main page should flushed before the inclusion of the page (the default is false). Note, however, that in JSP 1.1, flush was a required attribute and the only legal value was true.

```
<jsp:include page="relative-path-to-resource" flush="true" />
```

A News Headline Page

As an example of a typical use of `jsp:include`, consider the simple news summary page shown in Listing 13.1. Page developers can change the news items in the files Item1.html through Item3.html (Listings 13.2 through 13.4) without having to update the main news page. Figure 13–1 shows the result.

Notice that the included pieces are not complete Web pages. The included pages can be HTML files, plain text files, JSP pages, or servlets (but with JSP pages and servlets, only the output of the page is included, not the actual code). In all cases, however, the client sees only the *composite* result. So, if both the main page and the included pieces contain tags such as `DOCTYPE`, `BODY`, etc., the result will be illegal HTML because these tags will appear twice in the result that the client sees. With servlets and JSP, it is always a good habit to view the HTML source and submit the URL to an HTML validator (see Section 3.5, "Simple HTML-Building Utilities"). When `jsp:include` is used, this advice is even more important because beginners often erroneously design both the main page and the included page as complete HTML documents.

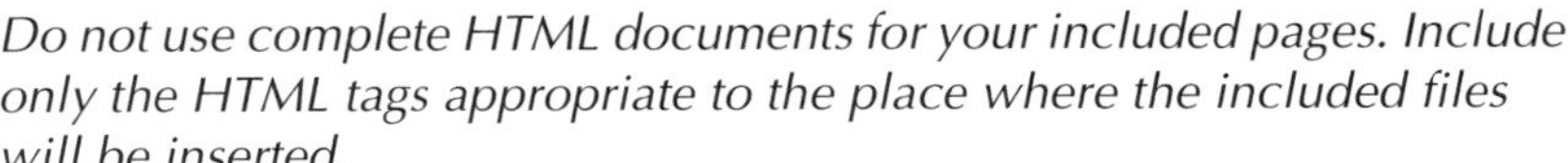

Core Approach

Do not use complete HTML documents for your included pages. Include only the HTML tags appropriate to the place where the included files will be inserted.

Listing 13.1 WhatsNew.jsp

```
<!DOCTYPE HTML PUBLIC "-//W3C//DTD HTML 4.0 Transitional//EN">
<HTML>
<HEAD>
<TITLE>What's New at JspNews.com</TITLE>
<LINK REL=STYLESHEET
      HREF="JSP-Styles.css"
      TYPE="text/css">
</HEAD>
<BODY>
<TABLE BORDER=5 ALIGN="CENTER">
  <TR><TH CLASS="TITLE">
      What's New at JspNews.com</TABLE>
```

Listing 13.1 WhatsNew.jsp *(continued)*

```
<P>
Here is a summary of our three most recent news stories:
<OL>
  <LI><jsp:include page="/WEB-INF/Item1.html" />
  <LI><jsp:include page="/WEB-INF/Item2.html" />
  <LI><jsp:include page="/WEB-INF/Item3.html" />
</OL>
</BODY></HTML>
```

Listing 13.2 /WEB-INF/Item1.html

```
<B>Bill Gates acts humble.</B> In a startling and unexpected
development, Microsoft big wig Bill Gates put on an open act of
humility yesterday.
<A HREF="http://www.microsoft.com/Never.html">More details...</A>
```

Listing 13.3 /WEB-INF/Item2.html

```
<B>Scott McNealy acts serious.</B> In an unexpected twist,
wisecracking Sun head Scott McNealy was sober and subdued at
yesterday's meeting.
<A HREF="http://www.sun.com/Imposter.html">More details...</A>
```

Listing 13.4 /WEB-INF/Item3.html

```
<B>Larry Ellison acts conciliatory.</B> Catching his competitors
off guard yesterday, Oracle prez Larry Ellison referred to his
rivals in friendly and respectful terms.
<A HREF="http://www.oracle.com/Mistake.html">More details...</A>
```

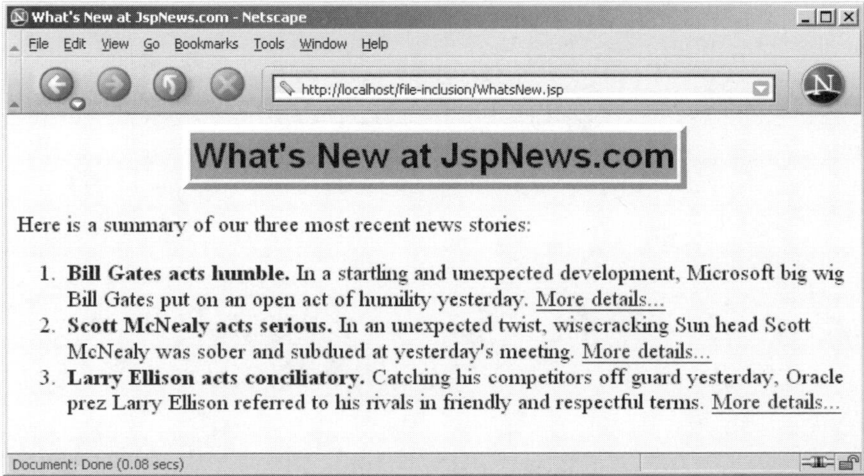

Figure 13–1 Including files at request time lets you update the individual files without changing the main page.

The jsp:param Element: Augmenting Request Parameters

The included page uses the same request object as the originally requested page. As a result, the included page normally sees the same request parameters as the main page. If, however, you want to add to or replace those parameters, you can use the `jsp:param` element (which has `name` and `value` attributes) to do so. For example, consider the following snippet.

```
<jsp:include page="/fragments/StandardHeading.jsp">
  <jsp:param name="bgColor" value="YELLOW" />
</jsp:include>
```

Now, suppose that the main page is invoked by means of http://host/path/MainPage.jsp?fgColor=RED. In such a case, the following list summarizes the results of various `getParameter` calls.

- **In main page (MainPage.jsp).** (Regardless of whether the `getParameter` calls are before or after the file inclusion.)
  - `request.getParameter("fgColor")` returns `"RED"`.
  - `request.getParameter("bgColor")` returns `null`.

- **In included page (StandardHeading.jsp).**
    - `request.getParameter("fgColor")` returns `"RED"`.
    - `request.getParameter("bgColor")` returns `"YELLOW"`.

If the main page receives a request parameter that is also specified with the `jsp:param` element, the value from `jsp:param` takes precedence only in the included page.

13.2 Including Files at Page Translation Time: The include Directive

You use the `include` directive to include a file in the main JSP document at the time the document is translated into a servlet (which is typically the first time it is accessed). The syntax is as follows:

```
<%@ include file="Relative URL" %>
```

Think of the `include` directive as a preprocessor: the included file is inserted character for character into the main page, then the resultant page is treated as a single JSP page. So, the fundamental difference between `jsp:include` and the `include` directive is the time at which they are invoked: `jsp:include` is invoked at request time, whereas the `include` directive is invoked at page translation time. However, there are more implications of this difference than you might first think. We summarize them in Table 13.1.

Table 13.1 Differences Between `jsp:include` and the `include` Directive

	`jsp:include` Action	**`include` Directive**
What does basic syntax look like?	`<jsp:include page="..." />`	`<%@ include file="..." %>`
When does inclusion occur?	Request time	Page translation time
What is included?	Output of page	Actual content of file
How many servlets result?	Two (main page and included page each become a separate servlet)	One (included file is inserted into main page, then that page is translated into a servlet)

Table 13.1 Differences Between `jsp:include` and the `include` Directive *(continued)*

	`jsp:include` Action	**`include` Directive**
Can included page set response headers that affect the main page?	No	Yes
Can included page define fields or methods that main page uses?	No	Yes
Does main page need to be updated when included page changes?	No	Yes
What is the equivalent servlet code?	`include` method of `RequestDispatcher`	None
Where is it discussed?	Section 13.1	Section 13.2 (this section)

There are many ramifications of the fact that the included file is inserted at page translation time with the `include` directive (`<%@ include ... %>`), not at request time as with `jsp:include`. However, there are two really important implications: maintenance and power. We discuss these two items in the following two subsections.

Maintenance Problems with the include Directive

The first ramification of the inclusion occurring at page translation time is that it is much more difficult to maintain pages that use the `include` directive than is the case with `jsp:include`. With the `include` directive (`<%@ include ... %>`), if the included file changes, all the JSP files that use it may need to be updated. Servers are required to detect when a JSP page changes and to translate it into a new servlet before handling the next request. Unfortunately, however, they are not required to detect when the included file changes, only when the main page changes. Servers are *allowed* to support a mechanism for detecting that an included file has changed (and then recompiling the servlet), but they are not *required* to do so. In practice, few do. So, with most servers, whenever an included file changes, *you* have to update the modification dates of each JSP page that uses the file.

This is a significant inconvenience; it results in such serious maintenance problems that the `include` directive should be used only in situations in which jsp:include would not suffice. Some developers have argued that using the include directive results in code that executes faster than it would with the jsp:include action. Although this may be true in principle, the performance difference is so small that it is difficult to measure, and the maintenance advantages of jsp:include are so great that it is virtually always preferred when both options are available. In fact, some developers find the maintenance burden of the include directive so onerous that they avoid it altogether. Perhaps this is an overreaction, but, at the very least, reserve the include directive for situations for which you really need the extra power it affords.

Core Approach

For file inclusion, use `jsp:include` whenever possible. Reserve the `include` directive (`<%@ include ... %>`) for cases in which the included file defines fields or methods that the main page uses or when the included file sets response headers of the main page.

Additional Power from the include Directive

If the include directive results in hard-to-maintain code, why would anyone want to use it? Well, that brings up the second difference between jsp:include and the include directive. The include directive is more powerful. With the include directive, the included file is permitted to contain JSP code such as response header settings and field definitions *that affect the main page*. For example, suppose snippet.jsp contained the following line of code:

```
<%! int accessCount = 0; %>
```

In such a case, you could do the following in the main page:

```
<%@ include file="snippet.jsp" %> <%-- Defines accessCount --%>
<%= accessCount++ %>               <%-- Uses accessCount --%>
```

With jsp:include, of course, this would be impossible because of the undefined accessCount variable; the main page would not translate successfully into a servlet. Besides, even if it could be translated without error, there would be no point; jsp:include includes the output of the auxiliary page, and snippet.jsp has no output.

Updating the Main Page

With most servers, if you use the `include` directive and change the included file, you also have to update the modification date of the main page. Some operating systems have commands that update the modification date without your actually editing the file (e.g., the Unix `touch` command), but a simple portable alternative is to include a JSP comment in the top-level page. Update the comment whenever the included file changes. For example, you might put the modification date of the included file in the comment, as below.

```
<%-- Navbar.jsp modified 9/1/03 --%>
<%@ include file="Navbar.jsp" %>
```

Core Warning

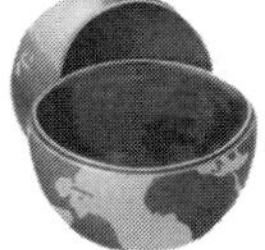

If you change an included JSP file, you may have to update the modification dates of all JSP files that use it.

XML Syntax for the include Directive

The XML-compatible equivalent of

```
<%@ include file="..." %>
```

is

```
<jsp:directive.include file="..." />
```

When this form is used, both the main page and the included file must use XML-compatible syntax throughout.

Example: Reusing Footers

As an example of a situation in which you would use the `include` directive instead of `jsp:include`, suppose that you have a JSP page that generates an HTML snippet containing a small footer that includes access counts and information about the most recent accesses to the current page. Listing 13.5 shows just such a page.

Now suppose you have several pages that want to have footers of that type. You could put the footer in WEB-INF (where it is protected from direct client access) and then have the pages that want to use it do so with the following.

```
<%@ include file="/WEB-INF/ContactSection.jsp" %>
```

Listing 13.6 shows a page that uses this approach; Figure 13–2 shows the result.

"Hold on!" you say, "Yes, ContactSection.jsp defines some instance variables (fields). And, if the main page *used* those instance variables, I would agree that you would have to use the `include` directive. But, in this particular case, the main page does not use the instance variables, so `jsp:include` should be used instead. Right?" Wrong. If you used `jsp:include` here, then all the pages that used the footer would see the same access count. You want each page that uses the footer to maintain a different access count. You do not want ContactSection.jsp to be its own servlet, you want ContactSection.jsp to provide code that will be part of each *separate* servlet that results from a JSP page that uses ContactSection.jsp. You need the `include` directive.

Listing 13.5 ContactSection.jsp

```
<%@ page import="java.util.Date" %>
<%-- The following become fields in each servlet that
     results from a JSP page that includes this file. --%>
<%!
private int accessCount = 0;
private Date accessDate = new Date();
private String accessHost = "<I>No previous access</I>";
%>
<P>
<HR>
This page &copy; 2003
<A HREF="http//www.my-company.com/">my-company.com</A>.
This page has been accessed <%= ++accessCount %>
times since server reboot. It was most recently accessed from
<%= accessHost %> at <%= accessDate %>.
<% accessHost = request.getRemoteHost(); %>
<% accessDate = new Date(); %>
```

Listing 13.6 SomeRandomPage.jsp

```
<!DOCTYPE HTML PUBLIC "-//W3C//DTD HTML 4.0 Transitional//EN">
<HTML>
<HEAD>
<TITLE>Some Random Page</TITLE>
<META NAME="author" CONTENT="J. Random Hacker">
<META NAME="keywords"
      CONTENT="foo,bar,baz,quux">
```

Listing 13.6 SomeRandomPage.jsp *(continued)*

```
<META NAME="description"
      CONTENT="Some random Web page.">
<LINK REL=STYLESHEET
      HREF="JSP-Styles.css"
      TYPE="text/css">
</HEAD>
<BODY>
<TABLE BORDER=5 ALIGN="CENTER">
  <TR><TH CLASS="TITLE">
      Some Random Page</TABLE>
<P>
Information about our products and services.
<P>
Blah, blah, blah.
<P>
Yadda, yadda, yadda.
<%@ include file="/WEB-INF/ContactSection.jsp" %>
</BODY></HTML>
```

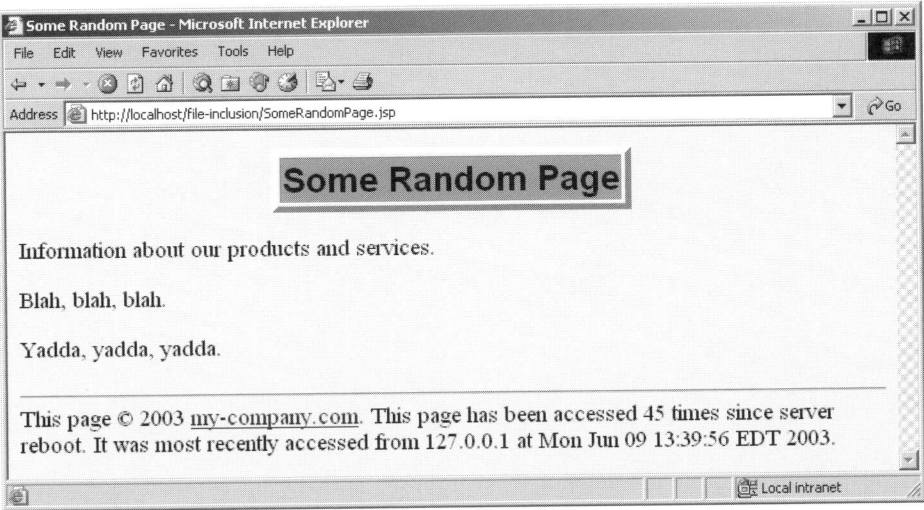

Figure 13–2 Result of SomeRandomPage.jsp. It uses the `include` directive so that it maintains access counts and most-recent-hosts entries separately from any other pages that use ContactSection.jsp.

13.3 Forwarding Requests with jsp:forward

You use `jsp:include` to combine output from the main page and the auxiliary page. Instead, you can use `jsp:forward` to obtain the complete output from the auxiliary page. For example, here is a page that randomly selects either page1.jsp or page2.jsp to output.

```
<% String destination;
   if (Math.random() > 0.5) {
     destination = "/examples/page1.jsp";
   } else {
     destination = "/examples/page2.jsp";
   }
%>
<jsp:forward page="<%= destination %>" />
```

To use `jsp:forward`, the main page must not have any output. This brings up the question, what benefit does JSP provide, then? The answer is, none! In fact, use of JSP is a hindrance in this type of situation because a real situation would be more complex, and complex code is easier to develop and test in a servlet than it is in a JSP page. We recommend that you completely avoid the use of `jsp:forward`. If you want to perform a task similar to this example, use a servlet and have it call the `forward` method of `RequestDispatcher`. See Chapter 15 for details.

13.4 Including Applets for the Java Plug-In

Early in the evolution of the Java programming language, the main application area was applets (Java programs embedded in Web pages and executed by Web browsers). Furthermore, most browsers supported the most up-to-date Java version. Now, however, applets are a very small part of the Java world, and the only major browser that supports the Java 2 platform (i.e., JDK 1.2–1.4) is Netscape 6 and later. This leaves applet developers with three choices:

- Develop the applets with JDK 1.1 or even 1.02 (to support *really* old browsers).
- Have users install version 1.4 of the Java Runtime Environment (JRE), then use JDK 1.4 for the applets.

- Have users install any version of the Java 2 Plug-in, then use Java 2 for the applets.

The first option is the one generally chosen for applets that will be deployed to the general public, because that option does not require users to install any special software. You need no special JSP syntax to use this option: just use the normal HTML `APPLET` tag. Just remember that **.class** files for applets need to go in the Web-accessible directories, not **WEB-INF/classes**, because it is the browser, not the server, that executes them. However, the lack of support for the Java 2 Platform imposes several restrictions on these applets:

- To use Swing, you must send the Swing files over the network. This process is time consuming and fails in Internet Explorer 3 and Netscape 3.x and 4.01–4.05 (which only support JDK 1.02), since Swing depends on JDK 1.1.
- You cannot use Java 2D.
- You cannot use the Java 2 collections package.
- Your code runs more slowly, since most compilers for the Java 2 platform are significantly improved over their 1.1 predecessors.

So, developers of complex applets for corporate intranets often choose one of the second two options.

The second option is best if the users all have Internet Explorer 6 (or later) or Netscape 6 (or later). With those browsers, version 1.4 of the JRE will replace the Java Virtual Machine (JVM) that comes bundled with the browser. Again, you need no special JSP syntax to use this option: just use the normal HTML `APPLET` tag. And again, remember that **.class** files for applets need to go in the Web-accessible directories, not **WEB-INF/classes**, because it is the browser, not the server, that executes them.

Core Approach

No matter what approach you use for applets, the applet .class files must go in the Web-accessible directories, not in WEB-INF/classes. The browser, not the server, uses them.

In large organizations, however, many users have earlier browser versions, and the second choice is not a viable option. So, to address this problem, Sun developed a browser plug-in for Netscape and Internet Explorer that lets you use the Java 2 platform in a variety of browser versions. This plug-in is available at **http://java.sun.com/products/plugin/** and also comes bundled with JDK 1.2.2 and later. Since the plug-in is quite large (several megabytes), it is not reasonable to expect users on the WWW at large to download and install it just to run your applets. On the other hand, it is a reasonable alternative for fast corporate intranets, especially since applets can automatically prompt browsers that lack the plug-in to download it.

Unfortunately, in some browsers, the normal `APPLET` tag will not work with the plug-in, since these older browsers are specifically designed to use only their built-in virtual machine when they see `APPLET`. Instead, you have to use a long and messy `OBJECT` tag for Internet Explorer and an equally long `EMBED` tag for Netscape. Furthermore, since you typically don't know which browser type will be accessing your page, you have to either include both `OBJECT` and `EMBED` (placing the `EMBED` within the `COMMENT` section of `OBJECT`) or identify the browser type at the time of the request and conditionally build the right tag. This process is straightforward but tedious and time consuming.

The `jsp:plugin` element instructs the server to build a tag appropriate for applets that use the plug-in. This element does not add any Java capabilities to the client. How could it? JSP runs entirely on the server; the client knows nothing about JSP. The `jsp:plugin` element merely simplifies the generation of the `OBJECT` or `EMBED` tags.

Core Note

The `jsp:plugin` element does not add any Java capability to the browser. It merely simplifies the creation of the cumbersome `OBJECT` and `EMBED` tags needed by the Java 2 Plug-in.

Servers are permitted some leeway in exactly how they implement `jsp:plugin` but most simply include both `OBJECT` and `EMBED`. To see exactly how your server translates `jsp:plugin`, insert into a page a simple `jsp:plugin` element with `type`, `code`, `width`, and `height` attributes as in the following example. Then, access the page from your browser and view the HTML source. For example, Listing 13.7 shows the HTML code generated by Tomcat for the following `jsp:plugin` element.

```
<jsp:plugin type="applet"
            code="SomeApplet.class"
            width="300" height="200">
</jsp:plugin>
```

Listing 13.7 Code Generated by Tomcat for `jsp:plugin`

```
<object classid="clsid:8AD9C840-044E-11D1-B3E9-00805F499D93"
        width="300" height="200"
        codebase="http://java.sun.com/products/plugin/1.2.2/jinst
all-1_2_2-win.cab#Version=1,2,2,0">
  <param name="java_code" value="SomeApplet.class">
  <param name="type" value="application/x-java-applet;">
<COMMENT>
<embed type="application/x-java-applet;" width="300" height="200"
       pluginspage="http://java.sun.com/products/plugin/"
       java_code="SomeApplet.class"
>
<noembed>
</COMMENT>
</noembed></embed>
</object>
```

The jsp:plugin Element

The simplest way to use `jsp:plugin` is to supply four attributes: `type`, `code`, `width`, and `height`. You supply a value of `applet` for the `type` attribute and use the other three attributes in exactly the same way as with the `APPLET` element, with two exceptions: the attribute names are case sensitive, and single or double quotes are always required around the attribute values. So, for example, you could replace

```
<APPLET CODE="MyApplet.class"
        WIDTH=475 HEIGHT=350>
</APPLET>
```

with

```
<jsp:plugin type="applet"
            code="MyApplet.class"
            width="475" height="350">
</jsp:plugin>
```

The `jsp:plugin` element has a number of other optional attributes. Most parallel the attributes of the `APPLET` element. Here is a full list.

- **`type`**
  For applets, this attribute should have a value of `applet`. However, the Java Plug-in also permits you to embed JavaBeans components in Web pages. Use a value of `bean` in such a case.

- **`code`**
  This attribute is used identically to the `CODE` attribute of `APPLET`, specifying the top-level applet class file that extends `Applet` or `JApplet`.
- **`width`**
  This attribute is used identically to the `WIDTH` attribute of `APPLET`, specifying the width in pixels to be reserved for the applet.
- **`height`**
  This attribute is used identically to the `HEIGHT` attribute of `APPLET`, specifying the height in pixels to be reserved for the applet.
- **`codebase`**
  This attribute is used identically to the `CODEBASE` attribute of `APPLET`, specifying the base directory for the applets. The `code` attribute is interpreted relative to this directory. As with the `APPLET` element, if you omit this attribute, the directory of the current page is used as the default. In the case of JSP, this default location is the directory in which the original JSP file resided, not the system-specific location of the servlet that results from the JSP file.
- **`align`**
  This attribute is used identically to the `ALIGN` attribute of `APPLET` and `IMG`, specifying the alignment of the applet within the Web page. Legal values are `left`, `right`, `top`, `bottom`, and `middle`.
- **`hspace`**
  This attribute is used identically to the `HSPACE` attribute of `APPLET`, specifying empty space in pixels reserved on the left and right of the applet.
- **`vspace`**
  This attribute is used identically to the `VSPACE` attribute of `APPLET`, specifying empty space in pixels reserved on the top and bottom of the applet.
- **`archive`**
  This attribute is used identically to the `ARCHIVE` attribute of `APPLET`, specifying a JAR file from which classes and images should be loaded.
- **`name`**
  This attribute is used identically to the `NAME` attribute of `APPLET`, specifying a name to use for interapplet communication or for identifying the applet to scripting languages like JavaScript.
- **`title`**
  This attribute is used identically to the very rarely used `TITLE` attribute of `APPLET` (and virtually all other HTML elements in HTML 4.0), specifying a title that could be used for a tool-tip or for indexing.

- **`jreversion`**
  This attribute identifies the version of the Java Runtime Environment (JRE) that is required. The default is 1.2.
- **`iepluginurl`**
  This attribute designates a URL from which the plug-in for Internet Explorer can be downloaded. Users who don't already have the plug-in installed will be prompted to download it from this location. The default value will direct the user to the Sun site, but for intranet use you might want to direct the user to a local copy.
- **`nspluginurl`**
  This attribute designates a URL from which the plug-in for Netscape can be downloaded. The default value will direct the user to the Sun site, but for intranet use you might want to direct the user to a local copy.

The jsp:param and jsp:params Elements

The `jsp:param` element is used with `jsp:plugin` in a manner similar to the way that `PARAM` is used with `APPLET`, specifying a name and value that are accessed from within the applet by `getParameter`. There are two main differences, however. First, since `jsp:param` follows XML syntax, attribute names must be lower case, attribute values must be enclosed in single or double quotes, and the element must end with `/>`, not just `>`. Second, all `jsp:param` entries must be enclosed within a `jsp:params` element.

So, for example, you would replace

```
<APPLET CODE="MyApplet.class"
        WIDTH=475 HEIGHT=350>
  <PARAM NAME="PARAM1" VALUE="VALUE1">
  <PARAM NAME="PARAM2" VALUE="VALUE2">
</APPLET>
```

with

```
<jsp:plugin type="applet"
            code="MyApplet.class"
            width="475" height="350">
  <jsp:params>
    <jsp:param name="PARAM1" value="VALUE1" />
    <jsp:param name="PARAM2" value="VALUE2" />
  </jsp:params>
</jsp:plugin>
```

The jsp:fallback Element

The `jsp:fallback` element provides alternative text to browsers that do not support `OBJECT` or `EMBED`. You use this element in almost the same way as you would use alternative text placed within an `APPLET` element. So, for example, you would replace

```
<APPLET CODE="MyApplet.class"
        WIDTH=475 HEIGHT=350>
  <B>Error: this example requires Java.</B>
</APPLET>
```

with

```
<jsp:plugin type="applet"
            code="MyApplet.class"
            width="475" height="350">
  <jsp:fallback>
    <B>Error: this example requires Java.</B>
  </jsp:fallback>
</jsp:plugin>
```

A jsp:plugin Example

Listing 13.8 shows a JSP page that uses the `jsp:plugin` element to generate an entry for the Java 2 Plug-in. Listing 13.9 shows the code for the applet itself (which uses Swing, Java 2D, and the auxiliary classes of Listings 13.10 through 13.12). Figure 13–3 shows the result.

Listing 13.8 PluginApplet.jsp

```
<!DOCTYPE HTML PUBLIC "-//W3C//DTD HTML 4.0 Transitional//EN">
<HTML>
<HEAD>
<TITLE>Using jsp:plugin</TITLE>
<LINK REL=STYLESHEET
      HREF="JSP-Styles.css"
      TYPE="text/css">
</HEAD>
<BODY>
<CENTER>
<TABLE BORDER=5>
  <TR><TH CLASS="TITLE">
      Using jsp:plugin</TABLE>
```

Listing 13.8 PluginApplet.jsp *(continued)*

```
<P>
<jsp:plugin type="applet"
            code="PluginApplet.class"
            width="370" height="420">
</jsp:plugin>
</CENTER></BODY></HTML>
```

Listing 13.9 PluginApplet.java

```
import javax.swing.*;

/** An applet that uses Swing and Java 2D and thus requires
 *  the Java Plug-in.
 */

public class PluginApplet extends JApplet {
  public void init() {
    WindowUtilities.setNativeLookAndFeel();
    setContentPane(new TextPanel());
  }
}
```

Listing 13.10 TextPanel.java

```
import java.awt.*;
import java.awt.event.*;
import javax.swing.*;

/** JPanel that places a panel with text drawn at various angles
 *  in the top part of the window and a JComboBox containing
 *  font choices in the bottom part.
 */

public class TextPanel extends JPanel
                       implements ActionListener {
  private JComboBox fontBox;
  private DrawingPanel drawingPanel;

  public TextPanel() {
    GraphicsEnvironment env =
      GraphicsEnvironment.getLocalGraphicsEnvironment();
```

Listing 13.10 TextPanel.java *(continued)*

```
    String[] fontNames = env.getAvailableFontFamilyNames();
    fontBox = new JComboBox(fontNames);
    setLayout(new BorderLayout());
    JPanel fontPanel = new JPanel();
    fontPanel.add(new JLabel("Font:"));
    fontPanel.add(fontBox);
    JButton drawButton = new JButton("Draw");
    drawButton.addActionListener(this);
    fontPanel.add(drawButton);
    add(fontPanel, BorderLayout.SOUTH);
    drawingPanel = new DrawingPanel();
    fontBox.setSelectedItem("Serif");
    drawingPanel.setFontName("Serif");
    add(drawingPanel, BorderLayout.CENTER);
  }

  public void actionPerformed(ActionEvent e) {
    drawingPanel.setFontName((String)fontBox.getSelectedItem());
    drawingPanel.repaint();
  }
}
```

Listing 13.11 DrawingPanel.java

```
import java.awt.*;
import java.awt.geom.*;
import javax.swing.*;

/** A window with text drawn at an angle. The font is
 *  set by means of the setFontName method.
 */

class DrawingPanel extends JPanel {
  private Ellipse2D.Double circle =
    new Ellipse2D.Double(10, 10, 350, 350);
  private GradientPaint gradient =
    new GradientPaint(0, 0, Color.red, 180, 180, Color.yellow,
                      true); // true means to repeat pattern
  private Color[] colors = { Color.white, Color.black };
```

Listing 13.11 DrawingPanel.java *(continued)*

```
  public void paintComponent(Graphics g) {
    super.paintComponent(g);
    Graphics2D g2d = (Graphics2D)g;
    g2d.setPaint(gradient);
    g2d.fill(circle);
    g2d.translate(185, 185);
    for (int i=0; i<16; i++) {
      g2d.rotate(Math.PI/8.0);
      g2d.setPaint(colors[i%2]);
      g2d.drawString("jsp:plugin", 0, 0);
    }
  }

  public void setFontName(String fontName) {
    setFont(new Font(fontName, Font.BOLD, 35));
  }
}
```

Listing 13.12 WindowUtilities.java

```
import javax.swing.*;
import java.awt.*;

/** A few utilities that simplify using windows in Swing. */

public class WindowUtilities {

  /** Tell system to use native look and feel, as in previous
   *  releases. Metal (Java) LAF is the default otherwise.
   */

  public static void setNativeLookAndFeel() {
    try {
      UIManager.setLookAndFeel
        (UIManager.getSystemLookAndFeelClassName());
    } catch(Exception e) {
      System.out.println("Error setting native LAF: " + e);
    }
  }

  ... // See www.coreservlets.com for remaining code.
}
```

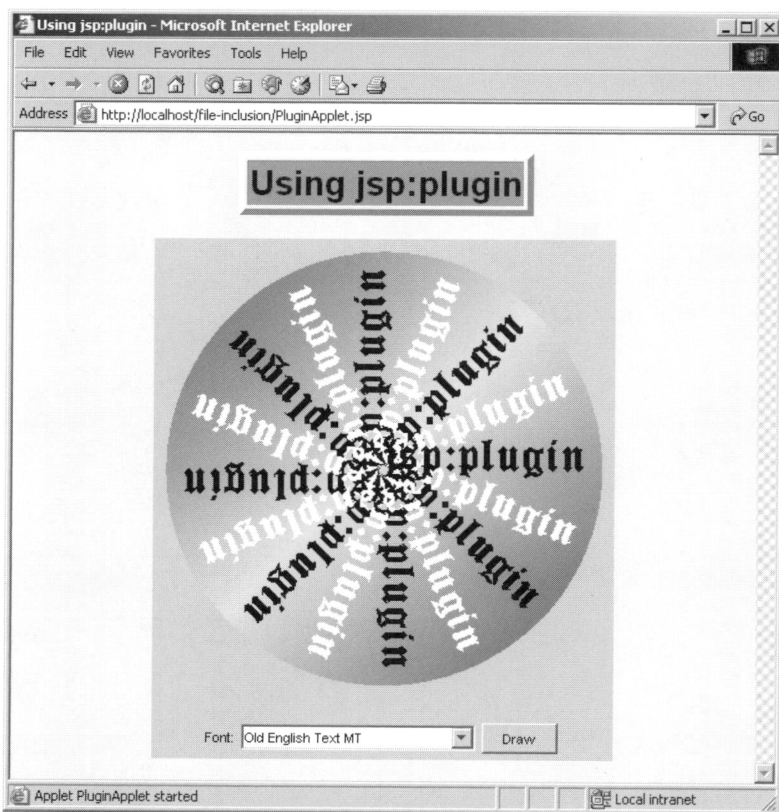

Figure 13–3 Result of PluginApplet.jsp in Internet Explorer with the JDK 1.4 plug-in.

Using JavaBeans Components in JSP Documents

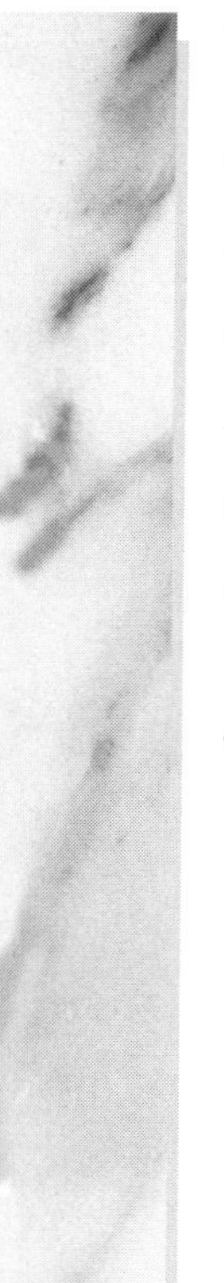

Topics in This Chapter

- Understanding the benefits of beans
- Creating beans
- Installing bean classes on your server
- Accessing bean properties
- Explicitly setting bean properties
- Automatically setting bean properties from request parameters
- Sharing beans among multiple servlets and JSP pages

Chapter

This chapter discusses the third general strategy for inserting dynamic content in JSP pages (see Figure 14–1): by means of JavaBeans components.

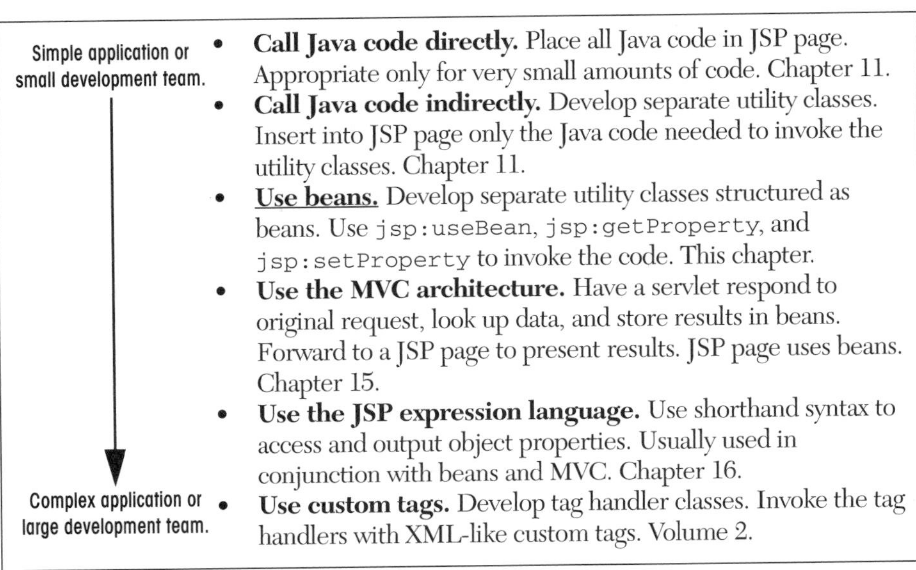

Figure 14–1 Strategies for invoking dynamic code from JSP.

14.1 Why Use Beans?

OK, so you already understand the benefit of using separate Java classes instead of embedding large amounts of code directly in JSP pages. As discussed in Section 11.3 (Limiting the Amount of Java Code in JSP Pages), separate classes are easier to write, compile, test, debug, and reuse. But what do beans provide that other classes do not? After all, beans are merely regular Java classes that follow some simple conventions defined by the JavaBeans specification; beans extend no particular class, are in no particular package, and use no particular interface.

Although it is true that beans are merely Java classes that are written in a standard format, there are several advantages to their use. With beans in general, visual manipulation tools and other programs can automatically discover information about classes that follow this format and can create and manipulate the classes without the user having to explicitly write any code. In JSP in particular, use of JavaBeans components provides three advantages over scriptlets and JSP expressions that refer to normal Java classes.

1. **No Java syntax.** By using beans, page authors can manipulate Java objects using only XML-compatible syntax: no parentheses, semicolons, or curly braces. This promotes a stronger separation between the content and the presentation and is especially useful in large development teams that have separate Web and Java developers.
2. **Simpler object sharing.** When you use the JSP bean constructs, you can much more easily share objects among multiple pages or between requests than if you use the equivalent explicit Java code.
3. **Convenient correspondence between request parameters and object properties.** The JSP bean constructs greatly simplify the process of reading request parameters, converting from strings, and putting the results inside objects.

14.2 What Are Beans?

As we said, beans are simply Java classes that are written in a standard format. Full coverage of JavaBeans is beyond the scope of this book, but for the purposes of use in JSP, all you need to know about beans are the three simple points outlined in the following list. If you want more details on beans in general, pick up one of the many books on the subject or see the documentation and tutorials at http://java.sun.com/products/javabeans/docs/.

- **A bean class must have a zero-argument (default) constructor.** You can satisfy this requirement either by explicitly defining such a constructor or by omitting all constructors, which results in a zero-argument constructor being created automatically. The default constructor will be called when JSP elements create beans. In fact, as we see in Chapter 15 (Integrating Servlets and JSP: The Model View Controller (MVC) Architecture), it is quite common for a servlet to create a bean, from which a JSP page merely looks up data. In that case, the requirement that the bean have a zero-argument constructor is waived.
- **A bean class should have no public instance variables (fields).** To be a bean that is accessible from JSP, a class should use accessor methods instead of allowing direct access to the instance variables. We hope you already follow this practice since it is an important design strategy in object-oriented programming. In general, use of accessor methods lets you do three things without users of your class changing their code: (a) impose constraints on variable values (e.g., have the `setSpeed` method of your `Car` class disallow negative speeds); (b) change your internal data structures (e.g., change from English units to metric units internally, but still have `getSpeedInMPH` and `getSpeedInKPH` methods); (c) perform side effects automatically when values change (e.g., update the user interface when `setPosition` is called).
- **Persistent values should be accessed through methods called `get`*`Xxx`* and `set`*`Xxx`*.** For example, if your `Car` class stores the current number of passengers, you might have methods named `getNumPassengers` (which takes no arguments and returns an `int`) and `setNumPassengers` (which takes an `int` and has a `void` return type). In such a case, the `Car` class is said to have a *property* named `numPassengers` (notice the lowercase `n` in the property name, but the uppercase `N` in the method names). If the class has a `get`*`Xxx`* method but no corresponding `set`*`Xxx`*, the class is said to have a read-only property named *`xxx`*.

  The one exception to this naming convention is with boolean properties: they are permitted to use a method called `is`*`Xxx`* to look up their values. So, for example, your `Car` class might have methods called `isLeased` (which takes no arguments and returns a `boolean`) and `setLeased` (which takes a `boolean` and has a `void` return type), and would be said to have a `boolean` property named `leased` (again, notice the lowercase leading letter in the property name).

Although you can use JSP scriptlets or expressions to access arbitrary methods of a class, standard JSP actions for accessing beans can only make use of methods that use the get*Xxx*/set*Xxx* or is*Xxx*/set*Xxx* naming convention.

14.3 Using Beans: Basic Tasks

You use three main constructs to build and manipulate JavaBeans components in JSP pages:

- **jsp:useBean.** In the simplest case, this element builds a new bean. It is normally used as follows:

```
<jsp:useBean id="beanName"
             class="package.Class" />
```

  If you supply a scope attribute (see Section 14.6, "Sharing Beans"), the jsp:useBean element can either build a new bean or access a preexisting one.

- **jsp:getProperty.** This element reads and outputs the value of a bean property. Reading a property is a shorthand notation for calling a method of the form get*Xxx*. This element is used as follows:

```
<jsp:getProperty name="beanName"
                 property="propertyName" />
```

- **jsp:setProperty.** This element modifies a bean property (i.e., calls a method of the form set*Xxx*). It is normally used as follows:

```
<jsp:setProperty name="beanName"
                 property="propertyName"
                 value="propertyValue" />
```

The following subsections give details on these elements.

Building Beans: jsp:useBean

The jsp:useBean action lets you load a bean to be used in the JSP page. Beans provide a very useful capability because they let you exploit the reusability of Java classes without sacrificing the convenience that JSP adds over servlets alone.

The simplest syntax for specifying that a bean should be used is the following.

```
<jsp:useBean id="name" class="package.Class" />
```

This statement usually means "instantiate an object of the class specified by `Class`, and bind it to a variable in `_jspService` with the name specified by `id`." Note, however, that you use the fully qualified class name—the class name with packages included. This requirement holds true regardless of whether you use `<%@ page import... %>` to import packages.

Core Warning

You must use the fully qualified class name for the `class` attribute of `jsp:useBean`.

So, for example, the JSP action

```
<jsp:useBean id="book1" class="coreservlets.Book" />
```

can normally be thought of as equivalent to the scriptlet

```
<% coreservlets.Book book1 = new coreservlets.Book(); %>
```

Installing Bean Classes

The bean class definition should be placed in the same directories where servlets can be installed, *not* in the directory that contains the JSP file. Just remember to use packages (see Section 11.3 for details). Thus, the proper location for individual bean classes is WEB-INF/classes/*subdirectoryMatchingPackageName*, as discussed in Sections 2.10 (Deployment Directories for Default Web Application: Summary) and 2.11 (Web Applications: A Preview). JAR files containing bean classes should be placed in the WEB-INF/lib directory.

Core Approach

Place all your beans in packages. Install them in the normal Java code directories: WEB-INF/classes/subdirectoryMatchingPackageName for individual classes and WEB-INF/lib for JAR files.

Using jsp:useBean Options: scope, beanName, and type

Although it is convenient to think of `jsp:useBean` as being equivalent to building an object and binding it to a local variable, `jsp:useBean` has additional options that make it more powerful. As we'll see in Section 14.6, you can specify a `scope` attribute that associates the bean with more than just the current page. If beans can be shared, it is useful to obtain references to existing beans, rather than always building a new object. So, the `jsp:useBean` action specifies that a new object is instantiated only if there is no existing one with the same `id` and `scope`.

Rather than using the `class` attribute, you are permitted to use `beanName` instead. The difference is that `beanName` can refer either to a class or to a file containing a serialized bean object. The value of the `beanName` attribute is passed to the `instantiate` method of `java.beans.Bean`.

In most cases, you want the local variable to have the same type as the object being created. In a few cases, however, you might want the variable to be declared to have a type that is a superclass of the actual bean type or is an interface that the bean implements. Use the `type` attribute to control this declaration, as in the following example.

```
<jsp:useBean id="thread1" class="mypackage.MyClass"
                          type="java.lang.Runnable" />
```

This use results in code similar to the following being inserted into the `_jspService` method.

```
java.lang.Runnable thread1 = new myPackage.MyClass();
```

A `ClassCastException` results if the actual class is not compatible with `type`. Also, you can use `type` without `class` if the bean already exists and you merely want to access an existing object, not create a new object. This is useful when you share beans by using the `scope` attribute as discussed in Section 14.6.

Note that since `jsp:useBean` uses XML syntax, the format differs in three ways from HTML syntax: the attribute names are case sensitive, either single or double quotes can be used (but one or the other *must* be used), and the end of the tag is marked with `/>`, not just `>`. The first two syntactic differences apply to all JSP elements that look like `jsp:`*`xxx`*. The third difference applies unless the element is a container with a separate start and end tag.

A few character sequences also require special handling in order to appear inside attribute values. To get `'` within an attribute value, use `\'`. Similarly, to get `"`, use `\"`; to get `\`, use `\\`; to get `%>`, use `%\>`; and to get `<%`, use `<\%`.

Accessing Bean Properties: jsp:getProperty

Once you have a bean, you can output its properties with `jsp:getProperty`, which takes a `name` attribute that should match the `id` given in `jsp:useBean` and a `property` attribute that names the property of interest.

Core Note

With `jsp:useBean`, the bean name is given by the `id` attribute. With `jsp:getProperty` and `jsp:setProperty`, it is given by the `name` attribute.

Instead of using `jsp:getProperty`, you could use a JSP expression and explicitly call a method on the object with the variable name specified by the `id` attribute. For example, assuming that the `Book` class has a `String` property called `title` and that you've created an instance called `book1` by using the `jsp:useBean` example given earlier in this section, you could insert the value of the `title` property into the JSP page in either of the following two ways.

```
<jsp:getProperty name="book1" property="title" />
<%= book1.getTitle() %>
```

The first approach is preferable in this case, since the syntax is more accessible to Web page designers who are not familiar with the Java programming language. If you create objects with `jsp:useBean` instead of an equivalent JSP scriptlet, be syntactically consistent and output bean properties with `jsp:getProperty` instead of the equivalent JSP expression. However, direct access to the variable is useful when you are using loops, conditional statements, and methods not represented as properties.

For you who are not familiar with the concept of bean properties, the standard interpretation of the statement "this bean has a property of type `T` called `foo`" is "this class has a method called `getFoo` that returns something of type `T`, and it has another method called `setFoo` that takes a `T` as an argument and stores it for later access by `getFoo`."

Setting Simple Bean Properties: jsp:setProperty

To modify bean properties, you normally use `jsp:setProperty`. This action has several different forms, but with the simplest form you supply three attributes: `name` (which should match the `id` given by `jsp:useBean`), `property` (the name of the property to change), and `value` (the new value). In Section 14.5 we present some alternative forms of `jsp:setProperty` that let you automatically associate a property with a request parameter. That section also explains how to supply values that are computed at request time (rather than fixed strings) and discusses the type conversion conventions that let you supply string values for parameters that expect numbers, characters, or boolean values.

An alternative to using the `jsp:setProperty` action is to use a scriptlet that explicitly calls methods on the bean object. For example, given the `book1` object shown earlier in this section, you could use either of the following two forms to modify the `title` property.

```
<jsp:setProperty name="book1"
                 property="title"
                 value="Core Servlets and JavaServer Pages" />
<% book1.setTitle("Core Servlets and JavaServer Pages"); %>
```

Using `jsp:setProperty` has the advantage that it is more accessible to the nonprogrammer, but direct access to the object lets you perform more complex operations such as setting the value conditionally or calling methods other than get*Xxx* or set*Xxx* on the object.

14.4 Example: StringBean

Listing 14.1 presents a simple class called `StringBean` that is in the `coreservlets` package. Because the class has no public instance variables (fields) and has a zero-argument constructor since it doesn't declare any explicit constructors, it satisfies the basic criteria for being a bean. Since `StringBean` has a method called `getMessage` that returns a `String` and another method called `setMessage` that takes a `String` as an argument, in beans terminology the class is said to have a `String` property called `message`.

Listing 14.2 shows a JSP file that uses the `StringBean` class. First, an instance of `StringBean` is created with the `jsp:useBean` action as follows.

```
<jsp:useBean id="stringBean" class="coreservlets.StringBean" />
```

After this, the `message` property can be inserted into the page in either of the following two ways.

```
<jsp:getProperty name="stringBean" property="message" />
<%= stringBean.getMessage() %>
```

The `message` property can be modified in either of the following two ways.

```
<jsp:setProperty name="stringBean"
                 property="message"
                 value="some message" />
<% stringBean.setMessage("some message"); %>
```

Please note that we do not recommend that you really mix the explicit Java syntax and the XML syntax in the same page; this example is just meant to illustrate the equivalent results of the two forms.

Core Approach

Whenever possible, avoid mixing the XML-compatible `jsp:useBean` tags with JSP scripting elements containing explicit Java code.

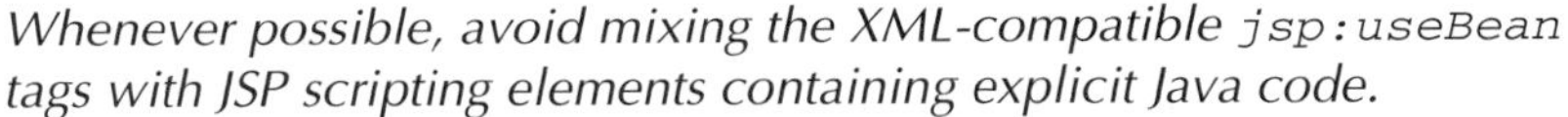

Figure 14–2 shows the result.

Listing 14.1 StringBean.java

```
package coreservlets;

/** A simple bean that has a single String property
 *  called message.
 */

public class StringBean {
  private String message = "No message specified";

  public String getMessage() {
    return(message);
  }

  public void setMessage(String message) {
    this.message = message;
  }
}
```

Listing 14.2 StringBean.jsp

```
<!DOCTYPE HTML PUBLIC "-//W3C//DTD HTML 4.0 Transitional//EN">
<HTML>
<HEAD>
<TITLE>Using JavaBeans with JSP</TITLE>
<LINK REL=STYLESHEET
      HREF="JSP-Styles.css"
      TYPE="text/css">
</HEAD>
<BODY>
<TABLE BORDER=5 ALIGN="CENTER">
  <TR><TH CLASS="TITLE">
      Using JavaBeans with JSP</TABLE>
<jsp:useBean id="stringBean" class="coreservlets.StringBean" />
<OL>
<LI>Initial value (from jsp:getProperty):
    <I><jsp:getProperty name="stringBean"
                        property="message" /></I>
<LI>Initial value (from JSP expression):
    <I><%= stringBean.getMessage() %></I>
<LI><jsp:setProperty name="stringBean"
                     property="message"
                     value="Best string bean: Fortex" />
    Value after setting property with jsp:setProperty:
    <I><jsp:getProperty name="stringBean"
                        property="message" /></I>
<LI><% stringBean.setMessage("My favorite: Kentucky Wonder"); %>
    Value after setting property with scriptlet:
    <I><%= stringBean.getMessage() %></I>
</OL>
</BODY></HTML>
```

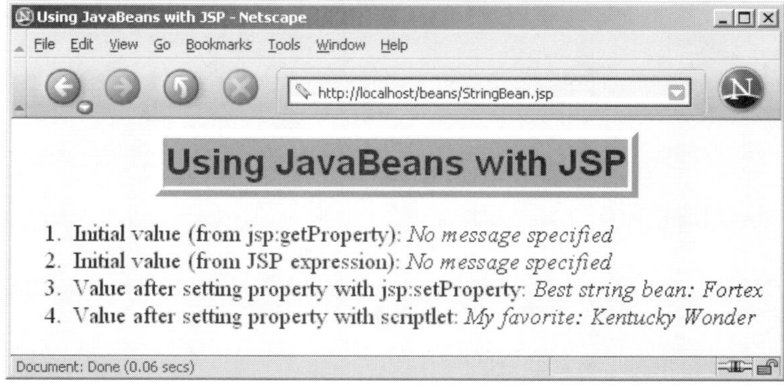

Figure 14–2 Result of StringBean.jsp.

14.5 Setting Bean Properties: Advanced Techniques

You normally use `jsp:setProperty` to set bean properties. The simplest form of this action takes three attributes: `name` (which should match the `id` given by `jsp:useBean`), `property` (the name of the property to change), and `value` (the new value).

For example, the `SaleEntry` class shown in Listing 14.3 has an `itemID` property (a `String`), a `numItems` property (an `int`), a `discountCode` property (a `double`), and two read-only properties, `itemCost` and `totalCost` (each of type `double`). Listing 14.4 shows a JSP file that builds an instance of the `SaleEntry` class by means of:

```
<jsp:useBean id="entry" class="coreservlets.SaleEntry" />
```

Listing 14.5 (Figure 14–3) gives the HTML form that collects the request parameters. The results are shown in Figure 14–4.

Once the bean is instantiated, using a request parameter to set the `itemID` is straightforward, as shown below.

```
<jsp:setProperty
    name="entry"
    property="itemID"
    value='<%= request.getParameter("itemID") %>' />
```

Notice that we used a JSP expression for the `value` attribute. Most JSP attribute values have to be fixed strings, but the `value` attribute of `jsp:setProperty` is permitted to be a request time expression. If the expression uses double quotes internally, recall that single quotes can be used instead of double quotes around attribute values and that `\'` and `\"` can be used to represent single or double quotes within an attribute value. In any case, the point is that it is *possible* to use JSP expressions here, but doing so requires the use of explicit Java code. In some applications, avoiding such explicit code is the main reason for using beans in the first place. Besides, as the next examples will show, the situation becomes much more complicated when the bean property is not of type `String`. The next two subsections will discuss how to solve these problems.

Listing 14.3 SaleEntry.java

```
package coreservlets;

/** Simple bean to illustrate the various forms
 *  of jsp:setProperty.
 */

public class SaleEntry {
  private String itemID = "unknown";
  private double discountCode = 1.0;
  private int numItems = 0;

  public String getItemID() {
    return(itemID);
  }

  public void setItemID(String itemID) {
    if (itemID != null) {
      this.itemID = itemID;
    } else {
      this.itemID = "unknown";
    }
  }

  public double getDiscountCode() {
    return(discountCode);
  }

  public void setDiscountCode(double discountCode) {
    this.discountCode = discountCode;
  }

  public int getNumItems() {
    return(numItems);
  }

  public void setNumItems(int numItems) {
    this.numItems = numItems;
  }

  // In real life, replace this with database lookup.
  // See Chapters 17 and 18 for info on accessing databases
  // from servlets and JSP pages.
```

Listing 14.3 SaleEntry.java *(continued)*

```
  public double getItemCost() {
    double cost;
    if (itemID.equals("a1234")) {
      cost = 12.99*getDiscountCode();
    } else {
      cost = -9999;
    }
    return(roundToPennies(cost));
  }

  private double roundToPennies(double cost) {
    return(Math.floor(cost*100)/100.0);
  }

  public double getTotalCost() {
    return(getItemCost() * getNumItems());
  }
}
```

Listing 14.4 SaleEntry1.jsp

```
<!DOCTYPE HTML PUBLIC "-//W3C//DTD HTML 4.0 Transitional//EN">
<HTML>
<HEAD>
<TITLE>Using jsp:setProperty</TITLE>
<LINK REL=STYLESHEET
      HREF="JSP-Styles.css"
      TYPE="text/css">
</HEAD>
<BODY>
<CENTER>
<TABLE BORDER=5>
  <TR><TH CLASS="TITLE">
      Using jsp:setProperty</TABLE>
<jsp:useBean id="entry" class="coreservlets.SaleEntry" />
<jsp:setProperty
    name="entry"
    property="itemID"
    value='<%= request.getParameter("itemID") %>' />
```

Listing 14.4 SaleEntry1.jsp *(continued)*

```
<%
int numItemsOrdered = 1;
try {
  numItemsOrdered =
    Integer.parseInt(request.getParameter("numItems"));
} catch(NumberFormatException nfe) {}
%>
<jsp:setProperty
    name="entry"
    property="numItems"
    value="<%= numItemsOrdered %>" />
<%
double discountCode = 1.0;
try {
  String discountString =
    request.getParameter("discountCode");
  discountCode =
    Double.parseDouble(discountString);
} catch(NumberFormatException nfe) {}
%>
<jsp:setProperty
    name="entry"
    property="discountCode"
    value="<%= discountCode %>" />
<BR>
<TABLE BORDER=1>
<TR CLASS="COLORED">
  <TH>Item ID<TH>Unit Price<TH>Number Ordered<TH>Total Price
<TR ALIGN="RIGHT">
  <TD><jsp:getProperty name="entry" property="itemID" />
  <TD>$<jsp:getProperty name="entry" property="itemCost" />
  <TD><jsp:getProperty name="entry" property="numItems" />
  <TD>$<jsp:getProperty name="entry" property="totalCost" />
</TABLE>
</CENTER></BODY></HTML>
```

Listing 14.5 SaleEntry1-Form.jsp

```
<!DOCTYPE HTML PUBLIC "-//W3C//DTD HTML 4.0 Transitional//EN">
<HTML>
<HEAD>
<TITLE>Invoking SaleEntry1.jsp</TITLE>
<LINK REL=STYLESHEET
      HREF="JSP-Styles.css"
      TYPE="text/css">
</HEAD>
<BODY>
<CENTER>
<TABLE BORDER=5>
  <TR><TH CLASS="TITLE">
      Invoking SaleEntry1.jsp</TABLE>
<FORM ACTION="SaleEntry1.jsp">
  Item ID: <INPUT TYPE="TEXT" NAME="itemID"><BR>
  Number of Items: <INPUT TYPE="TEXT" NAME="numItems"><BR>
  Discount Code: <INPUT TYPE="TEXT" NAME="discountCode"><P>
  <INPUT TYPE="SUBMIT" VALUE="Show Price">
</FORM>
</CENTER></BODY></HTML>
```

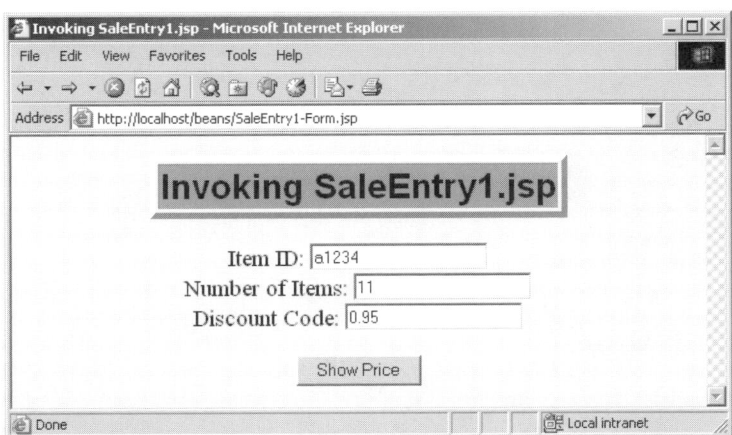

Figure 14–3 Front end to SaleEntry1.jsp.

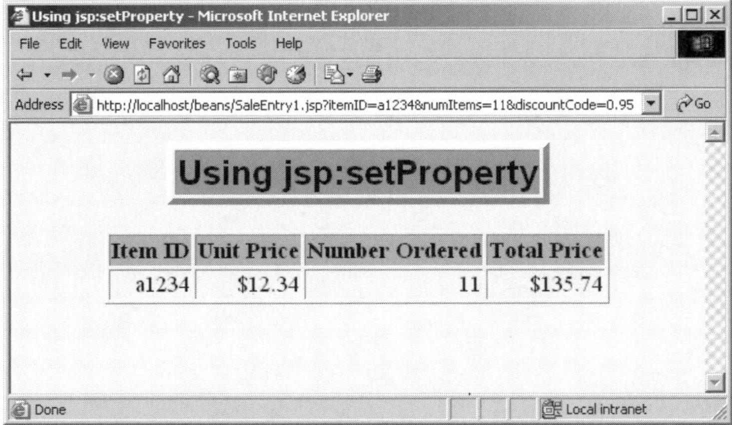

Figure 14–4 Result of SaleEntry1.jsp.

Associating Individual Properties with Input Parameters

Setting the `itemID` property is easy since its value is a `String`. Setting the `numItems` and `discountCode` properties is a bit more problematic since their values must be numbers whereas `getParameter` returns a `String`. Here is the somewhat cumbersome code required to set `numItems`.

```
<%
int numItemsOrdered = 1;
try {
  numItemsOrdered =
    Integer.parseInt(request.getParameter("numItems"));
} catch(NumberFormatException nfe) {}
%>
<jsp:setProperty
    name="entry"
    property="numItems"
    value="<%= numItemsOrdered %>" />
```

Fortunately, JSP has a nice solution to this problem. It lets you associate a property with a request parameter and automatically perform type conversion from strings to numbers, characters, and boolean values. Instead of using the `value` attribute, you use `param` to name an input parameter. The value of the named request parameter is automatically used as the value of the bean property, and type conversions from `String` to primitive types (`byte`, `int`, `double`, etc.) and wrapper classes (`Byte`, `Integer`, `Double`, etc.) are automatically performed. If the specified parameter is missing from the request, no action is taken (the system does not pass null to the associated property). So, for example, setting the numItems property can be simplified to:

```
<jsp:setProperty
     name="entry"
     property="numItems"
     param="numItems" />
```

You can simplify the code slightly if the request parameter name and the bean property name are the same. In that case, you can omit param as in the following example.

```
<jsp:setProperty
     name="entry"
     property="numItems" /> <%-- param="numItems" is assumed. --%>
```

We prefer the slightly longer form that lists the parameter explicitly. Listing 14.6 shows the relevant part of the JSP page reworked in this manner.

Listing 14.6 SaleEntry2.jsp

```
...
<jsp:useBean id="entry" class="coreservlets.SaleEntry" />
<jsp:setProperty
    name="entry"
    property="itemID"
    param="itemID" />
<jsp:setProperty
    name="entry"
    property="numItems"
    param="numItems" />
<jsp:setProperty
    name="entry"
    property="discountCode"
    param="discountCode" />
...
```

Associating All Properties with Request Parameters

Associating a property with a request parameter saves you the bother of performing conversions for many of the simple built-in types. JSP lets you take the process one step further by associating *all* properties with identically named request parameters. All you have to do is to supply "*" for the property parameter. So, for example, all three of the `jsp:setProperty` statements of Listing 14.6 can be replaced by the following simple line. Listing 14.7 shows the relevant part of the page.

```
<jsp:setProperty name="entry" property="*" />
```

Listing 14.7 SaleEntry3.jsp

```
...
<jsp:useBean id="entry" class="coreservlets.SaleEntry" />
<jsp:setProperty name="entry" property="*" />
...
```

This approach lets you define simple "form beans" whose properties correspond to the request parameters and get populated automatically. The system starts with the request parameters and looks for matching bean properties, not the other way around. Thus, no action is taken for bean properties that have no matching request parameter. This behavior means that the form beans need not be populated all at once; instead, one submission can fill in part of the bean, another form can fill in more, and so on. To make use of this capability, however, you need to share the bean among multiple pages. See Section 14.6 (Sharing Beans) for details. Finally, note that servlets can also use form beans, although only by making use of some custom utilities. For details, see Section 4.7 (Automatically Populating Java Objects from Request Parameters: Form Beans).

Although this approach is simple, three small warnings are in order.

- **No action is taken when an input parameter is missing.** In particular, the system does not supply `null` as the property value. So, you usually design your beans to have identifiable default values that let you determine if a property has been modified.
- **Automatic type conversion does not guard against illegal values as effectively as does manual type conversion.** In fact, despite the convenience of automatic type conversion, some developers eschew the automatic conversion, define all of their settable bean properties to be of type `String`, and use explicit `try`/`catch` blocks to handle malformed data. At the very least, you should consider the use of error pages when using automatic type conversion.
- **Bean property names and request parameters are case sensitive.** So, the property name and request parameter name must match exactly.

14.6 Sharing Beans

Up to this point, we have treated the objects that were created with `jsp:useBean` as though they were simply bound to local variables in the `_jspService` method (which is called by the `service` method of the servlet that is generated from the page). Although the beans are indeed bound to local variables, that is not the only behavior. They are also stored in one of four different locations, depending on the value of the optional `scope` attribute of `jsp:useBean`.

When you use `scope`, the system first looks for an existing bean of the specified name in the designated location. Only when the system fails to find a preexisting bean does it create a new one. This behavior lets a servlet handle complex user requests by setting up beans, storing them in one of the three standard shared locations (the request, the session, or the servlet context), then forwarding the request to one of several possible JSP pages to present results appropriate to the request data. For details on this approach, see Chapter 15 (Integrating Servlets and JSP: The Model View Controller (MVC) Architecture).

As described below, the `scope` attribute has four possible values: `page` (the default), `request`, `session`, and `application`.

- **`<jsp:useBean ... scope="page" />`**
  This is the default value; you get the same behavior if you omit the `scope` attribute entirely. The `page` scope indicates that, in addition to being bound to a local variable, the bean object should be placed in the `PageContext` object for the duration of the current request. Storing the object there means that servlet code can access it by calling `getAttribute` on the predefined `pageContext` variable.

  Since every page and every request has a different `PageContext` object, using `scope="page"` (or omitting `scope`) indicates that the bean is not shared and thus a new bean will be created for each request.

- **`<jsp:useBean ... scope="request" />`**
  This value signifies that, in addition to being bound to a local variable, the bean object should be placed in the `HttpServletRequest` object for the duration of the current request, where it is available by means of the `getAttribute` method.

  Although at first glance it appears that this scope also results in unshared beans, two JSP pages or a JSP page and a servlet will share request objects when you use `jsp:include` (Section 13.1), `jsp:forward` (Section 13.3), or the `include` or `forward` methods of `RequestDispatcher` (Chapter 15).

Storing values in the request object is common when the MVC (Model 2) architecture is used. For details, see Chapter 15.

- **`<jsp:useBean ... scope="session" />`**
  This value means that, in addition to being bound to a local variable, the bean will be stored in the `HttpSession` object associated with the current request, where it can be retrieved with `getAttribute`.

  Thus, this scope lets JSP pages easily perform the type of session tracking described in Chapter 9.
- **`<jsp:useBean ... scope="application" />`**
  This value means that, in addition to being bound to a local variable, the bean will be stored in the `ServletContext` available through the predefined `application` variable or by a call to `getServletContext`. The `ServletContext` is shared by all servlets and JSP pages in the Web application. Values in the `ServletContext` can be retrieved with the `getAttribute` method.

Creating Beans Conditionally

To make bean sharing more convenient, you can conditionally evaluate bean-related elements in two situations.

First, a `jsp:useBean` element results in a new bean being instantiated only if no bean with the same `id` and `scope` can be found. If a bean with the same `id` and `scope` *is* found, the preexisting bean is simply bound to the variable referenced by `id`.

Second, instead of

```
<jsp:useBean ... />
```

you can use

```
<jsp:useBean ...>statements</jsp:useBean>
```

The point of using the second form is that the statements between the `jsp:useBean` start and end tags are executed *only* if a new bean is created, *not* if an existing bean is used. Because `jsp:useBean` invokes the default (zero-argument) constructor, you frequently need to modify the properties after the bean is created. To mimic a constructor, however, you should make these modifications only when the bean is first created, not when an existing (and presumably updated) bean is accessed. No problem: multiple pages can contain `jsp:setProperty` statements between the start and end tags of `jsp:useBean`; only the page first accessed executes the statements.

For example, Listing 14.8 shows a simple bean that defines two properties: `accessCount` and `firstPage`. The `accessCount` property records cumulative access counts to any of a set of related pages and thus should be executed for all requests. The `firstPage` property stores the name of the first page that was accessed and thus should be executed only by the page that is first accessed. To enforce the distinction, we place the `jsp:setProperty` statement that updates the `accessCount` property in unconditional code and place the `jsp:setProperty` statement for `firstPage` between the start and end tags of `jsp:useBean`.

Listing 14.9 shows the first of three pages that use this approach. The source code archive at http://www.coreservlets.com/ contains the other two nearly identical pages. Figure 14–5 shows a typical result.

Listing 14.8 AccessCountBean.java

```
package coreservlets;

/** Simple bean to illustrate sharing beans through
 *  use of the scope attribute of jsp:useBean.
 */

public class AccessCountBean {
  private String firstPage;
  private int accessCount = 1;

  public String getFirstPage() {
    return(firstPage);
  }

  public void setFirstPage(String firstPage) {
    this.firstPage = firstPage;
  }

  public int getAccessCount() {
    return(accessCount);
  }

  public void setAccessCountIncrement(int increment) {
    accessCount = accessCount + increment;
  }
}
```

Listing 14.9 SharedCounts1.jsp

```
<!DOCTYPE HTML PUBLIC "-//W3C//DTD HTML 4.0 Transitional//EN">
<HTML>
<HEAD>
<TITLE>Shared Access Counts: Page 1</TITLE>
<LINK REL=STYLESHEET
      HREF="JSP-Styles.css"
      TYPE="text/css">
</HEAD>
<BODY>
<TABLE BORDER=5 ALIGN="CENTER">
  <TR><TH CLASS="TITLE">
      Shared Access Counts: Page 1</TABLE>
<P>
<jsp:useBean id="counter"
             class="coreservlets.AccessCountBean"
             scope="application">
  <jsp:setProperty name="counter"
                   property="firstPage"
                   value="SharedCounts1.jsp" />
</jsp:useBean>
Of SharedCounts1.jsp (this page),
<A HREF="SharedCounts2.jsp">SharedCounts2.jsp</A>, and
<A HREF="SharedCounts3.jsp">SharedCounts3.jsp</A>,
<jsp:getProperty name="counter" property="firstPage" />
was the first page accessed.
<P>
Collectively, the three pages have been accessed
<jsp:getProperty name="counter" property="accessCount" />
times.
<jsp:setProperty name="counter" property="accessCountIncrement"
                 value="1" />
</BODY></HTML>
```

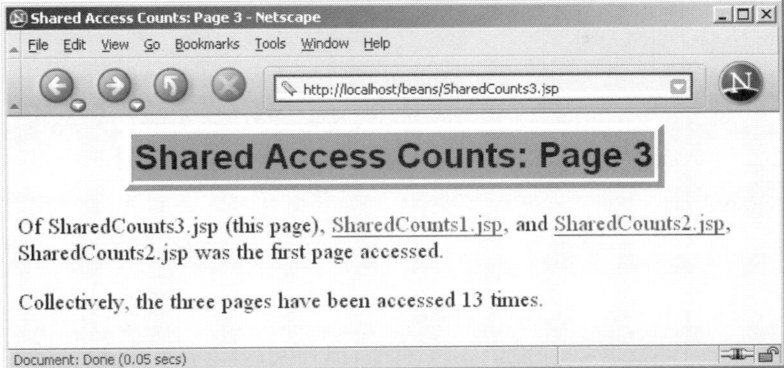

Figure 14–5 Result of a user visiting SharedCounts3.jsp. The first page visited by any user was SharedCounts2.jsp. SharedCounts1.jsp, SharedCounts2.jsp, and SharedCounts3.jsp were collectively visited a total of twelve times after the server was last started but before the visit shown in this figure.

14.7 Sharing Beans in Four Different Ways: An Example

In this section, we give an extended example that illustrates the various aspects of bean use:

- Using beans as utility classes that can be tested separately from JSP pages.
- Using unshared (page-scoped) beans.
- Sharing request-scoped beans.
- Sharing session-scoped beans.
- Sharing application-scoped (i.e., `ServletContext`-scoped) beans.

Before moving on to the examples, one caution is warranted. When you store beans in different scopes, be sure to use different names for each bean. Otherwise, servers can get confused and retrieve the incorrect bean.

Core Warning

Do not use the same bean name for beans stored in different locations. For every bean, use a unique value of `id` in `jsp:useBean`.

Building the Bean and the Bean Tester

The fundamental use of beans is as basic utility (helper) classes. We want to reiterate as strongly as possible: except for very short snippets, Java code that is directly inserted into JSP pages is harder to write, compile, test, debug, and reuse than regular Java classes.

For example, Listing 14.10 presents a small Java object that represents a food item with two properties: `level` and `goesWith` (i.e., four methods: `getLevel`, `setLevel`, `getGoesWith`, and `setGoesWith`). Perhaps this object is so simple that just looking at the source code suffices to show that it is implemented correctly. Perhaps. But how many times have you thought that before, only to uncover a bug later? In any case, a more complex class would surely require testing, so Listing 14.11 presents a test routine. Notice that the utility class represents a value in the application domain and is not dependent on any servlet- or JSP-specific classes. So, it can be tested entirely independently of the server. Listing 14.12 shows some representative output.

Listing 14.10 BakedBean.java

```
package coreservlets;

/** Small bean to illustrate various bean-sharing mechanisms. */

public class BakedBean {
  private String level = "half-baked";
  private String goesWith = "hot dogs";

  public String getLevel() {
    return(level);
  }

  public void setLevel(String newLevel) {
    level = newLevel;
  }

  public String getGoesWith() {
    return(goesWith);
  }

  public void setGoesWith(String dish) {
    goesWith = dish;
  }
}
```

Listing 14.11 BakedBeanTest.java

```
package coreservlets;

/** A small command-line program to test the BakedBean. */

public class BakedBeanTest {
  public static void main(String[] args) {
    BakedBean bean = new BakedBean();
    System.out.println("Original bean: " +
                       "level=" + bean.getLevel() +
                       ", goesWith=" + bean.getGoesWith());
    if (args.length>1) {
      bean.setLevel(args[0]);
      bean.setGoesWith(args[1]);
      System.out.println("Updated bean: " +
                         "level=" + bean.getLevel() +
                         ", goesWith=" + bean.getGoesWith());
    }
  }
}
```

Listing 14.12 Output of BakedBeanTest.java

```
Prompt> java coreservlets.BakedBeanTest gourmet caviar
Original bean: level=half-baked, goesWith=hot dogs
Updated bean: level=gourmet, goesWith=caviar
```

Using scope="page"—No Sharing

OK, after (and *only* after) we are satisfied that the bean works properly, we are ready to use it in a JSP page. The first application is to create, modify, and access the bean entirely within a single page request. For that, we use the following:

- **Create the bean:** use `jsp:useBean` with `scope="page"` (or no `scope` at all, since `page` is the default).
- **Modify the bean:** use `jsp:setProperty` with `property="*"`. Then, supply request parameters that match the bean property names.
- **Access the bean:** use `jsp:getProperty`.

Listing 14.13 presents a JSP page that applies these three techniques. Figures 14–6 and 14–7 illustrate that the bean is available only for the life of the page.

Listing 14.13 BakedBeanDisplay-page.jsp

```
<!DOCTYPE HTML PUBLIC "-//W3C//DTD HTML 4.0 Transitional//EN">
<HTML>
<HEAD>
<TITLE>Baked Bean Values: page-based Sharing</TITLE>
<LINK REL=STYLESHEET
      HREF="JSP-Styles.css"
      TYPE="text/css">
</HEAD>
<BODY>
<H1>Baked Bean Values: page-based Sharing</H1>
<jsp:useBean id="pageBean" class="coreservlets.BakedBean" />
<jsp:setProperty name="pageBean" property="*" />
<H2>Bean level:
<jsp:getProperty name="pageBean" property="level" /></H2>
<H2>Dish bean goes with:
<jsp:getProperty name="pageBean" property="goesWith" /></H2>
</BODY></HTML>
```

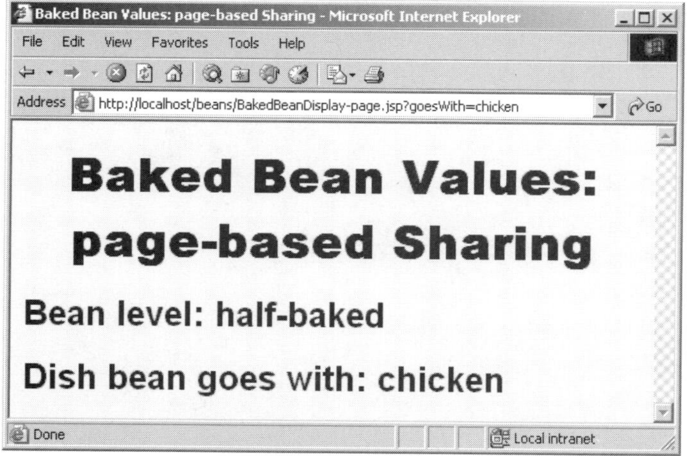

Figure 14–6 Initial request to BakedBeanDisplay-page.jsp—`BakedBean` properties persist within the page.

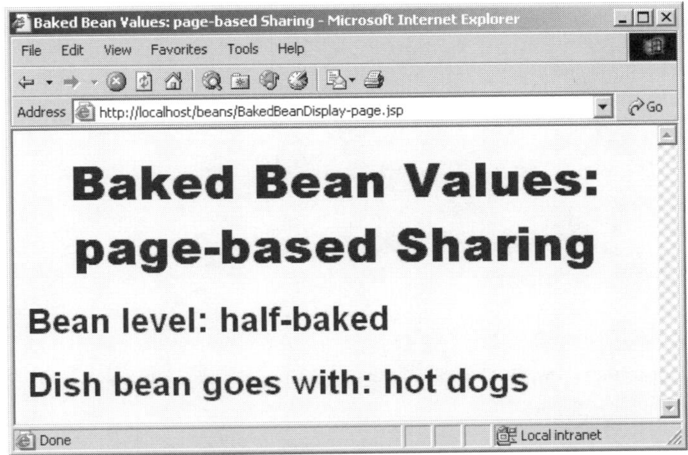

Figure 14–7 Subsequent request to BakedBeanDisplay-page.jsp—`BakedBean` properties do not persist between requests.

Using Request-Based Sharing

The second application is to create, modify, and access the bean within two different pages that share the same request object. Recall that a second page shares the request object of the first page if the second page is invoked with `jsp:include`, `jsp:forward`, or the `include` or `forward` methods of `RequestDispatcher`. To get the desired behavior, we use the following:

- **Create the bean:** use `jsp:useBean` with `scope="request"`.
- **Modify the bean:** use `jsp:setProperty` with `property="*"`. Then, supply request parameters that match the bean property names.
- **Access the bean in the first page:** use `jsp:getProperty`. Then, use `jsp:include` to invoke the second page.
- **Access the bean in the second page:** use `jsp:useBean` with the same `id` as on the first page, again with `scope="request"`. Then, use `jsp:getProperty`.

Listings 14.14 and 14.15 present a pair of JSP pages that applies these four techniques. Figures 14–8 and 14–9 illustrate that the bean is available in the second page but is not stored between requests.

Listing 14.14 BakedBeanDisplay-request.jsp

```
<!DOCTYPE HTML PUBLIC "-//W3C//DTD HTML 4.0 Transitional//EN">
<HTML>
<HEAD>
<TITLE>Baked Bean Values: request-based Sharing</TITLE>
<LINK REL=STYLESHEET
      HREF="JSP-Styles.css"
      TYPE="text/css">
</HEAD>
<BODY>
<H1>Baked Bean Values: request-based Sharing</H1>
<jsp:useBean id="requestBean" class="coreservlets.BakedBean"
             scope="request" />
<jsp:setProperty name="requestBean" property="*" />
<H2>Bean level:
<jsp:getProperty name="requestBean" property="level" /></H2>
<H2>Dish bean goes with:
<jsp:getProperty name="requestBean" property="goesWith" /></H2>
<jsp:include page="BakedBeanDisplay-snippet.jsp" />
</BODY></HTML>
```

Listing 14.15 BakedBeanDisplay-snippet.jsp

```
<H1>Repeated Baked Bean Values: request-based Sharing</H1>
<jsp:useBean id="requestBean" class="coreservlets.BakedBean"
             scope="request" />
<H2>Bean level:
<jsp:getProperty name="requestBean" property="level" /></H2>
<H2>Dish bean goes with:
<jsp:getProperty name="requestBean" property="goesWith" /></H2>
```

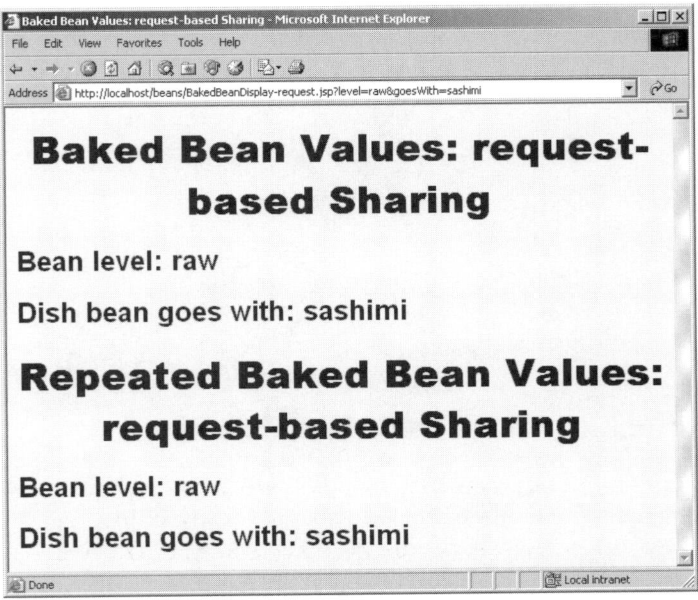

Figure 14–8 Initial request to BakedBeanDisplay-request.jsp—`BakedBean` properties persist to included pages.

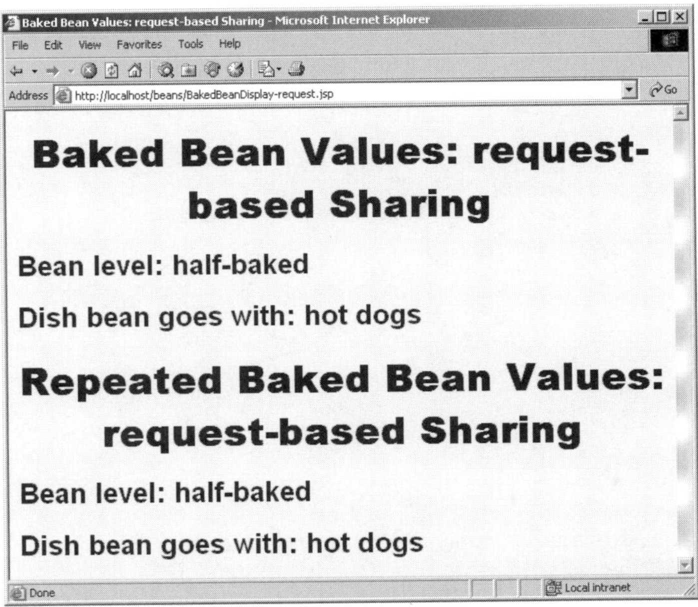

Figure 14–9 Subsequent request to BakedBeanDisplay-request.jsp—`BakedBean` properties do not persist between requests.

Using Session-Based Sharing

The third application involves two parts. First, we want to create, modify, and access the bean within a page. Second, if the *same* client returns to the page, he or she should see the previously modified bean. A classic case of session tracking. So, to get the desired behavior, we use the following:

- **Create the bean:** use `jsp:useBean` with `scope="session"`.
- **Modify the bean:** use `jsp:setProperty` with `property="*"`. Then, supply request parameters that match the bean property names.
- **Access the bean in the initial request:** use `jsp:getProperty` in the request in which `jsp:setProperty` is invoked.
- **Access the bean later:** use `jsp:getProperty` in a request that does not include request parameters and thus does not invoke `jsp:setProperty`. If this request is from the same client (within the session timeout), the previously modified value is seen. If this request is from a different client (or after the session timeout), a newly created bean is seen.

Listing 14.16 presents a JSP page that applies these techniques. Figure 14–10 shows the initial request. Figures 14–11 and 14–12 illustrate that the bean is available in the same session, but not in other sessions. Note that we would have gotten similar behavior if the `jsp:useBean` and `jsp:getProperty` code were repeated in multiple JSP pages: as long as the pages are accessed by the same client, the previous values will be preserved.

Listing 14.16 BakedBeanDisplay-session.jsp

```
<!DOCTYPE HTML PUBLIC "-//W3C//DTD HTML 4.0 Transitional//EN">
<HTML>
<HEAD>
<TITLE>Baked Bean Values: session-based Sharing</TITLE>
<LINK REL=STYLESHEET
      HREF="JSP-Styles.css"
      TYPE="text/css">
</HEAD>
<BODY>
<H1>Baked Bean Values: session-based Sharing</H1>
<jsp:useBean id="sessionBean" class="coreservlets.BakedBean"
             scope="session" />
```

Listing 14.16 BakedBeanDisplay-session.jsp *(continued)*

```
<jsp:setProperty name="sessionBean" property="*" />
<H2>Bean level:
<jsp:getProperty name="sessionBean" property="level" /></H2>
<H2>Dish bean goes with:
<jsp:getProperty name="sessionBean" property="goesWith" /></H2>
</BODY></HTML>
```

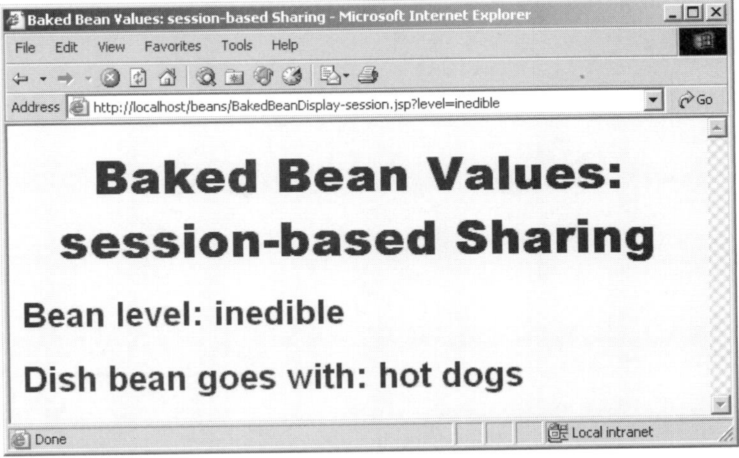

Figure 14–10 Initial request to BakedBeanDisplay-session.jsp.

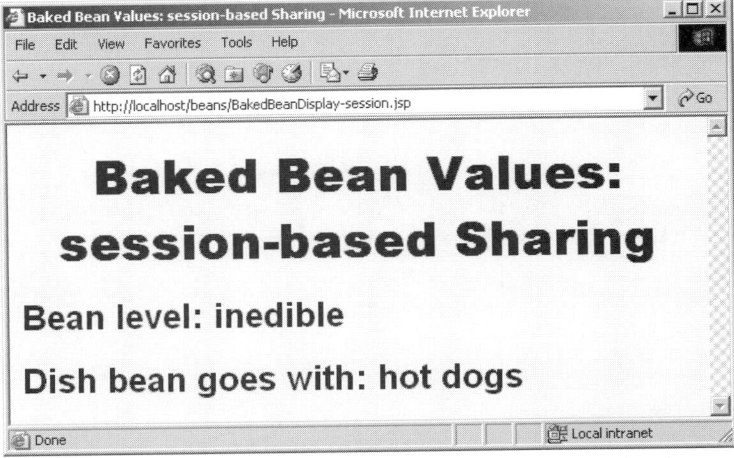

Figure 14–11 Subsequent request to BakedBeanDisplay-session.jsp—`BakedBean` properties persist between requests if the request is from the same client in the same session.

Figure 14–12 Subsequent request to BakedBeanDisplay-session.jsp—`BakedBean` properties do not persist between requests if the request is from a different client (as here) or is in a different session.

Using ServletContext-Based Sharing

The fourth and final application also involves two parts. First, we want to create, modify, and access the bean within a page. Second, if *any* client comes to the page later, he or she should see the previously modified bean. What else besides the `ServletContext` provides such global access? So, to get the desired behavior, we use the following:

- **Create the bean:** use `jsp:useBean` with `scope="application"`.
- **Modify the bean:** use `jsp:setProperty` with `property="*"`. Then, supply request parameters that match the bean property names.
- **Access the bean in the initial request:** use `jsp:getProperty` in the request in which `jsp:setProperty` is invoked.
- **Access the bean later:** use `jsp:getProperty` in a request that does not include request parameters and thus does not invoke `jsp:setProperty`. Whether this request is from the same client or a different client (regardless of the session timeout), the previously modified value is seen.

Listing 14.17 presents a JSP page that applies these techniques. Figure 14–13 shows the initial request. Figures 14–14 and 14–15 illustrate that the bean is available to multiple clients later. Note that we would have gotten similar behavior if the `jsp:useBean` and `jsp:getProperty` code were repeated in multiple JSP pages.

Listing 14.17 BakedBeanDisplay-application.jsp

```
<!DOCTYPE HTML PUBLIC "-//W3C//DTD HTML 4.0 Transitional//EN">
<HTML>
<HEAD>
<TITLE>Baked Bean Values: application-based Sharing</TITLE>
<LINK REL=STYLESHEET
      HREF="JSP-Styles.css"
      TYPE="text/css">
</HEAD>
<BODY>
<H1>Baked Bean Values: application-based Sharing</H1>
<jsp:useBean id="applicationBean" class="coreservlets.BakedBean"
             scope="application" />
<jsp:setProperty name="applicationBean" property="*" />
<H2>Bean level:
<jsp:getProperty name="applicationBean" property="level" /></H2>
<H2>Dish bean goes with:
<jsp:getProperty name="applicationBean" property="goesWith"/></
H2>
</BODY></HTML>
```

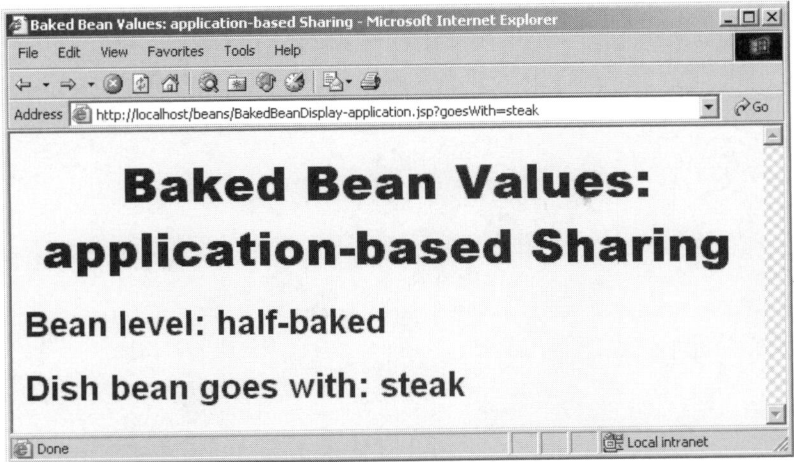

Figure 14–13 Initial request to BakedBeanDisplay-application.jsp.

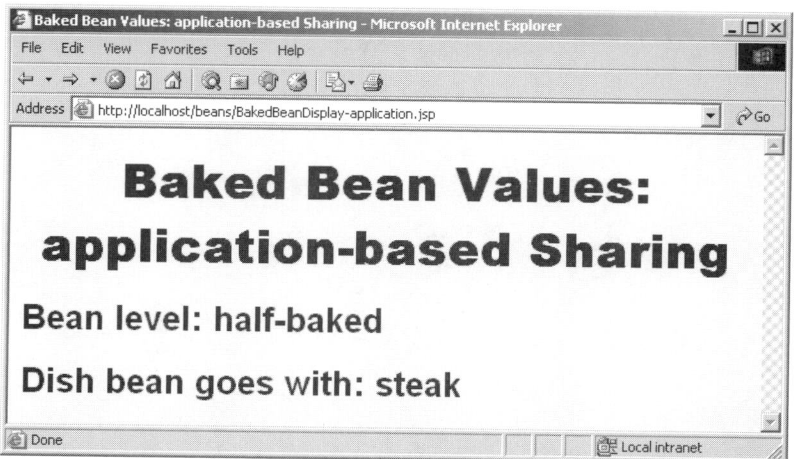

Figure 14–14 Subsequent request to BakedBeanDisplay-application.jsp—`BakedBean` properties persist between requests.

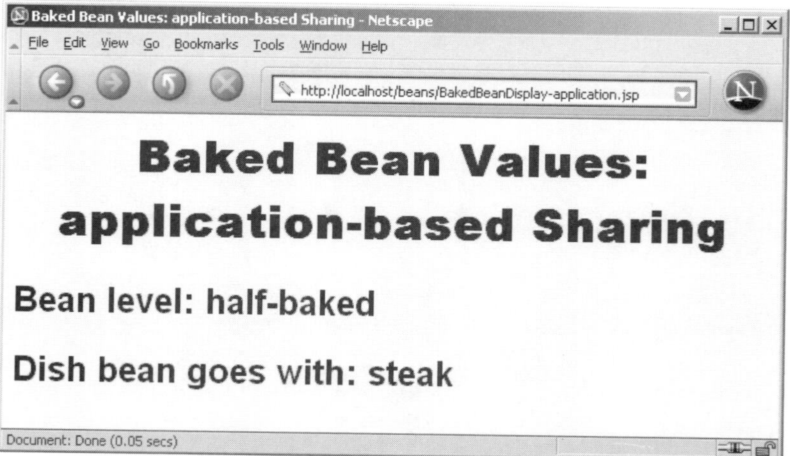

Figure 14–15 Subsequent request to BakedBeanDisplay-application—`BakedBean` properties persist between requests even if the request is from a different client (as here) or is in a different session.

Integrating Servlets and JSP: The Model View Controller (MVC) Architecture

Topics in This Chapter

- Understanding the benefits of MVC
- Using `RequestDispatcher` to implement MVC
- Forwarding requests from servlets to JSP pages
- Handling relative URLs
- Choosing among different display options
- Comparing data-sharing strategies
- Forwarding requests from JSP pages
- Including pages instead of forwarding to them

Chapter 15

Servlets are good at data *processing*: reading and checking data, communicating with databases, invoking business logic, and so on. JSP pages are good at *presentation*: building HTML to represent the results of requests. This chapter describes how to combine servlets and JSP pages to best make use of the strengths of each technology.

15.1 Understanding the Need for MVC

Servlets are great when your application requires a lot of real programming to accomplish its task. As illustrated earlier in this book, servlets can manipulate HTTP status codes and headers, use cookies, track sessions, save information between requests, compress pages, access databases, generate JPEG images on-the-fly, and perform many other tasks flexibly and efficiently. But, generating HTML with servlets can be tedious and can yield a result that is hard to modify.

That's where JSP comes in: as illustrated in Figure 15–1, JSP lets you separate much of the presentation from the dynamic content. That way, you can write the HTML in the normal manner, even using HTML-specific tools and putting your Web content developers to work on your JSP documents. JSP expressions, scriptlets, and declarations let you insert simple Java code into the servlet that results from the JSP page, and directives let you control the overall layout of the page. For more complex requirements, you can wrap Java code inside beans or even define your own JSP tags.

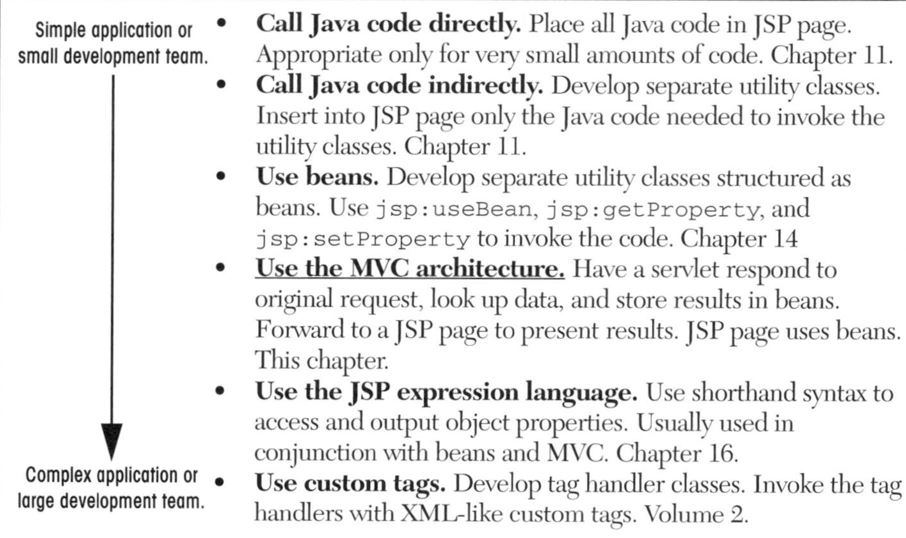

Figure 15–1 Strategies for invoking dynamic code from JSP.

Great. We have everything we need, right? Well, no, not quite. The assumption behind a JSP document is that it provides a *single* overall presentation. What if you want to give totally different results depending on the data that you receive? Scripting expressions, beans, and custom tags, although extremely powerful and flexible, don't overcome the limitation that the JSP page defines a relatively fixed, top-level page appearance. Similarly, what if you need complex reasoning just to determine the type of data that applies to the current situation? JSP is poor at this type of business logic.

The solution is to use *both* servlets and JavaServer Pages. In this approach, known as the Model View Controller (MVC) or Model 2 architecture, you let each technology concentrate on what it excels at. The original request is handled by a servlet. The servlet invokes the business-logic and data-access code and creates beans to represent the results (that's the *model*). Then, the servlet decides which JSP page is appropriate to present those particular results and forwards the request there (the JSP page is the *view*). The servlet decides what business logic code applies and which JSP page should present the results (the servlet is the *controller*).

MVC Frameworks

The key motivation behind the MVC approach is the desire to separate the code that creates and manipulates the data from the code that presents the data. The basic tools needed to implement this presentation-layer separation are standard in the servlet API and are the topic of this chapter. However, in very complex applications, a more elaborate MVC framework is sometimes beneficial. The most popular of these frameworks is Apache Struts; it is discussed at length in Volume 2 of this book. Although Struts is useful and widely used, you should not feel that you must use Struts in order to apply the MVC approach. For simple and moderately complex applications, implementing MVC from scratch with `RequestDispatcher` is straightforward and flexible. Do not be intimidated: go ahead and start with the basic approach. In many situations, you will stick with the basic approach for the entire life of your application. Even if you decide to use Struts or another MVC framework later, you will recoup much of your investment because most of your work will also apply to the elaborate frameworks.

Architecture or Approach?

The term "architecture" often connotes "overall system design." Although many systems are indeed designed with MVC at their core, it is not necessary to redesign your overall system just to make use of the MVC approach. Not at all. It is quite common for applications to handle some requests with servlets, other requests with JSP pages, and still others with servlets and JSP acting in conjunction as described in this chapter. Do not feel that you have to rework your entire system architecture just to use the MVC approach: go ahead and start applying it in the parts of your application where it fits best.

15.2 Implementing MVC with RequestDispatcher

The most important point about MVC is the idea of separating the business logic and data access layers from the presentation layer. The syntax is quite simple, and in fact you should be familiar with much of it already. Here is a quick summary of the required steps; the following subsections supply details.

1. **Define beans to represent the data.** As you know from Section 14.2, beans are just Java objects that follow a few simple conventions. Your first step is define beans to represent the results that will be presented to the user.
2. **Use a servlet to handle requests.** In most cases, the servlet reads request parameters as described in Chapter 4.
3. **Populate the beans.** The servlet invokes business logic (application-specific code) or data-access code (see Chapter 17) to obtain the results. The results are placed in the beans that were defined in step 1.

4. **Store the bean in the request, session, or servlet context.** The servlet calls `setAttribute` on the request, session, or servlet context objects to store a reference to the beans that represent the results of the request.
5. **Forward the request to a JSP page.** The servlet determines which JSP page is appropriate to the situation and uses the `forward` method of `RequestDispatcher` to transfer control to that page.
6. **Extract the data from the beans.** The JSP page accesses beans with `jsp:useBean` and a `scope` matching the location of step 4. The page then uses `jsp:getProperty` to output the bean properties. The JSP page does not create or modify the bean; it merely extracts and displays data that the servlet created.

Defining Beans to Represent the Data

Beans are Java objects that follow a few simple conventions. In this case, since a servlet or other Java routine (never a JSP page) will be creating the beans, the requirement for an empty (zero-argument) constructor is waived. So, your objects merely need to follow the normal recommended practices of keeping the instance variables private and using accessor methods that follow the get/set naming convention.

Since the JSP page will only access the beans, not create or modify them, a common practice is to define *value objects*: objects that represent results but have little or no additional functionality.

Writing Servlets to Handle Requests

Once the bean classes are defined, the next task is to write a servlet to read the request information. Since, with MVC, a servlet responds to the initial request, the normal approaches of Chapters 4 and 5 are used to read request parameters and request headers, respectively. The shorthand `populateBean` method of Chapter 4 can be used, but you should note that this technique populates a *form* bean (a Java object representing the form parameters), not a *result* bean (a Java object representing the results of the request).

Although the servlets use the normal techniques to read the request information and generate the data, they do not use the normal techniques to output the results. In fact, with the MVC approach the servlets do not create *any* output; the output is completely handled by the JSP pages. So, the servlets do not call `response.setContentType`, `response.getWriter`, or `out.println`.

Populating the Beans

After you read the form parameters, you use them to determine the results of the request. These results are determined in a completely application-specific manner. You might call some business logic code, invoke an Enterprise JavaBeans component, or query a database. No matter how you come up with the data, you need to use that data to fill in the value object beans that you defined in the first step.

Storing the Results

You have read the form information. You have created data specific to the request. You have placed that data in beans. Now you need to store those beans in a location that the JSP pages will be able to access.

A servlet can store data for JSP pages in three main places: in the `HttpServletRequest`, in the `HttpSession`, and in the `ServletContext`. These storage locations correspond to the three nondefault values of the `scope` attribute of `jsp:useBean`: that is, `request`, `session`, and `application`.

- **Storing data that the JSP page will use only in this request.** First, the servlet would create and store data as follows:

  ```
  ValueObject value = new ValueObject(...);
  request.setAttribute("key", value);
  ```

  Next, the servlet would forward the request to a JSP page that uses the following to retrieve the data.

  ```
  <jsp:useBean id="key" type="somePackage.ValueObject"
               scope="request" />
  ```

  Note that request *attributes* have nothing to do with request *parameters* or request *headers*. The request attributes are independent of the information coming from the client; they are just application-specific entries in a hash table that is attached to the request object. This table simply stores data in a place that can be accessed by both the current servlet and JSP page, but not by any other resource or request.
- **Storing data that the JSP page will use in this request and in later requests from the same client.** First, the servlet would create and store data as follows:

  ```
  ValueObject value = new ValueObject(...);
  HttpSession session = request.getSession();
  session.setAttribute("key", value);
  ```

Next, the servlet would forward to a JSP page that uses the following to retrieve the data:

```
<jsp:useBean id="key" type="somePackage.ValueObject"
             scope="session" />
```

- **Storing data that the JSP page will use in this request and in later requests from any client.** First, the servlet would create and store data as follows:

```
ValueObject value = new ValueObject(...);
getServletContext().setAttribute("key", value);
```

Next, the servlet would forward to a JSP page that uses the following to retrieve the data:

```
<jsp:useBean id="key" type="somePackage.ValueObject"
             scope="application" />
```

As described in Section 15.3, the servlet code is normally synchronized to prevent the data changing between the servlet and the JSP page.

Forwarding Requests to JSP Pages

You forward requests with the `forward` method of `RequestDispatcher`. You obtain a `RequestDispatcher` by calling the `getRequestDispatcher` method of `ServletRequest`, supplying a relative address. You are permitted to specify addresses in the WEB-INF directory; clients are not allowed to directly access files in WEB-INF, but the server is allowed to transfer control there. Using locations in WEB-INF prevents clients from inadvertently accessing JSP pages directly, without first going through the servlets that create the JSP data.

Core Approach

If your JSP pages only make sense in the context of servlet-generated data, place the pages under the WEB-INF directory. That way, servlets can forward requests to the pages, but clients cannot access them directly.

Once you have a `RequestDispatcher`, you use `forward` to transfer control to the associated address. You supply the `HttpServletRequest` and `HttpServlet-Response` as arguments. Note that the `forward` method of `RequestDispatcher` is quite different from the sendRedirect method of HttpServletRequest (Section 7.1). With forward, there is no extra response/request pair as with sendRedirect. Thus, the URL displayed to the client does not change when you use forward.

Core Note

When you use the forward method of RequestDispatcher, the client sees the URL of the original servlet, not the URL of the final JSP page.

For example, Listing 15.1 shows a portion of a servlet that forwards the request to one of three different JSP pages, depending on the value of the operation request parameter.

Listing 15.1 Request Forwarding Example

```
public void doGet(HttpServletRequest request,
                  HttpServletResponse response)
  throws ServletException, IOException {
  String operation = request.getParameter("operation");
  if (operation == null) {
    operation = "unknown";
  }
  String address;
  if (operation.equals("order")) {
    address = "/WEB-INF/Order.jsp";
  } else if (operation.equals("cancel")) {
    address = "/WEB-INF/Cancel.jsp";
  } else {
    address = "/WEB-INF/UnknownOperation.jsp";
  }
  RequestDispatcher dispatcher =
    request.getRequestDispatcher(address);
  dispatcher.forward(request, response);
}
```

Forwarding to Static Resources

In most cases, you forward requests to JSP pages or other servlets. In some cases, however, you might want to send requests to static HTML pages. In an e-commerce site, for example, requests that indicate that the user does not have a valid account name might be forwarded to an account application page that uses HTML forms to gather the requisite information. With GET requests, forwarding requests to a static HTML page is perfectly legal and requires no special syntax; just supply the address of the HTML page as the argument to getRequestDispatcher. However, since forwarded requests use the same request method as the original request, POST requests cannot be forwarded to normal HTML pages. The solution to this problem is to simply rename the HTML page to have a .jsp extension. Renaming somefile.html to somefile.jsp does not change its output for GET requests, but somefile.html cannot handle POST requests, whereas somefile.jsp gives an identical response for both GET and POST.

Redirecting Instead of Forwarding

The standard MVC approach is to use the forward method of RequestDispatcher to transfer control from the servlet to the JSP page. However, when you are using session-based data sharing, it is sometimes preferable to use response.sendRedirect.

Here is a summary of the behavior of forward.

- Control is transferred entirely on the server. No network traffic is involved.
- The user does not see the address of the destination JSP page and pages can be placed in WEB-INF to prevent the user from accessing them without going through the servlet that sets up the data. This is beneficial if the JSP page makes sense only in the context of servlet-generated data.

Here is a summary of sendRedirect.

- Control is transferred by sending the client a 302 status code and a Location response header. Transfer requires an additional network round trip.
- The user sees the address of the destination page and can bookmark it and access it independently. This is beneficial if the JSP is designed to use default values when data is missing. For example, this approach would be used when redisplaying an incomplete HTML form or summarizing the contents of a shopping cart. In both cases, previously created data would be extracted from the user's session, so the JSP page makes sense even for requests that do not involve the servlet.

Extracting Data from Beans

Once the request arrives at the JSP page, the JSP page uses `jsp:useBean` and `jsp:getProperty` to extract the data. For the most part, this approach is exactly as described in Chapter 14. There are two differences however:

- **The JSP page never creates the objects.** The servlet, not the JSP page, should create all the data objects. So, to guarantee that the JSP page will not create objects, you should use

  ```
  <jsp:useBean ... type="package.Class" />
  ```

  instead of

  ```
  <jsp:useBean ... class="package.Class" />.
  ```

- **The JSP page should not modify the objects.** So, you should use `jsp:getProperty` but not `jsp:setProperty`.

The scope you specify should match the storage location used by the servlet. For example, the following three forms would be used for request-, session-, and application-based sharing, respectively.

```
<jsp:useBean id="key" type="somePackage.SomeBeanClass"
             scope="request" />

<jsp:useBean id="key" type="somePackage.SomeBeanClass"
             scope="session" />

<jsp:useBean id="key" type="somePackage.SomeBeanClass"
             scope="application" />
```

15.3 Summarizing MVC Code

This section summarizes the code that would be used for request-based, session-based, and application-based MVC approaches.

Request-Based Data Sharing

With request-based sharing, the servlet stores the beans in the `HttpServlet-Request`, where they are accessible only to the destination JSP page.

Servlet

```
ValueObject value = new ValueObject(...);
request.setAttribute("key", value);
RequestDispatcher dispatcher =
  request.getRequestDispatcher("/WEB-INF/SomePage.jsp");
dispatcher.forward(request, response);
```

JSP Page

```
<jsp:useBean id="key" type="somePackage.ValueObject"
             scope="request" />
<jsp:getProperty name="key" property="someProperty" />
```

Session-Based Data Sharing

With session-based sharing, the servlet stores the beans in the `HttpSession`, where they are accessible to the same client in the destination JSP page or in other pages.

Servlet

```
ValueObject value = new ValueObject(...);
HttpSession session = request.getSession();
session.setAttribute("key", value);
RequestDispatcher dispatcher =
  request.getRequestDispatcher("/WEB-INF/SomePage.jsp");
dispatcher.forward(request, response);
```

JSP Page

```
<jsp:useBean id="key" type="somePackage.ValueObject"
             scope="session" />
<jsp:getProperty name="key" property="someProperty" />
```

Application-Based Data Sharing

With application-based sharing, the servlet stores the beans in the `ServletContext`, where they are accessible to any servlet or JSP page in the Web application. To guarantee that the JSP page extracts the same data that the servlet inserted, you should synchronize your code as below.

Servlet

```
synchronized(this) {
  ValueObject value = new ValueObject(...);
  getServletContext().setAttribute("key", value);
```

```
    RequestDispatcher dispatcher =
      request.getRequestDispatcher("/WEB-INF/SomePage.jsp");
    dispatcher.forward(request, response);
  }
```

JSP Page

```
<jsp:useBean id="key" type="somePackage.ValueObject"
             scope="application" />
<jsp:getProperty name="key" property="someProperty" />
```

15.4 Interpreting Relative URLs in the Destination Page

Although a servlet can forward the request to an arbitrary location on the same server, the process is quite different from that of using the `sendRedirect` method of `HttpServletResponse`. First, `sendRedirect` requires the client to reconnect to the new resource, whereas the `forward` method of `RequestDispatcher` is handled completely on the server. Second, `sendRedirect` does not automatically preserve all of the request data; `forward` does. Third, `sendRedirect` results in a different final URL, whereas with `forward`, the URL of the original servlet is maintained.

This final point means that if the destination page uses relative URLs for images or style sheets, it needs to make them relative to the servlet URL or the server root, not to the destination page's actual location. For example, consider the following style sheet entry:

```
<LINK REL=STYLESHEET
      HREF="my-styles.css"
      TYPE="text/css">
```

If the JSP page containing this entry is accessed by means of a forwarded request, `my-styles.css` will be interpreted relative to the URL of the *originating* servlet, not relative to the JSP page itself, almost certainly resulting in an error. The simplest solution to this problem is to give the full server path to the style sheet file, as follows.

```
<LINK REL=STYLESHEET
      HREF="/path/my-styles.css"
      TYPE="text/css">
```

The same approach is required for addresses used in `<IMG SRC=...>` and `<A HREF=...>`.

15.5 Applying MVC: Bank Account Balances

In this section, we apply the MVC approach to an application that displays bank account balances. The controller servlet (Listing 15.2) reads a customer ID and passes that to some data-access code that returns a `BankCustomer` value bean (Listing 15.3). The servlet then stores the bean in the `HttpServletRequest` object where it will be accessible from destination JSP pages but nowhere else. If the account balance of the resulting customer is negative, the servlet forwards to a page designed for delinquent customers (Listing 15.4, Figure 15–2). If the customer has a positive balance of less than $10,000, the servlet transfers to the standard balance-display page (Listing 15.5, Figure 15–3). Next, if the customer has a balance of $10,000 or more, the servlet forwards the request to a page reserved for elite customers (Listing 15.6, Figure 15–4). Finally, if the customer ID is unrecognized, an error page is displayed (Listing 15.7, Figure 15–5).

Listing 15.2 ShowBalance.java

```
package coreservlets;

import java.io.*;
import javax.servlet.*;
import javax.servlet.http.*;

/** Servlet that reads a customer ID and displays
 *  information on the account balance of the customer
 *  who has that ID.
 */

public class ShowBalance extends HttpServlet {
  public void doGet(HttpServletRequest request,
                    HttpServletResponse response)
      throws ServletException, IOException {
    BankCustomer customer =
      BankCustomer.getCustomer(request.getParameter("id"));
    String address;
    if (customer == null) {
      address = "/WEB-INF/bank-account/UnknownCustomer.jsp";
    } else if (customer.getBalance() < 0) {
      address = "/WEB-INF/bank-account/NegativeBalance.jsp";
      request.setAttribute("badCustomer", customer);
```

Listing 15.2 ShowBalance.java *(continued)*

```
    } else if (customer.getBalance() < 10000) {
      address = "/WEB-INF/bank-account/NormalBalance.jsp";
      request.setAttribute("regularCustomer", customer);
    } else {
      address = "/WEB-INF/bank-account/HighBalance.jsp";
      request.setAttribute("eliteCustomer", customer);
    }
    RequestDispatcher dispatcher =
      request.getRequestDispatcher(address);
    dispatcher.forward(request, response);
  }
}
```

Listing 15.3 BankCustomer.java

```
package coreservlets;

import java.util.*;

/** Bean to represent a bank customer. */

public class BankCustomer {
  private String id, firstName, lastName;
  private double balance;

  public BankCustomer(String id,
                      String firstName,
                      String lastName,
                      double balance) {
    this.id = id;
    this.firstName = firstName;
    this.lastName = lastName;
    this.balance = balance;
  }

  public String getId() {
    return(id);
  }

  public String getFirstName() {
    return(firstName);
  }
```

Listing 15.3 BankCustomer.java *(continued)*

```
  public String getLastName() {
    return(lastName);
  }

  public double getBalance() {
    return(balance);
  }

  public double getBalanceNoSign() {
    return(Math.abs(balance));
  }

  public void setBalance(double balance) {
    this.balance = balance;
  }

  // Makes a small table of banking customers.

  private static HashMap customers;

  static {
    customers = new HashMap();
    customers.put("id001",
                  new BankCustomer("id001",
                                   "John",
                                   "Hacker",
                                   -3456.78));
    customers.put("id002",
                  new BankCustomer("id002",
                                   "Jane",
                                   "Hacker",
                                   1234.56));
    customers.put("id003",
                  new BankCustomer("id003",
                                   "Juan",
                                   "Hacker",
                                   987654.32));
  }

  /** Finds the customer with the given ID.
   *  Returns null if there is no match.
   */

  public static BankCustomer getCustomer(String id) {
    return((BankCustomer)customers.get(id));
  }
}
```

Listing 15.4 NegativeBalance.jsp

```
<!DOCTYPE HTML PUBLIC "-//W3C//DTD HTML 4.0 Transitional//EN">
<HTML>
<HEAD>
<TITLE>You Owe Us Money!</TITLE>
<LINK REL=STYLESHEET
      HREF="/bank-support/JSP-Styles.css"
      TYPE="text/css">
</HEAD>
<BODY>
<TABLE BORDER=5 ALIGN="CENTER">
  <TR><TH CLASS="TITLE">
      We Know Where You Live!</TABLE>
<P>
<IMG SRC="/bank-support/Club.gif" ALIGN="LEFT">
<jsp:useBean id="badCustomer"
             type="coreservlets.BankCustomer"
             scope="request" />
Watch out,
<jsp:getProperty name="badCustomer" property="firstName" />,
we know where you live.
<P>
Pay us the
$<jsp:getProperty name="badCustomer" property="balanceNoSign" />
you owe us before it is too late!
</BODY></HTML>
```

Listing 15.5 NormalBalance.jsp

```
<!DOCTYPE HTML PUBLIC "-//W3C//DTD HTML 4.0 Transitional//EN">
<HTML>
<HEAD>
<TITLE>Your Balance</TITLE>
<LINK REL=STYLESHEET
      HREF="/bank-support/JSP-Styles.css"
      TYPE="text/css">
</HEAD>
<BODY>
<TABLE BORDER=5 ALIGN="CENTER">
  <TR><TH CLASS="TITLE">
      Your Balance</TABLE>
<P>
```

Listing 15.5 NormalBalance.jsp *(continued)*

```
<IMG SRC="/bank-support/Money.gif" ALIGN="RIGHT">
<jsp:useBean id="regularCustomer"
             type="coreservlets.BankCustomer"
             scope="request" />
<UL>
  <LI>First name: <jsp:getProperty name="regularCustomer"
                                   property="firstName" />
  <LI>Last name: <jsp:getProperty name="regularCustomer"
                                  property="lastName" />
  <LI>ID: <jsp:getProperty name="regularCustomer"
                           property="id" />
  <LI>Balance: $<jsp:getProperty name="regularCustomer"
                                 property="balance" />
</UL>
</BODY></HTML>
```

Figure 15–2 The `ShowCustomer` servlet with an ID corresponding to a customer with a negative balance.

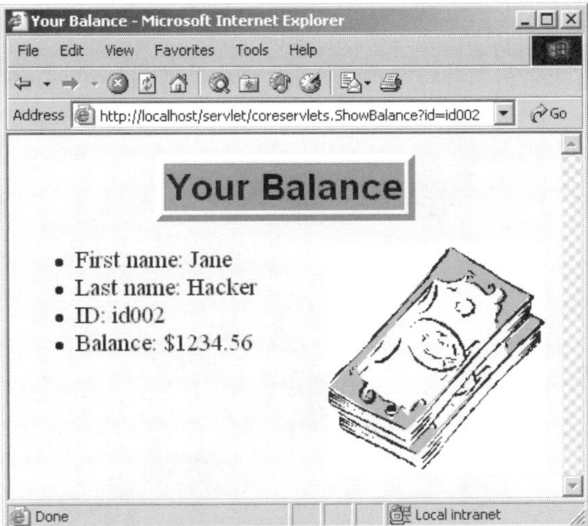

Figure 15–3 The ShowCustomer servlet with an ID corresponding to a customer with a normal balance.

Listing 15.6 HighBalance.jsp

```
<!DOCTYPE HTML PUBLIC "-//W3C//DTD HTML 4.0 Transitional//EN">
<HTML>
<HEAD>
<TITLE>Your Balance</TITLE>
<LINK REL=STYLESHEET
      HREF="/bank-support/JSP-Styles.css"
      TYPE="text/css">
</HEAD>
<BODY>
<TABLE BORDER=5 ALIGN="CENTER">
  <TR><TH CLASS="TITLE">
      Your Balance</TABLE>
<P>
<CENTER><IMG SRC="/bank-support/Sailing.gif"></CENTER>
<BR CLEAR="ALL">
<jsp:useBean id="eliteCustomer"
             type="coreservlets.BankCustomer"
             scope="request" />
It is an honor to serve you,
<jsp:getProperty name="eliteCustomer" property="firstName" />
<jsp:getProperty name="eliteCustomer" property="lastName" />!
```

Listing 15.6 HighBalance.jsp *(continued)*

```
<P>
Since you are one of our most valued customers, we would like
to offer you the opportunity to spend a mere fraction of your
$<jsp:getProperty name="eliteCustomer" property="balance" />
on a boat worthy of your status. Please visit our boat store for
more information.
</BODY></HTML>
```

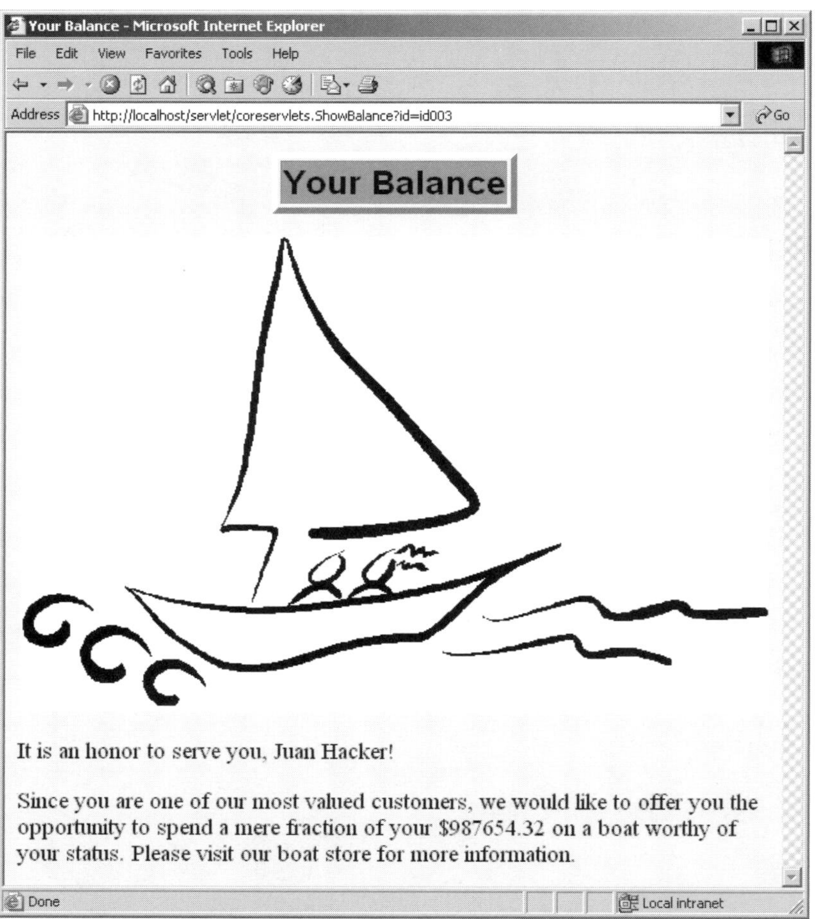

Figure 15–4 The `ShowCustomer` servlet with an ID corresponding to a customer with a high balance.

Listing 15.7 UnknownCustomer.jsp

```
<!DOCTYPE HTML PUBLIC "-//W3C//DTD HTML 4.0 Transitional//EN">
<HTML>
<HEAD>
<TITLE>Unknown Customer</TITLE>
<LINK REL=STYLESHEET
      HREF="/bank-support/JSP-Styles.css"
      TYPE="text/css">
</HEAD>
<BODY>
<TABLE BORDER=5 ALIGN="CENTER">
  <TR><TH CLASS="TITLE">
      Unknown Customer</TABLE>
<P>
Unrecognized customer ID.
</BODY></HTML>
```

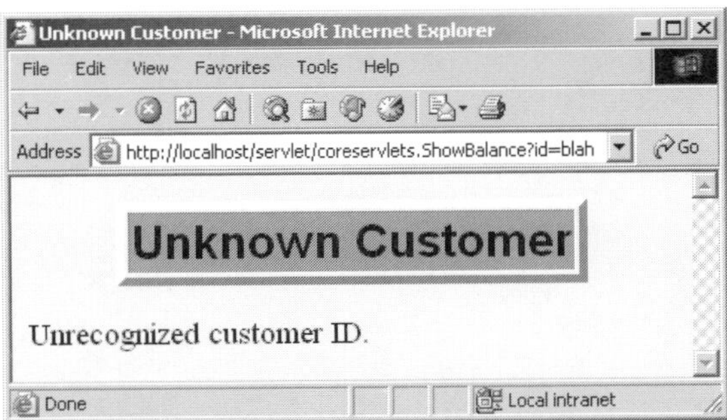

Figure 15–5 The `ShowCustomer` servlet with an unknown customer ID.

15.6 Comparing the Three Data-Sharing Approaches

In the MVC approach, a servlet responds to the initial request. The servlet invokes code that fetches or creates the business data, places that data in beans, stores the beans, and forwards the request to a JSP page to present the results. But, *where* does the servlet store the beans?

The most common answer is, in the request object. That is the only location to which the JSP page has sole access. However, you sometimes want to keep the results around for the same client (session-based sharing) or store Web-application-wide data (application-based sharing).

This section gives a brief example of each of these approaches.

Request-Based Sharing

In this example, our goal is to display a random number to the user. Each request should result in a new number, so request-based sharing is appropriate.

To implement this behavior, we need a bean to store numbers (Listing 15.8), a servlet to populate the bean with a random value (Listing 15.9), and a JSP page to display the results (Listing 15.10, Figure 15–6).

Listing 15.8 NumberBean.java

```
package coreservlets;

public class NumberBean {
  private double num = 0;

  public NumberBean(double number) {
    setNumber(number);
  }

  public double getNumber() {
    return(num);
  }

  public void setNumber(double number) {
    num = number;
  }
}
```

Listing 15.9 RandomNumberServlet.java

```
package coreservlets;

import java.io.*;
import javax.servlet.*;
import javax.servlet.http.*;

/** Servlet that generates a random number, stores it in a bean,
 *  and forwards to JSP page to display it.
 */
```

Listing 15.9 RandomNumberServlet.java *(continued)*

```
public class RandomNumberServlet extends HttpServlet {
  public void doGet(HttpServletRequest request,
                    HttpServletResponse response)
      throws ServletException, IOException {
    NumberBean bean = new NumberBean(Math.random());
    request.setAttribute("randomNum", bean);
    String address = "/WEB-INF/mvc-sharing/RandomNum.jsp";
    RequestDispatcher dispatcher =
      request.getRequestDispatcher(address);
    dispatcher.forward(request, response);
  }
}
```

Listing 15.10 RandomNum.jsp

```
<!DOCTYPE HTML PUBLIC "-//W3C//DTD HTML 4.0 Transitional//EN">
<HTML>
<HEAD>
<TITLE>Random Number</TITLE>
<LINK REL=STYLESHEET
      HREF="/bank-support/JSP-Styles.css"
      TYPE="text/css">
</HEAD>
<BODY>
<jsp:useBean id="randomNum" type="coreservlets.NumberBean"
             scope="request" />
<H2>Random Number:
<jsp:getProperty name="randomNum" property="number" />
</H2>
</BODY></HTML>
```

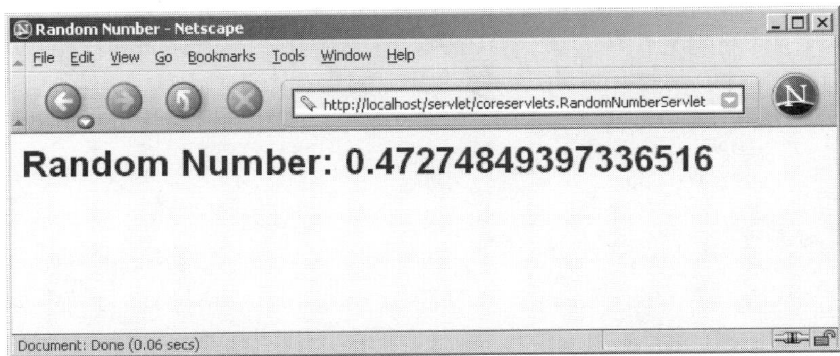

Figure 15–6 Result of RandomNumberServlet.

Session-Based Sharing

In this example, our goal is to display users' first and last names. If the users fail to tell us their name, we want to use whatever name they gave us previously. If the users do not explicitly specify a name and no previous name is found, a warning should be displayed. Data is stored for each client, so session-based sharing is appropriate.

To implement this behavior, we need a bean to store names (Listing 15.11), a servlet to retrieve the bean from the session and populate it with first and last names (Listing 15.12), and a JSP page to display the results (Listing 15.13, Figures 15–7 and 15–8).

Listing 15.11 NameBean.java

```
package coreservlets;

public class NameBean {
  private String firstName = "Missing first name";
  private String lastName = "Missing last name";

  public NameBean() {}

  public NameBean(String firstName, String lastName) {
    setFirstName(firstName);
    setLastName(lastName);
  }

  public String getFirstName() {
    return(firstName);
  }

  public void setFirstName(String newFirstName) {
    firstName = newFirstName;
  }

  public String getLastName() {
    return(lastName);
  }

  public void setLastName(String newLastName) {
    lastName = newLastName;
  }
}
```

Listing 15.12 RegistrationServlet.java

```
package coreservlets;

import java.io.*;
import javax.servlet.*;
import javax.servlet.http.*;

/** Reads firstName and lastName request parameters and forwards
 *  to JSP page to display them. Uses session-based bean sharing
 *  to remember previous values.
 */

public class RegistrationServlet extends HttpServlet {
  public void doGet(HttpServletRequest request,
                    HttpServletResponse response)
      throws ServletException, IOException {
    HttpSession session = request.getSession();
    NameBean nameBean =
      (NameBean)session.getAttribute("nameBean");
    if (nameBean == null) {
      nameBean = new NameBean();
      session.setAttribute("nameBean", nameBean);
    }
    String firstName = request.getParameter("firstName");
    if ((firstName != null) && (!firstName.trim().equals(""))) {
      nameBean.setFirstName(firstName);
    }
    String lastName = request.getParameter("lastName");
    if ((lastName != null) && (!lastName.trim().equals(""))) {
      nameBean.setLastName(lastName);
    }
    String address = "/WEB-INF/mvc-sharing/ShowName.jsp";
    RequestDispatcher dispatcher =
      request.getRequestDispatcher(address);
    dispatcher.forward(request, response);
  }
}
```

Listing 15.13 ShowName.jsp

```
<!DOCTYPE HTML PUBLIC "-//W3C//DTD HTML 4.0 Transitional//EN">
<HTML>
<HEAD>
<TITLE>Thanks for Registering</TITLE>
<LINK REL=STYLESHEET
      HREF="/bank-support/JSP-Styles.css"
      TYPE="text/css">
</HEAD>
<BODY>
<H1>Thanks for Registering</H1>
<jsp:useBean id="nameBean" type="coreservlets.NameBean"
             scope="session" />
<H2>First Name:
<jsp:getProperty name="nameBean" property="firstName" /></H2>
<H2>Last Name:
<jsp:getProperty name="nameBean" property="lastName" /></H2>
</BODY></HTML>
```

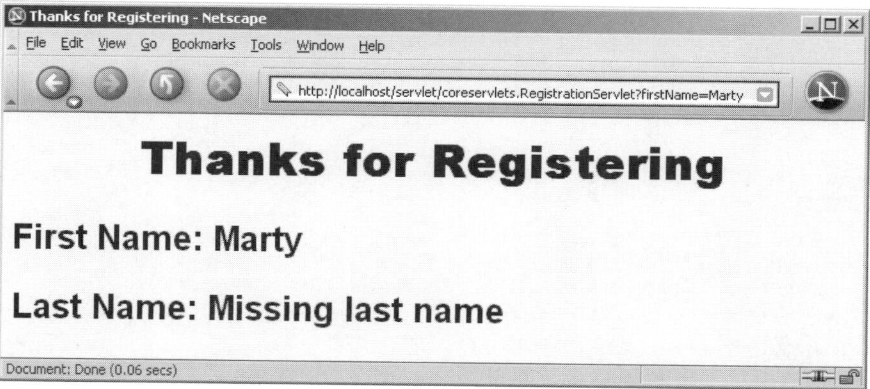

Figure 15–7 Result of `RegistrationServlet` when one parameter is missing and no session data is found.

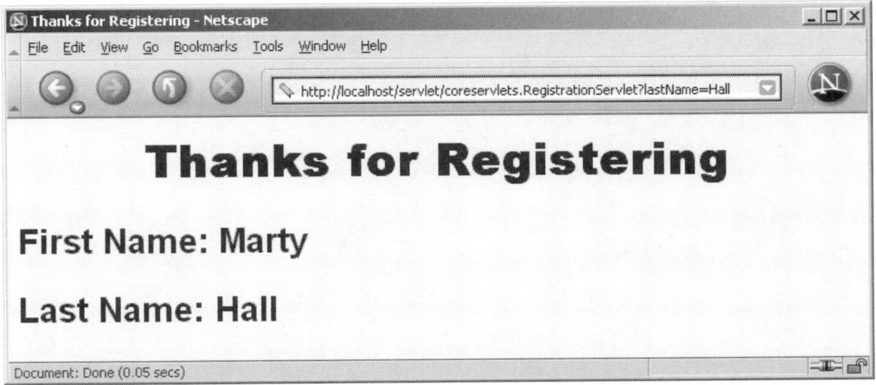

Figure 15–8 Result of `RegistrationServlet` when one parameter is missing and session data is found.

Application-Based Sharing

In this example, our goal is to display a prime number of a specified length. If the user fails to tell us the desired length, we want to use whatever prime number we most recently computed for *any* user. Data is shared among multiple clients, so application-based sharing is appropriate.

To implement this behavior, we need a bean to store prime numbers (Listing 15.14, which uses the `Primes` class presented earlier in Section 7.4), a servlet to populate the bean and store it in the `ServletContext` (Listing 15.15), and a JSP page to display the results (Listing 15.16, Figures 15–9 and 15–10).

Listing 15.14 PrimeBean.java

```
package coreservlets;

import java.math.BigInteger;

public class PrimeBean {
  private BigInteger prime;

  public PrimeBean(String lengthString) {
    int length = 150;
    try {
      length = Integer.parseInt(lengthString);
    } catch(NumberFormatException nfe) {}
    setPrime(Primes.nextPrime(Primes.random(length)));
  }
```

Listing 15.14 PrimeBean.java *(continued)*

```
  public BigInteger getPrime() {
    return(prime);
  }

  public void setPrime(BigInteger newPrime) {
    prime = newPrime;
  }
}
```

Listing 15.15 PrimeServlet.java

```
package coreservlets;

import java.io.*;
import javax.servlet.*;
import javax.servlet.http.*;

public class PrimeServlet extends HttpServlet {
  public void doGet(HttpServletRequest request,
                    HttpServletResponse response)
      throws ServletException, IOException {
    String length = request.getParameter("primeLength");
    ServletContext context = getServletContext();
    synchronized(this) {
      if ((context.getAttribute("primeBean") == null) ||
          (length != null)) {
        PrimeBean primeBean = new PrimeBean(length);
        context.setAttribute("primeBean", primeBean);
      }
      String address = "/WEB-INF/mvc-sharing/ShowPrime.jsp";
      RequestDispatcher dispatcher =
        request.getRequestDispatcher(address);
      dispatcher.forward(request, response);
    }
  }
}
```

Listing 15.16 ShowPrime.jsp

```
<!DOCTYPE HTML PUBLIC "-//W3C//DTD HTML 4.0 Transitional//EN">
<HTML>
<HEAD>
<TITLE>A Prime Number</TITLE>
<LINK REL=STYLESHEET
      HREF="/bank-support/JSP-Styles.css"
      TYPE="text/css">
</HEAD>
<BODY>
<H1>A Prime Number</H1>
<jsp:useBean id="primeBean" type="coreservlets.PrimeBean"
             scope="application" />
<jsp:getProperty name="primeBean" property="prime" />
</BODY></HTML>
```

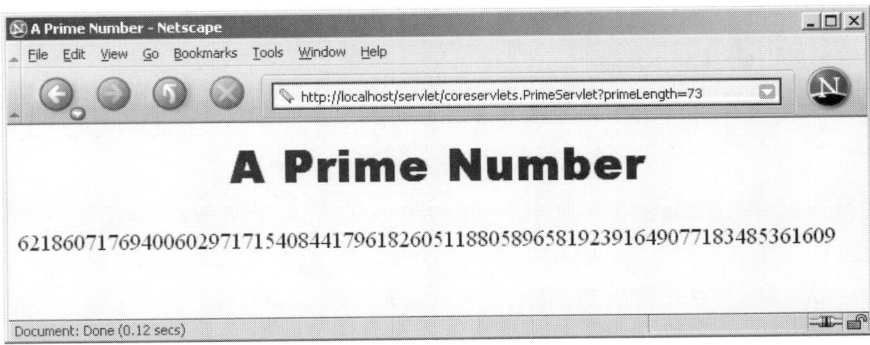

Figure 15–9 Result of `PrimeServlet` when an explicit prime size is given: a new prime of that size is computed.

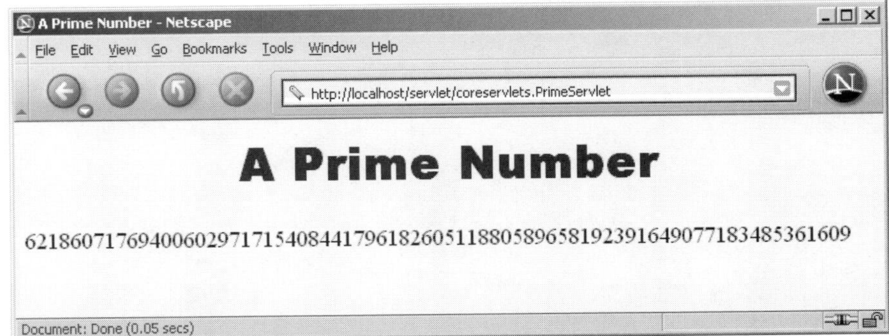

Figure 15–10 Result of `PrimeServlet` when no explicit prime size is given: the previous number is shown and no new prime is computed.

15.7 Forwarding Requests from JSP Pages

The most common request-forwarding scenario is one in which the request first goes to a servlet and the servlet forwards the request to a JSP page. The reason a servlet usually handles the original request is that checking request parameters and setting up beans requires a lot of programming, and it is more convenient to do this programming in a servlet than in a JSP document. The reason that the destination page is usually a JSP document is that JSP simplifies the process of creating the HTML content.

However, just because this is the *usual* approach doesn't mean that it is the *only* way of doing things. It is certainly possible for the destination page to be a servlet. Similarly, it is quite possible for a JSP page to forward requests elsewhere. For example, a request might go to a JSP page that normally presents results of a certain type and that forwards the request elsewhere only when it receives unexpected values.

Sending requests to servlets instead of JSP pages requires no changes whatsoever in the use of the `RequestDispatcher`. However, there is special syntactic support for forwarding requests from JSP pages. In JSP, the `jsp:forward` action is simpler and easier to use than wrapping `RequestDispatcher` code in a scriptlet. This action takes the following form:

```
<jsp:forward page="Relative URL" />
```

The `page` attribute is allowed to contain JSP expressions so that the destination can be computed at request time. For example, the following code sends about half the visitors to http://*host*/examples/page1.jsp and the others to http://*host*/examples/page2.jsp.

```
<% String destination;
   if (Math.random() > 0.5) {
     destination = "/examples/page1.jsp";
   } else {
     destination = "/examples/page2.jsp";
   }
%>
<jsp:forward page="<%= destination %>" />
```

The `jsp:forward` action, like `jsp:include`, can make use of `jsp:param` elements to supply extra request parameters to the destination page. For details, see the discussion of `jsp:include` in Section 13.2.

15.8 Including Pages

The `forward` method of `RequestDispatcher` relies on the destination JSP page to generate the *complete* output. The servlet is not permitted to generate any output of its own.

An alternative to `forward` is `include`. With `include`, the servlet can combine its output with that of one or more JSP pages. More commonly, the servlet still relies on JSP pages to produce the output, but the servlet invokes different JSP pages to create different *sections* of the page. Does this sound familiar? It should: the `include` method of `RequestDispatcher` is the code that the `jsp:include` action (Section 13.1) invokes behind the scenes.

This approach is most common when your servlets create portal sites that let users specify where on the page they want various pieces of content to be displayed. Here is a representative example.

```
String firstTable, secondTable, thirdTable;
if (someCondition) {
  firstTable = "/WEB-INF/Sports-Scores.jsp";
  secondTable = "/WEB-INF/Stock-Prices.jsp";
  thirdTable = "/WEB-INF/Weather.jsp";
} else if (...) { ... }
RequestDispatcher dispatcher =
  request.getRequestDispatcher("/WEB-INF/Header.jsp");
dispatcher.include(request, response);
dispatcher =
  request.getRequestDispatcher(firstTable);
dispatcher.include(request, response);
dispatcher =
  request.getRequestDispatcher(secondTable);
dispatcher.include(request, response);
dispatcher =
  request.getRequestDispatcher(thirdTable);
dispatcher.include(request, response);
dispatcher =
  request.getRequestDispatcher("/WEB-INF/Footer.jsp");
dispatcher.include(request, response);
```

Simplifying Access to Java Code: The JSP 2.0 Expression Language

Topics in This Chapter

- Motivating use of the expression language
- Invoking the expression language
- Disabling the expression language
- Preventing the use of classic scripting elements
- Understanding the relationship of the expression language to the MVC architecture
- Referencing scoped variables
- Accessing bean properties, array elements, `List` elements, and `Map` entries
- Using expression language operators
- Evaluating expressions conditionally

Chapter 16

JSP 2.0 introduced a shorthand language for evaluating and outputting the values of Java objects that are stored in standard locations. This expression language (EL) is one of the two most important new features of JSP 2.0; the other is the ability to define custom tags with JSP syntax instead of Java syntax. This chapter discusses the expression language; Volume 2 discusses the new tag library capabilities.

Core Warning

The JSP expression language cannot be used in servers that support only JSP 1.2 or earlier.

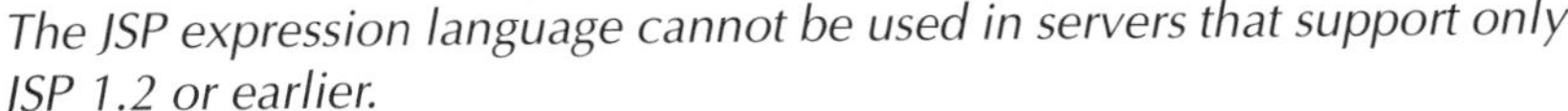

16.1 Motivating EL Usage

As illustrated in Figure 16–1, there are a number of different strategies that JSP pages can use to invoke Java code. One of the best and most flexible options is the MVC approach (see Chapter 15). In that approach, a servlet responds to the request; invokes the appropriate business logic or data access code; places the resultant data in beans; stores the beans in the request, session, or servlet context; and forwards the request to a JSP page to present the result.

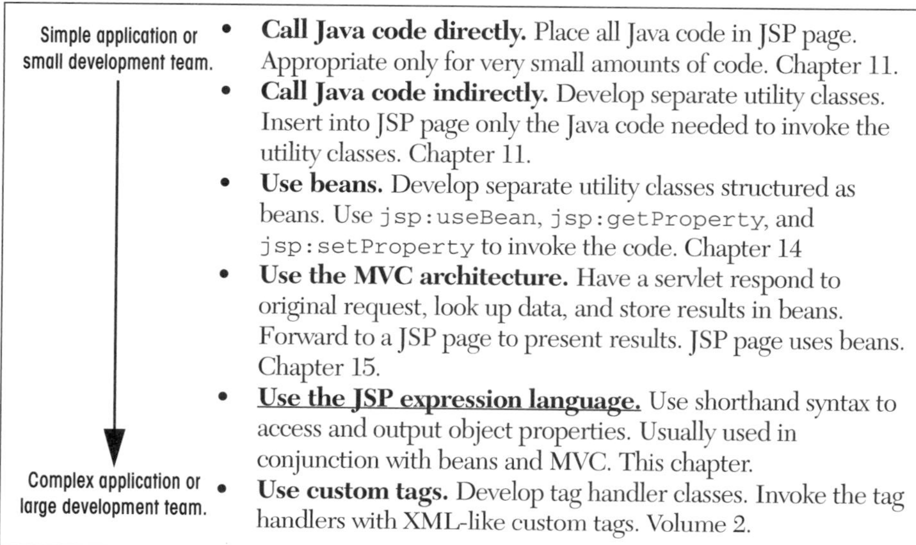

Figure 16–1 Strategies for invoking dynamic code from JSP.

The one inconvenient part about this approach is the final step: presenting the results in the JSP page. You normally use `jsp:useBean` and `jsp:getProperty`, but these elements are a bit verbose and clumsy. Furthermore, `jsp:getProperty` only supports access to simple bean properties; if the property is a collection or another bean, accessing the "subproperties" requires you to use complex Java syntax (precisely the thing you are often trying to avoid when using the MVC approach).

The JSP 2.0 expression language lets you simplify the presentation layer by replacing hard-to-maintain Java scripting elements or clumsy `jsp:useBean` and `jsp:getProperty` elements with short and readable entries of the following form.

```
${expression}
```

In particular, the expression language supports the following capabilities.

- **Concise access to stored objects.** To output a "scoped variable" (object stored with `setAttribute` in the `PageContext`, `HttpServletRequest`, `HttpSession`, or `ServletContext`) named `saleItem`, you use `${saleItem}`. See Section 16.5.
- **Shorthand notation for bean properties.** To output the `companyName` property (i.e., result of the `getCompanyName` method) of a scoped variable named `company`, you use `${company.companyName}`. To access the `firstName` property of the `president` property of a scoped variable named `company`, you use `${company.president.firstName}`. See Section 16.6.

- **Simple access to collection elements.** To access an element of an array, `List`, or `Map`, you use `${variable[indexOrKey]}`. Provided that the index or key is in a form that is legal for Java variable names, the dot notation for beans is interchangeable with the bracket notation for collections. See Section 16.7.
- **Succinct access to request parameters, cookies, and other request data.** To access the standard types of request data, you can use one of several predefined implicit objects. See Section 16.8.
- **A small but useful set of simple operators.** To manipulate objects within EL expressions, you can use any of several arithmetic, relational, logical, or empty-testing operators. See Section 16.9.
- **Conditional output.** To choose among output options, you do not have to resort to Java scripting elements. Instead, you can use `${test ? option1 : option2}`. See Section 16.10.
- **Automatic type conversion.** The expression language removes the need for most typecasts and for much of the code that parses strings as numbers.
- **Empty values instead of error messages.** In most cases, missing values or `NullPointerExceptions` result in empty strings, not thrown exceptions.

16.2 Invoking the Expression Language

In JSP 2.0, you invoke the expression language with elements of the following form.

```
${expression}
```

These EL elements can appear in ordinary text or in JSP tag attributes, provided that those attributes permit regular JSP expressions. For example:

```
<UL>
  <LI>Name: ${expression1}
  <LI>Address: ${expression2}
</UL>
<jsp:include page="${expression3}" />
```

When you use the expression language in tag attributes, you can use multiple expressions (possibly intermixed with static text) and the results are coerced to strings and concatenated. For example:

```
<jsp:include page="${expr1}blah${expr2}" />
```

This chapter will illustrate the use of expression language elements in ordinary text. Volume 2 of this book will illustrate the use of EL elements in attributes of tags that you write and tags that are provided by the JSP Standard Tag Library (JSTL) and JavaServer Faces (JSF) libraries.

Escaping Special Characters

If you want `${` to appear in the page output, use `\${` in the JSP page. If you want to use a single or double quote within an EL expression, use `\'` and `\"`, respectively.

16.3 Preventing Expression Language Evaluation

In JSP 1.2 and earlier, strings of the form `${...}` had no special meaning. So, it is possible that the characters `${` appear within a previously created page that is now being used on a server that supports JSP 2.0. In such a case, you need to deactivate the expression language in that page. You have four options for doing so.

- **Deactivating the expression language in an entire Web application.** You use a web.xml file that refers to servlets 2.3 (JSP 1.2) or earlier. See the first following subsection for details.
- **Deactivating the expression language in multiple JSP pages.** You use the `jsp-property-group` web.xml element to designate the appropriate pages. See the second following subsection for details.
- **Deactivating the expression language in individual JSP pages.** You use the `isELEnabled` attribute of the `page` directive. See the third following subsection for details.
- **Deactivating individual expression language statements.** In JSP 1.2 pages that need to be ported unmodified across multiple JSP versions (with no web.xml changes), you can replace `$` with `$`, the HTML character entity for `$`. In JSP 2.0 pages that contain both expression language statements and literal `${` strings, you can use `\${` when you want `${` in the output.

Remember that these techniques are *only* necessary when the page contains the sequence `${`.

Deactivating the Expression Language in an Entire Web Application

The JSP 2.0 expression language is automatically deactivated in Web applications whose deployment descriptor (i.e., WEB-INF/web.xml file) refers to servlet specification version 2.3 or earlier (i.e., JSP 1.2 or earlier). The web.xml file is discussed in great detail in the second volume of the book, but this volume provides a quick introduction in Section 2.11 (Web Applications: A Preview). For example, the following empty-but-legal web.xml file is compatible with JSP 1.2, and thus indicates that the expression language should be deactivated by default.

```
<?xml version="1.0" encoding="ISO-8859-1"?>
<!DOCTYPE web-app
  PUBLIC "-//Sun Microsystems, Inc.//DTD Web Application 2.3//EN"
  "http://java.sun.com/dtd/web-app_2_3.dtd">
<web-app>
</web-app>
```

On the other hand, the following web.xml file is compatible with JSP 2.0, and thus stipulates that the expression language should be activated by default. (Both of these web.xml files, like *all* code examples presented in the book, can be downloaded from the book's source code archive at http://www.coreservlets.com/).

```
<?xml version="1.0" encoding="ISO-8859-1"?>
<web-app xmlns="http://java.sun.com/xml/ns/j2ee"
         xmlns:xsi="http://www.w3.org/2001/XMLSchema-instance"
         xsi:schemaLocation=
           "http://java.sun.com/xml/ns/j2ee web-app_2_4.xsd"
         version="2.4">
</web-app>
```

Deactivating the Expression Language in Multiple JSP Pages

In a Web application whose deployment descriptor specifies servlets 2.4 (JSP 2.0), you use the `el-ignored` subelement of the `jsp-property-group` web.xml element to designate the pages in which the expression language should be ignored. Here is an example that deactivates the expression language for all JSP pages in the legacy directory.

```
<?xml version="1.0" encoding="ISO-8859-1"?>
<web-app xmlns="http://java.sun.com/xml/ns/j2ee"
         xmlns:xsi="http://www.w3.org/2001/XMLSchema-instance"
         xsi:schemaLocation=
           "http://java.sun.com/xml/ns/j2ee web-app_2_4.xsd"
         version="2.4">
  <jsp-property-group>
    <url-pattern>/legacy/*.jsp</url-pattern>
    <el-ignored>true</el-ignored>
  </jsp-property-group>
</web-app>
```

The `jsp-property-group` element is discussed in more detail in Volume 2 of this book.

Deactivating the Expression Language in Individual JSP Pages

To disable EL evaluation in an individual page, supply `false` as the value of the `isELEnabled` attribute of the `page` directive, as follows.

```
<%@ page isELEnabled="false" %>
```

Note that the `isELEnabled` attribute is new in JSP 2.0 and it is an error to use it in a server that supports only JSP 1.2 or earlier. So, you cannot use this technique to allow the same JSP page to run in either old or new servers without modification. Consequently, the `jsp-property-group` element is usually a better choice than the `isELEnabled` attribute.

Deactivating Individual Expression Language Statements

Suppose you have a JSP 1.2 page containing `${` that you want to use in multiple places. In particular, you want to use it in both JSP 1.2 Web applications and in Web applications that contain expression language pages. You want to be able to drop the page in any Web application without making *any* changes either to it or to the web.xml file. Although this is an unlikely scenario, it could happen, and none of the previously discussed constructs will serve the purpose. In such a case, you simply replace the `$` with the HTML character entity corresponding to the ISO 8859-1 value of `$` (36). So, you replace `${` with `${` throughout the page. For example,

```
&#36;{blah}
```

will portably display

```
${blah}
```

to the user. Note, however, that the character entity is translated to `$` by the *browser*, not by the *server*, so this technique will only work when you are outputting HTML to a Web browser.

Finally, suppose you have a JSP 2.0 page that contains both expression language statements and literal `${` strings. In such a case, simply put a backslash in front of the dollar sign. So, for example,

```
\${1+1} is ${1+1}.
```

will output

```
${1+1} is 2.
```

16.4 Preventing Use of Standard Scripting Elements

The JSP expression language provides succinct and easy-to-read access to scoped variables (Java objects stored in the standard locations). This capability eliminates much of the need for the explicit Java scripting elements described in Chapter 11. In fact, some developers prefer to use a no-classic-scripting-elements approach throughout their entire projects. You can use the `scripting-invalid` subelement of `jsp-property-group` to enforce this restriction. For example, the following **web.xml** file indicates that use of classic scripting elements in any JSP page will result in an error.

```
<?xml version="1.0" encoding="ISO-8859-1"?>
<web-app xmlns="http://java.sun.com/xml/ns/j2ee"
         xmlns:xsi="http://www.w3.org/2001/XMLSchema-instance"
         xsi:schemaLocation=
           "http://java.sun.com/xml/ns/j2ee web-app_2_4.xsd"
         version="2.4">
  <jsp-property-group>
    <url-pattern>*.jsp</url-pattern>
    <scripting-invalid>true</scripting-invalid>
  </jsp-property-group>
</web-app>
```

16.5 Accessing Scoped Variables

When you use the MVC approach (Chapter 15), a servlet invokes code that creates the data, then uses RequestDispatcher.forward or response.sendRedirect to transfer control to the appropriate JSP page. To permit the JSP page to access the data, the servlet needs to use setAttribute to store the data in one of the standard locations: the HttpServletRequest, the HttpSession, or the ServletContext.

Objects in these locations are known as "scoped variables," and the expression language has a quick and easy way to access them. You can also have scoped variables stored in the PageContext object, but this is much less useful because the servlet and the JSP page do not share PageContext objects. So, page-scoped variables apply only to objects stored earlier in the same JSP page, not to objects stored by a servlet.

To output a scoped variable, you simply use its name in an expression language element. For example,

```
${name}
```

means to search the PageContext, HttpServletRequest, HttpSession, and ServletContext (in that order) for an attribute named name. If the attribute is found, its toString method is called and that result is returned. If nothing is found, an empty string (not null or an error message) is returned. So, for example, the following two expressions are equivalent.

```
${name}
<%= pageContext.findAttribute("name") %>
```

The problems with the latter approach are that it is verbose and it requires explicit Java syntax. It is possible to eliminate the Java syntax, but doing so requires the following even more verbose jsp:useBean code.

```
<jsp:useBean id="name" type="somePackage.SomeClass" scope="...">
<%= name %>
```

Besides, with jsp:useBean, you have to know which scope the servlet used, and you have to know the fully qualified class name of the attribute. This is a significant inconvenience, especially when the JSP page author is someone other than the servlet author.

Choosing Attribute Names

To use the JSP expression language to access scoped variables, you must choose attribute names that would be legal as Java variable names. So, avoid dots, spaces, dashes, and other characters that are permitted in strings but forbidden in variable names.

Also, you should avoid using attribute names that conflict with any of the predefined names given in Section 16.8.

An Example

To illustrate access to scoped variables, the `ScopedVars` servlet (Listing 16.1) stores a `String` in the `HttpServletRequest`, another `String` in the `HttpSession`, and a `Date` in the `ServletContext`. The servlet forwards the request to a JSP page (Listing 16.2, Figure 16–2) that uses `${`*`attributeName`*`}` to access and output the objects.

Notice that the JSP page uses the same syntax to access the attributes, regardless of the scope in which they were stored. This is usually a convenient feature because MVC servlets almost always use unique attribute names for the objects they store. However, it is technically possible for attribute names to be repeated, so you should be aware that the expression language searches the `PageContext`, `HttpServletRequest`, `HttpSession`, and `ServletContext` *in that order*. To illustrate this, the servlet stores an object in each of the three shared scopes, using the attribute name `repeated` in all three cases. The value returned by `${repeated}` (see Figure 16–2) is the first attribute found when searching the scopes in the defined order (i.e., the `HttpServletRequest` in this case). Refer to Section 16.8 (Referencing Implicit Objects) if you want to restrict the search to a particular scope.

Listing 16.1 ScopedVars.java

```
package coreservlets;

/** Servlet that creates some scoped variables (objects stored
 *  as attributes in one of the standard locations). Forwards
 *  to a JSP page that uses the expression language to
 *  display the values.
 */

import java.io.*;
import javax.servlet.*;
import javax.servlet.http.*;
```

Listing 16.1 ScopedVars.java *(continued)*

```
public class ScopedVars extends HttpServlet {
  public void doGet(HttpServletRequest request,
                    HttpServletResponse response)
      throws ServletException, IOException {
    request.setAttribute("attribute1", "First Value");
    HttpSession session = request.getSession();
    session.setAttribute("attribute2", "Second Value");
    ServletContext application = getServletContext();
    application.setAttribute("attribute3",
                             new java.util.Date());
    request.setAttribute("repeated", "Request");
    session.setAttribute("repeated", "Session");
    application.setAttribute("repeated", "ServletContext");
    RequestDispatcher dispatcher =
      request.getRequestDispatcher("/el/scoped-vars.jsp");
    dispatcher.forward(request, response);
  }
}
```

Listing 16.2 scoped-vars.jsp

```
<!DOCTYPE HTML PUBLIC "-//W3C//DTD HTML 4.0 Transitional//EN">
<HTML>
<HEAD><TITLE>Accessing Scoped Variables</TITLE>
<LINK REL=STYLESHEET
      HREF="/el/JSP-Styles.css"
      TYPE="text/css">
</HEAD>
<BODY>
<TABLE BORDER=5 ALIGN="CENTER">
  <TR><TH CLASS="TITLE">
  Accessing Scoped Variables
</TABLE>
<P>
<UL>
  <LI><B>attribute1:</B> ${attribute1}
  <LI><B>attribute2:</B> ${attribute2}
  <LI><B>attribute3:</B> ${attribute3}
  <LI><B>Source of "repeated" attribute:</B> ${repeated}
</UL>
</BODY></HTML>
```

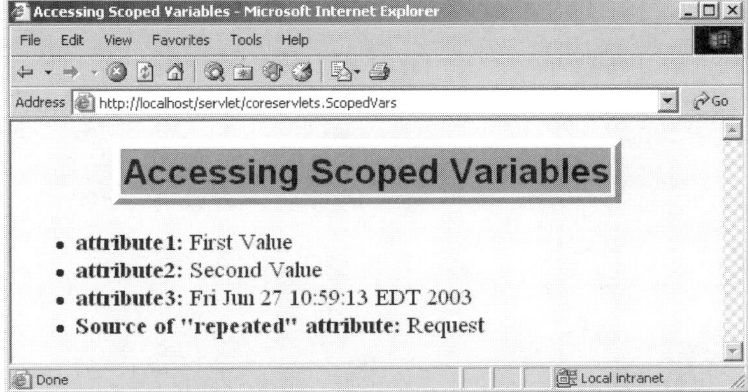

Figure 16–2 The JSP 2.0 expression language simplifies access to scoped variables: objects stored as attributes of the page, request, session, or servlet context.

16.6 Accessing Bean Properties

When you simply use `${name}`, the system finds the object named `name`, coerces it to a `String`, and returns it. Although this behavior is convenient, you rarely want to output *the actual object* that the MVC servlet stored. Rather, you typically want to output *individual properties* of that object.

The JSP expression language provides a simple but very powerful dot notation for accessing bean properties. To return the `firstName` property of a scoped variable named `customer`, you merely use `${customer.firstName}`. Although this form appears very simple, the system must perform reflection (analysis of the internals of the object) to support this behavior. So, assuming the object is of type `NameBean` and that `NameBean` is in the `coreservlets` package, to do the same thing with explicit Java syntax, you would have to replace

```
${customer.firstName}
```

with

```
<%@ page import="coreservlets.NameBean" %>
<%
NameBean person =
      (NameBean)pageContext.findAttribute("customer");
%>
<%= person.getFirstName() %>
```

Furthermore, the version with the JSP expression language returns an empty string if the attribute is not found, whereas the scripting element version would need additional code to avoid a NullPointerException in the same situation.

Now, JSP scripting elements are not the only alternative to use of the expression language. As long as you know the scope and fully qualified class name, you could replace

```
${customer.firstName}
```

with

```
<jsp:useBean id="customer" type="coreservlets.NameBean"
             scope="request, session, or application" />
<jsp:getProperty name="customer" property="firstName" />
```

However, the expression language lets you nest properties arbitrarily. For example, if the NameBean class had an address property (i.e., a getAddress method) that returned an Address object with a zipCode property (i.e., a getZipCode method), you could access this zipCode property with the following simple form.

```
${customer.address.zipCode}
```

There is no combination of jsp:useBean and jsp:getProperty that lets you do the same thing without explicit Java syntax.

Equivalence of Dot Notation and Array Notation

Finally, note that the expression language lets you replace dot notation with array notation (square brackets). So, for example, you can replace

```
${name.property}
```

with

```
${name["property"]}
```

The second form is rarely used with bean properties. However, it does have two advantages.

First, it lets you compute the name of the property at request time. With the array notation, the value inside the brackets can itself be a variable; with dot notation the property name must be a literal value.

Second, the array notation lets you use values that are illegal as property names. This is of no use when accessing bean properties, but it is very useful when accessing collections (Section 16.7) or request headers (Section 16.8).

An Example

To illustrate the use of bean properties, consider the BeanProperties servlet of Listing 16.3. The servlet creates an EmployeeBean (Listing 16.4), stores it in the request object with an attribute named employee, and forwards the request to a JSP page.

The EmployeeBean class has name and company properties that refer to NameBean (Listing 16.5) and CompanyBean (Listing 16.6) objects, respectively. The NameBean class has firstName and lastName properties and the CompanyBean class has companyName and business properties. The JSP page (Listing 16.7) uses the following simple EL expressions to access the four attributes:

```
${employee.name.firstName}
${employee.name.lastName}
${employee.company.companyName}
${employee.company.business}
```

Figure 16–3 shows the results.

Listing 16.3 BeanProperties.java

```
package coreservlets;

/** Servlet that creates some beans whose properties will
 *  be displayed with the JSP 2.0 expression language.
 */

import java.io.*;
import javax.servlet.*;
import javax.servlet.http.*;

public class BeanProperties extends HttpServlet {
  public void doGet(HttpServletRequest request,
                    HttpServletResponse response)
      throws ServletException, IOException {
    NameBean name = new NameBean("Marty", "Hall");
    CompanyBean company =
      new CompanyBean("coreservlets.com",
                      "J2EE Training and Consulting");
    EmployeeBean employee = new EmployeeBean(name, company);
    request.setAttribute("employee", employee);
    RequestDispatcher dispatcher =
      request.getRequestDispatcher("/el/bean-properties.jsp");
    dispatcher.forward(request, response);
  }
}
```

Listing 16.4 EmployeeBean.java

```
package coreservlets;

public class EmployeeBean {
  private NameBean name;
  private CompanyBean company;

  public EmployeeBean(NameBean name, CompanyBean company) {
    setName(name);
    setCompany(company);
  }

  public NameBean getName() { return(name); }

  public void setName(NameBean newName) {
    name = newName;
  }

  public CompanyBean getCompany() { return(company); }

  public void setCompany(CompanyBean newCompany) {
    company = newCompany;
  }
}
```

Listing 16.5 NameBean.java

```
package coreservlets;

public class NameBean {
  private String firstName = "Missing first name";
  private String lastName = "Missing last name";

  public NameBean() {}

  public NameBean(String firstName, String lastName) {
    setFirstName(firstName);
    setLastName(lastName);
  }

  public String getFirstName() {
    return(firstName);
  }
```

Listing 16.5 NameBean.java *(continued)*

```
  public void setFirstName(String newFirstName) {
    firstName = newFirstName;
  }

  public String getLastName() {
    return(lastName);
  }

  public void setLastName(String newLastName) {
    lastName = newLastName;
  }
}
```

Listing 16.6 CompanyBean.java

```
package coreservlets;

public class CompanyBean {
  private String companyName;
  private String business;

  public CompanyBean(String companyName, String business) {
    setCompanyName(companyName);
    setBusiness(business);
  }

  public String getCompanyName() { return(companyName); }

  public void setCompanyName(String newCompanyName) {
    companyName = newCompanyName;
  }

  public String getBusiness() { return(business); }

  public void setBusiness(String newBusiness) {
    business = newBusiness;
  }
}
```

Listing 16.7 bean-properties.jsp

```
<!DOCTYPE HTML PUBLIC "-//W3C//DTD HTML 4.0 Transitional//EN">
<HTML>
<HEAD><TITLE>Accessing Bean Properties</TITLE>
<LINK REL=STYLESHEET
      HREF="/el/JSP-Styles.css"
      TYPE="text/css">
</HEAD>
<BODY>
<TABLE BORDER=5 ALIGN="CENTER">
  <TR><TH CLASS="TITLE">
  Accessing Bean Properties
</TABLE>
<P>
<UL>
  <LI><B>First Name:</B> ${employee.name.firstName}
  <LI><B>Last Name:</B> ${employee.name.lastName}
  <LI><B>Company Name:</B> ${employee.company.companyName}
  <LI><B>Company Business:</B> ${employee.company.business}
</UL>
</BODY></HTML>
```

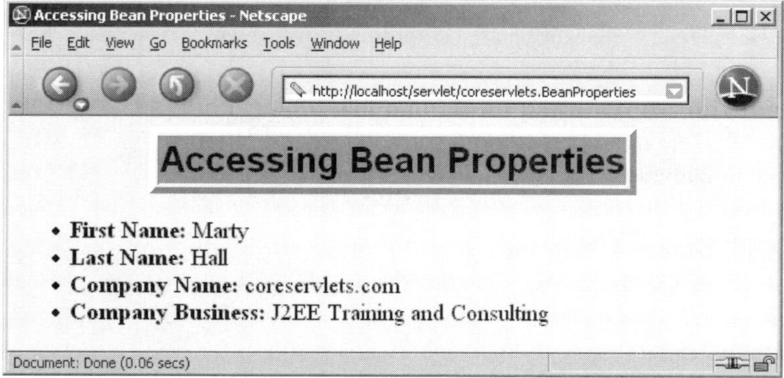

Figure 16–3 You use dots or array notation to access bean properties.

16.7 Accessing Collections

The JSP 2.0 expression language lets you access different types of collections in the same way: using array notation. For instance, if `attributeName` is a scoped variable referring to an array, `List`, or `Map`, you access an entry in the collection with the following:

```
${attributeName[entryName]}
```

If the scoped variable is an array, the entry name is the index and the value is obtained with `theArray[index]`. For example, if `customerNames` refers to an array of strings,

```
${customerNames[0]}
```

would output the first entry in the array.

If the scoped variable is an object that implements the `List` interface, the entry name is the index and the value is obtained with `theList.get(index)`. For example, if `supplierNames` refers to an `ArrayList`,

```
${supplierNames[0]}
```

would output the first entry in the `ArrayList`.

If the scoped variable is an object that implements the `Map` interface, the entry name is the key and the value is obtained with `theMap.get(key)`. For example, if `stateCapitals` refers to a `HashMap` whose keys are U.S. state names and whose values are city names,

```
${stateCapitals["maryland"]}
```

would return `"annapolis"`. If the `Map` key is of a form that would be legal as a Java variable name, you can replace the array notation with dot notation. So, the previous example could also be written as:

```
${stateCapitals.maryland}
```

However, note that the array notation lets you choose the key at request time, whereas the dot notation requires you to know the key in advance.

An Example

To illustrate the use of EL expressions to access collections, the `Collections` servlet (Listing 16.8) creates an array of strings, an `ArrayList`, and a `HashMap`. The servlet then forwards the request to a JSP page (Listing 16.9, Figure 16–4) that uses uniform array notation to access the elements of all three objects.

Purely numeric values are illegal as bean properties, so the array and `ArrayList` entries must be accessed with array notation. However, the `HashMap` entries could be accessed with either array or dot notation. We use array notation for consistency, but, for example,

```
${company["Ellison"]}
```

could be replaced with

```
${company.Ellison}
```

in Listing 16.9.

Listing 16.8 Collections.java

```
package coreservlets;

import java.util.*;

/** Servlet that creates some collections whose elements will
 *  be displayed with the JSP 2.0 expression language.
 *  <P>
 */

import java.io.*;
import javax.servlet.*;
import javax.servlet.http.*;

public class Collections extends HttpServlet {
  public void doGet(HttpServletRequest request,
                    HttpServletResponse response)
      throws ServletException, IOException {
    String[] firstNames = { "Bill", "Scott", "Larry" };
    ArrayList lastNames = new ArrayList();
    lastNames.add("Ellison");
    lastNames.add("Gates");
    lastNames.add("McNealy");
    HashMap companyNames = new HashMap();
    companyNames.put("Ellison", "Sun");
    companyNames.put("Gates", "Oracle");
    companyNames.put("McNealy", "Microsoft");
    request.setAttribute("first", firstNames);
    request.setAttribute("last", lastNames);
    request.setAttribute("company", companyNames);
    RequestDispatcher dispatcher =
      request.getRequestDispatcher("/el/collections.jsp");
    dispatcher.forward(request, response);
  }
}
```

Listing 16.9 collections.jsp

```
<!DOCTYPE HTML PUBLIC "-//W3C//DTD HTML 4.0 Transitional//EN">
<HTML>
<HEAD><TITLE>Accessing Collections</TITLE>
<LINK REL=STYLESHEET
      HREF="/el/JSP-Styles.css"
      TYPE="text/css">
</HEAD>
<BODY>
<TABLE BORDER=5 ALIGN="CENTER">
  <TR><TH CLASS="TITLE">
  Accessing Collections
</TABLE>
<P>
<UL>
  <LI>${first[0]} ${last[0]} (${company["Ellison"]})
  <LI>${first[1]} ${last[1]} (${company["Gates"]})
  <LI>${first[2]} ${last[2]} (${company["McNealy"]})
</UL>
</BODY></HTML>
```

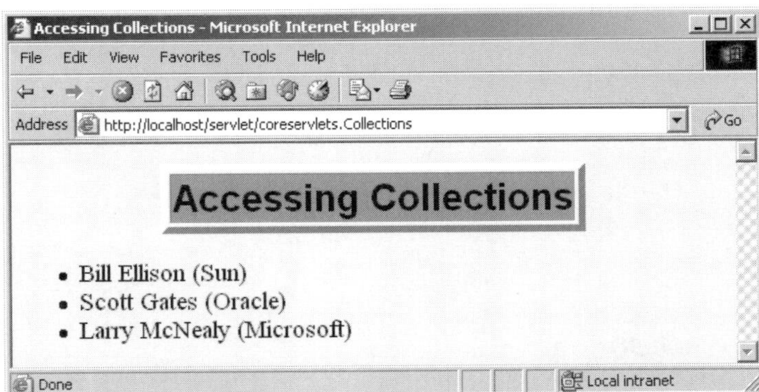

Figure 16–4 You use array notation or dots to access collections. Dots can be used only when the key is in a form that would be legal as a Java variable name.

16.8 Referencing Implicit Objects

In most cases, you use the JSP expression language in conjunction with the Model-View-Controller architecture (Chapter 15) in which the servlet creates the data and the JSP page presents the data. In such a scenario, the JSP page is usually only interested in the objects that the servlet created, and the general bean-access and collection-access mechanisms are sufficient.

However, the expression language is not restricted to use in the MVC approach; if the server supports JSP 2.0 and the **web.xml** file refers to servlets 2.4, the expression language can be used in any JSP page. To make this capability useful, the specification defines the following implicit objects.

pageContext

The `pageContext` object refers to the `PageContext` of the current page. The `PageContext` class, in turn, has `request`, `response`, `session`, `out`, and `servletContext` properties (i.e., `getRequest`, `getResponse`, `getSession`, `getOut`, and `getServletContext` methods). So, for example, the following outputs the current session ID.

```
${pageContext.session.id}
```

param and paramValues

These objects let you access the primary request parameter value (`param`) or the array of request parameter values (`paramValues`). So, for example, the following outputs the value of the `custID` request parameter (with an empty string, not `null`, returned if the parameter does not exist in the current request).

```
${param.custID}
```

For more information on dealing with request parameters, see Chapter 4.

header and headerValues

These objects access the primary and complete HTTP request header values, respectively. Remember that dot notation cannot be used when the value after the dot would be an illegal property name. So, for example, to access the `Accept` header, you could use either

```
${header.Accept}
```

or

```
${header["Accept"]}
```

But, to access the `Accept-Encoding` header, you must use

```
${header["Accept-Encoding"]}
```

For more information on dealing with HTTP request headers, see Chapter 5.

cookie

The `cookie` object lets you quickly reference incoming cookies. However, the return value is the `Cookie` object, not the cookie value. To access the value, use the standard `value` property (i.e., the `getValue` method) of the `Cookie` class. So, for example, either of the following outputs the value of the cookie named `userCookie` (or an empty string if no such cookie is found).

```
${cookie.userCookie.value}
${cookie["userCookie"].value}
```

For more information on using cookies, see Chapter 8.

initParam

The `initParam` object lets you easily access context initialization parameters. For example, the following outputs the value of the init param named `defaultColor`.

```
${initParam.defaultColor}
```

For more information on using initialization parameters, see Volume 2 of this book.

pageScope, requestScope, sessionScope, and applicationScope

These objects let you restrict where the system looks for scoped variables. For example, with

```
${name}
```

the system searches for `name` in the `PageContext`, the `HttpServlet-Request`, the `HttpSession`, and the `ServletContext`, returning the first match it finds. On the other hand, with

```
${requestScope.name}
```

the system only looks in the `HttpServletRequest`.

An Example

The JSP page of Listing 16.10 uses the implicit objects to output a request parameter, an HTTP request header, a cookie value, and information about the server. Figure 16–5 shows the results.

Listing 16.10 implicit-objects.jsp

```
<!DOCTYPE HTML PUBLIC "-//W3C//DTD HTML 4.0 Transitional//EN">
<HTML>
<HEAD><TITLE>Using Implicit Objects</TITLE>
<LINK REL=STYLESHEET
      HREF="/el/JSP-Styles.css"
      TYPE="text/css">
</HEAD>
<BODY>
<TABLE BORDER=5 ALIGN="CENTER">
  <TR><TH CLASS="TITLE">
  Using Implicit Objects
</TABLE>
<P>
<UL>
  <LI><B>test Request Parameter:</B> ${param.test}
  <LI><B>User-Agent Header:</B> ${header["User-Agent"]}
  <LI><B>JSESSIONID Cookie Value:</B> ${cookie.JSESSIONID.value}
  <LI><B>Server:</B> ${pageContext.servletContext.serverInfo}
</UL>
</BODY></HTML>
```

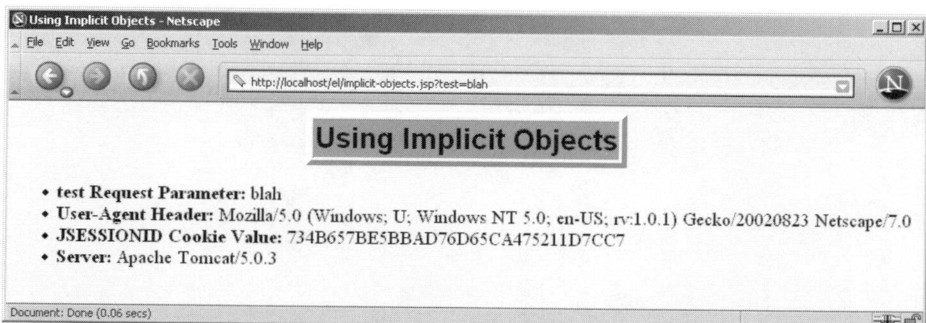

Figure 16–5 A number of scoped variables are defined automatically. These predefined variables are called "implicit objects."

16.9 Using Expression Language Operators

The JSP 2.0 expression language defines a number of arithmetic, relational, logical, and missing-value-testing operators. Although use of the operators often results in code that is a bit shorter than the equivalent Java code, you should keep in mind the main purpose of the expression language: to provide concise access to existing objects, usually in the context of the MVC architecture. So, we see little benefit in replacing long and complex scripting elements with only slightly shorter expression language elements. Both approaches are wrong; complex business- or data-access-logic does not belong in JSP pages at all. As much as possible, restrict the use of the expression language to *presentation* logic; keep the business logic in normal Java classes that are invoked by servlets.

Core Approach

Use the expression language operators for simple tasks oriented toward presentation logic (deciding how to present the data). Avoid using the operators for business logic (creating and processing the data). Instead, put business logic in regular Java classes and invoke the code from the servlet that starts the MVC process.

Arithmetic Operators

These operators are typically used to perform simple manipulation of values already stored in beans. Resist using them for complex algorithms; put such code in regular Java code instead.

+ and –

These are the normal addition and subtraction operators, with two exceptions. First, if either of the operands is a string, the string is automatically parsed to a number (however, the system does *not* automatically catch `NumberFormatException`). Second, if either of the operands is of type `BigInteger` or `BigDecimal`, the system uses the corresponding `add` and `subtract` methods.

*, /, and div

These are the normal multiplication and division operators, with a few exceptions. First, types are converted automatically as with the + and – operators. Second, the normal arithmetic operator precedence applies, so, for instance,

```
${ 1 + 2 * 3}
```

returns 7, not 9. You can use parentheses to change the operator precedence. Third, the / and `div` operators are equivalent; both are provided for the sake of compatibility with both XPath and JavaScript (ECMAScript).

% and mod

The `%` (or equivalently, `mod`) operator computes the modulus (remainder), just as with `%` in the Java programming language.

Relational Operators

These operators are most frequently used with either the JSP expression language conditional operator (Section 16.10) or with custom tags whose attributes expect boolean values (e.g., looping tags like those in the JSP Standard Tag Library—JSTL—as discussed in Volume 2 of this book).

== and eq

These two equivalent operators check whether the arguments are equal. However, they operate more like the Java `equals` method than the Java == operator. If the two operands are the same object, `true` is returned. If the two operands are numbers, they are compared with Java ==. If either operand is `null`, `false` is returned. If either operand is a `BigInteger` or `BigDecimal`, the operands are compared with `compareTo`. Otherwise, the operands are compared with `equals`.

!= and ne

These two equivalent operators check whether the arguments are different. Again, however, they operate more like the negation of the Java `equals` method than the Java != operator. If the two operands are the same object, `false` is returned. If the two operands are numbers, they are compared with Java !=. If either operand is `null`, `true` is returned. If either operand is a `BigInteger` or `BigDecimal`, the operands are compared with `compareTo`. Otherwise, the operands are compared with `equals` and the opposite result is returned.

< and lt, > and gt, <= and le, >= and ge

These are the standard arithmetic operators with two exceptions. First, type conversions are performed as with `==` and `!=`. Second, if the arguments are strings, they are compared lexically.

Logical Operators

These operators are used to combine results from the relational operators.

&&, and, ||, or, !, not

These are the standard logical AND, OR, and NOT operators. They operate by coercing their arguments to `Boolean`, and they use the normal Java "short circuit" evaluation in which the testing is stopped as soon as the result can be determined. `&&` and `and` are equivalent, `||` and `or` are equivalent, and `!` and `not` are equivalent.

The empty Operator

empty

This operator returns `true` if its argument is `null`, an empty string, an empty array, an empty `Map`, or an empty collection. Otherwise it returns `false`.

An Example

Listing 16.11 illustrates several of the standard operators; Figure 16–6 shows the result.

Listing 16.11 operators.jsp

```
<!DOCTYPE HTML PUBLIC "-//W3C//DTD HTML 4.0 Transitional//EN">
<HTML>
<HEAD><TITLE>EL Operators</TITLE>
<LINK REL=STYLESHEET
      HREF="/el/JSP-Styles.css"
      TYPE="text/css">
</HEAD>
<BODY>
<TABLE BORDER=5 ALIGN="CENTER">
  <TR><TH CLASS="TITLE">
  EL Operators
</TABLE>
```

Listing 16.11 operators.jsp *(continued)*

```
<P>
<TABLE BORDER=1 ALIGN="CENTER">
  <TR><TH CLASS="COLORED" COLSPAN=2>Arithmetic Operators
      <TH CLASS="COLORED" COLSPAN=2>Relational Operators
  <TR><TH>Expression<TH>Result<TH>Expression<TH>Result
  <TR ALIGN="CENTER">
    <TD>\${3+2-1}<TD>${3+2-1}  <%-- Addition/Subtraction --%>
    <TD>\${1&lt;2}<TD>${1<2}      <%-- Numerical comparison --%>
  <TR ALIGN="CENTER">
    <TD>\${"1"+2}<TD>${"1"+2}     <%-- String conversion --%>
    <TD>\${"a"&lt;"b"}<TD>${"a"<"b"} <%-- Lexical comparison --%>
  <TR ALIGN="CENTER">
    <TD>\${1 + 2*3 + 3/4}<TD>${1 + 2*3 + 3/4}  <%-- Mult/Div --%>
    <TD>\${2/3 &gt;= 3/2}<TD>${2/3 >= 3/2}         <%-- >= --%>
  <TR ALIGN="CENTER">
    <TD>\${3%2}<TD>${3%2}                   <%-- Modulo --%>
    <TD>\${3/4 == 0.75}<TD>${3/4 == 0.75} <%-- Numeric = --%>
  <TR ALIGN="CENTER">
    <%-- div and mod are alternatives to / and % --%>
    <TD>\${(8 div 2) mod 3}<TD>${(8 div 2) mod 3}
    <%-- Compares with "equals" but returns false for null --%>
    <TD>\${null == "test"}<TD>${null == "test"}

  <TR><TH CLASS="COLORED" COLSPAN=2>Logical Operators
      <TH CLASS="COLORED" COLSPAN=2><CODE>empty</CODE> Operator
  <TR><TH>Expression<TH>Result<TH>Expression<TH>Result
  <TR ALIGN="CENTER">
    <TD>\${(1&lt;2) && (4&lt;3)}<TD>${(1<2) && (4<3)} <%--AND--%>
    <TD>\${empty ""}<TD>${empty ""} <%-- Empty string --%>
  <TR ALIGN="CENTER">
    <TD>\${(1&lt;2) || (4&lt;3)}<TD>${(1<2) || (4<3)} <%--OR--%>
    <TD>\${empty null}<TD>${empty null} <%-- null --%>
  <TR ALIGN="CENTER">
    <TD>\${!(1&lt;2)}<TD>${!(1<2)}  <%-- NOT -%>
    <%-- Handles null or empty string in request param --%>
    <TD>\${empty param.blah}<TD>${empty param.blah}
</TABLE>
</BODY></HTML>
```

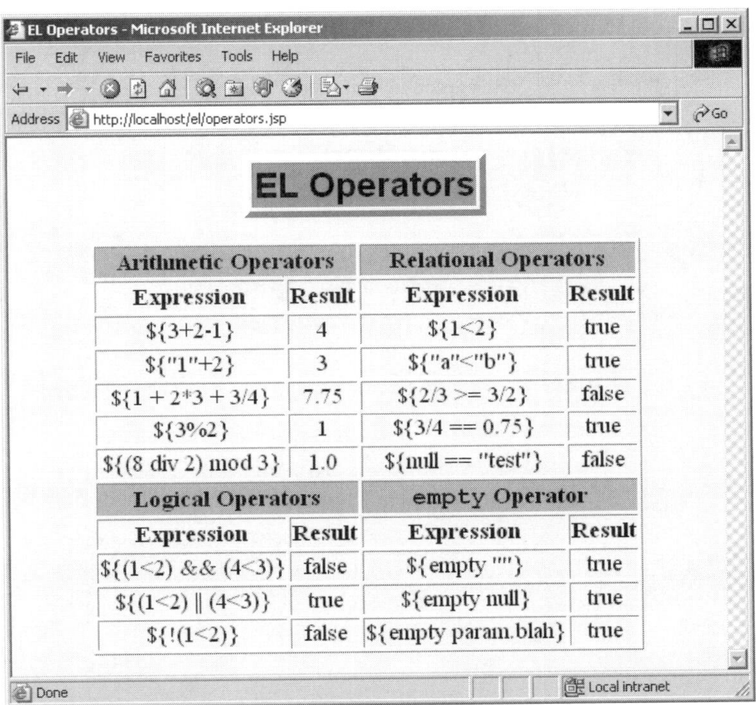

Arithmetic Operators		Relational Operators	
Expression	Result	Expression	Result
${3+2-1}	4	${1<2}	true
${"1"+2}	3	${"a"<"b"}	true
${1 + 2*3 + 3/4}	7.75	${2/3 >= 3/2}	false
${3%2}	1	${3/4 == 0.75}	true
${(8 div 2) mod 3}	1.0	${null == "test"}	false
Logical Operators		**empty Operator**	
Expression	Result	Expression	Result
${(1<2) && (4<3)}	false	${empty ""}	true
${(1<2) || (4<3)}	true	${empty null}	true
${!(1<2)}	false	${empty param.blah}	true

Figure 16–6 The expression language defines a small set of operators. Use them with great restraint; invoke business logic from servlets, not from JSP pages.

16.10 Evaluating Expressions Conditionally

The JSP 2.0 expression language does not, in itself, provide a rich conditional evaluation facility. That capability is provided by the `c:if` and `c:choose` tags of the JSP Standard Tag Library (JSTL) or by another custom tag library. (JSTL and the creation of custom tag libraries are covered in Volume 2 of this book.)

However, the expression language supports the rudimentary `?:` operator as in the Java, C, and C++ languages. For example, if `test` evaluates to `true`,

```
${ test ? expression1 : expression2 }
```

returns the value of `expression1`; otherwise, it returns the value of `expression2`. Just remember that the main purpose of the expression language is to simplify presentation logic; avoid using this technique for business logic.

An Example

The servlet of Listing 16.12 creates two `SalesBean` objects (Listing 16.13) and forwards the request to a JSP page (Listing 16.14) for presentation (Figure 16–7). However, if the total sales number is negative, the JSP page wants to use a table cell with a red background. If it is negative, the page wants to use a white background. Implementing this behavior is a presentation task, so the `?:` operator is appropriate.

Listing 16.12 Conditionals.java

```
package coreservlets;

/** Servlet that creates scoped variables that will be used
 *  to illustrate the EL conditional operator (xxx ? xxx : xxx).
 */

import java.io.*;
import javax.servlet.*;
import javax.servlet.http.*;

public class Conditionals extends HttpServlet {
  public void doGet(HttpServletRequest request,
                    HttpServletResponse response)
      throws ServletException, IOException {
    SalesBean apples =
      new SalesBean(150.25, -75.25, 22.25, -33.57);
    SalesBean oranges =
      new SalesBean(-220.25, -49.57, 138.25, 12.25);
    request.setAttribute("apples", apples);
    request.setAttribute("oranges", oranges);
    RequestDispatcher dispatcher =
      request.getRequestDispatcher("/el/conditionals.jsp");
    dispatcher.forward(request, response);
  }
}
```

Listing 16.13 SalesBean.java

```
package coreservlets;

public class SalesBean {
  private double q1, q2, q3, q4;

  public SalesBean(double q1Sales,
                   double q2Sales,
                   double q3Sales,
                   double q4Sales) {
    q1 = q1Sales;
    q2 = q2Sales;
    q3 = q3Sales;
    q4 = q4Sales;
  }

  public double getQ1() { return(q1); }

  public double getQ2() { return(q2); }

  public double getQ3() { return(q3); }

  public double getQ4() { return(q4); }

  public double getTotal() { return(q1 + q2 + q3 + q4); }
}
```

Listing 16.14 conditionals.jsp

```
<!DOCTYPE HTML PUBLIC "-//W3C//DTD HTML 4.0 Transitional//EN">
<HTML>
<HEAD><TITLE>Conditional Evaluation</TITLE>
<LINK REL=STYLESHEET
      HREF="/el/JSP-Styles.css"
      TYPE="text/css">
</HEAD>
<BODY>
<TABLE BORDER=5 ALIGN="CENTER">
  <TR><TH CLASS="TITLE">
  Conditional Evaluation
</TABLE>
<P>
<TABLE BORDER=1 ALIGN="CENTER">
  <TR><TH>
      <TH CLASS="COLORED">Apples
      <TH CLASS="COLORED">Oranges
```

Listing 16.14 conditionals.jsp *(continued)*

```
  <TR><TH CLASS="COLORED">First Quarter
      <TD ALIGN="RIGHT">${apples.q1}
      <TD ALIGN="RIGHT">${oranges.q1}
  <TR><TH CLASS="COLORED">Second Quarter
      <TD ALIGN="RIGHT">${apples.q2}
      <TD ALIGN="RIGHT">${oranges.q2}
  <TR><TH CLASS="COLORED">Third Quarter
      <TD ALIGN="RIGHT">${apples.q3}
      <TD ALIGN="RIGHT">${oranges.q3}
  <TR><TH CLASS="COLORED">Fourth Quarter
      <TD ALIGN="RIGHT">${apples.q4}
      <TD ALIGN="RIGHT">${oranges.q4}
  <TR><TH CLASS="COLORED">Total
      <TD ALIGN="RIGHT"
          BGCOLOR="${(apples.total < 0) ? "RED" : "WHITE" }">
      ${apples.total}
      <TD ALIGN="RIGHT"
          BGCOLOR="${(oranges.total < 0) ? "RED" : "WHITE" }">
      ${oranges.total}
</TABLE>
</BODY></HTML>
```

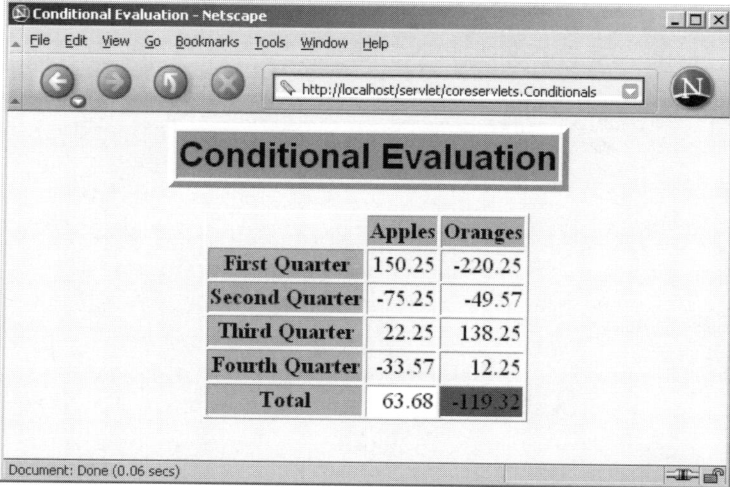

Figure 16–7 You can use the C-style `?:` operator to conditionally output different elements. However, the JSP Standard Tag Library (JSTL) is often a better alternative for this kind of conditional operation.

16.11 Previewing Other Expression Language Capabilities

This chapter summarizes most of the capabilities of the JSP 2.0 expression language. However, there are two capabilities that we did not discuss here: the use of the expression language in tag libraries and the use of expression language functions. We postpone coverage of these two capabilities to Volume 2 because they require techniques covered only in the second volume of the book.

Quick preview: expression language elements can be used in any custom tag attribute that allows request time expressions (i.e., whose `attribute` element specifies `true` for `rtexprvalue`). Functions correspond to public `static` methods in regular Java classes and are defined with the `function` element of the Tag Library Descriptor (TLD) file.

SUPPORTING TECHNOLOGY

Part III

ACCESSING DATABASES WITH JDBC

Topics in This Chapter

- Connecting to databases: the seven basic steps
- Simplifying JDBC usage: some utilities
- Using precompiled (parameterized) queries
- Creating and executing stored procedures
- Updating data through transactions
- Using JDO and other object-to-relational mappings

Chapter 17

JDBC provides a standard library for accessing relational databases. By using the JDBC API, you can access a wide variety of SQL databases with exactly the same Java syntax. It is important to note that although the JDBC API standardizes the approach for connecting to databases, the syntax for sending queries and committing transactions, and the data structure representing the result, JDBC does *not* attempt to standardize the SQL syntax. So, you can use any SQL extensions your database vendor supports. However, since most queries follow standard SQL syntax, using JDBC lets you change database hosts, ports, and even database vendors with minimal changes to your code.

DILBERT reprinted by permission of United Feature Syndicate, Inc.

Officially, JDBC is not an acronym and thus does not stand for anything. Unofficially, "Java DataBase Connectivity" is commonly used as the long form of the name.

Although a complete tutorial on database programming is beyond the scope of this chapter, we cover the basics of using JDBC in Section 17.1 (Using JDBC in General), presuming you are already familiar with SQL.

After covering JDBC basics, in Section 17.2 (Basic JDBC Examples) we present some JDBC examples that access a Microsoft Access database.

To simplify the JDBC code throughout the rest of the chapter, we provide some utilities for creating connections to databases in Section 17.3 (Simplifying Database Access with JDBC Utilities).

In Section 17.4 (Using Prepared Statements), we discuss prepared statements, which let you execute similar SQL statements multiple times; this can be more efficient than executing a raw query each time.

In Section 17.5 (Creating Callable Statements), we examine callable statements. Callable statements let you execute database stored procedures or functions.

In Section 17.6 (Using Database Transactions), we cover transaction management for maintaining database integrity. By executing changes to the database within a transaction, you can ensure that the database values are returned to their original state if a problem occurs.

In Section 17.7, we briefly examine object-to-relational mapping (ORM). ORM frameworks provide a complete object-oriented approach to manage information in a database. With ORM, you simply call methods on objects instead of directly using JDBC and SQL.

For advanced JDBC topics including accessing databases with custom JSP tags, using data sources with JNDI, and increasing performance by pooling database connections, see Volume 2 of this book. For more details on JDBC, see http://java.sun.com/products/jdbc/, the online API for `java.sql`, or the JDBC tutorial at http://java.sun.com/docs/books/tutorial/jdbc/.

17.1 Using JDBC in General

In this section we present the seven standard steps for querying databases. In Section 17.2 we give two simple examples (a command-line program and a servlet) illustrating these steps to query a Microsoft Access database.

Following is a summary; details are given in the rest of the section.

1. **Load the JDBC driver.** To load a driver, you specify the classname of the database driver in the `Class.forName` method. By doing so, you automatically create a driver instance and register it with the JDBC driver manager.

2. **Define the connection URL.** In JDBC, a connection URL specifies the server host, port, and database name with which to establish a connection.
3. **Establish the connection.** With the connection URL, username, and password, a network connection to the database can be established. Once the connection is established, database queries can be performed until the connection is closed.
4. **Create a `Statement` object.** Creating a `Statement` object enables you to send queries and commands to the database.
5. **Execute a query or update.** Given a `Statement` object, you can send SQL statements to the database by using the `execute`, `executeQuery`, `executeUpdate`, or `executeBatch` methods.
6. **Process the results.** When a database query is executed, a `ResultSet` is returned. The `ResultSet` represents a set of rows and columns that you can process by calls to `next` and various `get`*`Xxx`* methods.
7. **Close the connection.** When you are finished performing queries and processing results, you should close the connection, releasing resources to the database.

Load the JDBC Driver

The driver is the piece of software that knows how to talk to the actual database server. To load the driver, you just load the appropriate class; a `static` block in the driver class itself automatically makes a driver instance and registers it with the JDBC driver manager. To make your code as flexible as possible, avoid hard-coding the reference to the classname. In Section 17.3 (Simplifying Database Access with JDBC Utilities) we present a utility class to load drivers from a `Properties` file so that the classname is not hard-coded in the program.

These requirements bring up two interesting questions. First, how do you load a class without making an instance of it? Second, how can you refer to a class whose name isn't known when the code is compiled? The answer to both questions is to use `Class.forName`. This method takes a string representing a fully qualified classname (i.e., one that includes package names) and loads the corresponding class. This call could throw a `ClassNotFoundException`, so it should be inside a `try/catch` block as shown below.

```
try {
  Class.forName("connect.microsoft.MicrosoftDriver");
  Class.forName("oracle.jdbc.driver.OracleDriver");
  Class.forName("com.sybase.jdbc.SybDriver");
} catch(ClassNotFoundException cnfe) {
  System.err.println("Error loading driver: " + cnfe);
}
```

One of the beauties of the JDBC approach is that the database server requires no changes whatsoever. Instead, the JDBC driver (which is on the client) translates calls written in the Java programming language into the native format required by the server. This approach means that you have to obtain a JDBC driver specific to the database you are using and that you will need to check the vendor's documentation for the fully qualified class name to use.

In principle, you can use `Class.forName` for any class in your `CLASSPATH`. In practice, however, most JDBC driver vendors distribute their drivers inside JAR files. So, during development be sure to include the path to the driver JAR file in your `CLASSPATH` setting. For deployment on a Web server, put the JAR file in the WEB-INF/lib directory of your Web application (see Chapter 2, "Server Setup and Configuration"). Check with your Web server administrator, though. Often, if multiple Web applications are using the same database drivers, the administrator will place the JAR file in a common directory used by the server. For example, in Apache Tomcat, JAR files common to multiple applications can be placed in *install_dir*/common/lib.

Core Note

You can place your JDBC driver file (JAR file) in the WEB-INF/lib directory for deployment of your application. However, the administrator may choose to move the JAR file to a common library directory on the server.

Figure 17–1 illustrates two common JDBC driver implementations. The first approach is a JDBC-ODBC bridge, and the second approach is a pure Java implementation. A driver that uses the JDBC-ODBC bridge approach is known as a Type I driver. Since many databases support Open DataBase Connectivity (ODBC) access, the JDK includes a JDBC-ODBC bridge to connect to databases. However, you should use the vendor's pure Java driver, if available, because the JDBC-ODBC driver implementation is slower than a pure Java implementation. Pure Java drivers are known as Type IV. The JDBC specification defines two other driver types, Type II and Type III; however, they are less common. For additional details on driver types, see http://java.sun.com/products/jdbc/driverdesc.html.

In the initial examples in this chapter, we use the JDBC-ODBC bridge, included with JDK 1.4, to connect to a Microsoft Access database. In later examples we use pure Java drivers to connect to MySQL and Oracle9i databases.

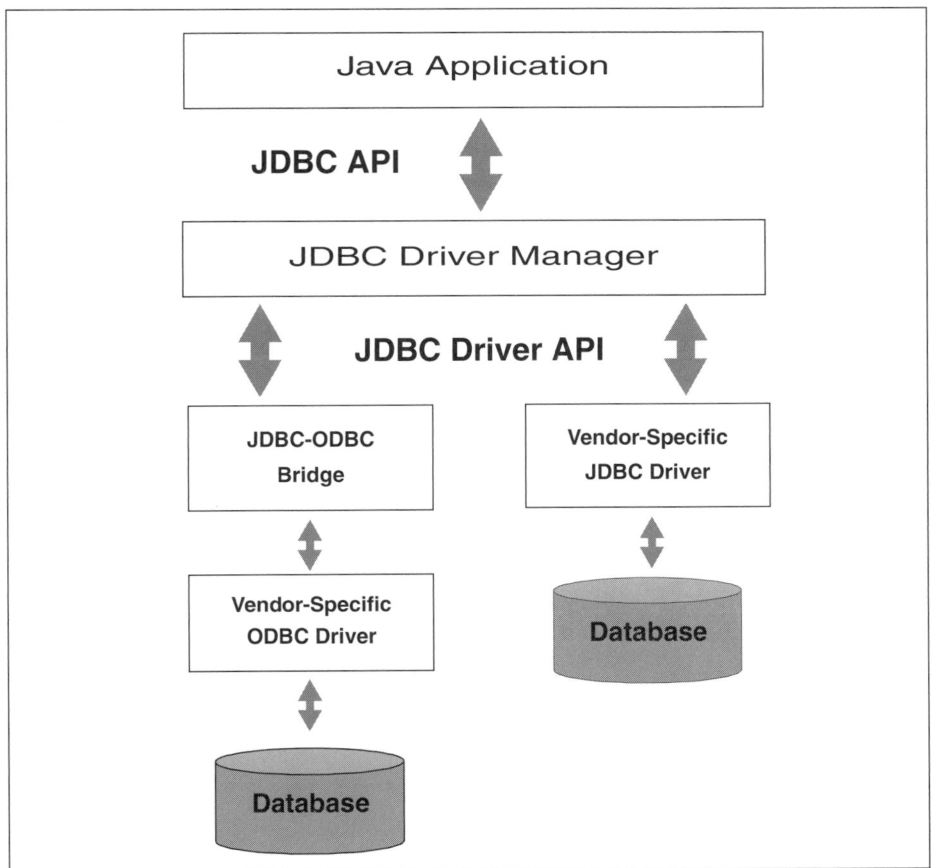

Figure 17–1 Two common JDBC driver implementations. JDK 1.4 includes a JDBC-ODBC bridge; however, a pure JDBC driver (provided by the vendor) yields better performance.

In Section 18.1 (Configuring Microsoft Access for Use with JDBC), we provide driver information for Microsoft Access. Driver information for MySQL is provided in Section 18.2 (Installing and Configuring MySQL), and driver information for Oracle is provided in Section 18.3 (Installing and Configuring Oracle9i Database). Most other database vendors supply free JDBC drivers for their databases. For an up-to-date list of these and third-party drivers, see http://industry.java.sun.com/products/jdbc/drivers/.

Define the Connection URL

Once you have loaded the JDBC driver, you must specify the location of the database server. URLs referring to databases use the `jdbc:` protocol and embed the server host, port, and database name (or reference) within the URL. The exact format is defined in the documentation that comes with the particular driver, but here are a few representative examples.

```
String host = "dbhost.yourcompany.com";
String dbName = "someName";
int port = 1234;
String oracleURL = "jdbc:oracle:thin:@" + host +
                   ":" + port + ":" + dbName;
String sybaseURL = "jdbc:sybase:Tds:" + host +
                   ":" + port + ":" + "?SERVICENAME=" + dbName;
String msAccessURL = "jdbc:odbc:" + dbName;
```

Establish the Connection

To make the actual network connection, pass the URL, database username, and database password to the `getConnection` method of the `DriverManager` class, as illustrated in the following example. Note that `getConnection` throws an `SQLException`, so you need to use a `try/catch` block. We're omitting this block from the following example since the methods in the following steps throw the same exception, and thus you typically use a single `try/catch` block for all of them.

```
String username = "jay_debesee";
String password = "secret";
Connection connection =
  DriverManager.getConnection(oracleURL, username, password);
```

The `Connection` class includes other useful methods, which we briefly describe below. The first three methods are covered in detail in Sections 17.4–17.6.

- **`prepareStatement.`** Creates precompiled queries for submission to the database. See Section 17.4 (Using Prepared Statements) for details.
- **`prepareCall.`** Accesses stored procedures in the database. For details, see Section 17.5 (Creating Callable Statements).
- **`rollback/commit.`** Controls transaction management. See Section 17.6 (Using Database Transactions) for details.
- **`close.`** Terminates the open connection.
- **`isClosed.`** Determines whether the connection timed out or was explicitly closed.

An optional part of establishing the connection is to look up information about the database with the `getMetaData` method. This method returns a `DatabaseMetaData` object that has methods with which you can discover the name and version of the database itself (`getDatabaseProductName`, `getDatabaseProductVersion`) or of the JDBC driver (`getDriverName`, `getDriverVersion`). Here is an example.

```
DatabaseMetaData dbMetaData = connection.getMetaData();
String productName =
  dbMetaData.getDatabaseProductName();
System.out.println("Database: " + productName);
String productVersion =
  dbMetaData.getDatabaseProductVersion();
System.out.println("Version: " + productVersion);
```

Create a Statement Object

A `Statement` object is used to send queries and commands to the database. It is created from the `Connection` using `createStatement` as follows.

```
Statement statement = connection.createStatement();
```

Most, but not all, database drivers permit multiple concurrent `Statement` objects to be open on the same connection.

Execute a Query or Update

Once you have a `Statement` object, you can use it to send SQL queries by using the `executeQuery` method, which returns an object of type `ResultSet`. Here is an example.

```
String query = "SELECT col1, col2, col3 FROM sometable";
ResultSet resultSet = statement.executeQuery(query);
```

The following list summarizes commonly used methods in the `Statement` class.

- **`executeQuery`.** Executes an SQL query and returns the data in a `ResultSet`. The `ResultSet` may be empty, but never `null`.
- **`executeUpdate`.** Used for `UPDATE`, `INSERT`, or `DELETE` commands. Returns the number of rows affected, which could be zero. Also provides support for Data Definition Language (DDL) commands, for example, `CREATE TABLE`, `DROP TABLE`, and `ALTER TABLE`.
- **`executeBatch`.** Executes a group of commands as a unit, returning an array with the update counts for each command. Use `addBatch` to add a command to the batch group. Note that vendors are not required to implement this method in their driver to be JDBC compliant.

- **`setQueryTimeout`.** Specifies the amount of time a driver waits for the result before throwing an `SQLException`.
- **`getMaxRows/setMaxRows`.** Determines the number of rows a `ResultSet` may contain. Excess rows are silently dropped. The default is zero for no limit.

In addition to using the methods described here to send arbitrary commands, you can use a `Statement` object to create parameterized queries by which values are supplied to a precompiled fixed-format query. See Section 17.4 (Using Prepared Statements) for details.

Process the Results

The simplest way to handle the results is to use the `next` method of `ResultSet` to move through the table a row at a time. Within a row, `ResultSet` provides various `get`*`Xxx`* methods that take a column name or column index as an argument and return the result in a variety of different Java types. For instance, use `getInt` if the value should be an integer, `getString` for a `String`, and so on for most other data types. If you just want to display the results, you can use `getString` for most of the column types. However, if you use the version of `get`*`Xxx`* that takes a column index (rather than a column name), note that columns are indexed starting at 1 (following the SQL convention), not at 0 as with arrays, vectors, and most other data structures in the Java programming language.

Core Warning

The first column in a `ResultSet` row has index 1, not 0.

Here is an example that prints the values of the first two columns and the first name and last name, for all rows of a `ResultSet`.

```
while(resultSet.next()) {
  System.out.println(resultSet.getString(1) + " " +
                     resultSet.getString(2) + " " +
                     resultSet.getString("firstname") + "  "
                     resultSet.getString("lastname"));
}
```

We suggest that when you access the columns of a `ResultSet`, you use the column name instead of the column index. That way, if the column structure of the table changes, the code interacting with the `ResultSet` will be less likely to fail.

Core Approach

Use the column name instead of the column index when accessing data in a `ResultSet`.

In JDBC 1.0, you can only move forward in the `ResultSet`; however, in JDBC 2.0, you can move forward (`next`) and backward (`previous`) in the `ResultSet` as well as move to a particular row (`relative`, `absolute`). In Volume 2 of this book, we present several custom tags that illustrate the JDBC 2.0 methods available in a `ResultSet`.

Be aware that neither JDBC 1.0 nor JDBC 2.0 provides a direct mechanism to determine the JDBC version of the driver. In JDBC 3.0, this problem is resolved by the addition of `getJDBCMajorVersion` and `getJDBCMinorVersion` methods to the `DatabaseMetaData` class. If the JDBC version is not clear from the vendor's documentation, you can write a short program to obtain a `ResultSet` and attempt a `previous` operation on the `ResultSet`. Since `resultSet.previous` is only available in JDBC 2.0 and later, a JDBC 1.0 driver would throw an exception at this point. See Section 18.4 (Testing Your Database Through a JDBC Connection) for an example program that performs a nonrigorous test to determine the JDBC version of your database driver.

The following list summarizes useful `ResultSet` methods.

- **`next/previous`.** Moves the cursor to the next (any JDBC version) or previous (JDBC version 2.0 or later) row in the `ResultSet`, respectively.
- **`relative/absolute`.** The `relative` method moves the cursor a relative number of rows, either positive (up) or negative (down). The `absolute` method moves the cursor to the given row number. If the absolute value is negative, the cursor is positioned relative to the end of the `ResultSet` (JDBC 2.0).
- **`get`*`Xxx`*.** Returns the value from the column specified by the column name or column index as an *Xxx* Java type (see `java.sql.Types`). Can return 0 or `null` if the value is an SQL `NULL`.
- **`wasNull`.** Checks whether the last `get`*`Xxx`* read was an SQL `NULL`. This check is important if the column type is a primitive (`int`, `float`, etc.) and the value in the database is 0. A zero value would be indistinguishable from a database value of `NULL`, which is also returned as a 0. If the column type is an object (`String`, `Date`, etc.), you can simply compare the return value to `null`.
- **`findColumn`.** Returns the index in the `ResultSet` corresponding to the specified column name.

- **`getRow`.** Returns the current row number, with the first row starting at 1 (JDBC 2.0).
- **`getMetaData`.** Returns a `ResultSetMetaData` object describing the `ResultSet`. `ResultSetMetaData` gives the number of columns and the column names.

The `getMetaData` method is particularly useful. Given only a `ResultSet`, you have to know the name, number, and type of the columns to be able to process the table properly. For most fixed-format queries, this is a reasonable expectation. For ad hoc queries, however, it is useful to be able to dynamically discover high-level information about the result. That is the role of the `ResultSetMetaData` class: it lets you determine the number, names, and types of the columns in the `ResultSet`.

Useful `ResultSetMetaData` methods are described below.

- **`getColumnCount`.** Returns the number of columns in the `ResultSet`.
- **`getColumnName`.** Returns the database name of a column (indexed starting at 1).
- **`getColumnType`.** Returns the SQL type, to compare with entries in `java.sql.Types`.
- **`isReadOnly`.** Indicates whether the entry is a read-only value.
- **`isSearchable`.** Indicates whether the column can be used in a `WHERE` clause.
- **`isNullable`.** Indicates whether storing `NULL` is legal for the column.

`ResultSetMetaData` does *not* include information about the number of rows; however, if your driver complies with JDBC 2.0, you can call `last` on the `ResultSet` to move the cursor to the last row and then call `getRow` to retrieve the current row number. In JDBC 1.0, the only way to determine the number of rows is to repeatedly call `next` on the `ResultSet` until it returns `false`.

Core Note

`ResultSet` and `ResultSetMetaData` do not directly provide a method to return the number of rows returned from a query. However, in JDBC 2.0, you can position the cursor at the last row in the `ResultSet` by calling `last`, and then obtain the current row number by calling `getRow`.

Close the Connection

To close the connection explicitly, you would do:

```
connection.close();
```

Closing the connection also closes the corresponding `Statement` and `ResultSet` objects.

You should postpone closing the connection if you expect to perform additional database operations, since the overhead of opening a connection is usually large. In fact, reusing existing connections is such an important optimization that the JDBC 2.0 API defines a `ConnectionPoolDataSource` interface for obtaining pooled connections. Pooled connections are discussed in Volume 2 of this book.

17.2 Basic JDBC Examples

In this section, we present two simple JDBC examples that connect to the Microsoft Access Northwind database (shown in Figure 17–2) and perform a simple query. The Northwind database is included in the samples section of Microsoft Office. To configure the Northwind database for access from JDBC, see Section 18.1.

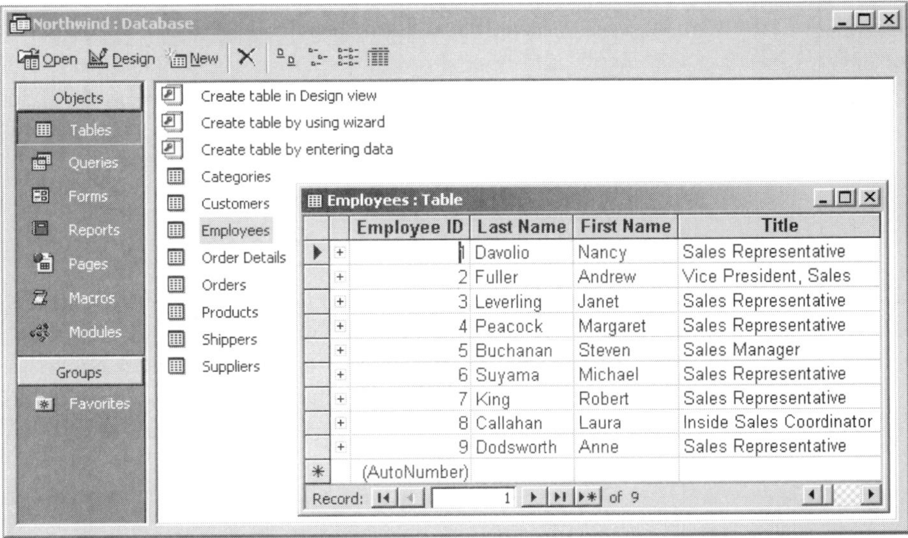

Figure 17–2 Microsoft Access Northwind sample database showing the first four columns of the Employees table. See Section 18.1 for information on using this database.

Northwind is a good database for testing and experimentation since it is already installed on many systems and since the JDBC-ODBC bridge for connecting to Microsoft Access is already bundled in the JDK. However, Microsoft Access is not intended for serious online databases. For production purposes, a higher-performance option like MySQL (see Section 18.2), Oracle9i (see Section 18.3), Microsoft SQL Server, Sybase, or DB2 is far better.

The first example, Listing 17.1, presents a standalone class called `NorthwindTest` that follows the seven steps outlined in the previous section to display the results of querying the `Employee` table.

The results for the `NorthwindTest` are shown in Listing 17.2. Since `NorthwindTest` is in the `coreservlets` package, it resides in a subdirectory called **coreservlets**. Before compiling the file, set the `CLASSPATH` to include the directory *containing* the **coreservlets** directory. See Section 2.7 (Set Up Your Development Environment) for details. With this setup, simply compile the program by running `javac NorthwindTest.java` from within the **coreservlets** subdirectory (or by selecting "build" or "compile" in your IDE). To run `NorthwindTest`, you need to refer to the full package name with `java` **`coreservlets.`**`NorthwindTest`.

The second example, Listing 17.3 (`NorthwindServlet`), connects to the database from a servlet and presents the query results as an HTML table. Both Listing 17.1 and Listing 17.3 use the JDBC-ODBC bridge driver, `sun.jdbc.odbc.JdbcOdbcDriver`, included with the JDK.

Listing 17.1 NorthwindTest.java

```
package coreservlets;

import java.sql.*;

/** A JDBC example that connects to the MicroSoft Access sample
 *  Northwind database, issues a simple SQL query to the
 *  employee table, and prints the results.
 */

public class NorthwindTest {
  public static void main(String[] args) {
    String driver = "sun.jdbc.odbc.JdbcOdbcDriver";
    String url = "jdbc:odbc:Northwind";
    String username = ""; // No username/password required
    String password = ""; // for desktop access to MS Access.
    showEmployeeTable(driver, url, username, password);
  }

  /** Query the employee table and print the first and
   *  last names.
   */
```

Listing 17.1 NorthwindTest.java *(continued)*

```
  public static void showEmployeeTable(String driver,
                                       String url,
                                       String username,
                                       String password) {
    try {
      // Load database driver if it's not already loaded.
      Class.forName(driver);
      // Establish network connection to database.
      Connection connection =
        DriverManager.getConnection(url, username, password);
      System.out.println("Employees\n" + "==========");
      // Create a statement for executing queries.
      Statement statement = connection.createStatement();
      String query =
        "SELECT firstname, lastname FROM employees";
      // Send query to database and store results.
      ResultSet resultSet = statement.executeQuery(query);
      // Print results.
      while(resultSet.next()) {
        System.out.print(resultSet.getString("firstname") + " ");
        System.out.println(resultSet.getString("lastname"));
      }
      connection.close();
    } catch(ClassNotFoundException cnfe) {
      System.err.println("Error loading driver: " + cnfe);
    } catch(SQLException sqle) {
      System.err.println("Error with connection: " + sqle);
    }
  }
}
```

Listing 17.2 NorthwindTest Result

```
Prompt> java coreservlets.NorthwindTest

Employees
==========
Nancy Davolio
Andrew Fuller
Janet Leverling
Margaret Peacock
Steven Buchanan
Michael Suyama
Robert King
Laura Callahan
Anne Dodsworth
```

For the second example, `NorthwindServlet` (Listing 17.3), the information for performing the query is taken from an HTML form, NorthwindForm.html, shown in Listing 17.4. Here, you can enter the query into the form text area before submitting the form to the servlet. The servlet reads the driver, URL, username, password, and the query from the request parameters and generates an HTML table based on the query results. The servlet also demonstrates the use of `DatabaseMetaData` to look up the product name and product version of the database. The HTML form is shown in Figure 17–3; Figure 17–4 shows the result of submitting the form. For this example, the HTML form and servlet are located in the Web application named `jdbc`. For more information on creating and using Web applications, see Section 2.11.

Listing 17.3 NorthwindServlet.java

```
package coreservlets;

import java.io.*;
import java.sql.*;
import javax.servlet.*;
import javax.servlet.http.*;

/** A simple servlet that connects to a database and
 *  presents the results from the query in an HTML
 *  table. The driver, URL, username, password,
 *  and query are taken from form input parameters.
 */

public class NorthwindServlet extends HttpServlet {
  public void doPost(HttpServletRequest request,
                     HttpServletResponse response)
      throws ServletException, IOException {
    response.setContentType("text/html");
    PrintWriter out = response.getWriter();
    String docType =
      "<!DOCTYPE HTML PUBLIC \"-//W3C//DTD HTML 4.0 " +
      "Transitional//EN\"\n";
    String title = "Northwind Results";
    out.print(docType +
              "<HTML>\n" +
              "<HEAD><TITLE>" + title + "</TITLE></HEAD>\n" +
              "<BODY BGCOLOR=\"#FDF5E6\"><CENTER>\n" +
              "<H1>Database Results</H1>\n");
    String driver = request.getParameter("driver");
    String url = request.getParameter("url");
    String username = request.getParameter("username");
```

Listing 17.3 NorthwindServlet.java *(continued)*

```
    String password = request.getParameter("password");
    String query = request.getParameter("query");
    showTable(driver, url, username, password, query, out);
    out.println("</CENTER></BODY></HTML>");
  }

  public void showTable(String driver, String url,
                        String username, String password,
                        String query, PrintWriter out) {
    try {
      // Load database driver if it's not already loaded.
      Class.forName(driver);
      // Establish network connection to database.
      Connection connection =
        DriverManager.getConnection(url, username, password);
      // Look up info about the database as a whole.
      DatabaseMetaData dbMetaData = connection.getMetaData();
      out.println("<UL>");
      String productName =
        dbMetaData.getDatabaseProductName();
      String productVersion =
        dbMetaData.getDatabaseProductVersion();
      out.println("  <LI><B>Database:</B> " + productName +
                  "  <LI><B>Version:</B> " + productVersion +
                  "</UL>");
      Statement statement = connection.createStatement();
      // Send query to database and store results.
      ResultSet resultSet = statement.executeQuery(query);
      // Print results.
      out.println("<TABLE BORDER=1>");
      ResultSetMetaData resultSetMetaData =
        resultSet.getMetaData();
      int columnCount = resultSetMetaData.getColumnCount();
      out.println("<TR>");
      // Column index starts at 1 (a la SQL), not 0 (a la Java).
      for(int i=1; i <= columnCount; i++) {
        out.print("<TH>" + resultSetMetaData.getColumnName(i));
      }
      out.println();
      // Step through each row in the result set.
      while(resultSet.next()) {
        out.println("<TR>");
```

Listing 17.3 NorthwindServlet.java *(continued)*

```
        // Step across the row, retrieving the data in each
        // column cell as a String.
        for(int i=1; i <= columnCount; i++) {
          out.print("<TD>" + resultSet.getString(i));
        }
        out.println();
      }
      out.println("</TABLE>");
      connection.close();
    } catch(ClassNotFoundException cnfe) {
      System.err.println("Error loading driver: " + cnfe);
    } catch(SQLException sqle) {
      System.err.println("Error connecting: " + sqle);
    } catch(Exception ex) {
      System.err.println("Error with input: " + ex);
    }
  }
}
```

Listing 17.4 NorthwindForm.html

```
<!DOCTYPE HTML PUBLIC "-//W3C//DTD HTML 4.0 Transitional//EN">
<HTML>
<HEAD>
<TITLE>Simple Query Form</TITLE>
<LINK REL=STYLESHEET
      HREF="JSP-Styles.css"
      TYPE="text/css">
</HEAD>
<BODY>
<H2>Query Input:</H2>
<FORM ACTION="/jdbc/servlet/coreservlets.NorthwindServlet"
      METHOD="POST">
<TABLE>
  <TR><TD>Driver:
      <TD><INPUT TYPE="TEXT" NAME="driver"
                 VALUE="sun.jdbc.odbc.JdbcOdbcDriver" SIZE="35">
  <TR><TD>URL:
      <TD><INPUT TYPE="TEXT" NAME="url"
                 VALUE="jdbc:odbc:Northwind" SIZE="35">
  <TR><TD>Username:
      <TD><INPUT TYPE="TEXT" NAME="username">
```

Listing 17.4 NorthwindForm.html *(continued)*

```
  <TR><TD>Password:
      <TD><INPUT TYPE="PASSWORD" NAME="password">
  <TR><TD VALIGN="TOP">Query:
      <TD><TEXTAREA ROWS="5" COLS="35" NAME="query"></TEXTAREA>
  <TR><TD COLSPAN="2" ALIGN="CENTER"><INPUT TYPE="SUBMIT">
</TABLE>
</FORM>
</BODY></HTML>
```

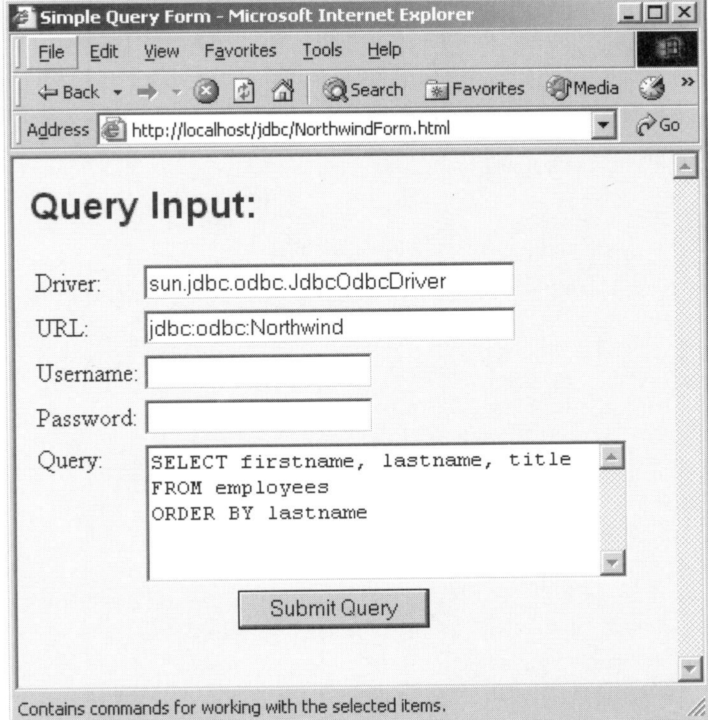

Figure 17–3 NorthwindForm.html: front end to servlet that queries the Northwind database.

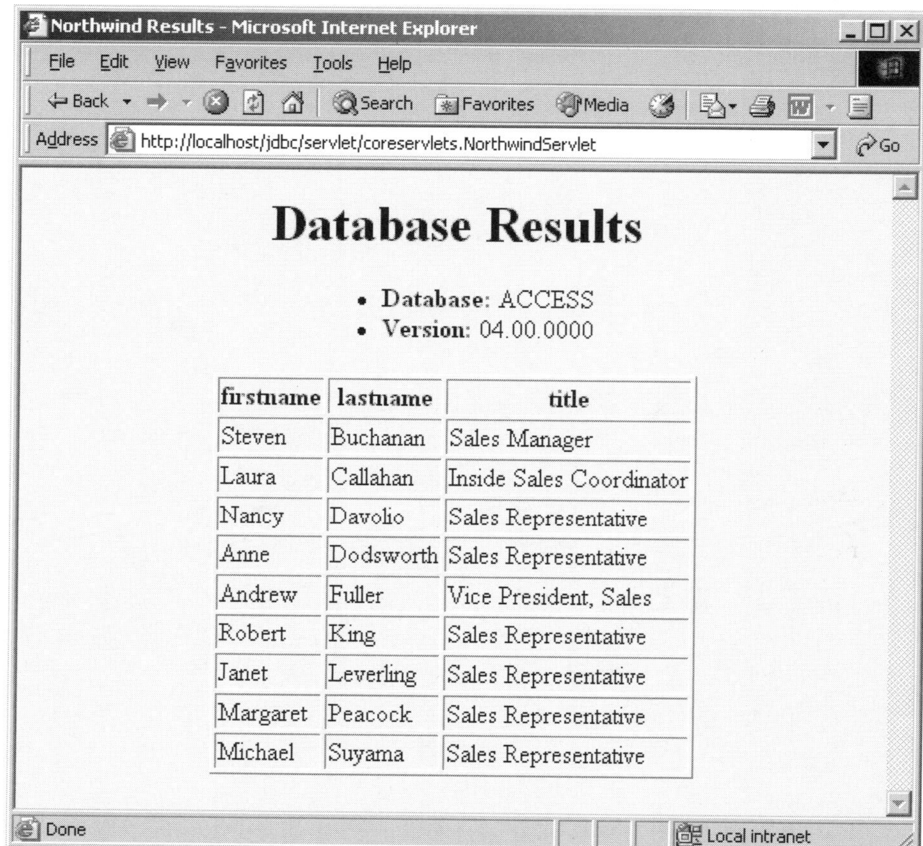

Figure 17–4 Result of querying the Northwind database.

In the preceding example, the HTML table was generated from the query results within a servlet. In Volume 2 of this book, we present various custom tags to generate the HTML table from the query results in the JSP page itself. Furthermore, if your development model favors JSP, the JSP Standard Tag Library (JSTL) provides an `sql:query` action to query a database and store the query result in a scoped variable for processing on the JSP page. JSTL is also covered in Volume 2 of this book.

17.3 Simplifying Database Access with JDBC Utilities

In this section, we present a couple of helper classes that are used throughout this chapter to simplify coding. These classes provide basic functionality for loading drivers and making database connections.

For example, the `DriverUtilities` class (Listing 17.5) simplifies the building of a URL to connect to a database. To build a URL for MySQL, which is in the form

```
String url = "jdbc:mysql://host:3306/dbname";
```

you first need to load the vendor data by calling `loadDrivers`. Then, call `makeURL` to build the URL, as in

```
DriverUtilities.loadDrivers();
String url =
  DriverUtilities.makeURL(host, dbname, DriverUtilities.MYSQL);
```

where the host, database name, and vendor are dynamically specified as arguments. In this manner, the database URL does not need to be hard-coded in the examples throughout this chapter. More importantly, you can simply add information about your database to the `loadDrivers` method in `DriverUtilities` (and a constant to refer to your driver, if desired). Afterwards, the examples throughout this chapter should work for your environment.

As another example, the `ConnectionInfoBean` class (Listing 17.9) provides a utility method, `getConnection`, for obtaining a `Connection` to a database. Thus, to obtain a connection to the database, replace

```
Connection connection = null;
try {
  Class.forName(driver);
  connection = DriverManager.getConnection(url, username,
                                           password);
} catch(ClassNotFoundException cnfe) {
  System.err.println("Error loading driver: " + cnfe);
} catch(SQLException sqle) {
  System.err.println("Error connecting: " + sqle);
}
```

with

```
Connection connection =
  ConnectionInfoBean.getConnection(driver, url,
                                   username, password);
```

If an `SQLException` occurs while the connection is being acquired, `null` is returned.

We define four utility classes in this section.

1. **`DriverUtilities`**
   This class, shown in Listing 17.5, loads explicitly coded driver information about various database vendors. It then provides methods for obtaining the driver class for a vendor (`getDriver`) and creating a URL (`makeURL`), given the host, database name, and vendor. We provide driver information for Microsoft Access, MySQL, and Oracle databases, but you can easily update the class for your environment.
2. **`DriverUtilities2`**
   This class, shown in Listing 17.6, extends `DriverUtilities` (Listing 17.5) and overrides `loadDrivers` to obtain the driver information from an XML file. A representative XML file is shown in drivers.xml, Listing 17.7.
3. **`DriverInfoBean`**
   The `DriverInfoBean` class, shown in Listing 17.8, encapsulates driver information for a specific vendor (used by `DriverUtilities`, Listing 17.5). The bean contains a keyword (vendor name), a brief description of the driver, the driver classname, and a URL for connecting to a database.
4. **`ConnectionInfoBean`**
   This class, shown in Listing 17.9, encapsulates information for connection to a *particular* database. The bean encapsulates a name for the connection, a brief description of the connection, the driver class, the URL to connect to the database, the username, and the password. In addition, the bean provides a `getConnection` method to directly obtain a `Connection` to a database.

Listing 17.5 DriverUtilities.java

```
package coreservlets;

import java.io.*;
import java.sql.*;
import java.util.*;
import coreservlets.beans.*;
```

Listing 17.5 DriverUtilities.java *(continued)*

```
/** Some simple utilities for building JDBC connections to
 *  databases from different vendors. The drivers loaded are
 *  hard-coded and specific to our local setup. You can
 *  either modify the loadDrivers method and recompile or
 *  use <CODE>DriverUtilities2</CODE> to load the driver
 *  information for each vendor from an XML file.
 */

public class DriverUtilities {
  public static final String MSACCESS = "MSACCESS";
  public static final String MYSQL = "MYSQL";
  public static final String ORACLE = "ORACLE";

  // Add constant to refer to your database here ...

  protected static Map driverMap = new HashMap();

  /** Load vendor driver information. Here we have hard-coded
   *  driver information specific to our local setup.
   *  Modify the values according to your setup.
   *  Alternatively, you can use <CODE>DriverUtilities2</CODE>
   *  to load driver information from an XML file.
   *  <P>
   *  Each vendor is represented by a
   *  <CODE>DriverInfoBean</CODE> that defines a vendor
   *  name (keyword), description, driver class, and URL. The
   *  bean is stored in a driver map; the vendor name is
   *  used as the keyword to retrieve the information.
   *  <P>
   *  The url variable should contain the placeholders
   *  [$host] and [$dbName] to substitute for the <I>host</I>
   *  and <I>database name</I> in <CODE>makeURL</CODE>.
   */

  public static void loadDrivers() {
    String vendor, description, driverClass, url;
    DriverInfoBean info = null;

    // MSAccess
    vendor = MSACCESS;
    description = "MS Access 4.0";
    driverClass = "sun.jdbc.odbc.JdbcOdbcDriver";
    url = "jdbc:odbc:[$dbName]";
    info = new DriverInfoBean(vendor, description,
                              driverClass, url);
    addDriverInfoBean(info);
```

Listing 17.5 DriverUtilities.java *(continued)*

```
    // MySQL
    vendor = MYSQL;
    description = "MySQL Connector/J 3.0";
    driverClass = "com.mysql.jdbc.Driver";
    url = "jdbc:mysql://[$host]:3306/[$dbName]";
    info = new DriverInfoBean(vendor, description,
                              driverClass, url);
    addDriverInfoBean(info);

    // Oracle
    vendor = ORACLE;
    description = "Oracle9i Database";
    driverClass = "oracle.jdbc.driver.OracleDriver";
    url = "jdbc:oracle:thin:@[$host]:1521:[$dbName]";
    info = new DriverInfoBean(vendor, description,
                              driverClass, url);
    addDriverInfoBean(info);

    // Add info on your database here...
  }

  /** Add information (<CODE>DriverInfoBean</CODE>) about new
   *  vendor to the map of available drivers.
   */

  public static void addDriverInfoBean(DriverInfoBean info) {
    driverMap.put(info.getVendor().toUpperCase(), info);
  }

  /** Determine if vendor is represented in the loaded
   *  driver information.
   */

  public static boolean isValidVendor(String vendor) {
    DriverInfoBean info =
      (DriverInfoBean)driverMap.get(vendor.toUpperCase());
    return(info != null);
  }

  /** Build a URL in the format needed by the
   *  database drivers. In building of the final URL, the
   *  keywords [$host] and [$dbName] in the URL
   *  (looked up from the vendor's <CODE>DriverInfoBean</CODE>)
   *  are appropriately substituted by the host and dbName
   *  method arguments.
   */
```

Listing 17.5 DriverUtilities.java *(continued)*

```
  public static String makeURL(String host, String dbName,
                               String vendor) {
    DriverInfoBean info =
      (DriverInfoBean)driverMap.get(vendor.toUpperCase());
    if (info == null) {
      return(null);
    }
    StringBuffer url = new StringBuffer(info.getURL());
    DriverUtilities.replace(url, "[$host]", host);
    DriverUtilities.replace(url, "[$dbName]", dbName);
    return(url.toString());
  }

  /** Get the fully qualified name of a driver. */

  public static String getDriver(String vendor) {
    DriverInfoBean info =
      (DriverInfoBean)driverMap.get(vendor.toUpperCase());
    if (info == null) {
      return(null);
    } else {
      return(info.getDriverClass());
    }
  }

  /** Perform a string substitution, where the first "match"
   *  is replaced by the new "value".
   */

  private static void replace(StringBuffer buffer,
                              String match, String value) {
    int index = buffer.toString().indexOf(match);
    if (index > 0) {
      buffer.replace(index, index + match.length(), value);
    }
  }
}
```

In `DriverUtilities`, driver information for each vendor (Microsoft Access, MySQL, and Oracle9i) is explicitly coded into the program. If you are using a different database, you will need to modify `DriverUtilities` to include your driver information and then recompile the code. Since this approach may not be convenient, we include a second program, `DriverUtilities2` in Listing 17.6, that reads the driver information from an XML file. Then, to add a new database vendor to your program, you simply edit the XML file. An example XML file, drivers.xml, is given in Listing 17.7

When using `DriverUtilites2` in a command-line application, place the driver file, drivers.xml, in the working directory from which you started the application. Afterwards, call `loadDrivers` with the complete filename (including path).

For a Web application, we recommend placing drivers.xml in the WEB-INF directory. You may want to specify the filename as a context initialization parameter in web.xml (for details, see the chapter on web.xml in Volume 2 of this book). Also, remember that from the servlet context you can use `getRealPath` to determine the physical path to a file relative to the Web application directory, as shown in the following code fragment.

```
ServletContext context = getServletContext();
String path = context.getRealPath("/WEB-INF/drivers.xml");
```

JDK 1.4 includes all the necessary classes to parse the XML document, drivers.xml. If you are using JDK 1.3 or earlier, you will need to download and install a SAX and DOM parser. Xerces-J by Apache is an excellent parser and is available at http://xml.apache.org/xerces2-j/. Most Web application servers are already bundled with an XML parser, so you may not need to download Xerces-J. Check the vendor's documentation to determine where the parser files are located and include them in your `CLASSPATH` for compiling your application. For example, Tomcat 4.x includes the parser JAR files (xercesImpl.jar and xmlParserAPI.jar) in the *install_dir*/common/endorsed directory.

Note that if you are using servlets 2.4 (JSP 2.0) in a fully J2EE-1.4-compatible server, you are guaranteed to have JDK 1.4 or later.

Listing 17.6 DriverUtilities2.java

```
package coreservlets;

import java.io.*;
import java.util.*;
import javax.xml.parsers.*;
import org.w3c.dom.*;
import org.xml.sax.*;
import coreservlets.beans.*;

/** Extends <CODE>DriverUtilities</CODE> to support the
 *  loading of driver information for different database vendors
 *  from an XML file (default is drivers.xml). Both DOM and
 *  JAXP are used to read the XML file.  The format for the
 *  XML file is:
```

Listing 17.6 DriverUtilities2.java *(continued)*

```
 *  <P>
 *  <PRE>
 *    &lt;drivers&gt;
 *      &lt;driver&gt;
 *        &lt;vendor&gt;ORACLE&lt;/vendor&gt;
 *        &lt;description&gt;Oracle&lt;/description&gt;
 *        &lt;driver-class&gt;
 *          oracle.jdbc.driver.OracleDriver
 *        &lt;/driver-class&gt;
 *        &lt;url&gt;
 *          jdbc:oracle:thin:@[$host]:1521:[$dbName]
 *        &lt;/url&gt;
 *      &lt;/driver&gt;
 *      ...
 *    &lt;drivers&gt;
 *  </PRE>
 *  <P>
 *  The url element should contain the placeholders
 *  [$host] and [$dbName] to substitute for the host and
 *  database name in makeURL.
 */

public class DriverUtilities2 extends DriverUtilities {
  public static final String DEFAULT_FILE = "drivers.xml";

  /** Load driver information from default XML file,
   *  drivers.xml.
   */

  public static void loadDrivers() {
    DriverUtilities2.loadDrivers(DEFAULT_FILE);
  }

  /** Load driver information from specified XML file. Each
   *  vendor is represented by a <CODE>DriverInfoBean</CODE>
   *  object and stored in the map, with the vendor name as
   *  the key. Use this method if you need to load a
   *  driver file other than the default, drivers.xml.
   */

  public static void loadDrivers(String filename) {
    File file = new File(filename);
    try {
      InputStream in = new FileInputStream(file);
      DocumentBuilderFactory builderFactory =
        DocumentBuilderFactory.newInstance();
```

Listing 17.6 DriverUtilities2.java *(continued)*

```
      DocumentBuilder builder =
        builderFactory.newDocumentBuilder();
      Document document = builder.parse(in);
      document.getDocumentElement().normalize();
      Element rootElement = document.getDocumentElement();
      NodeList driverElements =
        rootElement.getElementsByTagName("driver");
      // Build DriverInfoBean for each vendor
      for(int i=0; i<driverElements.getLength(); i++) {
        Node node = driverElements.item(i);
        DriverInfoBean info =
          DriverUtilities2.createDriverInfoBean(node);
        if (info != null) {
          addDriverInfoBean(info);
        }
      }
    } catch(FileNotFoundException fnfe) {
      System.err.println("Can't find " + filename);
    } catch(IOException ioe) {
      System.err.println("Problem reading file: " + ioe);
    } catch(ParserConfigurationException pce) {
      System.err.println("Can't create DocumentBuilder");
    } catch(SAXException se) {
      System.err.println("Problem parsing document: " + se);
    }
  }

  /** Build a DriverInfoBean object from an XML DOM node
   *  representing a vendor driver in the format:
   *  <P>
   *  <PRE>
   *    &lt;driver&gt;
   *      &lt;vendor&gt;ORACLE&lt;/vendor&gt;
   *      &lt;description&gt;Oracle&lt;/description&gt;
   *      &lt;driver-class&gt;
   *         oracle.jdbc.driver.OracleDriver
   *      &lt;/driver-class&gt;
   *      &lt;url&gt;
   *        jdbc:oracle:thin:@[$host]:1521:[$dbName]
   *      &lt;/url&gt;
   *    &lt;/driver&gt;
   *  </PRE>
   */
```

Listing 17.6 DriverUtilities2.java *(continued)*

```
  public static DriverInfoBean createDriverInfoBean(Node node) {
    Map map = new HashMap();
    NodeList children = node.getChildNodes();
    for(int i=0; i<children.getLength(); i++) {
      Node child = children.item(i);
      String nodeName = child.getNodeName();
      if (child instanceof Element) {
        Node textNode = child.getChildNodes().item(0);
        if (textNode != null) {
          map.put(nodeName, textNode.getNodeValue());
        }
      }
    }
    return(new DriverInfoBean((String)map.get("vendor"),
                              (String)map.get("description"),
                              (String)map.get("driver-class"),
                              (String)map.get("url")));
  }
}
```

Listing 17.7 drivers.xml

```
<?xml version="1.0"?>
<!--
Used by DriverUtilities2. Here you configure information
about your database server in XML. To add a driver, include
a vendor keyword, description, driver-class, and URL.
For general use, the host and database name should not
be included in the URL; a special notation is required
for the host and database name. Use [$host] as a
placeholder for the host server and [$dbName] as a placeholder
for the database name. Specify the actual host and database name
when making a call to makeUrl (DriverUtilities). Then, the
appropriate strings will be substituted for [$host]
and [$dbName] before the URL is returned.
-->
<drivers>
  <driver>
    <vendor>MSACCESS</vendor>
    <description>MS Access</description>
    <driver-class>sun.jdbc.odbc.JdbcOdbcDriver</driver-class>
    <url>jdbc:odbc:[$dbName]</url>
  </driver>
```

Listing 17.7 drivers.xml *(continued)*

```
  <driver>
    <vendor>MYSQL</vendor>
    <description>MySQL Connector/J 3.0</description>
    <driver-class>com.mysql.jdbc.Driver</driver-class>
    <url>jdbc:mysql://[$host]:3306/[$dbName]</url>
  </driver>
  <driver>
    <vendor>ORACLE</vendor>
    <description>Oracle</description>
    <driver-class>oracle.jdbc.driver.OracleDriver</driver-class>
    <url>jdbc:oracle:thin:@[$host]:1521:[$dbName]</url>
  </driver>
</drivers>
```

Listing 17.8 DriverInfoBean.java

```
package coreservlets.beans;

/** Driver information for a vendor.  Defines the vendor
 *  keyword, description, driver class, and URL construct for
 *  connecting to a database.
 */

public class DriverInfoBean {
  private String vendor;
  private String description;
  private String driverClass;
  private String url;

public class DriverInfoBean {
  private String vendor;
  private String description;
  private String driverClass;
  private String url;

  public DriverInfoBean(String vendor,
                        String description,
                        String driverClass,
                        String url) {
    this.vendor = vendor;
    this.description = description;
    this.driverClass = driverClass;
    this.url = url;
  }
```

Listing 17.8 DriverInfoBean.java *(continued)*

```
  public String getVendor() {
    return(vendor);
  }

  public String getDescription() {
    return(description);
  }

  public String getDriverClass() {
    return(driverClass);
  }

  public String getURL() {
    return(url);
  }
}
```

Listing 17.9 ConnectionInfoBean.java

```
package coreservlets.beans;

import java.sql.*;

/** Stores information to create a JDBC connection to
 *  a database. Information includes:
 *  <UL>
 *     <LI>connection name
 *     <LI>description of the connection
 *     <LI>driver classname
 *     <LI>URL to connect to the host
 *     <LI>username
 *     <LI>password
 *  </UL>
 */

public class ConnectionInfoBean {
  private String connectionName;
  private String description;
  private String driver;
  private String url;
  private String username;
  private String password;
```

Listing 17.9 ConnectionInfoBean.java *(continued)*

```
  public ConnectionInfoBean() { }

  public ConnectionInfoBean(String connectionName,
                            String description,
                            String driver,
                            String url,
                            String username,
                            String password) {
    setConnectionName(connectionName);
    setDescription(description);
    setDriver(driver);
    setURL(url);
    setUsername(username);
    setPassword(password);
  }

  public void setConnectionName(String connectionName) {
    this.connectionName = connectionName;
  }

  public String getConnectionName() {
    return(connectionName);
  }

  public void setDescription(String description) {
    this.description = description;
  }

  public String getDescription() {
    return(description);
  }

  public void setDriver(String driver) {
    this.driver = driver;
  }

  public String getDriver() {
    return(driver);
  }

  public void setURL(String url) {
    this.url = url;
  }

  public String getURL() {
    return(url);
  }
```

Listing 17.9 ConnectionInfoBean.java *(continued)*

```
  public void setUsername(String username) {
    this.username = username;
  }

  public String getUsername() {
    return(username);
  }

  public void setPassword(String password) {
    this.password = password;
  }

  public String getPassword() {
    return(password);
  }

  public Connection getConnection() {
    return(getConnection(driver, url, username, password));

  }

  /** Create a JDBC connection or return null if a
   *  problem occurs.
   */

  public static Connection getConnection(String driver,
                                         String url,
                                         String username,
                                         String password) {

    try {
      Class.forName(driver);
      Connection connection =
        DriverManager.getConnection(url, username,
                                    password);
      return(connection);
    } catch(ClassNotFoundException cnfe) {
      System.err.println("Error loading driver: " + cnfe);
      return(null);
    } catch(SQLException sqle) {
      System.err.println("Error connecting: " + sqle);
      return(null);
    }
  }
}
```

17.4 Using Prepared Statements

If you are going to execute similar SQL statements multiple times, using parameterized (or "prepared") statements can be more efficient than executing a raw query each time. The idea is to create a parameterized statement in a standard form that is sent to the database for compilation before actually being used. You use a question mark to indicate the places where a value will be substituted into the statement. Each time you use the prepared statement, you simply replace the marked parameters, using a `setXxx` call corresponding to the entry you want to set (using 1-based indexing) and the type of the parameter (e.g., `setInt`, `setString`). You then use `executeQuery` (if you want a `ResultSet` back) or `execute`/`executeUpdate` to modify table data, as with normal statements.

For instance, in Section 18.5, we create a `music` table summarizing the price and availability of concerto recordings for various classical composers. Suppose, for an upcoming sale, you want to change the price of all the recordings in the `music` table. You might do something like the following.

```
Connection connection =
  DriverManager.getConnection(url, username, password);
String template =
  "UPDATE music SET price = ? WHERE id = ?";
PreparedStatement statement =
  connection.prepareStatement(template);
float[] newPrices = getNewPrices();
int[] recordingIDs = getIDs();
for(int i=0; i<recordingIDs.length; i++) {
  statement.setFloat(1, newPrices[i]);  // Price
  statement.setInt(2, recordingIDs[i]); // ID
  statement.execute();
}
```

The performance advantages of prepared statements can vary significantly, depending on how well the server supports precompiled queries and how efficiently the driver handles raw queries. For example, Listing 17.10 presents a class that sends 100 different queries to a database, using prepared statements, then repeats the same 100 queries, using regular statements. On one hand, with a PC and fast LAN connection (100 Mbps) to an Oracle9i database, prepared statements took only about 62 percent of the time required by raw queries, averaging 0.61 seconds for the 100 queries as compared with an average of 0.99 seconds for the regular statements (average of 5 runs). On the other hand, with MySQL (Connector/J 3.0) the prepared statement times were nearly identical to the raw queries with a fast LAN connection, with only about an 8 percent reduction in query time. To get performance numbers for your setup, download DriverUtilities.java from http://www.coreservlets.com/, add information about your drivers to it, then run the `PreparedStatements` program yourself. To create the `music` table, see Section 18.5.

Be cautious though: a prepared statement does not always execute faster than an ordinary SQL statement. The performance improvement can depend on the particular SQL command you are executing. For a more detailed analysis of the performance for prepared statements in Oracle, see http://www.oreilly.com/catalog/jorajdbc/chapter/ch19.html.

However, performance is not the only advantage of a prepared statement. Security is another advantage. We recommend that you always use a prepared statement or stored procedure (see Section 17.5) to update database values when accepting input from a user through an HTML form. This approach is strongly recommended over the approach of building an SQL statement by concatenating strings from the user input values. Otherwise, a clever attacker could submit form values that look like portions of SQL statements, and once those were executed, the attacker could inappropriately access or modify the database. This security risk is often referred to as an SQL Injection Attack. In addition to removing the risk of a such an attack, a prepared statement will properly handle embedded quotes in strings and handle noncharacter data (e.g., sending a serialized object to a database).

Core Approach

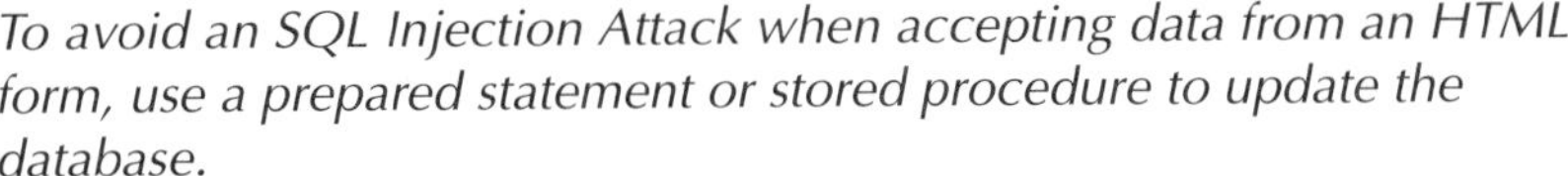

To avoid an SQL Injection Attack when accepting data from an HTML form, use a prepared statement or stored procedure to update the database.

Listing 17.10 PreparedStatements.java

```
package coreservlets;

import java.sql.*;
import coreservlets.beans.*;

/** An example to test the timing differences resulting
 *  from repeated raw queries vs. repeated calls to
 *  prepared statements. These results will vary dramatically
 *  among database servers and drivers. With our setup
 *  and drivers, Oracle9i prepared statements took only 62% of
 *  the time that raw queries required, whereas MySQL
 *  prepared statements took nearly the same time as
 *  raw queries, with only an 8% improvement.
 */
```

Listing 17.10 PreparedStatements.java *(continued)*

```
public class PreparedStatements {
  public static void main(String[] args) {
    if (args.length < 5) {
      printUsage();
      return;
    }
    String vendor = args[4];
    // Use DriverUtilities2.loadDrivers() to load
    // the drivers from an XML file.
    DriverUtilities.loadDrivers();
    if (!DriverUtilities.isValidVendor(vendor)) {
      printUsage();
      return;
    }
    String driver = DriverUtilities.getDriver(vendor);
    String host = args[0];
    String dbName = args[1];
    String url =
      DriverUtilities.makeURL(host, dbName, vendor);
    String username = args[2];
    String password = args[3];
    // Use "print" only to confirm it works properly,
    // not when getting timing results.
    boolean print = false;
    if ((args.length > 5) && (args[5].equals("print"))) {
      print = true;
    }
    Connection connection =
      ConnectionInfoBean.getConnection(driver, url,
                                       username, password);
    if (connection != null) {
      doPreparedStatements(connection, print);
      doRawQueries(connection, print);
    }
    try {
      connection.close();
    } catch(SQLException sqle) {
      System.err.println("Problem closing connection: " + sqle);
    }
  }

  private static void doPreparedStatements(Connection conn,
                                           boolean print) {
    try {
      String queryFormat =
        "SELECT id FROM music WHERE price < ?";
```

Listing 17.10 PreparedStatements.java *(continued)*

```
      PreparedStatement statement =
        conn.prepareStatement(queryFormat);
      long startTime = System.currentTimeMillis();
      for(int i=0; i<100; i++) {
        statement.setFloat(1, i/4);
        ResultSet results = statement.executeQuery();
        if (print) {
          showResults(results);
        }
      }
      long stopTime = System.currentTimeMillis();
      double elapsedTime = (stopTime - startTime)/1000.0;
      System.out.println("Executing prepared statement " +
                         "100 times took " +
                         elapsedTime + " seconds.");
    } catch(SQLException sqle) {
      System.err.println("Error executing statement: " + sqle);
    }
  }

  public static void doRawQueries(Connection conn,
                                  boolean print) {
    try {
      String queryFormat =
        "SELECT id FROM music WHERE price < ";
      Statement statement = conn.createStatement();
      long startTime = System.currentTimeMillis();
      for(int i=0; i<100; i++) {
        ResultSet results =
          statement.executeQuery(queryFormat + i/4);
        if (print) {
          showResults(results);
        }
      }
      long stopTime = System.currentTimeMillis();
      double elapsedTime = (stopTime - startTime)/1000.0;
      System.out.println("Executing raw query " +
                         "100 times took " +
                         elapsedTime + " seconds.");
    } catch(SQLException sqle) {
      System.err.println("Error executing query: " + sqle);
    }
  }
```

Listing 17.10 PreparedStatements.java *(continued)*

```
  private static void showResults(ResultSet results)
      throws SQLException {
    while(results.next()) {
      System.out.print(results.getString(1) + " ");
    }
    System.out.println();
  }

  private static void printUsage() {
    System.out.println("Usage: PreparedStatements host " +
                       "dbName username password " +
                       "vendor [print].");
  }
}
```

The preceding example illustrates how to create a prepared statement and set parameters for the statement in a command-line program. For Web development, you may want to submit prepared statements to the database from a JSP page. If so, the JSP Standard Tag Library (JSTL—see Volume 2 of this book) provides an `sql:query` action to define a prepared statement for submission to the database and an `sql:param` action to specify parameter values for the prepared statement.

17.5 Creating Callable Statements

With a `CallableStatement`, you can execute a stored procedure or function in a database. For example, in an Oracle database, you can write a procedure or function in PL/SQL and store it in the database along with the tables. Then, you can create a connection to the database and execute the stored procedure or function through a `CallableStatement`.

A stored procedure has many advantages. For instance, syntax errors are caught at compile time instead of at runtime; the database procedure may run much faster than a regular SQL query; and the programmer only needs to know about the input and output parameters, not the table structure. In addition, coding of the stored procedure may be simpler in the database language than in the Java programming language because access to native database capabilities (sequences, triggers, multiple cursors) is possible.

One disadvantage of a stored procedure is that you may need to learn a new database-specific language (note, however, that Oracle8i Database and later support stored procedures written in the Java programming language). A second disadvantage is that the business logic of the stored procedure executes on the database server instead of on the client machine or Web server. The industry trend has been to move as much business logic as possible from the database and to place the business logic in JavaBeans components (or, on large systems, Enterprise JavaBeans components) executing on the Web server. The main motivation for this approach in a Web architecture is that the database access and network I/O are often the performance bottlenecks.

Calling a stored procedure in a database involves the six basic steps outlined below and then described in detail in the following subsections.

1. **Define the call to the database procedure.** As with a prepared statement, you use special syntax to define a call to a stored procedure. The procedure definition uses escape syntax, where the appropriate `?` defines input and output parameters.
2. **Prepare a `CallableStatement` for the procedure.** You obtain a `CallableStatement` from a `Connection` by calling `prepareCall`.
3. **Register the output parameter types.** Before executing the procedure, you must declare the type of each output parameter.
4. **Provide values for the input parameters.** Before executing the procedure, you must supply the input parameter values.
5. **Execute the stored procedure.** To execute the database stored procedure, call `execute` on the `CallableStatement`.
6. **Access the returned output parameters.** Call the corresponding `get`*`Xxx`* method, according to the output type.

Define the Call to the Database Procedure

Creating a `CallableStatement` is somewhat similar to creating a `PreparedStatement` (see Section 17.4, "Using Prepared Statements") in that special SQL escape syntax is used in which the appropriate `?` is replaced with a value before the statement is executed. The definition for a procedure takes four general forms.

- **Procedure with no parameters.**
  `{ call` *`procedure_name`* `}`
- **Procedure with input parameters.**
  `{ call` *`procedure_name`*`(?, ?, ...) }`
- **Procedure with an output parameter.**
  `{ ? call` *`procedure_name`* `}`
- **Procedure with input and output parameters.**
  `{ ? = call` *`procedure_name`*`(?, ?, ...) }`

In each of the four procedure forms, the *`procedure_name`* is the name of the stored procedure in the database. Also, be aware that a procedure can return more than one output parameter and that the indexed parameter values begin with the output parameters. Thus, in the last procedure example above, the first *input* parameter is indexed by a value of 2 (not 1).

Core Note

If the procedure returns output parameters, then the index of the input parameters must account for the number of output parameters.

Prepare a CallableStatement for the Procedure

You obtain a `CallableStatement` from a `Connection` with the `prepareCall` method, as below.

```
String procedure = "{ ? = call procedure_name( ?, ? ) }";
CallableStatement statement =
  connection.prepareCall(procedure);
```

Register the Output Parameter Types

You must register the JDBC type of each output parameter, using `register-OutParameter`, as follows,

```
statement.registerOutParameter(n, type);
```

where *n* corresponds to the ordered output parameter (using 1-based indexing), and *type* corresponds to a constant defined in the `java.sql.Types` class (`Types.FLOAT`, `Types.DATE`, etc.).

Provide Values for the Input Parameters

Before executing the stored procedure, you replace the marked input parameters by using a `setXxx` call corresponding to the entry you want to set and the type of parameter (e.g., `setInt`, `setString`). For example,

```
statement.setString(2, "name");
statement.setFloat(3, 26.0F);
```

sets the first input parameter (presuming one output parameter) to a `String`, and the second input parameter to a `float`. Remember that if the procedure has output parameters, the index of the input parameters starts from the first output parameter.

Execute the Stored Procedure

To execute the stored procedure, simply call `execute` on the `CallableStatement` object. For example:

```
statement.execute();
```

Access the Output Parameters

If the procedure returns output parameters, then after you call `execute`, you can access each corresponding output parameter by calling `getXxx`, where `Xxx` corresponds to the type of return parameter (`getDouble`, `getDate`, etc.). For example,

```
int value = statement.getInt(1);
```

returns the first output parameter as a primitive `int`.

Example

In Listing 17.11, the `CallableStatements` class demonstrates the execution of an Oracle stored procedure (technically, a function, since it returns a value) written for the `music` table (see Section 18.5 for setting up the `music` table). You can create the `discount` stored procedure in the database by invoking our `CallableStatements` class and specifying `create` on the command line. Doing so calls the `createStoredFunction` method, which submits the procedure (a long string) to the database as an SQL update. Alternatively, if you have Oracle SQL*Plus, you can load the procedure directly from **discount.sql**, Listing 17.12. See Section 18.5 for information on running the SQL script in SQL*Plus.

The stored procedure `discount` modifies the `price` entry in the `music` table. Specifically, the procedure accepts two input parameters, `composer_in` (the composer to select in the `music` table) and `discount_in` (the percent by which to discount the price). If the `discount_in` is outside the range 0.05 to 0.50, then a value of `-1` is returned; otherwise, the number of rows modified in the table is returned from the stored procedure.

Listing 17.11 CallableStatements.java

```
package coreservlets;

import java.sql.*;
import coreservlets.beans.*;
```

Listing 17.11 CallableStatements.java *(continued)*

```
/** An example that executes the Oracle stored procedure
 *  "discount". Specifically, the price of all compositions
 *  by Mozart in the "music" table are discounted by
 *  10 percent.
 *  <P>
 *  To create the stored procedure, specify a command-line
 *  argument of "create".
 */

public class CallableStatements {
  public static void main(String[] args) {
    if (args.length < 5) {
      printUsage();
      return;
    }
    String vendor = args[4];
    // Change to DriverUtilities2.loadDrivers() to force
    // loading of vendor drivers from default XML file.
    DriverUtilities.loadDrivers();
    if (!DriverUtilities.isValidVendor(vendor)) {
      printUsage();
      return;
    }
    String driver = DriverUtilities.getDriver(vendor);
    String host = args[0];
    String dbName = args[1];
    String url =
      DriverUtilities.makeURL(host, dbName, vendor);
    String username = args[2];
    String password = args[3];

    Connection connection =
      ConnectionInfoBean.getConnection(driver, url,
                                       username, password);
    if (connection == null) {
      return;
    }

    try {
      if ((args.length > 5) && (args[5].equals("create"))) {
        createStoredFunction(connection);
      }
      doCallableStatement(connection, "Mozart", 0.10F);
    } catch(SQLException sqle) {
      System.err.println("Problem with callable: " + sqle);
```

Listing 17.11 CallableStatements.java *(continued)*

```
    } finally {
      try {
        connection.close();
      } catch(SQLException sqle) {
        System.err.println("Error closing connection: " + sqle);
      }
    }
  }

  private static void doCallableStatement(Connection connection,
                                          String composer,
                                          float discount)
      throws SQLException {
    CallableStatement statement = null;
    try {
      connection.prepareCall("{ ? = call discount( ?, ? ) }");
      statement.setString(2, composer);
      statement.setFloat(3, discount);
      statement.registerOutParameter(1, Types.INTEGER);
      statement.execute();
      int rows = statement.getInt(1);
      System.out.println("Rows updated: " + rows);
    } catch(SQLException sqle) {
      System.err.println("Problem with callable: " + sqle);
    } finally {
      if (statement != null) {
        statement.close();
      }
    }
  }

  /** Create the Oracle PL/SQL stored procedure "discount".
   *  The procedure (technically, a PL/SQL function, since a
   *  value is returned), discounts the price for the specified
   *  composer in the "music" table.
   */

  private static void createStoredFunction(
                        Connection connection)
      throws SQLException {
    String sql = "CREATE OR REPLACE FUNCTION discount " +
                 "  (composer_in IN VARCHAR2, " +
                 "   discount_in IN NUMBER) " +
                 "RETURN NUMBER " +
                 "IS " +
```

Listing 17.11 CallableStatements.java *(continued)*

```
                    "  min_discount CONSTANT NUMBER:= 0.05; " +
                    "  max_discount CONSTANT NUMBER:= 0.50; " +
                    "BEGIN " +
                    "  IF discount_in BETWEEN min_discount " +
                    "                AND max_discount THEN " +
                    "    UPDATE music " +
                    "    SET price = price * (1.0 - discount_in) "+
                    "    WHERE composer = composer_in; " +
                    "    RETURN(SQL%ROWCOUNT); " +
                    "  ELSE " +
                    "    RETURN(-1); " +
                    "  END IF; " +
                    "END discount;";
    Statement statement = null;
    try {
      statement = connection.createStatement();
      statement.executeUpdate(sql);
    } catch(SQLException sqle) {
      System.err.println("Problem creating function: " + sqle);
    } finally {
      if (statement != null) {
        statement.close();
      }
    }
  }

  private static void printUsage() {
    System.out.println("Usage: CallableStatement host " +
                       "dbName username password " +
                       "vendor [create].");
  }
}
```

Listing 17.12 discount.sql (PL/SQL function for Oracle)

```
/* Discounts the price of all music by the specified
 * composer, composer_in. The music is discounted by the
 * percentage specified by discount_in.
 *
 * Returns the number of rows modified, or -1 if the discount
 * value is invalid.
 */
```

Listing 17.12 discount.sql (PL/SQL function for Oracle) *(continued)*

```
CREATE OR REPLACE FUNCTION discount
  (composer_in IN VARCHAR2, discount_in IN NUMBER)
RETURN NUMBER
IS
  min_discount CONSTANT NUMBER:= 0.05;
  max_discount CONSTANT NUMBER:= 0.50;
BEGIN
  IF discount_in BETWEEN min_discount AND max_discount THEN
    UPDATE music
    SET price = price * (1.0 - discount_in)
    WHERE composer = composer_in;
    RETURN(SQL%ROWCOUNT);
  ELSE
    RETURN(-1);
  END IF;
END discount;
```

17.6 Using Database Transactions

When a database is updated, by default the changes are permanently written (or *committed*) to the database. However, this default behavior can be programmatically turned off. If autocommitting is turned off and a problem occurs with the updates, then each change to the database can be backed out (or rolled back to the original values). If the updates execute successfully, then the changes can later be permanently committed to the database. This approach is known as *transaction management*.

Transaction management helps to ensure the integrity of your database tables. For example, suppose you are transferring funds from a savings account to a checking account. If you first withdraw from the savings account and then deposit into the checking account, what happens if there is an error after the withdrawal but before the deposit? The customer's accounts will have too little money, and the banking regulators will levy stiff fines. On the other hand, what if you first deposit into the checking account and then withdraw from the savings account, and there is an error after the deposit but before the withdrawal? The customer's accounts will have too much money, and the bank's board of directors will fire the entire IT staff. The point is, no matter how you order the operations, the accounts will be left in an inconsistent state if one operation is committed and the other is not. You need to guarantee that either both operations occur or that neither does. That's what transaction management is all about.

The default for a database connection is autocommit; that is, each executed statement is automatically committed to the database. Thus, for transaction management you first need to turn off autocommit for the connection by calling `setAutoCommit(false)`.

Typically, you use a `try/catch/finally` block to properly handle the transaction management. First, you should record the autocommit status. Then, in the `try` block, you should call `setAutoCommit(false)` and execute a set of queries or updates. If a failure occurs, you call `rollback` in the `catch` block; if the transactions are successful, you call `commit` at the end of the `try` block. Either way, you reset the autocommit status in the `finally` block.

Following is a template for this transaction management approach.

```
Connection connection =
  DriverManager.getConnection(url, username, password);
boolean autoCommit = connection.getAutoCommit();
Statement statement;
try {
  connection.setAutoCommit(false);
  statement = connection.createStatement();
  statement.execute(...);
  statement.execute(...);
  ...
  connection.commit();
} catch(SQLException sqle) {
  connection.rollback();
} finally {
  statement.close();
  connection.setAutoCommit(autoCommit);
}
```

Here, the statement for obtaining a connection from the `DriverManager` is outside the `try/catch` block. That way, `rollback` is not called unless a connection is successfully obtained. However, the `getConnection` method can still throw an `SQLException` and must be thrown by the enclosing method or be caught in a separate `try/catch` block.

In Listing 17.13, we add new recordings to the `music` table as a transaction block (see Section 18.5 to create the `music` table). To generalize the task, we create a `TransactionBean`, Listing 17.14, in which we specify the connection to the database and submit a block of SQL statements as an array of strings. The bean then loops through the array of SQL statements, executes each one of them, and if an `SQLException` is thrown, performs a `rollback` and rethrows the exception.

Listing 17.13 Transactions.java

```
package coreservlets;

import java.sql.*;
import coreservlets.beans.*;

/** An example to demonstrate submission of a block of
 *  SQL statements as a single transaction. Specifically,
 *  four new records are inserted into the music table.
 *  Performed as a transaction block so that if a problem
 *  occurs, a rollback is performed and no changes are
 *  committed to the database.
 */

public class Transactions {
  public static void main(String[] args) {
    if (args.length < 5) {
      printUsage();
      return;
    }
    String vendor = args[4];
    // Change to DriverUtilities2.loadDrivers() to load
    // vendor drivers from an XML file instead of loading
    // hard-coded vendor drivers in DriverUtilities.
    DriverUtilities.loadDrivers();
    if (!DriverUtilities.isValidVendor(vendor)) {
      printUsage();
      return;
    }
    String driver = DriverUtilities.getDriver(vendor);
    String host = args[0];
    String dbName = args[1];
    String url =
      DriverUtilities.makeURL(host, dbName, vendor);
    String username = args[2];
    String password = args[3];
    doTransactions(driver, url, username, password);
  }

  private static void doTransactions(String driver,
                                     String url,
                                     String username,
                                     String password) {
```

Listing 17.13 Transactions.java *(continued)*

```
    String[] transaction =
    { "INSERT INTO music VALUES " +
      " ( 9, 'Chopin',        'No. 2 in F minor',  100, 17.99)",
      "INSERT INTO music VALUES " +
      " (10, 'Tchaikovsky',  'No. 1 in Bb minor', 100, 24.99)",
      "INSERT INTO music VALUES " +
      " (11, 'Ravel',         'No. 2 in D major',  100, 14.99)",
      "INSERT INTO music VALUES " +
      " (12, 'Schumann',      'No. 1 in A minor',  100, 14.99)"};
    TransactionBean bean = new TransactionBean();
    try {
      bean.setConnection(driver, url, username, password);
      bean.execute(transaction);
    } catch (SQLException sqle) {
      System.err.println("Transaction failure: " + sqle);
    } finally {
      bean.close();
    }
  }

  private static void printUsage() {
    System.out.println("Usage: Transactions host " +
                       "dbName username password " +
                       "vendor.");
  }
}
```

Listing 17.14 TransactionBean.java

```
package coreservlets.beans;

import java.io.*;
import java.sql.*;
import java.util.*;
import coreservlets.*;

/** Bean for performing JDBC transactions. After specifying
 *  the connection, submit a block of SQL statements as a
 *  single transaction by calling execute. If an SQLException
 *  occurs, any prior statements are automatically rolled back.
 */
```

Listing 17.14 TransactionBean.java *(continued)*

```
public class TransactionBean {
  private Connection connection;

  public void setConnection(Connection connection) {
    this.connection = connection;
  }

  public void setConnection(String driver, String url,
                            String username, String password) {
    setConnection(ConnectionInfoBean.getConnection(
                      driver, url, username, password));
  }

  public Connection getConnection() {
    return(connection);
  }

  public void execute(List list) throws SQLException {
    execute((String[])list.toArray(new String[list.size()]));
  }

  public void execute(String transaction)
      throws SQLException {
    execute(new String[] { transaction });
  }

  /** Execute a block of SQL statements as a single
   *  transaction.  If an SQLException occurs, a rollback
   *  is attempted and the exception is thrown.
   */

    public void execute(String[] transaction)
      throws SQLException {
    if (connection == null) {
      throw new SQLException("No connection available.");
    }
    boolean autoCommit = connection.getAutoCommit();
    try {
      connection.setAutoCommit(false);
      Statement statement = connection.createStatement();
      for(int i=0; i<transaction.length; i++) {
        statement.execute(transaction[i]);
      }
      statement.close();
    } catch(SQLException sqle) {
      connection.rollback();
      throw sqle;
```

Listing 17.14 TransactionBean.java *(continued)*

```
      } finally {
        connection.commit();
        connection.setAutoCommit(autoCommit);
      }
    }

    public void close() {
      if (connection != null) {
        try {
          connection.close();
        } catch(SQLException sqle) {
          System.err.println(
            "Failed to close connection: " + sqle);
        } finally {
          connection = null;
        }
      }
    }
  }
```

The preceding example demonstrates the use of a bean for submitting transactions to a database. This approach is excellent for a servlet; however, in a JSP page, you may want to use the `sql:transaction` action available in the JSP Standard Tag Library (JSTL). See Volume 2 of this book for details on JSTL.

17.7 Mapping Data to Objects by Using ORM Frameworks

Because of the need to easily move data back and forth from a database to a Java object, numerous vendors have developed frameworks for mapping objects to relational databases. This is a powerful capability since object-oriented programming and relational databases have always had an impedance mismatch: objects understand both state and behavior and can be traversed through relationships with other objects, whereas relational databases store information in tables but are typically related through primary keys.

Table 17.1 summarizes a few popular object-to-relational mapping (ORM) frameworks. Numerous other ORM frameworks are available. For a comparison of Java-based ORM products, see http://c2.com/cgi-bin/wiki?ObjectRelationalTool-

Comparison. Another excellent source for ORM frameworks and tutorials is located at http://www.javaskyline.com/database.html. (Remember that the book's source code archive at http://www.coreservlets.com/ contains up-to-date links to all URLs mentioned in the book.)

Table 17.1 Object-to-Relational Mapping Frameworks

Framework	URL
Castor	http://castor.exolab.org/
CocoBase	http://www.cocobase.com/
FrontierSuite	http://www.objectfrontier.com/
Kodo JDO	http://www.solarmetric.com/
ObJectRelationalBridge	http://db.apache.org/ojb/
TopLink	http://otn.oracle.com/products/ias/toplink/

Many, but not all, of these frameworks support the API for Java Data Objects (JDO). The JDO API provides a complete object-oriented approach to manage objects that are mapped to a persistent store (database). Detailed coverage of ORM frameworks and JDO is beyond the scope of this book. However, we provide a brief summary to show the power that JDO provides. For more information on JDO, see the online material at http://java.sun.com/products/jdo/ and http://jdocentral.com/. In addition, you can refer to *Core Java Data Objects* by Sameer Tyagi et al.

In JDO frameworks, the developer must provide XML-based metadata for each Java class that maps to the relational database. The metadata defines the persistent fields in each class and the potential role of each field relative to the database (e.g., the primary key). Once the metadata and source code for each Java class are defined, the developer must run a framework utility to generate the necessary JDO code to support persistence of the object's fields in the persistent store (database).

JDO framework utilities take one of two approaches to modify a Java class in support of the persistent store: the first approach is to modify the source code before compiling, the second approach is to modify the bytecode (.class file) after compiling the source code. The second approach is more common because it simplifies the maintenance of the source code—the generated database code is never seen by the developer.

In the case of a JDO implementation for an SQL database, the framework utility generates all the necessary code required by the JDO persistence manager to `INSERT` new rows in the database, as well as to perform `UPDATE` and `DELETE` operations for persisting modifications to the data. The developer is not required to write any SQL or JDBC code; the framework utility generates all the necessary code, and the persistence manager generates all the necessary communication with the database. Once the framework is set up, the developer simply needs to create objects and understand the JDO API.

Listing 17.15 shows Music.jdo, an example of how metadata for the `Music` class (Listing 17.16) is defined for SolarMetric's Kodo JDO implementation. The XML file Music.jdo maps the `Music` class to a table in the database by using an `extension` element with a `key` attribute of `table` and a `value` attribute of `music`. It is not necessary that the database already have a table named `music`; in fact, the Kodo framework creates all tables necessary in the database for the persistent storage, possibly using modified table names. The `name` attribute simply defines a mapping for the framework.

The .jdo file further designates a `field` element for each field in the class that must be persisted in the database. Each `field` element defines an `extension` element to map a field in the class to a column in the database table, where the `value` attribute clarifies the name of the database column. The `extension` elements are vendor specific, so be sure to consult the documentation of your JDO vendor for the proper values for the `key` attribute.

The `PersistenceManager` class provides access to the persistent store (database). For example, Listing 17.17 shows how to insert fields associated with new objects into the persistent store with the `makePersistentAll` method. Changes to the persistent store are managed as a transaction and must be placed between calls to the `begin` and `commit` methods of the `Transaction` class. Thus, to insert the fields associated with a `Music` object into the database, you simply call the appropriate `setXxx` methods on the `Music` object and then invoke the `makePersistentAll` method within a transaction. The JDO persistence manager automatically creates and executes the SQL statements to commit the data to the database. In a similar manner, the deletion of fields associated with a `Music` object is handled through the `makeDeletePersistent` method of `PersistenceManager`. For more complicated interaction with the persistent store, JDO provides a `Query` class to execute queries and return the results as a `Collection` of objects.

Lastly, the location of the database, the username, the password, and other system-specific information is read from system properties (specified by Listing 17.18 in this example).

Listing 17.15 Music.jdo

```
<?xml version="1.0"?>
<!DOCTYPE jdo PUBLIC
"-//Sun Microsystems, Inc.//DTD Java Data Objects Metadata 1.0//EN"
"http://java.sun.com/dtd/jdo_1_0.dtd">
<jdo>
  <package name="coreservlets.jdo">
    <class name="Music" >
      <extension vendor-name="kodo"
                 key="table" value="music"/>
      <extension vendor-name="kodo"
                 key="lock-column" value="none"/>
      <extension vendor-name="kodo"
                 key="class-column" value="none"/>
      <field name="id" primary-key="true">
        <extension vendor-name="kodo"
                   key="data-column" value="id"/>
      </field>
      <field name="composer">
        <extension vendor-name="kodo"
                   key="data-column" value="composer"/>
      </field>
      <field name="concerto">
        <extension vendor-name="kodo"
                   key="data-column" value="concerto"/>
      </field>
      <field name="available">
        <extension vendor-name="kodo"
                   key="data-column" value="available"/>
      </field>
      <field name="price">
        <extension vendor-name="kodo"
                   key="data-column" value="price"/>
      </field>
    </class>
  </package>
</jdo>
```

Listing 17.16 Music.java

```
package coreservlets.jdo;

 /** Music object corresponding to a record in a database.
  *  A Music object/record provides information about
  *  a concerto that is available for purchase and
  *  defines fields for the ID, composer, concerto,
  *  items available, and sales price.
  */

public class Music {
  private int id;
  private String composer;
  private String concerto;
  private int available;
  private float price;

  public Music() { }

  public Music(int id, String composer, String concerto,
               int available, float price) {
    setId(id);
    setComposer(composer);
    setConcerto(concerto);
    setAvailable(available);
    setPrice(price);
  }

  public void setId(int id) {
    this.id = id;
  }

  public int getId() {
    return(id);
  }

  public void setComposer(String composer) {
    this.composer = composer;
  }

  public String getComposer() {
    return(concerto);
  }

  public void setConcerto(String concerto) {
    this.concerto = concerto;
  }
```

Listing 17.16 Music.java *(continued)*

```
  public String getConcerto() {
    return(composer);
  }

  public void setAvailable(int available) {
    this.available = available;
  }

  public int getAvailable() {
    return(available);
  }

  public void setPrice(float price) {
    this.price = price;
  }

  public float getPrice() {
    return(price);
  }
}
```

Listing 17.17 PopulateMusicTable.java

```
package coreservlets.jdo;

import java.util.*;
import java.io.*;
import javax.jdo.*;

/** Populate database with music records by using JDO.
 */
public class PopulateMusicTable {
  public static void main(String[] args) {
    // Create seven new music objects to place in the database.
    Music[] objects = {
      new Music(1, "Mozart", "No. 21 in C# minor", 7, 24.99F),
      new Music(2, "Beethoven", "No. 3 in C minor", 28, 10.99F),
      new Music(3, "Beethoven", "No. 5 Eb major", 33, 10.99F),
      new Music(4, "Rachmaninov", "No. 2 in C minor", 9, 18.99F),
      new Music(5, "Mozart", "No. 24 in C minor", 11, 21.99F),
      new Music(6, "Beethoven", "No. 4 in G", 33, 12.99F),
      new Music(7, "Liszt", "No. 1 in Eb major", 48, 10.99F)
    };
```

Listing 17.17 PopulateMusicTable.java *(continued)*

```
    // Load properties file with JDO information. The properties
    // file contains ORM Framework information specific to the
    // vendor and information for connecting to the database.
    Properties properties = new Properties();
    try {
      FileInputStream fis =
        new FileInputStream("jdo.properties");
      properties.load(fis);
    } catch(IOException ioe) {
      System.err.println("Problem loading properties file: " +
                         ioe);
      return;
    }

    // Initialize manager for persistence framework.
    PersistenceManagerFactory pmf =
      JDOHelper.getPersistenceManagerFactory(properties);
    PersistenceManager pm = pmf.getPersistenceManager();

    // Write the new Music objects to the database.
    Transaction transaction = pm.currentTransaction();
    transaction.begin();
    pm.makePersistentAll(objects);
    transaction.commit();
    pm.close ();
  }
}
```

Listing 17.18 jdo.properties

```
# Configuration information for Kodo JDO Framework and
# MySQL database.
javax.jdo.PersistenceManagerFactoryClass=
  com.solarmetric.kodo.impl.jdbc.JDBCPersistenceManagerFactory
javax.jdo.option.RetainValues=true
javax.jdo.option.RestoreValues=true
javax.jdo.option.Optimistic=true
javax.jdo.option.NontransactionalWrite=false
javax.jdo.option.NontransactionalRead=true
javax.jdo.option.Multithreaded=true
javax.jdo.option.MsWait=5000
javax.jdo.option.MinPool=1
javax.jdo.option.MaxPool=80
```

Listing 17.18 jdo.properties *(continued)*

```
javax.jdo.option.IgnoreCache=false
javax.jdo.option.ConnectionUserName: brown
javax.jdo.option.ConnectionURL: jdbc:mysql://localhost/csajsp
javax.jdo.option.ConnectionPassword: larry
javax.jdo.option.ConnectionDriverName: com.mysql.jdbc.Driver
com.solarmetric.kodo.impl.jdbc.WarnOnPersistentTypeFailure=true
com.solarmetric.kodo.impl.jdbc.SequenceFactoryClass=
  com.solarmetric.kodo.impl.jdbc.schema.DBSequenceFactory
com.solarmetric.kodo.impl.jdbc.FlatInheritanceMapping=true
com.solarmetric.kodo.EnableQueryExtensions=false
com.solarmetric.kodo.DefaultFetchThreshold=30
com.solarmetric.kodo.DefaultFetchBatchSize=10
com.solarmetric.kodo.LicenseKey=5A8A-D98C-DB5F-6070-6000
```

Configuring MS Access, MySQL, and Oracle9i

Topics in This Chapter

- Configuring a DSN to connect to Microsoft Access
- Installing and configuring MySQL
- Creating databases and users in MySQL
- Installing and configuring Oracle9i
- Using the Database Configuration Assistant to create a database in Oracle9i
- Manually creating a database in Oracle9i
- Creating users in Oracle9i
- Testing your database through a JDBC connection
- Determining the JDBC version of your database driver
- Setting up the example `music` table

Chapter 18

In this chapter, we provide details for configuring three popular databases for use with JDBC: Microsoft Access, MySQL, and Oracle9i.

The first database, Microsoft Access, is an excellent database for practice and experimentation because the Java SDK (or JDK) already includes the appropriate JDBC driver and many developers already have Access installed. However, you would be unlikely to use Microsoft Access for serious applications, since it is not designed to handle a large number of concurrent connections. For details on configuring Microsoft Access, see Section 18.1.

The second database, MySQL, is a production-quality database and probably the best free option. In Section 18.2 we provide details for installing and configuring MySQL. In addition, we provide information for downloading and using the appropriate MySQL JDBC driver in your Web applications.

The third database, Oracle9i, though not free, is an excellent production database. See Section 18.3 for details on installing and configuring Oracle9i. The installation and database creation process is quite lengthy. However, Oracle9i is widely used in industry, so taking the time to gain experience with the product is well worth the effort. After the installation and database creation, we provide information for installing the correct Oracle JDBC driver for use with various versions of the Java SDK.

Lastly, we provide programs to test your database and load the example database table used in this book.

18.1 Configuring Microsoft Access for Use with JDBC

If you have Microsoft Office, Microsoft Access and the required Open DataBase Connectivity (ODBC) driver are probably already installed on your machine. So, although we don't recommend Microsoft Access for a high-end production Web site, we think that Microsoft Access is excellent for learning and testing JDBC code. For instance, the examples in Chapter 17 connect to the preinstalled Northwind database of Microsoft Access. For a production site, you should use a more robust product like Oracle9i, DB2, Sybase, Microsoft SQL Server, or MySQL.

To connect to a Microsoft Access database from the Java platform, you can use the JDBC-ODBC bridge, `sun.jdbc.odbc.JdbcOdbcDriver`, included with the JDK. The bridge permits JDBC to communicate with the database by using ODBC, without requiring a native-format driver. However, you will need to configure an ODBC Data Source Name (DSN) to map a name to a physical database.

The URL to connect to a Microsoft Access database does not specify a host. Instead, the URL points to a DSN, for example, `jdbc:odbc:`*`dsn`*., where *`dsn`* is the name of the database assigned through the ODBC DSN wizard. Note that the Sun driver, `sun.jdbc.odbc.JdbcOdbcDriver`, is not fully compliant with JDBC 2.0 and thus does not support all the advanced JDBC features introduced in JDBC 2.0. However, it is more than adequate for the capabilities discussed in this chapter. You can find JDBC 2.0 drivers for Microsoft Access at http://industry.java.sun.com/products/jdbc/drivers/.

For your application to connect to a database on a server, ODBC Version 3.x needs to be installed on that server. Fortunately, ODBC is installed with many Microsoft products. If you don't have ODBC, you can easily install it separately on your system. ODBC is bundled with Microsoft Data Access Components (MDAC). See http://www.microsoft.com/data/download.htm for the correct MDAC version to install on your system.

Configuring a System DSN through the ODBC Administration Tool requires four steps, which we outline here and describe in detail in the subsections following the outline.

1. **Select a System DSN from the ODBC Data Source Administrator.** The Data Source Administrator, located in the system Administrative Tools, allows you to create a new data source name.
2. **Select a driver for the new System DSN.** Multiple ODBC database drivers are available to map to your DSN. Most likely, you will select the Microsoft Access Driver.

3. **Select a data source.** Locate and select the database file on your computer as the data source for your ODBC connection. Here, you also specify the name of the source to use when connecting to the ODBC driver.
4. **Select OK to accept the new DSN.** Selecting OK completes the configuration of the ODBC System data source. Afterwards, you can connect to the data source from Java through the JDBC-ODBC bridge.

Select a System DSN from the ODBC Data Source Administrator

On Windows 2000, you can configure the data sources (ODBC) by selecting Start, Settings, then Control Panel. Next, select Administrative Tools and then Data Sources. Lastly, select the System DSN tab, and select Add to create a new DSN. Other versions of Windows are similar; for instance, on Windows XP, the steps are identical except that you select the Control Panel directly from the Start menu. Figure 18–1 shows the System DSN tab in the ODBC Data Source Administrator window.

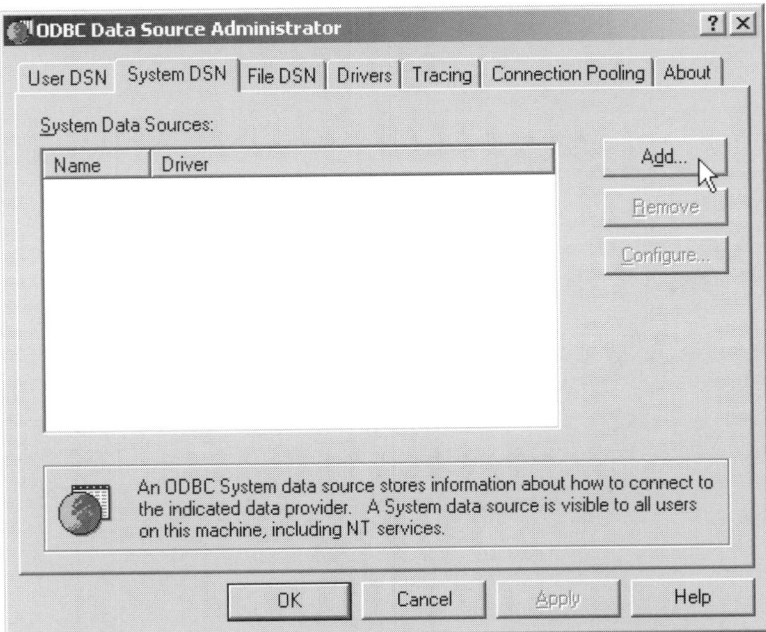

Figure 18–1 First window displayed when you are configuring an ODBC data source. Select the System DSN tab and then click the Add button to create a new DSN.

Select a Driver for the New System DSN

In the Create New Data Source window, Figure 18–2, choose the Microsoft Access Driver (*.mdb) and then select Finish.

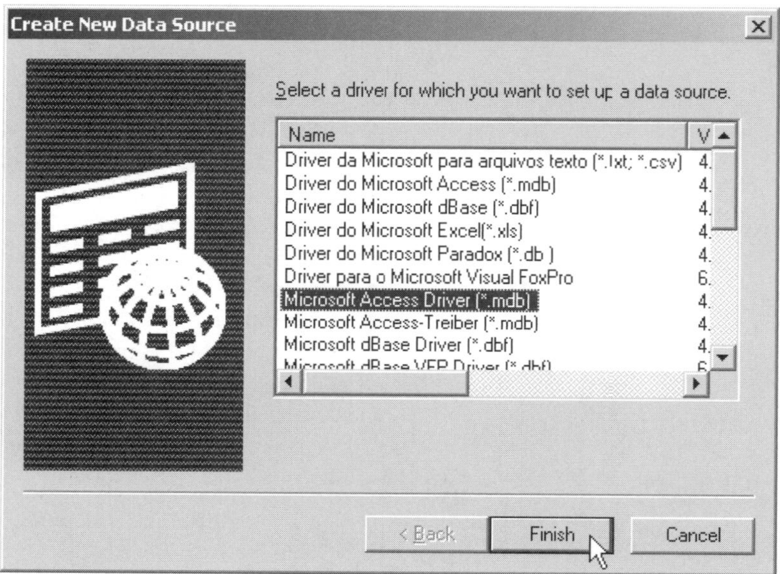

Figure 18–2 Second window presented when you are creating a System DSN. Before continuing the configuration, choose the driver for the data source by clicking Finish.

Select a Data Source

In the ODBC Microsoft Access Setup window, enter a data source name (with an optional description). The DSN will be the same name used in the JDBC URL, `jdbc:odbc:`*`dsn`*. For example, if you choose `Test` as the DSN, you would supply `"jdbc:odbc:Test"` as the first argument to `DriverManager.getConnection`. Next, click the Select button, as shown in Figure 18–3, to select the physical database file to bind to the data source name. After that step, click the OK button.

If you are using the Northwind sample database provided with Microsoft Access, the location of the database file is most likely C:\Program Files\Microsoft Office\Office\Samples\Northwind.mdb or something very similar, depending on the version of Microsoft Access you have installed. If the Northwind file is not available, you may need to install the sample database by opening Microsoft Access and selecting the Northwind Sample Database from the opened window. Alternatively, you can download the sample database from http://office.microsoft.com/downloads/2000/Nwind2K.aspx.

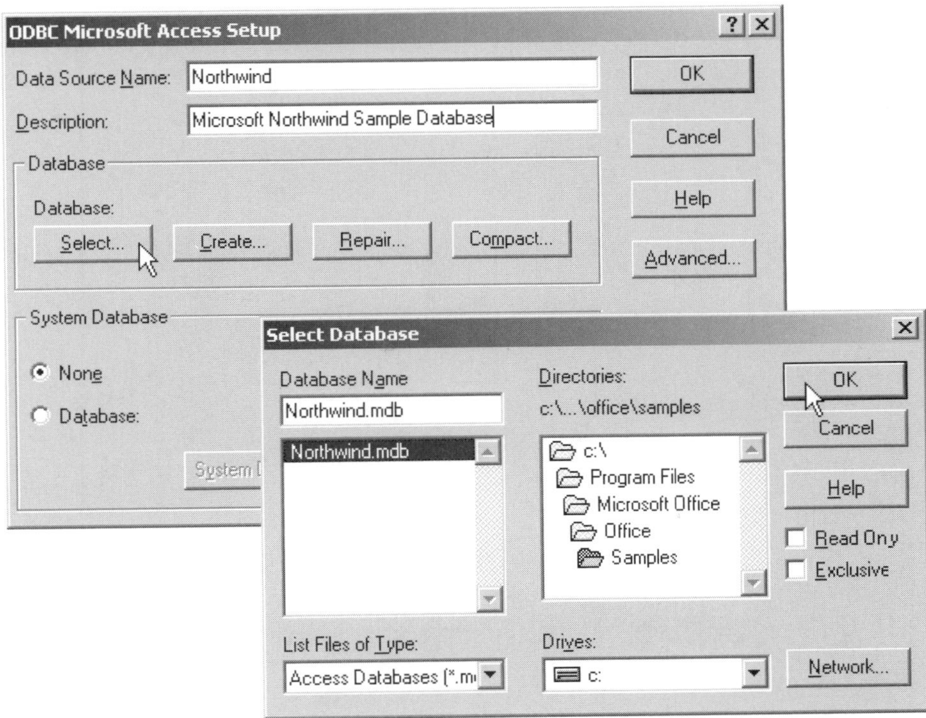

Figure 18–3 Third window for setting up a System DSN to a Microsoft Access database. Specify the name of the data source (with an optional description) and then select the physical database file to bind to the source name.

Select OK to Accept the New DSN

At this point, the newly defined DSN should be listed in the System DSN tab, as shown in Figure 18–4. Finish the configuration by clicking the OK button.

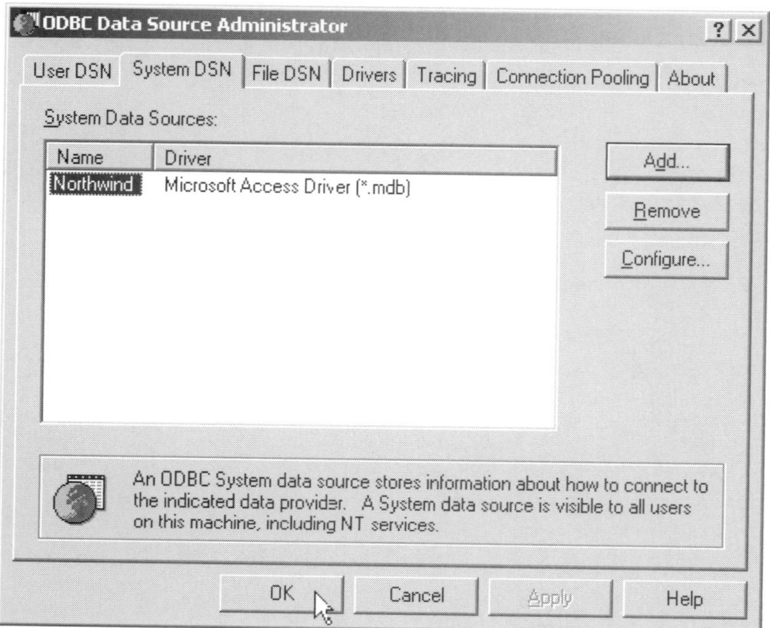

Figure 18–4 Fourth window presented after you have added a new system data source. Click OK to accept the change.

18.2 Installing and Configuring MySQL

MySQL is a popular and free open source database available for Unix (Solaris, Linux, etc.), MacOS, and Windows. When this book went to press, Version 4.0 was the current stable version of MySQL. Version 4.0 of MySQL does not support stored procedures and a few other advanced database features, but it is free and has surprisingly high performance.

Below are details for downloading and installing MySQL on Windows. These instructions provide the minimal installation for MySQL. For security issues (e.g., setting the root password) and postconfiguration guidelines, see the instructions at http://www.mysql.com/documentation/mysql/bychapter/. The online documentation also provides installation instructions for Unix (including Linux) and MacOS.

To use MySQL, you must install the product, set up a database, and configure users' rights. Here, we outline the four steps required to set up MySQL, followed by a detailed description of the steps.

1. **Download and install MySQL.** Download MySQL from http://www.mysql.com/downloads/ and install as a service.
2. **Create a database.** Add a new database to MySQL by entering a simple `CREATE DATABASE` command.
3. **Create a user.** To create a user, use `GRANT` to assign database privileges to the user.
4. **Install the JDBC driver.** Download the appropriate driver for MySQL, bundled as a JAR file. During development, include the JAR file in your `CLASSPATH`. For deployment, place the JAR file in the WEB-INF/lib directory of your Web application.

Download and Install MySQL

You can download MySQL from http://www.mysql.com/downloads/. Download `mysql-4.0.xx-win.zip` (or later), unzip, and run the **setup.exe** program to install MySQL. We recommend installing MySQL in the C:\mysql directory. Note that before installing MySQL on Windows, you must log in to the computer with administrative rights.

Core Warning

To install MySQL on Windows NT/2000/XP, you must have local administrator rights on the machine.

On Windows NT/2000/XP, to configure MySQL as a service, run the following command in DOS from the C:\mysql\bin directory.

```
C:\mysql\bin> mysqld-max-nt --install
```

For more details, see the online documentation at http://www.mysql.com/documentation/.

Create a Database

Before creating a database, you must start the MySQL server. You can start the service from the command line by entering the `net start` command as shown.

```
C:\mysql\bin> net start MySql
```

If the server is already running, you will receive a warning message.

Next, to create a new database, start the MySQL monitor as the `root` user by using the following command.

```
C:\mysql\bin> mysql.exe --user=root
```

Then create the database by entering the `CREATE DATABASE` command as follows.

```
mysql> CREATE DATABASE database_name;
```

where *database_name* is the name of the database you want to create. For the code in this chapter, we created a database named `csajsp`. To see a listing of the current databases, enter the following command.

```
mysql> SHOW DATABASES;
```

If you prefer graphical interfaces over command-line utilities, use MySQL Control Center for managing your server. MySQL Control Center is available at http://www.mysql.com/downloads/mysqlcc.html.

Create a User

You can create a user at the same time you grant privileges to that user. To grant a user access to the database from the local host, use the command

```
mysql> GRANT ALL PRIVILEGES ON database.* TO user@localhost
       IDENTIFIED BY 'password';
```

where *database* is the name of the database and *user* is the name of the new user. To grant the user rights to the database from other client machines, use the command

```
mysql> GRANT ALL PRIVILEGES ON database.* TO user@"%"
       IDENTIFIED BY 'password';
```

where `@"%"` acts as a wildcard for access to the database from any client machine. If you have problems creating new users, check that you started the MySQL monitor as the `root` user.

Install the JDBC Driver

Two JDBC drivers are commonly used to access MySQL: MySQL Connector/J and the Caucho Resin driver.

MySQL recommends the MySQL Connector/J driver, which is available at http://www.mysql.com/products/connector-j/. In our examples, we use version 3.0 of the Connector/J driver. The driver is bundled in a JAR file named mysql-connector-java-3.0.6-stable-bin.jar with a class name of `com.mysql.jdbc.Driver`. The

URL to use with the MySQL Connector/J driver is jdbc:mysql://host:3306/*dbName*, where *dbName* is the name of the database on the MySQL server.

Caucho Resin also provides a MySQL driver at http://www.caucho.com/projects/jdbc-mysql/index.xtp. The driver is bundled in the JAR file named caucho-jdbc-mysql-2.1.0.jar with a class name of `com.caucho.jdbc.mysql.Driver`. The URL to use with the Caucho Resin driver is jdbc:mysql-caucho://host:3306/*dbName*, where, again, *dbName* is the name of the database on the MySQL server.

Neither driver is fully JDBC 2.0 compliant since MySQL is not fully ANSI SQL-92 compliant.

For development, place the JAR file in your `CLASSPATH`; for deployment, place the JAR file in the Web application's WEB-INF/lib directory. However, if multiple applications on the server are using MySQL databases, the Web administrator may choose to move the JAR file to a common lib directory on the container. For example, with Tomcat 4.x, JAR files used by multiple applications can be placed in the *install_dir*/common/lib directory.

18.3 Installing and Configuring Oracle9i Database

Oracle9i Database is a high-volume, production database deployed in many corporate enterprises for both Internet and intranet applications. Oracle9i Database provides all the functionality you would expect in a production database server, including stored procedures, views, triggers, enhanced security, and data recovery.

Three different editions of Oracle9i Database Release 2 are available from Oracle, as described below. Oracle9i includes a large family of products (including Oracle9i Application Server and Oracle9i Developer Suite), but in the remaining sections we use "Oracle9i" to refer to Oracle9i Database.

- **Enterprise Edition.** Oracle9i Enterprise Edition delivers an efficient, reliable solution for both Internet and intranet applications. The Enterprise Edition is suitable for high-volume transaction processing and data warehousing. The Enterprise Edition includes a preconfigured database, networking services, database management tools, and utilities. In addition, multiple product options are licensable with the Enterprise Edition.
- **Standard Edition.** Oracle9i Standard Edition is a scaled-down version of the Enterprise Edition and can be licensed only for servers with a maximum of four processors. The Standard Edition is suitable for workgroup, department, intranet, and Internet applications. The Standard Edition includes a preconfigured database, networking

services, database management tools, and utilities; however, the Standard Edition does not support all features available in the Enterprise Edition.

- **Personal Edition.** Oracle9i Personal Edition is suitable for a single-user, desktop environment. The Personal Edition is intended for educational purposes, providing a cost-effective, yearly licensing fee. The Personal Edition supports all the features and options available in the Enterprise Edition, with the exception of Oracle Real Application Clusters.

For a more detailed summary of the three Oracle9i Database editions, see http://otn.oracle.com/products/oracle9i/pdf/9idb_rel2_prod_fam.pdf.

To use Oracle9i, you must install the product, set up a database, and configure users' rights. In this section we provide information for downloading and installing Oracle9i Release 2 on Windows XP. For other platforms, you can find platform-specific installation instructions at http://otn.oracle.com/docs/products/oracle9i/. Below, we outline the four steps required to set up an Oracle9i, followed by a detailed description of each step.

1. **Download and install Oracle9i.** Download Oracle9i Database Release 2 from http://otn.oracle.com/software/products/oracle9i/ and install by using the Oracle Universal Installer.
2. **Create a database.** Typically, a database is created during the installation of Oracle9i; however, if Oracle9i is already installed on the computer you are using, you can create a new database manually or use the Database Configuration Assistant.
3. **Create a user.** To access the database from a Web application, you need to create a new user and then grant connection and table rights to the user.
4. **Install the JDBC driver.** To access an Oracle database from a Web application, download the appropriate JDBC driver from http://otn.oracle.com/software/tech/java/sqlj_jdbc/. During development, include the JAR file in your `CLASSPATH`. For deployment, place the JAR file in the WEB-INF/lib directory of your Web application.

Download and Install Oracle9i

You can download Oracle9i Database Release 2 from http://otn.oracle.com/software/products/oracle9i/. A registration is required for download of Oracle software; however, the registration is free. Be sure to read the license agreement if you plan on using Oracle9i for production purposes. Oracle products are free to download for a 30-day evaluation period. After 30 days, you must purchase a license.

In the following instructions, we show you how to install Oracle9i Database Release 2 Personal Edition on the Windows XP platform. For installation instructions for other platforms, see the documentation at http://otn.oracle.com/docs/products/oracle9i/.

Oracle9i Database Release 2 for Windows NT/2000/XP is bundled in three ZIP files: 92010NT_Disk1.zip (612,802,971 bytes), 92010NT_Disk2.zip (537,604,934 bytes), and 92010NT_Disk3.zip (254,458,106 bytes). The same install files are used for the Enterprise, Standard, and Personal editions. Follow the instructions on the download page and unzip the three files into corresponding directories named Disk1, Disk2, and Disk3. Alternatively, instead of downloading the software, you can purchase a CD pack at http://oraclestore.oracle.com/.

Oracle recommends the following minimum hardware requirements: Pentium 266, 256 Mbytes of RAM, and approximately 3 Gbytes of disk space for an NTFS partition. Exact requirements are available at http://otn.oracle.com/docs/products/oracle9i/doc_library/release2/A95493-01/html/reqs.htm.

Following are the instructions to install Oracle9i Database Personal Edition on the C:\ drive of a Windows XP computer. To perform this installation, you must log in to the machine with local administrator rights.

Core Warning

To install Oracle9i on Windows NT/2000/XP, you must have local administrator rights on the machine.

Steps to Install Oracle9i

1. **Start the Oracle Universal Installer.** You can start the Oracle Universal Installer 2.2 from the setup.exe program located in the Disk1 directory. If the installer fails to start, try the setup.exe program located in the Disk1\install\win32 directory. When you start the installer, you will momentarily see the copyright screen, followed by a Welcome screen as shown Figure 18–5. Click the Next button.

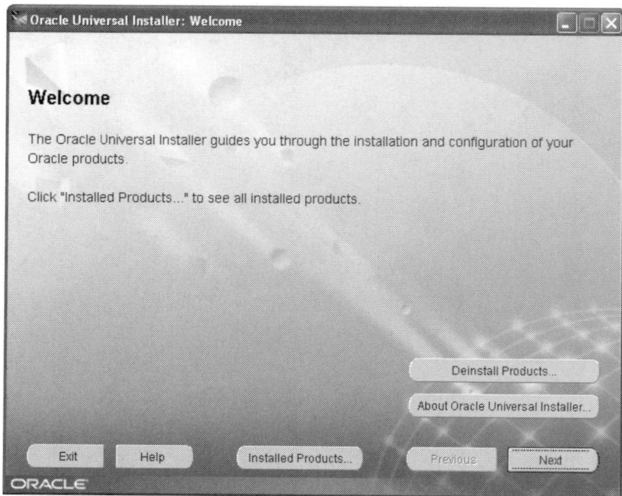

Figure 18–5 Second Oracle install window: Welcome message.

2. **Specify file locations.** On the third screen displayed (Figure 18–6), you specify the location of the installation program and the directory on which to install Oracle9i. Accept the default values. The Oracle Home, `OraHome92`, is used in the name for all Oracle services created during the installation process. Click Next to continue.

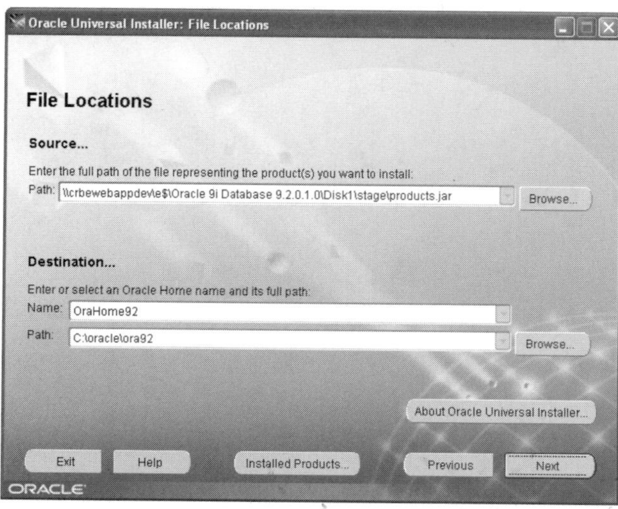

Figure 18–6 Third Oracle install window: summarizes the location of source and destination files for the installation process.

3. **Select a product to install.** On the fourth screen displayed (Figure 18–7), you select which product to install. Accept the default product, Oracle9i Database, and then click Next.

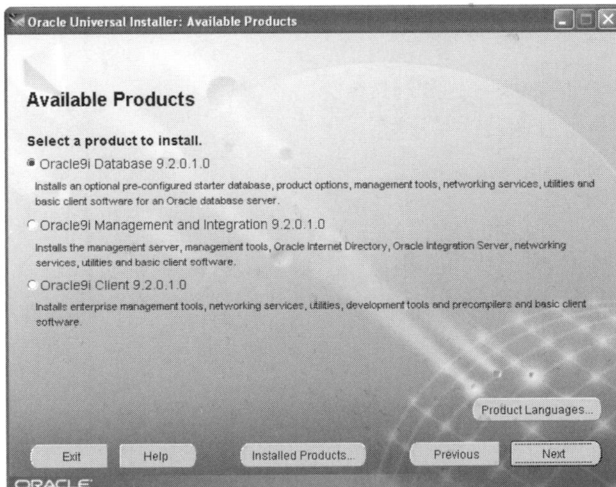

Figure 18–7 Fourth Oracle install window: for selecting a product to install.

4. **Select the installation type.** On the fifth screen displayed (Figure 18–8), you select the database edition to install. For a single-user environment, we recommend the Personal Edition, which requires 2.53 Gbytes of disk space on Windows XP. For more details on the three editions, see http://otn.oracle.com/products/oracle9i/pdf/9idb_rel2_prod_fam.pdf. Click Next.

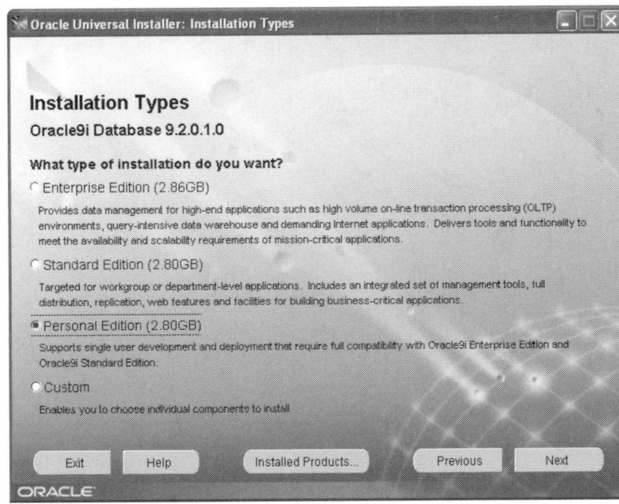

Figure 18–8 Fifth Oracle install window: for selecting an installation type. For a single user, select the Personal Edition.

5. **Select a database configuration.** On the sixth screen displayed (Figure 18–9), you specify the database configuration. We recommend the default selection, General Purpose, because the installation process for this selection automatically creates a starter database. Accept the default database configuration and click Next.

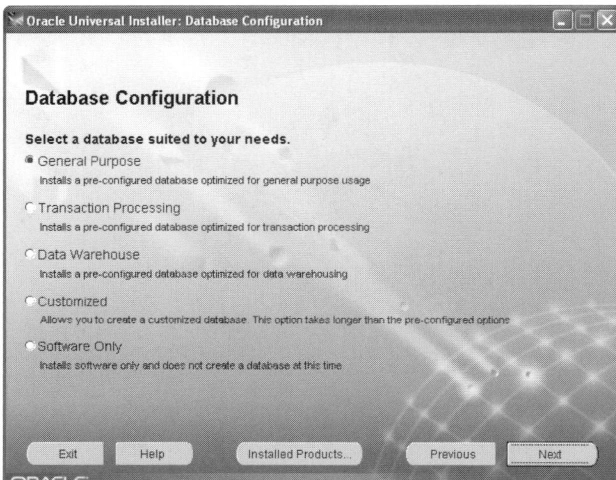

Figure 18–9 Sixth Oracle install window: for selecting a database configuration.

6. **Specify the port for the Oracle MTS Recovery Service.** On the seventh screen displayed (Figure 18–10), you specify the port for the Oracle MTS Recovery Service, which is automatically installed with Oracle Services for Microsoft Transaction Server. This service helps resolve requests for distributed transaction coordinated by the Microsoft DTC (MS DTC exposes COM objects that allow clients to initiate and participate in coordinated transactions across multiple connections to various data stores). You might not use this capability, so simply accept the default port number of 2030 and click Next.

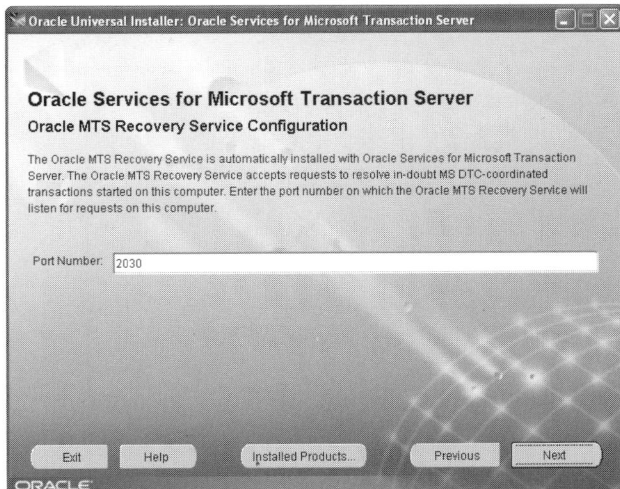

Figure 18–10 Seventh Oracle install window: for specifying a port for the Oracle MTS Recovery Service.

7. **Provide a database system identification (SID).** On the eighth screen displayed (Figure 18–11), you uniquely identify your database. Oracle configuration and utility tools use the SID to identify the database to operate upon. For the JDBC examples presented in this book, we suggest a Global Database Name of `csajsp.coreservlets.com`. Entering this name will autogenerate a SID of `csajsp`. Click Next.

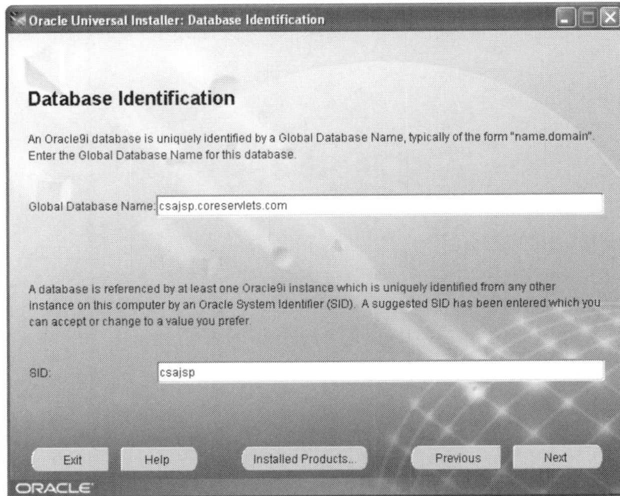

Figure 18–11 Eighth Oracle install window: for specifying the name of the global database and SID.

8. **Specify a database location.** The ninth screen displayed (Figure 18–12) defines the physical location of the database. In a production environment, Oracle recommends placing the database on a disk other than the one on which the Oracle9i software is installed. In a development environment, you might have only a single disk available. We used the default suggested location, C:\oracle\oradata. Click Next.

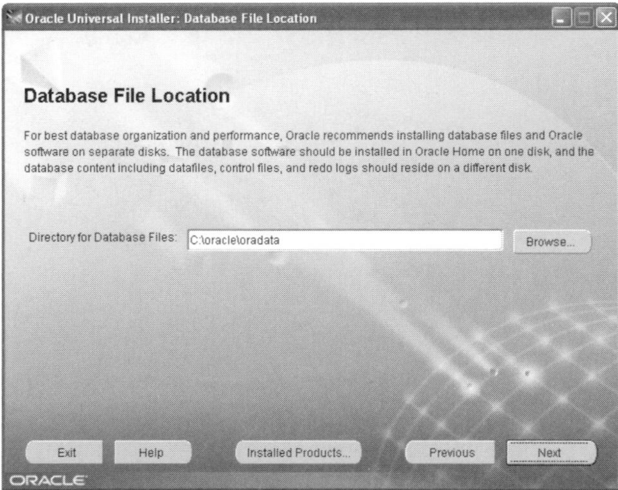

Figure 18–12 Ninth Oracle install window: for specifying the physical location of the database.

9. **Specify a default character set.** On the tenth screen displayed (Figure 18–13), you select a character set for your database. Accept the default character set in accordance with the language setting of the operating system.

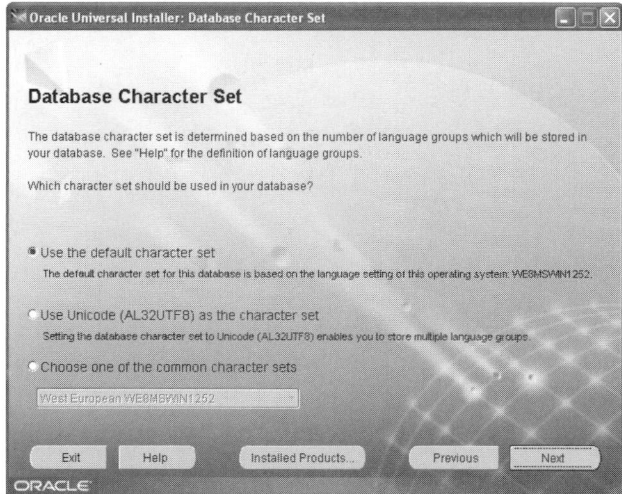

Figure 18–13 Tenth Oracle install window: for selecting the default character set to use for the database.

10. **Review list of products.** The eleventh screen displayed (Figure 18–14) summarizes which Oracle products are about to be installed on the computer. After reviewing this list, click the Install button.

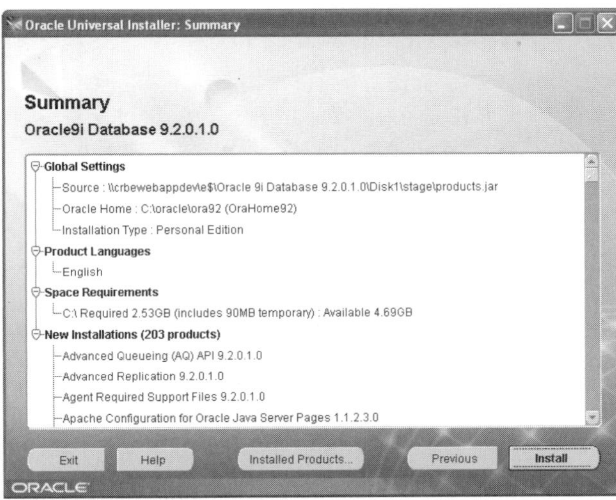

Figure 18–14 Eleventh Oracle install window: summarizes the products to be installed on the computer.

11. **Install Oracle9i.** At this point, the Oracle Universal Installer will install Oracle9i. The installer (Figure 18–15) indicates the progress of the installation and provides a brief message about each component as it is installed. All installation activity is recorded to a log file located at C:\Program Files\Oracle\Inventory\logs. You can examine the log file for details if the installation fails.

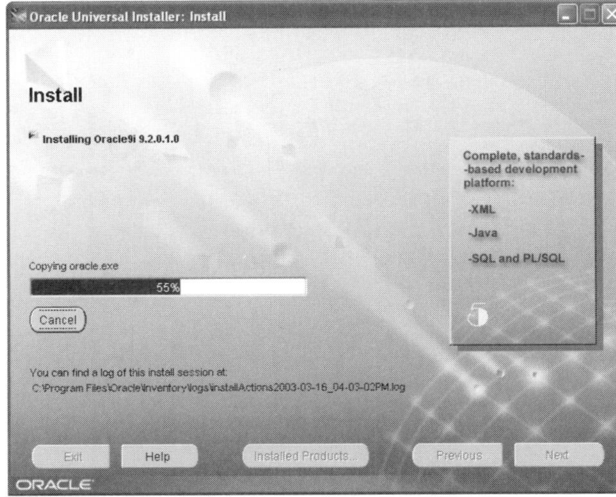

Figure 18–15 Twelfth Oracle install window: during the installation of the Oracle components.

12. **Install configuration tools.** After the core Oracle9i software is installed, you can optionally install configuration tools to manage your database. We recommend that you install the configuration tools. Click Next. Progress of the tool installations is indicated by the Oracle Universal Installer, as shown in Figure 18–16.

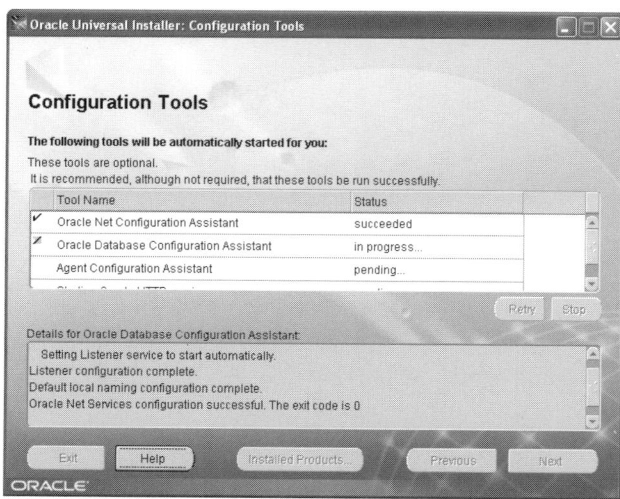

Figure 18–16 Thirteenth Oracle install window: during the installation of configuration tools.

13. **Specify passwords.** After the configuration tools are installed, the Database Configuration Assistant will prompt you for new `SYS` and `SYSTEM` passwords to manage the database (Figure 18–17). The default passwords used in many Oracle database products are `change_on_install` for `SYS` and `manager` for `SYSTEM`. Don't use these commonly known passwords. After specifying new passwords, click OK.

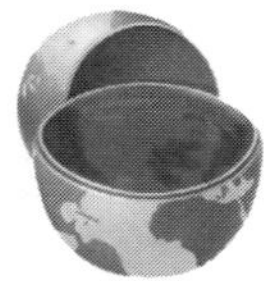

Core Warning

The default passwords for the `SYS` *and* `SYSTEM` *administrative accounts are commonly known. For secure administration of your database, specify different passwords.*

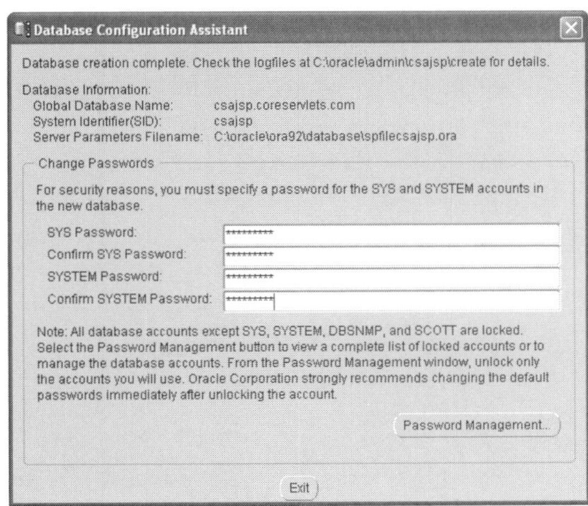

Figure 18–17 Fourteenth Oracle install window: for specifying passwords. Use the Database Configuration Assistant to specify a password for the `SYS` and `SYSTEM` administrative accounts.

14. **Complete the installation.** The last screen displayed (Figure 18–18) is the end of the installation process. At this point, Oracle9i Database Release 2 is successfully installed on your computer with a starter database named `csajsp`. Click Exit to end the Oracle Universal Installer program.

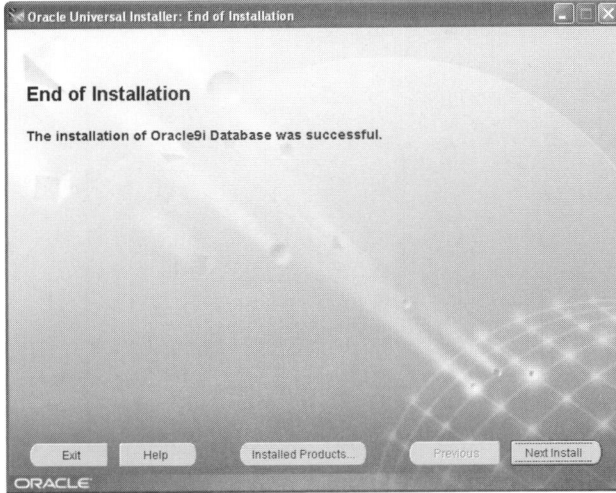

Figure 18–18 Fifteenth Oracle install window: completes the installation of Oracle9i.

Create a Database

Typically, you would create a starter database during installation of Oracle9i. However, if Oracle9i is already installed on the computer you are using, you may want to create a new database. You have two choices for creating a new database. The first choice is to use the Oracle Database Configuration Assistant, which is a graphical configuration tool. The second choice is to manually create the database. To give a better understanding of Oracle9i, we present both approaches for creating a new database. As with the Oracle9i installation, you must have local Windows administrative rights to create a new database.

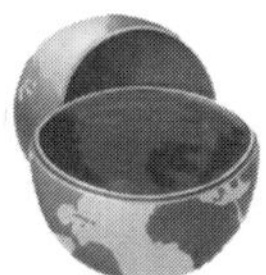

Core Warning

To create a new Oracle9i database on Windows NT/2000/XP, you must have local administrator rights on the machine.

Create a Database with the Configuration Assistant

The process to create a new database is complicated, so Oracle strongly recommends using the Database Configuration Assistant (DBCA). Following are the steps to create a database with the DBCA.

1. **Start the Oracle Database Configuration Assistant.** The DBCA is included with the Oracle9i database installation. To start the DBCA on Windows XP, from the Start menu, select Start, then Programs, then Oracle - OraHome92, then Configuration and Migration Tools, and last, Database Configuration Assistant. When the DBCA starts, a Welcome screen is displayed, as shown in Figure 18–19. Click Next.

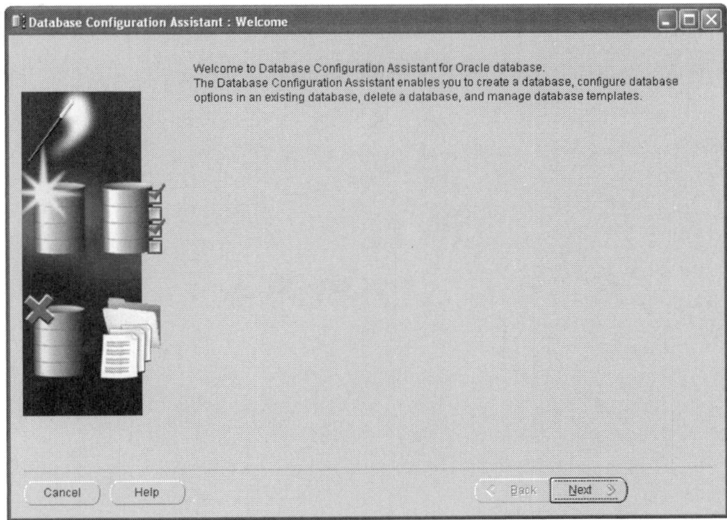

Figure 18–19 First DBCA window: Welcome message.

2. **Select an operation.** On the second screen displayed (Figure 18–20), you select an operation to perform. Select the first option: Create a database. Click Next.

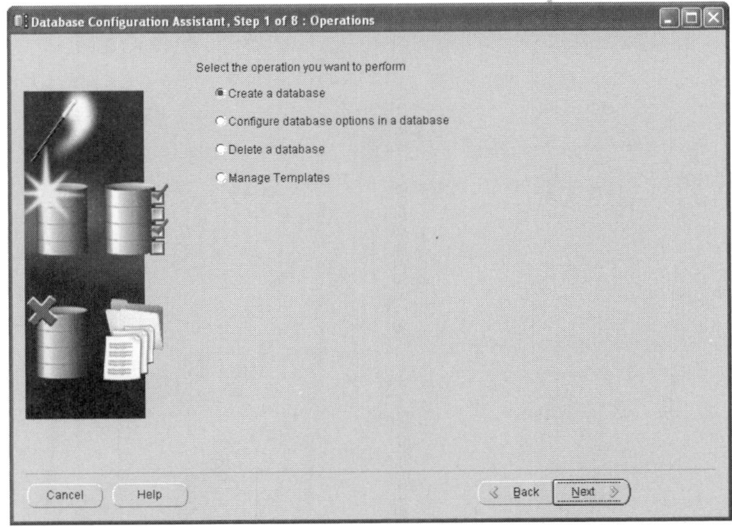

Figure 18–20 Second DBCA window: for selecting an operation to perform.

3. **Select a database template.** On the third screen displayed (Figure 18–21), you select a template for creating the database. Select the template for a new database. Click Next.

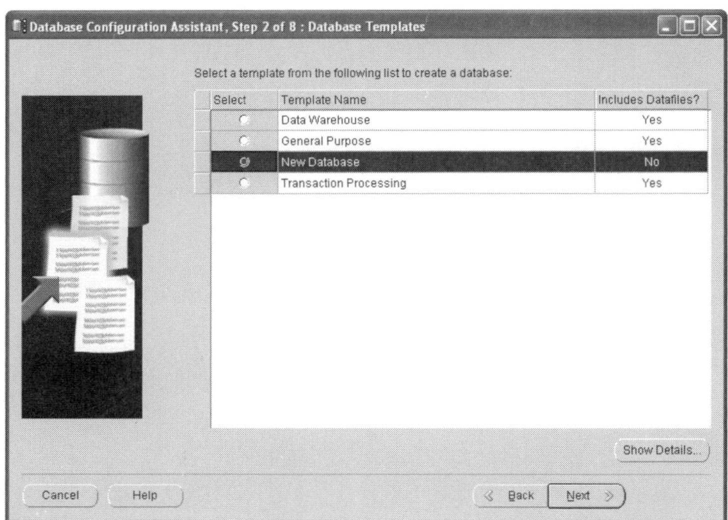

Figure 18–21 Third DBCA window: for selecting a database template.

4. **Provide a database identification.** On the fourth screen displayed (Figure 18–22), you specify a Global Database Name and SID to identify your new database. Oracle configuration and utility tools use the SID to identify the database to operate upon. For the JDBC examples presented in this book, we suggest a Global Database Name of `csa-jsp.coreservlets.com`. Entering this choice will autogenerate a SID of `csajsp`. Click Next.

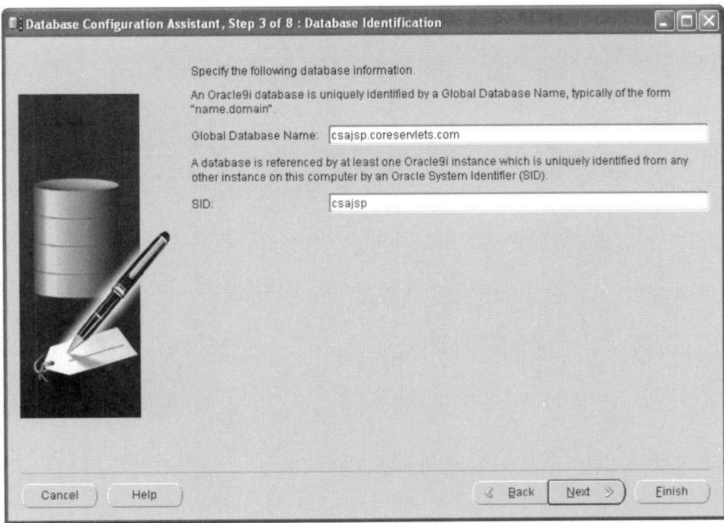

Figure 18–22 Fourth DBCA window: for specifying the name of the global database and SID.

5. **Select the database features to install.** On the fifth screen displayed (Figure 18–23), you select the features you want to configure for use in your database. To create a simple database for testing, you do not need the optional features; uncheck each of them. If you are prompted with a question to confirm deletion of an associated tablespace, answer Yes. Also, select the Standard database features button and uncheck the four options. Click Next.

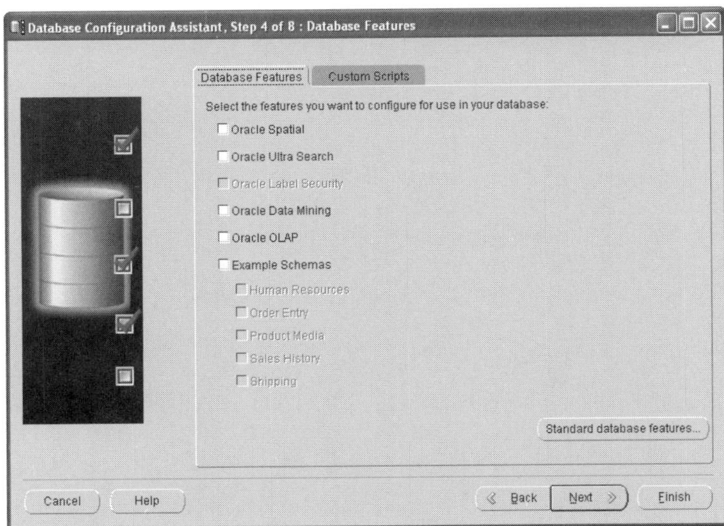

Figure 18–23 Fifth DBCA window: for selecting the database features to install.

6. **Select a database connection option.** On the sixth screen displayed (Figure 18–24), you select the mode in which you want your database to operate. Select the Dedicated Server Mode option. Click Next.

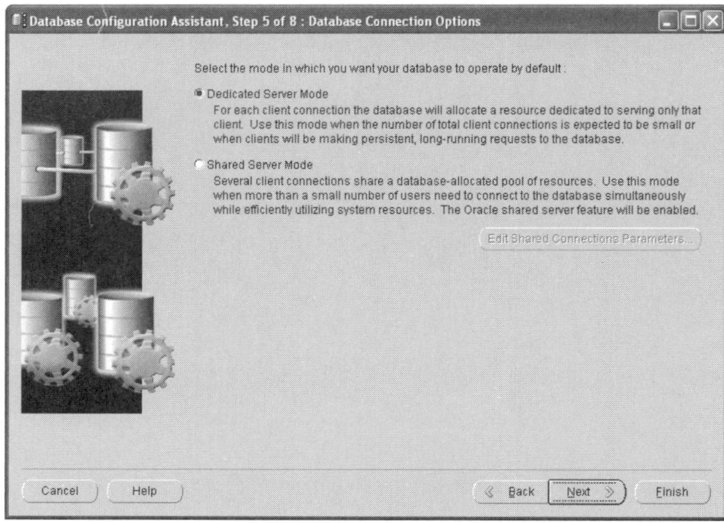

Figure 18–24 Sixth DBCA window: for selecting the operational mode of the database.

7. **Specify initialization parameters.** On the seventh screen displayed (Figure 18–25), you can customize the database. The default parameters are sufficient, so you don't need to customize any of the tab settings. Click Next.

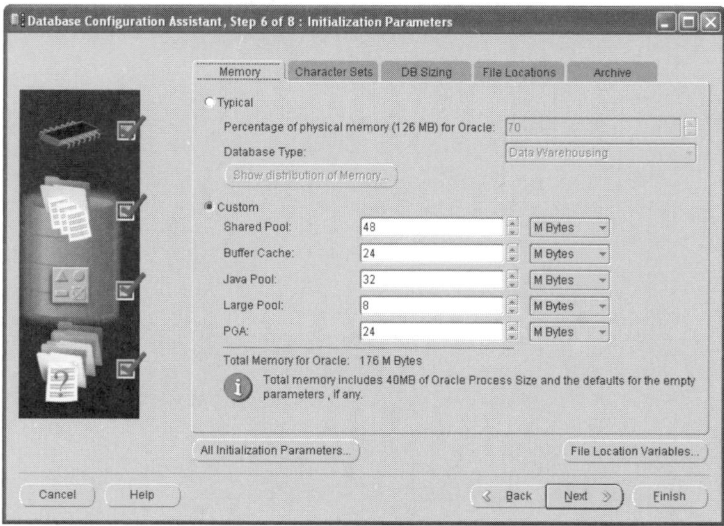

Figure 18–25 Seventh DBCA window: for specifying database initialization parameters.

8. **Specify storage parameters.** On the eighth screen displayed (Figure 18–26) you specify storage parameters for the database creation. The default storage files and locations are sufficient and require no modification. Click Next.

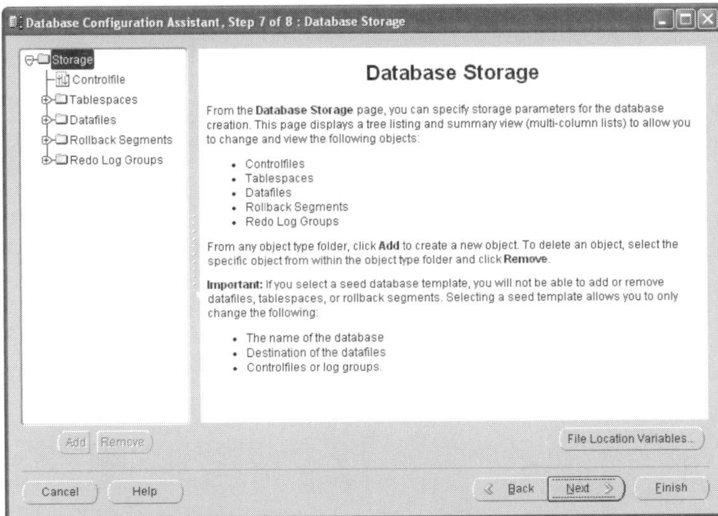

Figure 18–26 Eighth DBCA window: for specifying database storage parameters.

9. **Select database creation options**. On the ninth screen displayed (Figure 18–27), you specify the database creation options. Here, you simply want to create a new database, so check the Create Database option. Click Next.

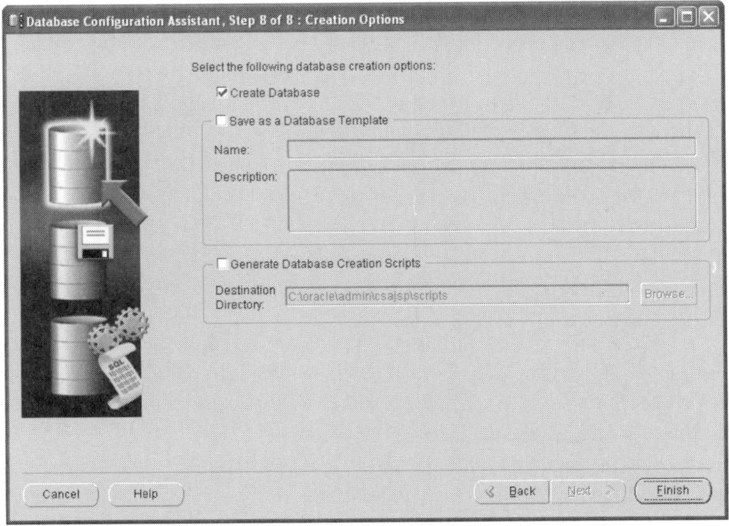

Figure 18–27 Ninth DBCA window: for selecting database creation options.

10. **Review the database configuration.** At this point, the DBCA presents a summary of all the selected options to create the database, as shown in Figure 18–28. After you have reviewed the options, click OK.

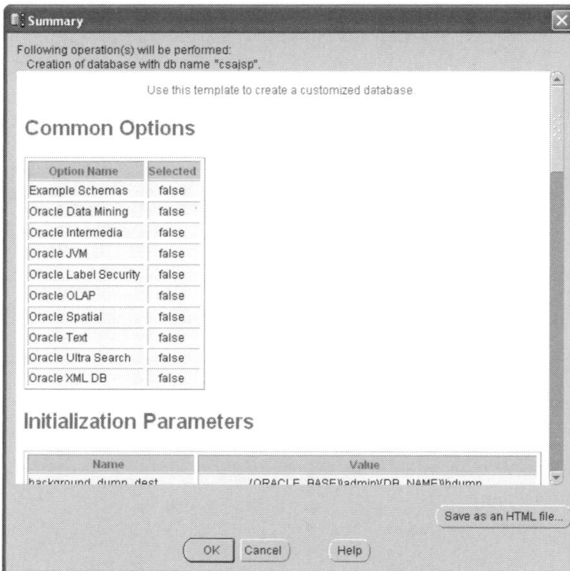

Figure 18–28 Tenth DBCA window: summarizes the configuration options before the database is created.

11. **Monitor the database creation process.** The eleventh screen displayed (Figure 18–29) indicates activities as the database is created. You can monitor this process if so desired.

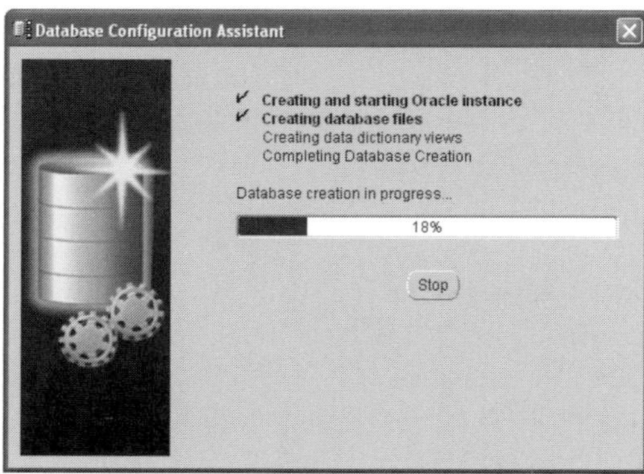

Figure 18–29 Eleventh DBCA window: during the creation of the database.

12. **Specify passwords.** After the database is installed, the Database Configuration Assistant will prompt you for `SYS` and `SYSTEM` passwords to manage the database (Figure 18–30). After specifying new passwords, click OK to complete the database creation process.

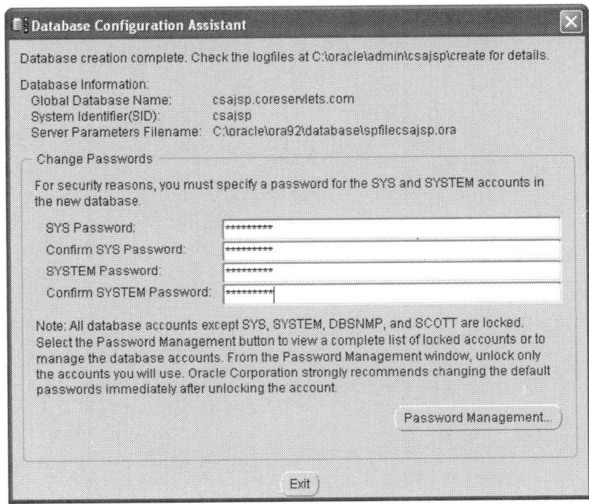

Figure 18–30 Twelfth DBCA window: for specifying the `SYS` and `SYSTEM` administrative passwords.

Create a Database Manually

You usually use the Database Configuration Assistant (described in the previous subsection) to create new databases. However, for more complete control of the process, you occasionally want to do it manually. This section describes that manual process. The following list briefly outlines the steps to manually create an Oracle9i database. Detailed instructions follow the list.

1. **Set up database directories.** Before you can create a new database, you must first set up the necessary directories for both administrative and database files.
2. **Create an initialization parameter file.** An initialization parameter file is required for configuration and startup of the database. In addition to other information, the parameter file contains information about the block size and the number of processes permitted.
3. **Create a password file.** A password file containing user authorization information is required for management of the database. Administrators can be authenticated either through a password file or through OS system groups. For this configuration, we use a password file.

4. **Create a service for the database.** On Windows NT/2000/XP, the database runs as a service. This approach prevents the database from shutting down when the administrator logs off the computer.
5. **Declare the `ORACLE_SID` value.** The `ORACLE_SID` is an environment variable to declare which database to use when running Oracle tools, such as SQL*Plus.
6. **Connect to the Oracle service as `SYSDBA`.** To manage and create a database from SQL*Plus, you must connect to the Oracle service as the system database administrator (`SYSDBA`).
7. **Start the database instance.** Starting the instance initializes the memory and processes to permit creation and management of a database. If the database instance is not started, the database cannot be created.
8. **Create the database.** Issue a command in SQL*Plus to create the database, allocating log and temp files.
9. **Create a user tablespace.** The tablespace stores the tables created by a user of the database.
10. **Run scripts to build data dictionary views.** Two scripts, catalog.sql and catproc.sql, must be run to set up views and synonyms in the database. The first script, catproc.sql, also configures the database for use with PL/SQL.

Next, we provide detailed information about each step.

Set Up Database Directories

Before creating a new database, set up the directories for both the administrative and database files. Assuming that Oracle9i is installed on the C:\ drive, create the following directories:

```
C:\oracle\admin\csajsp
C:\oracle\admin\csajsp\bdump
C:\oracle\admin\csajsp\cdump
C:\oracle\admin\csajsp\pfile
C:\oracle\admin\csajsp\udump
C:\oracle\oradata\csajsp
```

The bdump directory holds alert and trace files on behalf of background processes. The cdump directory stores a core dump file should the Oracle server fail and be unrecoverable. The udump directory holds trace files used on behalf of a user process. The oradata\csajsp directory contains the physical database.

Create an Initialization Parameter File

For the database to start up, Oracle must read an initialization parameter file. The parameters in this file initialize many of the memory and process settings of the Oracle instance. The standard naming convention for an initialization parameter file is init*SID*.ora, where *SID* is the system identifier for the database.

An instance is a combination of the memory and background processes associated with the database. A significant component of the instance is the System Global Area (SGA) that is allocated when the instance is started. The SGA is a memory area that stores and processes data retrieved from the physical database.

Core Note

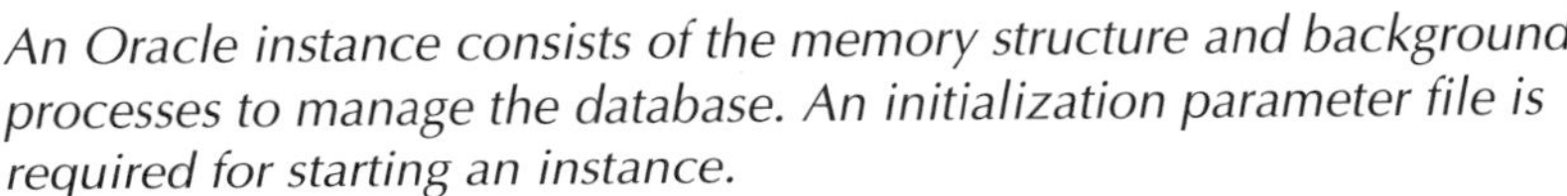

An Oracle instance consists of the memory structure and background processes to manage the database. An initialization parameter file is required for starting an instance.

In practice, most database administrators simply copy and modify an existing parameter file when they need to create a new database. Listing 18.1 presents an example initialization parameter file that creates a database named `csajsp` on Windows XP. Place this file in the C:\oracle\admin\csajsp\pfile directory.

For more information on initialization parameters, see Chapter 1 of the online Oracle9i Database Reference at http://download-west.oracle.com/docs/cd/B10501_01/server.920/a96536/toc.htm. The minimum parameters that must be specified in an initialization parameter file are `background_dump_dest`, `compatible`, `control_files`, `db_block_buffers`, `db_name`, `shared_pool_size`, and `user_dump_dest`.

Listing 18.1 initCSAJSP.ora (database initialization parameter file)

```
# Initialization parameter file for Oracle9i database
# on Windows XP.

# Database Identification
db_domain=coreservlets.com
db_name=csajsp

# Instance Identification
instance_name=csajsp
```

Listing 18.1 initCSAJSP.ora (database initialization parameter file) *(continued)*

```
# Cache and I/O
db_block_size=8192
db_cache_size=25165824
db_file_multiblock_read_count=16

# Cursors and Library Cache
open_cursors=300

# Diagnostics and Statistics
background_dump_dest=C:\oracle\admin\csajsp\bdump
core_dump_dest=C:\oracle\admin\csajsp\cdump
timed_statistics=TRUE
user_dump_dest=C:\oracle\admin\csajsp\udump

# File Configuration
control_files=("C:\oracle\oradata\csajsp\CONTROL01.CTL",
               "C:\oracle\oradata\csajsp\CONTROL02.CTL",
               "C:\oracle\oradata\csajsp\CONTROL03.CTL")

# Job Queues
job_queue_processes=10

# MTS
dispatchers="(PROTOCOL=TCP) (SERVICE=csajspXDB)"

# Miscellaneous
aq_tm_processes=1
compatible=9.2.0.0.0

# Optimizer
hash_join_enabled=TRUE
query_rewrite_enabled=FALSE
star_transformation_enabled=FALSE

# Pools
java_pool_size=33554432
large_pool_size=8388608
shared_pool_size=50331648

# Processes and Sessions
processes=150

# Redo Log and Recovery
fast_start_mttr_target=300
```

Listing 18.1 initCSAJSP.ora (database initialization parameter file) *(continued)*

```
# Security and Auditing
remote_login_passwordfile=EXCLUSIVE

# Sort, Hash Joins, Bitmap Indexes
pga_aggregate_target=25165824
sort_area_size=524288

# System Managed Undo and Rollback Segments
undo_management=AUTO
undo_retention=10800
undo_tablespace=undotbs
```

Create a Password File

If the initialization parameter REMOTE_LOGIN_PASSWORDFILE is set to EXCLUSIVE, a password file must be created to authenticate administrators that have SYSDBA privileges. Connecting to an Oracle service with SYSDBA privileges gives the administrator unrestricted ability to perform any operation on the database. Using a password file to authenticate the administrator provides the greatest level of security.

Use the ORAPWD command-line tool to create a password file. The command accepts three arguments: FILE, which specifies the location and filename of the password file; PASSWORD, which specifies the password to assign to user SYS for administering the database; and ENTRIES, which specifies the maximum number of users to whom you intend to grant SYSDBA privileges for administering the database (the user SYS already has SYSDBA privileges).

For example, the following command,

```
Prompt> ORAPWD FILE="C:\oracle\ora92\DATABASE\PWDcsajsp.ora"
               PASSWORD=csajspDBA ENTRIES=5
```

creates the password file named PWDcsajsp.ora, with csajspDBA as the SYS user password to administrate the database. The ENTRIES value of 5 defines a total of 5 users (administrators) with SYSDBA privileges in the password file.

By convention, for Oracle9i, the password file is placed in the C:\oracle\ora92\DATABASE directory and the name of the password file is PWD*database*.ora, where ***database*** is the name (SID) of the database associated with the password file.

Create an Oracle Service for the Database

Before creating the database on Windows NT/2000/XP, you need to create an Oracle service to run the database. Creating an Oracle service avoids process termination of the database when the administrator logs out of the computer. To accomplish this step, use the `oradim` command-line utility.

Assuming that the SID for your database is `csajsp` and the initialization parameter file is initCSAJSP.ora, located in C:\oracle\admin\csajsp\pfile, use the following command to create the Oracle service.

```
Prompt> oradim -NEW -SID CSAJSP -STARTMODE MANUAL
          -PFILE "C:\oracle\admin\csajsp\pfile\initCSAJSP.ora"
```

This command will create a service named `OracleServiceCSAJSP`, configured to start up manually. When first created, however, the service should start. To check that the service has started, issue the following command.

```
Prompt> net start OracleServiceCSAJSP
```

If you want the database service to start when the computer is rebooted, change the service startup type to automatic. To change the startup type on Windows XP, go to the Start menu, then Control Panel, then Performance and Maintenance, then Administrative Tools, Services, then right-click the service to change and select Properties. Next, simply change the Startup type from the available dropdown list.

Declare the `ORACLE_SID` Value

The `ORACLE_SID` is an environment variable used by various Oracle tools (e.g., SQL*Plus) to identify which database to operate upon. To set the `ORACLE_SID` to the `csajsp` database, enter the following command.

```
Prompt> set ORACLE_SID=csajsp
```

Note that there should be no spaces around the equal (=) character.

Connect to the Oracle Service as `SYSDBA`

The next step is to use SQL*Plus to connect to the database service as a system DBA (`SYSDBA`) before creating the new database. First, start SQL*Plus with the `nolog` option, as below.

```
Prompt> SQLPLUS /nolog
```

Then, connect to the Oracle service as `SYSDBA`, using the following command,

```
SQL> CONNECT SYS/password AS SYSDBA
```

where *password* is the SYS password you specified when creating the password file earlier. Note: by your setting of the ORACLE_SID environment variable, SQL*Plus automatically knows the database service in which to connect (OracleService-CSAJSP, in this case).

Start the Oracle Instance

The Oracle instance must be started to create a new database. To start the instance without mounting the database, issue the following command in SQL*Plus.

```
SQL> STARTUP NOMOUNT
                PFILE="C:\oracle\admin\csajsp\pfile\initCSAJSP.ora"
```

The PFILE must refer to the file containing the initialization parameters for the database. Starting the instance in NOMOUNT creates the SGA and starts background processes. However, the database cannot be accessed. Typically, you start a database in NOMOUNT only during creation of the database or during maintenance of the database (e.g., creating control files).

Create the Database

To create a new database, you issue the CREATE DATABASE SQL command in SQL*Plus. Listing 18.2 provides a CREATE DATABASE command to create the csajsp database on a Windows NT/2000/XP platform. To create the database, simply type (cut and paste) this command to SQL*Plus. Or alternatively, you can create the database by running the create_csajsp.sql script from SQL*Plus. To execute the script, use the following command.

```
SQL> @create_csajsp.sql
```

Note that you may need to specify the full path after the @ for SQL*Plus to find the script.

Execution of this command (or script) creates the csajsp database in the C:\oracle\oradata\csajsp directory and automatically creates two user accounts, SYS and SYSTEM, to administer the database. SYS is the owner of the database dictionary (information about structure and users of the database), and SYSTEM is the owner of additional tables and views used by Oracle tools.

If the database creation fails, examine the alert log file, C:\oracle\admin\csajsp\bdump\alert_csajsp.log, for errors. Correct the problem, delete all the files in the C:\oracle\oradata\csajsp directory, and reissue the command.

Listing 18.2 create_csajsp.sql

```
/* SQL command to create an Oracle9i database named csajsp. */

CREATE DATABASE csajsp
  USER SYS IDENTIFIED BY csajspDBA
  USER SYSTEM IDENTIFIED BY csajspMAN
  LOGFILE
    GROUP 1 ('C:\oracle\oradata\csajsp\redo01.log') SIZE 100M,
    GROUP 2 ('C:\oracle\oradata\csajsp\redo02.log') SIZE 100M,
    GROUP 3 ('C:\oracle\oradata\csajsp\redo03.log') SIZE 100M
  MAXLOGFILES 5
  MAXDATAFILES 100
  MAXINSTANCES 1
  CHARACTER SET WE8MSWIN1252
  NATIONAL CHARACTER SET AL16UTF16
  DATAFILE 'C:\oracle\oradata\csajsp\system01.dbf'
    SIZE 325M REUSE
    AUTOEXTEND ON NEXT 10240K MAXSIZE UNLIMITED
    EXTENT MANAGEMENT LOCAL
  DEFAULT TEMPORARY TABLESPACE temp
    TEMPFILE 'C:\oracle\oradata\csajsp\temptbs01.dbf'
    SIZE 20M REUSE
    EXTENT MANAGEMENT LOCAL
  UNDO TABLESPACE undotbs
    DATAFILE 'C:\oracle\oradata\csajsp\undotbs01.dbf'
    SIZE 200M REUSE
      AUTOEXTEND ON NEXT 5120K MAXSIZE UNLIMITED;
```

Create a User Tablespace

Before users can store information in a database, you must create a tablespace for them. All tables created by the user are placed in the tablespace. To create a user tablespace, enter the following command in SQL*Plus.

```
SQL> CREATE TABLESPACE users
       DATAFILE 'C:\oracle\oradata\csajsp\users01.dbf'
       SIZE 15M REUSE
       AUTOEXTEND ON NEXT 1280K MAXSIZE UNLIMITED
       EXTENT MANAGEMENT LOCAL;
```

This command creates a tablespace named `users` with an initial size of 15 Mbytes. The data is physically stored in the file users01.dbf.

Run Scripts to Build Data Dictionary Views

The last step in creating the database is to run the catalog.sql and catproc.sql scripts from SQL*Plus. Enter the full path to the script preceded by an `@`.

```
SQL> @C:\oracle\rdbms\admin\catalog.sql
SQL> @C:\oracle\rdbms\admin\catproc.sql
```

The catalog.sql script creates views and synonyms for the data dictionary tables. The catproc.sql script runs all scripts required or used with Oracle PL/SQL. Both of these scripts generate considerable output, which can be ignored; error messages may occur as tables and views are first dropped before being created.

Create a User

To access the database from a Web application, you'll need to create a new user with the appropriate rights. From SQL*Plus, enter the following `CREATE USER` command,

```
SQL> CREATE USER username IDENTIFIED BY password
        DEFAULT TABLESPACE users
        QUOTA UNLIMITED ON users
        TEMPORARY TABLESPACE temp;
```

where *`username`* is the login name for the new user and *`password`* is the password for the new user. The default tablespace is where tables created by the user are placed, and the `QUOTA` clause grants unlimited use to store information in the `users` tablespace. If a `QUOTA` is not specified for the default tablespace, then the user cannot create any tables. A temporary tablespace is also assigned to the user for sorting data if required by the SQL query.

Next, you need to grant the new user rights to connect to the database service and to create new tables. Issue the following SQL*Plus command,

```
SQL> GRANT CREATE SESSION, CREATE TABLE
        TO username;
```

where *`username`* is the user requiring access to the database. Granting the `CREATE TABLE` privilege also enables the user to drop tables.

Install the JDBC Driver

In our JDBC examples, we use the Oracle Thin JDBC driver, which establishes a direct TCP connection to the Oracle database server. Oracle JDBC drivers are downloadable from http://otn.oracle.com/software/tech/java/sqlj_jdbc/. Download the appropriate version, bundled as classes12.zip (for use with JDK 1.2 and JDK 1.3) or ojdbc14.jar (for use with the JDK 1.4) and place it in your `CLASSPATH` for development and in your application's WEB-INF/lib directory for deployment.

If multiple applications on the Web server access Oracle databases, the Web administrator may choose to move the JAR file to a common directory on the container. For example, with Tomcat, JAR files used by multiple applications can be placed in the *install_dir*/common/lib directory.

If your Web application server does not recognize ZIP files located in the WEB-INF/lib directory, you can change the extension of the file to .jar; ZIP and JAR compression algorithms are compatible (JAR files simply include a manifest with metainformation about the archive). However, some developers choose to unzip the file and then create an uncompressed JAR file by using the `jar` tool with the `-0` command option. Both compressed and uncompressed JAR files are supported in a `CLASSPATH`, but classes from an uncompressed JAR file can load faster. See http://java.sun.com/j2se/1.4.1/docs/tooldocs/tools.html for platform-specific documentation on the Java archive tool.

As a final note, if security is also important in your database transmissions, see http://download-west.oracle.com/docs/cd/B10501_01/java.920/a96654/advanc.htm, for ways to encrypt traffic over your JDBC connections. To encrypt the traffic from the Web server to the client browser, use SSL (for details, see the chapters on Web application security in Volume 2 of this book).

18.4 Testing Your Database Through a JDBC Connection

After installing and configuring your database, you will want to test your database for JDBC connectivity. In Listing 18.3, we provide a program to perform the following database tests.

- Establish a JDBC connection to the database and report the product name and version.
- Create a simple "authors" table containing the ID, first name, and last name of the two authors of *Core Servlets and JavaServer Pages, Second Edition*.
- Query the "authors" table, summarizing the ID, first name, and last name for each author.
- Perform a nonrigorous test to determine the JDBC version. Use the reported JDBC version with caution: the reported JDBC version does not mean that the driver is certified to support all classes and methods defined by that JDBC version.

Since `TestDatabase` is in the `coreservlets` package, it must reside in a subdirectory called coreservlets. Before compiling the file, set the `CLASSPATH` to include the directory *containing* the coreservlets directory. See Section 2.7 (Set Up

Your Development Environment) for details. With this setup, simply compile the program by running `javac TestDatabase.java` from within the **coreservlets** subdirectory (or by selecting "build" or "compile" in your IDE). However, to run `TestDatabase`, you need to refer to the full package name as shown in the following command,

```
Prompt> java coreservlets.TestDatabase host dbName
            username password vendor
```

where *host* is the hostname of the database server, *dbName* is the name of the database you want to test, *username* and *password* are those of the user configured to access the database, and *vendor* is a keyword identifying the vendor driver.

This program uses the class `DriverUtilities` from Chapter 17 (Listing 17.5) to load the vendor's driver information and to create a URL to the database. Currently, `DriverUtilities` supports Microsoft Access, MySQL, and Oracle databases. If you use a different database vendor, you will need to modify `DriverUtilities` and add the vendor information. See Section 17.3 (Simplifying Database Access with JDBC Utilities) for details.

The following shows the output when `TestDatabase` is run against a MySQL database named `csajsp`, using the MySQL Connector/J 3.0 driver.

```
Prompt> java coreservlets.TestDatabase localhost
            csajsp brown larry MYSQL

Testing database connection ...

Driver: com.mysql.jdbc.Driver
URL: jdbc:mysql://localhost:3306/csajsp
Username: brown
Password: larry
Product name: MySQL
Product version: 4.0.12-max-nt
Driver Name: MySQL-AB JDBC Driver
Driver Version: 3.0.6-stable ( $Date: 2003/02/17 17:01:34 $,
$Revision: 1.27.2.1
3 $ )

Creating authors table ... successful

Querying authors table ...
+-------------+-------------+-------------+
| id          | first_name  | last_name   |
+-------------+-------------+-------------+
| 1           | Marty       | Hall        |
| 2           | Larry       | Brown       |
+-------------+-------------+-------------+
```

```
Checking JDBC version ...

JDBC Version: 3.0
```

Interestingly, the MySQL Connector/J 3.0 driver used with MySQL 4.0.12 reports a JDBC version of 3.0. However, MySQL is not fully ANSI SQL-92 compliant and the driver cannot be JDBC 3.0 certified. Therefore, you should always check the vendor's documentation closely for the JDBC version and always thoroughly test your product before releasing to production.

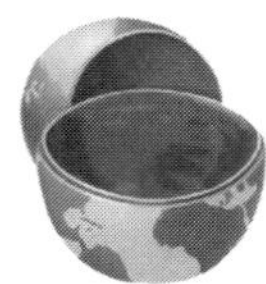

Core Warning

The JDBC version reported by `DatabaseMetaData` *is unofficial. The driver is not necessarily certified at the level reported. Check the vendor documentation.*

Listing 18.3 TestDatabase.java

```
package coreservlets;

import java.sql.*;

/** Perform the following tests on a database:
 *  <OL>
 *  <LI>Create a JDBC connection to the database and report
 *      the product name and version.
 *  <LI>Create a simple "authors" table containing the
 *      ID, first name, and last name for the two authors
 *      of Core Servlets and JavaServer Pages, 2nd Edition.
 *  <LI>Query the "authors" table for all rows.
 *  <LI>Determine the JDBC version. Use with caution:
 *      the reported JDBC version does not mean that the
 *      driver has been certified.
 *  </OL>
 */

public class TestDatabase {
  private String driver;
  private String url;
  private String username;
  private String password;
```

Listing 18.3 TestDatabase.java *(continued)*

```
public TestDatabase(String driver, String url,
                    String username, String password) {
  this.driver = driver;
  this.url = url;
  this.username = username;
  this.password = password;
}

/** Test the JDBC connection to the database and report the
 *  product name and product version.
 */

public void testConnection() {
  System.out.println();
  System.out.println("Testing database connection ...\n");
  Connection connection = getConnection();
  if (connection == null) {
    System.out.println("Test failed.");
    return;
  }
  try {
    DatabaseMetaData dbMetaData = connection.getMetaData();
    String productName =
      dbMetaData.getDatabaseProductName();
    String productVersion =
      dbMetaData.getDatabaseProductVersion();
    String driverName = dbMetaData.getDriverName();
    String driverVersion = dbMetaData.getDriverVersion();
    System.out.println("Driver: " + driver);
    System.out.println("URL: " + url);
    System.out.println("Username: " + username);
    System.out.println("Password: " + password);
    System.out.println("Product name: " + productName);
    System.out.println("Product version: " + productVersion);
    System.out.println("Driver Name: " + driverName);
    System.out.println("Driver Version: " + driverVersion);
  } catch(SQLException sqle) {
    System.err.println("Error connecting: " + sqle);
  } finally {
    closeConnection(connection);
  }
  System.out.println();
}
```

Listing 18.3 TestDatabase.java *(continued)*

```
/** Create a simple table (authors) containing the ID,
 *  first_name, and last_name for the two authors of
 *  Core Servlets and JavaServer Pages, 2nd Edition.
 */

public void createTable() {
  System.out.print("Creating authors table ... ");
  Connection connection = getConnection();
  if (connection == null) {
    System.out.println("failure");
    return;
  }
  try {
    String format =
      "(id INTEGER, first_name VARCHAR(12), " +
      " last_name VARCHAR(12))";
    String[] rows = { "(1, 'Marty', 'Hall')",
                      "(2, 'Larry', 'Brown')" };
    Statement statement = connection.createStatement();
    // Drop previous table if it exists, but don't get
    // error if not. Thus, the separate try/catch here.
    try {
      statement.execute("DROP TABLE authors");
    } catch(SQLException sqle) {}
    String createCommand =
      "CREATE TABLE authors " + format;
    statement.execute(createCommand);
    String insertPrefix =
      "INSERT INTO authors VALUES";
    for(int i=0; i<rows.length; i++) {
      statement.execute(insertPrefix + rows[i]);
    }
    System.out.println("successful");
  } catch(SQLException sqle) {
    System.out.println("failure");
    System.err.println("Error creating table: " + sqle);
  } finally {
    closeConnection(connection);
  }
  System.out.println();
}
```

Listing 18.3 TestDatabase.java *(continued)*

```
/** Query all rows in the "authors" table. */

public void executeQuery() {
  System.out.println("Querying authors table ... ");
  Connection connection = getConnection();
  if (connection == null) {
    System.out.println("Query failed.");
    return;
  }
  try {
    Statement statement = connection.createStatement();
    String query = "SELECT * FROM authors";
    ResultSet resultSet = statement.executeQuery(query);
    ResultSetMetaData resultSetMetaData =
      resultSet.getMetaData();
    int columnCount = resultSetMetaData.getColumnCount();
    // Print out columns
    String[] columns = new String[columnCount];
    int[] widths = new int[columnCount];
    for(int i=1; i <= columnCount; i++) {
      columns[i-1] = resultSetMetaData.getColumnName(i);
      widths[i-1] = resultSetMetaData.getColumnDisplaySize(i);
    }
    System.out.println(makeSeparator(widths));
    System.out.println(makeRow(columns, widths));
    // Print out rows
    System.out.println(makeSeparator(widths));
    String[] rowData = new String[columnCount];
    while(resultSet.next()) {
      for(int i=1; i <= columnCount; i++) {
        rowData[i-1] = resultSet.getString(i);
      }
      System.out.println(makeRow(rowData, widths));
    }
    System.out.println(makeSeparator(widths));
  } catch(SQLException sqle) {
    System.err.println("Error executing query: " + sqle);
  } finally {
    closeConnection(connection);
  }
  System.out.println();
}
```

Listing 18.3 TestDatabase.java *(continued)*

```
/** Perform a nonrigorous test for the JDBC version.
 *  Initially, a last() operation is attempted for
 *  JDBC 2.0. Then, calls to getJDBCMajorVersion and
 *  getJDBCMinorVersion are attempted for JDBC 3.0.
 */

public void checkJDBCVersion() {
  System.out.println();
  System.out.println("Checking JDBC version ...\n");
  Connection connection = getConnection();
  if (connection == null) {
    System.out.println("Check failed.");
    return;
  }
  int majorVersion = 1;
  int minorVersion = 0;
  try {
    Statement statement = connection.createStatement(
                            ResultSet.TYPE_SCROLL_INSENSITIVE,
                            ResultSet.CONCUR_READ_ONLY);
    String query = "SELECT * FROM authors";
    ResultSet resultSet = statement.executeQuery(query);
    resultSet.last(); // JDBC 2.0
    majorVersion = 2;
  } catch(SQLException sqle) {
    // Ignore - last() not supported
  }
  try {
    DatabaseMetaData dbMetaData = connection.getMetaData();
    majorVersion = dbMetaData.getJDBCMajorVersion(); // JDBC 3.0
    minorVersion = dbMetaData.getJDBCMinorVersion(); // JDBC 3.0
  } catch(Throwable throwable) {
    // Ignore - methods not supported
  } finally {
    closeConnection(connection);
  }
  System.out.println("JDBC Version: " +
                     majorVersion + "." + minorVersion);
}

// A String of the form "|  xxx |  xxx |  xxx |"

private String makeRow(String[] entries, int[] widths) {
  String row = "|";
  for(int i=0; i<entries.length; i++) {
    row = row + padString(entries[i], widths[i], " ");
```

Listing 18.3 TestDatabase.java *(continued)*

```
      row = row + " |";
    }
    return(row);
  }

  // A String of the form "+------+-----+------+"

  private String makeSeparator(int[] widths) {
    String separator = "+";
    for(int i=0; i<widths.length; i++) {
      separator += padString("", widths[i] + 1, "-") + "+";
    }
    return(separator);
  }

  private String padString(String orig, int size,
                           String padChar) {
    if (orig == null) {
      orig = "<null>";
    }
    // Use StringBuffer, not just repeated String concatenation
    // to avoid creating too many temporary Strings.
    StringBuffer buffer = new StringBuffer(padChar);
    int extraChars = size - orig.length();
    buffer.append(orig);
    for(int i=0; i<extraChars; i++) {
      buffer.append(padChar);
    }
    return(buffer.toString());
  }

  /** Obtain a new connection to the database or return
   *  null on failure.
   */

  public Connection getConnection() {
    try {
      Class.forName(driver);
      Connection connection =
        DriverManager.getConnection(url, username,
                                    password);
      return(connection);
    } catch(ClassNotFoundException cnfe) {
      System.err.println("Error loading driver: " + cnfe);
      return(null);
```

Listing 18.3 TestDatabase.java *(continued)*

```
    } catch(SQLException sqle) {
      System.err.println("Error connecting: " + sqle);
      return(null);
    }
  }

  /** Close the database connection. */

  private void closeConnection(Connection connection) {
    try {
      connection.close();
    } catch(SQLException sqle) {
      System.err.println("Error closing connection: " + sqle);
      connection = null;
    }
  }

  public static void main(String[] args) {
    if (args.length < 5) {
      printUsage();
      return;
    }
    String vendor = args[4];
    // Change to DriverUtilities2.loadDrivers() to
    // load the drivers from an XML file.
    DriverUtilities.loadDrivers();
    if (!DriverUtilities.isValidVendor(vendor)) {
      printUsage();
      return;
    }
    String driver = DriverUtilities.getDriver(vendor);
    String host = args[0];
    String dbName = args[1];
    String url =
      DriverUtilities.makeURL(host, dbName, vendor);
    String username = args[2];
    String password = args[3];

    TestDatabase database =
      new TestDatabase(driver, url, username, password);
    database.testConnection();
    database.createTable();
    database.executeQuery();
    database.checkJDBCVersion();
  }
```

Listing 18.3 TestDatabase.java *(continued)*

```
  private static void printUsage() {
    System.out.println("Usage: TestDatabase host dbName " +
                       "username password vendor.");
  }
}
```

18.5 Setting Up the music Table

The JDBC examples in this book use the `Employees` table from the Microsoft Access Northwind database (see Section 17.2) and the custom `music` table, shown in Table 18.1.

Table 18.1 Music Table

ID	COMPOSER	CONCERTO	AVAILABLE	PRICE
1	Mozart	No. 21 in C# minor	7	24.99
2	Beethoven	No. 3 in C minor	28	10.99
3	Beethoven	No. 5 Eb major	33	10.99
4	Rachmaninov	No. 2 in C minor	9	18.99
5	Mozart	No. 24 in C minor	11	21.99
6	Beethoven	No. 4 in G	33	12.99
7	Liszt	No. 1 in Eb major	48	10.99

The `music` table summarizes the price and availability of concerto recordings for various classical composers. To create the `music` table in your database, you can run either of the two programs CreateMusicTable.java or create_music_table.sql, as explained in the following subsections.

Using CreateMusicTable.java to Create the music Table

The Java program CreateMusicTable.java, for creating the `music` table, is shown in Listing 18.4. Since `CreateMusicTable` is in the `coreservlets` package, the file must reside in a subdirectory called coreservlets. Before compiling the file, set the

CLASSPATH to include the directory *containing* the **coreservlets** directory (see Section 2.7, "Set Up Your Development Environment") and compile the program by running javac CreateMusicTable.java from within the **coreservlets** subdirectory. However, to create the music table, you must refer to the full package name when executing CreateMusicTable, as shown in the following command,

```
Prompt> java coreservlets.CreateMusicTable host dbName
            username password vendor
```

where *host* is the hostname of the database server, *dbName* is the name of the database in which to load the table, *username* and *password* are those of the user configured to access the database, and *vendor* is a keyword identifying the vendor driver (MSACCESS, MYSQL, ORACLE). Thus, if running MySQL on the local host with a database name of csajsp, you might enter the command

```
Prompt> java coreservlets.CreateMusicTable localhost
            CSAJSP brown larry MYSQL
```

where brown is the username and larry is the password to access the database.

This program uses two classes from Chapter 17: DriverUtilities in Listing 17.5 and ConnectionInfoBean in Listing 17.9. DriverUtilities loads the driver information and creates a URL to the database. ConnectionInfoBean stores connection information to a database and can create a database connection. Currently, DriverUtilities supports Microsoft Access, MySQL, and Oracle databases. If using a different database vendor, you must modify DriverUtilities and add your specific vendor information. See Section 17.3 (Simplifying Database Access with JDBC Utilities) for details.

Listing 18.4 CreateMusicTable.java

```
package coreservlets;

import java.sql.*;
import coreservlets.beans.*;

/** Create a simple table named "music" in the
 *  database specified on the command line. The driver
 *  for the database is loaded from the utility class
 *  DriverUtilities.
 */
```

Listing 18.4 CreateMusicTable.java *(continued)*

```
public class CreateMusicTable {
  public static void main(String[] args) {
    if (args.length < 5) {
      printUsage();
      return;
    }
    String vendor = args[4];
    // Change to DriverUtilities2.loadDrivers() to
    // load the drivers from an XML file.
    DriverUtilities.loadDrivers();
    if (!DriverUtilities.isValidVendor(vendor)) {
      printUsage();
      return;
    }
    String driver = DriverUtilities.getDriver(vendor);
    String host = args[0];
    String dbName = args[1];
    String url =
      DriverUtilities.makeURL(host, dbName, vendor);
    String username = args[2];
    String password = args[3];
    String format =
      "(id INTEGER, composer VARCHAR(16), " +
      " concerto VARCHAR(24), available INTEGER, " +
      " price FLOAT)";
    String[] rows = {
      "(1, 'Mozart',       'No. 21 in C# minor',  7, 24.99)",
      "(2, 'Beethoven',    'No. 3 in C minor',   28, 10.99)",
      "(3, 'Beethoven',    'No. 5 Eb major',     33, 10.99)",
      "(4, 'Rachmaninov', 'No. 2 in C minor',     9, 18.99)",
      "(5, 'Mozart',       'No. 24 in C minor',  11, 21.99)",
      "(6, 'Beethoven',    'No. 4 in G',         33, 12.99)",
      "(7, 'Liszt',        'No. 1 in Eb major',  48, 10.99)" };
    Connection connection =
      ConnectionInfoBean.getConnection(driver, url,
                                       username, password);
    createTable(connection, "music", format, rows);
    try {
      connection.close();
    } catch(SQLException sqle) {
      System.err.println("Problem closing connection: " + sqle);
    }
  }
```

Listing 18.4 CreateMusicTable.java *(continued)*

```
  /** Build a table with the specified format and rows. */

  private static void createTable(Connection connection,
                                  String tableName,
                                  String tableFormat,
                                  String[] tableRows) {
    try {
      Statement statement = connection.createStatement();
      // Drop previous table if it exists, but don't get
      // error if not. Thus, the separate try/catch here.
      try {
        statement.execute("DROP TABLE " + tableName);
      } catch(SQLException sqle) {}
      String createCommand =
        "CREATE TABLE " + tableName + " " + tableFormat;
      statement.execute(createCommand);
      String insertPrefix =
        "INSERT INTO " + tableName + " VALUES";
      for(int i=0; i<tableRows.length; i++) {
        statement.execute(insertPrefix + tableRows[i]);
      }
    } catch(SQLException sqle) {
      System.err.println("Error creating table: " + sqle);
    }
  }

  private static void printUsage() {
     System.out.println("Usage: CreateMusicTable host dbName " +
                        "username password vendor.");
  }
}
```

Using create_music_table.sql to Create the music Table

The SQL script, create_music_table.sql, for creating the `music` table is shown in Listing 18.5. If the database vendor provides a utility to run SQL commands, you can run this script to create the `music` table.

For a MySQL database, you can run the MySQL monitor and execute the SQL script, as shown.

```
mysql> SOURCE create_music_table.sql
```

For details on starting MySQL monitor, see Section 18.2. If the script is not located in the same directory in which you started MySQL monitor, you must specify the full path to the script.

For an Oracle database, you can run SQL*Plus and execute the SQL script by using either of the following two commands.

```
SQL> START create_music_table.sql
```

or

```
SQL> @create_music_table.sql
```

For details on starting SQL*Plus, see Section 18.3. Again, if the script is not located in the same directory in which you started SQL*Plus, you must specify the full path to the script.

Listing 18.5 create_music_table.sql

```
/* SQL script to create music table.
 *
 * From MySQL monitor run:
 *   mysql> SOURCE create_music_table.sql
 *
 * From Oracle9i SQL*Plus run:
 *   SQL> START create_music_table.sql
 *
 * In both cases, you may need to specify the full
 * path to the SQL script.
 */

DROP TABLE music;
CREATE TABLE music (
  id INTEGER,
  composer VARCHAR(16),
  concerto VARCHAR(24),
  available INTEGER,
  price FLOAT);
INSERT INTO music
  VALUES (1, 'Mozart', 'No. 21 in C# minor', 7, 24.99);
```

Listing 18.5 create_music_table.sql *(continued)*

```
INSERT INTO music
  VALUES (2, 'Beethoven', 'No. 3 in C minor', 28, 10.99);
INSERT INTO music
  VALUES (3, 'Beethoven', 'No. 5 Eb major', 33, 10.99);
INSERT INTO music
  VALUES (4, 'Rachmaninov', 'No. 2 in C minor', 9, 18.99);
INSERT INTO music
  VALUES (5, 'Mozart', 'No. 24 in C minor', 11, 21.99);
INSERT INTO music
  VALUES (6, 'Beethoven', 'No. 4 in G', 33, 12.99);
INSERT INTO music
  VALUES (7, 'Liszt', 'No. 1 in Eb major', 48, 10.99);
COMMIT;
```

Creating and Processing HTML Forms

Topics in This Chapter

- Data submission from forms
- Text controls
- Push buttons
- Check boxes and radio buttons
- Combo boxes and list boxes
- File upload controls
- Server-side image maps
- Hidden fields
- Groups of controls
- Tab ordering
- A Web server for debugging forms

Chapter 19

HTML forms provide a simple and reliable user interface to collect data from the user and transmit the data to a servlet or other server-side program for processing. In this chapter we present the standard form controls defined by the HTML 4.0 specification. However, before covering each control, we first explain how the form data is transmitted to the server when a `GET` or `POST` request is made.

We also present a mini Web server that is useful for understanding and debugging the data sent by your HTML forms. The server simply reads all the HTTP data sent to it by the browser, then returns a Web page with those lines embedded within a `PRE` element. We use this server throughout the examples in this chapter to show the form control data that is sent to the server when the HTML form is submitted.

To use forms, you'll need to remember where to place regular HTML files to make them accessible to the Web server. This location varies from server to server, as discussed in Chapter 2 and the Appendix. Below, we review the location for HTML files in the default Web application for Tomcat, JRun, and Resin.

Default Web Application: Tomcat

- **Main Location.**
  install_dir/webapps/ROOT
- **Corresponding URL.**
  http://*host*/*SomeFile*.html
- **More Specific Location (Arbitrary Subdirectory).**
  install_dir/webapps/ROOT/*SomeDirectory*

- **Corresponding URL.**
  http://*host*/*SomeDirectory*/*SomeFile*.html

Default Web Application: JRun

- **Main Location.**
  install_dir/servers/default/default-ear/default-war
- **Corresponding URL.**
  http://*host*/*SomeFile*.html
- **More Specific Location (Arbitrary Subdirectory).**
  install_dir/servers/default/default-ear/default-war/*SomeDirectory*
- **Corresponding URL.**
  http://*host*/*SomeDirectory*/*SomeFile*.html

Default Web Application: Resin

- **Main Location.**
  install_dir/doc
- **Corresponding URL.**
  http://*host*/*SomeFile*.html
- **More Specific Location (Arbitrary Subdirectory).**
  install_dir/doc/*SomeDirectory*
- **Corresponding URLs.**
  http://*host*/*SomeDirectory*/*SomeFile*.html

The server's default Web application is useful for practice and learning, but when you deploy real-life applications, you will almost certainly use custom Web applications; see Section 2.11 for details.

19.1 How HTML Forms Transmit Data

HTML forms let you create a variety of user interface controls to collect input in a Web page. Each of the controls typically has a name and a value, where the name is specified in the HTML and the value comes either from user input or from a default value in the HTML. The entire form is associated with the URL of a program that will process the data, and when the user submits the form (usually by pressing a button), the names and values of the controls are sent to the designated URL as a string of the form

```
name1=value1&name2=value2...&nameN=valueN
```

This string can be sent to the designated program in one of two ways: GET or POST. The first method, an HTTP GET request, appends the form data to the end of the specified URL after a question mark. The second method, HTTP POST, sends the data after the HTTP request headers and a blank line. In the following examples, we show explicitly how the data is sent to the server for both GET and POST requests.

For example, Listing 19.1 (HTML code) and Figure 19–1 (typical result) show a simple form with two textfields. The HTML elements that make up this form are discussed in detail in the rest of this chapter, but for now note a couple of things. First, observe that one textfield has a name of firstName and the other has a name of lastName. Second, note that the GUI controls are considered text-level (inline) elements, so you need to use explicit HTML formatting to make sure that the controls appear next to the text describing them. Finally, notice that the FORM element designates http://localhost:8088/SomeProgram as the URL to which the data will be sent.

Before submitting the form, we started a server program called EchoServer on port 8088 of our local machine. EchoServer, shown in Section 19.12, is a mini Web server used for debugging. No matter what URL is specified and what data is sent to EchoServer, it merely returns a Web page showing all the HTTP information sent by the browser. As shown in Figure 19–2, when the form is submitted with Joe in the first textfield and Hacker in the second, the browser simply requests the URL http://localhost:8088/SomeProgram?firstName=Joe&lastName=Hacker.

Listing 19.1 GetForm.html

```
<!DOCTYPE HTML PUBLIC "-//W3C//DTD HTML 4.0 Transitional//EN">
<HTML>
<HEAD>
  <TITLE>A Sample Form Using GET</TITLE>
</HEAD>
<BODY BGCOLOR="#FDF5E6">
<CENTER>
<H2>A Sample Form Using GET</H2>
<FORM ACTION="http://localhost:8088/SomeProgram">
  First name:
  <INPUT TYPE="TEXT" NAME="firstName" VALUE="Joe"><BR>
  Last name:
  <INPUT TYPE="TEXT" NAME="lastName" VALUE="Hacker"><P>
  <INPUT TYPE="SUBMIT"> <!-- Press this button to submit form -->
</FORM>
</CENTER>
</BODY></HTML>
```

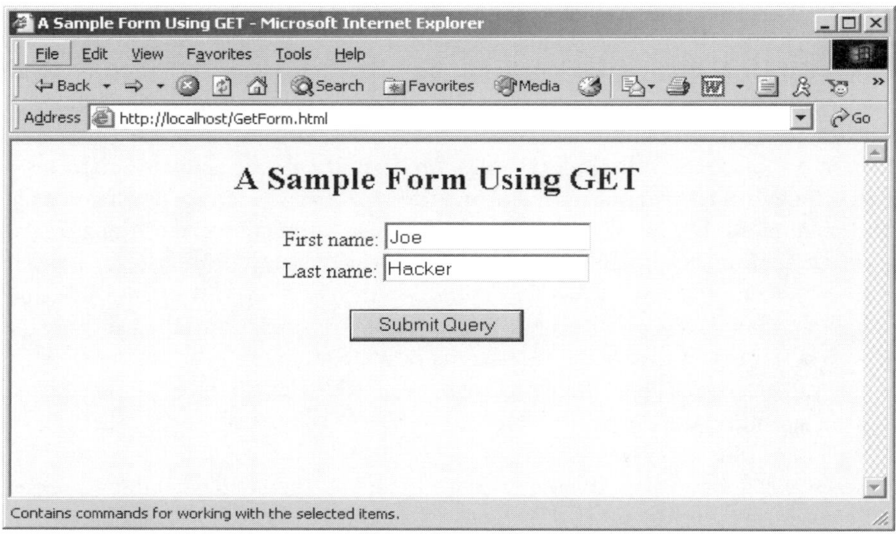

Figure 19–1 Initial result of GetForm.html.

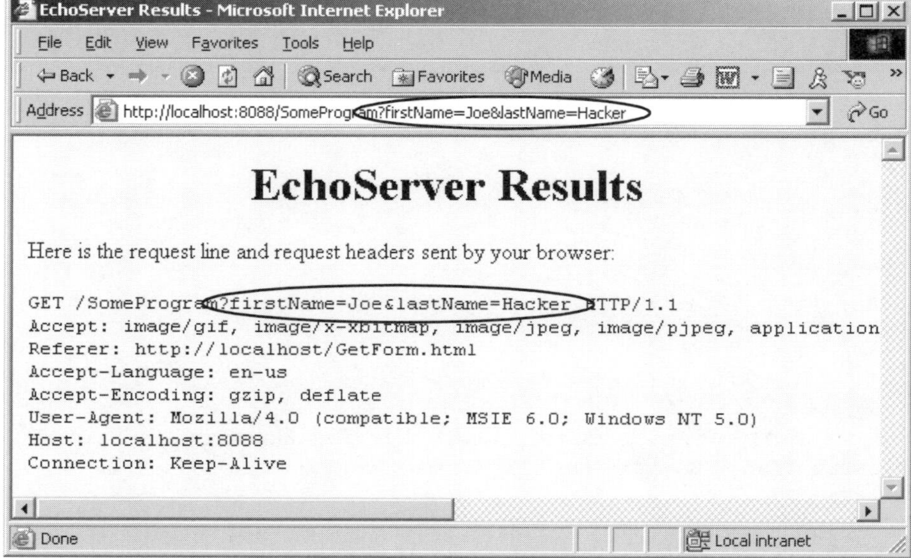

Figure 19–2 HTTP request sent by Internet Explorer 6.0 when submitting GetForm.html.

Listing 19.2 (HTML code) and Figure 19–3 (typical result) show a variation that uses `POST` instead of `GET`. As shown in Figure 19–4, submitting the form with textfield values of `Joe` and `Hacker` results in the line `firstName=Joe&lastName=Hacker` being sent to the browser on a separate line after the HTTP request headers and a blank line.

That's the general idea behind HTML forms: GUI controls gather data from the user, each control has a name and a value, and a string containing all the name/value pairs is sent to the server when the form is submitted. Extracting the names and values on the server is straightforward in servlets: that subject is covered in Chapter 4 (Handling the Client Request: Form Data). The commonly used form controls are covered in the following sections.

Listing 19.2 PostForm.html

```
<!DOCTYPE HTML PUBLIC "-//W3C//DTD HTML 4.0 Transitional//EN">
<HTML>
<HEAD>
  <TITLE>A Sample Form Using POST</TITLE>
</HEAD>
<BODY BGCOLOR="#FDF5E6">
<CENTER>
<H2>A Sample Form Using POST</H2>
<FORM ACTION="http://localhost:8088/SomeProgram"
      METHOD="POST">
  First name:
  <INPUT TYPE="TEXT" NAME="firstName" VALUE="Joe"><BR>
  Last name:
  <INPUT TYPE="TEXT" NAME="lastName" VALUE="Hacker"><P>
  <INPUT TYPE="SUBMIT">
</FORM>
</CENTER>
</BODY></HTML>
```

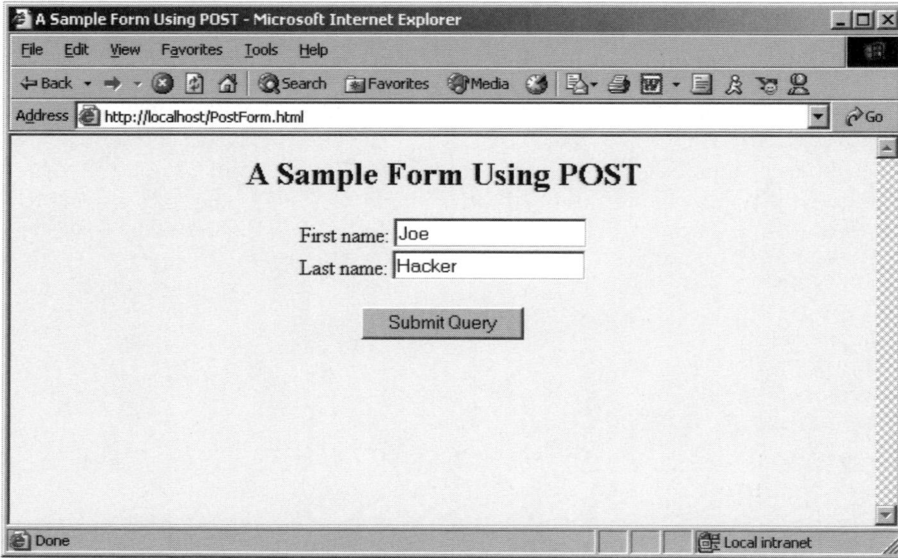

Figure 19–3 Initial result of PostForm.html.

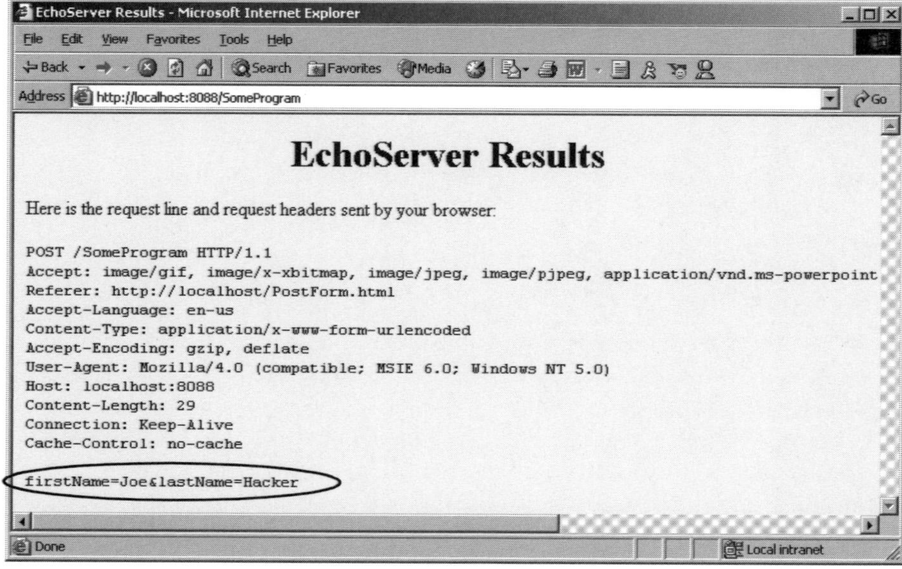

Figure 19–4 HTTP request sent by Internet Explorer 6.0 when submitting PostForm.html.

19.2 The FORM Element

HTML forms allow you to create a set of data input elements associated with a particular URL. Each of these elements is typically given a name in the HTML source code, and each has a value based on the original HTML or user input. When the form is submitted, the names and values of all active elements are collected into a string with = between each name and value and with & between each name/value pair. This string is then transmitted to the URL designated by the FORM element. The string is either appended to the URL after a question mark or sent on a separate line after the HTTP request headers and a blank line, depending on whether GET or POST is used as the submission method. This section covers the FORM element itself, used primarily to designate the URL and to choose the submission method. The following sections cover the various user interface controls that can be used within forms.

HTML Element: **`<FORM ACTION="..." ...> ... </FORM>`**
Attributes: ACTION, METHOD, ENCTYPE, TARGET, ONSUBMIT, ONRESET, ACCEPT, ACCEPT-CHARSET

The FORM element creates an area for data input elements and designates the URL to which any collected data will be transmitted. For example:

```
<FORM ACTION="http://some.isp.com/someWebApp/SomeServlet">
  FORM input elements and regular HTML
</FORM>
```

The rest of this section explains the attributes that apply to the FORM element: ACTION, METHOD, ENCTYPE, TARGET, ONSUBMIT, ONRESET, ACCEPT, and ACCEPT-CHARSET. Note that we do not discuss attributes like STYLE, CLASS, and LANG that apply to general HTML elements, but only those that are specific to the FORM element.

ACTION

The ACTION attribute specifies the URL of the server-side program that will process the FORM data (e.g., http://www.whitehouse.gov/servlet/schedule-fund-raiser). If the server-side program is located on the same server from which the HTML form was obtained, we recommend using a relative URL instead of an absolute URL for the action. This approach lets you move both the form and the servlet to a different host without editing either. This is an important consideration since you typically develop and test on one machine and then deploy on another. For example,

```
ACTION="/servlet/schedule-fund-raiser"
```

Core Approach

If the servlet or JSP page is located on the same server as the HTML form, use a relative URL in the `ACTION` attribute.

In addition, you can specify an email address to which the `FORM` data will be sent (e.g., mailto:audit@irs.gov). Some ISPs do not allow ordinary users to create server-side programs, or they charge extra for this privilege. In such a case, sending the data by email is a convenient option when you create pages that need to collect data but not return results (e.g., for accepting orders for products). You must use the `POST` method (see `METHOD` in the following subsection) when using a mailto URL.

Also, note that the `ACTION` attribute is not required for the `FORM` element. If you omit `ACTION`, the form data is sent to the same URL as the form itself. See Section 4.8 for an example of the use of this self-submission approach.

METHOD

The `METHOD` attribute specifies how the data will be transmitted to the HTTP server. When `GET` is used, the data is appended to the end of the designated URL after a question mark. For an example, see Section 19.1 (How HTML Forms Transmit Data). `GET` is the default and is also the method that is used when the user types a URL into the address bar or clicks on a hypertext link. When `POST` is used, the data is sent on a separate line. Either `GET` or `POST` could be preferable, depending on the situation.

Since `GET` data is part of the URL, the advantages of `GET` are that you can do the following:

- **Save the results of a form submission.** For example, you can submit data and bookmark the resultant URL, send it to a colleague by email, or put it in a normal hypertext link. The ability to bookmark the results page is the main reason google.com, yahoo.com, and other search engines use `GET`.
- **Type data in by hand.** You can test servlets or JSP pages that use `GET` simply by entering a URL with the appropriate data attached. This ability is convenient during initial development.

Since `POST` data is *not* part of the URL, the advantages of `POST` are that you can do the following:

- **Transmit large amounts of data.** Many browsers limit URLs to a few thousand characters, making `GET` inappropriate when your form must send a large amount of data. Since HTML forms let you upload files from the client machine (see Section 19.7), sending multiple megabytes of data is quite commonplace. Only `POST` can be used for this task.
- **Send binary data.** Spaces, carriage returns, tabs, and many other characters are illegal in URLs. If you upload a large binary file, it would be a time-consuming process to encode all the characters before transmission and decode them on the other end.
- **Keep the data private from someone looking over the user's shoulder.** HTML forms let you create password fields in which the data is replaced by asterisks on the screen. However, using a password field is pointless if the data is displayed in clear text in the URL, letting snoopers read it by peering over the user's shoulder or by scrolling through the browser's history list when the user leaves the computer unattended. Note, however, that `POST` alone provides no protection from someone using a packet sniffer on the network connection. To protect against this type of attack, use SSL (https:// connections) to encrypt the network traffic. For more information on using SSL in Web applications, see the chapters on Web application security in Volume 2 of this book.

To read `GET` or `POST` data from a servlet, you call

```
request.getParameter("name")
```

where `name` is the value of the `NAME` attribute of the input element in the HTML form. For additional details, see Chapter 4 (Handling the Client Request: Form Data). Note that, if needed, you can also use `request.getInputStream` to read the `POST` data directly, as below.

```
int length = request.getContentLength();
if (length > SOME_MAXSIZE) {
  throw new IOException("Possible denial of service attack");
}
byte[] data = new byte[length];
ServletInputStream inputStream = request.getInputStream();
int read = inputStream.readLine(data, 0, length);
```

ENCTYPE

This attribute specifies the way in which the data will be encoded before being transmitted. The default is `application/x-www-form-urlencoded`. The encoding, as specified by the World Wide Web Consortium, is UTF-8, except that the client converts each space into a plus sign (+) and each other nonalphanumeric character into a percent sign (%) followed by the two hexadecimal digits representing that character in the browser's character set. These transformations are in addition to placing an equal sign (=) between entry names and values and an ampersand (&) between the pairs.

For example, Figure 19–5 shows a version of GetForm.html (Listing 19.1) where "`Larry (Java Hacker?)`" is entered for the first name. As can be seen in Figure 19–6, this entry is sent as "`Larry+%28Java+Hacker%3F%29`". That's because spaces become plus signs, 28 is the ASCII value (in hex) for a left parenthesis, 3F is the ASCII value of a question mark, and 29 is a right parenthesis.

Note that, unless otherwise specified, `POST` data is also encoded as `application/x-www-form-urlencoded`.

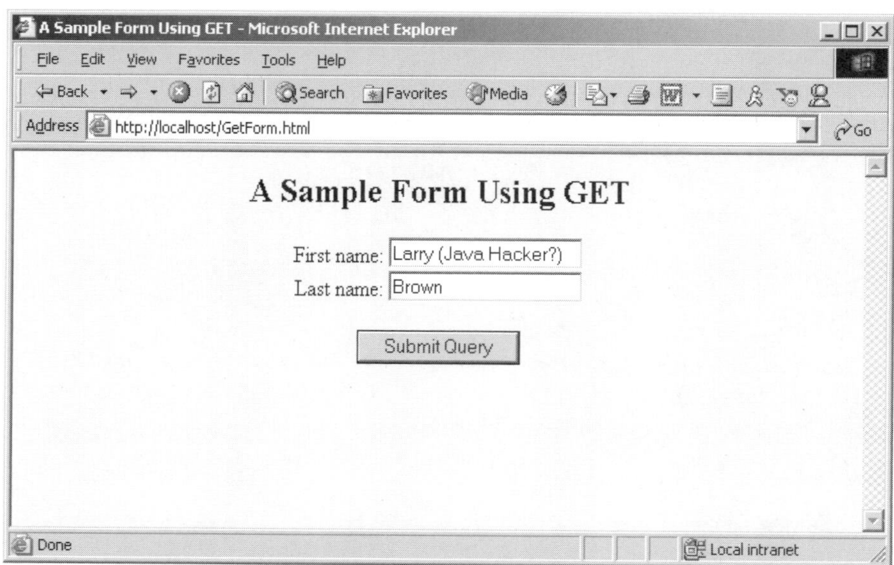

Figure 19–5 Customized result of GetForm.html.

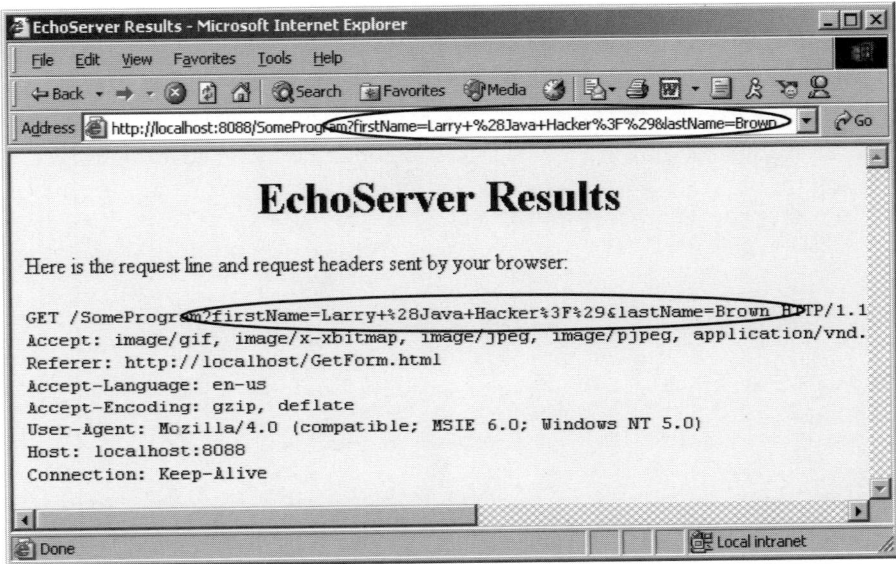

Figure 19–6 HTTP request sent by Internet Explorer 6.0 when submitting **GetForm.html** with the data shown in Figure 19–5.

Most recent browsers support an additional `ENCTYPE` of `multipart/form-data`. This encoding transmits each field as a separate part of a MIME-compatible document. To use this `ENCTYPE`, you must specify `POST` as the method type. This encoding sometimes makes it easier for the server-side program to handle complex data, and it is required when you are using file upload controls to send entire documents (see Section 19.7). For example, Listing 19.3 shows a form that differs from **GetForm.html** (Listing 19.1) only in that

```
<FORM ACTION="http://localhost:8088/SomeProgram">
```

has been changed to

```
<FORM ACTION="http://localhost:8088/SomeProgram"
      ENCTYPE="multipart/form-data" METHOD="POST">
```

Figures 19–7 and 19–8 show the results.

Listing 19.3 MultipartForm.html

```
<!DOCTYPE HTML PUBLIC "-//W3C//DTD HTML 4.0 Transitional//EN">
<HTML>
<HEAD>
  <TITLE>Using ENCTYPE="multipart/form-data"</TITLE>
</HEAD>
<BODY BGCOLOR="#FDF5E6">
<CENTER>
<H2>Using ENCTYPE="multipart/form-data"</H2>
<FORM ACTION="http://localhost:8088/SomeProgram"
      ENCTYPE="multipart/form-data" METHOD="POST">
  First name:
  <INPUT TYPE="TEXT" NAME="firstName" VALUE="Joe"><BR>
  Last name:
  <INPUT TYPE="TEXT" NAME="lastName" VALUE="Hacker"><P>
  <INPUT TYPE="SUBMIT">
</FORM>
</CENTER>
</BODY></HTML>
```

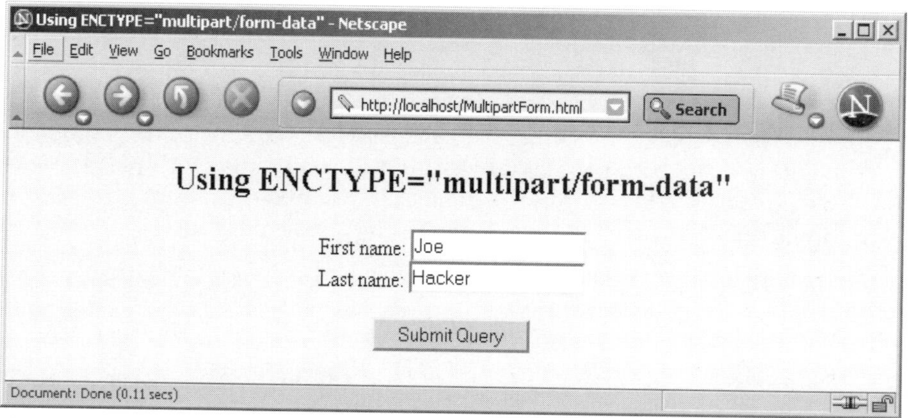

Figure 19–7 Initial result of MultipartForm.html.

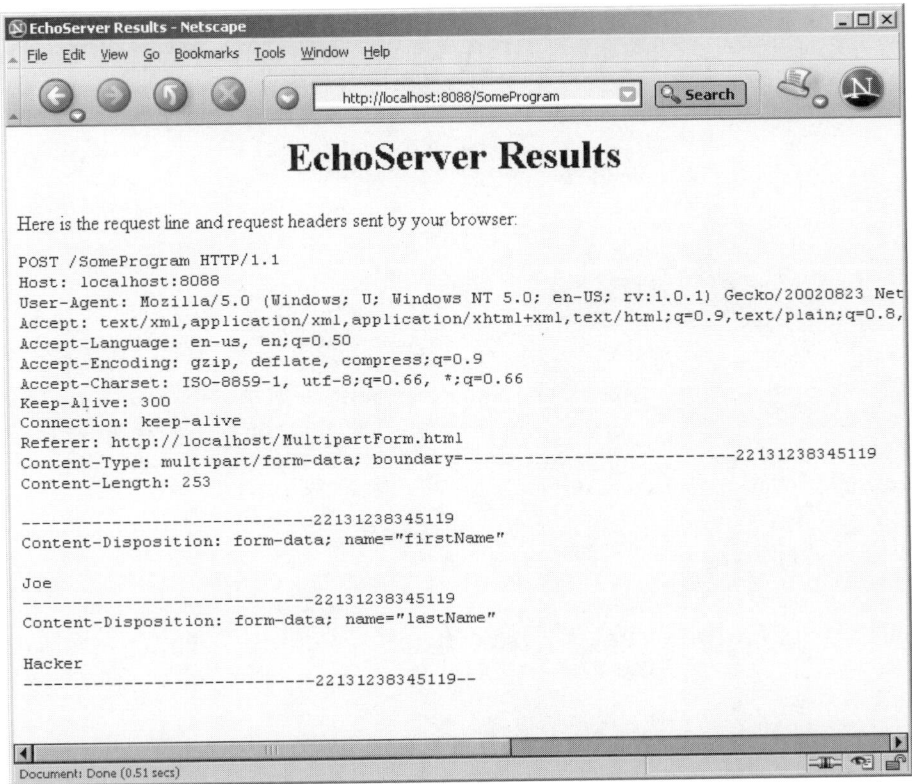

Figure 19–8 HTTP request sent by Netscape 7.0 when submitting MultipartForm.html.

TARGET

The `TARGET` attribute is used by frame-capable browsers to determine which frame cell should be used to display the results of the servlet, JSP page, or other program handling the form submission. The default is to display the results in whatever frame cell contains the form being submitted.

ONSUBMIT and ONRESET

These attributes are used by JavaScript to attach code that should be evaluated when the form is submitted or reset. For `ONSUBMIT`, if the expression evaluates to `false`, the form is not submitted. This case lets you invoke JavaScript code on the client that checks the format of the form field values before they are submitted, prompting the user for missing or illegal entries.

ACCEPT and ACCEPT-CHARSET

These attributes are new in HTML 4.0 and specify the MIME types (`ACCEPT`) and character encodings (`ACCEPT-CHARSET`) that must be accepted by the servlet or other program processing the form data. The MIME types listed in `ACCEPT` can also be used by the client to limit which file types are displayed to the user for file upload elements.

19.3 Text Controls

HTML supports three types of text-input elements: textfields, password fields, and text areas. Each is given a name, and the value is taken from the content of the control. The name and value are sent to the server when the form is submitted, which is typically done by means of a submit button (see Section 19.4).

Textfields

HTML Element: **`<INPUT TYPE="TEXT" NAME="..." ...>`**
(No End Tag)

Attributes: `NAME` (required), `VALUE`, `SIZE`, `MAXLENGTH`, `ONCHANGE`, `ONSELECT`, `ONFOCUS`, `ONBLUR`, `ONKEYDOWN`, `ONKEYPRESS`, `ONKEYUP`

This element creates a single-line input field in which the user can enter text, as illustrated earlier in Listings 19.1, 19.2, and 19.3. For multiline fields, see `TEXTAREA` in the following subsection. `TEXT` is the default `TYPE` in `INPUT` forms, although it is recommended for clarity that `TEXT` be supplied explicitly. You should remember that the normal browser word-wrapping applies inside `FORM` elements, so use appropriate HTML markup to ensure that the browser will not separate the descriptive text from the associated textfield.

Core Approach

Use explicit HTML constructs to group textfields with their descriptive text.

Netscape 7.0 and Internet Explorer 6.0 submit the form when the user presses Enter while the cursor is in a textfield and the form has a SUBMIT button (see Section 19.4 for details on a SUBMIT button). However, this behavior is not dictated by the HTML specification, and other browsers behave differently.

Core Warning

Don't rely on the browser submitting the form when the user presses Enter while in a textfield. Always include a button or image map that submits the form explicitly.

To prevent the form from being submitted when the user presses Enter in a textfield, use a BUTTON input with an onClick event handler instead of a SUBMIT button. For example, you may want to use

```
<INPUT TYPE="BUTTON" VALUE="Check Values"
       onClick="submit()">
```

instead of

```
<INPUT TYPE="SUBMIT">
```

to submit your form.

The following subsections describe the attributes that apply specifically to textfields. Attributes that apply to general HTML elements (e.g., STYLE, CLASS, ID) are not discussed. The TABINDEX attribute, which applies to *all* form elements, is discussed in Section 19.11 (Tab Order Control).

NAME

The NAME attribute identifies the textfield when the form is submitted. In standard HTML, the attribute is required. Because data is always sent to the server in the form of name/value pairs, no data is sent for form controls that have no NAME.

VALUE

A VALUE attribute, if supplied, specifies the *initial* contents of the textfield. When the form is submitted, the *current* contents are sent; these can reflect user input. If the textfield is empty when the form is submitted, the form data simply consists of the name and an equal sign (e.g., name1=value1&**textfieldname=**&name3=value3).

SIZE

This attribute specifies the width of the textfield, based on the average character width of the font being used. If text beyond this size is entered, the textfield scrolls to accommodate it. This could happen if the user enters more characters than SIZE number or enters SIZE number of wide characters (e.g., capital W) when a proportional-width font is being used. Netscape and Internet Explorer 6.0 automatically use a proportional font in textfields. Unfortunately, you cannot change the font by embedding the INPUT element in a FONT or CODE element. However, you can use cascading style sheets to change the font of input elements. For example, the following style sheet (placed in the HEAD section of the HTML page) will display the text for all INPUT elements as 12pt Futura (assuming that the Futura font is installed on the client machine).

```
<style type="text/css">
INPUT {
 font-size : 12pt;
 font-family : Futura;
}
</style>
```

Core Approach

By default, Netscape and Internet Explorer display INPUT elements in a proportional font. To change the font for INPUT elements, use style sheets.

MAXLENGTH

MAXLENGTH gives the maximum number of *allowable* characters. This number is in contrast to the number of *visible* characters, which is specified through SIZE. However, note that users can always override this; for GET requests, they can type data directly in the URL and for POST requests they can write their own HTML form. So, the server-side program should not rely on the request containing the appropriate amount of data.

ONCHANGE, ONSELECT, ONFOCUS, ONBLUR, ONDBLDOWN, ONKEYPRESS, and ONKEYUP

These attributes are used only by browsers that support JavaScript. They specify the action to take when the mouse leaves the textfield after a change has occurred, when the user selects text in the textfield, when the textfield gets the input focus, when the textfield loses the input focus, and when individual keys are pressed or released, respectively.

Password Fields

HTML Element: `<INPUT TYPE="PASSWORD" NAME="..." ...>`
(No End Tag)

Attributes: `NAME` (required), `VALUE`, `SIZE`, `MAXLENGTH`, `ONCHANGE`, `ONSELECT`, `ONFOCUS`, `ONBLUR`, `ONKEYDOWN`, `ONKEYPRESS`, `ONKEYUP`

Password fields are created and used just like textfields, except that when the user enters text, the input is not echoed; instead, some obscuring character, usually an asterisk, is displayed (see Figure 19–9). Obscured input is useful for collecting data such as credit card numbers or passwords that the user would not want shown to people who may be near his computer. The regular, unobscured text (clear text) is transmitted as the value of the field when the form is submitted.

Since `GET` data is appended to the URL after a question mark, you should always use `POST` with a password field so that a bystander cannot read the unobscured password from the URL display at the top of the browser. In addition, for security during transmission of data, you should consider using SSL, which encrypts the data. For more information on using SSL, see the chapters on Web application security in Volume 2 of this book.

Core Approach

To protect the user's privacy, always use `POST` *when creating forms that contain password fields. For additional security, transmit the data by using* ***https://****, which uses SSL to encrypt the data.*

NAME, VALUE, SIZE, MAXLENGTH, ONCHANGE, ONSELECT, ONFOCUS, ONBLUR, ONKEYDOWN, ONKEYPRESS, and ONKEYUP

Attributes for password fields are used in exactly the same manner as with textfields.

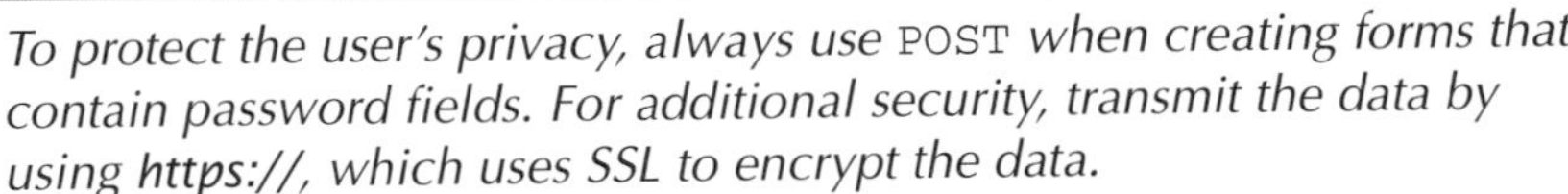

Figure 19–9 A password field created by means of `<INPUT TYPE="PASSWORD" ...>`.

Text Areas

HTML Element: `<TEXTAREA NAME="..." ROWS=xxx COLS=yyy> ... </TEXTAREA>`

Attributes: NAME (required), ROWS (required), COLS (required), WRAP (nonstandard), ONCHANGE, ONSELECT, ONFOCUS, ONBLUR, ONKEYDOWN, ONKEYPRESS, ONKEYUP

The TEXTAREA element creates a multiline text area; see Figure 19–10. The element has no VALUE attribute; instead, text between the start and end tags is used as the initial content of the text area. The initial text between <TEXTAREA ...> and </TEXTAREA> is treated similarly to text inside the now-obsolete XMP element. That is, white space in this initial text is maintained, and HTML markup between the start and end tags is taken literally, except for character entities such as <, ©, and so forth, which are interpreted normally. Unless a custom ENCTYPE is used in the form (see Section 19.2, "The FORM Element"), characters, including those generated from character entities, are URL-encoded before being transmitted. That is, spaces become plus signs and other nonalphanumeric characters become %*XX*, where *XX* is the numeric value of the character in hex.

NAME

This attribute specifies the name that will be sent to the server.

ROWS

ROWS specifies the number of visible lines of text. If more lines of text are entered, a vertical scrollbar will be added to the text area.

COLS

COLS specifies the visible width of the text area, based on the average width of characters in the font being used. In Netscape 7.0 and Internet Explorer 6.0, if the text on a single line contains more characters than the specified width allows, the text is wrapped to the next line. However, if a single word has more characters than the specified width, Internet Explorer 6.0 wraps the word to the next line and Netscape 7.0 adds a horizontal scrollbar to keep the word on one line. Other browsers may behave differently.

ONCHANGE, ONSELECT, ONFOCUS, ONBLUR, ONKEYDOWN, ONKEYPRESS, and ONKEYUP

These attributes apply only to browsers that support JavaScript; they specify code to be executed when certain conditions arise. ONCHANGE handles the situation in which the input focus leaves the text area after it has changed, ONSELECT describes what to do when text in the text area is selected by the user, ONFOCUS and ONBLUR specify what to do when the text area acquires or loses the input focus, and the remaining attributes determine what to do when individual keys are typed.

Listing 19.4 creates a text area with 5 visible rows that can hold about 30 characters per row. The result is shown in Figure 19–10.

Listing 19.4 Example of a TEXTAREA form control

```
<CENTER>
<P>
Enter some HTML:<BR>
<TEXTAREA NAME="HTML" ROWS=5 COLS=30>
Delete this text and replace
with some HTML to validate.
</TEXTAREA>
<CENTER>
```

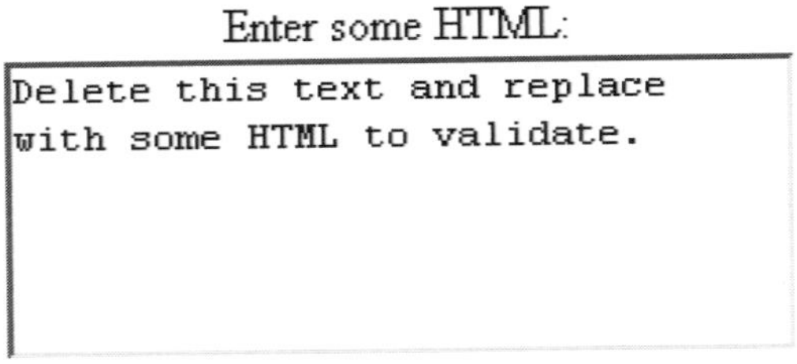

Enter some HTML:

Delete this text and replace
with some HTML to validate.

Figure 19–10 A text area in Netscape 7.0.

19.4 Push Buttons

Push buttons are used for two main purposes in HTML forms: to submit forms and to reset the controls to the values specified in the original HTML. Browsers that use JavaScript can also use buttons for a third purpose: to trigger arbitrary JavaScript code.

Traditionally, buttons have been created by the INPUT element used with a TYPE attribute of SUBMIT, RESET, or BUTTON. In HTML 4.0, the BUTTON element was introduced and is supported by Internet Explorer 6.0 and Netscape 7.0. This new element lets you create buttons with multiline labels, images, font changes, and the like. However, earlier browsers may not support the `BUTTON` element.

Submit Buttons

HTML Element: `<INPUT TYPE="SUBMIT" ...>` (No End Tag)

Attributes: `NAME`, `VALUE`, `ONCLICK`, `ONDBLCLICK`, `ONFOCUS`, `ONBLUR`

When a submit button is clicked, the form is sent to the servlet or other server-side program designated by the `ACTION` parameter of the `FORM`. Although the action can be triggered in other ways, such as the user clicking on an image map, most forms have at least one submit button. Submit buttons, like other form controls, adopt the look and feel of the client operating system, so will look slightly different on different platforms. Figure 19–11 shows a submit button on Windows 2000 Professional, created by

```
<INPUT TYPE="SUBMIT">
```

Submit Query

Figure 19–11 A submit button with the default label.

NAME and VALUE

Most input elements have a name and an associated value. When the form is submitted, the names and values of active elements are concatenated to form the data string. If a submit button is used simply to initiate the submission of the form, the button's name can be omitted and it does not contribute to the data string that is sent. If a name *is* supplied, then only the name and value of the button that was actually clicked are sent. This capability lets you use more than one button and detect which one is pressed. The label is used as the value that is transmitted. Supplying an explicit `VALUE` will change the default label.

For instance, Listing 19.5 creates a textfield and two submit buttons, shown in Figure 19–12. If, for example, the first button is selected, the data string sent to the server would be `Item=256MB+SIMM&`**`Add`**`=Add+Item+to+Cart`.

Listing 19.5 Example of `SUBMIT` input controls

```
<CENTER>
Item:
<INPUT TYPE="TEXT" NAME="Item" VALUE="256MB SIMM"><BR>
<INPUT TYPE="SUBMIT" NAME="Add"
       VALUE="Add Item to Cart">
<INPUT TYPE="SUBMIT" NAME="Delete"
       VALUE="Delete Item from Cart">
</CENTER>
```

Figure 19–12 Submit buttons with user-defined labels.

Note that when the form data is submitted to a servlet, `request.getParameter` returns `null` for buttons that were not pressed. So, you could use a simple check for `null`, as below, to determine which button was selected.

```
if (request.getParameter("Add") != null) {
  doCartAdditionOperation(...);
} else if (request.getParameter("Delete") != null) {
  doCartDeletionOperation(...);
}
```

ONCLICK, ONDBLCLICK, ONFOCUS, and ONBLUR

These nonstandard attributes are used by JavaScript-capable browsers to associate JavaScript code with the button. The `ONCLICK` and `ONDBLCLICK` code is executed when the button is pressed, the `ONFOCUS` code when the button gets the input focus, and the `ONBLUR` code when the button loses the focus. If the code attached to a button returns `false`, the submission of the form is suppressed. HTML attributes are not case sensitive, and these attributes are traditionally called `onClick`, `onDblClick`, `onFocus`, and `onBlur` by JavaScript programmers.

HTML Element: `<BUTTON TYPE="SUBMIT" ...> HTML Markup </BUTTON>`

Attributes: NAME, VALUE, ONCLICK, ONDBLCLICK, ONFOCUS, ONBLUR

This alternative way of creating submit buttons lets you use arbitrary HTML markup for the content of the button. This element lets you have multiline button labels, button labels with font changes, image buttons, and so forth. Listing 19.6 gives a few examples, with results shown in Figure 19–13.

NAME, VALUE, ONCLICK, ONDBLCLICK, ONFOCUS, and ONBLUR

These attributes are used in the same way as with `<INPUT TYPE="SUBMIT" ...>`.

Listing 19.6 ButtonElement.html

```
<!DOCTYPE HTML PUBLIC "-//W3C//DTD HTML 4.0 Transitional//EN">
<HTML>
<HEAD>
  <TITLE>The BUTTON Element</TITLE>
</HEAD>
<BODY BGCOLOR="WHITE">
<CENTER>
<H2>The BUTTON Element</H2>
<FORM ACTION="http://localhost:8088/SomeProgram">
<BUTTON TYPE="SUBMIT">Single-line Label</BUTTON>
  
<BUTTON TYPE="SUBMIT">Multi-line<BR>label</BUTTON>
<P>
<BUTTON TYPE="SUBMIT">
<B>Label</B> with <I>font</I> changes.
</BUTTON>
<P>
<BUTTON TYPE="SUBMIT">
<IMG SRC="images/Java-Logo.gif" WIDTH="110" HEIGHT="101"
     ALIGN="LEFT" ALT="Java Cup Logo">
Label<BR>with image
</BUTTON>
</FORM>
</CENTER>
</BODY></HTML>
```

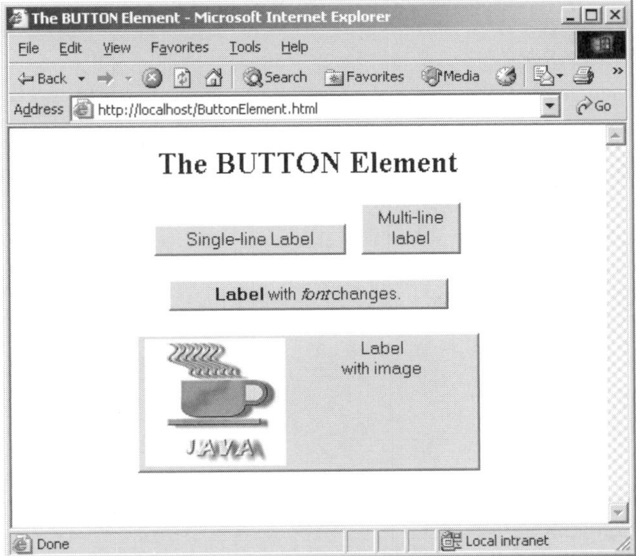

Figure 19–13 Submit buttons created with the `BUTTON` element.

Reset Buttons

HTML Element: `<INPUT TYPE="RESET" ...>` (No End Tag)

Attributes: `VALUE`, `NAME`, `ONCLICK`, `ONDBLCLICK`, `ONFOCUS`, `ONBLUR`

Reset buttons serve to reset the values of all items in the form to those specified in the original `VALUE` parameters. Their value is never transmitted as part of the form's contents.

VALUE

The `VALUE` attribute specifies the button label; "Reset" is the default.

NAME

Because reset buttons do not contribute to the data string transmitted when the form is submitted, they are not named in standard HTML. However, JavaScript permits a `NAME` attribute to be used to simplify reference to the element.

ONCLICK, ONDBLCLICK, ONFOCUS, and ONBLUR

These nonstandard attributes are used by JavaScript-capable browsers to associate JavaScript code with the button. The `ONCLICK` and `ONDBLCLICK` code is executed when the button is pressed, the `ONFOCUS` code when the button gets the input focus, and the ONBLUR code when it loses the focus. HTML attributes are not case sensitive, and these attributes are traditionally called onClick, onDblClick, onFocus, and onBlur by JavaScript programmers.

HTML Element: **<BUTTON TYPE="RESET" ...>**
HTML Markup
</BUTTON>

Attributes: VALUE, NAME, ONCLICK, ONDBLCLICK, ONFOCUS, ONBLUR

This alternative way of creating reset buttons lets you use arbitrary HTML markup for the content of the button. All attributes are used identically to those in <INPUT TYPE="RESET" ...>.

JavaScript Buttons

HTML Element: **<INPUT TYPE="BUTTON" ...>** **(No End Tag)**

Attributes: NAME, VALUE, ONCLICK, ONDBLCLICK, ONFOCUS, ONBLUR

This element is recognized only by browsers that support JavaScript. It creates a button with the same visual appearance as a SUBMIT or RESET button and allows the author to attach JavaScript code to the ONCLICK, ONDBLCLICK, ONFOCUS, or ONBLUR attributes. The name/value pair associated with a JavaScript button is not transmitted as part of the data when the form is submitted. Arbitrary code can be associated with the button, but one of the most common uses is to verify that all input elements are in the proper format before the form is submitted to the server. For instance, the following creates a button that, when activated, calls the validateForm function.

```
<INPUT TYPE="BUTTON" VALUE="Check Values"
       onClick="validateForm()">
```

HTML Element: **<BUTTON TYPE="BUTTON" ...>**
HTML Markup
</BUTTON>

Attributes: NAME, VALUE, ONCLICK, ONDBLCLICK, ONFOCUS, ONBLUR

This alternative way of creating JavaScript buttons lets you use arbitrary HTML markup for the content of the button. All attributes are used identically to those in <INPUT TYPE="BUTTON" ...>.

19.5 Check Boxes and Radio Buttons

Check boxes and radio buttons are useful controls for allowing the user to select among a set of predefined choices. Although check boxes can be selected or deselected individually, radio buttons can be grouped so that only a single member of the group can be selected at a time.

Check Boxes

HTML Element: `<INPUT TYPE="CHECKBOX" NAME="..." ...>` **(No End Tag)**

Attributes: `NAME` (required), `VALUE`, `CHECKED`, `ONCLICK`, `ONFOCUS`, `ONBLUR`

This input element creates a check box whose name/value pair is transmitted *only* if the check box is checked when the form is submitted. For instance, the following code results in the check box shown in Figure 19–14.

```
<P>
<INPUT TYPE="CHECKBOX" NAME="noEmail" CHECKED>
Check here if you do <I>not</I> want to
get our email newsletter
```

☑ Check here if you do *not* want to get our email newsletter

Figure 19–14 An HTML check box.

Note that the descriptive text associated with the check box is normal HTML, and care should be taken to guarantee that it appears next to the check box. Thus, the `<P>` in the preceding example ensures that the check box isn't part of the previous paragraph.

Core Approach

Paragraphs inside a `FORM` are filled and wrapped just like regular paragraphs. So, be sure to insert explicit HTML markup to keep input elements with the text that describes them.

NAME

This attribute supplies the name that is sent to the server. The NAME attribute is required for standard HTML check boxes but is optional when used with JavaScript.

VALUE

The VALUE attribute is optional and defaults to on. Recall that the name and value are sent to the server only if the check box is checked when the form is submitted. For instance, in the preceding example, noEmail=on would be added to the data string since the box is checked, but nothing would be added if the box was unchecked. As a result, servlets, JSP pages, or other server-side programs often check only for the existence of the check box name (e.g., that request.getParameter returns non-null), ignoring its value.

CHECKED

If the CHECKED attribute is supplied, then the check box is initially checked when the associated Web page is loaded. Otherwise, it is initially unchecked.

ONCLICK, ONFOCUS, and ONBLUR

These attributes supply JavaScript code to be executed when the button is clicked, receives the input focus, and loses the focus, respectively.

Radio Buttons

HTML Element: **<INPUT TYPE="RADIO" NAME="..."**
VALUE="..." ...> **(No End Tag)**

Attributes: NAME (required), VALUE (required), CHECKED, ONCLICK, ONFOCUS, ONBLUR

Radio buttons differ from check boxes in that only a single radio button in a given group can be selected at any one time. You indicate a group of radio buttons by providing all of them with the same NAME. Only one button in a group can be depressed at a time; selecting a new button when one is already selected results in the previous choice becoming deselected. The value of the one selected is sent when the form is submitted. Although radio buttons technically need not appear near to each other, this proximity is almost always recommended.

An example of a radio button is shown in Listing 19.7. Because input elements are wrapped as part of normal paragraphs, a DL list is used to make sure that the buttons appear under each other in the resultant page and are indented from the heading above them. Figure 19–15 shows the result. In this case, creditCard=java would get sent as part of the form data when the form is submitted.

Listing 19.7 Example of a radio button group

```
<DL>
  <DT>Credit Card:
  <DD><INPUT TYPE="RADIO" NAME="creditCard" VALUE="visa">
      Visa
  <DD><INPUT TYPE="RADIO" NAME="creditCard" VALUE="mastercard">
      Master Card
  <DD><INPUT TYPE="RADIO" NAME="creditCard"
             VALUE="java" CHECKED>
      Java Smart Card
  <DD><INPUT TYPE="RADIO" NAME="creditCard" VALUE="amex">
      American Express
  <DD><INPUT TYPE="RADIO" NAME="creditCard" VALUE="discover">
      Discover
</DL>
```

Credit Card:
- ○ Visa
- ○ Master Card
- ◉ Java Smart Card
- ○ American Express
- ○ Discover

Figure 19–15 Radio buttons in HTML.

NAME

Unlike the NAME attribute of most input elements, this NAME attribute is shared by multiple elements. All radio buttons associated with the same name are grouped logically so that no more than one can be selected at any given time. Note that attribute values are case sensitive, so the following would result in two radio buttons that are *not* in the same group.

```
<INPUT TYPE="RADIO" NAME="Foo" VALUE="Value1">
<INPUT TYPE="RADIO" NAME="FOO" VALUE="Value2">
```

Core Warning

Be sure the NAME attribute of each radio button in a logical group matches that of the other group members exactly, including case.

VALUE

The VALUE attribute supplies the value that gets transmitted with NAME when the form is submitted. It doesn't affect the appearance of the radio button. Instead, normal text and HTML markup are placed around the radio button, just as with check boxes.

CHECKED

If the CHECKED attribute is supplied, then the radio button is initially checked when the associated Web page is loaded. Otherwise, it is initially unchecked.

ONCLICK, ONFOCUS, and ONBLUR

These attributes specify JavaScript code to be executed when the button is clicked, receives the input focus, and loses the focus, respectively.

19.6 Combo Boxes and List Boxes

A SELECT element presents a set of options to the user. If only a single entry can be selected and no visible size has been specified, the options are presented in a combo box (drop-down menu); list boxes are used when multiple selections are permitted or a specific visible size has been specified. The choices themselves are specified by OPTION entries embedded in the SELECT element. The typical format is as follows:

```
<SELECT NAME="Name" ...>
  <OPTION VALUE="Value1">Choice 1 Text
  <OPTION VALUE="Value2">Choice 2 Text
  ...
  <OPTION VALUE="ValueN">Choice N Text
</SELECT>
```

The HTML 4.0 specification also defines OPTGROUP (with a single attribute of LABEL) to enclose OPTION elements to create cascading menus.

HTML Element: `<SELECT NAME="..." ...> ... </SELECT>`

Attributes: NAME (required), SIZE, MULTIPLE, ONCLICK, ONFOCUS, ONBLUR, ONCHANGE

SELECT creates a combo box or list box for selecting among choices. You specify each choice with an OPTION element enclosed between <SELECT ...> and </SELECT>.

NAME

NAME identifies the form to the servlet, JSP page, or other server-side program.

SIZE

SIZE gives the number of visible rows. If SIZE is used, the SELECT menu is usually represented as a list box instead of a combo box. A combo box is the normal representation when neither SIZE nor MULTIPLE is supplied.

MULTIPLE

The MULTIPLE attribute specifies that multiple entries can be selected simultaneously. If MULTIPLE is omitted, only a single selection is permitted. From a servlet, you would use `request.getParameterValues` to obtain an array of the entries selected in the list. For example, the code

```
String[] listValues = request.getParameterValues("language");
if (listValues != null) {
  for(int i=0; i<listValues.length; i++) {
    String value = listValues[i];
    ...
  }
}
```

would allow you to process all values selected in a list named `language` (see Listing 19.8). Be aware that the order of the values in the returned array may not correspond to the order of the values displayed in the list.

Core Approach

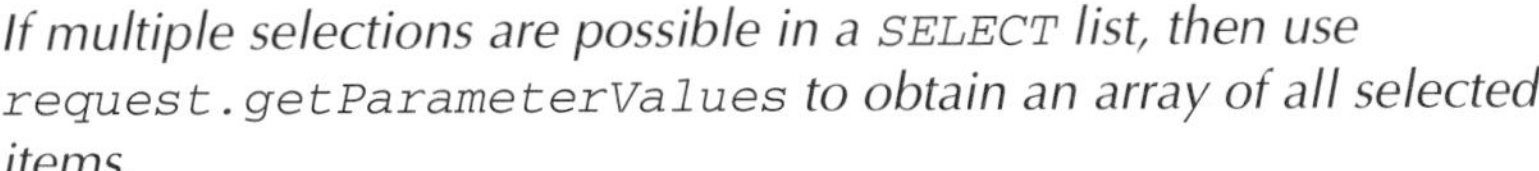

If multiple selections are possible in a `SELECT` list, then use `request.getParameterValues` to obtain an array of all selected items.

ONCLICK, ONFOCUS, ONBLUR, and ONCHANGE

These nonstandard attributes are supported by browsers that understand JavaScript. They indicate code to be executed when the entry is clicked, gains the input focus, loses the input focus, and loses the focus after having been changed, respectively.

HTML Element: `<OPTION ...>` (End Tag Optional)

Attributes: SELECTED, VALUE

This element specifies the menu choices; it is valid only inside a SELECT element.

VALUE

`VALUE` gives the value to be transmitted with the `NAME` of the `SELECT` menu if the current option is selected. This is *not* the text that is displayed to the user; that is specified by separate HTML markup listed after the `OPTION` tag.

SELECTED

If present, `SELECTED` specifies that the particular menu item shown is selected when the page is first loaded.

Listing 19.8 creates a menu of programming language choices. Because only a single selection is allowed and no visible `SIZE` is specified, it is displayed as a combo box. Figures 19–16 and 19–17 show the initial appearance and the appearance after the user activates the menu by clicking on it. If the entry `Java` is active when the form is submitted, then `language=java` is sent to the server-side program. Notice that it is the `VALUE` attribute, not the descriptive text, that is transmitted.

Listing 19.8 Example of a `SELECT` menu

```
Favorite language:
<SELECT NAME="language">
  <OPTION VALUE="c">C
  <OPTION VALUE="c++">C++
  <OPTION VALUE="java" SELECTED>Java
  <OPTION VALUE="lisp">Lisp
  <OPTION VALUE="perl">Perl
  <OPTION VALUE="smalltalk">Smalltalk
</SELECT>
```

Favorite language: Java

Figure 19–16 A `SELECT` element displayed as a combo box (drop-down menu).

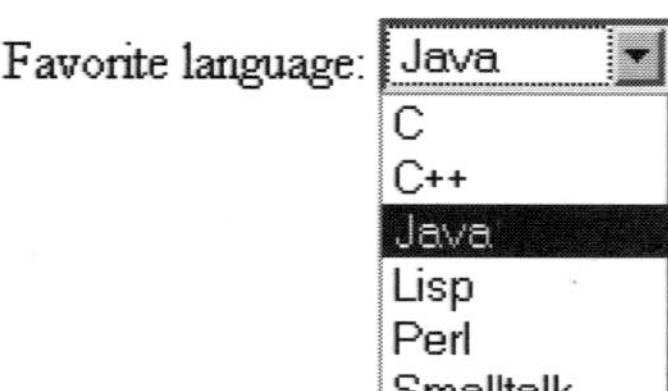

Figure 19–17 Choosing options from a `SELECT` menu.

The second example shows a SELECT element rendered as a list box. If more than one entry is active when the form is submitted, then more than one value is sent, listed as separate entries (repeating NAME). For instance, in the example shown in Listing 19.9 (Figure 19–18), `language=java&language=perl` gets added to the data being sent to the server. Multiple entries that share the same name is the reason servlet authors need to be familiar with the `getParameterValues` method of `HttpServletRequest` in addition to the more common `getParameter` method. See Chapter 4 (Handling the Client Request: Form Data) for details.

Listing 19.9 Example of a SELECT menu that permits selection of multiple options

```
Languages you know:<BR>
<SELECT NAME="language" MULTIPLE>
  <OPTION VALUE="c">C
  <OPTION VALUE="c++">C++
  <OPTION VALUE="java" SELECTED>Java
  <OPTION VALUE="lisp">Lisp
  <OPTION VALUE="perl" SELECTED>Perl
  <OPTION VALUE="smalltalk">Smalltalk
</SELECT>
```

Languages you know:

Figure 19–18 A SELECT element that specifies MULTIPLE or SIZE results in a list box.

HTML Element: `<OPTGROUP ...> ... </OPTGROUP>`

Attributes: `LABEL` (required)

This element, supported by Netscape 7.0 and Internet Explorer 6.0, permits grouping of menu choices. It is valid only inside a `SELECT` element.

LABEL

`LABEL` gives the text to display for the group of menu choices. Netscape and Internet Explorer display the label in bold text, using an oblique font.

Listing 19.10 creates a menu of server-side language choices. Here the menu choices are categorized into two groups by the `OPTGROUP` element. The first group is Common Servlet Languages, and the second group is Common CGI Languages. Figure 19–19 shows the displayed menu with `Java` selected for the common CGI language. For this selection the request data sent to the server is `language=java`. Be aware that no additional information is sent to the server by Netscape and Internet Explorer to indicate which `OPTGROUP` choice was selected. As a result, you should use unique values for all the menu choices, regardless of group.

Core Approach

When using multiple `OPTGROUP` elements, ensure that all `OPTION`s use a unique name for the `VALUE`.

Listing 19.10 Example of a `SELECT` menu categorized into two groups with the `OPTGROUP` element

```
Server-side Languages:
<SELECT NAME="language">
  <OPTGROUP LABEL="Common Servlet Languages">
    <OPTION VALUE="java1">Java
  </OPTGROUP>
  <OPTGROUP LABEL="Common CGI Languages">
    <OPTION VALUE="c">C
    <OPTION VALUE="c++">C++
    <OPTION VALUE="java2">Java
    <OPTION VALUE="perl">Perl
    <OPTION VALUE="vb">Visual Basic
</OPTGROUP>
</SELECT>
```

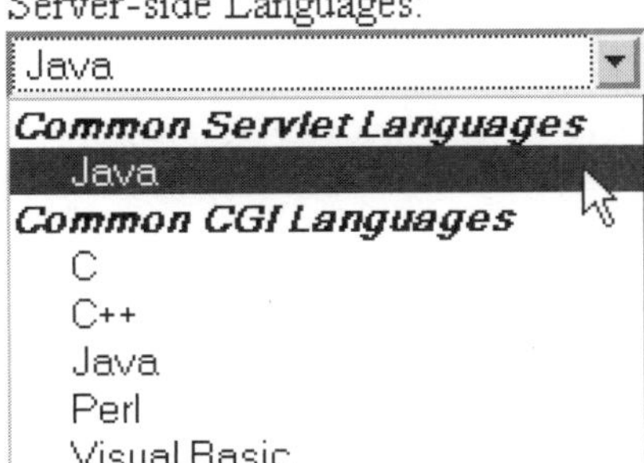

Figure 19–19 A SELECT element using OPTGROUP to group menu choices in Netscape 7.0.

19.7 File Upload Controls

HTML Element: `<INPUT TYPE="FILE" ...>` (No End Tag)

Attributes: NAME (required), VALUE (ignored), SIZE, MAXLENGTH, ACCEPT, ONCHANGE, ONSELECT, ONFOCUS, ONBLUR (nonstandard)

This element results in a filename textfield next to a Browse button. Users can enter a path directly in the textfield or click on the button to bring up a file selection dialog that lets them interactively choose the path to a file. When the form is submitted, the *contents* of the file are transmitted as long as an ENCTYPE of `multipart/form-data` was specified in the initial FORM declaration. For multipart data, you also need to specify POST as the method type. This element provides a convenient way to make user-support pages, with which the user sends a description of a problem along with any associated data or configuration files.

Core Approach

Always specify `ENCTYPE="multipart/form-data"` and `METHOD="POST"` in forms with file upload controls.

Unfortunately, the servlet API provides no high-level tools to read uploaded files; you have to call `request.getInputStream` and parse the request yourself. Fortunately, numerous third-party libraries are available for this task. One of the most popular is from the Jakarta Commons library; for details, see http://jakarta.apache.org/commons/fileupload/.

NAME

The NAME attribute identifies the textfield to the server-side program.

VALUE

For security reasons, this attribute is ignored; only the end user can specify a filename. Otherwise, a malicious HTML author could steal client files by specifying a filename and then using JavaScript to automatically submit the form when the page is loaded.

SIZE and MAXLENGTH

The SIZE and MAXLENGTH attributes are used the same way as in textfields, specifying the number of visible and maximum allowable characters, respectively.

ACCEPT

The ACCEPT attribute is intended to be a comma-separated list of MIME types used to restrict the available filenames. However, very few browsers support this attribute.

ONCHANGE, ONSELECT, ONFOCUS, and ONBLUR

These attributes are used by browsers that support JavaScript to specify the action to take when the mouse leaves the textfield after a change has occurred, when the user selects text in the textfield, when the textfield gets the input focus, and when the textfield loses the input focus, respectively.

For example, the code in Listing 19.11 creates a file upload control. Figure 19–20 shows the initial result, and Figure 19–21 shows a typical pop-up window that results when the Browse button is activated.

Listing 19.11 Example of a file upload control

```
<FORM ACTION="http://localhost:8088/SomeProgram"
      ENCTYPE="multipart/form-data" METHOD="POST">
Enter data file below:<BR>
<INPUT TYPE="FILE" NAME="fileName">
</FORM>
```

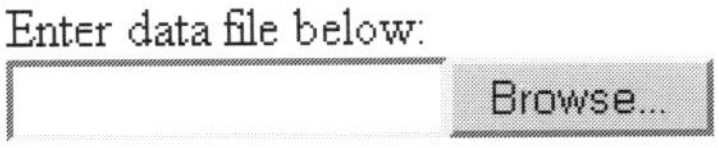

Enter data file below:

Browse...

Figure 19–20 Initial look of a file upload control.

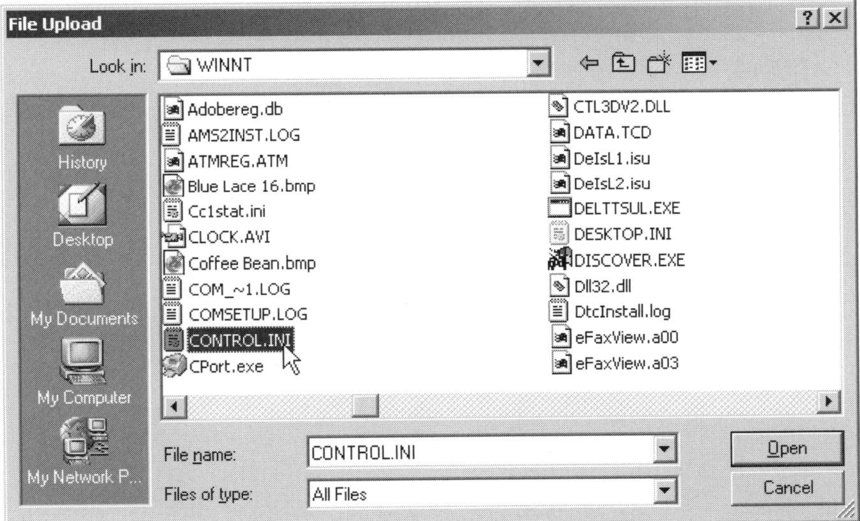

Figure 19–21 A file chooser resulting from the user clicking on Browse in a file upload control on Windows 2000 Professional.

19.8 Server-Side Image Maps

In standard HTML, an element called `MAP` lets you associate URLs with various regions of an image; then, when the image is clicked in one of the designated regions, the browser loads the appropriate URL. This form of mapping is known as a *client-side image map*, since the determination of which URL to contact is made on the client and no server-side program is involved. HTML also supports *server-side image maps* that can be used within HTML forms. With such maps, an image is drawn; when the user clicks on the image, the coordinates of the click are sent to a server-side program.

Client-side image maps are simpler and more efficient than server-side ones and should be used when all you want to do is associate a fixed set of URLs with some predefined image regions. However, server-side image maps are appropriate if the URL needs to be computed (e.g,. for weather maps), the regions change frequently, or other form data needs to be included with the request. This section discusses two approaches to server-side image maps.

IMAGE—Standard Server-Side Image Maps

The usual way to create server-side image maps is by means of an `<INPUT TYPE="IMAGE" ...>` element inside a form.

HTML Element: `<INPUT TYPE="IMAGE" ...>` (No End Tag)

Attributes: `NAME` (required), `SRC`, `ALIGN`

This element displays an image that, when clicked, sends the form to the servlet or other server-side program specified by the enclosing form's `ACTION`. The name itself is not sent; instead, *name*`.x=`*xpos* and *name*`.y=`*ypos* are transmitted, where *xpos* and *ypos* are the coordinates of the mouse click relative to the upper-left corner of the image.

NAME

The `NAME` attribute identifies the textfield when the form is submitted.

SRC

`SRC` designates the URL of the associated image.

ALIGN

The `ALIGN` attribute has the same options (`TOP`, `MIDDLE`, `BOTTOM`, `LEFT`, `RIGHT`) and default (`BOTTOM`) as the `ALIGN` attribute of the `IMG` element and is used in the same way.

Listing 19.12 shows a simple example in which the form's `ACTION` specifies the `EchoServer` developed in Section 19.12. Figures 19–22 and 19–23 show the results before and after the image is clicked.

Listing 19.12 ImageMap.html

```
<!DOCTYPE HTML PUBLIC "-//W3C//DTD HTML 4.0 Transitional//EN">
<HTML>
<HEAD>
  <TITLE>The IMAGE Input Control</TITLE>
</HEAD>
<BODY>
<H1 ALIGN="CENTER">The IMAGE Input Control</H1>
Which island is Java? Click and see if you are correct.
<FORM ACTION="http://localhost:8088/GeographyTester">
  <INPUT TYPE="IMAGE" NAME="map" SRC="images/indonesia.gif">
</FORM>
Of course, image maps can be implemented <B>in</B>
Java as well. :-)
</BODY></HTML>
```

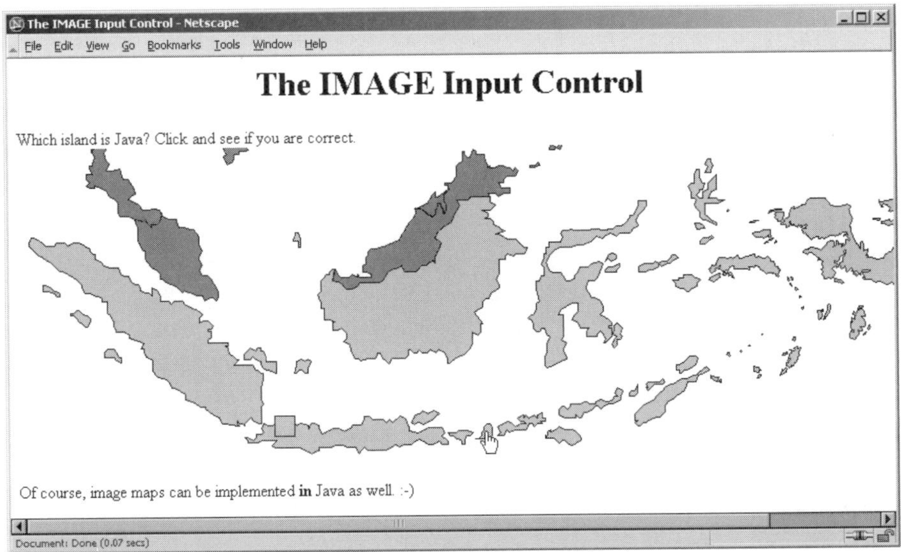

Figure 19–22 An `IMAGE` input control with `NAME="map"`.

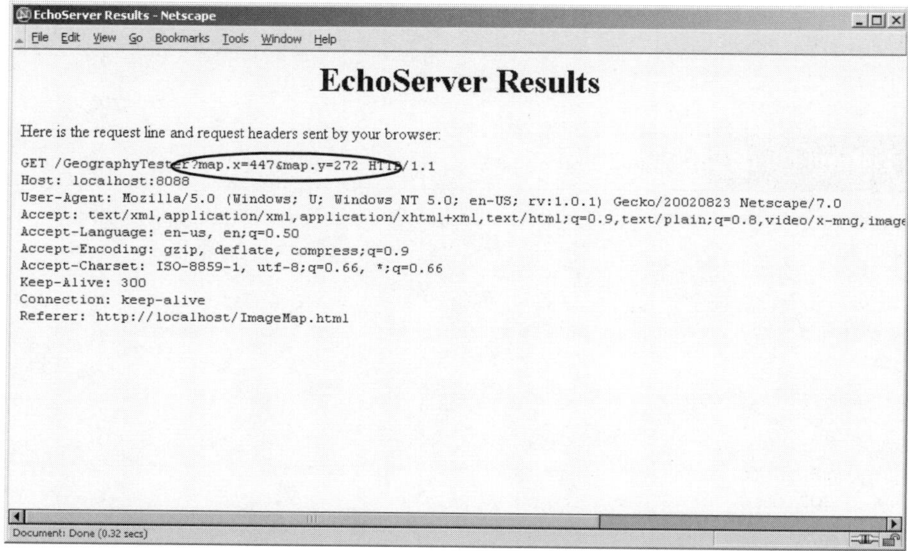

Figure 19–23 Clicking on the image at (447, 272) submits the form and adds `map.x=447&map.y=272` to the form data.

ISMAP—Alternative Server-Side Image Maps

`ISMAP` is an optional attribute of the `IMG` element and can be used in a manner similar to the `<INPUT TYPE="IMAGE" ...>` `FORM` entry. `ISMAP` is not actually a `FORM` element at all, but it can still be used for simple connections to servlets or other server-side programs. If an image with `ISMAP` is inside a hypertext link, then clicking on the image results in the coordinates of the click being sent to the specified URL. Coordinates are separated by commas and are specified in pixels relative to the top-left corner of the image.

For instance, Listing 19.13 embeds an image that uses the `ISMAP` attribute inside a hypertext link to http://localhost:8088/ChipTester, which is answered by the mini HTTP server developed in Section 19.12. Figure 19–24 shows the initial result, which is identical to what would have been shown had the `ISMAP` attribute been omitted. However, when the mouse button is pressed 270 pixels to the right and 189 pixels below the top-left corner of the image, the browser requests the URL http://localhost:8088/ChipTester?270,189 (as is shown in Figure 19–25).

If a server-side image map is used simply to select among a static set of destination URLs, then a client-side `MAP` element is a much better option because the server doesn't have to be contacted just to decide which URL applies. If the image map is intended to be mixed with other input elements, then the `IMAGE` input type is preferred instead. However, for a stand-alone image map in which the URL associated with a region changes frequently or requires calculation, an image with ISMAP is a reasonable choice.

Listing 19.13 IsMap.html

```
<!DOCTYPE HTML PUBLIC "-//W3C//DTD HTML 4.0 Transitional//EN">
<HTML>
<HEAD>
  <TITLE>The ISMAP Attribute</TITLE>
</HEAD>
<BODY>
<H1 ALIGN="CENTER">The ISMAP Attribute</H1>
<H2>Select a pin:</H2>
<A HREF="http://localhost:8088/ChipTester">
<IMG SRC="images/chip.gif" WIDTH=495 HEIGHT=200 ALT="Chip"
     BORDER=0 ISMAP></A>
</BODY></HTML>
```

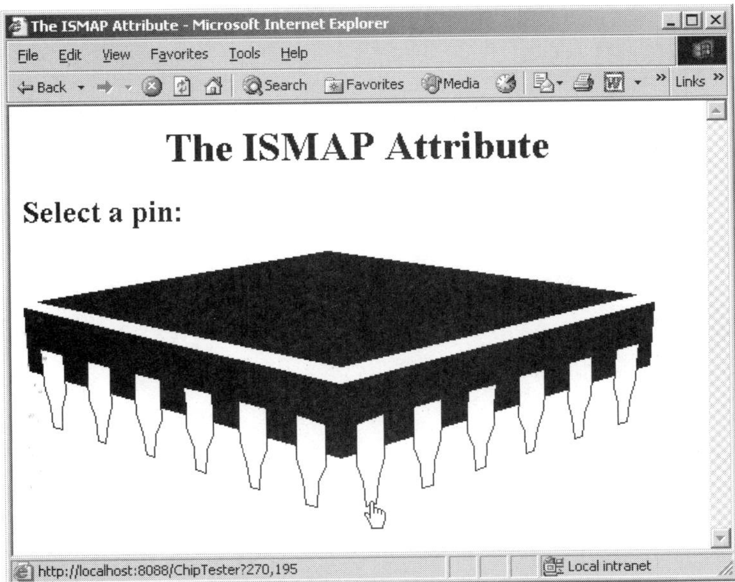

Figure 19–24 Setting the ISMAP attribute of an IMG element inside a hypertext link changes what happens when the image is selected.

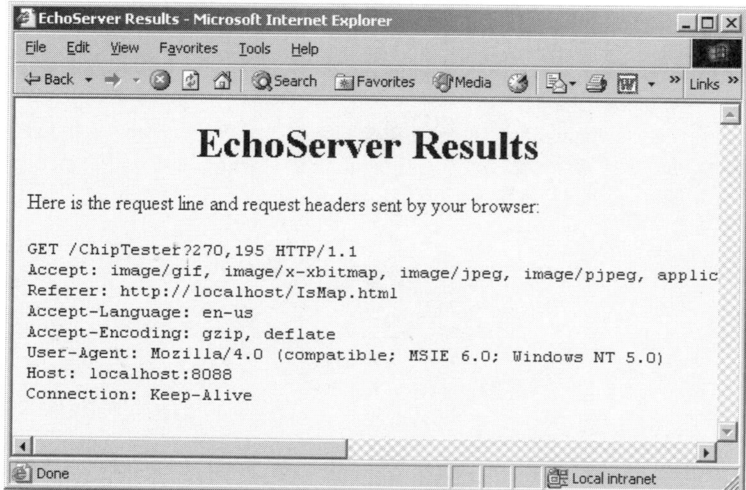

Figure 19–25 When an `ISMAP` image is selected, the coordinates of the selection are transmitted with the URL.

19.9 Hidden Fields

Hidden fields do not affect the appearance of the page that is presented to the user. Instead, they store fixed names and values that are sent unchanged to the server, regardless of user input. Hidden fields are typically used for three purposes:

- **Tracking the user.** As the user moves around within the site, user IDs in hidden fields can be used to track which pages the user has visited or to indicate the selections made by the user. In practice, servlet authors typically rely on the servlet session tracking API rather than attempting to implement session tracking at this low level. For details on session tracking, see Chapter 9.
- **Providing predefined input to a server-side program.** When a variety of static HTML pages act as front ends to the same program on the server, predefined hidden fields can help provide information about the requesting source page. For example, an online store might pay commissions to people who refer customers to their site. In this scenario, the referring page could let visitors search the store's catalog by means of a form, but embed a hidden field giving its referral ID.

- **Storing contextual information in pages that are dynamically generated.** For example, in a table listing the items in a shopping cart, you can place a hidden field in each row to identify the particular item ID. In this manner, the user can modify the number of items ordered and, when submitted to the server-side program, the hidden field will identify the item being modified. The user never needs to see the item ID on the HTML page.

Note that the term "hidden" does not mean that the field cannot be discovered by the user, since it is clearly visible in the HTML source. Because there is no reliable way to "hide" the HTML that generates a page, authors are cautioned not to use hidden fields to embed passwords or other sensitive information.

HTML Element: `<INPUT TYPE="HIDDEN" NAME="..." VALUE="...">` (No End Tag)

Attributes: `NAME` (required), `VALUE`

This element stores a name and a value, but no graphical element is created in the browser. The name/value pair is added to the form data when the form is submitted. For instance, with the following example, `itemID=brown001` will always get sent with the form data.

```
<INPUT TYPE="HIDDEN" NAME="itemID" VALUE="brown001">
```

19.10 Groups of Controls

HTML 4.0 defines the `FIELDSET` element, with an associated `LEGEND`, that can be used to visually group controls within a form. Note that the `FIELDSET` element works only in Netscape 6 and later and Internet Explorer 6 and later.

HTML Element: `<FIELDSET> ... </FIELDSET>`

Attributes: None.

This element is used as a container to enclose controls and, optionally, a `LEGEND` element. It has no attributes beyond the universal ones for style sheets, language, and so forth. Listing 19.14 gives an example, with the result shown in Figure 19–26.

Listing 19.14 Fieldset.html

```
<!DOCTYPE HTML PUBLIC "-//W3C//DTD HTML 4.0 Transitional//EN">
<HTML>
<HEAD>
  <TITLE>Grouping Controls</TITLE>
</HEAD>
<BODY BGCOLOR="#FDF5E6">
<H2 ALIGN="CENTER">Grouping Controls</H2>
<FORM ACTION="http://localhost:8088/SomeProgram">
<FIELDSET>
<LEGEND>Group One</LEGEND>
Field 1A: <INPUT TYPE="TEXT" NAME="field1A" VALUE="Field A"><BR>
Field 1B: <INPUT TYPE="TEXT" NAME="field1B" VALUE="Field B"><BR>
Field 1C: <INPUT TYPE="TEXT" NAME="field1C" VALUE="Field C"><BR>
</FIELDSET>
<FIELDSET>
<LEGEND ALIGN="RIGHT">Group Two</LEGEND>
Field 2A: <INPUT TYPE="TEXT" NAME="field2A" VALUE="Field A"><BR>
Field 2B: <INPUT TYPE="TEXT" NAME="field2B" VALUE="Field B"><BR>
Field 2C: <INPUT TYPE="TEXT" NAME="field2C" VALUE="Field C"><BR>
</FIELDSET>
</FORM>
</BODY></HTML>
```

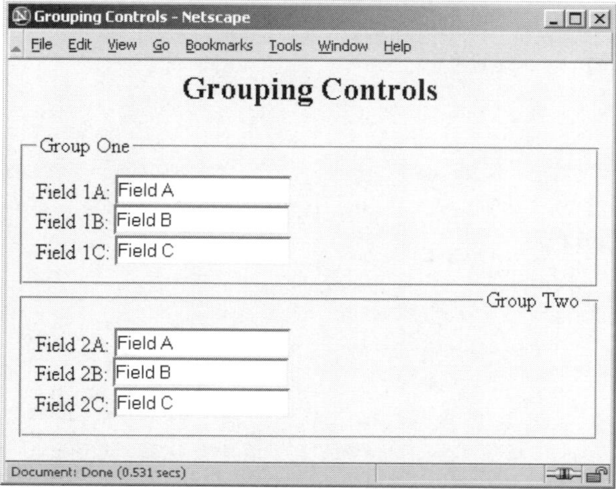

Figure 19–26 The `FIELDSET` element lets you visually group related controls shown in Netscape 7.0.

HTML Element: `<LEGEND> ... </LEGEND>`
Attributes: `ALIGN`

This element places a label on the etched border that is drawn around the group of controls; it is legal only within an enclosing FIELDSET.

ALIGN

This attribute controls the position of the label. Legal values are TOP, BOTTOM, LEFT, and RIGHT, with TOP being the default. In Figure 19–26, the first group has the default legend alignment, and the second group stipulates ALIGN="RIGHT". In HTML, style sheets are often a better way to control element alignment since they permit a single change to be propagated to multiple pages.

19.11 Tab Order Control

HTML 4.0 defines a TABINDEX attribute that can be used in any of the visual HTML elements. The TABINDEX value is an integer, and it controls the order in which elements receive the input focus when the TAB key is pressed.

In Listing 19.15 we present three textfields, field1, field2, and field3. Here, the TABINDEX attribute is set such that the tab order is from field1 to field3, and then finally to field2. The HTML page is displayed in Figure 19–27.

Typically, the implied tab order used by the browser is top-to-bottom, left-to-right. If a nonstandard order is important in your application, you should explicitly declare a tab order.

Listing 19.15 Tabindex.html

```
<!DOCTYPE HTML PUBLIC "-//W3C//DTD HTML 4.0 Transitional//EN">
<HTML>
<HEAD>
  <TITLE>Controlling TAB Order</TITLE>
</HEAD>
<BODY BGCOLOR="#FDF5E6">
<H2 ALIGN="CENTER">Controlling TAB Order</H2>
<FORM ACTION="http://localhost:8088/SomeProgram">
Field 1 (first tab selection):
<INPUT TYPE="TEXT" NAME="field1" TABINDEX=1><BR>
Field 2 (third tab selection):
<INPUT TYPE="TEXT" NAME="field2" TABINDEX=3><BR>
Field 3 (second tab selection):
<INPUT TYPE="TEXT" NAME="field3" TABINDEX=2><BR>
</FORM>
</BODY></HTML>
```

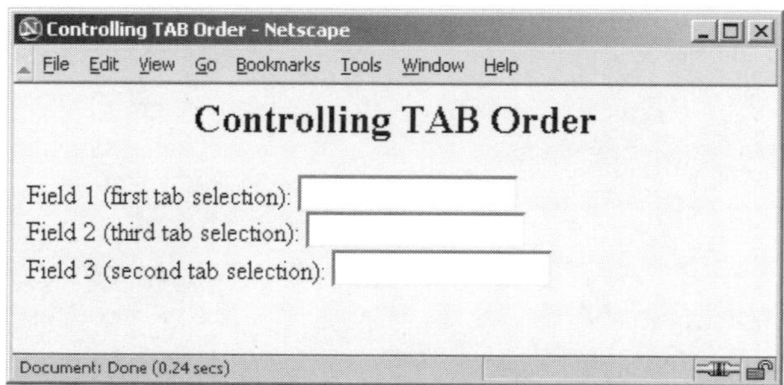

Figure 19–27 Repeatedly pressing the TAB key cycles the input focus among the first, third, and second text fields, in that order (as dictated by `TABINDEX`).

19.12 A Debugging Web Server

This section presents a mini "Web server" that is useful when you are trying to understand the behavior of HTML forms. We used it for many of the examples earlier in the chapter. The server simply reads all the HTTP data sent to it by the browser, then returns a Web page with those lines embedded within a `PRE` element.

This server is also useful for debugging servlets. When something goes wrong, the first task is to determine if the problem lies in the way in which you collect data or the way in which you process it. The `WebClient` program of Section 3.6 lets you see the raw data resulting from the server-side program; `EchoServer` lets you see the raw data transmitted by the client form.

Starting the `EchoServer` on, say, port 8088 of your local machine, then changing your forms to specify **http://localhost:8088/** lets you see if the data being collected is in the format you expect. In addition to seeing the sent form data, `EchoServer` also shows the HTTP request headers sent from the browser.

EchoServer

Listing 19.16 presents the top-level server code. You typically run `EchoServer` from the command line, specifying a port to listen on, or accepting the default port of 8088. `EchoServer` then accepts repeated HTTP requests from clients, packaging all HTTP data sent to it inside a Web page that is returned to the client. In most cases, the server reads until a blank line is received, indicating the end of `GET`, `HEAD`, or most other types of HTTP requests. In the case of `POST`, however, the server checks the `Content-Length` request header and reads that many bytes beyond the blank line.

Listings 19.17 and 19.18 present some utility classes that simplify networking. The `EchoServer` is built on top of them.

Listing 19.16 EchoServer.java

```
import java.net.*;
import java.io.*;
import java.util.*;

/** A simple HTTP server that generates a Web page showing all
 *  the data that it received from the Web client (usually
 *  a browser). To use this server, start it on the system of
 *  your choice, supplying a port number if you want something
 *  other than port 8088. Call this system server.com. Next,
 *  start a Web browser on the same or a different system, and
 *  connect to http://server.com:8088/whatever. The resultant
 *  Web page will show the data that your browser sent. For
 *  debugging in a servlet or other server-side program, specify
 *  http://server.com:8088/whatever as the ACTION of your HTML
 *  form. You can send GET or POST data; either way, the
 *  resultant page will show what your browser sent.
 */

public class EchoServer extends NetworkServer {
  protected int maxRequestLines = 50;
  protected String serverName = "EchoServer";

  /** Supply a port number as a command-line
   *  argument. Otherwise, use port 8088.
   */

  public static void main(String[] args) {
    int port = 8088;
    if (args.length > 0) {
      try {
        port = Integer.parseInt(args[0]);
      } catch(NumberFormatException nfe) {}
    }
    new EchoServer(port, 0);
  }

  public EchoServer(int port, int maxConnections) {
    super(port, maxConnections);
    listen();
  }
```

Listing 19.16 EchoServer.java *(continued)*

```
  /** Overrides the NetworkServer handleConnection method to
   *  read each line of data received, save it into an array
   *  of strings, then send it back embedded inside a PRE
   *  element in an HTML page.
   */

  public void handleConnection(Socket server)
      throws IOException{
    System.out.println
        (serverName + ": got connection from " +
         server.getInetAddress().getHostName());
    BufferedReader in = SocketUtil.getReader(server);
    PrintWriter out = SocketUtil.getWriter(server);
    String[] inputLines = new String[maxRequestLines];
    int i;
    for (i=0; i<maxRequestLines; i++) {
      inputLines[i] = in.readLine();
      if (inputLines[i] == null) // Client closed connection.
        break;
      if (inputLines[i].length() == 0) { // Blank line.
        if (usingPost(inputLines)) {
          readPostData(inputLines, i, in);
          i = i + 2;
        }
        break;
      }
    }
    printHeader(out);
    for (int j=0; j<i; j++) {
      out.println(inputLines[j]);
    }
    printTrailer(out);
    server.close();
  }

  // Send standard HTTP response and top of a standard Web page.
  // Use HTTP 1.0 for compatibility with all clients.

  private void printHeader(PrintWriter out) {
    out.println
      ("HTTP/1.0 200 OK\r\n" +
       "Server: " + serverName + "\r\n" +
       "Content-Type: text/html\r\n" +
       "\r\n" +
       "<!DOCTYPE HTML PUBLIC " +
         "\"-//W3C//DTD HTML 4.0 Transitional//EN\">\n" +
```

Listing 19.16 EchoServer.java *(continued)*

```
        "<HTML>\n" +
        "<HEAD>\n" +
        "  <TITLE>" + serverName + " Results</TITLE>\n" +
        "</HEAD>\n" +
        "\n" +
        "<BODY BGCOLOR=\"#FDF5E6\">\n" +
        "<H1 ALIGN=\"CENTER\">" + serverName +
          " Results</H1>\n" +
        "Here is the request line and request headers\n" +
        "sent by your browser:\n" +
        "<PRE>");
  }

  // Print bottom of a standard Web page.

  private void printTrailer(PrintWriter out) {
    out.println
      ("</PRE>\n" +
       "</BODY>\n" +
       "</HTML>\n");
  }

  // Normal Web page requests use GET, so this server can simply
  // read a line at a time. However, HTML forms can also use
  // POST, in which case we have to determine the number of POST
  // bytes that are sent so we know how much extra data to read
  // after the standard HTTP headers.

  private boolean usingPost(String[] inputs) {
    return(inputs[0].toUpperCase().startsWith("POST"));
  }

  private void readPostData(String[] inputs, int i,
                            BufferedReader in)
      throws IOException {
    int contentLength = contentLength(inputs);
    char[] postData = new char[contentLength];
    in.read(postData, 0, contentLength);
    inputs[++i] = new String(postData, 0, contentLength);
  }

  // Given a line that starts with Content-Length,
  // this returns the integer value specified.
```

Listing 19.16 EchoServer.java *(continued)*

```
  private int contentLength(String[] inputs) {
    String input;
    for (int i=0; i<inputs.length; i++) {
      if (inputs[i].length() == 0)
        break;
      input = inputs[i].toUpperCase();
      if (input.startsWith("CONTENT-LENGTH"))
        return(getLength(input));
    }
    return(0);
  }

  private int getLength(String length) {
    StringTokenizer tok = new StringTokenizer(length);
    tok.nextToken();
    return(Integer.parseInt(tok.nextToken()));
  }
}
```

Listing 19.17 NetworkServer.java

```
import java.net.*;
import java.io.*;

/** A starting point for network servers. You'll need to
 *  override handleConnection, but in many cases listen can
 *  remain unchanged. NetworkServer uses SocketUtil to simplify
 *  the creation of the PrintWriter and BufferedReader.
 */

public class NetworkServer {
  private int port, maxConnections;

  /** Build a server on specified port. It will continue to
   *  accept connections, passing each to handleConnection until
   *  an explicit exit command is sent (e.g., System.exit) or
   *  the maximum number of connections is reached. Specify
   *  0 for maxConnections if you want the server to run
   *  indefinitely.
   */
```

Listing 19.17 NetworkServer.java *(continued)*

```
public NetworkServer(int port, int maxConnections) {
  setPort(port);
  setMaxConnections(maxConnections);
}

/** Monitor a port for connections. Each time one is
 *  established, pass resulting Socket to handleConnection.
 */

public void listen() {
  int i=0;
  try {
    ServerSocket listener = new ServerSocket(port);
    Socket server;
    while((i++ < maxConnections) || (maxConnections == 0)) {
      server = listener.accept();
      handleConnection(server);
    }
  } catch (IOException ioe) {
    System.out.println("IOException: " + ioe);
    ioe.printStackTrace();
  }
}

/** This is the method that provides the behavior to the
 *  server, since it determines what is done with the
 *  resulting socket. <B>Override this method in servers
 *  you write.</B>
 *  <P>
 *  This generic version simply reports the host that made
 *  the connection, shows the first line the client sent,
 *  and sends a single line in response.
 */

protected void handleConnection(Socket server)
    throws IOException{
  BufferedReader in = SocketUtil.getReader(server);
  PrintWriter out = SocketUtil.getWriter(server);
  System.out.println
    ("Generic Network Server: got connection from " +
     server.getInetAddress().getHostName() + "\n" +
     "with first line '" + in.readLine() + "'");
  out.println("Generic Network Server");
  server.close();
}
```

Listing 19.17 NetworkServer.java *(continued)*

```
  /** Gets the max connections server will handle before
   *  exiting. A value of 0 indicates that server should run
   *  until explicitly killed.
   */

  public int getMaxConnections() {
    return(maxConnections);
  }

  /** Sets max connections. A value of 0 indicates that server
   *  should run indefinitely (until explicitly killed).
   */

  public void setMaxConnections(int maxConnections) {
    this.maxConnections = maxConnections;
  }

  /** Gets port on which server is listening. */

  public int getPort() {
    return(port);
  }

  /** Sets port. <B>You can only do before "connect" is
   *  called.</B> That usually happens in the constructor.
   */

  protected void setPort(int port) {
    this.port = port;
  }
}
```

Listing 19.18 SocketUtil.java

```
import java.net.*;
import java.io.*;

/** A shorthand way to create BufferedReaders and
 *  PrintWriters associated with a Socket.
 */

public class SocketUtil {
  /** Make a BufferedReader to get incoming data. */
```

Listing 19.18 SocketUtil.java *(continued)*

```
  public static BufferedReader getReader(Socket s)
      throws IOException {
    return(new BufferedReader(
       new InputStreamReader(s.getInputStream())));
  }

  /** Make a PrintWriter to send outgoing data.
   *  This PrintWriter will automatically flush stream
   *  when println is called.
   */

  public static PrintWriter getWriter(Socket s)
      throws IOException {
    // Second argument of true means autoflush.
    return(new PrintWriter(s.getOutputStream(), true));
  }
}
```

Server Organization and Structure

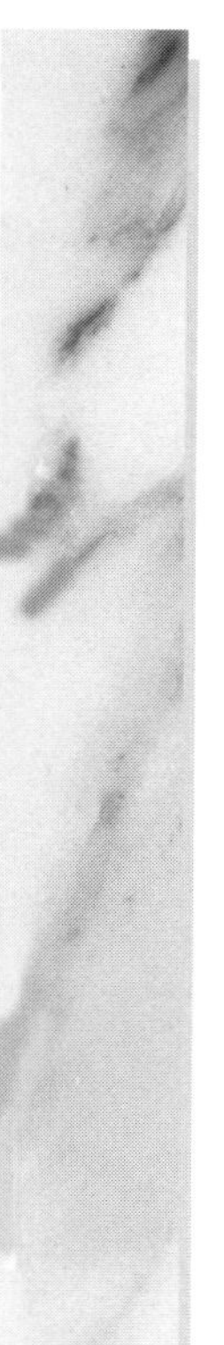

Topics in This Appendix

- URLs for downloading the software
- Addresses for bookmarking the API
- Steps for configuring the server
- Procedures for setting up your development environment
- Directories for files in the default Web application
- Directories for files in custom Web applications
- Directories for autogenerated servlet code

Appendix

This appendix summarizes the various files and directories used by Tomcat, JRun, and Resin. It also reminds you how to download and configure the server software.

Tomcat

For details, see Section 2.4. Updated information on configuring Tomcat is available at http://www.coreservlets.com/.

Downloading the Software

- http://jakarta.apache.org/tomcat/. Click on Binaries and choose the latest release version of either Tomcat 5 (servlets 2.4 and JSP 2.0) or Tomcat 4 (servlets 2.3 and JSP 1.2). Unzip into the location of your choice, hereafter referred to as *install_dir*.

Bookmarking the Servlet and JSP APIs

Tomcat bundles the documentation and links to it on the server homepage. Bookmark the version on disk so you can access it even when Tomcat is not running.

Tomcat 4

- **Servlet and JSP APIs:** *install_dir*/webapps/tomcat-docs/servletapi/index.html

Tomcat 5

- **Servlet API:** *install_dir*/webapps/tomcat-docs/servletapi/index.html
- **JSP API:** *install_dir*/webapps/tomcat-docs/jspapi/index.html

Configuring the Server

- **Set the `JAVA_HOME` variable.** Have it list the base Java installation directory, not the bin subdirectory.
- **Specify the server port.** Edit *install_dir*/conf/server.xml and change the value of the `port` attribute of the `Connector` element from 8080 to 80.
- **Enable servlet reloading.** Edit *install_dir*/conf/server.xml and add the following to the top of the `Service` element: `<DefaultContext reloadable="true"/>`
- **Enable the ROOT context.** Uncomment the following line in *install_dir*/conf/server.xml: `<Context path="" docBase="ROOT" debug="0"/>` Some versions of Tomcat 5 are missing the trailing slash; if so, add it.
- **Turn on the invoker servlet.** Uncomment the invoker servlet's `servlet` and `servlet-mapping` elements in *install_dir*/conf/web.xml.

Setting Up Your Development Environment

- **Create a development directory.** Develop code there; copy to the server's deployment directory for testing.
- **Set your `CLASSPATH`.** Have it include *install_dir*/common/lib/servlet.jar, your main development directory, and "." (the current working directory).
- **Make shortcuts to start and stop the server.** In your development directory, make shortcuts to *install_dir*/bin/startup.bat and *install_dir*/bin/shutdown.bat. Double-click them to start and stop the server. Use startup.sh and shutdown.sh on Unix/Linux.

Using the Default Web Application

The main location is *install_dir*/webapps/ROOT. Create *install_dir*/webapps/ROOT/WEB-INF/classes if the classes directory does not already exist. You have to enable the ROOT context to use the default Web application (see the preceding section on configuring the server).

Packageless Servlets

- **Code:** *install_dir*/webapps/ROOT/WEB-INF/classes
- **URL:** http://*host*/servlet/*ServletName*

Packaged Servlets

- **Code:** *install_dir*/webapps/ROOT/WEB-INF/classes/*packageName*
- **URL:** http://*host*/servlet/*packageName.ServletName*

Packaged Beans and Utility Classes

- *install_dir*/webapps/ROOT/WEB-INF/classes/*packageName*

JAR Files

- *install_dir*/webapps/ROOT/WEB-INF/lib

HTML and JSP Pages (Not In Subdirectories)

- **Code Location:** *install_dir*/webapps/ROOT
- **URL:** http://*host*/*filename*

HTML and JSP Pages (In Subdirectories)

- **Code Location:** *install_dir*/webapps/ROOT/*directoryName*
- **URL:** http://*host*/*directoryName*/*filename*

Using Custom Web Applications

Create a Web application directory in *install_dir*/webapps. The directory should have a WEB-INF subdirectory, a web.xml file in WEB-INF (copy the one from ROOT), and a WEB-INF/classes subdirectory. Instead of a regular directory, you can also use a WAR file (JAR file with file extension renamed from .jar to .war) with this structure. In the following, we use *webappName* to refer to the name of the directory (or the base name of the WAR file, minus .war). See Section 2.11 for details.

Packageless Servlets

- **Code Location:**
  install_dir/webapps/*webappName*/WEB-INF/classes
- **Default URL:**
  http://*host*/*webappName*/servlet/*ServletName*
- **Custom URL:**
  http://*host*/*webappName*/*AnyName*
  (designate */AnyName* with `servlet` and `servlet-mapping` elements in web.xml)

Packaged Servlets

- **Code Location:**
  install_dir/webapps/*webappName*/WEB-INF/classes/*packageName*
- **Default URL:**
  http://*host*/*webappName*/servlet/*packageName.ServletName*
- **Custom URL:**
  http://*host*/*webappName*/*AnyName*
  (designate */AnyName* with `servlet` and `servlet-mapping` elements in web.xml)

Packaged Beans and Utility Classes

- *install_dir*/webapps/*webappName*/WEB-INF/classes/*packageName*

JAR Files

- *install_dir*/webapps/*webappName*/WEB-INF/lib

HTML and JSP Pages (Not In Subdirectories)

- **Code Location:** *install_dir*/webapps/*webappName*
- **URL:** http://*host*/*webappName*/*filename*

HTML and JSP Pages (In Subdirectories)

- **Code Location:** *install_dir*/webapps/*webappName*/*directoryName*
- **URL:** http://*host*/*webappName*/*directoryName*/*filename*

Viewing Autogenerated Code for JSP Pages

You can view the servlet code that Tomcat generates from your JSP pages.

- **Default Web Application:**
  install_dir/work/Standalone/localhost/_
- **Custom Web Applications:**
  install_dir/work/Standalone/localhost/*webAppName*

JRun

For details, see Section 2.5.

Downloading the Software

- http://www.macromedia.com/software/jrun/. Follow the instructions for obtaining the free trial version.

Bookmarking the Servlet and JSP APIs

You can access the APIs online; you can also download them to your machine for faster access.

Servlets 2.3 and JSP 1.2

- **Online Documentation:**
  http://jakarta.apache.org/tomcat/tomcat-4.1-doc/servletapi/
- **Download Documentation:**
  http://java.sun.com/products/jsp/download.html

Servlets 2.4 and JSP 2.0

- **Servlet 2.4 Documentation (Online):**
  http://jakarta.apache.org/tomcat/tomcat-5.0-doc/servletapi/
- **JSP 2.0 Documentation (Online):**
  http://jakarta.apache.org/tomcat/tomcat-5.0-doc/jspapi/
- **Servlet 2.4 and JSP 2.0 Documentation (Download):**
  http://java.sun.com/products/jsp/download.html

Configuring the Server

Run the installation wizard and specify the following:

- **The serial number.** Leave it blank for the free development server.
- **User restrictions.** Limit the use of JRun to your account or make it available to anyone on your system.
- **The SDK installation location.** Specify the base Java directory, not the bin subdirectory.
- **The server installation directory.** Accept the default in most cases.
- **The administrator username and password.** Pick any values you want, but write them down for later use.
- **The autostart capability.** Do *not* identify JRun as a Windows service.

After completing the installation, go to the Start menu, select Programs, select Macromedia JRun 4, and choose JRun Launcher. Select the admin server and press Start. Next, open a browser and enter the URL http://localhost:8000/. Log in with the username and password you specified during installation, then select Services under the default server in the left-hand pane. Next, choose WebService, change the port from 8100 to 80, press Apply, and stop and restart the server.

Setting Up Your Development Environment

- **Create a development directory.** Develop code there; copy to the server's deployment directory for testing.
- **Set your CLASSPATH.** Have it include *install_dir*/lib/jrun.jar, your main development directory, and "." (the current working directory).
- **Make shortcuts to start and stop the server.** Go to the Start menu, select Programs, select Macromedia JRun 4, right-click on the JRun Launcher icon, and select Copy. Then go to your development directory, right-click in the window, and select Paste Shortcut (not just Paste). There is no separate shutdown icon; the JRun Launcher lets you both start and stop the server.

Using the Default Web Application

The main location is *install_dir*/servers/default/default-ear/default-war.

Packageless Servlets

- **Code:** *install_dir*/servers/default/default-ear/default-war/WEB-INF/classes
- **URL:** http://*host*/servlet/*ServletName*

Packaged Servlets

- **Code:** *install_dir*/servers/default/default-ear/default-war/WEB-INF/classes/*packageName*
- **URL:** http://*host*/servlet/*packageName.ServletName*

Packaged Beans and Utility Classes

- *install_dir*/servers/default/default-ear/default-war/WEB-INF/classes/*packageName*

JAR Files

- *install_dir*/servers/default/default-ear/default-war/WEB-INF/lib

HTML and JSP Pages (Not In Subdirectories)

- **Code Location:** *install_dir*/servers/default/default-ear/default-war
- **URL:** http://*host*/*filename*

HTML and JSP Pages (In Subdirectories)

- **Code Location:** *install_dir*/servers/default/default-ear/default-war/*directoryName*
- **URL:** http://*host*/*directoryName*/*filename*

Using Custom Web Applications

Create a Web application directory in *install_dir*/servers/default. The directory should have a WEB-INF subdirectory, a web.xml file in WEB-INF (copy the one from the default Web application), and a WEB-INF/classes subdirectory. Instead of a regular directory, you can also use a WAR file (JAR file with file extension renamed from .jar to .war) with this structure. In the following, we use ***webappName*** to refer to the name of the directory (or the base name of the WAR file, minus .war). See Section 2.11 for details.

Packageless Servlets

- **Code Location:** *install_dir*/servers/default/*webappName*/WEB-INF/classes
- **Default URL:** http://*host*/*webappName*/servlet/*ServletName*
- **Custom URL:** http://*host*/*webappName*/*AnyName*
(designate /*AnyName* with `servlet` and `servlet-mapping` elements in web.xml)

Packaged Servlets

- **Code Location:** *install_dir*/servers/default/*webappName*/WEB-INF/classes/*packageName*
- **Default URL:** http://*host*/*webappName*/servlet/*packageName.ServletName*
- **Custom URL:** http://*host*/*webappName*/*AnyName*
(designate /*AnyName* with `servlet` and `servlet-mapping` elements in web.xml)

Packaged Beans and Utility Classes

- *install_dir*/servers/default/*webappName*/WEB-INF/classes/*packageName*

JAR Files

- *install_dir*/servers/default/*webappName*/WEB-INF/lib

HTML and JSP Pages (Not In Subdirectories)

- **Code Location:** *install_dir*/servers/default/*webappName*
- **URL:** http://*host*/*webappName*/*filename*

HTML and JSP Pages (In Subdirectories)

- **Code Location:** *install_dir*/servers/default/*webappName*/*directoryName*
- **URL:** http://*host*/*webappName*/*directoryName*/*filename*

Viewing Autogenerated Code for JSP Pages

You can view the servlet code that JRun generates from your JSP pages. However, JRun does not save the .java files unless you change the `keepGenerated` element from `false` to `true` in *install_dir*/servers/default/SERVER-INF/default-web.xml.

- **Default Web Application:**
  install_dir/servers/default/default-ear/default-war/WEB-INF/jsp
- **Custom Web Applications:**
  install_dir/servers/default/*webappName*/WEB-INF/jsp

Resin

For details, see Section 2.6.

Downloading the Software

- http://caucho.com/resin/. Click on the download link at the bottom of the page and follow the instructions.

Bookmarking the Servlet and JSP APIs

You can access the APIs online; you can also download them to your machine for faster access.

Servlets 2.3 and JSP 1.2

- **Online Documentation:**
  http://jakarta.apache.org/tomcat/tomcat-4.1-doc/servletapi/
- **Download Documentation:**
  http://java.sun.com/products/jsp/download.html

Servlets 2.4 and JSP 2.0

- **Servlet 2.4 Documentation (Online):**
  http://jakarta.apache.org/tomcat/tomcat-5.0-doc/servletapi/
- **JSP 2.0 Documentation (Online):**
  http://jakarta.apache.org/tomcat/tomcat-5.0-doc/jspapi/
- **Servlet 2.4 and JSP 2.0 Documentation (Download):**
  http://java.sun.com/products/jsp/download.html

Configuring the Server

Unzip Resin into the directory of your choice (hereafter referred to as *install_dir*) and perform the following two steps:

1. **Set the `JAVA_HOME` variable.** Set this variable to list the base Java installation directory, not the `bin` subdirectory.
2. **Specify the port.** Edit *install_dir*/conf/resin.conf and change the value of the `port` attribute of the `http` element from 8080 to 80.

Setting Up Your Development Environment

- **Create a development directory.** Develop code there; copy to the server's deployment directory for testing.
- **Set your `CLASSPATH`.** Have it include *install_dir*/lib/jsdk23.jar, your main development directory, and "." (the current working directory).
- **Make shortcuts to start and stop the server.** Right-click on *install_dir*/bin/httpd.exe, and select Copy. Then go to your development directory, right-click in the window, and select Paste Shortcut (not just Paste). There is no separate shutdown icon; invoking httpd.exe results in a popup window with a Quit button that lets you stop the server.

Using the Default Web Application

The main location is *install_dir*/doc.

Packageless Servlets

- **Code:** *install_dir*/doc/WEB-INF/classes
- **URL:** http://*host*/servlet/*ServletName*

Packaged Servlets

- **Code:** *install_dir*/doc/WEB-INF/classes/*packageName*
- **URL:** http://*host*/servlet/*packageName.ServletName*

Packaged Beans and Utility Classes

- *install_dir*/doc/WEB-INF/classes/*packageName*

JAR Files

- *install_dir*/doc/WEB-INF/lib

HTML and JSP Pages (Not In Subdirectories)

- **Code Location:** *install_dir*/doc
- **URL:** http://*host*/*filename*

HTML and JSP Pages (In Subdirectories)

- **Code Location:** *install_dir*/doc/*directoryName*
- **URL:** http://*host*/*directoryName*/*filename*

Using Custom Web Applications

Create a Web application directory in *install_dir*/webapps. The directory should have a WEB-INF subdirectory, a web.xml file in WEB-INF (copy the one from the default Web application), and a WEB-INF/classes subdirectory. Instead of a regular directory, you can also use a WAR file (JAR file with file extension renamed from .jar to .war) with this structure. In the following, we use *webappName* to refer to the name of the directory (or the base name of the WAR file, minus .war). See Section 2.11 for details.

Packageless Servlets

- **Code Location:** *install_dir*/webapps/*webappName*/WEB-INF/classes
- **Default URL:** http://*host*/*webappName*/servlet/*ServletName*
- **Custom URL:** http://*host*/*webappName*/*AnyName*
  (designate /*AnyName* with `servlet` and `servlet-mapping` elements in web.xml)

Packaged Servlets

- **Code Location:**
  install_dir/webapps/*webappName*/WEB-INF/classes/*packageName*
- **Default URL:**
  http://*host*/*webappName*/servlet/*packageName.ServletName*
- **Custom URL:**
  http://*host*/*webappName*/*AnyName*
  (designate /*AnyName* with `servlet` and `servlet-mapping` elements in web.xml)

Packaged Beans and Utility Classes

- *install_dir*/webapps/*webappName*/WEB-INF/classes/*packageName*

JAR Files

- *install_dir*/webapps/*webappName*/WEB-INF/lib

HTML and JSP Pages (Not In Subdirectories)

- **Code Location:** *install_dir*/webapps/*webappName*
- **URL:** http://*host*/*webappName*/*filename*

HTML and JSP Pages (In Subdirectories)

- **Code Location:** *install_dir*/webapps/*webappName*/*directoryName*
- **URL:** http://*host*/*webappName*/*directoryName*/*filename*

Viewing Autogenerated Code for JSP Pages

You can view the servlet code that Resin generates from your JSP pages.

- **Default Web Application:** *install_dir*/doc/WEB-INF/work
- **Custom Web Applications:** *install_dir*/webapps/*webappName*/WEB-INF/work

Index

A

B

H

I

J

S

W

X

Z

Prentice Hall Professional Technical Reference
http://www.phptr.com/
Prentice Hall PTR InformIT InformIT Online Books Financial Times Prentice Hall ft.com PTG Interactive Reuters
Tomorrow's Solutions for Today's Professionals
Prentice Hall Professional Technical Reference
PRENTICE HALL PTR
Browse Book Series What's New User Groups Alliances Special Sales Contact Us
Search | Help | Home
Quick Search
PTR Favorites
Find a Bookstore
Book Series
Special Interests
Newsletters
Press Room
International
Best Sellers
Solutions Beyond the Book
Shopping Bag
Keep Up to Date with
PH PTR Online
We strive to stay on the cutting edge of what's happening in professional computer science and engineering. Here's a bit of what you'll find when you stop by www.phptr.com:
What's new at PHPTR? We don't just publish books for the professional community, we're a part of it. Check out our convention schedule, keep up with your favorite authors, and get the latest reviews and press releases on topics of interest to you.
Special interest areas offering our latest books, book series, features of the month, related links, and other useful information to help you get the job done.
User Groups Prentice Hall Professional Technical Reference's User Group Program helps volunteer, not-for-profit user groups provide their members with training and information about cutting-edge technology.
Companion Websites Our Companion Websites provide valuable solutions beyond the book. Here you can download the source code, get updates and corrections, chat with other users and the author about the book, or discover links to other websites on this topic.
Need to find a bookstore? Chances are, there's a bookseller near you that carries a broad selection of PTR titles. Locate a Magnet bookstore near you at www.phptr.com.
Subscribe today! Join PHPTR's monthly email newsletter! Want to be kept up-to-date on your area of interest? Choose a targeted category on our website, and we'll keep you informed of the latest PHPTR products, author events, reviews and conferences in your interest area.
Visit our mailroom to subscribe today! http://www.phptr.com/mail_lists